Teaching English
as a Second or Foreign Language

Teaching English as a Second or Foreign Language

Second Edition

Marianne Celce-Murcia, Editor
University of California, Los Angeles

HEINLE & HEINLE PUBLISHERS
A Division of Wadsworth, Inc.
Boston, Massachusetts 02116

In loving memory of Gottle Luise

Director: Laurie E. Likoff
Full-Service Manager: Michael Weinstein
Production Coordinator: Cynthia Funkhouser
Text Design Adaptation: Princeton Editorial Associates
Cover Design: Caliber Design Planning
Compositor: TCSystems
Printer and Binder: Malloy Lithographing

NEWBURY HOUSE
A division of HarperCollins Publishers

Language Science
Language Teaching
Language Learning

For permission to use copyrighted material, grateful acknowledgment is made to the copyright holders on pp. v and vi, which are hereby made part of this copyright page.

Teaching English as a Second or Foreign Language, Second Edition

Library of Congress Cataloging-in-Publication Data

Teaching English as a second or foreign language / Marianne Celce
—Murcia.—2nd ed.
   p. cm.
  Includes bibliographical references and index.

   1. English language—Study and teaching—Foreign speakers.
I. Celce-Murcia, Marianne.
PE1128.A2T44   1991
428'.007—dc20   91-2549
                             CIP

ISBN 0-8384-2860-6

98 97   9 8

Credits

We are grateful to the following publishers for permission to reproduce their materials in the following chapters:

"English for Specific Purposes (ESP)," Ann M. Johns:
p. 68: Swales, J. (1971/1974). Explanation of Present Simple. *Writing Scientific English*. London: Nelson. Reprinted with permission.
p. 69: Trimble, L. (1985). Rhetorical Process Chart. *English for Science and Technology: A Discourse Approach*. Cambridge: Cambridge University Press. Reprinted with permission.
"Listening Comprehension in Second/Foreign Language Instruction," Joan Morley:
pp. 94, 96, 98: Davis, P. and Rinvolucri, M. (1988). Selection from *Dictation, New Methods and New Possibilities*. Cambridge: Cambridge University Press. Reprinted with permission.
p. 98: Morley, J. (1972). Selection from *Improving Aural Comprehension*. Ann Arbor: The University of Michigan Press. Reprinted with permission.
pp. 96–97: Morley, J. (1984). Selection from *Listening and Language Learning in ESL*. Englewood Cliffs, NJ: Prentice Hall Regents. Reprinted with permission.
p. 101: Numrich, C./National Public Radio (1987). White Plains, NY: Longman. From *Consider the Issues: Developing Critical Listening and Critical Thinking Skills*, by Carol Numrich/National Public Radio. Copyright © 1987 by Longman Publishing Group. Reprinted with permission of Longman Publishing Group.
pp. 94–98: Schecter, Sandra (1984). Selection from *Listening Tasks*. Cambridge: Cambridge University Press. Reprinted with permission.
pp. 94–98: Ur, Penny (1984). Selection from *Teaching Listening Comprehension*. Cambridge: Cambridge University Press. Reprinted with permission.
"A synthesis of Methods for Interactive Listening," Pat Wilcox Peterson:
p. 110: Nagle, S. J. and Sanders, S. L. (1986). A Model of Listening Comprehension Processing in the Adult Language Learner. From Comprehension Theory and Second Language Pedagogy. *TESOL Quarterly*, *20:1*, 19. Reprinted with permission.
"Academic Reading and the ESL/EFL Teacher," Fraida Dubin and David Bycina:
pp. 210–212, 214: Zeilik, M. and Gausted, J. (1983). New York: HarperCollins Publishers Inc. Excerpts from *Astronomy: The Cosmic Perspective*. Copyright © 1983 by Michael Zeilik and John Gausted. Reprinted with permission of HarperCollins Publishers Inc.
"Grammar in Writing," Jan Frodesen:
p. 274: Raimes, A. (1988). New York: St. Martin's Press. Selection from *Grammar Troublespots: An Editing Guide for ESL Students*. Copyright © 1988 St. Martin's Press, Inc. Reprinted with permission.
"Vocabulary Learning and Teaching," Bernard D. Seal:
p. 303: Seal, B. (1988). Selection from *Vocabulary Builder 2*. London: Longman. Reprinted with permission.
"Teaching Language Through Context," Marguerite Ann Snow:
pp. 323, 324, 325: Chamberlain, P., Quinn, M. E., Spanos, G. (1988). Selection from *Strategies for Integrating Language and Content: Science*. This strategy sheet was developed by Patricia Chamberlain, Mary Ellen Quinn, and George

Spanos at a seminar on Methods of Integrating Language and Content Instruction held at the Center for Applied Linguistics. Reprinted with permission.

"Experimental Language Learning," Janet L. Eyring: pp. 357, 358, 359. Arnold, N. et al. (1987). How to Write an Autobiography. *Integrating Styles and Skills: An approach to Lesson Planning for the ESL Classroom*. Arlington Public Schools, ESOL/HILT Program and Center for Applied Linguistics (ERIC Reproduction Services No. ED 292 292). Reprinted with permission.

Acknowledgments

Many colleagues, students, and friends have been of invaluable assistance in the preparation of this volume. My greatest debt is to all the colleagues who graciously accepted my invitation to contribute chapters. The breadth and depth of their expertise makes this volume truly unique.

I am extremely grateful to Donna Brinton, Cara Wallis, and Carlos Galdamez for assistance in preparing the cumulative list of references. Likewise, the index could not have been prepared without the dedicated work of Sandra Gill.

Both Laurie Likoff and Cindy Funkhouser of Newbury House were most helpful and supportive in bringing this large volume to completion.

Finally, I would like to mention that I have incorporated in this second edition many of the suggestions for improving the first edition that readers, students, and colleagues have graciously shared with me over the years. I am also grateful to Susan Parks of the University of Montreal and Bill Harshbarger of the University of Washington for their comments and suggestions on the first draft of this second edition: the suggestions, in many cases, led to useful revisions and improvements.

Contents

Foreword

This volume, the second edition of *Teaching English as a Second or Foreign Language,* represents my effort to put together a comprehensive introduction to the profession of teaching English to speakers of other languages. (This was the same objective my late colleague Lois McIntosh and I had in mind when we began working on the first edition [1979] 15 years ago.) I set out with the goal of maintaining a balance between theory and practice—between providing needed background information and relevant research, on the one hand, and providing many practical classroom suggestions and resources for teachers, on the other. I also wanted to cover all of the areas that are considered critical to successful language instruction: knowledge of teaching methods, background on and strategies for teaching the language skills, new ways to integrate the skills, an understanding of important student factors, and additional information helpful to a teacher's performance and growth. I have tried to produce an introduction to the field that would be of sufficient depth and breadth to be suitable for students with some previous teaching experience, yet straightforward enough not to needlessly bewilder the novice.

There is a complementary volume I have edited on more theoretical topics, such as language acquisition, language policy, interlanguage analysis, cognitive style, attitude and motivation research, language and culture (i.e., Celce-Murcia, *Beyond Basics: Issues and Research in TESOL,* 1985). These topics are also important if the teacher wants to have a complete and balanced background in ESL/EFL. However, these topics are of less immediate practicality than the ones included in this basic volume since they are often concerned with abstract procedures or with research areas that have not yet yielded clear-cut answers or solutions, but which promise to bring us useful insights in the future.

Two factors motivated me to undertake this task. First of all, I feel that there still is a paucity of fully satisfactory introductory ESL/EFL methods texts; this continues to make both the teaching and the learning of basic ESL skills and concepts somewhat difficult. There are many individual texts and volumes dealing exclusively with methods and approaches, or speaking skills, or reading, or writing. However, there are only a few comprehensive textbooks available to help with the challenges involved in teaching a basic and comprehensive methods course. The continuing need for such a text, along with colleagues' exhorting me to prepare an updated second edition, was, therefore, my primary motivation in preparing this second edition.

A second motivating factor was the belief that no one person or two people could, on their own, hope to write an adequate introduction to ESL/EFL. The field has simply become too vast. What I did as editor was to prepare a reasonable outline for the text and a pedagogically motivated format for the chapters. I then approached appropriate individuals for contributions. In a few cases (i.e., Prator, Larsen-Freeman, Peck, and Cohen), I asked the author who had contributed a specific chapter to the first edition to prepare the revision; in most cases, however, the authors of the first-edition chapters were unavailable or could not be located, so I approached colleagues who I felt were specialists in an area and who were interested in communicating with prospective teachers about their area of specialization. In addition to the wide range of specialists whose contributions I was fortunate to solicit for this project, a remarkable number of my present and former graduate students have contributed to this second edition, and this is a source of great personal and professional satisfaction.

A total of 36 authors have contributed to the 32 chapters in this textbook. I thought the reader might like to know something about the background and experience of the contributors, so I have included a short biographical statement on each of the 36 in the section following this introduction.

With the exception of two chapters (i.e., the ones by Prator and Celce-Murcia) none of the chapters in the present collection has previously been published, and the two mentioned have undergone revisions. Thirty chapters have been written especially for this textbook. Each chapter concludes with a set of discussion questions, a number of suggested related activities, and some suggestions for further reading directed toward those who get interested in a given chapter's content and who want to find out more about the topic. A unified bibliography of all the references cited and an index come at the end of the book.

Although it is designed primarily as a textbook for a preservice TESL/TEFL methods course, I hope that this book will also be a useful reference and guide for individuals who are teaching ESL or EFL without having had specific training and for practicing teachers who received their training some time ago.

As for instructors planning to use this book as the core text for a methodology course, I would advise them not to attempt covering every single chapter during one academic term. I advise, instead, that they be selective and use the chapters most relevant to the preparation of their students as teachers.

In trying to make the text comprehensive, I admit to having made it too long for one course. I know of one setting where sections I, IV, and V constitute one course and sections II and III a second course. One colleague has written that he prefers to emphasize sections I, IV, and V in his methods course, whereas another colleague writes that she uses sections II and III as the core of her methods course. Different instructors and different training programs emphasize different things. This is understandable.

I personally like to give students options when assigning chapters to read. For example, after everyone has read and discussed the five chapters in Part I, students can select chapters that best meet their current or anticipated future needs:

- Read either one of the two chapters on listening.
- Read any two of the three chapters on speaking.
- Read any two of the four chapters on reading and so on.

Another approach I have used is to ask everyone to skim a particular section of the book (or subsection in Part II) but then to let students form pairs or small groups that are responsible for presenting and leading discussion on individual chapters. (The instructor should, of course, provide a model and explicit guidelines for what is expected in such a presentation.)

The textbook chapters that are not covered in a course as a result of needs analysis and careful selection then become useful reference material for the teacher in training, whose interests and needs and target students may well change after completion of the methods course and the training program. If one goes overseas or works in a somewhat remote area, it is useful to have one comprehensive reference for language methodology. I have attempted here to compile and edit such a reference.

It goes without saying that I welcome comments and feedback on this edition. We all have much to learn from each other.

Contributors

Robert W. Blair (Ph.D., Indiana University, 1964) is Professor of Linguistics at Brigham Young University. He is the author-editor of *Innovative Approaches to Language Teaching* (Newbury House, 1982), with a second edition of this book in preparation. In addition to his being an experimentalist in alternative language teaching approaches, Professor Blair's teaching and research interests include language acquisition, sociolinguistics, and native languages of North and South America. He has published grammars and dictionaries on several Amerindian languages.

Donna M. Brinton (M.A., University of California, Los Angeles, 1981) is Administrative Coordinator of ESL courses and a lecturer for the TESL/Applied Linguistics Department at UCLA. In her capacity as lecturer she teaches various courses in TESL methodology, and media, and supervises the field practicum. Ms. Brinton has published a number of articles on curriculum issues and teacher training, and is a coauthor of two books in the field: *Getting Along: English Grammar and Writing* (Prentice-Hall, 1982) and *Content-Based Second Language Instruction* (Newbury House, 1989). Prior to joining the TESL faculty at UCLA, Ms. Brinton taught general English and ESP courses to adult learners in Germany.

David Bycina (M.A., University of Hawaii at Manoa, 1983) is Supervisor of Instruction at the American Language Institute, University of Southern California. In addition to his master's degree, he also holds a British Royal Society of Arts Certificate in Teaching English as a Foreign Language. He has taught EFL in Germany and Japan as well as ESL in the United States. He has contributed articles and reviews to a variety of publications and is coauthor, with Jack Richards, of *Person to Person* (Oxford University Press, Vol. 1, 1984; Vol. 2, 1985).

Marianne Celce-Murcia (Ph.D., University of California, Los Angeles, 1972) is Professor of TESL and Applied Linguistics at UCLA, where since 1972 she has been teaching grammar and discourse and also language methodology and materials development. Professor Celce-Murcia has worked outside the United States in Nigeria (1964–1966), Egypt (1980), and Canada (1983), and has served TESOL as Associate Convention Chair, Editorial Advisory Board member, and Executive Board member-at-large. She is editor of *Beyond Basics: Issues and Research in TESOL*

(1985) and coauthor with Diane Larsen-Freeman of *The Grammar Book: An ESL/EFL Teacher's Course* (1983), both with Newbury House. She is also coauthor with Sharon Hilles of *Techniques and Resources in Teaching Grammar*, Oxford University Press, (1988).

Craig Chaudron (Ph.D., University of Toronto, 1982) is Associate Professor in the Department of English as a Second Language, University of Hawaii at Manoa. He has taught ESL/EFL and Applied Linguistics in Europe and Canada, and at several U.S. universities. He was Director of the Center for Second Language Classroom Research, University of Hawaii, for three years, and has published in the areas of classroom research, second language acquisition, research methods, and listening comprehension. He is currently coeditor of *Applied Linguistics*.

Andrew D. Cohen (Ph.D., Stanford University, 1973) is Professor of Language Education in the School of Education, Hebrew University, Jerusalem, Israel. He has also taught in the ESL section at UCLA (1972—1975, 1980—1981). Professor Cohen has published numerous articles in the fields of language learning, teaching, and testing. His books include *Testing Language Ability in the Classroom* (1980), *A Sociolinguistic Approach to Bilingual Education* (1975), and *Language Learning: Insights for Learners, Teachers, and Researchers* (1990) all with Newbury House.

JoAnn Crandall (Ph.D., Georgetown University, 1982) is Vice President and Director of International and Corporate Education at the Center for Applied Linguistics in Washington, D.C., where she has been involved in a number of teacher education, curriculum development, and technical assistance projects in ESL. She has served as Director of the Language and Orientation Resource Center, an information clearinghouse and technical assistance center for refugees; directed training of trainers projects for the Peace Corps for Sri Lanka, Thailand, Nepal, and China; conducted needs assessments of English language teaching in Central America and Indonesia; and directed curriculum developments projects in adult vocational ESL and elementary content-based ESL. She has served on the Executive Board of TESOL as Affiliate Representative, First Vice President, and President (1987–1988), and as Chair of the Long Range Planning and Policy Committee.

Graham Crookes (Ph.D., University of Hawaii, 1988) is Assistant Professor in the Department of English as a Second Language, University of Hawaii at Manoa. He has taught ESL and Applied Linguistics in England, Malaysia, Japan, and the United States, and has published in *TESOL Quarterly, Applied Linguistics,* and *Studies in Second Language Acquisition*. His research interests include teacher training, materials and syllabus design, and classroom research.

Fraida Dubin (Ph.D., University of California, Los Angeles, 1971) is Associate Professor in the Department of Higher, Adult, and Professional Education at the University of Southern California. She has been a teacher trainer, program director, course designer, and materials writer both in California, her native state, and in other parts of the world: India, Greece, Iran, Israel, Botswana, and Hungary. She has coauthored and coedited books for teachers: *Facilitating Language Learning* (McGraw-Hill, 1977), *Course Design* (Cambridge University Press, 1986), and *Teaching Second Language Reading for Academic Purposes* (Addison-Wesley, 1986). She has also coauthored textbooks for students: *It's Time to Talk* (Prentice-Hall, 1977) and, with Addison-Wesley, *Reading by All Means* (1981), *Three Easy Pieces* (1984), and *Reading on Purpose* (1987). Her focus as an author and researcher is on the uses of language and literacy in society.

D. Scott Enright (Ph.D., Stanford University, 1982) is an Associate Professor of Educational Foundations, Early Childhood Education, and Applied Linguistics/ESL at Georgia State University in Atlanta, where he teaches TESL methods and qualitative research methodology. He is a former bilingual elementary school teacher in Kindergarten—Grade 2. His research and writing interests center on children's classroom language use and on home—school language connections. He is a member of TESOL's Executive Board and a former editor of the Brief Reports and Summaries section of the *TESOL Quarterly*. His publications include *Children and ESL: Integrating Perspectives*, coedited with Pat Rigg (TESOL, 1986) and *Integrating English: Developing English Language and Literacy in the Multilingual Classroom*, coauthored with Mary Lou McCloskey (Addison-Wesley, 1988).

Janet L. Eyring (Ph.D., University of California, Los Angeles, 1989) is Assistant Professor in the Foreign Languages and Literatures Department at California State University, Fullerton. Prior to that she had taught ESL for ten years in various settings: adult schools, binational centers, refugee projects, and university programs. She did research work on the effects of "project work" instruction in a university setting for her dissertation in Applied Linguistics at UCLA. Other interests include teaching literacy, grammar, writing, culture in the ESL classroom, intercultural communication, and curriculum development.

Jan Frodesen (Ph.D., University of California, Los Angeles, 1991) is a lecturer in the Writing Programs at UCLA. As a teaching assistant at UCLA from 1984 to 1989, she taught composition to both native and nonnative English speakers. Her prior composition teaching experience includes three years of high school English. She has also taught intensive ESL as a graduate teaching fellow at the University of Oregon and vocational ESL to American immigrants and refugees in New York City. Her interests include discourse analysis, composition theory and pedagogy, and ESL curriculum development.

Janet M. Goodwin (M.A., University of California, Los Angeles, 1983) is a lecturer in ESL at UCLA, where she has served as intermediate ESL/oral skills supervisor since 1986. She has previously taught EFL/ESP in Germany and intensive ESL at the Experiment in International Living in Brattleboro, Vermont. As a Fulbright Lecturer, she also trained EFL teachers in Italy from 1983 to 1985. She has presented professional papers at state and national TESOL conventions on pronunciation, oral proficiency testing, the foreign TA issue, in-service teacher training, the use of dialog journals in TESL, and reading.

Wayne W. Haverson (Ed.D., University of Northern Colorado, 1975) is a Professor of Postsecondary Education and the Coordinator of Graduate Programs in the School of Education at Oregon State University, where he teaches courses in English as a second language methodology and adult literacy. He has served as the Staff Development Coordinator for the Oregon Adult Basic Education and Refugee Programs, a regional trainer for the Center for Applied Linguistics Refugee Technical Assistance Program, and a member of the Mainstream English Language Training project. A frequent presenter at regional and national conferences, Dr. Haverson has presented invited papers and workshops in Canada, Thailand, Japan, Hong Kong, the Philippines and the Netherlands. The author of numerous articles on ESL literacy, Professor Haverson's has most recently published *Celebration: Festivities for Reading*, coauthored with his wife, Susan.

Barbara Hawkins (Ph.D., University of California, Los Angeles, 1988) is a Staff Associate/Resource Teacher at Encinita Elementary School in Rosemead, California. In her position, she is involved with on-site teacher training in reading and language arts for teachers of both ESL and monolingual English students. She is also responsible for the development and execution of the programs for the federally funded Chapter I Reading/Writing Laboratory at the school. She has taught ESL in the United States in grades K–12, and at the university level as well. She has also taught EFL in Spain for two years (1975—1977). Her areas of interest are second language acquisition and education; the relationship involving language, cognition, and social knowledge; discourse analysis; classroom interaction; and the metalinguistic awareness of children.

Sharon Hilles (Ph.D., University of California, Los Angeles, 1989) is Assistant Professor of English at California Polytechnic University, Pomona. During the past 12 years she has taught ESL at all levels in Los Angeles area adult schools and served as ESL Department Chair at Belmont Adult School. She has also taught composition and trained ESL teachers at UCLA. She is coauthor of *Techniques and Resources in Teaching Grammar* (Oxford University Press, 1988) and has published several articles on second language acquisition. Her research and teaching interests include second language acquisition, ethnographic research, and second language teaching methodology and pedagogy.

Thom Hudson (Ph.D., University of California, Los Angeles, 1989) is Assistant Professor of English as a Second Language at the University of Hawaii, Manoa. From fall 1987 to summer 1989, he was a Fulbright Professor at the Universidad de Guadalajara, Mexico (UdeG), and was the UCLA Chief of Party directing the Reading English for Science and Technology Project in the Faculty of Chemical Engineering at the UdeG. Previously (1978–1981), Dr. Hudson worked as an EFL materials writer, teacher, and coordinator for the Curriculum Development Project of the Centre for Developing English Language Teaching at Ain Shams University in Cairo, Egypt. In addition to these two projects, Dr. Hudson has also worked as a language test developer and Program Director for National Education Corporation, International, and as an ESL teacher at UCLA and elsewhere. His research interests include language testing, reading, curriculum and materials development, and English for Specific Purposes.

Ann M. Johns (Ph.D., University of Southern California, 1979) is a Professor of Academic Skills and Linguistics at San Diego State University and coeditor of *English for Specific Purposes: An International Journal*. She has led ESP teacher training institutes in Egypt, China, and Pakistan, as well at her own university, where she also directs the Writing-Across-the-Curriculum Program and an Adjunct English-for-Academic-Purposes Project for linguistically diverse freshman students. Professor John's recent research and publications have focused upon student summarizing skills, the teaching of EAP reading and writing, issues in empowering students in a university culture, and features of text coherence. On the topic of coherence, she has coedited a volume entitled *Coherence: Research and Pedagogical Perspectives* for TESOL (1989).

Barbara Kroll (Ph.D., University of Southern California, 1982) is an Assistant Professor of English and linguistics in the Department of English at California State University, Northridge, where she is also involved in the training of teaching assistants for the freshman composition program. She previously taught in the TESL/Applied Linguistics Programs at UCLA, the Department of Linguistics at the University of California, Santa Barbara, and the Department of ESL at the University of Hawaii. She began her ESL/EFL career as a teacher of English language skills at Ben-Gurion University of the Negev (1970–1974) in Beersheva, Israel. Dr. Kroll has given frequent conference presentations at the local, state, national, and international level, most often discussing issues in the teaching of writing. She has recently edited *Second Language Writing: Research Insights for the Classroom* (Cambridge University Press, 1990), an anthology of articles for writing researchers and teachers in training.

Diane Larsen-Freeman (Ph.D., University of Michigan, 1975) is a Senior Faculty Member in the M.A.T. Program at the School for International Training in Brattleboro, Vermont. From 1975 to 1978 she was an Assistant Professor of English in the ESL Section at UCLA. Prior to teaching at UCLA, Dr. Larsen-Freeman taught EFL for two years in Malaysia as a Peace Corps volunteer and then for two years at the University of Michigan's English Language Institute. Her publications include *Discourse Analysis and Second Language Research* (Newbury House, 1980), *The Grammar Book: An ESL/EFL Teacher's Course* (with M. Celce-Murcia) (Newbury House 1983), *Techniques and Principles in Language Teaching* (Oxford University Press, 1986), and *An Introduction to Second Language Acquisition Research* (with M. Long) (Longman, 1990). Dr. Larsen-Freeman is currently editing a grammar series for ESL/EFL students (Newbury House). From 1980 to 1985 Dr. Larsen-Freeman was editor of the journal *Language Learning*.

Anne Lazaraton (M.A., University of California, Los Angeles, 1985) is a doctoral candidate in Applied Linguistics at UCLA. She has taught ESL and science in the Kingdom of Tonga as a Peace Corps volunteer and English for Academic Purposes to university students in California. She has published and presented papers on discourse analysis, oral proficiency testing, and research methodology. Along with Evelyn Hatch she has coauthored *The Research Manual: Design and Statistics for Applied Linguistics* (Newbury House, 1990). In 1985 she was the chairperson for the Los Angeles Second Language Research Forum held at UCLA.

Brian Lynch (Ph.D., University of California, Los Angeles, 1987) is Assistant Adjunct Professor of TESL/Applied Linguistics at the University of California, Los Angeles, where he also serves as Academic Director of ESL Service Courses. From fall 1985 to summer 1987, he was a Fulbright Professor at the Universidad de Guadalajara (UdeG), Mexico, and was the UCLA Chief of Party for the initial two years of the Reading English for Science and Technology Project in the Faculty of Chemical Engineering at the UdeG. Dr. Lynch has also worked as a teacher and researcher for the Guangzhou English Language Center (GELC) at Zhongshan University (August 1980 to July 1981). In addition to this EFL experience, Dr. Lynch worked as a language test developer for National Education Corporation, International, and as an ESL teacher at UCLA. His research interests include language testing, program evaluation, reading, and English for Specific Purposes.

Mary McGroarty (Ph.D., Stanford University, 1982) is Associate Professor in the Applied Linguistics Program of the English Department at Northern Arizona University. She was previously a member of the TESL/Applied Linguistics faculty at UCLA for six years and has worked with several language education programs in the United States and abroad. Her research and teaching interests include theoretical and pedagogic aspects of bilingualism, the nature of language skills, and cultural influences on language learning and teaching. She has published in the *TESOL Quarterly*, the *NABE Journal*, the *Canadian Modern Language Review*, and several anthologies.

Joan Morley (M.A., University of Michigan, 1968) is Associate Professor of Linguistics and former Deputy Director of the English Language Institute. She has specialized in instructional research and the development of materials and methodologies for learners of English as a Second Language. Her interests include Applied Linguistics and language learning and teaching, both theory and practice, with an emphasis on aspects of aural comprehension, oral communication, pronunciation, and self-access self-study instructional modules; she has published a number of articles and books in these areas. Her Linguistics specialty is English Phonetics and Phonology. She was TESOL Second Vice President (1976–1977) and Chair of the 11th Annual TESOL

Convention, TESOL '77 in Miami Beach. She was TESOL President (1986–1987) and served three terms on the TESOL Executive Board for a total of 10 years.

Elite Olshtain (Ph.D., University of California, 1979) teaches Second Language Acquisition, Discourse Analysis, and Classroom Oriented Research at the School of Education and the Department of Linguistics at Tel Aviv University, where she served as department head for 10 years. From 1984 to 1989 she was Head of Teacher Education at Tel Aviv University. Professor Olshtain has coordinated teams of material developers in TEFL, the Teaching of Hebrew, French, and Arabic as Foreign Languages, and Computer Courseware. From 1978 to 1984 she worked with an in-service program designed to prepare Italian teachers of English as teacher trainers. She has trained language teachers in various countries, such as the United States, Israel, Italy, Spain, Mexico, and Brazil. She has published professional articles in journals and anthologies and is coauthor (with Fraida Dubin) of *Facilitating Language Learning* (McGraw-Hill, 1977), *Reading by All Means* (Addison-Wesley, 1981), *Three Easy Pieces* (Addison-Wesley, 1984), *Reading on Purpose* (Addison-Wesley, 1986), and *Course Design* (Cambridge University Press, 1986).

Sabrina Peck (Ph.D., University of California, Los Angeles, 1985) is Assistant Professor of Elementary Education at California State University, Northridge. She spent four years as an elementary school teacher in Boston and in St. Croix, U.S. Virgin Islands. She taught EFL to high school students and directed an EFL teachers' seminar for two summers in Peru. In 1986 she designed and directed the Spanish for Social Workers program at the UCLA School of Social Welfare. Her publications include *Second Language Acquisition Studies* (Newbury House, 1983), coedited with Kathleen Bailey and Michael Long, as well as articles dealing with child second language acquisition, ESL methods, and Spanish for social workers.

Pat Wilcox Peterson (Ph.D., University of Minnesota, 1989) is Assistant Professor in the Foreign Language Department at Mankato State University in Minnesota. Her dissertation examined nonnative speakers' ability to use both top-down and bottom-up processing strategies in comprehending academic lectures. She has coauthored (with Jean Sims) a listening comprehension text, *Better Listening Skills* (Prentice-Hall, 1981) and has also published four books with the U.S. Information Agency on grammar review, elementary writing skills, and ESP (a reader and an anthology on curriculum and program development). Professor Peterson has also published several articles on content-based language teaching, which is another of her interests.

Clifford H. Prator (Ph.D., University of Michigan, 1939) was a Professor of English at UCLA, where for almost thirty years he was responsible for the direction of all ESL work. He has also been instrumental in the development of the Philippine Center for Language Study in Manila, the Instituto Colombo-Americano in Bogota, and the Center for Developing English Language Teaching at Ain Shams University in Cairo, Egypt. In 1967-1968 he was Field Director of the survey of Language Use and Language Teaching in Eastern Africa, sponsored by the Ford Foundation. As Professor Emeritus at UCLA since 1979, his major interests have been the training of teacher-specialists in ESL and questions of language policy. His *Manual of American English Pronunciation* (Holt, Rinehart & Winston, 1985) and the *English Language Policy Survey of Jordan*, of which he was a coauthor (Center for Applied Linguistics, 1975) are perhaps his best known publications. He has been awarded the Philippine Legion of Honor for his services to Philippine education.

Katherine Barnhouse Purgason (M.A., University of Pittsburgh, 1980) is a doctoral candidate in Applied Linguistics at UCLA. She has been training teachers in the TESOL program at William

Carey International University in Pasadena, California since 1982. In 1986 she taught TEFL methodology at Gazi University, Ankara, Turkey, as a Fulbright lecturer. Under the auspices of Oberlin College's Shansi program for international educational exchange, she taught EFL from 1975 to 1977 in Seoul, Korea, and from 1980 to 1982 in Shanxi, People's Republic of China. She has given presentations on English for Specific Purposes at state and national TESL conventions. Her research interests include teacher training, curriculum development, and distance education.

Heidi Riggenbach (Ph.D., University of California, Los Angeles, 1989) is an Assistant Professor of Applied Linguistics at the University of Washington, Seattle. She taught ESL in China for the UCLA/China exchange program in 1982–1984, and in 1987–1988 was awarded a Fulbright lectureship in Penang, Malaysia, where she taught courses in methodology and linguistics at the Universiti Sains Malaysia. Her publications have been in the areas of materials development, language pedagogy, and discourse analysis.

Janice Schreck (Ph.D., University of Illinois, 1981) is Director of Educational Evaluation for the Consortium for Learning, Evaluation, and Research. She previously was a faculty member in the College of Education at the University of Illinois, where she taught psychometrics, reading methodology, and instructional design. She has developed and implemented individualized reading programs for university-level ESOL programs in the United States and abroad and has also taught in Africa and the Middle East. She has designed and taught courses for major U.S. corporations in computer-based learning and delivery, served as a consultant to both public and private educational agencies in instructional design and development, and evaluated educational software both during developmental phases and after publication.

Richard Schreck (Ph.D., University of Illinois, 1978) is Director of International Programs at the University of Maryland, University College, where he administers international academic programs as well as cross-cultural training for both U.S. and foreign corporations involved in international business and management. He previously taught in the Division of ESL at the University of Illinois and the ELI at the University of Michigan, and additionally served as director of UCLA's programs at the Centre for Developing English Language Teaching at Ain Shams University in Cairo, Egypt, and as Associate Director of the Language and Culture Center at the University of Houston. He has published and presented papers on various aspects of Computer-Assisted Language Learning (CALL) and was editor of On Line, the TESOL Newsletter's column on CALL.

Bernard D. Seal (M.A., University of California, Los Angeles, 1981) is a supervisor at the American Language Institute, University of Southern California, where his work involves teaching ESL, teacher training, materials and curriculum development, and course supervision. An author of several ESL textbooks, Mr. Seal has a long-standing interest in the teaching of vocabulary. In 1987 and 1988, Longman published his two vocabulary textbooks: *Vocabulary Builder 1* and *Vocabulary Builder 2*, which are now also available in American editions. His other interests include the use of video in ESL, techniques in the teaching of oral communication skills, strategies for the independent language learner, and adjunct course design. He is editing a content-based college ESL series for Newbury House.

Alexandra Skierso (M.A., University of California, Los Angeles, 1979) is currently working in educational administration at UCLA. Previously, she had taught EFL at the Division of English Auxiliary Studies at Tel Aviv University, Israel, and while there served as curriculum developer for the 1,000 students in the intermediate EFL course in the fall of 1979.

Marguerite Ann Snow (Ph.D., University of California, Los Angeles, 1985) is an Assistant Professor of Education in the TESOL Programs at California State University, Los Angeles, where she teaches courses in the theory and methods of second language learning and teaching. In 1985 she had a Fulbright fellowship to Hong Kong and more recently has trained English teachers in Hungary. Her interests include teacher training, ESL methods, content-based instruction, and immersion foreign language education. She is coauthor with Donna Brinton and Marjorie B. Wesche of *Content-Based Second Language Instruction* (Newbury House, 1989).

Susan L. Stern (Ph.D., University of California, Los Angeles, 1985), is Professor of English as a Second Language at Irvine Valley College in Irvine, California. She has also taught a variety of ESL courses at the University of California, Irvine (1986–1990) and at UCLA (1976–1980), and worked as a project coordinator in testing research and development for the International Division of National Education Corporation (1984–1985). Her primary research interests are the teaching of literature in ESL/EFL, drama/role playing in second language learning, and oral communication.

I
Teaching Methodology

In this section of the textbook Celce-Murcia first gives an overview of nine approaches to language teaching that have made a mark on the teaching of English as a second or foreign language. Then, in the next chapter, Prator identifies and discusses his candidates for the three foundations of ESL methodology; he also gives background on the growth and consolidation of the TESOL profession in the United States. Blair's chapter introduces the reader to an impressive array of innovative methods that have been proposed for teaching second and foreign languages. The chapter by Crookes and Chaudron discusses classroom research and its implications for developing a principled approach to classroom language teaching, while the chapter by Johns introduces the reader to the English-for-Specific-Purposes movement along with its many influences on general English language teaching.

Taken collectively, I feel that these five chapters give the reader a good idea of where the field is, and where it may be headed.

Language Teaching Approaches:

An Overview[1]

Marianne Celce-Murcia

INTRODUCTION

The field of second (or foreign) language teaching has undergone many fluctuations and dramatic shifts over the years. As opposed to physics or chemistry, where progress is more or less steady until a major discovery causes a radical theoretical revision (Kuhn, 1970), language teaching is a field where fads and heroes have come and gone in a manner fairly consistent with the kinds of changes that occur in youth culture. I believe that one reason for the frequent changes that have been taking place until recently is the fact that very few language teachers have even the vaguest sense of history about their profession and are unclear concerning the historical bases of the many methodological options they currently have at their disposal. It is hoped that this brief and necessarily oversimplified survey will encourage many language teachers to learn more about the origins of their profession. Such knowledge will give some healthy perspective in evaluating the so-called innovations or new approaches

to methodology that will continue to emerge over time.

PRE-20TH-CENTURY TRENDS: A BRIEF SURVEY

Prior to this century, language teaching methodology vacillated between two types of approaches: one type of approach which focused on *using* a language (i.e., speaking and understanding), the other type which focused on *analyzing* a language (i.e., learning the grammatical rules).

Both the Classical Greek and Medieval Latin periods were characterized by an emphasis on teaching people to use foreign languages. The classical languages, first Greek and then Latin, were used as *lingua francas*. Higher learning was given only in these languages all over Europe. They were also used very widely in philosophy or religion, politics, and business. Thus the educated elite became fluent speakers, readers, and writers of the appropriate classical language. We can

3

assume that the teachers or tutors used informal and direct approaches to convey the form and meaning of the language they were teaching and that they used aural-oral techniques with no language textbooks per se, but rather a small stock of hand-copied written manuscripts of some sort, perhaps a few texts in the target language, or crude dictionaries that listed equivalent words in two or more languages side by side.

Later during the Renaissance the formal study of the grammars of Greek and Latin became popular through the mass production made possible by the invention of the printing press. In the case of Latin, it was discovered that the grammar of the classical texts was different from that of the Latin being used as a *lingua franca*—the latter subsequently being labeled Vulgate Latin, i.e., the Latin of the common people. Eventually major differences developed between the Classical Latin described in the Renaissance grammars, which became the formal object of instruction in schools, and the Latin being used for everyday purposes. This occurred at the same time that Latin was being abandoned as a *lingua franca*. (No one was speaking Classical Latin anymore, and various European vernaculars had begun to rise in respectability and popularity.) Thus in retrospect, strange as it may seem, the Renaissance preoccupation with the formal study of Classical Latin may have contributed to the demise of Latin as a *lingua franca* in Western Europe.

Since the European vernaculars had increased in prestige and utility, it is not surprising that people in one country or region began to find it necessary and useful to learn the language of another country or region. Thus the focus in language study shifted back to utility rather than analysis during the 17th century. Perhaps the most famous language teacher and methodologist of this period is Jan Comenius, a Czech, who published books about his teaching techniques between 1631 and 1658. Some of the techniques that he used and espoused were the following:

- Use imitation instead of rules to teach a language.
- Have your students repeat after you.
- Use a limited vocabulary initially.
- Help your students practice reading and speaking.
- Teach language through pictures to make it meaningful.

Thus, Comenius, for the first time, made explicit an inductive approach to learning a foreign language, the goal of which was to teach use rather than analysis of the language being taught.

Comenius's views held sway for some time; however, by the beginning of the 19th century the systematic study of the grammar of Classical Latin and of classical texts had once again taken over in schools and universities throughout Europe. The analytical grammar-translation approach became firmly entrenched, as a method for teaching not only Latin but modern languages as well. It was perhaps best codified in the work of Karl Ploetz, a German scholar, who had a tremendous influence on the language teaching profession during his lifetime and afterwards (he died in 1881).

True to form, however, the swinging of the pendulum continued. By the end of the 19th century the Direct Method, which once more stressed the ability to use rather than to analyze a language as the goal of language instruction, had been established as a viable alternative. Gouin, a Frenchman, began to publish in 1880 concerning his work with the Direct Method. He had been influenced by an older friend, the German philosopher-scientist Alexander von Humboldt, who had expressed the following notion:

A language cannot be taught. One can only create conditions for learning to take place.

The Direct Method crossed the Atlantic in the early 20th century when de Sauzé, a disciple of Gouin, came to Cleveland, Ohio in order to see to it that all foreign language instruction in the public schools there reflected the Direct Method.

De Sauzé's endeavor was not completely successful (in Cleveland or elsewhere) since there were too few foreign language teachers who were fluent speakers of the language they were teaching. This later led the Modern Language Association of America to endorse the Reading Approach to language teaching, since given the skills and limitations of most language teachers, the most one could reasonably expect is that students would come away from the study of a foreign language with an ability to read the target language—with emphasis on some of the great works of literature that had been produced in the language.

The Reading Approach, as reflected in the work of Michael West (1941) and others, held sway until the 1940s, when World War II once more made it imperative for the U.S. military to teach foreign language learners how to speak and understand a language quickly and efficiently. At this time, the U.S. government hired linguists to help teach languages and develop materials: The audiolingual approach, which drew heavily on structural linguistics and behavioral psychology, was born. In Britain the same historical pressures gave rise to the Situational Approach (e.g., Pittman, 1963), which drew on Firthian Linguistics and the experience of Britain's language educators with oral approaches to foreign language teaching. Although somewhat influenced by, but less dogmatic than, its American counterpart (i.e., the Audiolingual Approach), the Situational Approach advocated organizing structures around situations that would provide the learner with maximum opportunity to practice the target language, with "practice" nonetheless often meaning little more than choral repetition.

NINE 20TH-CENTURY APPROACHES TO LANGUAGE TEACHING

In addition to the Grammar-Translation Approach, the Direct Approach,[2] the Reading Approach, Audiolingualism, and the Situational Approach—whose historical development we have now sketched out briefly—

there are four other discernible approaches to foreign language teaching that have been widely used during this era, the final quarter of the 20th century. Thus, there are nine approaches altogether that I shall be referring to:

1. Grammar-Translation Approach
2. Direct Approach
3. Reading Approach
4. Audiolingualism (U.S.)
5. Situational Approach (Brit.)
6. Cognitive Approach
7. Affective-Humanistic Approach
8. Comprehension-Based Approach
9. Communicative Approach

However, before specifying the features of each approach, I would like to digress a moment to clarify some terminology that is crucial to this discussion. Namely, what do we mean by the terms "approach," "method," and "technique"? Are these terms synonymous? If not, how do they differ? Anthony (1963) has provided a useful set of definitions for our purposes. An *approach* to language teaching is something that reflects a certain model or research paradigm—a theory, if you like. This term is the broadest of the three. A *method,* on the other hand, is a set of procedures, i.e., a system that spells out rather precisely how to teach a language. Methods are more specific than approaches but less specific than techniques. Methods are typically compatible with one (or sometimes two) approaches. A *technique* is a classroom device or activity and thus represents the narrowest term of the three concepts. Some techniques are widely used and found in many methods (e.g., imitation and repetition); however, some techniques are specific to or characteristic of a given method (e.g., using cuisinaire rods = the Silent Way). See Blair's discussion of the Silent Way in the following chapter.

At this point I would like to outline each of the nine approaches listed above. In addition, I will note any special proficiency or role that the teacher is expected (or not expected) to fulfill.

1. **Grammar-Translation Approach** (an extension of the approach used to teach classical languages to the teaching of modern languages).
   a. Instruction is given in the native language of the students.
   b. There is little use of the target language.
   c. Focus is on grammatical parsing, i.e., the form and inflection of words.
   d. There is early reading of difficult classical texts.
   e. A typical exercise is to translate sentences from the target language into the mother tongue.
   f. The result of this approach is usually an inability on the part of the student to use the language for communication.
   g. The teacher does not have to be able to speak the target language.
2. **Direct Approach** (a reaction to the grammar-translation approach and its failure to produce learners who could use the foreign language they had been studying).
   a. No use of the mother tongue is permitted (i.e., teacher does not need to know the students' native language).
   b. Lessons begin with dialogs and anecdotes in modern conversational style.
   c. Actions and pictures are used to make meanings clear.
   d. Grammar is learned inductively.
   e. Literary texts are read for pleasure and are not analyzed grammatically.
   f. The target culture is also taught inductively.
   g. The teacher must be a native speaker or have nativelike proficiency in the target language.
3. **Reading Approach** (a reaction to the impracticality of the direct approach; reading was viewed as the most usable skill to have in a foreign language since not many people traveled abroad around 1930; also, few teachers could use a foreign language well enough to use a direct approach in class).
   a. Only the grammar useful for reading comprehension is taught.
   b. Vocabulary is controlled at first (based on frequency and usefulness) and then expanded.
   c. Translation is once more a respectable classroom procedure.
   d. Reading comprehension is the only language skill emphasized.
   e. The teacher does not need to have good oral proficiency in the target language.
4. **Audiolingualism** (a reaction to the reading approach and its lack of emphasis on oral-aural skills; this approach became dominant in the United States during the 1940s, 1950s, and 1960s; it takes much from the direct approach but adds features from structural linguistics and behavioral psychology).
   a. Lessons begin with dialogs.
   b. Mimicry and memorization are used, based on the assumption that language is habit formation.
   c. Grammatical structures are sequenced and rules are taught inductively.
   d. Skills are sequenced: listening, speaking—reading, writing postponed.
   e. Pronunciation is stressed from the beginning.
   f. Vocabulary is severely limited in initial stages.
   g. A great effort is made to prevent learner errors.
   h. Language is often manipulated without regard to meaning or context.
   i. The teacher must be proficient only in the structures, vocabulary, etc. that s/he is teaching since learning activities and materials are carefully controlled.
5. **Situational Approach** (a reaction to the reading approach and its lack of

emphasis on oral-aural skills; this approach was dominant in Britain during the 1940s, 1950s, and 1960s; it draws much from the direct approach but adds features from Firthian Linguistics and the emerging professional field of language pedagogy).

a. The spoken language is primary.
b. All language material is practiced orally before being presented in written form (reading and writing are taught only after an oral base in lexical and grammatical forms has been established).
c. Only the target language should be used in the classroom.
d. Efforts are made to ensure that the most general and useful lexical items are presented.
e. Grammatical structures are graded from simple to complex.
f. New items (lexical and grammatical) are introduced and practiced situationally (e.g., at the post office, at the bank, at the dinner table).

6. **Cognitive Approach** (a reaction to the behaviorist features of the audiolingual approach).

a. Language learning is viewed as rule acquisition, not habit formation.
b. Instruction is often individualized; learners are responsible for their own learning.
c. Grammar must be taught but it can be taught deductively (rules first, practice later) and/or inductively (rules can either be stated after practice or left as implicit information for the learners to process on their own).
d. Pronunciation is de-emphasized; perfection is viewed as unrealistic.
e. Reading and writing are once again as important as listening and speaking.
f. Vocabulary instruction is important, especially at intermediate and advanced levels.
g. Errors are viewed as inevitable, something that should be used constructively in the learning process.
h. The teacher is expected to have good general proficiency in the target language as well as an ability to analyze the target language.

7. **Affective-Humanistic[3] Approach** (a reaction to the general lack of affective considerations in both audiolingualism and cognitive code).

a. Respect is emphasized for the individual (each student, the teacher) and for his/her feelings.
b. Communication that is meaningful to the learner is emphasized.
c. Instruction involves much work in pairs and small groups.
d. Class atmosphere is viewed as more important than materials or methods.
e. Peer support and interaction is needed for learning.
f. Learning a foreign language is viewed as a self-realization experience.
g. The teacher is viewed as a counselor or facilitator.
h. The teacher should be proficient in the target language and the student's native language since translation may be used heavily in the initial stages to help students feel at ease; later it is gradually phased out.

8. **Comprehension-Based Approach** (an outgrowth of research in first language acquisition, which led some language methodologists to assume that second or foreign language learning is very similar to first language acquisition).

a. Listening comprehension is very important and is viewed as the basic skill that will allow speaking, reading, and writing to develop spontaneously over time given the right conditions.
b. Learners should begin by listening to meaningful speech and by responding nonverbally in

meaningful ways before they produce any language themselves.

c. Learners should not speak until they feel ready to do so; this results in better pronunciation than when the learner is forced to speak immediately.

d. Learners progress by being exposed to meaningful input that is just one step beyond their level of competence.

e. Rule learning may help learners monitor (or become aware of) what they do, but it will not aid their acquisition or spontaneous use of the target language.

f. Error correction is seen as unnecessary and perhaps even counterproductive; the important thing is that the learners can understand and can make themselves understood.

g. If the teacher is not a native speaker (or near-native), appropriate materials such as audiotapes and videotapes must be available to provide the appropriate input for the learners.

9. **Communicative Approach** (grew out of the work of anthropological linguists (e.g., Hymes, 1972) and Firthian linguists (e.g., Halliday, 1973), who view language first and foremost as a system for communication).

a. It is assumed that the goal of language teaching is learner ability to communicate in the target language.

b. It is assumed that the content of a language course will include semantic notions and social functions, not just linguistic structures.

c. Students regularly work in groups or pairs to transfer (and, if necessary, negotiate) meaning in situations where one person has information that the other(s) lack.

d. Students often engage in role-play or dramatization to adjust their use of the target language to different social contexts.

e. Classroom materials and activities are often authentic to reflect real-life situations and demands.

f. Skills are integrated from the beginning; a given activity might involve reading, speaking, listening, and perhaps also writing (this assumes the learners are educated and literate).

g. The teacher's role is primarily to facilitate communication and only secondarily to correct errors.

h. The teacher should be able to use the target language fluently and appropriately.

To sum up, we can see that certain features of several of the first five approaches outlined above arose in reaction to perceived inadequacies or impracticalities in an earlier approach or approaches. The four more recently developed approaches also do this to some extent; however, each one is grounded on a slightly different theory or view of how people learn second or foreign languages, or how people use languages, and each has a central point around which everything else revolves:

Cognitive Approach: Language is rule-governed cognitive behavior (not habit formation).

Affective-Humanistic Approach: Learning a foreign language is a process of self-realization and of relating to other people.

Comprehension Approach: Language acquisition occurs if and only if the learner comprehends meaningful input.

Communicative Approach: The purpose of language (and thus the goal of language teaching) is communication.

These four more recent approaches are not necessarily in conflict or totally incompatible since it is not impossible to conceive of an integrated approach which would include attention to rule formation, affect, comprehension, and communication and which would view the learner as someone who thinks, feels, understands, and has something to say. In fact, many teachers would find such an approach, if well conceived and well integrated, to be very attractive.

A NOTE ON APPROACH, METHOD, AND SYLLABUS TYPE

We now understand that an approach is general (e.g., Cognitive), that a method is a specific set of procedures more or less compatible with an approach (e.g., Silent Way), and that a technique is a very specific type of learning activity used in one or more methods (e.g., using rods to cue and facilitate language practice). Historically, an approach or method also tends to be used in conjunction with a syllabus, which is an inventory of things the learner should master; this inventory is sometimes presented in a recommended sequence and is used to design courses and teaching materials.

What sort of syllabuses have been used with the approaches discussed above? Most of them have used—implicitly or explicitly—a structural syllabus, which consists of a list of grammatical inflections and constructions that the teacher is expected to teach and the learner is expected to master. The Grammar-Translation Approach, the Direct Approach, the Audiolingual Approach, the Cognitive Approach, and even some methods following the Comprehension Approach have all employed a structural syllabus. In other words, teachers and textbook writers following these approaches have organized their language courses and language-teaching materials around grammar points.

In contrast to the structural syllabus, the Reading Approach is text based, and this kind of language course is organized around texts and vocabulary items with only minor consideration given to grammar.

In the Situational Approach, there is often a dual-objective syllabus in which various situations are specified for instruction (e.g., the post office, a restaurant, a bus, the doctor's office, etc.) along with some of the structures and the vocabulary that one might need to produce language in these situations.

In the Communicative Approach, one type of syllabus is organized around notions (meanings such as spatial location, age, degree) and functions (social transactions and interactions such as asking for information or complimenting someone). In this syllabus format (Wilkins, 1976), grammar and vocabulary are quite secondary, being taught not in and of themselves, but only insofar as they help express the notions and functions that are in focus. Some adherents of the Communicative Approach, however, reject any sort of atomistic syllabus, whether structural or notional functional. They advocate instead a communicative syllabus (i.e., a process-based or task-based syllabus) in which real-world tasks and materials are used to design language courses (see Yalden, 1983).

The Affective-Humanistic Approach has produced the most radical syllabus type—the learner-generated syllabus. Thus, in methods like Community Language Learning (see the following chapter by Blair) and Project Work (see the chapter by Eyring), the learners decide what they want to learn in—and do with—the target language.

CONCLUSION

What is the solution for the ESL/EFL teacher, given the abundance of current and future approaches? The only way to make wise decisions is to learn more about the specific methods available (see Blair, this volume). This chapter has just scratched the surface. Further information is available in books, in journal articles, at professional conferences, and at professional workshops. There are also four other things the teacher has to do to make a good decision concerning the choice of an approach or method (or a combination of these):

1. Assess student needs: Why should they be learning English? For what purpose?
2. Examine instructional constraints: time (hours per week, days per week, weeks per term); class size (nature of enrollment); materials (set syllabus and text—or completely open to teacher); physical factors (classroom size, AV support).
3. Determine needs, attitudes, and aptitudes of individual students to the extent that this is possible (see Peck, this volume).

Having done all these, the teacher will be in a position to derive useful techniques or principles by studying all the available approaches and methods. Clifford Prator, a former professor and current colleague of mine, sums up the professional ESL teacher's responsibility nicely:

Adapt; don't adopt.

A teacher is certainly in a better position to follow this advice if s/he is familiar with the history and the state of the art of our profession. References are provided below to aid the reader in the attainment of these objectives.

NOTES

1. Earlier versions of this chapter were published in the *Mextesol Journal* (Celce-Murcia, 1980) and *Practical English Teaching* (Celce-Murcia, 1981). This is an updated version based on many sources, notably Madsen (1979), Prator with Celce-Murcia (1979), and Kelly (1969). I am also grateful to Bob Blair for his feedback on an earlier version of this chapter.

2. The term "Direct Method" is more widely used than "Direct Approach"; however, the former is a misnomer, since it is really an approach, not a method, if we follow Anthony's terminology.

3. The term "humanistic" has two meanings. One meaning refers to the humanities (i.e., literature, history, philosophy). The other refers to that branch of psychology concerned with the role of the socioaffective domain in human behavior. It is the latter meaning that is being referred to here. However, see Stevick (1990) for an even broader perspective on humanism in language teaching.

QUESTIONS FOR DISCUSSION

1. What has been the attitude toward the teaching of (a) pronunciation, (b) grammar, (c) vocabulary in the nine approaches discussed in this chapter? Has there been a swinging of the pendulum? Why or why not?

2. What changes have occurred regarding the position of spoken language and written language in the various approaches? Why?

3. Which of these approaches have you personally experienced as a language learner? What were your impressions and what is your assessment of the effectiveness of the approach or method?

4. Which approach do you, as a teacher, feel most comfortable with? Why?

SUGGESTED ACTIVITIES

1. Select an integrated skills ESL/EFL text that you have used or expect to use. Examine its contents to determine which approach it seems to follow most closely. Support your decision with examples. Discuss any mixing of approaches that you observe.

2. Examine any English language proficiency test —standardized or otherwise. See if you can detect a methodological bias in the test. Support your conclusion(s) with examples.

3. What kinds of language learners do you teach (or expect to teach)? Be as specific as possible. Which approach would serve such a population best? Why?

SUGGESTIONS FOR FURTHER READING

Teachers interested in the history of the language teaching profession should consult:

Howatt, A. P. R. (1884)
A History of English Language Teaching. Oxford: Oxford University Press.

Kelly, L. G. (1969)
Twenty-five Centuries of Language Teaching. New York: Newbury House.

Teachers interested in the current state of the art in Language Teaching methodology should consult:

Larsen-Freeman, D. (1986)
Techniques and Principles in Language Teaching. Oxford: Oxford University Press.

Richards, J. C., and Rodgers, T. S. (1986)
Approaches and Methods in Language Teaching. New York: Cambridge University Press.

Stern, H. H. (1983)
Fundamental Concepts of Language Teaching. Oxford: Oxford University Press.

Cornerstones of Method and Names for the Profession[1]

Clifford H. Prator

THE SEARCH FOR A METHODOLOGY

A first dip into the literature on methods of teaching foreign languages is likely to be a puzzling, even a disheartening, experience. Conscientious teachers-to-be would presumably hope to find there a coherent system of ideas, built up in an orderly fashion by the contributions of successive generations of authorities who made every effort to base their recommendations on experimental evidence and scientific fact. What novices actually discover, if they sample the works on the subject written over the last 50 years, is something quite different.

In fact, the most striking feature of the history of language instruction, especially in the United States, appears to be the great diversity of the methodologies that have been propounded. At relatively brief intervals one highly touted "method" or "approach" has succeeded another in the favor of educators, and the proponents of each have tended to deny the validity of all that preceded. The use of the mother tongue in the foreign language classroom has been successively empha-sized, banned, required, and barely tolerated. The ability to speak the foreign tongue was once regarded as irrelevant. Then came the Direct Method, which made speaking its primary aim. But this was followed by the Reading Approach, whose proponents believed that the only language skill which could really be taught within the available time was reading. And later the triumphant Aural-Oral or Audiolingual Approach once again insisted on the primacy of speech. There have been similarly violent swings of the pendulum with regard to many other elements of language teaching: the role of rules, the use of phonetic symbols, vocabulary control, and the like.

New teachers will probably also be struck by the highly individualistic tone of much methodological literature. They will note that prophets have arisen—Gouin, De Sauzé, Berlitz, West, Kaulfers, Ogden, Fries, among others—who have built up large and often blindly enthusiastic groups of followers and who have been able to impose their somewhat closed systems of thought on a generation or more of disciples by their personal prestige and authority. Unlike the prophets of the Bible, however, these prophets of the language teaching profession have developed no coherent body of doctrine; indeed, their dominant ideas are to some extent mutually exclusive.

As these facts become clear to students, they are left with a series of deeply disturbing questions. Why does the pendulum swing so widely and rapidly from one extreme to another? Why have language teachers been able to achieve so little balance and continuity in their work? Is progress possible if it is continually necessary to begin over again? What reason is there to believe that the currently approved methodology will last any longer than have its predecessors? In short, in what is one to have faith, and why?

LANGUAGE TEACHING, AN ART OR A SCIENCE?

To judge by its pattern of development, language instruction has up to the present been rather more of an art than a science. That is to say, it has been largely intuitive, dependent on the personal skill and convictions of the teacher, and hence particularly subject to fads and abrupt about-faces. It has hardly been possible to see in it the characteristics of a systematically arranged body of knowledge developed through the use of time-tested and generally accepted methods.

Perhaps this is to some extent inevitable; the element of human nature and behavior, precisely the element that is most difficult to treat with scientific rigor, is so prominent in language teaching that it can probably never be made entirely explicable in scientific terms. The new teacher would do well, as a matter of principle, to distrust any methodologist who claims that enough is now known about the process of learning a language to permit the teaching of it in an absolutely scientific way.

Yet few thoughtful teachers would be willing to take the opposite position, that their profession is purely an art, basically unanalyzable and unteachable, to be improved only through the exercise of greater personal gifts of insight and imagination. In today's world, any educators worthy of the name are deeply uncomfortable if they cannot believe that their work bears some demonstrable relationship to established scientific fact. They cannot be happy in a situation where they can justify their actions only by their confidence in their own abilities, or by an appeal to the prestige of authority. They need a more durable and confidence-inspiring basis on which to build their work than the pronouncements of a single prophet.

The answer to the question that stands at the beginning of this section seems, then, to be that language teaching must be both an art *and* a science. To the extent that it remains an art, it permits individual teachers to exercise such personal gifts as they may be endowed with. To the extent that it can be related to a science or sciences and thus itself become an applied science, it can be developed in a coherent way, be given continuity, and be taught.

The most successful teacher will always be something of an artist. But the art will be enhanced rather than destroyed if it is exercised within a framework of scientifically established guidelines. Therein lies the possibility of faith.

THE CORNERSTONES OF METHOD

The belief that it is necessary to relate language teaching to an established scientific discipline is certainly not new. Indeed, it has been an important feature of several of the later methods and approaches mentioned above. Until recently, however, there has been little agreement as to *which* discipline or disciplines are the essential ones. West, and particularly the Americans associated with him in developing the Reading Approach, looked almost exclusively to psychologists for guidance. Kaulfers tried to bring something of the aims and subject matter of the social sciences into language instruction. Ogden and Richards found the ideas which led to their Basic English in semantics and logic. Fries based his concept of English teaching on structural linguistics. Since these leaders of the profession were looking in different directions for their inspiration, it is hardly surprising that their common interest in a scientific approach failed to result in compatible methods.

It is only during the last few years that the realization has begun to emerge that past methodologies, in general, have been too narrowly based, that more than one cornerstone is necessary for the development of a type of teaching which will be both flexible enough to meet the manifold language needs of modern society and sufficiently scientific to avoid the abrupt about-faces that have characterized previous language instruction. It is an encouraging fact that this realization has not been the work of any one individual but appears to have forced itself almost simultaneously upon a large number of the leaders of the profession on both sides of the Atlantic. The fact is encouraging because it seems to hold out the promise of a methodology that will not harden into a closed system but will remain open to new ideas arising from the advances made in several related scientific disciplines.

The emerging consensus among methodologists arises from a set of relationships so fundamental and self-evident that they may be regarded as axiomatic. The basic elements in any teaching situation are the teacher, the subject matter, the learner, and the aims of instruction. These elements are related to one another in a way very similar to the terms of an equation. As in any question, the value of the first term—in this case the behavior of the teacher—should vary as different values are assigned to the other terms.

This is, of course, another way of stating that *methods of language teaching should be based on at least three cornerstones*: (a) what is known about the nature of the language, (b) what is known about the nature of the learner, (c) the aims of instruction.

The science which analyzes the nature of language in general as well as that of particular languages is linguistics. The science that has studied the processes of human learning deeply is psychology. The aims of instruction are not scientifically determined but depend on the needs felt by the society and the individual at a given moment; a number of scientific and humanistic disciplines can, however, throw some light on these needs.

LANGUAGE TEACHING AND LINGUISTICS

Though there are still some skeptics, most creative methodologists now agree, then, that one of the cornerstones on which language instruction must be built—perhaps the most useful one—is the science that deals with the nature of language itself: linguistics. Of the various branches of linguistics, that which treats most directly the kind of problems which teachers must concern themselves with, at least in the elementary stages of instruction, is *synchronic* or *descriptive* linguistics. *Diachronic* or *historical* linguistics deals with the development of languages, chiefly written languages, over long periods of time and with the discovery of the genetic relationships among them. Descriptive linguistics, on the other hand, was developed in order to provide a rigorous method for analyzing living languages as they are used today. Since little has been written in the majority of such tongues, the descriptivists have learned to work with them directly in their spoken form.

Though descriptive linguistics is now known and cultivated in many parts of the world, it has had its stronghold in the United States, and Americans like to credit Bloomfield with having brought it to the dignity of a science by the publication of *Language* in 1933. The first large-scale attempt to apply linguistics to the teaching of English to speakers of other languages was made at the University of Michigan accompanying and following the appearance of Fries's *Teaching and Learning English as a Foreign Language* in 1945.

In spite of the irrefutable logic of establishing a close relationship between methods of teaching language, on the one hand, and the best established body of facts available about language, on the other, the battle to convince teachers of the necessity for such an orientation has been long and arduous, and only partially won.

Much of the resistance has been due, without doubt, to the very dogmatism and excessiveness of the claims that some linguists have felt confident enough to make. The less cautious among them have allowed to be seen their belief that linguistics can supply all the needed answers and that language instruction can be regarded as a mere appendage of descriptive linguistics. Not content with their basic role as analysts of language, and with having teachers look to their science as a source of ideas, some of which might be applicable to instructional purposes, they have sometimes urged that their techniques should be taken into the classroom practically unchanged. There have been those who argued that a Ph.D. in linguistics was a perfectly adequate—indeed, the only adequate—preparation for a specialist in language instruction, even if the degree work was organized without reference to teaching. There has even been a tendency to substitute the phrase "applied linguistics" for "language teaching" as the name of the profession.[2]

As any people who have spent many years of their lives training and supervising teachers know, however, the best linguists are not necessarily the best language teachers. Quite the reverse may often be true. Some of the teachers of English to speakers of other languages who have been most undeniably successful know, regrettably, little or nothing about linguistic science. And some of the most brilliant graduate students of linguistics seem hopelessly inept as apprentice teachers. What can be safely asserted is no more than that teachers who have the firmest grasp of the fundamentals of linguistics, all other things being equal, will probably be the most effective in their work.

The chief disadvantage of an exclusive relationship between language teaching and linguistics is that the latter, by definition, casts very little light on the human element in the language teaching equation, the nature of the learner. That element is, however, much too important to be slighted. Perhaps the best way to convince oneself of the truth of this statement is to attempt to use in a classroom situation certain of the materials that have been developed directly by narrowly oriented linguists who lacked classroom experience. Such materials—with their pages of drill on meaningless sounds, their excessive reliance on unfamiliar terminology and symbolism, their disconnected sentences unrelated to reality, their indifference to true communication—may be sound linguistically, but they are certainly no models of teachability.

Nevertheless, it would not be fair to lay at the door of linguists all the blame for the many troubles that have attended their *affaire de coeur* with language teachers. The teachers themselves, in large numbers, have been perfectly willing to forget what their experience has taught them and to adopt uncritically everything the linguists had to offer, without testing, without looking elsewhere for additional guidance. In other words, they seem to have given up any idea they may once have had of standing on their own feet as creative scholars with a basically independent profession of their own to develop.[3]

In the current state of affairs, then, the relationship between linguistics and language teaching is confused and even somewhat paradoxical. On the one hand, the many teachers in the United States who reject linguistics as mechanical and unnecessary, as well as many abroad who hardly know of its existence, need to be convinced that the tie is essential. On the other hand, there is the necessity to caution teachers against the dangers of a relationship that can be too dependent and too exclusive. In doing both things, the methodologist must try to make the difference between a theoretical science and an applied art-science, between unquestioning adoption and judicious application, crystal-clear.

LANGUAGE TEACHING AND PSYCHOLOGY

No such ambivalence is involved in the relations between language teachers and psychologists. These were, by and large, relatively slight during the two decades between 1940 and 1960, roughly the period of greatest linguistic hegemony. During the 15 years preceding 1940, however, they had been close and beneficial. Perhaps because of the very wide range of problems with which psychologists are concerned, the latter seem never to have developed the feeling of possessiveness about language instruction that has been shown at times by linguists.

The years 1925 to 1940 were those of the Reading Approach. The methodologists responsible for its popularity—West and his followers in the British Commonwealth, and the American and Canadian Committees on Modern Languages in North America—were determined to reduce the role of guesswork in language teaching. They hoped, as we still hope today, to be able to replace guesswork by experimental evidence. They therefore invited as many psychologists as they could interest to participate with them in their work.

The result was an explosive increase in the amount of evaluative experimentation dealing with the teaching of languages. In fact, a large proportion of the total literature on such experiments dates from this period, much of it still quite pertinent.[4] But with the advent of linguistically oriented language teaching, this literature came to be neglected. It was the product of a group that had approved of the reading aim and hence was suspect to the champions of the Aural-Oral Approach.

Thus, with the repudiation of the reading aim came an unfortunate tendency to minimize the potential relevance of psychology to language instruction. Actually, there was little if any demonstrable connection between the work of the psychologists who collaborated with the American and Canadian Committees on Modern Languages and the fact that the Committees concluded that an ability to read was the only foreign language skill likely to be achieved under the conditions then prevailing in North American schools. Critics of the Reading Approach have pointed out more than once that the evidence gathered clearly did not support the recommendations made in the name of the Committees.[5] The role of the psychologists in the matter was essentially neutral.

There were more substantial reasons, however, for doubting that psychology had a great deal of help to offer foreign language teachers, reasons arising from the state of the science in general and from its methods of developing learning theory in particular. For one thing, psychologists were divided in rapidly changing schools, each of which disputed the validity of their rivals' analysis of mental and behavioral processes. The behaviorists were attempting to discredit the introspective method; the gestalt group approved of introspection but were unwilling to accept Thorndike's connectionism.[6] Confusing differences in terminology made it very difficult for an outsider to decide whether or not the plethora of investigation had indeed established a modicum of fact.

For reasons obvious to the psychologists, experiments dealing with learning theory were carried out mostly with animals; to apply the results to human learning it would have been necessary to extrapolate. When the experimental subjects were human, they were set to performing tasks which bore no resemblance a language teacher could see to the kinds of activities central to studying a foreign tongue: tasks such as learning to associate pairs of nonsense words or to distinguish between sounds of varying intensity and pitch. Joint attempts by teachers and psychologists to measure the effectiveness of one method of language teaching against another in an actual classroom situation over an extended period of time proved inconclusive because of lack of clarity in the definition of methods, inability to control variables, and insufficient rigor of design.[7]

But these objections have become less valid in recent years. The area of agreement among psychologists regarding the nature of learning seems to have grown progressively larger as new theorists have deliberately attempted to work out a synthesis of the controversial points and thus act as a bridge between schools of thought. "While it remains true that research findings will be somewhat differently expressed and explained within different theoretical frameworks, the findings themselves are fairly solid," says a Columbia professor who set himself the job of explaining "what psychology we can trust." He was able to prepare a list of 50 propositions about children and learning with which he thought few knowledgeable psychologists of any school of thought would disagree (Watson, 1961, p. 1).

It is also encouraging that more and more psychologists are becoming specifically interested in language learning and even in foreign language learning. One major cause of this is certainly the fact that there has been a perceptible shift of the center of gravity of linguistics itself toward psychology. The generative-transformational approach to the analysis of language, which has become dominant since the appearance of Chomsky's *Syntactic Structures* in 1957, is very much concerned with the possibility that there may be a direct connection between grammatical rules and a human being's competence to produce speech. Analysis of this kind has given psychologists for the first time a linguistic model whose validity can perhaps be tested experimentally. A new term, "psycholinguistics" (apparently dating from about 1950), has come into wide use to describe the work of those whose investigations are carried out in the border area between psychology and linguistics. Methodologists and language teachers generally have been impressed by the value and relevance of these investigations and are showing unmistakable

signs of renewed confidence in the helpfulness of psychologists.

The trend toward a rapproachement may have begun in 1955, when Carroll demonstrated that a leading educational psychologist can also be an excellent linguist by publishing his survey of linguistics and related disciplines. It was greatly strengthened by the passage of the National Defense Education Act (NDEA), which made available funds both for linguistic analysis and for psychological experimentation. In 1959 under NDEA auspices, a Conference on Psychological Experiments Related to Second-Language Learning was held at the University of California, Los Angeles. The research designed or suggested there was later carried out by investigators all over the country.[8] Especially favorable attention has been attracted by Berko's work (1958) on the child's learning of English morphology, which was widely popularized in a series of films on language teaching, and by Lambert's investigation (1961) at McGill of the roles of attitudes and motivation in foreign language learning. By 1961 enough material on psycholinguistics had accumulated to make possible the publication of a sizable anthology under that title by Saporta (1961).

The great interest in programmed learning gave impetus toward a reestablishment of the former close working relationship between language teachers and psychologists. Much of the development of programmed materials for language instruction—see Lane (1964)—has been based on the theoretical foundation supplied by Skinner (1957), leader of the strict behaviorists.

One of the foremost benefits that should accrue from such a close working relationship is a reawakening of the scientific spirit among language teachers. To be sure, the latter have tried hard at the urging of the linguists to be more scientific in their analysis of language itself, but this has been accompanied by an unmistakable tendency to accept on faith the linguists' dictums regarding methodology. There is an obvious need for more experimental testing of such tenets as "never are the students assigned a lesson in advance for silent study before coming to class," and "reading in the foreign language . . . is deliberately postponed until the structure of the new language is firmly grasped, and it may never become an important part of the study" (Fries, 1945, p. 7).

Though much past experimentation has been inconclusive, we seem at least to have learned *why* this has been the case. It should be possible through joint effort to devise experiments which would involve the acquisition of skills or the answering of questions that any teacher would regard as directly pertinent to foreign language instruction. And there appears to be no reason why these could not be carried out with sufficient rigor to satisfy the most exacting psychologist. Carroll believes that a particularly helpful type of experimentation that is now entirely feasible would be one designed not merely to differentiate two methods of instruction in terms of their overall results, but also to reveal *the conditions under which each method succeeds best* (1955, pp. 178–179, 187–189).

Even in its present state of development, learning theory is a valuable counterpoise to linguistic theory. In a study that should be widely read, *The Psychologist and the Foreign-Language Teacher*, Rivers (1964) shows how each major assumption of the Audiolingual Approach can be checked and often rendered more accurate and sophisticated by a confrontation with appropriate psychological literature.

But the greatest benefit to be hoped for is undoubtedly a better understanding of and a stronger emphasis on the human element in the language teaching equation. Language learners are, in the main, rational human beings. They seem to be proud of their ability to analyze data and make generalizations. They do not normally enjoy speaking unless they understand what they are saying, but they do get great satisfaction from communicating their thoughts through speech. They like their sentences to come out in logical sequence, and hope that they bear some relationship to the real world around them. They are easily baffled by new names for old things or abstract representations of the concrete. They are deeply averse to the performance of tasks that seem meaningless to them. They dislike endless mechanical repetitions. They come in many different shapes and sizes, and appear to learn things in various ways. No matter what they are forced to do, they do not learn at all unless they want to do so. Language teachers have been in grave danger of losing sight of some of these apparent truths. Only the psychologists could perhaps tell us whether they are really facts, or merely beliefs held to be self-evident.

One must add that, if the necessary humanization is to be effected, it will probably not be through the influence of the Skinnerian behaviorists, with their view that a person is the mere site of verbal behavior rather than one of its causes. Contacts with this group may be of value in other ways, but their view of language and people does not seem to lead in the direction of greater feeling for the learner as an element of language teaching.[9] Fortunately, there are many other behaviorists who believe—along with other psychologists such as the gestalt group and even some of Pavlov's countrymen[10]—that the speaker does play a significant role in the generation of human speech.

THE AIMS OF LANGUAGE INSTRUCTION

Of the three cornerstones of method—whether it be in the teaching of English to speakers of other languages or in any other type of foreign language teaching—the aims of instruction are in one sense the most important. That is to say, in the teaching situation it is the methods used, more than any other factor, that determine the results achieved. And if results do not coincide with objectives, the teaching is at least partially unsuccessful. In any given classroom the teacher should have as clear an idea as possible of what s/he wants to accomplish and should choose the techniques and materials accordingly.

The aims of instruction are thus an overriding consideration. If they conflict with methodological conclusions drawn from another source, then these latter must be disregarded to the extent that they cannot be reconciled with the aims set up. A class made up of students who need, above all else, to learn to pronounce English well so as to become radio announcers can serve as an example. Because of the very definite nature of these students' needs, objectives can be precisely formulated in terms of a scientific skill. How shall the class spend its time? The teacher may have learned in a phonetics course that the ability to pronounce English depends primarily on being able to recognize one English sound as different from another. S/he may therefore be tempted to conclude that all classes in oral English, including this one, should be devoted to hearing and discrimination drills. But the teacher's objectives point in another direction, toward having the class spend its time in actually pronouncing English of the sort used by radio announcers. In this case, a reconciliation is certainly possible, since there is clear justification for both types of activity: Both can be included in the class hour, but most time should be given to the type which most resembles the terminal behavior prescribed by the objectives.

Should any serious consideration of methods not begin, then, with the drawing up of a generally acceptable statement of objectives from which the most promising teaching techniques could be deduced in a step-by-step analysis? This is indeed the way the planning for any particular class or any single meeting of a class should begin. It would not be a very useful procedure for a textbook on methods of teaching English, however.

The difficulty lies in drawing up a statement that will win general acceptance. Language teachers have argued endlessly about objectives. Shall we aim at a speaking knowledge, a reading knowledge, or both? Shall we work toward a nativelike perfection in pronunciation or content ourselves with

reasonable intelligibility? Is it enough to develop practical language skills, or must we also impart an understanding of how language works? Should literature be taught for appreciation alone or for the insights it can give into a new culture? The list of questions could be prolonged almost indefinitely.

To gain even a moderate degree of acceptance, a statement of objectives would have to be so general, so vague, so devoid of any indication of priorities as to be practically worthless as a basis for methodological decisions. Total agreement could probably be achieved on nothing more definite than that all those enrolled in English classes should learn English.

This is another way of saying that *instructional aims are useful as an indication of method only to the extent that they are specific.* Many general methodological principles can be deduced from the nature of language and some from what we know about the nature of the learner but none from the aims of instruction *en masse.* Objectives can play their dominant role only under circumstances which permit their being clearly defined; they should ensure the modification of general methods in specific situations.

There is no intention here to suggest that, in refusing to agree on aims, language teachers are simply being perverse or stubborn. The chief reason they cannot agree is that languages must be taught for a great variety of purposes and there is never enough class time to achieve all the ends that would be desirable. The needs for English felt around the world today, and hence the reasons for teaching it, are particularly diverse and pressing. In the United States it is taught to give children a mastery sufficient to enable them to obtain a complete education in American schools, to make it possible for adult immigrants to function effectively in a new society, to put foreign students in a position to cope with university lectures and examinations, to familiarize pilots with a few spoken expressions so they can land a plane safely. Overseas still other aims are pursued, equally valid and sometimes prescribed by law.

The clearest conclusion to be drawn from a study of the aims of teaching English to speakers of other languages is *the necessity for variety and flexibility of methods.*

There is much evidence that English teachers have tended to forget or ignore the overriding importance of specific objectives. Methods calculated to achieve one objective have been used in an attempt to achieve some other avowed or implicit objective that was quite different. Most new foreign students in American universities badly need help in learning to read rapidly and to express their thoughts in writing. Yet the only English courses provided for them in many institutions offer a diet made up almost exclusively of oral pattern practice and pronunciation drills. The justification given for this anomaly would presumably be that a mastery of the spoken language is an essential prerequisite to learning to read and write it. However sound such a principle may be in the abstract, when applied to this concrete case to the exclusion of all other considerations it leaves teachers in the absurd position of never knowing whether or not they are making progress toward their reading-and-writing objectives. They hope so, but mere hope is not sufficient. If a course aims to improve mastery of all the different language skills, it should include some practice in all of them.

Similar anomalies arise when textbooks developed to achieve a specific set of objectives are taken over and used with students whose needs are altogether different. At the English Language Institute of the University of Michigan, a series of texts was produced to meet the highly specialized needs of a group of adult Latin Americans living on campus and studying the language full time so as to be able to enroll in an American university.[11] Because of their success in their original setting and their prestige, these texts were widely adopted, often without modification, for use in many parts of the world at various levels of instruction by students with very disparate needs. The explanation usually given

was that they were the best available. In each such situation, a clear formulation of immediate and ultimate objectives would have enabled the teachers to see the extent and nature of the risk they were running and to plan the modifications necessary to make their work fully productive.

Teachers must often be reminded that aims, and hence methods and materials, do and must vary. There is no one method, immutable, universal, and eternal.

TESL, TEFL, TEAL, AND TESOL

One of the clearest and most significant examples of the necessity for such modification stems from the differences between the objectives of teaching English as a second language and teaching it as a foreign language. In conclusion, then, it seems useful to try to clear up certain difficulties of terminology.

Those who teach English to students who speak some other language as their mother tongue have never found it easy to label their own profession. If they simply call themselves "teachers of English," they run the risk of having people think their work is no different from that of any other teacher of English in American or British schools, a very common and harmful confusion. But the attempt to find a more meaningful descriptive phrase always seems to produce terms that are either too long for current use (like that which stands at the beginning of this paragraph) or are awkward, ambiguous, or fraught with undesirable connotations.

The first phrase to gain currency in this country was "teachers of English as a *foreign* language," often abbreviated to TEFL. It was soon realized, however, that people like the Filipinos or the Nigerians, who receive most of their education through the medium of English and use it extensively in their everyday life even though it is not their mother tongue, do not like to think of the language as something foreign or alien to their culture.

To meet this objection, "teachers of English as a *second* language" (TESL) was proposed and became quite popular. "Second" was intended to mean simply that English was not the first language the students learned in point of time. It was thought that no word could be freer of emotional overtones than a colorless numerical term. Unfortunately, "second" turned out to have connotations of unimportance, especially when people began making the easy mistake of saying "secondary" instead of "second." Furthermore, it was objected that English might actually be the third or fourth language of students in a so-called second language situation; therefore, what was really needed was a phrase meaning any language other than the first.

In Canada, particularly in British Columbia, the acronym TEAL has long stood for Teachers of English as an Additional Language. This professional label avoids some of the unfortunate connotations of the word "second" in TESL. It also reflects a positive aspect of Canada's national language policy, which is to encourage maintenance of the mother tongue for immigrants as well as indigenous non-English speakers.

In recent years still other terms have been suggested such as "teachers of English to speakers of other languages" (TESOL) and "teachers of English to non-English speakers" (TENES).[12] So far, no one appears to have discovered undesirable connotations in the first of these, but its meaning is certainly not completely clear: "Speakers of other languages" seems to include any Americans who have learned to speak a foreign language in addition to English. The second, "teachers of English to non-English speakers," is awkward and one cannot be sure whether the reference is to speakers who are not English or to those who do not speak it. And how long do "non-English speakers" remain such? Are they still to be referred to in the same way in intermediate and advanced classes?

It seems quite possible that the best solution of the problem may lie, not in attempting to win acceptance for one of the possible alternative terms as a general label and rejecting the others, but in assigning specific and much-needed meanings to those that are already best established. Undesirable connotations may disappear if the several different denotations can be made sufficiently clear.

There is already considerable precedent, especially in the United Kingdom, for assigning such a specialized meaning to "teachers of English as a *second* language." They are those who teach it in systems *where English is the partial or universal medium of instruction for other subjects in the curriculum*. On the other hand, "teachers of English as a *foreign* language" are those who work in systems *where instruction in other subjects is not normally given in English*. In this sense English is typically taught as a second language to Africans in Kenya or to Spanish-speaking children in the American Southwest, and as a foreign language in France. The distinction is thus based on the uses to which the language is to be put, on ultimate objectives. As was pointed out at the beginning of this section, this is a useful and important distinction. It also seems to be a reasonably clear one.

If specific meanings are assigned to "teachers of English as a second language" and "teachers of English as a foreign language," then there is still need for a term which can be applied to both groups jointly but which will distinguish them from those who teach English to children for whom it is the mother tongue. Such a term is useful, for example, in the name of a professional association which embraces both former groups. Faced with this problem, those who organized such an association decided to use "teachers of English to speakers of other languages" (TESOL) as a name which would include all teachers who teach English to students who speak another language as their mother tongue.

SUMMARY AND CONCLUSION

As this chapter indicates, there exist controversies in our profession ranging from the search for a reasonable language teaching methodology to the search for an appropriate professional name. Three "cornerstones" that are parts of the foundation in the development of any acceptable methodology have been proposed, with the third viewed as somehow being more basic than the other two:

1. *Linguistics*: the nature of language in general, and also the English language and the languages(s) of the learners in particular.
2. *Psychology*: the nature of the learner, the nature of the teaching/learning process.
3. *The aims of instruction*: i.e., what things must the learner be able to do in or with English?

Current intellectual trends, which encourage the development of syllabi based on needs, and which encourage interdisciplinary research as well as healthy skepticism with respect to doctrinaire proposals, suggest that our profession is coming of age and will perhaps make better progress in the future than it has in the past.

Various names (and acronyms) that have been suggested as professional labels have been listed and discussed; of these, the following appear to have gained relatively permanent acceptance:

TEFL (Teaching/Teachers of English as a Foreign Language): used in educational situations where instruction in other subjects is not normally given in English.

TESL (Teaching/Teachers of English as a Second Language): used in educational situations where English is the partial or universal medium of instruction for other subjects.

TEAL (Teaching/Teachers of English as an Additional Language): used in parts of Canada in lieu of TESL to stress the benefits of first-language maintenance.

TESOL (Teaching/Teachers of English to Speakers of Other Languages): a cover-term for teachers working in any of the above situations.

This relative consensus in terminology is also a healthy development.

NOTES

1. This chapter, with a few minor changes, reflects a paper written by the author in 1964–1965 while he was on sabbatical leave. It is included here because the editor feels it is timeless in nature and contains much valuable information not found elsewhere in the literature. The other chapters in this section provide the more current reviews of language methodology that language teachers in training require.

2. There is a clear need for the term "applied linguistics" when it is properly used. Each year new possibilities of applying linguistics are being discovered in a large number of fields: machine translation, information retrieval, the analysis of literature, literacy campaigns, the treatment of aphasia, among others. But to equate "applied linguistics" with "language teaching" is a gross misuse of the term. Linguistics may be applied for many purposes, and certainly much more is involved in language teaching than the application of linguistics.

3. The attempt to sort out the respective roles of linguists and language teachers has given rise to much impassioned writing on both sides. For an example of excessive linguistic claims see Cornelius (1953). A typical protest from an indignant teacher is that of Heise (1961).

4. This material was analyzed in some detail by Coleman and Fife (1933–1949).

5. The Committees' formal report was made by Coleman (1929). The lack of correlation between recommendations and data was pointed out by Mercier (1930), Carroll (1955, p. 172), and others.

6. A concise survey of the various schools of psychology at midcentury was made by Woodworth (1948) and an analysis of the different approaches to learning theory by Hilgard (1956).

7. The most extensive such attempt was the Investigation of the Teaching of a Second Language reported by Agard and Dunkel (1948), and briefly assessed by Carroll (1955, pp. 177–179). A characteristic linguist's reaction to psychological experimentation dealing with language learning is that of Lado (1964, pp. 35–45).

8. The conference report was prepared by Pimsleur (1959). Research completed by the end of 1964 is listed by the National Defense Language Development Program, U.S. Office of Education (1964).

9. See Chomsky's review (1959) of Skinner's *Verbal Behavior*.

10. See Chapters I and II of Belyayev (1964).

11. English Language Institute (1943).

12. Ohannessian (1965) suggests that the original appearance of the first of these expressions was in her

Interim Bibliography on the Teaching of English to Speakers of Other Languages (1960) and that the second originated with Harold B. Allen's 1966 *Survey of the Teaching of English to Non-English Speakers*.

DISCUSSION QUESTIONS

1. When certain of the profession are referred to in the early parts of this article as "prophets," what meaning is attached to this term? Do you think the use of this word is justifiable?

2. Is it desirable that language instruction should become entirely explicable in scientific terms?

3. Do you agree that "the aims of instruction are not scientifically determined but depend on the needs felt by the society and the individual at a given moment"?

4. Why does the Skinnerian psychologists' view that people are the site of verbal behavior rather than one of its causes make it unlikely that they will contribute to the humanization of language teaching?

5. Can you explain the decision to consider the three cornerstones of method in the particular order followed in this section?

6. Do you think it is ever true that the best way to learn a given skill is to practice a different but related skill?

SUGGESTED ACTIVITIES

1. Ask several TESOL or other language teachers about specific ways in which a knowledge of linguistics or psychology has been helpful in their work, and try to find out their judgment as to the relative value to them of the two sciences. Report your findings to the class.

2. Conduct a poll among your fellow students in order to determine (a) the expression they prefer as a general label for all those that teach English to students who speak another language as their mother tongue and (b) the chief reason for their preference.

SUGGESTIONS FOR FURTHER READING

Belyayev, B. V. (1964)
The Psychology of Teaching Foreign Languages (translated from the Russian). New York: Macmillan.

> Summarizes many interesting Soviet experiments that have pedagogical relevance to the teaching of foreign languages.

Fries, C. C. (1945)
Teaching and Learning English as a Foreign Language. Ann Arbor: University of Michigan Press.

> The earliest American exposition of language teaching methodology that follows the principles of structural linguistics. It was a classic (a "Bible" of sorts) up until the early 1960s.

Mackey, W. (1965)
Language Teaching Analysis (Chapter 5). Bloomington, Indiana and London: Indiana University Press.

> This is a clear and concise overview of the interplay of language analysis and method, of the development of language teaching; it also describes 15 types of methods and reflects on what methods are made of.

Rivers, W. (1964)
The Psychologist and the Foreign Language Teacher. Chicago: University of Chicago Press.

> Focuses on the influence that various schools of psychology have had on language teaching methodology.

Stern, H. H. (1983)
Fundamental Concepts of Language Teaching. Oxford: Oxford University Press.

> A more recent and extremely comprehensive overview of language teaching that takes linguistic, social, psychological, and educational factors into consideration.

Innovative Approaches

Robert W. Blair

INTRODUCTION

As far back as the history of language instruction goes, conscientious teachers have sought new and better ways to facilitate and accelerate language learning. Challenging questions have always confronted them: What else can we do in our language instruction programs, beyond or beside what we are already doing, to promote more efficient learning for more learners? What principles, beyond or beside those we now base our teaching on, could better guide our instructional approaches? Which of the present assumptions that underlie what we teach and how we teach might be faulty? What new techniques, new insights, new ideas, new emphases, new aims, or new twists could increase the rate and quality of learning of our students? On what established or emerging body of scientific knowledge can we confidently base our next-generation methodology? Are we asking the right questions? Are we looking in the right places for answers?

Advice has come from many disciplines, each piece defensible if not wholly convincing to all. And we have responded to the logic and persuasion of these by incorporating their suggestions in one way or another into our developing concepts and practices of language instruction. The educational psychologist advised: "Look to sound principles of instruction," and we experimented more consciously with various instructional models. The descriptive linguist advised: "Look to a better description of the structure of language," and we experimented with alternative ways of describing linguistic structure.

The sociolinguist advised: "Teach language through its functional use," and we experimented with replacing our formal linguistic syllabus with a notional-functional syllabus targeted on projected communication needs of learners. The expert in child language development advised: "Look to the natural model of first language acquisition," and we experimented with changes to bring instruction in line with what we found there. The humanist advised: "Center your teaching in the learner and teach the whole man," and we began experimenting more consciously with ways that reflect that compelling view. From the perspective of many other reputable sources, some scientific, others intuitive, came suggestions, some of which stimulated tremendous excitement as we tried to devise better ways of fostering learning in classrooms, seeking ever better formulas based on true principles.

Along the way, to be sure, some few zealots advertised claims for their unique, all-purpose method that were worthy of headlines in the *National Enquirer*, but unbiased observation suggests there is not yet a single, comprehensive formula or a known body of principles which, if followed, can satisfy all tastes and assure uniform success for all teachers and learners. More attractive to most members of the language teaching profession has been the soft-spoken, pragmatic eclectic who advises that teaching is an art, not a science; one must just take the best of all approaches, the techniques and ideas and strategies found to be most congenial, and blend them into a workable formula that suits the realities of the particular teaching situation. Looking back from the vantage point of the late 1980s we can see that all methods have their rationale and supporters. In short, all methods work! Yet not all methods work equally efficiently for all learners and for all teachers and for all situations and for all purposes. All methods have limitations.

It is my purpose here to briefly look at certain of the more unconventional approaches that have attracted the attention of the profession in recent years, to discuss in what ways these contrast with the mainstream approaches, and to show reason for interest in them, in what they are exploring, in what they accomplish, in the assumptions that underlie them, and in the principles and ideas that guide them.

MAKING SENSE OUT OF A DELUGE OF CREATIVITY

Since the 1960s, mainstream approaches in America have been characterized in some of the literature as being (a) "audiolingual," (b) "cognitive," or (c) an eclectic combination of these. Such a simplistic characterization, it is now seen, covers over some important dimensions of learning, but this is a convenient representation of a mid-1960s American view of the two extremes of a supposed continuum: on the one side, there was "pure" or "classical" audiolingualism, in which language was viewed largely as a definable set of structures with lexical exponents, which could be learned inductively, pattern by pattern, by means of a rigorously planned and carefully executed program of instruction based on the laws of conditioning and reinforcement; and on the "cognitive" side, language was viewed as essentially rule-governed behavior; and (adult) language learning, it was thought, could be significantly aided by a well-laid-out, systematic approach that explained the rules and gave practice in their conscious use.

From the literature and from conference papers and presentations during the past three decades we have clear evidence of a quiet, marvelous ferment of creative activity. New pathways to learning have been explored and remarkably innovative ways of fostering language learning have emerged. And we can only assume that the public documentation of language teaching innovations represents but a fraction of what has been and is actually going on. Within this great variety of ideas, most but not all fit well into the mainstream of long-established, conventional approaches. It is the few that do not fit into mainstream thinking and practice, the ones that challenge conventional wisdom and explore far-out pathways, that are the focus of this chapter.

It is obvious that any discussion of unconventional approaches can be made meaningful only if their innovations can be reduced to a representative sample—and perhaps to a discussion of only the most convention-challenging of the new departures, those whose rationale and whose degree of success have caused many to reconsider conventional assumptions and even reexamine some of our most fundamental beliefs.

It is safe to say that each of the "innovative" approaches discussed below emerged as a reaction to conventional assumptions about such things as the structure of the various components of language or of the various kinds of text; about how language is processed in the brain and how it is used in interpersonal communication; about the nature of human learning in general and of language learning in particular; about the nature of the younger or older language learner and such parameters as memory, emotion, readiness, motivation, and perception. Also the "innovative" approaches emerged as reactions against conventional notions about what are the most effective course objectives and emphases, course content, course pathway choices and teaching procedures, and even about what it is legitimate to do in the course of teaching languages.

It would be convenient, if it were only possible, to make a list of issues on which all advocates of the conventional approaches and all advocates of the more unconventional approaches have been and are yet uncompromisingly opposed, and then on each point at issue discuss the conflicting rationales of the opposing views. Such a list is not possible because, for one thing, individually and collectively we in the profession are constantly learning from our own and each other's experience as well as from our different views of how various research findings might apply to language teaching. In the passage of years we individually and collectively sort through these, and enough of us shift position on various issues that the formerly sharp contrasts are no longer so sharply drawn. Nevertheless, in discussing the recent evolution of unconventional approaches, it will be instructive to set these and their assumptions and rationales against the recent historical background of more conventional thinking about language teaching. We will begin with comprehension-based approaches.

COMPREHENSION-BASED APPROACHES

Total physical response (J. J. Asher)

Delayed oral response (V. A. Postovsky)

Draw the picture

Optimal habit reinforcement and "The Learnables" (H. Winitz)

The natural approach (T. Terrell)

Diglot-weave input

Approaches which focus on establishing receptive skills first (listening comprehension in particular; but to some extent also reading comprehension) and do not attempt specifically to train oral production—oral fluency being expected to emerge naturally and gradually out of the data base established through ample comprehension experience of the right kind—are called Comprehension-Based Approaches or Comprehension-Based Learning (CBA or CBL).

Two fundamental assumptions which conventional wisdom has held about adult language learning but with which proponents of CBL took issue are (1) that "talk" was the stuff of language, and that learning to talk must therefore be the immediate and primary aim in language learning; (2) that by focusing on talking, the learner will not only acquire fluency and accuracy in talking but will, in the process, gain the concomitant receptive skills.

In questioning these assumptions, proponents of CBL have given cogent arguments for beginning with the almost exclusive promotion of receptive skills. One of their arguments goes like this: The two processes, sending and receiving, entail quite different tasks, and certainly involve different levels of mental processing. Of the two, transmission entails by far the more complex mental processing, so to focus on training students in speaking a new langauage from the first is to take a much steeper and more tortuous road than to focus on giving them first a massive amount of experience in learning to comprehend spoken discourse.

Another argument for CBL goes as follows: In natural language acquisition, learners go through a preproduction phase or silent period—in effect, a sorting-out period. Sifting through massive input, and following an inner "syllabus," they gradually extract chunks and pieces they are motivated to use for their immediate communication needs. For a considerable time they make do with a faulty but gradually improving mastery of the native system. As they enter increasingly into verbal interaction with fluent speakers of the language, this brings more "negotiated" input directed at them and near their level of understanding—which input then feeds acquisition.

The conclusion that CBL advocates take from these (and other) arguments is that just as there is a natural progression in a child's acquisition of motor skills, so also there is a natural progression in the development of communication skills, reception being the foundation for production. By following this natural pathway of learning, language training gains significant advantages. Some of the advantages claimed for CBL over conventional classroom approaches are the following:

- lower learner anxiety
- lower drain on the learner's cognitive faculties
- increased time and concentration on comprehension tasks
- cleaner exposure to the language, hearing only the authentic model
- increased rate of language input per unit of time
- increased amount of language data processed per unit of time
- broader variety of learners who "take to it"
- more encouragement of a variety of acquisition strategies
- intellectual capacity and study habits better directed
- quicker comprehension attainment
- higher comprehension attainment

Total Physical Response

A comprehensive history of language teaching methods in America would document the considerable interest in and exploration of "natural" or "direct" methods before and after the turn of the 20th century. Guoin, Berlitz, Sweet, and others in the 19th century, Jespersen, de Sauzé, Palmer, and others in the first third of our century reacted against the formal, highly contrived foreign language curricula and methods typical of their period of history, and developed ideas that have come down to our day as part of the heritage of quality language teaching.

Within the present period of focus (1960–1989) a particularly notable impetus to comprehension approaches was given near the beginning of this period by James J. Asher, a talented young research psychologist at San Jose State University. Taken up with the astonishing genius of children in learning a second language, he observed that, as is evident to everyone, during the preproduction period children apparently learn to understand a great deal long before they try to say much. What Asher next observed was more astute: the door of understanding is first opened as children respond meaningfully to a particular type of input—namely, directives

in context-clear situations that invite an action response rather than a verbal response. Their early social interaction is through a physical response to invitations for movement, such as "Hey, come on!" "Let's run" "Throw the ball" "Okay, boys line up on this side, girls on that side." Whether the directive is translated into some L1 equivalent, whether it is repeated back, or whether a verbal rejoinder is voiced ("Yeah!" "Okay!") is not critical to learning; what really counts, he reasoned, is that the request be galvanized immediately into action, that the asked-for physical response take place and be visible, so that both parties in the communication can see at once how the message was understood. The mechanism is short and simple: (1) the directive, (2) the hearing and interpretation of the directive, (3) the overt action, and then immediately (4) the visible confirmation or disconfirmation of comprehension.

From his reflection on this particular mechanism of natural language acquisition, Asher hypothesized that kinetic, physically active response, rather than merely cognitive or vocal response, to "translate" language input could be the major contributing factor accounting for the rapidity of language acquisition in children. Furthermore, he saw the implications of his hypothesis for a principled language teaching approach.

By the mid-1960s, he had developed an approach to language training which came to be known as the strategy of Total Physical Response (TPR). The approach has been adapted to varied situations throughout America and abroad, but the core concept of TPR remains unchanged. At the start of TPR training a teacher plays "Follow the leader" or "Do what I do," modeling a couple of actions (e.g., *Stand up! Sit down!*) the first time or two in calling for those actions. This enables the learners to infer (and "perform") the tie between the command and the desired action. Commands for single actions quickly give way to commands for two or three actions in sequence (*Stand up, walk to the sofa, and sit down*), and then to yet more complicated actions, sometimes involving imaginary scenarios (*John, sit in the car, turn the key, look around, and honk the horn twice*). For certain effect, some teachers occasionally turn TPR into the game "Simon says . . ." (or "The sergeant says . . ."). Some, after a vocabulary and sentence structure base has been erected, add truth conditions or contingencies and other features into the mix: *If today is Friday, Maria will jump up and clap her hands.* Or (after participants have been assigned a "pecking order"),

Private Hernandez, Sergeant Beltono wants you to stand up, but Major Lopez wants you to kneel down, so what are you going to do? Good choice, you knelt down.

Instruction in how to do or make things through a succession of connected activities—for example, how to make borsch soup, how to create a doll out of a sock, or how to do a particular dance step—lends itself easily to TPR, as does a point-by-point description of an action sequence such as the following.

You are going to buy a pair of skates. They cost $5. Look in your purse for your wallet. It isn't there. Look again. It is not there. Recall that you put it in your coat pocket. Reach in your right coat pocket. It is not there. You are worried. Reach in your left coat pocket. Good! There is your wallet. Take it out, open it, and pull out a $5 bill. Hand over the $5. Put on the skates and skate away.

The simplicity, logic, and power of TPR has stimulated the development of syllabuses for teaching various languages. Perhaps the most complete publication on it is Asher (1977), an excerpt of which appears also in Blair (1982).

A criticism some have voiced against TPR is that it deals with language in too general a way and fails to train students to perform "survival" functions, such as exchanging greetings, asking directions, and ordering a meal. But proponents of TPR do not accept as the proper aim of beginning language training the teaching of in-country survival language. The basic principle of a comprehension approach, it must be remembered, says that to begin by pushing production cuts against the grain of natural acquisition. What TPR offers is a less demanding, more leisurely route to the acquisition of comprehension skills which properly underlie the natural acquisition of full-blown communication skills.

Problem-Solving Tasks as Variations on a Theme

Identify the Box. It is easy to see that TPR is a kind of progressive problem-solving game in which learners demonstrate through observable actions their comprehension of

Touch the box in which there is a woman standing behind a table.

In which box are there three men, one tall and two short?

Figure 1

increasingly longer and more complex instructions. Other types of problem-solving tasks that call for more subtle action (such as pointing or touching or pressing a computer key to make a choice among alternatives) are very close in spirit to TPR. Elementary school workbooks often contain problem-solving tasks which are excellent for comprehension training. The key instructional principle is to provide immediate feedback on whether each choice made is correct or not. For a couple of examples of this sort of problem-solving task, see Figure 1 at the bottom of page 27.

Delayed Oral Response (V. A. Postovsky)

Valerian A. Postovsky was, as much as anyone, a pioneer in exploring the CBL model and justifying its rationale. In the late 1960s as an Instructional Program Developer in Russian at the Defense Language Institute (DLI) in Monterey, California, he sought a methodology that would be more congruous with both the nature of the L1 acquisition process and the known study habits and inclinations of DLI students. Language acquisition research had made clear by that time that the principle mechanisms of L1 acquisition are not vocal imitation of model utterances, correction of mistakes, and similar methods, but these, along with heavy memorization tasks, grammar explanation, and structural drill, dominated the methodology used in DLI instruction. Aware of Asher's experimentation with an approach to language training strictly through listening-comprehension, Postovsky began experimenting with the same principle, which he came to call "delayed oral response" (Postovsky, 1970, 1974). His experiments with this model led to results that encouraged him to develop and test a program that presented Russian through problem-solving tasks with multiple-choice responses—essentially the same as "identify the boxes" but automated for self-instruction. As four "pictures" were presented on the screen of a teaching machine, the learner heard the "problem" voiced in spoken Russian and responded by touching one of the four pictures displayed on the screen; if the choice was correct, the program automatically put the next task up on the screen; if the program did not go to the next task, the student knew he had to make another choice. The progression was carefully controlled so that in each "problem" there was never more than one unknown.

Draw the Picture

Another kind of problem-solving task that is close to the spirit of TPR gives instructions for drawing a simple picture. For example:

Draw a big circle. Inside the circle quickly draw a small house with a chimney. There is smoke coming out of the chimney. Draw the smoke. Behind the house is a tree. Quickly draw the tree. Now draw a car at the top of the tree. Look at the picture on p. 10. Does your picture have all the elements of this picture? What was the first thing you drew, point to it. What was the last thing you drew?

Optimal Habit Reinforcement and "The Learnables" (H. Winitz)

Harris Winitz, a professor of speech science and psychology at the University of Missouri, became interested in comprehension-based learning and its implications for language teaching in the early 1970s. His experimentation with the model (which he called Optimal Habit Reinforcement) led to significant publications about its assumptions and performance (Winitz 1975, 1981), and also to the development of "The Learnables," a self-instructional program consisting of audiocassettes with accompanying picture books, which follows the principles of CBL.

It is interesting to note that after experimenting with alternative modes of overt response to the picture stimuli, Winitz concluded that a covert response was satisfactory, so in "The Learnables" no feedback is given to the learners, no confirmation or disconfirmation of their responses. They simply look at the picture, listen to the brief corresponding script, and decide whether they comprehend. If not, they can rewind the cassette a bit and go through the buildup material again.

The Natural Approach (T. Terrell)

Perhaps the most fully developed of the comprehension-based approaches is Tracy D. Terrell's Natural Approach (Krashen & Terrell, 1983; Terrell, 1976, 1981). A fundamental assumption underlying it is that learners of any age are able to take in speech input—if most of it is comprehensible—and discover its system without having it arbitrarily broken down for them and spoon-fed. The approach therefore supplies a high amount of input made comprehensible through pictures, actions, and situational, grammatical, and lexical transparency. It respects the initial preproduction period, expecting speech to emerge not from artificial practice but from motivated language use, progressing from early single-word responses up to more and more coherent discourse. Interpersonal and personal negotiation of meaning rather than attention to grammatical correctness is fostered for an extended period, and the learning activities are designed for learner comfort and enjoyment.

It is with Terrell's policy of not bringing attention to student production errors that many take issue, claiming that it may promote the early attainment of fluency but only at the cost of accuracy. Some feel strongly about this, raising the claim that once bad habits are established, they are not easily eradicated. Once a low level of interlanguage is used repeatedly and successfully in communication situations, it "fossilizes." So dangerous and real is this threat of fossilization, these critics claim, that no matter what treatment is administered later, there is little hope for these method-crippled learners ever to rise from their sad affliction. Apparently these critics believe that the only protection against gross fossilization is an approach which right from the beginning guides the learner systematically through a training program focused on linguistic correctness.

Diglot-Weave Input

A significant part of a teacher's task in CBL is to supply learners with voluminous comprehensible input. Beyond the commonly used ways mentioned of providing large amounts of comprehensible input, there has been experimentation with some innovative ways which are capable of providing high-grade comprehensible input in massive amounts. One of those involves code switching, or, in its pedagogical application, diglot-weave input. Best known for the promotion of this concept is the work of Robins Burling (1966, 1978, 1983), an anthropologist at the University of Michigan who developed a diglot-weave model for an experimental class in reading French. Taking the text of a French novel, Burling changed its lexical and grammatical expression in the early pages to a form of English heavily influenced by French syntax, yet understandable. Then, page by page, he modified the text by adding more French features, but never so many as to hinder the comprehensibility of the text. His students could read the novel at near normal speed with full understanding, even though it gradually went from basically English to basically French.

An oral application of the diglot-weave principle was made by Rudy Lentulay (1976), a professor of Russian at Bryn Mawr University, when he was invited to teach a class in Russian for 20 minutes two days a week to kindergarten children. At first he hesitated to accept the invitation, wondering what he could teach them under such a limited schedule. By chance, he had just finished reading Anthony Burgess's novel *A Clockwork Orange*, in which the teenage characters use Russian words as slang. From this came the idea of making a word game that small children could play, so he accepted the job and created a novel approach to teaching a language orally. Each week he told a different story, sprinkling Russian words in wherever the context made their meaning clear and engaging the children in talk about the story, all in English except for where the new Russian words were called for. The game was this: Once a new expression was started in circulation, the children were expected to use it in place of its English equivalent thereafter. The "trick" was to catch the teacher or a pupil using an English word or phrase where the Russian equivalent was called for. Before the end of the term he was telling stories with mostly Russian words, and the children were understanding and able to play the game.

Here is the first part of an English-Spanish diglot-weave story, modeled on one Lentulay told. It is to be presented with the aid of pictures and mime.

A *Cuento* About a Smashed *Ventana*

*Would you like me to tell you a **cuento**? **Oquei,** let me tell you **un cuento** about some naughty **muchachos**—some **muchachos** and some **muchachas**—who were playing with a **pelota** in **la calle** near **una casa.** Look, in this **dibujo** you can see **la casa. Mi cuento** is about **una** glass **ventana** on **la segunda** story **de la casa.***

*Besides being about some **muchachos** playing **pelota en la calle** near **una casa** with glass **ventanas,** this **cuento** is about **un hombre** who is **el** owner **de la casa.** This **hombre** is not out **en la calle** with **los muchachos. No.** He is **en** his **casa** on **la segunda** floor when **el cuento** begins. And **el cuento** is about **una** kind **mujer** who is walking down **la calle** toward **la casa** and looks up and **ve** what happens. I can tell you now, **el hombre en la casa** gets **muy enojado** at **los muchachos,** and **la mujer** is shocked when she looks up and **ve** what happens.*

The novelty of mixing two languages so as to artifically increase comprehensibility of course shocks those who are on the side of accuracy above all and who fear that taking such liberties can only lead to a "pidginized" corruption of the authentic language. They question the legitimacy of code switching as a pedagogical device or the use of any text that is not a model of native use. Others see in diglot-weave texts a promising vehicle for providing beginners with massive amounts of comprehensible input and are not convinced that dire consequences will result.

PRODUCTION-BASED LEARNING

Silent way (C. Gattegno)
Sheltered initiation language learning (Z. Bar-Lev)
Outreach learning (T. Brewster, E. Brewster, and D. Larson)

The three approaches to be considered next are more radical than CBL in that their advocates do not accept the hypothesis that speech emerges naturally out of comprehension, nor do they accept the proposition that research on language acquisition in natural acquisition environments is more relevant to the question of how to improve language teaching than are other areas of research. While agreeing that language acquisition research is relevant to formal language teaching, they reject applications that have been proposed. Limits of space allow only a glance at three innovative approaches which push production from the first and thus go against a basic principle of CBL. Since all three agree in denying learners a silent period, it is important to ask how that is justified.

Meticulous research has shown that the initial preproduction period observed in language acquirers may not be so vocally passive or strictly receptive as had been assumed. In a classic study Michael Halliday showed that months before acquiring any words or structures in the language of their environment, babies use, in social interaction and in private reflection, a functional vocal communication system to satisfy social or personal needs. He suggested that the child's efforts to communicate and its use of a prelanguage (i.e., a preverbal communication system) in social interaction serve as a map or tool for learning how to make sense of input and how to "make meaning" and convey it to others. So it is in pushing its limited communication resources to accomplish functional ends that the baby gradually discovers and learns to use more and more features of the more powerful environmental language.

Applied to language teaching, this can be taken to suggest that it may not be such a bad idea to encourage learners to attempt verbal communication before any appreciable foundation of comprehension is laid. Of course, it is nothing new to coax out verbal production right from the first. Conventional language instruction has done this all along without a prespeech phase. What is new in the "production-based approaches" we will look at next is how they proceed.

Silent Way Learning (SWL)

Of the three, the best known, no doubt for its strikingly innovative teacher strategies, is Caleb Gattegno's Silent Way Learning (Gattegno 1963, 1976). This method does not begin, as one might assume from its name, with the learners sitting silently while the teacher provides verbal input; rather it begins with the teacher being silent or at least holding verbal input to a bare minimum while eliciting and subtly reinforcing verbal output from the learners. Production is typically elicited at first with the aid of "scatter charts" of words and affixes, Cuisenaire Rods (small wooden or plastic blocks of various sizes and colors, called "rods" for short), language-specific "Fidel Charts," which color-code all pronunciation possibilities uniformly, regardless of spelling, and gestural cues and other kinds of hints. All of these unusual features of SWL are used to make pronunciation, vocabulary, and structures available for the learners to discover and test in use.

I cannot give more than a hint of the unusual instructional procedures used in SWL. Learning proceeds mainly as the learners try their tongues at speech, testing hypotheses of meaning, form, and function, getting subtle confirmation or disconfirmation of these, and then revising or extending their hypotheses or pursuing others. Each learner chooses what s/he will say and the level of complexity s/he will use to say it. The card-

inal principle the teacher must follow is phrased in four words: *Subordinate teaching to learning*. Knowing that even the most efficient learning takes time, the teacher attends only to the measures of progress, not of perfection. The teacher must use each learner's production to determine what language or guidance inputs to make.

In the first minute of instruction learners find that much more is demanded of them than in other formal learning settings. They find they must give utmost attention to the learning tasks set before them, for the instructor will not deal with their structural errors or their forgetting of a word by modeling the correct form; rather s/he will throw them back on their own inner resources, forcing awareness by self-discovery and making them build their own "inner criteria" of correctness. Just as in learning to play the violin one cannot get the notes from anyone else, so also in learning to speak a language, learners must independently acquire a visceral feeling of how it feels and sounds to perform "in tune" and with a full, sure voice of their own. Information can readily be transferred, but skill cannot. SWL classes quickly find that their instructor offers neither praise nor criticism and does not allow questions or even recourse to the native language. S/he corrects and guides by means of gestures and silent lip movements, focusing the learner's attention on just the portion of a word or phrase needing improvement. Always the instructor respects the learners' capacity to learn and to be patient in learning how to make meaning come from their own lips in acceptable form. The instructor invites the learners to assume responsibility for their learning, to take the active role—in short, to become robust, self-reliant, creative learners, independent of the teacher and patient in working out the structural principles of the language on their own. The motivation for this is the belief that the more the teacher does what the learners can do for themselves, the less they will do for themselves. Where it becomes evident that a learner is hung up on a word or a structure and needs momentary help beyond the silent, gestural hints available from the teacher, a classmate may offer his or her solution. The felicitous result of this is a classroom atmosphere free of competition, one that promotes group cooperation and mutual support. Denied their anticipated strategies of mimicry and guided drills, the learners, in exploring what they can do with the pieces of the language they discover and put into use, find that they are able to create innumerable meaningful utterances of their own whose meaning they contextualize through reference to objects before them.

If one aim of comprehension approaches could be encapsulated in a few words, these might be: "From much, little" or "Know much, say little," referring to the fact that the massive input one receives in CBL translates, early on, into a relatively limited capability to say much even though one may understand a great deal. In contrast, one of the aims of SWL is the reverse of that: "From little, much," or "Know a little, say much," referring to the fact that from the meager input learners receive they are urged to make as much of it as they can, to push their communication envelope outward. Progress toward mastery of a language depends in large part on the demands the learner places on his or her interlanguage, particularly as these address real communication needs. Those learners are most likely to succeed who, at whatever level of interlanguage, best exploit the limited language resources they have, applying what they know to new and wider contexts. As a matter of fact, in primary or secondary language acquisition, children, who are the most adept language learners of all, consistently do this.

Obviously SWL does not set out to provide new immigrants the language they need to apply for a job or ask for a bus schedule by telephone, nor is it aimed at supplying this summer's tour group to Spain a repertoire of useful expressions for conceivable social encounters there. If its aims are compared with those of Competency-Based Language Training (a prominent bandwagon at present), which aims to equip learners right up front with language that fits imagined social interchange scenarios, SWL with its at-first generic language seems irrelevant to any social purpose. Consider, for example, a typical utterance—one of scores of thousands at her command—spoken spontaneously, fluently, confidently, and accurately by a novice language learner only four clock hours into the language. It accurately describes a complex configuration of rods. "This is a red rod; it is standing upright at the end of a blue rod, which is lying next to an orange rod."

Judged on its own terms, SWL scores very high. Under its instruction the learners work on getting a feel of the language, its diction, rhythm, and melody; they work on assimilating words and absorbing and expanding the set of rules that enable them to say things they are motivated to say; they work on developing fluency, control, and confidence in using the language. There is plenty to work on, say SWL advocates, without having to worry right away about coping with two-way social interchanges or getting around in a foreign country.

Despite its acknowledged irrelevance to normal social discourse in the beginning stage, and its concentration on building linguistic rather than communicative competence first, many learners find the experience of SWL marvelously exciting. I found it absolutely electrifying, unlike any classroom learning I had experienced before. I had never been more alert and receptive to input than when learning Serbian by SWL. I enjoyed the exhilaration of self-created, internally motivated discourse and self-discovered rules that guided my creation of meaningful word strings. What I was able to do with the language in a short time was, I felt, phenomenal and immensely satisfying. I scarcely noticed that I was not taught how to introduce myself or dialog with anyone.

Since my first experience as a learner under SWL, I have explored its powers also from the other side of the desk. Within the very first three-hour session I have witnessed learners of Russian, Chinese, and other languages spontaneously create (and clearly understand) long strings representing the equivalent of "Take a blue rod and a red rod; give the red rod to me and the blue rod to him." I have watched faces light up with the excitement of discovery. On the other hand, I have also seen discouraged faces and found that not everyone takes to Silent Way Learning with equal relish. But that, of course, is not a problem unique to SWL. There is no method and no teacher that succeeds in satisfying all learners all the time. Whether SWL enables a higher percentage of learners to learn more efficiently or gain more satisfaction than other approaches is not known. But if the value of beginning language classes everywhere were measured by the percentage of dropouts, low achievers, dissatisfied students, and those who fail to become independent learners against the percentage of those who experience satisfaction with the speed, ease, and pleasure of their learning, I would guess that SWL would achieve high ratings.

Of course, there have been many criticisms of SWL, some well taken, some inane: "It's too slow." "It's too ambitious." "It's not based on accepted theory." "It won't work without a gifted teacher." "It's too focused on structure." "It's too limiting." "It intimidates some learners." "It won't work in a large class." An even "It's nothing new!"

From these and from the counterarguments raised by the defenders of SWL one can see that there are sensitive and complex issues here which cannot yet be settled by an appeal to universally agreed-upon principles or theory. If the theory behind comprehension approaches were all the truth and nothing but the truth, there would be no way to account for the known successes of SWL—or any other approach not founded on that theory. Clearly, the impressive success of this production-based approach raises interesting questions.

Sheltered Initiation Language Learning

The next in line for discussion is, unfortunately, not widely known and has as yet no official name. I refer to it here as Sheltered Initiation Language Learning (SILL). The idea of SILL is quite different from that of the sheltered classroom concept (see Snow, this volume). The creation of Zev Bar-Lev, professor of linguistics at San Diego State University, its startling methodological assumptions, instructional procedures, and degree of success present as bold a challenge to prevalent language acquisition theory as do those of SWL.

To begin with, Bar-Lev notes that the spontaneous speech of most learners, even after considerable training in the best-taught classrooms, is typically marked by gross errors; more than that, the learners often speak with tentativeness, hesitation, and stumbling, as if groping for words and testing the grammatical machinery to grind them out—and this even though they may be able to read books and understand spoken discourse quite well. In diagnosing this pathology and looking for ways to combat it, Bar-Lev specifically rejects the assumptions that fluent speech will eventually emerge naturally out of extended comprehension experience of the right kind and that learners gain by delaying ambitious oral production for a time. SILL prompts meaningful, ambitious oral creations in the first hours of instruction.

In rejecting the major postulates of CBL, in aiming first for ease of learning, and in starting with generic rather than function-specific language, Bar-Lev lines up with Gattegno. But here the relationship of SWL and SILL ends; on observation they do not look at all alike. For one thing, SILL uses teaching strategies that are markedly interventionist, the antithesis of SWL strategies. But an even more marked difference comes from Bar-Lev's rejection of the following assumption which Gattegno—and almost everyone else who has taught or studied a language—accepts as fundamental:

From first to last, the target of all language instruction must be always and only the authentic adult model: native pronunciation, normal spelling, standard grammar, culturally appropriate pragmatics, etc. To foster the production of language that departs from the native model is unsanctioned, illegitimate, unthinkable and unforgivable!

Bar-Lev's heresy proposes that learners be sheltered at first from a deluge of grammatical, orthographic, phonetic, and semantic details so that they can concentrate on producing fluid, uninhibited speech. (Actually there is precedent for this heresy in such reductionist strategies as that of Basic English and Neoispano, and some support for it in writings on the implications of pidginization and creolization for language acquisition by John Schumann, Roger Andersen, and others. It should be noted here, however, that in SILL the progressive levels of interlanguage are controlled in such a way that there is no characteristic of pidginization; there are no necessary ungrammaticalities.) Bar-Lev has learners enter a language through ingeniously contrived, grammatically progressive, planned interlanguage levels of the language. Each lesson is a level of the prelanguage rather than a chunk of the standard language, and each level contains a selected vocabulary and a restricted grammar. (Of course, all beginning language courses present a more or less sheltered version of the language at first; Bar-Lev just takes the notion of sheltering much further than anyone else. He argues that even if we could present the full picture of such complex things as English definite article usage, our students would come up with a distortion of it or fail to apply it. We can teach and drill all the details of article usage until we are blue in the face, yet we know very well that most learners of English will not from that point on incorporate what we "taught" them into their interlanguage.)

What are the expected long-term results of introducing learners to a sheltered version of the language? It is expected that the gifted students will in time learn to speak no less accurately or fluently than under conventional training, but students who would not acquire either accuracy or fluency at all will be able to speak fluently—though without grammatical accuracy. Furthermore, these students would *enjoy* the language-learning experience. All would speak with less hesitancy and self-correction than they would under normal training.

What is the most notable early effect of teaching a sheltered version of a language? Within a short time, beginners are able to string words together into sentences and discourses of surprising length and complexity—and without errors that would jar a native listener. In fact, during the first hours after beginning instruction in a sheltered language, learners are creating story plots on their own. Picture a learner in her fourth hour of German spontaneously composing and telling an original story plot of the following level of ambitiousness:

The policeman comes to the house. The policeman says to the mother: "The fish is not good." The mother says: "The fish is good." The mother runs into the street and eats the fish. The mother is dead and the policeman says: "The fish is not good."

Within a few hours of SILL training, students become fluent narrators of such stories and are able to ask and answer simple questions such as "Who runs into the street?" Viewed from the perspective of the standard language, the learners' production may contain errors, buy they are not likely to be so noticeable as those of much more advanced learners in other approaches. In fluency and ambitiousness in sustained speech, though, SILL is most impressive—which is what it is from the first: fluent, ambitious, bold, risk-taking communication. SILL pushes learners to express themselves without vacillation even when they are unsure of the exact word or the precise form. *Midphrase hesitation is the demon.* For an extended period their performance is evaluated only on content, volume, and fluency of delivery.

One key to fluency is to start with uncluttered simplicity of form, taking as target a reduced rule-density language; another is to produce creative narration in one's own confident form of speech, blessed by the teacher's encouragement and not threatened by authoritarian correction based on native norms—or even the "norms" of the sheltered language. Bar-Lev uses both keys. To him, rendering an impromptu melody expressively on a piano with one finger is a better starting point than executing a piece miserably with ten.

He reminds us that the "tool-sharpening" theory of foreign language instruction, whereby students sharpen their grammar tools for a few semesters in preparation for later use of them, simply does not work for many students. Despite all the emphasis on nativelike accuracy of form, no curriculum has yet succeeded in getting learners to produce ambitious speech spontaneously without errors. All language learners speak imperfectly, even after years of study. What Bar-Lev wants to do is lead learners more quickly to optimal imperfection and to put them at peace with their imperfections.

Actually, most of the "errors" his learners make (errors if matched against the standard norm, which is not the immediate target) are the kind that are minimally confusing to native listeners. These are what he calls "optimal errors." He gives evidence to show that the fluent speech of SILL learners, sprinkled as it is with "optimal errors," is observably cleaner and nearer the native model than the hesitant and imperfect speech of learners trained, for example, in a "natural approach." Learning the full standard form of a language in a simulated natural acquisition environment does not result in optimal learning, Bar-Lev maintains. Just as the artist can improve the appearance of nature, so the SILL teacher can bring about something closer to optimal learning for the language learner.

A principle Bar-Lev uses in devising SILL curriculum—reminiscent of SWL—is to go for learnability above functionality at first. There is no rush to prepare students to cope with conceivable in-country survival situations. Of greater value is to create rewarding

and enjoyable learning experiences that show how much one can learn to communicate in a very short time and how exciting and satisfying such a learning experience can be.

Criticism of SILL is predictable. First of all, because in SILL (as also in SWL) learnability takes precedence over relevancy, and enjoyment and ease of learning over strict functionality, the same objections made to SWL will be brought against SILL. But SILL faces even stiffer resistance because of the liberties it allows with language form. There is something in all of us, it seems, that at first resists the idea of teaching students less than the full-blown truth about the forms of language. To counter that objection, Bar-Lev points out that fossilization of grammatical form and pronunciation is less to be feared than fossilization of habits of hesitation and vacillation. While adults are less flexible than children, under proper conditions they are able to correct their errors and bring their speech more and more closely in line with the norm as they progress in handling communication situations.

There is one other major criticism raised against the strategies Bar-Lev uses in SILL. As mentioned, in the interest of facilitating early fluency, he selects and sequences words and structures with an eye to their learnability as well as their communicative value; and then to aid in the learning of these, he uses mnemonic devices, pictures, flash cards, and other "scaffolding" strategies. For example, the first word presented in his book *Automatic Hebrew* is "elephant." It is presented by means of a cartoon of an elephant emerging out of a half-peeled banana. The Hebrew word for elephant sounds much like the English word "peel," so through association of the sound "peel" with the meaning "elephant" (an association aided by the clever cartoon image that codes both the sound and the meaning), the learner's task is rendered easy. The word now "has a handle on it." After practicing recall of the word a few times with the help of the mnemonic handle, the learner can access it directly; but if for some reason the word does not come to mind automatically when needed, s/he can resort to the mnemonic image to "find its handle."

Such temporary scaffolding is not unique to SILL, and it is not known to what extent teachers may introduce it themselves in class, but it is rarely seen in language teaching materials, and almost never used to such advantage as in SILL. Critics of such strategies grant that memory hooks may appear to facilitate recall at first, but claim that in the long run such artificial intervention is burdensome and counterproductive, for in the linguistic sign there must be only a direct connection between sound and symbol.

Again from the arguments pro and con SILL, it is clear that the issues are sensitive and complex, and furthermore that even though Bar-Lev's experimentation with such radical alternatives challenges conventional wisdom, it merits serious consideration. In any case, future explanations or theories of formal language learning will, I submit, need to account for the manifest success of SILL.

Outreach Learning

The next approach, which I call Outreach Learning, is based on two books written to guide learners who must learn a language on their own in a foreign setting. The first one is *Language Acquisition Made Practical* by E. Thomas Brewster and Elizabeth S. Brewster (1976); the later one is *Guidelines for Barefoot Language Learning* by Donald N. Larson (1984). Courses which use these books in lieu of a language textbook require each student in the course to select a language to learn for which there is a community of speakers nearby. They are then expected to set about learning the language on their own through interaction with native speakers, following the program and principles set forth in the books. The classroom is used only as a base from which learning in the community is launched. The basic thrust of the course is to help the students find that they can best con-

trol their own learning, and that the community of native speakers is the best possible learning resource.

Language teachers are generally not familiar with Outreach Learning, perhaps because it is not much concerned with language teaching in classrooms. It merits discussion here, however, because it takes into account important things about language learning that are seldom addressed in other approaches—most notably the critical social dimensions of learning a language. The approach is built on the foundational principle that, at least for people taking up residence in a foreign country, language learning involves joining a new social group, becoming an insider. The main challenge is not "How do I learn a language?"; it is "How do I become a functioning person in a new social group in a foreign culture?" The authors of Outreach Learning stress the fact that language acquisition is a social, not an academic activity—i.e. that social factors tower over instructional ones in shaping learning, and that if we ignore the myriad natural forces that shape communicative competence we may cause a pathology of results that is typical of language learned in classrooms. A teacher's or a learner's preoccupation with the mechanics of language form gets in the way of the natural forces of the mind, the personality, and the socializing and acculturative drives that motivate and channel one's progress in becoming an insider and forming bonds with cospeakers. Even the kind of pseudo-communication practiced in role-plays in many classrooms is bereft of the social and psychological reality needed to make learning optimal. In many ways, the authors insist, an academic approach runs counter to fundamental facts about language acquisition. Speech emerges not from listening comprehension training or production practice, but from the process of repeated, motivated, meaningful interaction with native speakers whose group one aspires to join.

In Outreach Learning, learners, with the help of a language consultant, work out a first text they can use to begin to establish social relationships with people in the community. The short text is a formulaic template composed of a greeting, a statement or two, and a farewell, but most importantly, one that provides a slot or two where prepared monolog scripts can be inserted later. It is what the learners then do with this text that counts most: They go out into the community and use the text over and over again in establishing contact with people, inviting these people to help them, to support them in learning the language, to become conversational partners with them. It is the social use of texts *together with* the forming of bonds with native speakers in the community that serves as the driving force of the approach. The task assignment from the first day is to meet dozens of people, in shops, homes, wherever one can find a comfortable moment to reach out to them with a warm handshake and smile and words that communicate interest in them. If Spanish were the language chosen, perhaps the first day's text would be:

---

(1) Hola.   *(2) Estoy aprendiendo espanol*   *(3) Se muy poco.*   *(4) Adios.*

(1) Hello.   *(2) I'm learning Spanish.*   *(3) I know very little.*   *(4) Good-bye.*

This much, plus some formulaic statements each day, such as "yes," "good," "please," "thanks," supply the minimum tools for engaging native speakers from the first day on in meaningful, if rudimentary, conversation.

The second day, an expanded text is worked up with the help of a language consultant. It might be something like this (plus another wild-card statement or two):

---

(1) Hola.   *(2) Me llamo Marlo Jones.*   *(3) Mucho gusto.*

(1) Hello.   *(2) My name is Marlo Jones.*   *(3) Nice to meet you.*

(4) Estoy aprendiendo una rima.   *(5) Paso manana, oquei?*   *(6) Adios.*

(4) I'm learning a poem.   *(5) I'll come by tomorrow, okay?*   *(6) Good-bye.*

By the third day, if not sooner, the learner can use that slightly expanded text as a frame for a short "discourse," a poem, joke, proverb, or anecdote worked up as a monolog. For example:

---

(1) Good morning.	*Buenos dias.*
(2) I've learned part of the poem.	*He aprendido una parte de la rima.*
(3) May I tell it to you?	*Me permite contarsela?*
I DON'T KNOW WHEN,	*NO SE CUANDO,*
I DON'T KNOW WHO,	*NO SE QUIEN,*
I DON'T ANYTHING	*NO SE NADA*
VERY WELL . . .	*MUY BIEN . . .*
(4) There's more. I forgot the rest.	*Hay mas. Se me olvido el resto.*
(5) I'll tell you it tomorrow, okay?	*Manana so lo dire, oquei?*
(6) Good-bye.	*Adios.*

Each day old friends are contacted and new friends are made, and the learners interact more capably each time, conversing and discoursing at a level they control. In a short time, other performatives besides monolog pieces can be added—for example, yes-no questions: "Do you like Chicago?" and then alternative questions: "Do you like Chicago or Miami better?" And a little later, information questions: "Where were you born?" Learners don't have years, months, weeks, or even days to rehearse dialogs and communicative functions or to master paradigms and patterns before using the language in the real world; they have only a small part of a day! And from that day on, their assignment is to reach out to people, expressing themselves with whatever they can put together, learning to cope with their inadequacies in self-expression and to tolerate the discomfort of understanding little of what is said to them. But from that first day on, every word they express in genuine person-to-person communication is emotionally charged and becomes personally meaningful as it contributes to their relationship with real persons. Every trip to the store, the bus stop, or the post office, gives an opportunity for "a language lesson" from a friend. Learning the language comes as a product of meeting the increasing communication demands that attend the process of becoming an insider. The difference between learning through this approach and learning in even the best classroom environment may be compared, someone has commented, to the difference between looking at maps or pictures of a place and actually being there.

The above is of course a very gross characterization of what Outreach Learning entails, but it is enough to give an idea of the principles that motivate it and of its initial steps and direction. Perhaps because it aims at deschooling language learning, its unique prescriptions have received little attention in the literature on language teaching, but for many teachers the prescriptions are quite suggestive: get learners out into the community and give them the task of making many friends who will help them as cospeakers of

English. Help them work out discourses of increasing complexity which they can insert in their conversations with these friends and make them accountable for the number and quality of contacts they make. Then get out of their way!

HUMANISTIC AND PSYCHOSUGGESTIVE APPROACHES

> Values-clarification and problem-posing approaches (Galyean, Freire)
>
> Suggestopedia (Lozanov)
>
> Counseling-learning community language learning (Curran)

The ideal of language teaching for communicative competence would be to provide massive comprehensible input under conditions of zero resistance, so that learners could turn *all* input into intake and have *all* intake accessible for output. Such an ideal has stimulated experimentation not only with learner-external dimensions of the learning environment (input and output) but also with learner-internal dimensions (the learner as receiver and processor of input, producer of output, and participant in a community of learners and speakers). An increasing number of members of the language teaching community are taking this long-neglected dimension as the focus of their work, seeking ways to increase learner receptivity to input and reduce learner anxiety about producing communicative output.

Focus on this dimension has come about in response to an important set of questions: How can differences between the learning efficiency of ordinary learners and of extraordinary learners be explained? What are the limits on the learning efficiency of ordinary adults? Why do limits exist? What can be done to push limits back? Can instruction be designed so as to tap more successfully the learning power of the mind and eliminate psychological barriers that block learning and inhibit production?

Partial motivation for such questions is

the abundant evidence that some otherwise ordinary people are capable of performing seemingly extraordinary feats of learning. For example, people with "photographic memory" can recall complicated visual images; speed-readers can absorb information from a written page at many times the normal rate; some people who cannot read music can play hundreds of pieces by heart; some illiterate singers can memorize a new ballad of great length and complexity on hearing it one time only. Then there is the oft-heard claim that we use only a fraction of the learning capacity of our brain, and the suggestion that what keeps us from exploiting our learning potential is a variety of cultural and psychological resistance factors which place artificial limits on information processing: "Hearing, we do not hear; seeing we do not see." Of the various metaphors applied to this composite of resistance factors, the most current one is "filters" (more specifically, affective, cognitive, input, and output filters). The effect of the set of input filters is to block input from becoming intake; the effect of the set of output filters is to inhibit intake from becoming output. The psychological and neurological components that produce the effect called filtering are not yet well understood, but the metaphor seems to be a useful one. As learners find how to "lower their filters," it is suggested, they become able to process more input as intake and access more intake as output.

A growing number of language teachers concern themselves now with the question of how to lower the affective filters. Common advice for this is still: keep the lessons pleasant, fun, and nonthreatening; smile and give lots of encouragement, and similar admonitions. But these are cliches. There are more interesting attempts to deal with the affective filters.

Values-Clarification and Problem-Posing Approaches

Certain words are commonly associated with approaches which take aim on lowering the filters: whole-person, humanistic, holis-

tic, new dimensions, accelerated, suggestopedic, and many others. A values-clarification approach is an example of one of these. The principal assumption behind it is that the most efficient learning is that which promotes self-understanding and self-realization, that language learners experience least resistance to learning when they use language to look within and talk about themselves and the immediate community and events surrounding them in ways that can lead to personal insight or values clarification. A values-clarification approach, then, prescribes a kind of instruction in which the topic is the self in relation to other persons, states, and events. Here is a sample of the kind of exchange in which a learner is engaged in talk about herself and others in the community.

T: *Betty, my eyes are closed but you are the focus of my mind's eye. What do you imagine I am seeing?*
B: *My face smiling at you.*
T: *What else am I seeing?*
B: *My pink sweater and brown skirt.*
T: *What kind of person is it I am seeing?*
B: *A teenager who is a little shy but full of fun.*
T: *Now in my mind's eye I am looking at Roger, seated next to you. What do you imagine I am seeing?*
B: *Someone who is confident and serious. A good athlete. A nice guy.*

Here is an even more personal sample (from Galyean, 1982).

On the board I have written a model sentence. . . . You are to supply your own answers. The purpose of this exercise is to help you think about similarities and differences between things you did as a child and those you do now. See what patterns, if any, you discover. In what ways have you changed? Remained the same? Do you think you are making free choices or are you trapped by past patterns of behavior?

> *When I was a child I used to play* _____ *but now I play* _____.
>
> *When I was a child I used to read* _____ *but now I read* _____.

*When I was a child I used to wonder about
_____ but now I wonder about
_____.*

*When I was a child I used to look forward to
_____ but now I look forward to
_____.*

Such activities as these may at first seem to be merely language exercises; however, because of the personal significance of their content, they can serve as lead-ins to discussions that can bring out perceptions and insights of personal interest. The students are not role-playing but are being themselves. It is not a game; there is nothing artificial about it. They have something genuine to say, something that matters to them. And in the pleasure and excitement of speaking and hearing "language from within" they drop their defenses and lower their affective filter. Anyway, that is what is hoped for in a values-clarification approach. A good start on the literature on this is found in Galyean (1982) and Moskowitz (1978).

A "problem-posing approach" aims also for self-understanding, but at a personal and community level deeper than in values-clarification approaches. The father of problem-posing as an educational approach is Paulo Freire, a Brazilian social critic and education reformer whose revolutionary work for the education of impoverished peasants in northeastern Brazil brought him international renown. Freire's approach involved first helping these people "grasp the reality of their oppression," raising their political consciousness of issues and problems in the circumstances of their lives, and seeing that they are not helpless and impotent but can make themselves agents in changing their political, economic, social, and cultural circumstances. Literacy is motivated and purposeful, for it gives them a powerful tool by which they can bring about change. This "conscientization" and politicization was initiated through problem-posing, together with the dialog which rose out of it, resulting in a new vision of life's possibilities which could be brought about through concerted community

action. The intended culmination of the conscientization was always community action.

Such education and political involvement was not for the domestication of people or the transfer of knowledge or skill, Freire stated; it was for the humanization and liberation of the oppressed. The acquisition and use of literacy then came as a by-product of the conscientization and politicization process. The childish primers used in conventional literacy programs were useless, their vocabulary and subject matter being powerless to evoke discussion of the situation, the needs, and the potential power of the oppressed community, and therefore irrelevant to the needs of radical education. In Freirian literacy campaigns, words, pictures, and ideas are selected for inclusion for their political, economic, social, and cultural implications and their power to evoke dialog about realities and needed change. A word or concept such as *favela* ("slum"), for example, would be a candidate for dialog, since it is evocative of the grim circumstances and critical needs of the poor and oppressed.

Used in ESL training in the United States, the Problem-Posing Approach is still recognizable. Dialog is generally promoted by pictures or other evocative stimuli plus problem-posing questions:

"What do you see in this picture? Is there any problem you can discern? What are the people doing? Why are they doing that? Does what they are doing make sense to you? What do you see could be long-range consequences of such actions?"

The teacher or discussion moderator, like Phil Donahue on TV, never proposes solutions but only attempts to draw out responses from the learners and, if necessary, to moderate the discussion by giving cognitive or affective feedback:

I understand you to be saying you don't like to work in a smoke-filled room. You believe tobacco smoke can be injurious to non-smokers, but you don't know what you can do to get smokers to respect your position. Is that right?

This first step, then, is *problem identification*. The next step is *reflection and research*, often from the points of view of both the native culture and the target culture. In this, learners collaborate on tasks such as conducting research out of class on aspects and perceptions of the problem.

The third step is *action toward solving the problem*. The students make decisions about what action to take to mitigate the problem, and then proceed to take that action, which might be to write letters to the editor, solicit high-level support, or other methods. Following that, there may be a *summative review and practice* during which key linguistic pragmatic items used in the problem-identification, reflection-research, and action steps are gone over.

The primary intent of the moderator (teacher) is to bring about conscientization and emotional involvement in the issues discussed, and to see those subsequently raised to concerted action responses. To the extent that learners become deeply involved personally and communally in the communication process on matters that affect their lives and on which their action can have influence, they will experience increased readiness to learn what is perceived as needed. A start on other sources of information on this approach can be found in Freire (1970a, 1973) and Crawford-Lange (1987).

Suggestopedia

One can imagine a number of ways, other than the above, that might be used to stimulate learning readiness or subdue psychological resistance to learning: hypnosis, subliminal messages, meditative relaxation, guided imagery, soft slow-beat music, electrical or sound impulses, creative art. Actually, all of these and more are being experimented with in the investigation of learning resistance and the search for more effective means to increase it. A major influence in encouraging if not legitimizing such experimentation has been the research of Giorgi Lozanov (1978, 1982, 1988), beginning in

the 1960s, with music therapy, relaxation, and other suggestological means of enhancing learning readiness. A Bulgarian physician and psychotherapist, Lozanov first used the rapid memorization of foreign vocabulary as the test vehicle of his experimentation with suggestology, concluding that the experimental techniques used, aimed at relaxing the subjects and fostering hope and trust in their own powers of learning massive amounts quickly and easily, made possible a phenomenal rate of learning—up to a thousand words in an hour, reportedly, or (as advertised) "from five to fifty times the normal rate!" Then he experimented with higher-order language learning, producing, it was claimed, equally dramatic results.

Suggestopedia, as he called his pedagogical application of "the science of suggestology" (of which hypnosis is one branch), aims specifically at neutralizing learning inhibitions and de-suggesting false limitations that cultural norms impose on learning. He rejected the paradoxical but increasingly popular solution to instructional impotence: "Less is more, slow is fast." He would demonstrate that by artfully enhancing learner receptivity, "much more can be much more, and much faster can be much faster!" Was it possible that suggestopedia could bring about learning superconductivity, a perfect state of learning receptiveness enabling learners to process massive input into intake with no forgetting? That was the aim, and some of Lozanov's experiments, it was claimed, had come close to achieving it.

As can be expected, such claims were met generally with skepticism, particularly when the Lozanov Method was swept up by the media and sensationalized, then commercialized. The only way to see for oneself how this marvelous new way of teaching and learning actually worked was to take an expensive workshop. So in the language teaching profession generally, suggestopedia was looked at as a sensationalized, mysterious, costly, and highly questionable new gimmick, something not sanctioned, not legitimate, and imagined to be as far removed from

American-style language teaching as yoga, hypnosis, sleep learning and the like. Those who read Lozanov's writings on suggestopedia found them to be characterized more by an intimidating jargon associated with medical science and psychotherapy than by clarity of exposition. Yet in many countries of eastern and western Europe, in South Africa and North America and elsewhere, some experimentalists began seriously to explore ideas and techniques associated initially with suggestopedia. By the late 1980s, in its various international transformations, it had been given new dimensions and new names: Accelerated Learning, SuperLearning, Power Learning, Integrated Learning, Right-Brain Learning, Psychopedia, Language in New Dimensions, and others, but for most language teachers in America it remains yet today wrapped in mystery.

In my view, the most important product of Lozanov's research, though, was not a new model for language teaching or even a higher baseline for the measurement of success, but rather an increased realization (1) that language instruction research must look beyond manipulating the external dimensions of the learning environment, (2) that extremely important psychological and cultural variables in the learning environment which had not been understood or addressed previously are open to experimentation, and (3) that suggestology and perhaps other ways of dealing with the psyche of learners provide fresh ideas and tools. The increased readiness of the community of language teaching specialists to consider such alternatives as these today is due, I think, to the growing acceptance of the filters hypothesis and an increased readiness to believe that there may be more effective ways to deal with the filters than we had supposed.

There is not space here to adequately describe the procedures of "classical" suggestopedia or of any of its later versions or transformations, but a hint of what one part of one form of it entails will suggest how extraordinary some of its procedures are. The instructional setting suggests a living room more than a classroom. The learners sit in easy chairs. The teacher is lively, dynamic, confident, yet sensitive, and speaks only the target language, which suggests that the learners do the same. In the first three-hour meeting, all learners choose a new name and nationality, after which they are given a fictional autobiography. By means of song, imitation, and play, the learners are enabled to introduce themselves to each other and assume their new roles. Then over the next two days, the teacher twice presents a script that is many pages long, each time with a different aim and a different learning setup; these script performances, called "concert sessions," are accompanied by music. In the first of these, the "active concert session," the music is emotional, and the tone of the artistic presentation reflects the character of the music, as if the reader were part of the orchestra. The use of musical, dramatic, and visual art are marked characteristics of Lozanov's teaching. The learners have the script in two languages arranged in short phrases on opposite sides of the page. After the concert session come various kinds of elaboration activities, including group or choral reading of parts of the script, singing and playing games as a group, and such. The second day the script is performed again, this time in a "pseudopassive concert session," where a state of wakeful relaxation is artfully stimulated. This reading is accompanied by music of a different tone and mood, generally baroque-style. Following that, the learners (in their new identities) are aided again in elaborating the script in various ways. This may include narrating an event or anecdote, or creating an original story, using the language in the script.

Being a teacher, a learner, and an observer of classes using various versions of suggestopedia has been for me a delightful and instructive experience. There is more joviality and camaraderie in this form of learning than in any other I know of. The concert sessions do indeed, for many, induce wakeful relaxation which seems to have positive effect on learning: input slips in without notice, many have reported, so that one has the sensation of not having learned much at all, yet in the elaboration activities many things are found to have lodged in the mind, seemingly learned without cost!

Counseling-Learning Community Language Learning

Of all approaches to language learning, I think the most underrated is Counseling-Learning Community Language Learning (C-L CLL). I can only suppose that the reason it is so underrated is that on the surface level, at first glance, one part of its procedure may look so simple and transparent that some teachers have taken the part for the whole and perceive it as merely a ready technique, requiring neither text nor preparation, which they can add to their collection of free-time activities. All that may seem to be required is a teacher to translate student utterances slowly and clearly so that they can repeat the words phrase by phrase. This perception of C-L CLL is woefully shallow and distorted. To be sure, one aspect of the approach may require translation and repetition, but to take this small part for the whole is like taking a sophisticated computer to be only an old-fashioned typewriter.

Interestingly, as was the case of almost all the other innovative approaches mentioned above, C-L CLL was developed by someone who had no training as a language teacher but chose language as a vehicle for experimentation with learning and the promotion of learning. Charles A. Curran was a Catholic priest and a professor of clinical psychology at Loyola University (Chicago), where he wrote and conducted research on the application of principles of clinical psychology to education. Trained by Carl Rogers in clinical psychology, he saw in traditional educational philosophy and practice the cause of many learner discomforts and learning pathologies. He theorized that inept learning and consequent negative feelings and behaviors may be brought about by depersonalized ways of teaching which split head from heart and individual from community—that is, ways which address the individual learner's intellect alone to the neglect of other dimensions of the self-in-community. He felt that teachers are unaware of what depersonalized instruction does to resistant learners. He took as his main concern the deep-level interpersonal dynamics of the teacher–learner relationship and the teaching-learning process and concluded that the kind of healthy growth which learning can represent must involve the whole, integrated person of the learner: intellect, emotions, values, and personality—all related to the same integrated features in the teacher and in every other person taking part in the community of learners.

In his philosophy of holistic learning and education as well as in his blaming the traditional, depersonalized methods of instruction for causing learning pathologies, Curran is at one with other proponents of humanistic education, but in his prescriptions of what to do to promote optimal, joyful, therapeutic learning, he is unique. He adds, I believe, a profound new dimension to a comprehension of the learning and teaching process, a dimension which cannot be reduced to a set of classroom procedures or techniques, but which requires that a teacher use effective ways of deeply understanding learners in their struggle to learn. These ways parallel those found in the dynamics of an effective counselor–client relationship as viewed by Rogers. As genuine understanding and support is given according to the principles of Rogerian counseling, the learner finds that he or she can talk honestly and openly within the group about the learning experience, feeling confident of being understood, and through receiving and sensing this understanding, can dissipate negative factors that block the way to learning.

One thing observers of one of the main activities of a C-L CLL class may notice is that there is no visible textbook, prepared lesson plan, or even defined objectives. Rather, there is a group of learners, sitting in a circle, who themselves initiate conversation (in the native or the target language), the proper target-language form of which they are aided in producing by one or more fluent speakers outside the circle ("angels on the shoulder" I call them). Observers will note that in a short time the learners generate a massive amount of unrestricted, self-motivated target-language data, some or all of which is recorded as it comes from their lips. A postsession debriefing may involve instruction dealing with the form and substance of the material generated in the session.

What casual observers of a C-L CLL class are likely to misunderstand and underrate is the vital function of the reflection sessions in which the learners (clients) are invited to talk about the learning experience they have just gone through, and the teacher (counselor) reflects back to them an understanding of the experience they have shared. Observers with no background in clinical psychology are likely to fail to appreciate the important role this interchange plays in the learning dynamics, and will likely underestimate the effect this can have on opening the learning pathways. However, if observers happen to attend only a very beginning class and then the same class several weeks later, they will likely be surprised at the quickness, confidence, and communicative ability that the learners have acquired. Recommended as good first sources on C-L CLL are Rardin et al. (1988) and Curran (1976).

CONCLUSION

Developments in language teaching come about, at least in part, as probing questions are researched and alternative answers are explored. Most of this chapter was devoted to describing some recent answers to questions such as those posed at the beginning. Clearly, the work of Asher, Bar-Lev, Brewster and Brewster, Burling, Curran, Freire, Galyean, Gattegno, Larson, Lozanov, Postovsky, and Terrell discussed above has contributed meaningfully to the current dialog about language teaching and learning. The contributions of most of these pioneers is discussed in several books that treat language

teaching methodology since 1960: Blair (1982), Larsen-Freeman (1986), Oller and Richard-Amato (1983), Richard-Amato (1988), Richards and Rodgers (1986). An excellent summary of many of the issues involved in innovative methods is found in Breen (1987b, 1987c).

It is impossible, of course, to predict how the work of these explorers, individually or collectively, will affect language teaching in the future, or how it will contribute to an emerging "paradigm shift" in how the community of language education specialists view their world, but it cannot be denied that the work of the innovators constitutes a challenge to conventional thinking about language teaching. As the process and the results of alternative models are researched and compared to those of more conventional models, it will be interesting to see what the data will show.

DISCUSSION QUESTIONS

1. How can the CBL viewpoint "From much, little" be compatible with Gattegno's "From little, much"?

2. Is the immediate fostering of ambitious communication efforts counterproductive to the acquisition of fluency and accuracy? Is it not like trying to force a baby to walk before it can crawl?

3. Is premature, faulty production potentially deleterious to the eventual emergence of fluent and accurate speech?

4. Would you justify or condemn the following in language teaching? Why?

a. Code switching as a pedagogical device ("diglot-weave")
b. Initially simplifying the language code
c. Relaxed learning (as with suggestopedia)
d. Frequent use of mnemonic aids

5. Of what value have experiments with radically innovative approaches been? Have they enlarged our vision? Increased our understanding? Do you see them as contributing to the emergence of a new and better model of learning?

6. According to one or another view of language acquisition, risk taking and conversational interaction play a major part in language acquisition. What implications do you think they have for language teaching?

SUGGESTED ACTIVITIES

1. Select one of the approaches discussed in this chapter and debate its assumptions and their application to language teaching.

2. Language teachers are divided on a number of issues, the following among them. Take a side and debate the strengths of your position and the weakness of the other.

    a. Elicit speech from the beginning.
    b. Delay speech to provide a comprehension-building period.

    a. Place initial emphasis on learners' getting the forms right.
    b. Place initial emphasis on learners' inferencing meaning.

    a. Encourage only reproduction of modeled discourse.
    b. Encourage production of original, ambitious discourse.

    a. Teach exclusively for in-country "survival" proficiency at first.
    b. Teach essentially for enjoyment and ease of learning at first.

    a. Push for mastery of all points in a proficiency-based syllabus.
    b. Expect mostly incidental learning in a process-based syllabus.

3. Describe a particular group of beginning-level language learners that you are familiar with. What is their age, educational level, and cultural background? For what purpose do they need to learn the new language? How much do they need to learn? How urgent are their needs? Now decide which method or combination of methods described in this chapter might be effective with this group of learners.

SUGGESTIONS FOR FURTHER READING

Blair, R. W., ed (1982)
Innovative approaches to language teaching. New York: Newbury House.

Bowen, J. D., H. Madsen, and A. Hilferty (1985)
TESOL Techniques and Procedures. New York: Newbury House.

Larsen-Freeman, D. (1986)
Techniques and principles in language teaching. New York: Oxford University Press.

Long, M. H., and J. C. Richards, eds. (1987)
Methodology in TESOL: A Book of Readings. New York: Newbury House.

Moskowitz, G. (1978)
Caring and Sharing in the Foreign Language Class: A Source-Book on Humanistic Techniques. New York: Newbury House.

Oller, J., and P. Richard-Amato, eds. (1983)
Methods That Work. New York: Newbury House.

Richard-Amato, P. (1988)
Making It Happen. New York: Longman.

Richards, J., and T. Rodgers (1986)
Approaches and Methods in Language Teaching. New York: Cambridge University Press.

Stevick, E., (1976)
Memory, Meaning and Method. New York: Newbury House.

Winitz, H. (1981)
The Comprehension Approach. New York: Newbury House.

Guidelines for Classroom Language Teaching[1]

Graham Crookes and Craig Chaudron

INTRODUCTION

Knowledge concerning what goes on in the classroom between teacher and students is obviously the core area of information pertaining to formal second language (SL) teaching and learning. Although knowledge of out-of-class aspects of SL teaching such as needs analysis, curriculum design, lesson planning, materials design, and evaluation are necessary for a truly professional operation, at times when these must be dealt with minimally (as when teaching under difficult circumstances), so long as there is a teacher working with a group of students, the essence of classroom SL teaching is present, and SL learning is possible.

In this chapter we identify and discuss some of the more important characteristics and principles of this interaction, most of which derive from a logical analysis of the classroom teaching situation.[2] Our conception of the teacher is someone faced with a great number of decisions to be made at every moment of classroom instruction. In some cases, research findings can guide those decisions. In many others, research can inform professional judgment, but decisions must be based on feel rather than knowledge. However, the decision will be aided by a knowledge of the conceptually determined range of alternatives available.

When a second language is to be taught, a number of major steps must be taken, in terms of which the chapter is organized. First, elements of the language must be brought into the classroom and presented by the teacher to students.[3] Or, if language is not presented, then a skill, a learning strategy, or some aspect of the use of language will be set out for consideration. Second, that which has been presented must in addition be learned, and the teacher has to arrange matters and events to bring this about. The teacher selects learning activities and facilitates their utilization. Third, by the very nature of learning, information must be provided to learners concerning their success—the teacher must provide knowledge of results, i.e., correction, or feedback, to the students. Fourth, all of these processes take place in a social milieu, and because of the way language functions between individuals, the processes cannot be totally separated from the social climate which develops among students and between teacher and students. Finally, although the processes immediately adjacent in time to the lesson (teachers' lesson planning and teachers' evaluation of the students' success, i.e., testing) are dealt with elsewhere in this book, one more process which is very close to the lesson itself will be discussed here. Conscientious SL teachers usually come out of a class asking themselves "how the class went"—which is to say, they engage in a process of self-evaluation. We believe that this is a vital process for professional self-development, and one which needs to be explicitly structured into SL teachers' routines. We include it here as it is an integral part of efficient SL classroom skills.

LANGUAGE PRESENTATION

Meta-planning for Lesson Objectives

Which elements of a lesson are undertaken depends on the objectives a teacher has in mind to be attained by the lesson. (Such objectives need not be the orthodox "behavioral" objectives, it should be noted.) They are then the result of lesson planning, which Purgason's chapter discusses. However, in general terms, the first element of a lesson is often the first component of the traditional "present-practice-evaluate" sequence which constitutes many teachers' understanding of basic lesson structure, both within and outside SL teaching.

Though this is not always necessary, particularly if the lesson is intended mainly to practice material already partially learned, let us assume for present purposes that a teacher has selected a particular element of language, or aspect of language learning, to be presented as the first major stage of a class period. There are then two main classes of choices to be made: those concerning the physical characteristics of the presentation, that is, materials, use of audiovisual (AV) equipment, etc., and those concerning the conceptual aspects of the presentation, i.e., deductive or inductive, via rules or analogies, and so on. The former are considered in the following section, the latter in the section after that.

Modalities (Materials, AV)

The increasing quantity and quality of published ESL materials means that teachers are less and less thrown entirely on their own resources, which is undoubtedly a good thing.[4] Without materials, the average teacher is probably even more likely than usual to succumb to the tendency to dominate the classroom by taking up class time. However, there is increasing recognition[5] of SL learning as a process of skill acquisition (O'Malley, Chamot, & Walker, 1987), which implies the importance of practice—that is, output, rather than mere input (cf. Harmer's 1983 "balanced activities" approach). Teachers thus need to remain aware that they are not in the classroom to fill up the time with the sound of their own voices, but to arrange matters so that their students do the talking (or writing, or listening). Particularly in EFL rather than ESL situations, class time is so valuable that we believe the teacher should get offstage as soon as possible consistent with an adequate presentation of material, and the giving of clear instructions for some practice exercise. (See the section "Class organization.")

Assuming that the instructor decides that a given teaching objective calls for some support in the way of materials, what then? The major resource is of course the textbook. In addition, other teaching aids fall into two categories (Celce-Murcia, 1979): nontechnical aids, and technical (projected) aids (not counting the students themselves, who can of course play a stimulating role in the presentation stages of the lesson). The former are the chalkboard, realia, flashcards, magazine pictures, charts, and so on. The latter include the overhead projector, audiotape, and videotape. Both types of aids are considered elsewhere in this book (see the chapter by Brinton), so we will not discuss them in detail here, except to point out that although it is obvious that, for example, visual support of a presentation can aid its comprehensibility, by contextualizing the language involved, in most cases the utility of such aids appears rarely to have been thought important enough for SL-related investigation (as opposed to prescription). Whether or not to use them, therefore, is usually a matter for individual judgment, supported by general considerations. Does their use in a given circumstance aid comprehension, for example; does it stimulate more student talk than would have otherwise occurred; above all, does their use constitute an efficient use of class time, particularly taking into account the teacher time required to produce them, or the logistics of setting up and later removing the equipment? It is also a matter where teachers in general would benefit from some careful teacher investigation and report concerning success and failure in practice.

Perhaps because of the complexity of the question, a similar research vacuum surrounds the question of how actually to use a textbook. For the untrained teacher, a good textbook can stand for a syllabus and training program, while an experienced teacher will not hesitate to use the text as an aid, adopting parts, adapting other elements (cf. Stevick, 1971), and dispensing with it completely under some circumstances. The utility of the average textbook for a typical present-day ESL course is normally unquestioned (but see Allwright, 1981, and O'Neill, 1982, for positions on both sides of this point). The complexity of most textbooks defies specific suggestions, but we would urge teachers to remember that most textbooks are the product of the pressures of the market, as imperfectly interpreted through the interaction of publisher and materials writer. As Ariew (1982) mentions, this is why texts (in a given period of time) are often very much alike; market pressures, however, are not the same as educational pressures. What sells may not be what works; what works may not necessarily have a format which book-publishing companies can utilize or produce. Above all, therefore, a critical stance is called for (see also Richards, 1984).

With regard to the presentation stage, some general points can be made. The main one is that the instructor is, in fact, rather free from constraints despite the various procedures suggested by the teachers' notes typically accompanying the text. Texts designed for beginning and intermediate learners commonly present the material of each unit via a dialog, and the teacher is often instructed to have the students "do" the dialog. This will likely involve having the class as a whole, or in large sections, repeat the dialog in unison, possibly moving on then to partial memorization. Perhaps an equally efficient procedure for some classes would be to have students pair off and read the dialog aloud, while the

teacher circulates and checks individual performance. The point is that teachers have full right and responsibility to utilize the material in whatever way seems appropriate. However, we hope they will make use of the findings that SL research suggests can be applied here.

For example, recent work has stressed the role of attention and awareness in SL learning (Schmidt, 1990), and the importance of drawing the learner's attention to certain characteristics of the language which might otherwise be missed (Rutherford, 1987). It follows, therefore, that the teacher should usually present the text or illustrative material with an immediate focus on what the target points are. On the other hand, research over the last decade has made clear that SL learning does not take place in a simple linear fashion, with one linguistic element simply being added to the next. In the syntactic domain, learners proceed at different speeds through fairly regular sequences (Pienemann & Johnston, 1987, inter alia). In particular, it is unlikely that structural target points will be internalized by many in the class after one exposure. Consequently, the presentation phase with regard to a particular aspect of language should almost certainly come up on other occasions, in other lessons. The accurate description of SL learning as the learning of a cognitive skill (O'Malley et al., 1987) implies the appropriateness of an initial presentation, and the inevitability of a first stage of use (the "cognitive stage") which is errorful and difficult for the learner. Movement toward automaticity will require a great deal of active, realistic practice in the use of the target language, which may not be particularly susceptible to general error correction. Again, at the presentation stage, it is relevant to consider what little is known about the learner's development of control over the pragmatic aspects of the SL. This is facilitated by an emphasis on realistic, communicative language use in the classroom from an early stage, and also by developing the metalinguistic language needed to talk about this aspect of language (Henriksen, 1988; Kasper & House, 1981).

As a final comment, though we have used the generally accepted term "textbook" throughout this section, looking to the future, it may be that the textbook as such will become obsolete. As desktop publishing becomes increasingly available, and particularly with increased availability of optical readers (which can input pictorial material directly into word-processed material), it seems likely that in-house materials will become increasingly used. The advantages with regard to personalization and localization of materials are clear; such materials can also be tailored to meet the needs and strengths of the teachers of a given school or program (Dubin & Olshtain, 1986).

Rule Presentations

A great deal of research in the 1960s was directed at the question of whether and when to present explicit second language grammar rules to students (Levin, 1972). The upshot of those studies was that explicit grammar instruction was not consistently superior in the long run to other practices. As a result, the various communicatively oriented language teaching methods and prescriptions in recent years have de-emphasized the use of explicit grammar rule presentation, and even a concern for grammatically based materials (see, e.g., Krashen, 1982; Larsen-Freeman, 1986; Richards & Rodgers, 1986). However, recent research on second language acquisition has again raised the question (Harley, 1988; Long, 1988; Rutherford, 1987; Rutherford & Sharwood Smith, 1988), both because sequences of acquisition might be affected by the order of presentation of particular forms (e.g., Tomasello & Herron, 1988; Zobl, 1985) and because students' attention to form may enhance their performance (at least in the short run, e.g., Harley, 1989; Hulstijn & Hulstijn, 1984; Mitchell, Parkinson, & Johnstone, 1981; cf. also the discussion in Chaudron, 1988). Furthermore, rule presentation need not be limited to grammar points. As more and more language curricula include the

functional and sociolinguistic or pragmatic aspects of second language use, teachers need to be conversant with the appropriate rules of use and should be prepared to present these to students as they begin to study a given topic.

Effective language teachers should therefore not only be aware of developments in knowledge about acquisitional sequences, but they should be able to provide pedagogically comprehensible, accurate descriptions of second language grammar rules and rules of use when appropriate. Some such provision is often made in the text or materials, with graphic displays of paradigms (e.g., the conjugation of "to be," the assignment of relative pronouns depending on case, the sequence of prenominal determiners and adjectives, when to say "Hello," "Hi," and "How's it goin' ").

Nevertheless, the teachers' presentation of rules will normally involve reformulations for their students' specific problems and degree of understanding, as Færch (1986) suggests. Teachers should have at the ready descriptions of typical rule applications with illustrations (such as when and how to use "some" versus "any"), and associated practice exercises. After observing several classrooms, Færch (1986) found that a typical sequence in teacher rule-presentation involved, first, a "Problem formulation," next, an "Induction," with the teacher eliciting student opinions, and then the teacher's "Rule-formulation," followed optionally by further "Exemplification" by the teacher or students. Alert teachers will adapt this typical pattern to their circumstances, either shortening the sequence if a rule is judged to be quickly learned, or developing more student-generated ideas and interaction if the students have difficulty with it.

Despite the probable usefulness of rule presentations in many instances, teachers should nonetheless stay closely abreast of current research on second language acquisition, in order to understand which sorts of rules are reasonably learned and controlled, and which are not.

Explanations

As a follow-up to the presentation of rules, teachers need to be prepared at all times during instruction not only to respond to students' questions, providing explanations of the learning points, but also to react to learners' problems (see later section, "Correction and Feedback"), clarifying for the learners the possible source of their problems, and "explaining" possible solutions. Obviously, such explanations will not always be phrased in terms of the target grammar, functions, or use, for they may involve study habits, psychological operations with language, or physical behaviors (such as how to place the tongue to pronounce /θ/).

Although explanations are frequent and important, little research has been focused directly on how teachers provide them. Eisenstein (1980) provides a characterization of some of the factors to be considered in giving grammar explanations: whether a grammatical description should be explicit or not; whether a rule is isolated or not; whether the explanation involves a deductive or inductive presentation; who gives the explanation—the teacher, text, or another student; whether the language is abstract or not; and whether the explanation is provided orally or in writing. On the basis of classroom observation and analysis, Chaudron (1982) outlines a variety of features of teachers' discourse that were used to clarify and explain (sometimes implicitly) teachers' vocabulary use. The most explicitly explanatory of these included repetition and emphasis in pronunciation, analysis of morphology, provision of antonyms and synonyms, nonverbal demonstrations, verbal examples and collocations, descriptions of characteristics or typical situations for use of a term, translations, paraphrases, and use of definitions.

Following Chaudron's approach, Yee & Wagner (1984) developed a discourse model of teachers' vocabulary and grammar explanations. Their model (reproduced in Chaudron, 1988, p. 88) contains several major segments (a framing stage, a focusing stage, the explanation itself, and a restatement), with several subcategories as optional features (e.g., with or without mention of the topic item, metastatements, teacher solicits of students, examples), and at each stage, they point out that comprehension checks by the teacher are optional. An example of their model in a brief grammar explanation is the following:

Teacher:	Can we say "these" in a tag?	Focus + solicit
	You can't use the word "these" in a tag.	Explanation + explicit rule
	What do we need to use?	+ solicit

Clearly, teachers should pay attention to the clarity and sufficiency of their explanations, especially to the extent of student comprehension. Just as with general teacher feedback, teachers should never assume that their explanations are understood or "learned." Students need to be given the opportunity to demonstrate comprehension, and preferably not merely by solicitation of a "yes" or a nod. We will discuss student responsiveness more below, under question types and wait time.

TASKS

Clearly, to aid discussion and communication among teachers (as well as for the sake of comparative research), it is useful to have a set of terms to describe similar teaching procedures. Therefore, in the following sections we will utilize the terms "activity" and "task," looking in particular at the characteristics of these that are important for successful control over teaching and learning.

Subsections of a Lesson— the Activity

Probably the most commonly used and general term for the units of which a lesson consists is "activity." Most teachers, in discussing their lesson plans and behaviors, will use this word, although specific activities often have particular names. Surprisingly, however, through the years there has been remarkably little standardization of either a definition or a delineation of the set of possible language teaching activities. The term rarely if ever appears indexed in the classic language teaching methodology texts and is not an entry in the *Longman Dictionary of Applied Linguistics* (Richards, Platt, & Weber, 1985), although it is named as an alternative to the entry for "task." We do not propose here to explore fully the breadth of possibilities, or distinguish definitively among the uses of the terms "activity," "exercise," or "task." In fact, however, much recent analysis of SL classrooms, materials, and syllabi has utilized the last term to discuss those less-controlled activities which produce realistic use of the SL. These have also characterized the *communicative approaches*[6] whose upsurge marks the current era of SL teaching. In order to discuss both the controlled and freer types of classroom learning procedures we will on this occasion utilize "activity" as a broader term, with "task" applying to a separable element of a lesson, which is primarily geared to practicing language presented earlier (or otherwise learned), usually involving students working with each other, and which has a specific objective (see below).

In much early work on language teaching, the concern was on the nature of skill use, drill types (e.g., Politzer, 1970), and eventually types of communicative interaction (referred to as activities by Paulston & Bruder, 1976). Thus, fairly extensive taxonomies of drill types were detailed, on a continuum from "controlled" to "free" (i.e., with respect to the degree of teacher versus student control), or "mechanical" to "meaningful," to "communicative." The frequent dictum is that, for a specific learning point, learners need to develop from more controlled and mechanical to more free and communicative behaviors. Therefore, a classification of activity types along such a continuum sets the

options from which the teacher can select a given sequence within a lesson.

Unfortunately, very little classroom research has involved a consistent system of description upon which to base comparisons of the communicative degree of activities (though see the teacher attitude/opinion surveys of Swaffar, Arens, & Morgan, 1982, and Nunan, 1988a). For example, Fröhlich, Spada, and Allen (1985) do not specify the set of activities they used to segment their classroom analyses. Mitchell et al. (1981) also only analyze a small set of "language" activities as segments of lessons (e.g., "translation," "real FL," "transposition," "imitation"), which they propose interact with class groupings, topics, skills areas, and modes of teacher involvement. Nunan (1988) cites a 1985 study by K. Eltis and B. Low which polled 445 teachers on the perceived usefulness of teaching activities, and the following ranking was found (from high to low usefulness):

> students working in pairs/small groups
> role-play
> language games
> reading topical articles
> students making oral presentations
> cloze exercises
> using video materials
> students repeating teacher cue (drill)
> exercise in free writing
> setting and correcting homework
> listening and note taking
> repeating and learning dialogs
> students reading aloud in class
> exercises in conference writing
> (adapted from Nunan, 1988, p. 89)

In recent classroom observation work by Chaudron and Valcárcel (1988), a tentative list of activity types has been developed. We display this list grouped according to three degrees of teacher versus student control over the performance of the activity, although, like other practitioners, we recognize that factors such as the topic and the teacher's goals can influence the degree of control. Teachers should be familiar with each of these types, and pay attention to the various discussions in the literature of their benefits and disadvantages.

Controlled—Teacher Has Basic Control Over Processes

Warm-up: mimes, dance, song, jokes, play. This activity has the purpose of getting the students stimulated, relaxed, motivated, attentive, or otherwise engaged and ready for the classroom lesson, not necessarily related to the target language.

Setting: Focusing in on lesson topic. Either verbal or nonverbal evocation of the context that is relevant to the lesson point; by way of questioning or miming or picture presentation, possibly tape recording of situations and people, teacher directs attention to the upcoming topic.

Organizational: managerial structuring of lesson or class activities. Includes reprimanding of students and other disciplinary action, organization of class furniture and seating, etc., general procedures for class interaction and performance, structure and purpose of lesson, etc.

Content explanation: explanation of lesson content and grammar or other rules and points. Phonology, grammar, lexis, sociolinguistics, or whatever is being ''taught.''

Role play demonstration: use of selected students or teacher to illustrate the procedures(s) to be applied in the lesson segment to follow. Includes brief illustration of language or other content to be incorporated.

Dialogue/Narrative presentation: reading or listening passage presented for passive reception. No implication of student production or other identification of specific target forms or functions (students may be asked to ''understand'').

Dialogue/Narrative recitation: reciting a previously known or prepared text, either in unison or individually.

Reading aloud: reading directly from a given text.

Checking: teacher either circulating or guiding the correction of students' work, providing feedback as an activity rather than within another activity.

Question-answer, display: activity involving prompting of student responses by means of display questions (i.e., teacher or questioner already knows the response or has a very limited set of expectations for the appropriate response). Distinguished from referential questions by means of the likelihood of the questioner's knowing the response, and the speaker's being aware of that fact.

Drill: typical language activity involving fixed patterns of teacher and student responding and prompting, usually with repetition, substitution, and other mechanical alterations. Typically with little meaning attached.

Translation: student or teacher provision of L1 or L2 translations of given text.

Dictation: student writing down orally presented text.

Copying: student writing down text presented visually.

Identification: student picking out and producing/labeling or otherwise identifying a specific target form, function, definition, or other lesson-related item.

Recognition: student identifying forms, etc., as in Identification, but without producing language as response (i.e., checking off items, drawing symbols, rearranging pictures).

Review: teacher-led review of previous week/month/ or other period as a formal summary and type of test of student recall and performance.

Testing: formal testing procedures to evaluate student progress.

Meaningful drill: drill activity involving responses with meaningful choices, as in reference to different information. Distinguished from Information Exchange by the regulated sequence and general form of responses.

Semicontrolled

Brainstorming: a special form of preparation for the lesson, like Setting, which involves free, undirected contributions by the students and teacher on a given topic, to generate multiple associations without linking them; no explicit analysis or interpretation by the teacher.

Story-telling (especially when student-generated): not necessarily lesson-based, lengthy presentation of story or event by teacher or student (may overlap with Warm-up or Narrative recitation). May be used to maintain attention, motivation, or as lengthy practice).

Question-answer, referential: activity involving prompting of responses by means of referential questions (i.e., the questioner does not know beforehand the response information). Distinguished from Question-answer, Display.

Cued narrative/Dialog: student production of narrative or dialog following cues from miming, cue cards, pictures, or other stimuli related to narrative/dialog (e.g., metalanguage requesting functional acts).

Information transfer: application from one mode (e.g., visual) to another (e.g., writing), which involves some transformation of the information (e.g., student fills out diagram while listening to description). Distinguished from Identification in that the student is expected to transform and reinterpret the language or information.

Information exchange: task involving two-way communication as in information gap exercises, when one or both parties (or a larger group) must share information to achieve some goal. Distinguished from Question-answer, Referential in that sharing of information is critical for the resolution of task.

Wrap-up: brief teacher or student produced summary of point and/or items that have been practiced or learned.

Narration/exposition: presentation of a story or explanation derived from prior stimuli. Distinguished from Cued Narrative because of lack of immediate stimulus.

Preparation: student study, silent reading, pair planning and rehearsing, preparing for later activity. Usually a student-directed or -oriented project.

Free

Role-play: relatively free acting out of specified roles and functions. Distinguished from Cued Dialogues by the fact that cueing is provided only minimally at the beginning, and not during the activity.

Games: various kinds of language game activity, if not like other previously defined activities (e.g., board and dice games making words).

Report: report of student-prepared exposition on books, experiences, project work, without immediate stimulus, and elaborated on according to student interests. Akin to Composition in writing mode.

Problem solving: activity involving specified problem and limitations of means to resolve it; requires cooperative action on part of participants in small or large group.

Drama: planned dramatic rendition of play, skit, story, etc.

Simulation: activity involving complex interaction between groups and individuals based on simulation of real-life actions and experiences.

Discussion: debate or other form of grouped discussion of specified topic, with or without specified sides/positions prearranged.

Composition: as in Report (verbal), written development of ideas, story, or other exposition.

A propos: conversation or other socially oriented interaction/speech by teacher, students, or even visitors, on general real-life topics. Typically authentic and genuine.

Task Types and Parameters

In the list above, the headings "Free" and "Semicontrolled" cover a number of activities which have been discussed elsewhere as "tasks." Since more information has been collected on them than on other classroom activities, they are considered separately in this section.

It might be thought that the construction of a list of possible task types from which a teacher could select was one of the most fundamental jobs for writers on SL pedagogy, one long since completed. Surprisingly, though, SL methodologists have only recently started dealing with general principles of communicative materials design (e.g., Nunan, 1989; Wright, 1987; with a precursor in Breen, Candlin, & Waters, 1979). So there exist in the literature various descriptors, and various definitions of task, some quite promising, but without much in the way of evidence of their utility. To begin with, there is no one agreed-upon description, though there is substantial overlap in the definitions which are in use. We list them so that a general impression can be gained, as it is not our intent to legislate a single form here.

one of a set of sequenceable, differentiable and problem-posing activities which involve learners in some self-reliant selection among a range of variably available cognitive and communicative strategies applied to existing or acquired knowledge in the exploration and attainment of a variety of pre-specified or emergent goals

via a range of procedures, desirably independently with other learners in some social milieu.—Candlin (1984)

a piece of work undertaken for oneself or for others, freely or for some reward . . . by "task" is meant the hundred and one things people do in everyday life, at work, at play, and in between.—Long (1985, p. 89)

a task is . . . any structural language learning endeavor which has a particular objective, appropriate content, a specified working procedure, and a range of outcomes for those who undertake the task . . . [it refers] to a range of workplans which have the overall purpose of facilitating language learning—from the simple and brief exercise type to more complex and lengthy activities such as group problem-solving simulations and decision-making.—Breen (1987a, p. 23)

One of a set of differentiated, sequenceable goal-directed activities drawing on a range of cognitive and communicative procedures relatable to the acquisition of pre-genre and genre skills appropriate to a foreseen or emerging sociorhetorical situation.—Swales (1990b)

the smallest unit of classroom work which involves learners in comprehending, manipulating, producing or interacting in the target language. Minimally, tasks will contain some form of data or input (this might be verbal, e.g., a dialogue or reading passage, or non-verbal, e.g., a picture sequence). The task will also have (implicitly or explicitly) a goal and roles for teachers and learners.—Nunan (1989, p. 5)

A wide variety of text types are in use as the stimulus material for tasks. Nunan (1989) refers to the following forms:

speech	writing
dialogs	public notices and
monologs	signs
interviews	diary extracts
conversations	postcards
aural descriptions	poems, songs, and
and narratives	rhymes
descriptions of	newspaper headlines
processes	short stories
media extracts	instructions and
public	directions
announcements	telephone directories
games and puzzles	junk mail
picture strips	textbook/journal
photo essays	extracts
	invitations

Our purpose in citing this taxonomy here is simply to alert teachers to the fact that almost anything can be used as the basis of a task. In many SL teaching situations, use of a wide variety of texts (written and spoken) is justified, since part of developing learners' skill is ensuring that they become familiar with as wide a range of text types as possible.

Some of the terms given in the lists above also have been used occasionally as task descriptors, but they are too superficial for this purpose. More useful are statements concerning the possible, desirable, or minimal units of a task. Nunan (1988a) would identify them as goals, data, activities, and roles; Candlin (1987) refers to input, roles, settings (classroom or out-of-class), actions (procedures and subtasks), monitoring (degree of supervision), outcomes, and feedback (evaluation). Outside the SL field, the classroom-research based work of Doyle (1979, 1980, 1983) has been quite influential, and antedates most SL-related statements on task components. His position on the parameters or components of a task has been summarized as follows:

> a task is comprised of several elements. One element is *content,* the subject matter to be taught. . . . A second element of a task is *materials,* the things that [can be] observe[d] and manipulate[d]. A third element of the task is *activity* . . . the things that the teacher and student will be doing during the lesson. . . . A fourth element is *goals,* the teacher's general aim for the task. . . . A fifth element is the *student,* especially his [sic] abilities, needs, and interests. The last element is the *social context* of instruction. (our emphasis; Shavelson & Stern, 1981, p. 478)

Doyle's position seems relatively well founded, but it is definitely oriented to the non-SL classroom; more recent SL-oriented positions are primarily based on perceived ease of use and conceptual analysis. Future investigation must further substantiate their adequacy. We hope that these statements provide a general idea of the concept being considered here. However, we recognize that their utility is restricted by the very limited amount of research on which they are based at present. Because of the long-term nature of SL learning, on the one hand, and the short-term nature of many observations of SL learning in the classroom, it is at present difficult to demonstrate that a given task or classroom arrangement is better than another. Nevertheless, we can direct attention to some aspects of, for example, the discourse generated by a particular arrangement, and argue that in the light of what we know about SL learning, or about learning in general, such an arrangement is (or is not) desirable.

Relevant Characteristics

Several of the characteristics to be discussed focus on the provision of *comprehensible input,* as indicated by markers of interactional modification. It has been argued that language which is comprehensible to the SL learner (and at an appropriate level) will be of high utility for learning purposes, and that indicators of such discourse are those deviations from normal talk which are used to clarify misunderstandings or problems in communication (see Long, 1980). The role of practice in SL development has also been emphasized, and Swain (1985) has referred to this as the *output hypothesis.* This would suggest that task characteristics which require learners to produce more complex constructions than they would otherwise use should be valuable (see Crookes & Schmidt, 1990; Duff, 1986). If teachers are aware of these factors, they can make more informed decisions about what material to select or to develop themselves (for more detailed discussion see Chaudron, 1988; Crookes, 1986).

The task characteristic on which most work has been done to date has been termed *information structure* (an aspect of "information transfer" activities—see list above under "Subsections of a lesson"). Information gap tasks may be designed so that each participant holds different information which must be shared verbally in order for the task to be successfully completed. Such a "two-way task" can be compared to one in which verbal information transfer is also necessary for task completion, but where the information is allocated solely to one participant, who is required to convey it to the other. Long (1980) showed that two-way tasks produce more interactional modification (repetitions, expansions, confirmation checks) than do one-way tasks, for native speaker-nonnative speaker (NS-NNS) dyads. Studies by Doughty and Pica (1986, Pica & Doughty, 1985) give further support for the differences discovered between one-way versus two-way tasks with respect to talk between nonnative speakers.

A second characteristic of tasks, which is in a sense complementary to the one-/two-way distinction, is *shared assumptions*. Some studies suggest that the extensive shared background information available in some two-way tasks may work against calling forth more negotiation of meaning. It may be (as Gass & Varonis, 1985, argue) that if both participants in an information-gap task have a very clear idea of the structure of one another's information, there will be less likelihood of partial or complete meaning breakdowns. Similarly (as Gaies, 1982, suggests), if both participants are well acquainted with each other, they will be able to manage communication difficulties without the need for extensive negotiation that is probably useful for language acquisition. This may also apply to the availability of visual support for a task. In an investigation of the degree to which three different tasks produced changes in learners' interlanguages, Crookes and Rulon (1988) found that of two problem-solving tasks, the one which was less productive of immediately observable IL development was that in which the task provided visual support to both members of the dyad. Even though the pictures used were not identical, they were versions of the same picture, differing only in certain limited features. This effect of shared assumptions is further supported by non-SL work: in research on young children's production of oral narrative (in their first language, English) on different tasks, investigators found that "in summary . . . telling an original story elicited a greater quantity of language and somewhat more mature language structures than the other tasks, although each task yielded slightly different structures" (Nurss & Hough, 1985, p. 283).

A third feature which has been posited as likely to be relevant is *recycling*. If the discourse generated by a task requires the same linguistic material to be used repeatedly, such a conversation would be potentially more useful to the NNS than one in which many items occurred once only. However, the sole attempt to investigate this so far (Crookes & Rulon, 1985) used "discourse topic" as an indicator of recycling, but found that different topics may contain the same linguistic items, possibly because this unit of analysis was too large. The question would still seem worthy of further investigation, nevertheless.

A fourth possible factor is *convergence*, which derives from the work of Duff (1986). Many communicative tasks available on the ESL materials market require participants to "reach a mutually acceptable solution" (Duff, 1986, p. 150), often in solving some values clarification problem (for an early example, see Cole, 1970). Also quite common now are materials which require students to take a stand on one or another side of an issue, and argue their positions (e.g., Alexander, Kingsbury & Chapman, 1978). The former type may be termed a "convergent task type," the latter a "divergent task type" (Duff, 1986, p. 150). Duff found that the discourse which these two types of task produce have different characteristics. Specifically, her results show that convergent tasks lead to frequent exchange of turns and more communication units, whereas divergent tasks lead to longer turns of greater syntactic complexity. If convergent tasks may produce more questions and shorter turns, it might be assumed that more comprehensible input is available in the discourse which accompanies their performance. Alternatively, if emphasis is being placed on output and the role of practice, divergent tasks may be more highly valued, although "the extended discourse (long turns) in [divergent tasks] reduces opportunities for negotiation of input . . . coupled with the greater syntactic complexity of [discussion], this reduces . . . the amount of comprehensible input available" (Duff, 1986, p. 170).

The factors covered in this section constitute what we hope is only the beginning of investigations into the utility of SL classroom materials. We hope that by being aware of those factors which have been investigated, as well as the things for which no evidence can legitimately be claimed (despite publishers' promotional claims), teachers will find it easier to make the best possible decisions when designing or selecting SL tasks.

FACILITATION

As we mentioned earlier, and as is taken for granted in most current SL pedagogical prescriptions, a major role of the instructor is to arrange matters so the material presented gets used and thereby learned. This is, of course, far more critical in the learning of a cognitive skill, where practice assumes major dimensions, than in the learning of most school subjects, where declarative knowledge (Anderson, 1982; O'Malley et al., 1987) is being presented, and where clear presentation may be sufficient in itself to ensure learning (cf. West, 1960). We need, therefore, to give some consideration to such matters as the overall organization of the classroom, the nature and dynamics of teacher–student and student–student interaction, and the interface between these matters and the selection of classroom learning tasks.

Class Organization

The way in which a classroom is organized can have a significant influence on language learning processes. The key participants for describing classroom organization are the following: the teacher, the teacher aide or trainee, the individual student and groupings of students, the class as a whole, the language presentational materials used (e.g., textbook, AV media), and any visitors or outsiders. Combinations of these result in particular structures in class organization (sometimes referred to as "participant organization," cf. van Lier, 1988).

The dominant view of second language classroom processes today favors a great amount of student-centered learning instead of the traditional teacher-dominated classroom (Nunan, 1988a). The teacher-dominated classroom ("teacher-fronted") is characterized by the teacher's speaking most of the time, leading activities, and constantly passing judgment on student performance, whereas in a highly student-centered classroom, students will be observed working individually or in pairs and small groups, each on distinct tasks and projects. The most extreme sort of student-centered learning (known as "autonomous learning"— Henner-Stanchina, 1976), of course, is conducted entirely separately from the classroom environment, as individual learning projects are carried out in the target language community, and intermittent, perhaps infrequent, contacts are made with the teacher on an as-needed basis.

Learner-centered instruction has the benefits of greater individualization of learning objectives, increased student opportunities to perform (whether receptively or productively) with the target language, increased personal sense of relevance and achievement, and, in fact, a relieving of the teacher's constant supervision of all students. Furthermore, students often will pay more attention and learn better from one another, since their performances and processes of negotiation of meaning are more closely adapted to one another's level of ability. Teachers should thus be prepared to develop fewer teacher-dominated activities and tasks, while remaining conscious of their students' need for guidance in setting objectives, for appropriate models of and feedback about the target language, and for constructive and supportive evaluation of their progress.

In general, the most appropriate and effective classroom organization is therefore pair and group work. Contrary to a popular negative view of the outcomes of learner-dominated activities, classroom-centered research has demonstrated that at the same time that students have many more opportunities to employ the target language, they manage to perform equally successfully in terms of grammatical accuracy as when the teacher is leading discussion (Pica & Doughty 1985; cf. discussion in Chaudron, 1988, pp. 150–152). We will therefore focus briefly on the management of group work in second language classes.

Group Work

Pica and Doughty (e.g., 1985) looked at *interactional modification* in teacher-fronted versus student-only group decision-making discussions, comparing complete classes plus a teacher with small groups minus a teacher. On the one-way task used in this study, they did not find differences, but when they used a two-way task they found more interactional modifications did occur in the group situation. As mentioned above, this does not directly consider learning, but rather a factor which should facilitate it (i.e., negotiation of meaning via changes in the structure of discourse).

One of the earliest studies to provide evidence in favor of SL group work was that of Long, Adams, McLean, and Castaños (1976), who found NNS participants in a dyadic discussion task utilizing a wider range of language than NNSs in a larger, teacher-fronted group engaged in discussing the same question. This referred to what kinds of remarks students made, whether or not they initiated changes of topic, and in general whether or not they used a wide range of language functions. It was also suggested that a large group situation might cause students' utterances to be briefer and less complex, as opposed to the more relaxed atmosphere provided by the small group.

These findings are probably consistent with the practical experience of many teachers, who may well have found that students, particularly those from Asian cultures, are reluctant to speak in front of the whole class, but are much more forthcoming in smaller groups. Obviously, this has implications for the utility of the group setting, from both a "pedagogical" and a "psycho-

linguistic" point of view (Long & Porter, 1985). Concerning the former, it is a better use of class time. For the latter, since output is probably very important for SL learning, situations which permit or encourage only one- or two-word responses are less desirable than those which allow more complex speech, or more risk taking in terms of the use of unfamiliar, as yet unautomatized language.

Assuming the general utility of group work, there are other, lower-level questions to consider. An elementary matter is group size, and at least one study exists to support the elementary observation that participants in larger groups speak less (Liski & Puntanen, 1983). More details on which teachers may base decisions about this factor come from a study (Antony, 1986) of the discourse of NNS groups of two to five in size performing "task-based consensus activities."

Group size does not seem greatly to affect the number of wpm (words per minute) of the group as a whole, so smaller groups likely generate more wpm per student. Larger groups, however, seem to introduce new ideas more quickly and have more simultaneous starts and more brief overlaps. So while smaller groups may provide more practice in speaking, larger groups may well provide more valuable input (Antony, 1986, p. 5).

While SL teaching in the last decade has emphasized group work, a related development in mainstream education has focused on "cooperative learning," which adds consideration of reward structures and sometimes team competition to the characteristics of SL group work. Its applicability to the SL classroom has just begun to be investigated. For example, Bejarano (1987) conducted a large-scale longitudinal study of cooperative learning organization in EFL classes in Israel, and reported superior results for the experimental groups. Although the findings in this study are not as clear-cut as claimed (cf. Chaudron, Crookes, & Long, 1988; Zhang, 1988), students in the cooperative learning groups maintained equivalent performance to those in regular EFL classrooms, despite starting at a lower level of ability.

There is a large number of possible arrangements for cooperative learning tasks in language classrooms, and second language teachers need to be familiar with the basic principles of this type of organization. Three essential elements are identified by Bossert (1988): (1) Students are told to work together, (2) reward contingencies are arranged to encourage this, (3) tasks are constructed which can only be completed if learners work together. Obviously, point 1 is simple to carry out. Point 2 requires a little more planning. It is possible to allocate rewards to groups as wholes. Some forms of cooperative learning allow groups to compete against other groups, in which case rewards may be allocated in inverse proportion to those of other (successful) groups. The third point is probably the one to which most attention has been given in SL work, since task interdependence is a major feature of information-gap tasks and related activities. In these cases, students know only one piece of the solution to a puzzle or information required to solve a problem, and must communicate it to others in their group. More typical of mainstream cooperative learning and less common in current SL materials is the possibility that task interdependence can be fostered by assigning special functions to group members—for example, chairperson, checker, gofer. (See Johnson, Johnson, Holubec, & Roy, 1984; cf. Jacobs, 1988, for discussion of SL applications of this approach.)

In addition to group size and the shared cooperative goals of group work, it should be recognized that group work results in greater diversity of performance from one group to another. This fact suggests that just as individuals contribute to a group, the different groups in a classroom can be linked through different tasks and roles, and shared responsibilities, to generate whole-class tasks and objectives. Although competitive models can be employed in this way (as in one of Bejarano's treatment groups), this view points rather toward whole-class cooperative learning projects.

Aspects of the Teacher-Fronted Class

Although we emphasize the relative productivity of the small group over the teacher-fronted class, teachers sometimes need to operate in a "lock-step" mode. There are a few general characteristics of teacher–student interaction which can fairly easily be manipulated under those conditions, to the advantage of SL learning. One is question type, and another is wait time.

Question Types

A number of studies (Brock, 1986; Dinsmore, 1985; Early, 1985; Long & Sato, 1983; Long et al., 1984; Nunan, 1986; Pica & Long, 1986) have shown that ESL teachers' classroom questioning patterns are typically different from those used by native speakers conversing casually with adult nonnative speakers. SL teachers ask more *display* questions (those to which the questioner already knows the answer) than do ordinary NSs talking to NNSs. The latter usually use *referential* questions (those to which the questioner does *not* already know the answer). This may be because teachers have a tendency to act as if the SL was information which they must transmit to the students, thus leading them to test whether it has been understood by using display questions.

There are reasons to be concerned over this pattern. First of all, there is general acceptance of the idea that the model of the target language provided by the teacher in the classroom should not deviate greatly from that likely to be encountered in real life. Second, if teacher–student interaction is predominantly by way of display questions, relatively little real communication is going on. As Long and Crookes (1987, p. 181) observe, "display questions by definition preclude students attempting to communicate new, unknown information. They tend to set the focus of the entire exchanges they initiate on accuracy rather than meaning. The teacher (and usually the student) already knows what the other is saying or trying to say, so there is no meaning left to negotiate."

Without negotiation of meaning it is questionable whether students addressed by a teacher are actually receiving useful input, in terms of its being appropriate to their current level of comprehension and/or language development. Furthermore, less complex language is likely to be produced by learners who know that the teacher is only asking the question to check their knowledge, rather than really wanting a proper and complete answer to a real question.

A further distinction is relevant, between *closed* referential questions (questions to which the speaker does not know the answer, but to which there is either only one or a very limited set of possible answers) and *open* referential questions (questions to which the speaker does not know the answer, and to which a large [infinite] variety of answers are possible). Long et al. (1984) found that open referential questions produced more complex student responses than did closed referential questions (with complexity measured by number of words per student turn).

Wait-Time

Wait-time refers to the pause which follows a teacher question either to an individual student or to the whole class, which lasts until either a student answers or the teacher adds a comment or poses another question. It can also apply to the period between one student's answer to a question and the response of the teacher or another student. Wait-time has been the subject of a substantial number of investigations over the last 20 years, mostly outside the SL field. These have found that wait-times can be altered by teachers, but tend to be short, around one second (e.g., Rowe, 1969; for review see Tobin, 1987). Also, when wait-time is increased to three to five seconds, there is improvement in learning, and in the quality of classroom discourse. The principal SL study of wait-time (Long et al., 1984), found that increased wait-time after teacher questions resulted in longer

SL student utterances. It did not result in more utterances per student turn, however, which may have been due to the low level of the students on whom the study was conducted, or possibly an interaction between cognitive level of questions and wait-time. When asking "harder" questions, teachers tended to wait longer anyway, but the difficulty of such questions was not always compensated for by proportionately longer wait-time. We advance the matter of wait-time here as an example of a classroom procedure which is very easy to manipulate, and one which warrants further classroom investigation. Teachers might want to try the effects of simply waiting longer as they interact with their SL students, knowing that their findings, if communicated, could aid their colleagues and further substantiate (or perhaps disprove) the potential of increased wait-time in SL teaching.

CORRECTION AND FEEDBACK

In earlier sections on rule presentations and explanation, we noted that a focus on formal aspects of the SL had again become a concern of methodologists and practitioners. Error correction and feedback have typically been considered to be part of such a focus. However, as Chaudron notes in his review of feedback in language teaching (1988; see also Chaudron, 1986, for a review of feedback on writing):

In any communicative exchange, speakers derive from their listeners information on the reception and comprehension of their message. . . . From the language teacher's point of view, the provision of feedback . . . is a major means by which to inform learners of the accuracy of both their formal target language production and their other classroom behavior and knowledge. From the learners' point of view, the use of feedback in repairing their utterances, and involvement in repairing their interlocutors' utterances, may constitute the most potent source of improvement in both target language development and other subject matter knowledge. (pp. 132–133)

Thus, there is no reason to associate feedback and correction solely with a formal focus. Nevertheless, approaches to language teaching will vary in the degree to which the teacher is considered to be the source of "correcting" behavior. A traditional notion is that the teacher or materials provide a correction of every (important) learner error, while a more current view would emphasize the importance of learners obtaining feedback (and possible correction) only when the meanings they attempt to convey are not understood, and even then, the feedback should be a natural outcome of the communicative interaction (often between learners). Even in the most learner-centered instruction, learners need feedback in order to differentiate between acceptable and unacceptable target language use.

Communicative language teaching materials must provide opportunities for learners to recognize the communicative effectiveness of their target language productions (in the form of feedback and repairing of misunderstood speech), for example, when correct description of pictures in a two-way information gap task is the only source of success on the task. Regrettably, research on the effects of teacher feedback on development of accuracy in learner-centered tasks has not been conducted (but see Crookes & Rulon, 1985, for feedback in NS-NNS dyadic tasks).

The provision of feedback, or even "corrections," does not mean that the information provided must be stated in formalized grammatical or other descriptive terms. The teacher has many options available (Allwright, 1975; Chaudron, 1977; Long, 1977), from simply indicating lack of comprehension, or otherwise signaling the fact of an error, and getting the learner to self-correct (see discussion of learner-oriented correction in Chaudron, 1988; Long & Porter, 1985), to the most elaborate grammatical explanation and drill of correct forms.

Teachers will most frequently make the mistake of thinking that by providing a correct "model," by repeating student statements with some slight change in the grammatical form, learners will perceive the correction and incorporate it into their developing gram-

mars. Such feedback is likely to be perceived by the learner not as a *formal* change, but rather as a confirmation, rephrasing, or clarification of the functional meaning. As a hypothetical example:

Student: *I can no go back home today early.*
Teacher: *You can't go home early today?*
Student: *No.*

If there is in fact reason to provide formal feedback in such a case, it helps to focus on the specific correction by emphasizing and isolating the modeled forms (Chaudron, 1977); "I *can't* go home," or "*early today.*" On the other hand, this practice may still be less effective than one of getting learners to self-correct (see Herron & Tomasello, 1988), or having other learners assist in corrections. Peer correction has the potential advantage of being set at the right level of development in the learner's interlanguage grammar. If there are further grounds for ensuring that a correction be understood, teachers should make an effort to *verify* comprehension and ability to produce an appropriate form (preferably supplied by the learner or peers), by means of a follow-up elicitation. Caution must be maintained, however, in not resorting to extensive drills in such cases.

Moreover, a recent study of learners of French as a SL suggests that provision of correct forms may be more effective if learners are induced to produce an incorrect form before having it "corrected." Tomasello and Herron (1988) induced certain errors by presenting exceptions to rules and either indicating or not indicating that they were exceptions. Those students who were corrected after producing overgeneralized forms of the exceptions were superior on tests of the forms than students who were simply shown the exceptions in contrast to the rules.

An important limitation on the effectiveness of feedback and correction, especially with respect to grammatical development, is the natural order of development of a given structure or function. Ultimately, teachers must remain current with findings of research in second language acquisition, in order to be knowledgeable about fixed sequences of acquisition, for it is unlikely that any sort of error correction or feedback can radically influence these.

CLASSROOM CLIMATE

As teachers we cannot ignore the fact that classroom SL learning has a social dimension. It might be assumed that all practitioners are aware of this, and also that all SL teachers will strive to arrange for a relaxed, supportive environment in order to promote learning. However, it is desirable to ask what evidence we have to support this position, or if it is only an assumption (cf. Brumfit, 1981; Moskowitz, 1978). It certainly has not always been assumed to be an accurate statement, as a glance at the prescriptions for SL classrooms of 20 years ago will quickly show. In addition, the position that such an environment favors learning is not accepted across all cultures (particularly non-Western educational systems). Culturally determined student expectations, the individual teacher's personality, and the interaction between these two impose limitations on the social climate of the classroom. Nevertheless, teachers have some flexibility as to what choices they make.

In recent years there have been two streams of discussion in this area directly connected to SL learning. One is that broadly associated with the label "humanistic approaches." In this area are the so-called innovative methods such as Counseling-Learning and Suggestopedia. The training needed to utilize these techniques according to the full prescriptions of their founders is more extensive than most SL teachers have time for, and the evidence for their success has not been forthcoming (cf. Wagner & Tilney, 1983). The second strand here is the less doctrinaire position associated in particular with Schumann (1978) and Krashen (e.g., 1982). Krashen in particular has posited an "affective filter," which must be lowered if successful unconscious SL development is to take place. However, these positions have suffered from

a general lack of direct support (McLaughlin, 1987a; Schumann, 1986).

Meanwhile, for the last 20 years or more, mainstream educational researchers have been investigating the topic of classroom climate, or classroom environment, in non-SL classes (Fraser, 1986). Their results have not been particularly clear-cut, either. Observational measures of positive affect correlate poorly with achievement, which may have to do with the fact that praise, a major component of such measures, is distributed inconsistently across high- and low-achieving pupils. Teachers thus may need to reconsider the tendency to use "Good!" far too often, and inconsistently, even though they may accept the need for a positive classroom climate in general (cf. Soar & Soar, 1975). More usefully (and as might be expected), negative affect correlates significantly, and negatively, with achievement. More well-defined results come from student self-report measures of learning environment (e.g., the Learning Environment Inventory [LEI], Walberg, 1968). Since these investigations are concerned with students' *perception* of classes, a distinction has been made between the previous aspect of this topic, "classroom climate," and that implied here, "classroom psychological environment." The latter is keyed to such concepts as students' familiarity with each other, enjoyment of classwork, physical environment, influence on class activities, familiarity with course goals, organization of the course material, and its speed of coverage. The validity of the LEI is indicated by research which finds it to be a better predictor of in-class achievement than IQ measures, and there is also evidence for the measure's cross-linguistic and cross-cultural validity (Anderson & Walberg, 1974).

How then does one achieve a positive learning environment? The moves one should make seem straightforward, but in the press of so many other considerations (the section of the textbook to be covered, tests to be administered, activities to do) they can sometimes be lost sight of. We can remind teachers of a number of fairly obvious points, some of which derive from research using the LEI—others from recent developments in the study of motivation.[7]

It would appear desirable, then, to arrange matters so that the class is cohesive, with students as far as possible knowing each other, and being assured that the teacher knows them. As has often been suggested in SL pedagogy (e.g., Bailey & Celce-Murcia, 1979), there is value in ice-breaking activities at the beginning of a class—short questionnaires which must be filled in about a fellow student, or simple games which require each person to enquire about others' names and backgrounds are fine for this. The teacher must also make an effort to know names and backgrounds (seating plans and the same short questionnaires will be useful here). Interpersonal skills will be needed to ensure that there is an absence of friction, that students mix with each other, and that there are neither cliques nor perceived teacher "favorites." Related factors which may also be important are how enthusiastic the teacher appears, and whether s/he appears happy, and uses humor in the classroom (Moskowitz & Hayman, 1974).

The importance of a good physical environment shows up in mainstream educational research (Walberg, 1985) and in comments on SL classrooms (Bailey & Celce-Murcia, 1979). It has often been observed that the SL instructor typically has limited control over the teaching environment, but we would urge teachers first to push their degree of control in this area to the maximum, particularly concerning seating arrangements, and second to monitor and be sensitive to changing aspects of the classroom environment (noise, temperature, light). Obviously, the bright, clean classroom with relevant pictures on the walls, and movable, comfortable chairs with some support for writing on, is the ideal to be striven for.

Then there are aspects of the way the course is conducted which contribute to a favorable classroom environment. Course goals should be known by the participants. Even if it is only an ordinary conversation class, they should be made explicit and referred to. (This will also aid teacher planning and evaluation.) Whatever rules may be necessary for the class to run smoothly should be spelled out and adhered to—prompt attendance, no smoking, and so on. As is obvious (but not always easy to achieve), the material should be appropriate to the level of the students, well organized, and coverable at a comfortable speed.

Finally, let us consider some motivational factors (see also Keller, 1983). An important area here is interest. Taking the content of the class as a given, the instructor can work on keeping up interest by personalizing instruction—making connections between the material and individual students, or to him- or herself. It is also important to use a wide range of activities, so that classes vary in format.

According to motivation theories, we all have personal needs for achievement, affiliation, and power. In a classroom context that means we like to succeed, we like to make connections with others, and we like to have control over our own learning situation. Consequently, the instructor should ensure that learning activities are pitched at an appropriate level. Success will engender confidence and higher expectations of future success (sometimes called expectancy). This should lead to a greater degree of effort in future work. Then, the instructor should choose activities and tasks which facilitate the establishing of relationships between students. In addition, s/he should allow a measure of choice, or control, over what is done in the classroom by the students.

Satisfaction can be worked toward particularly by attending to the motivating qualities of the activities selected and the rewards given in the class. As far as possible, it is desirable to choose learning activities which have "task-endogeneous rewards"—that is, they are fun to do in and of themselves. If external rewards are to be given with these activities, they should be unexpected, noncontingent on performance. Students will also be more satisfied if they are given feedback when they can use it, which may be not only after a response, but just before the next opportunity to practice.

TEACHER SELF-EVALUATION

It is natural for conscientious teachers to ask themselves whether a lesson (or a course) was successful. Consciously or unconsciously, they probably do so during any given element of teaching. However, one is more likely to be reflective at the end of a day, or a lesson, than during it, simply because of one's cognitive limitations—it is very hard to make a balanced judgment while in the midst of teaching, because there are too many factors to attend to simultaneously. On the other hand, once the class is over, it is also difficult to make an unbiased assessment, since the data needed to do so are absent—there is only the memory of a very complex situation, which fades quickly. Yet how can teachers plan for future classes, or find aspects of their teaching skills to improve, if they do not assess themselves? Formative self-evaluation is needed as the basis for change and development, rather than summative evaluation from outside, which is often done on the basis of a single lesson. We need to find a way for teachers to reflect on their teaching, and then go about improving it (cf. Cruickshank, 1987).

For present purposes, we suggest a model for this process based on Fleming, Fleming, Oksman, & Roach (1984), who have formalized the fairly commonsense procedures that need to be undertaken under four headings: (1) focusing, (2) monitoring, (3) appraising, and (4) reacting. In the first stage, the individual using this model has to decide what the main areas of job functioning are to be, and how they are to be examined. This might mean referring to a position description, or to any previous external supervisor's evaluation of performance. Other organizational information, such as guidelines for practice or regular procedures to be followed, might be relevant. This process can obviously cover all aspects of a teacher's performance, both in class and out of class, but we will concentrate on in-class activity. In doing this first step, the teacher will decide what data to collect and how to collect it. For self-evaluation of regular teaching, audiotape is the easiest data-collection procedure. It is a straightforward matter to bring a small tape recorder to class, place it on a table, and set it going. Quite soon, students and teacher will ignore it. More adventurous teachers may wish to explore the use of videotape, where in fact again both students and teachers will rapidly ignore the equipment. This source of data could be combined with observation by fellow teachers, and even, in some situations, written comments from students.

The second stage in most cases would be to review the tapes outside of class, and possibly to transcribe some of them, or some portions of them. Then, third, they need to be subjected to analysis, or appraisal. The teacher may decide to use one of the widely available classroom observation schemes which cover all aspects of class interaction, or simply focus on a particular element, such as use of praise (see Chaudron, 1988; Long, 1983b). If the latter, the item or behavior focused on should presumably follow from those aspects of the individual's performance identified in the first "focusing" stage of the process.

One possible system to start from in analyzing performance could be the self-evaluation checklist of Bailey and Celce-Murcia (1979), with the teacher extending it to fit his/her personal teaching concerns. However, we recommend that before completing any such checklist, the teacher should first list the main objectives of a given lesson, in at least three categories: target language learning objectives (e.g., plurals of nouns, acts of apologizing), learning skills objectives (e.g., asking peers or teacher for clarification, studying rules), and personal or social attitudes objectives (e.g., appreciating others' point of view, understanding the cultural connotations of target language use). We also note that while the checklist items concerning variety are important, other aspects of a lesson should be considered, such as *clarity* of teacher presentation, and appropriate *sequencing* of lesson activities and tasks.

Finally, if the self-evaluation process is to have an effect, the teacher must consciously decide how to react to the information—whether change is needed, and how it can be achieved. Fleming et al. (1984) point out that this phase is one where it may be beneficial to consult colleagues, because options for effecting change may not always be obvious. The practitioner may also need to consider whether a change is feasible or essential, and to evaluate its likely effect on other aspects of the class or the teacher's procedures. Finally, if substantial change is desired, it may be useful to draw up a checklist for professional development in this area, which might set as goals the development of materials, seeking regular observation and coaching from a trusted colleague, or a determination to alter one's allocation of time outside the class to allow for a search for professional resources relevant to an identified teaching problem.

The primary reason for taking the sort of steps suggested above is to actually improve one's own practice. However, an additional incentive might come from the fact that a documented plan for self-evaluation is likely to contribute positively to any outside supervisors' evaluation.

CONCLUSIONS

In discussing the topic of principles of SL classroom teaching, we find vast areas of ignorance where there should be knowledge. On the one hand, teachers should know what relatively firm information does exist, and where there is room for investigation. This should obviously aid their difficult decision making. Moreover, as the SL profession develops, more teachers are qualified to conduct their own research, or to collaborate with researchers on investigations, as is increasingly done elsewhere in education (Billups & Rauth, 1987; Klinghammer, 1987;

Mohr & MacLean, 1987; Neubert & Binko, 1987). We are also seeing increased recognition of the importance of action research (Argyris, Putnam, & Smith, 1985), which starts with the teachers' own problems and concerns.

On the other hand, teaching will always be a series of judgment calls—the real-time cognitive complexity of the task means it will never be just a science, and will ever remain something of an art (cf. Clark & Lampert, 1986; Leinhardt & Greeno, 1986). It has been the purpose of this chapter to help the judgment calls to be educated, informed ones, through the teacher's combined use of knowledge and educated professional reflection.

NOTES

1. We are grateful to the following people for their assistance in the preparation of this chapter. Beverly Edge, Rosarió Albuquerque, Juana Marin, Marisol Valcárcel and her team in Murcia, Mercedes Verdú, and Julio Roca. Portions of this chapter were also made possible through grants and support of the Social Science Research Institute, University of Hawaii, the Research Corporation of the University of Hawaii, and the Comité Conjunto Hispano-Norteamericano para la Cooperación Cultural y Educativa, Madrid. We also acknowledge the valuable basis provided by the article on this topic in the previous edition (Bailey & Celce-Murcia, 1979), from which we have noticeably drawn several of our ideas.

2. Our discussion is traditional to the extent that we will not deal with approaches to SL teaching which involve going outside the classroom (e.g., Ashworth, 1985; Fried-Booth, 1982, 1986).

3. What "size" the elements are is not at issue here. That is to say, we are not concerned with whether the units presented are structural, functional, or the language of a given pedagogical task, in an unanalyzed whole.

4. It should be remembered that some less traditional approaches do not require a text per se (e.g., the Silent Way, Counseling-Learning).

5. We might say re-recognition, as the idea is not a new one—see e.g., West (1960).

6. We should point out that we are deliberately avoiding the word "method" here—we do not accept its general validity as a term of art or analysis (cf. Richards, 1984).

7. It may be said that these are also supported by common sense; but as this is an elusive concept which continues to change from one generation to another, we feel it is desirable to be able to support its prescriptions with evidence where possible.

DISCUSSION QUESTIONS

1. Why should the ESL teacher be concerned about keeping up with the results of classroom research and second language acquisition?

2. Do you agree that teachers should make their lesson objectives clear to their students? Can you think of situations in which this would be inappropriate? Why?

3. How much do you think presentation, explanation, and discussion of rules for language use have a place in the SL classroom? What underlying view of language and language learning supports your view?

4. Discuss the ways in which one might investigate what is the most effective way of giving feedback (or correction). What data would you collect, and how would you identify successful correction?

5. Discuss ways in which a teacher with a multicultural group of students can best maintain a positive classroom climate, promoting student interest and motivation.

SUGGESTED ACTIVITIES

1. With several other teachers draw up a list of teaching behaviors or techniques that you think are important in your own teaching situation. Then observe each other, using a checklist of these behaviors as a guide. On the basis of your colleagues' observations, which of these do you think you need to improve or alter? Draw up a plan for how you would achieve this change in your teaching.

2. Prepare and compare a minilesson—as a group, select a specific point of language form or function, rule of conversation, or other social use of English. Individually develop a sequence of activities that you might use to present, develop, and evaluate this point, and then compare your suggestions. Develop a jointly agreed-upon way of teaching this point and practice it with one another. A useful alternative way of practicing this

would be for each one to teach the point in a language unknown to the others in the group. Discuss your feelings on once again being a second language learner.

3. Select a unit from a currently available ESL textbook. Identify ways in which it is not appropriate to your current teaching situation (e.g., wrong level, inappropriate cultural content or interest level for your students, orientation toward small/large groups). What sort of changes do you think would improve the unit?

SUGGESTIONS FOR FURTHER READING

Bossert, S. T. (1988)
Cooperative Activities in the Classroom. In E. Z. Rothkopf, (ed.), *Review of Research in Education* (vol. 15). Washington, DC: American Educational Research Association.
Provides thorough coverage of what is known about all types of cooperative learning in regular classroom situations.

Chaudron, C. (1988)
Second Language Classrooms. Cambridge: Cambridge University Press.
At present the most comprehensive survey of the state of knowledge of SL classroom research. It should be read in small bites.

Cruickshank, D. R. (1987)
Reflective Teaching. Reston, VA: Association of Teacher Educators.
A very accessible book, which intends to aid teachers to become more knowledgeable about their own practice, and encourages them to become lifelong students of teaching and learning.

Harmer, J. (1983)
The Practice of English Language Teaching. London: Longman.
One of the best of the practical guides to SL teaching (apart from the present volume) on the market. It has a British perspective, knowledge of which can broaden the SL teacher's horizons.

Neubert, G. A., & Binko, J. B. (1987)
Teach-Probe-Revise: A Model for Initiating Classroom Research. *The Teacher Educator, 22*(1), 9–17.
Presents a simple and straightforward model

which enables teachers to add an investigatory technique to their classroom teaching. This enables them to make use of research findings, test them, and add new information to existing knowledge so as to aid other teachers.

O'Neill, R. (1982)
Why Use Textbooks? *ELT Journal, 36*(2), 104–111. This down-to-earth article is one of the few recent comprehensive considerations of just why we bother with materials.

English for Specific Purposes (ESP)

Its History and Contributions

Ann M. Johns

ESP: WHAT IS IT?

English for Specific Purposes (ESP), by far the largest contributor to the international movement dealing with languages for specific purposes, comprises a diverse group of teachers and curriculum designers dedicated to the proposition that all language teaching must be designed for the specific learning and language use purposes of identified groups of students. The movement's practitioners can most commonly be found among those teaching adults, who have more easily identifiable needs than do children, and among those teaching abroad, where contact with first language speakers is often not readily available. Therefore, for teachers in English-speaking countries who plan to work overseas, a knowledge of ESP and its rationale is essential. However, ESP is also important in North America; for there, it is closely allied to content-based instruction for primary and secondary immigrant students, and to survival and vocational programs for adults who are not native speakers of English.

HISTORICAL PERSPECTIVE

Almost 30 years ago, ESL/EFL practitioners in many parts of the world began to convene in order to discuss the development of systematic analyses of student needs, particularly as they related to the features of the English that students must employ in the "real world." The practitioners asked, "What will our students be doing with English when they finish our classes?" (e.g., reading technical manuals, listening to academic lectures, selling products). "What are the characteristics of the language they need in order to succeed?" and "What are the best methods available for answering these questions?" Since that time, ESP advocates have continued to insist that curricula should be based upon the most systematic, accurate, and empirical measures of student needs and of the language required by the tasks they must perform outside of the classroom.

In the first phase of its history (the 1960s and the early 1970s), ESP researchers and teachers concentrated on the sentence-level

67

characteristics of the types of English identified as useful to their students. Researchers completed extensive analyses of the lexical and grammatical features of academic and professional registers such as the language of electrical engineering and the language of the law. They discovered, among many other things, that the English of Science and Technology (EST) favors the present simple tense, the passive, and noun compounds; they also discovered that business letters contain a set format, many formulaic expressions, a limited vocabulary, and a limited set of conjunctions. After careful analyses of identified spoken or written discourse, practitioners organized their grammar-based curricula around the features of these special registers. One of the most famous of the published volumes to appear during this period was Swales's *Writing Scientific English* (1971), where chapters are based principally upon the grammatical forms most commonly found in the scientific English register. The following, taken from the Swales text, contains an explanation of modals in this register and sentences from the exercise which follows:

After the Present Simple, the most common verb forms in scientific English are those which contain modals. The most frequent modals are:

Group 1: *can, may, might, could*
Group 2: *will*
Group 3: *should, must, have to*

Modals are used with the base form of the verb to give extra meaning to the sentence. In spoken English, it is very difficult to say exactly what these extra meanings are. In scientific English, it is easier.

The modals in group 1 are frequently used to make statements of possibility and probability. Consider:

- *The glass bottle breaks when dropped. (Every time this type of bottle is dropped from this height onto this surface it breaks: approximately 98–100% chance of breaking.)*
- *A bottle can break when dropped. (A good chance that it will break: approximately 40–70% probability.)*

- *The bottle may break when dropped. (Some chance that it will break: 20–40% probability.)*
- *The bottle could/might break when dropped. (A small chance: approximately 5–20% probability.)*
- *The bottle cannot break when dropped. (Almost no chance: 0–2% probability.)*

Exercise 16: Complete these sentences qualifying the main verbs with modals. The first one has been done.

1. *Death occurs if the body temperature rises to 44°C.*
   (a) *Death can occur if the body temperature rises to 43°C.*
   (b) *Death_____if the body temperature rises to 42.5°C.*
   (c) *Death_____if the temperature rises to 42°C . . . (Swales, 1971, pp. 33–34)*

Though Swales's book is one of the best known from this period, there were, and continue to be, many more published and unpublished curricula based upon a sentence-level analysis of English registers.

As time has passed, there have been modernizing influences on register analysis, such as those which integrate grammatical form with rhetorical function. In 1981, for example, a seminal article by Tarone and her colleagues examined the function of the passive in a single genre (astrophysics papers). Noting that "one of the most salient grammatical features of the register of English for Science and Technology (EST) as compared to registers of 'general English' is its relatively frequent use of the passive" (Tarone, Dwyer, Gillette, & Icke, 1981, p. 123), these researchers first examined the frequency of the passive within a single scientific field (astrophysics) and within a single genre (journal papers), and then performed a rhetorical analysis "to determine the systematic functions of the passive voice, as opposed to active, within the text as a whole" (Tarone et al., 1981, p. 124). The researchers found that writers of astrophysics journal articles use the passive when (a) they are following established procedures rather than discussing their own procedural choices, (b) they are discussing others' work in contrast to their own, (c) they are referring to their own future research, or (d) they wish to front (i.e., topicalize) certain information in sentences. This important article and the many which follow it break new ground in two ways: They move away from mere counting of linguistic features to asking *why* particular features are employed, and they begin to consider differences within general ESP registers, in this case, among scientific disciplines and among genres within these disciplines. The effect of these changes upon research direction and curriculum development has been major. Never again could mere counts of grammatical and lexical features in registers be considered sufficient for understanding language use or for development of ESP curricula.

In this second phase of ESP (late 1970s and early 1980s), then, the focus of register analyses became more rhetorical. In addition to publishing articles following from the Tarone et al. (1981) work, researchers and practitioners began to examine the organization and functions of entire discourses at a number of levels of abstraction. One of the best known of these inquiries originated with the Washington State ESP Group, consisting of Trimble, Selinker, Lackstrom, and Bley-Vroman. A current discussion of their English for Science and Technology (EST) register studies appears in Trimble's *EST: A Discourse Approach* (1985), in which the Rhetorical Process Chart for the levels of abstraction in scientific discourse is found (Chart 3.1).

Influenced by the focus upon function and purpose in discourse, other ESP researchers investigated the rhetorical moves, or macropurposes, within spoken and written language. Swales, for example, examined 48 scientific articles from a number of disciplines for the characteristic moves in their introductions (1981), finding that there are generally four:

Move One: *Establishing the field by:*
 a. *Showing centrality of the topic, or*

CHART 3.1
EST Rhetorical Process Chart

Level	Description of level
A. *The objectives of the total discourse*	EXAMPLES: 1. Detailing an experiment 2. Making a recommendation 3. Presenting new hypotheses or theory 4. Presenting other types of EST information
B. *The genereal rhetorical functions that develop the objectives of Level A*	EXAMPLES: 1. Stating purpose 2. Reporting past research 3. Stating the problem 4. Presenting information on apparatus used in an experiment— a) Description b) Operation 5. Presenting information on experimental procedures
C. *The specific rhetorical functions that develop the general rhetorical functions of Level B*	EXAMPLES: 1. Description: physical, function, and process 2. Definition 3. Classification 4. Instructions 5. Visual-verbal relationships
D. *The rhetorical techniques that provide relationships within and between the rhetorical units of Level C*	EXAMPLES: I. Orders 1. Time order 2. Space order 3. Causality and result II. Patterns 1. Causality and result 2. Order of importance 3. Comparison and contrast 4. Analogy 5. Exemplification 6. Illustration

(Trimble, 1985, p. 11)

 b. *Stating current knowledge of the topic, or*
 c. *Ascribing key characteristics.*
Move Two: *Summarizing previous research*
 a. *Indicating a gap, or*
 b. *Question raising, or*
 c. *Extending a finding.*

Move Four: Introducing present research by
  a. *Stating the purpose of the research, or*
  b. *Describing briefly present research.*

After several years of research, Swales and his colleagues have discovered some variability among scientific disciplines (Swales & Najjar, 1987), but they contend that student production of appropriate rhetorical moves may be more important to expert acceptance of ESL text than is employment of standard English grammar (Swales, 1990a). Researchers have also made another, related discovery: that there are major discrepancies between advice given in teaching manuals and expert text occurring in the real world (Swales & Najjar, 1987). This discrepancy between actual practice and pedagogical rules will continue to be of concern to ESP practitioners as it provides important questions for future research and curriculum (Huckin & Pesante, 1988).

Others have also been concerned with discourse moves, in both spoken and written language. Neu (1986), for example, studied rhetorical moves in oral discourse—specifically, the language of American-English business negotiations. Her data indicate that there are four successive moves in this discourse when it is initiated by American-English speakers: (a) an opening/exchange, (b) mention of the first price, (c) bargaining and other discussion of prices, and (d) a closing. In Europe, a concern with rhetorical moves by speakers of several languages, as well as for other features in negotiation, has increased as the Common Market becomes more integrated (Ulijn & Gorter, 1986). The discourse-based phase of register analysis continues to be fruitful as it absorbs new theories and research methodologies which appear in the literature.

A third, overlapping phase in ESP integrates the discoveries of Phase 1, in which linguistic features of registers were counted, and Phase 2, which explored the rhetorical elements of discourse. In this third phase, researchers have concentrated upon systematic analyses of the *target situations* in which students are found to be employing spoken English, in an attempt to make the following central to a "notional-functional" curriculum: (a) the communicative purposes of the speaker/writer, (b) the setting for language use, and (c) the mode of communication and language use (see Munby, 1978). In this approach, the basis for curricular scope and sequence comes from the particular communicative purposes (or "functions") of a speaker within a specified context. All other features of language (e.g., grammar and vocabulary) are subsumed under these purposes. Therefore in Notional-Functional Syllabuses, instead of having textbook units which are organized grammatically (as in Phase 1), such as "The Present Perfect," or which consider the purposes of written discourse (e.g., "Article Introductions" or "The Sales Letter"), as in Phase 2, there are chapter headings such as "Agreeing and Disagreeing" or "Paying Compliments." Within the chapters, students are provided with sample dialogs taking place in different contexts among different people, thereby exemplifying the language which realizes a speaker's communicative purposes within a specified context. A large number of textbooks are based upon Notional-Functional syllabus design. Among those published in the United States are Bodman and Lanzano's *No Hot Water Tonight* (1975), for "survival English," and Richards and Bycina's *Person to Person* (Book 2, 1985), a conversation book for intermediate-level students who share a relatively high level of education. Many other ESL textbooks emphasize the "functional nature of communication," a catchword in the marketing of teaching materials.

Recently, a fourth phase, with a considerably different focus, has been introduced to ESP from studies in psycholinguistics and elsewhere. Rather than centering on the discourse, the communicative situation, or the learner's communicative purposes, the focus of this phase is upon the *strategies* which learners employ to acquire the target language. With this emphasis, needs assessment concentrates upon activities or procedures which lead to effective thinking and learning. The foremost proponents of this learner-centered ESP approach are Hutchinson and Waters (1987), who maintain that

. . . our concern in ESP is not with language use—though this will help define our course objectives. Our concern is with language learning. We cannot simply assume that describing and exemplifying what people do with language will enable someone to learn it. If that were so, we would need to do no more than read a grammar book and a dictionary. . . . A truly valid approach to ESP must be based on an understanding of the processes of language learning. (p. 14)

Though Hutchinson and Waters have drawn heavily upon earlier, language-based ESP studies, their focus on factors influencing student learning is quite different. Among the factors which they consider essential to syllabus design are (a) measurement and use of learner's existing knowledge, (b) learner interest in the material presented, (c) how learners store and retrieve information, and (d) active learner involvement (1987, p. 119). According to these practitioners, then, it is the activities in the classroom, not the language of a context or the communicative purposes of the learners, which should be the first concern in developing classroom materials.

Thus, ESP continues to develop and expand throughout the world, influenced by the major theoretical and applied schools of linguistics.

SUBCATEGORIES OF ESP

As ESP expanded during its 30-year history and an increasing number of ESP textbooks and references appeared, it became necessary to identify subcategories of the movement according to the real-life situations in which specific groups of learners employ the language. Strevens (1977) provided the most famous model of the categories of ESP, which has been updated and Americanized here:

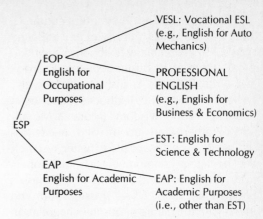

Not all of the subcategories of ESP have received the same amount of attention and study. In his valuable retrospective, Swales (1985) points out that Academic English for Science and Technology (EST) has been the best developed and most frequently taught of these, for: "EST is the senior branch of ESP—senior in age, larger in volume of publications and greater in number of practitioners employed" (1985, p. x).

There are a number of reasons for this EST concentration. First, many ESP students throughout the world are scientists and engineers, principally because the vast majority of scientific papers and books are printed in English (Baldauf & Jernudd, 1983). Second, in many ways, it is easier, or at least less confusing, to study science and the scientific disciplines than it is to study business or the humanities, because science, especially at the discourse level, is more regular across languages—e.g., there are many similarities, at every level, between scientific English registers and those of scientific Spanish (Widdowson, 1981).

Other areas of ESP have also been well studied with a number of curricula resulting. An example in the United States is the Vocational ESL Movement (VESL), which has produced a large number of special-purpose curricula for prevocational and on-site situations, especially for refugee populations. One of the best collections discussing this work is a special VESL issue (3, 2) of the *ESP Journal* (1984), edited by Burkart and Crandall.

The English of Business and Economics (EBE) has the longest history of any ESP area (Yates, 1977) and many textbooks have been produced to assist business people to speak and write Business English. Until recently, however, most EBE textbooks have been based upon "folk-wisdom" (Moran & Moran, 1985) rather than upon valid needs assessments. The prospect for better research and pedagogy is improving as practitioners explore the use of case studies in EBE classes (Piotrowski, 1986; Uber-Grosse, 1988) and investigate the nature of business negotiation (Neu, 1986; Ulijn & Gorter, 1986).

CONTRIBUTIONS OF ESP

Needs Analysis

ESP's greatest contribution to language teaching has been its insistence upon careful and extensive needs and task analyses for curriculum design. Before the inception of ESP, and even today, there has been a tendency for teachers and curriculum designers, especially of "general English" classes, to "intuit" the needs and future language uses of students, rather than to attempt to discover them. ESP practitioners maintain that intuitions do not always serve our students well. Instead of guessing at student needs, ESP practitioners contend that we must constantly develop new techniques for examining the tasks students have to perform in English, for understanding the target situations in which they will operate, for analyzing the discourse of the target situations, and for determining student learning strategies. Only in this way can ESL/EFL curricula and classroom organization be valid.

Until recently, ESP needs analyses, outlined carefully by Munby (1978) and others, were completed before the development of classroom materials. One influential example of such precourse analysis was completed by Richterich and Chancerel (1978) for the Council of Europe, which exploited three sources of precourse needs indicators: the students themselves (i.e., their perceived needs and proficiencies), the students' employer(s), and the teaching organization, including the proficiencies of the teachers as well as local organizational constraints. From their studies came the *Threshold Level* materials, which continue to form a basis for teaching English and other languages in Europe. In the United States, needs assessments have included extensive surveys of experts to determine what tasks students must undertake in a particular language use context. Since the early 1980s, for example, teachers of English for Academic Purposes (EAP) students have been asking academic faculty to rank the importance of the four skills in their classrooms (Johns, 1981), to identify the approaches to writing required of students in specific disciplines (West & Byrd, 1982) and to identify the tasks (e.g., summary/critique) which students must perform (Horowitz, 1986). Vocational ESL (VESL) precourse needs assessments also abound. An excellent synthesis of the work in this area appears in Prince (1984), which explores these questions: "What approach should we take to needs assessment in 'workplace English'?" "How do we identify needs with a given approach?" "How do we evaluate our needs assessment?"

In the last 10 years or so, needs assessments have become increasingly more sophisticated, under the influence of new methodologies, new foci, and new assumptions. Kennedy (1986), breaking with the tradition of precourse needs assessment, advocated a process approach to syllabus design in which formative and summative evaluation of teaching materials by students and faculty become essential to the continuing development of an ESP curriculum. Ramani and her colleagues (Ramani, Chacko, Singh, & Glendinning, 1988) use qualitative methodologies to establish needs. Working in the Indian Institute of Science (Bangalore), this group has employed principles of ethnography to determine the elements of a new academic purposes curriculum. Rather than examining language itself, these researchers observed the students in their natural academic environment, interviewing "key informant" students several times to determine their communicative practices, needs, and problems. Then they interviewed the subject specialists to identify the particular difficulties students were having with the content and practices of the classroom. Finally, they evaluated the information they had gathered and designed a curriculum around it.

A related, but more casual qualitative needs assessment, one which is accessible to the average teacher, was undertaken recently by a methodology student who was concerned with English that her "survival" students needed in a grocery store. After following shoppers around a supermarket for several days, she concluded that the only English students needed to succeed there was spoken at the cash register ("May I cash a personal check?"), and that names and prices of fruits and vegetables, which she had been so carefully teaching, were unnecessary, at least at the beginning level.

So far, the needs assessments discussed have relied upon teachers and experts as the final decision-makers in course design. However, as learner-centered curricula become more common, involvement of students becomes increasingly central. Johns (1990), for example, assigns journal writing to academic students, a tool to encourage them in a systematic study of the academic situation and its rules, in order to appreciate the important linguistic and pragmatic constraints of the target culture. From these student assessments of rules, conventions, and the language to which they are exposed, she develops an English for Academic Purposes course.

As can be seen from this brief discussion, ESP practitioners are continuously involved in attempts to improve their approaches to needs assessment; the literature is filled with proposals for new methodologies and critiques of existing ones. Because they believe in careful and extensive analyses, ESP practitioners often reprimand the so-called general English community for developing and publishing materials which are too broad and therefore inappropriate for any single student group, and for touting curricula which are not based on a careful assessment of the language, tasks, and culture of a target situation.

Materials Design

A second major ESP contribution is its work in syllabus or curriculum design. It can be argued that most of the creative work in developing materials for ESL/EFL classrooms originates with ESP practitioners, people concerned with appropriate discourse and activities for specific populations. Earlier in this chapter, the Notional-Functional—or "Communicative"—Syllabus Design was mentioned. This approach to the organization of curricula, which has influenced much of language teaching, represents a major paradigm shift from materials for which grammatical elements are the focus. Under the Notional-Functional Syllabus, the scope and sequence of the materials depend upon the purposes (i.e., communicative functions) of the speakers and writers who will be using the curricular materials. This "communicative" approach has been widely adopted, and is, as mentioned earlier, the basis for a large number of current textbooks.

However, there are those who contend that the Notional-Functional syllabus is limiting and fragmented. Widdowson (1979), for example, points out that like grammatical syllabuses, Notional-Functional curricula isolate bits of discourse (e.g., sentences which show "agreement") and therefore do not give students the full richness of the language in various contexts. Widdowson notes:

What such a (notional functional) syllabus does not do is to represent language as discourse, and since it does not it cannot possibly in its present form account for communicative competence—because communicative competence is not a compilation of items in memory, but a set of strategies or creative procedures for realizing the value of linguistic elements in contexts of use, an ability to make sense as a participant in discourse, whether spoken or written, by shared knowledge of code resources and rules of language use. (1979, p. 253)

In order to overcome the isolation of features characteristic of Notional-Functional and grammatical syllabuses, three others syllabus types have been developed by ESP advocates: the task-based, the project-based, and the process-based. Candlin and Murphy (1986) are the two names most closely identified with the task-based syllabus, though a number of other people have completed research and developed lessons based on this concept. Task-based syllabus designs are of two types. For the first type, the researcher identifies a number of tasks which students must perform in a target situation (e.g., business negotiation, or completion of a laboratory project) and builds the syllabus upon task assignment, including the study of those elements which prove to be most difficult for learners. McKenna (1987), for example, investigated successful student question-raising in large academic lectures and built a syllabus around this essential skill. Jacobson (1986) followed ESL students through a physics laboratory procedure to determine the steps which gave them the greatest difficulty.

A second type of task-based syllabus begins with the learning process involved in the completion of a task. Krahnke (1987), using the students' development of a guidebook to their school as a task example, describes this approach in the following manner:

Tasks are not static; that is, they should involve a process of information manipulation and development. They should also involve informational content that the language learners do not have at the beginning of the task. Another characteristic of tasks is that they require the student to apply cognitive processes of evaluation, selection, combination, modification or supplementation (so-called "higher-order" thinking skills) to a combination of new and old information. In task-based instruction, language is not taught, per se, but is supplied as needed for the completion of the task. (1987, pp. 57–58)

The final sentence of the Krahnke quote typifies both approaches to task-based instruction, for in these syllabuses, it is the task itself which gives students incentives and direction and provides them with the necessary language for study. Thus, in this design type, teachers should select tasks appropriate to both student future use and learning activation, not necessarily for the level, type, or authenticity of the language involved.

Project-based syllabuses are closely related to task-based, differing principally in terms of scope of the teaching units and the nature of the tasks involved. Whereas in task-based syllabuses the task possibilities do not always require a completed, visible product (e.g., as in the completion of a negotiation), project-based curricula result in one or more tangible products. Herbolich's (1979b) "box kites" project, developed at the University of Kuwait, is an excellent example of this syllabus type. In order to teach manual writing, Herbolich and his colleagues decided that students should actually construct something (a) which was relatively new to them and which had no available manual instructions, (b) which was related to their field (engineering), and (c) which encouraged them to learn the discourse features relevant to manual writing. After some research and trial and error, each student produced a kite, recording the manual instructions for doing so as he went along. The project therefore entailed two products, the kite and the manual, the latter of which was necessary for the teaching of manual writing.[1]

A third category of recent ESP materials design is the process-based syllabus, best identified with Breen (1984). This is the most radical in that the product or task is the syllabus itself, and the process for developing the syllabus is determined, for the most part, by the students. In this approach, preliminary decisions are made by the teacher before the course begins about how participation should take place in the classroom, the procedure (i.e., what tasks should be undertaken and in what order), and the subject matter. However, throughout the course, major changes in the curricula are instituted, through contractual agreement between the students and the teacher. The advantages of the process-type syllabus are obvious: The teacher and students can change the syllabus in major or minor ways throughout the course, resulting in a course suitable to students needs. Nonetheless, there are disadvantages: In the wrong hands, a process syllabus becomes chaotic. The teacher can ask, "So, what do you want to do today?" a question unprepared teachers have been asking for years.

Authenticity

The issue of authenticity, a third contribution of the ESP movement, is closely allied to decisions about needs assessment and curriculum design. Traditionally in ESP, authenticity referred to student needs, as indicated by the students themselves and the real language of the contexts in which students produce and understand English (see Munby, 1978; Richterich & Chancerel, 1978). For the traditional ESP practitioner, there was no simplification of real discourse for pedagogical purposes; instead, authentic, unmodified oral and written texts were provided for students at every proficiency level (T. F. Johns, 1974, p. 8).

This reliance on authenticity of discourse has led to providing real lectures for English for Academic Purposes students instead of canned or simplified ones; it has led to authentic readings from real textbooks or instructional manuals; it has led to requiring students to become involved in authentic situations in which they are exposed to real, unpredictable, spoken discourse. Many published textbooks include authentic discourse; in fact, without the claim to authenticity, ESP materials would lose some of their marketability.

However, with the student-centered ESP principles of Hutchinson and Waters (1987) cited earlier, and with the emphasis upon the learning process rather than the written or spoken product, a new definition for authenticity has arisen, a definition which considers the authenticity of strategies and activities instead of the authenticity of discourse. Widdowson explains this authenticity in the following manner:

A process-oriented approach accepts from the outset that the language data given to the learner will not be preserved in store intact but will be used in the mental mill. Hence the language content of the course is selected not because it is representative of what the learner will have to deal with after the course is over but because it is likely to activate strategies for learning as the course progresses. (1981, p. 5)

This perspective on authenticity integrates well with task-based, project-based, and process-based syllabuses, since in each of these syllabus types, the activities which stimulate learning and higher-order thinking are essential to the success of the learner and curriculum.

ESP AND THE FUTURE

It is difficult to predict the future of the English for Specific Purposes Movement. Because it relies on authenticity of text and context and careful needs assessment, the movement's character is largely dependent upon the necessity for English use in various parts of the world. It is therefore the responsibility of those who advocate the principles of ESP to remain flexible and current so that they may understand the needs of new students and the discourse of new pedagogical settings.

NOTE

1. See Swales (1985) for further comments on this project and the virtues and pitfalls in project work.

DISCUSSION QUESTIONS

1. The author contends that "all English language teaching must be designed for the specific learning and language use purposes of identified groups of students," i.e., that all effective language teaching is ESP. Do you agree with this contention, or do you believe that there is a single "common core" of English that all students should study? If you accept the second argument, of what should this common core consist? Are there certain groups of students who might require a common core and others who do not?

2. The author notes that traces of all phases of ESP's history remain in language teaching. Is this

true? Can you find evidence in textbooks of grammatical and functional features of social registers? How much evidence of discourse study do textbooks present?

3. The author discusses several definitions of authenticity: of student needs, of discourse, of tasks, and of activities. If you were a curriculum designer, which of these views of authenticity would take precedence in your design? Discuss in some detail how you would go about establishing authenticity of this type in your curriculum.

4. Hutchinson and Waters (1987) provide a list of five features for student-centered ESP classrooms which might apply to any language classroom at any level (pp. 33–35). Is this list complete? If not, what might be added? Select one of these points and discuss in specific terms how you might apply it in developing classroom activities.

5. Have you had any experiences with ESP or Languages for Specific Purposes (LSP) as a student or as a teacher? Do you see the ESP experience as something different from other types of language learning experiences? If so, how? Were the texts different? Were the activities different? Was there more focus upon student needs or learning strategies?

6. Several areas of language teaching/learning are not dealt with by the author, e.g., testing. What are the problems and possibilities in testing in an ESP class? Are these issues common in all testing or does ESP present unusual challenges?

7. One important tenet of current ESP teaching is that what students experience in a classroom should be transferable to "real" English language situations. Students should be able to replicate activities or language in the world to demonstrate to themselves the utility of ESP training. Can you think of ways in which activities, texts, or experiences can be structured for maximum transferability?

SUGGESTED ACTIVITIES

1. Peruse the selections in Swales's *Episodes in ESP* (1985), containing 15 chapters on ESP milestones. Does Swales's history of ESP parallel the four phases discussed in this chapter? What developments in ESP does Swales include which are not in this discussion? Read carefully one or two of the Swales chapters and summarize for the class what these selections contributed to the ESP movement.

2. According to the author, "The greatest contribution of ESP to language teaching has been its insistence upon careful and extensive needs and task analyses before and during the development of a curriculum." Select a group of students who are at present attending an ESL class or who will be doing so in the future. Using articles from the *English for Specific Purposes* journal, if possible, design an extensive needs assessment for that group: determining who should be asked about needs (e.g., students, instructors, employers), how needs information should be gathered, how questions about the language used should be asked (e.g., about features of discourse, about language functions), and what types of observations should be made (see, e.g., Ramani et al., 1988). Design a questionnaire for a single group of people (e.g., academic instructors) who are able to identify these students' needs. For assistance in this effort, consult Bridgeman and Carlson (1984) or Horowitz (1986).

3. Select one task (e.g., the completion of an essay examination, or understanding and carrying out instructions) which your students must perform. If possible, observe some students carrying out this task—or ask students to observe and record themselves, if possible. Then develop a task-based lesson, emerging from the findings of the minitask analysis. The emphasis in the lesson should be upon the aspects of the task or language required which present particular problems for the students.

4. Survey one of the volumes of *The Annual Review of Applied Linguistics* listed in the "Suggestions for Further Reading." Select one or two articles and report on their topics and conclusions to the class.

SUGGESTIONS FOR FURTHER READING

References of Historical Interest

Kennedy, C. and R. Bolitho (1984)
English for Specific Purposes. London: Macmillan.

Robinson, P. (1980)
ESP: English for Specific Purposes. Englewood Cliffs, New Jersey: Prentice-Hall.

Selinker, L., E. Tarone, and V. Hanzeli, eds. (1981)
English for Academic and Technical Purposes: Studies in Honor of Louis Trimble. New York: Newbury House.

Swales, J. (1985)
Episodes in ESP. Englewood Cliffs, New Jersey: Prentice-Hall.

Swales, J. M., and H. Mustafa, eds. (1984)
English for Specific Purposes in the Arab World. Birmingham: University of Aston.

Trimble, L. (1985)
English for Science and Technology: A Discourse Approach, Cambridge: CUP.

Waters, A., ed. (1982)
Issues in ESP. Lancaster Practical Papers in English Language Education, 5, 1982.

References Indicating Ongoing Trends

Annual Review of Applied Linguistics, 7, 1986. Language and the Professions.

Annual Review of Applied Linguistics, 10, 1989. ESP and Communicative Syllabus Design.

English for Specific Purposes: An International Journal (3 issues per year) (Ann M. Johns and John Swales, eds.). Pergamon Journals, Maxwell House, Fairview Park, Elmsford, NY 10523.

English Language Research Journal, 1987, Issue No. 1. Genre Analysis and ESP, University of Birmingham, England.

ESP: State of the Art (M. L. Tickoo, ed.), 1988. SEAMEO Regional English Language Centre, Singapore, Anthology Series 21.

Hutchinson, T., and A. Waters (1987)
English for Specific Purposes: A Learner-Centered Approach. Cambridge: Cambridge University Press.

UNESCO/ALSED-LSP Newsletter, LSP Centre, Copenhagen School of Economica, Fabrikvej 7, DK-2000, Copenhagen, Denmark.

II
Language Skills
A. Listening

Until recently the skill of listening comprehension had been neglected both with regard to its place in language methodology and with regard to the development of techniques and materials for teaching the listening skill per se. As Morley's chapter points out, listening comprehension is now felt to be a necessary preliminary to oral proficiency, as well as an important skill in its own right. The need to prepare learners, from the start, to understand speakers of English, speaking at a normal rate, in a normal manner, is now one of the major goals of ESL/EFL instruction. Morley describes for the teacher some techniques and activities for achieving this important goal in both interactional (e.g., conversation) and transactional (e.g., lecture) settings. In Peterson's chapter the development of listening skills in a second language is directly linked with a psycholinguistic model of cognitive processing. Peterson presents a taxonomy that shows us at what stage of development a learner can benefit from practice with different kinds of listening activities: bottom-up, top-down, or interactive.

Listening Comprehension in Second/Foreign Language Instruction

Joan Morley

Ideas about language learning and language teaching have been changing in some fundamental ways during the last two decades. In fact, in retrospect, the following themes that dominated the Second AILA Conference at Cambridge in 1969 seem to have been near prophetic in pointing toward future trends in a "new era" of second/foreign language education:

- a new focus on the individual learner as the central element in the complex process of second language acquisition
- a focus on the so-called receptive skills of reading and listening, long regarded as 'passive' skills, as much more complex processes
- an emerging notion that listening comprehension may be the key fundamental skill that has not been adequately understood
- a desire to bring students into closer contact with 'real' language as it is used in the real world by people communicating successfully with each other.

(Pimsleur & Quinn, 1971)

Since 1969 there have, indeed, been significant paradigm shifts in learning theory, linguistic theory, and instructional models, with an important movement from a primary focus on teaching and a teacher-centered classroom to an increasing concern with learning and a learner-centered classroom. At the same time there has been a shift from a major emphasis on structure to an emphasis that includes attention to language function and communication.

While every facet of language study has been influenced by these changes, none has been affected more dramatically than listening comprehension. The status of listening began to change from one of neglect to one of increasing importance, as the instructional programs of the 1970s expanded their pragmatic skills-focus on reading, writing, and speaking, to include listening. And during the 1980s new instructional frameworks that featured functional language and communicative approaches also gave special attention to listening. Today, attention to listening in second language development is becoming an important topic of study in both theory and pedagogy, but much work remains to be done. As a research focus, although listening is well recognized as a critical dimension in language learning, it remains one of the least understood processes. And as a focus of instruction, listening continues to be underrated in many programs, and some of the recommended methods and techniques, as well as some of the published materials, continue to be based on outdated models of language learning and teaching. G. Brown (1987) observed that a significant number of published courses on listening comprehension and classroom practices in many schools in many countries continue to demonstrate that listening is often regarded as the least important skill and that the instructional heritage of the early 1960s approach "is still alive and kicking" (1987, p. 12).

The first part of this chapter looks at some general aspects of listening and language learning. (See Peterson in this volume for additional information.) The second part presents some principles and guidelines for developing (or adapting) listening comprehension activities and materials. Lesson suggestions are given for class and small group or pair work, and for individualized self-study using equipment in the classroom, at home, or in different kinds of language laboratory settings. Example lesson segments are included.

LISTENING AND LANGUAGE LEARNING

The Importance of Listening

As Rivers, long an advocate for more attention to listening comprehension, observed: "Speaking does not of itself constitute communication unless what is said is comprehended by another person." "Teaching the comprehension of spoken speech is therefore of primary importance if the communication aim is to be reached" (1966, pp. 196, 204).

Listening is used far more than any other single language skill in normal daily life. On average, we can expect to listen twice as much as we speak, four times more than we read, and five times more than we write. (Rivers, 1981; Weaver, 1972) The importance of listening cannot be underestimated; it is imperative that it not be treated trivially in second and foreign language curricula.

Emerging Recognition of the Importance of Listening in Second/Foreign Language Study

Yet many of us still take listening for granted, often with little conscious awareness of our performance as listeners. Weaver (1972) commented on the elusiveness of our listening awareness: "After all, listening is neither so dramatic nor so noisy as talking. The talker is the center of attention for all listeners. His behavior is overt and vocal, and he hears and notices his own behavior, whereas listening activity often seems like merely being there—doing nothing" (pp. 12–13).

Much of the language teaching field, too, took listening for granted until relatively recent times (but see Gouin, 1880; Nida, 1953; Palmer, 1917; Sweet, 1899). Modern-day arguments for listening comprehension began to be voiced in the mid-1960s by Rivers (1966), as noted above, by Newmark and Diller, and by Belasco. Newmark and Diller (1964) underscored "the need for the systematic development of listening comprehension *not only as a foundation for speaking, but also as a skill in its own right*" (p. 20). Belasco (1971) expressed his concerns very clearly: "I was rudely jolted by the realization that it is possible to develop so-called 'speaking ability' and yet be virtually incompetent in understanding the spoken language. . . . [students] were learning to audio-comprehend certain specific dialogues and drills . . . but could not understand [the language] out of the mouths of native speakers" (pp. 4–5). But as Blair (1982) observed, special attention to listening "just didn't 'sell' . . ." until recent times.

Three Perspectives on Listening and Language Instruction

In English language teaching programs of the 1940s, 1950s, and 1960s the predominant British model of situational language teaching and the predominant American model of audiolingual methodology accorded little attention to listening beyond its role in the learner's imitation of dialogs, or grammar and pronunciation drills. And in the language learning theory of the times, little importance was attributed to listening beyond sound recognition/discrimination and the prosodic patterning of spoken language as involved in memorization and habit formation. Listening was regarded as a "passive" skill along with reading, and was simply taken for granted.

However, slowly and steadily over the last 20 years more and different kinds of attention have been given to listening comprehension. Today, instructional procedures can be divided into (at least) three different types. Each uses the term "listening" from its particular perspective on the nature of language learning and the role of listening in the process: (1) *listening to repeat* (i.e., imitate and memorize), as in the above-mentioned situational and audiolingual models of instruction; (2) *listening to "understand"* (i.e., comprehension of meaning as a communicative language function), or as Newmark and Diller noted (above), the development of listening comprehension as a skill in its own right; (3) *listening as the primary focus in the "comprehension approach"* to second/foreign language learning.

Listening to Repeat

Listening and repeating are key components in both audiolingual and situational instruction, and these models continue to be used in a number of programs. Listening/repeating is also a technique used for pronunciation work in other kinds of instructional formats. Here the learner is asked to listen, in order to "hear" a model (e.g., a sentence, a phrase, a word, a sound) and in order to reproduce it. Since this kind of processing can be done *below* the level of propositional language structuring, the development of "listening-with-understanding" may or may not be a signficant by-product of such "hearing-and-pattern-matching" routines. As documented in Belasco's paper (above) and as summarized in the following comment by Terrell (1982), evidence suggests more likely not: "Students in an audiolingual approach usually have excellent pronunciation, can repeat dialogues and use memorized prefabricated patterns in conversation. They can do pattern drills, making substitutions and changing morphemes using various sorts of agreement rules. What they very often cannot do, is participate in a normal conversation with a native speaker" (1982, p. 121).

Listening to Understand

The instructional focus here is on helping learners develop listening "as-a-skill-in-its-own-right" in order to understand the meaning of spoken language quickly and accurately, comfortably and confidently, in a variety of settings. Core coursebooks gave limited attention to listening comprehension, and very few specialized listening instructional materials were available until the early 1970s (*five* texts only, by personal count in 1971). In contrast, what began as a few books in the early 1970s became a virtual avalanche as dozens of texts and tape programs, audio or video, were published (something above 150 available now), with more added every year. By and large, the materials published over the last 20 years have featured one (or both) of two basic types of expected student response: (1) the question-oriented response model, (2) the task-oriented response model.

The Question-Oriented Response Model. Here students are asked to listen to an oral text (e.g., a sentence, a dialog/conversation, a paragraph reading, a talk or "lecturette"), then answer a series of factual ("quiz-style") comprehension questions on the content in order to "prove" that they have understood. Questions are true-false, multiple choice, fill-in-the-blank, short answer, and similar question types borrowed from traditional reading techniques. Follow-up activities often include work with grammar (e.g., rewriting sentences changing tense, person, or some other element) or vocabulary exercises based on the aural text. Beyond this kind of language manipulation, students are not asked to "do" anything functional with the information. The efficacy of this model, in both listening and reading instruction, has been called into serious question on a number of counts. These include the following: The focus is on "testing," not teaching; essentially this model seems to call for memorization of information and, in fact, it may be more a test of memory, or previous knowledge, or good guessing ability, than a measure of meaningful comprehension; this model features neither authentic functions nor genuine communicative outcomes; overall it has little true motivational value and may be perceived by students as a boring activity and simply another vehicle for studying grammar and vocabulary.

The Task-Oriented Response Model. In this model, language tasks are set for students to complete, either individually or in small-group collaborations. Basically, the tasks are structured so that they make use of the information provided in the spoken text, not as an end in itself, but as a resource to use in order to achieve a communicative task outcome. Task-based formats have developed rapidly in recent years in both research and pedagogy. "Task" is used here in Johnson's sense (Brumfit & Johnson, 1979, p. 22), in which task-oriented teaching is defined as teaching which employs "actual meaning" by focusing on tasks to be mediated through language, and where success or failure is judged in terms of whether or not the tasks are performed. The primary lesson goal is to provide learners with guided listening task experiences. In addition, lessons often include a

focus on helping learners to develop language learning strategies, both general ones and listening-specific ones. (See Peterson in this volume.)

Listening as the Primary Focus in the "Comprehension Approach" to Second/Foreign Language Learning

Beginning in the mid-1960s and continuing into the 1970s, several language researchers-teachers developed instructional programs that featured two things: early attention to listening comprehension and a delay in oral production. Winitz (1981) defined it as follows: "In the comprehension approach a new system of learning is not really advocated. The instructional format is to extend the teaching interval of one component of training, comprehension, while delaying instruction or experience in speaking, reading, writing . . . the comprehension approach is cognitive in orientation. As used here, cognitive is defined as a system that gives students the opportunity to engage in problem-solving, the personal discovery of grammatical rules" (1981, p. xvii). Continuing attention to comprehension approaches to language acquisition throughout the 1970s and 1980s resulted in several special systems of instruction, including Asher (1965, 1969), Total Physical Response; Postovsky (1970, 1974), Delay in Oral Practice at the Beginning of Second Language Learning; Winitz and Reeds (1973), Rapid Acquisition of a Foreign Language by the Avoidance of Speaking; Terrell (1977, 1982; Terrell, Genzmer, Nicolai, & Tschirner, 1988), A Natural Approach to the Acquisition and Learning of a Language. (See Blair in this volume.)

Teaching and materials development will reflect whichever of the above perspectives a given textbook writer, teacher, or teacher trainer has adopted as a part of a personal theoretical and pedagogical "belief system". The author's beliefs (which may or may not be stated directly) about theory and practice in language learning and teaching should be one of the first evaluative focuses in textbook analysis. In analyzing the listening activities of either a core coursebook or a supplementary text, keep in mind that materials can be modified and adapted if their procedures and/or student response model are not to your liking. Bamford (1982) and Richards (1983) both present good suggestions for materials adaptation.

Some Dimensions of Language and the Listening Act

Listening, a Dynamic Process, Not a Passive State

Listening along with reading has had a traditional label of "passive skill." Nothing could be further from the truth. Anderson and Lynch (1988) reject a conceptualization of listening as a "passive act," calling it a "listener-as-tape-recorder" explanation of listening. They argue that such a perspective on listening fails to account for the interpretations listeners make as they "hear" the spoken text according to their own purposes for listening, their expectations, and their own store of background knowledge.

Implications for Instruction. One of the obvious implications for instruction is to bring students to an understanding that listening is *not* a passive skill, but one that not only is active but very demanding. This can be done gradually as a part of listening activity work, especially activities that are in the task-based and communicative outcomes mode, where the "work" can be rather enjoyable in a problem-solving and discovery-process format. Learners can come to realize that just as it is "work" to become better readers, writers, and speakers in a second language, listening skill, too, doesn't happen magically or as an overnight phenomenon.

In another direction, in your contacts with school personnel, it may be necessary to work toward dispelling the false notion—the "myth"—that listening is a passive skill. A false characterization of listening and reading

as the "passive" skills of language still remains as a conventional wisdom in some quarters. Administrators readily see the need for reading and writing coursework, but the case for listening instruction may have to be made.

Listening, in Three Active Communicative Modes

Every day we engage in communicative listening in one way or another most of our waking hours. Probably the first mode that comes to mind is listening in *two-way communication,* or "interactive" listening. Here the reciprocal "speech chain" (Denes & Pinson, 1963) of speaker/listener is obvious to us. Here there are two (or more) active participants who take turns in speaker-role and listener-role as the face-to-face (or telephone) interaction moves along. A second mode is listening in *one-way communication.* Auditory input often seems to surround us as we move through the day. The input comes from a variety of sources: conversations overheard; public address announcements; recorded messages (including telephone-answering machines); the media (e.g., radio, television, films); instructional situations of all kinds; public performances (e.g., lectures, religious services, plays, operas, musicals, concerts). As we hear speakers but cannot "interact," we often "talk to ourselves" in a "reactive" self-dialog manner, as we consider what we hear. We may subvocalize or even vocalize responses as we react to what we hear. The third communicative mode— *self-dialog communication*—is one in which we may not be aware of our *internal* roles as "speaker" and "listener/reactor" *in our own thought processes.* Sometimes we recreate language internally and "listen" again as we retell and relive communicative interludes. Sometimes we simply attend to our own internal language, which we produce as we think through alternatives, plan strategies, and make decisions—all by "talking to ourselves" and "listening to ourselves." Notice that listening is *not* a passive experience in any of these three communicative modes. All are highly active participatory experiences.

Implications for Instruction. Second/ foreign language learners need to have instructional opportunities in both two-way and one-way communicative modes, as will be illustrated in the second part of this chapter. Self-dialog communication may be something to discuss with students and to encourage them to use in the other modes, as well as a mode in its own right.

Listening and Language Function, Interactional and Transactional Discourse

Brown and Yule (1983a) suggest dividing language functions into two major divisions: language for interactional purposes and language for transactional purposes. They note that these two terms correspond to Halliday's terms "interpersonal" and "ideational" (Halliday, 1970, p. 143).

Interactional Language Function. Here the purpose is to further social relationships and express personal attitudes. Interactional language is listener-oriented more than message-oriented, focuses more on person than on information, and has as an important objective: the establishment and maintenance of cordial social relationships. Indirectness and vagueness are tolerated as role relationships are negotiated. There is a premium on establishing peer solidarity and working out the delicate nuances of turn-taking in the interaction. Some features of interactional language use are talking about "safe" topics (such as weather, the immediate environment), much shifting of topics with a great deal of agreement on them, expressing opinions, maintaining "face" and respecting "face," identifying with the concerns of the other person, and, in general, "being nice" to the other person and a little less careful about detail. Brown and Yule comment that "a great deal of ordinary every-

day conversation appears to consist of one individual commenting on something which is present to both him and his listener . . . a great deal of casual conversation contains phrases and echoes of phrases which appear more to be intended as contributions to a conversation than to be taken as instances of information-giving."

Transactional Language Function. Here the purpose is to convey factual or propositional information. Transactional language is message-oriented, with a focus on content and a concern for "getting things done in the real world." There is a premium on language clarity and precision. Some features of transactional language are instructing, giving directions, explaining, describing, ordering, inquiring, requesting, relating, checking on the correctness of details, and verifying of understanding. Brown and Yule comment: "Speakers typically go to considerable trouble to make what they are saying clear when a transaction is involved, and may contradict the listener if he appears to have misunderstood. When the *message* is the reason for speaking, then the message must be understood" (1983a, p. 13).

Implications for Instruction. Teachers need to make students aware of these two language functions and to provide practice experiences for both. Sometimes transitions between transactional or "business-type" talk and interactional or "social talk" are clear moves from one dimension to the other, but sometimes the strands in an interaction are not so obvious; sometimes they are intertwined. Students need guidance and practice in learning how to recognize and how to respond appropriately, as will be illustrated in the second part of the chapter.

Listening and Language Processing, Bottom-Up and Top-Down

In accounting for the complex nature of processing spoken language it has been hypothesized that "bottom-up" and "top-down" modes work together in a combined cooperative process. (See Peterson in this volume for more information.)

Bottom-Up Processing. This mode of the processing of language information is evoked by an external source, that is, by the incoming language data itself. Bottom-up comprehension of speech, then, refers to the part of the process in which the "understanding" of incoming language is worked out proceeding from sounds, into words, into grammatical relationship and lexical meaning, and so on. The composite meaning of the "message" is arrived at based on the incoming language data.

Top-Down Processing. Here the processing of language information comes from an internal source. That is, it is evoked from a bank of prior knowledge and global expectations. These include expectations about language and expectations about the "world." Learners bring to bear on the task of "understanding" the incoming speech, prior information which allows them to predict on the basis of context—both the preceding linguistic context and the situation-and-topic and setting-and-participants context—what the incoming "message" at any point can be expected to be and how the "pieces" fit into the "whole." Chaudron and Richards (1986) note: "Top-down processing involves prediction and inferencing on the basis of hierarchies of facts, propositions, and expectations, and it enables the listener or the reader to bypass some aspects of bottom-up processing. On encountering the topic of 'going to the dentist,' for example, we refer to knowledge about the participants in the situation, their roles and purposes, and the typical procedures adopted by dentists, and their consequences" (1986, pp. 114–115).

Implications for Instruction. As with language function, students need awareness of these two kinds of language processing and practice opportunities for both. Many published materials focus heavily on one or the other of these processes, without referring to them by these names, of course. In the Michigan materials *Improving Aural Comprehension* (Morley, 1972), which is a task-structured problem-solving listening program intended for teens and adults (focused on graded listening experiences in processing specific kinds of notional information—e.g., numerical, time, space—and using that information immediately for problem solving), can be included under the rubric of bottom-up work. (See a lesson segment on pages 98–99 in this chapter.) Another Michigan text, *Films for EFL Practice* (Morley, 1973) focuses on top-down areas, including predicting, inferencing, explaining, contrasting and comparing, causal relationships, and attending to other similar language tasks. (See a lesson segment on pages 100–101 in this chapter.)

Taking dual perspectives into account, Richards (1990) proposes a model of materials design for second language listening comprehension that combines *language functions* (interactional and transaction) and *language processes* (top-down and bottom-up). He observes that the extent to which one or the other *process* (top-down or bottom-up) dominates is determined by (a) the *purpose* (transactional or interactional) for listening, (b) the kind of background knowledge which can be applied to the task, and (c) the degree of familiarity listeners have with the topic of discourse. He gives illustrations of different formats, concluding:

Too often, listening texts require students to adopt a single approach in listening, one which demands a detailed understanding of the content of a discourse and the recognition of every word and structure that occurs in a text. Students should not be required to respond to interactional discourse as if it were being used for a transactional purpose, nor should they be expected to use a bottom-up approach to an aural text if a top-down one is more appropriate. (p. 83)

Richards uses the two language *functions* and the two language *processes* to construct the following four-part grid, which allows for a listening activity to be classified according to the demands of the *function* for listening and the *process* which can be expected to be most prominently involved.

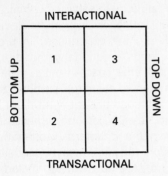

INTERACTIONAL

BOTTOM UP
TOP DOWN

| 1 | 3 |
| 2 | 4 |

TRANSACTIONAL

Richards gives an example for each of the four cells as follows. In the bottom-up mode:

1. Listening closely to a joke (interactive) in order to know "when to laugh."
2. Listening closely to instructions (transactive) during a first driving lesson.

In the top-down mode:

3. Listening casually to cocktail party "talk" (interactive).
4. Experienced air traveler listening casually to verbal air safety instructions (transactive) which have been heard many times before.

Other examples of interactional uses are greetings, small talk, jokes, compliments, and passing the time of day with friends or with encounters with strangers. Other examples of transactional uses are instructions, descriptions, lectures, news broadcasts.

Richards notes that in many situations *both* interactional and transactional purposes are involved. In particular, it is suggested that effective classroom participation requires both: *interactional* to interact with teacher and other students while accomplishing class tasks, and *transactional* to assimilate new information, construct new concepts, and acquire new skills.

Listening, Affect, and Attitudes

Listening can be defined broadly as "everything that impinges on the human processing which mediates between sound and the construction of meaning. . . ." Moreover, "everything that impinges . . ." includes the important dimension of the *affective information,* which is an integral part of real-world communication.

In developing activities and materials for listening instruction, it is essential to consider the *affective domain* which encompasses attitudes, emotions, and feelings. In this section, the focus turns to how attitudinal and emotional information is conveyed, both *linguistically* and *nonlinguistically,* and some of the attitudinal language functions that second language learners need to experience in instructional listening materials.

Linguistic and Nonlinguistic Cues to Affect

As an old folk adage says: "It's not *what* you say, it's *how* you say it!" But how can SL listeners learn to recognize and interpret aspects of the "how" as well as the "what" in both two-way and one-way oral communication? How can they become skilled at processing *non*linguistic as well as linguistic affective information?

In *two-way* interactive communication "messages" are conveyed in at least three ways: a *linguistic* dimension and two *nonlinguistic* dimensions: paralinguistic and extralinguistic. In one-way communication the visual cues of extralinguistic information may be missing, and the listener must rely on the linguistic and paralinguistic information.

Linguistic Messages. Meanings begin in people. In truth: "Meanings aren't in words, meanings are in people." But sometimes meanings don't come across clearly, and we hear speakers protest, "But that's not what I said." In an attempt to convey an "intended" meaning, speakers choose words and arrange them into sentences (or "part" sentences) and groups of sentences in larger pieces of mono-log or dialog discourse patterns.

The words chosen and both the intrasen-tential and intersentential arrangements of them map "affect" onto the linguistic infor-mation. Speakers may or may not be con-scious of the nature and/or the strength of the affective coloring; on the other hand, they may use it with careful design.

Examples: That was an (interesting/excellent/ good/fair/so-so/terrible) movie. I like him a lot but . . . Even though she's my best friend . . .

Clearly, affective interpretation must be a part of listening comprehension activities. This means that instructional experiences must be contextualized and must reflect real-world situations and feeling, tasks, and outcomes.

Paralinguistic Messages. In another di-mension, the way words, sentences, and groups of sentences in spoken language are programmed *vocally* enables them to carry information about how they are to be inter-preted as the vocal features transmit *the speaker's attitude toward what he or she is saying.* In the realm of intonation in particu-lar, early on Pike (1945) drew attention to attitudinal intonation patterns, and the work by Brazil, Coulthard, and Johns (1980) and Brown, Currie, and Kenworthy (1980) has ex-plored a variety of aspects of intonation and discourse. The vocal elements that map affec-tive information onto the "word" message are those beyond the more-or-less basic/ neutral stress, rhythm, and intonation pat-terns. They include a broad spectrum of vocal qualities, including rate-rhythm-stress features, tonal variations, and more. In truth: "It's not just *what* you say, it's *how* you say it".

Brown (1977) has an excellent chapter on paralinguistic features, including a matrix of variables, which makes a useful framework for studying a number of vocal parameters.

See also Stanley (1978) for a discussion of vocal features.

Extralinguistic Messages. Speakers also convey meaning through body language. That is, simultaneous "physical" messages are being transmitted alongside the "word" and "vocal" information and must be inter-preted by the listener. Once again, the speaker may or may not be fully aware of this aspect of his or her communication. Elements involved here include body postures, body movements, body and hand gestures, facial expressions, facial gestures, eye contact, and spatial use by the communicators. The con-ventional folk wisdom here is "It's not just what you *say*, it's what you *do*," and most importantly, it's a "wisdom" that varies with languages and cultures.

Intellectual, Emotional, and Moral Attitudes

As noted above, an important part of communication is the expression and com-prehension of attitudes. Van Ek (1976), in a Council of Europe volume that gives a full specification of the objectives and item in-ventories of their language project, lists six basic language functions. Three focus on atti-tudes: intellectual, emotional, and moral atti-tudes. The other three are imparting and seek-ing factual information, getting things done (suasion), and socializing. These are all areas for consideration in developing listening comprehension instructional materials, and it is important to alert learners to the interweav-ing of *interactional* and *transactional* talk (as discussed on p. 86) and the combining of fact and opinion, of content and value judgements.

Intellectual Attitudes. Included here are expression and comprehension of the follow-ing kinds of intellectual attitudes: agreement/ disagreement; denying something; accepting/ declining something; a variety of types of inquiry; dealing with knowing, forgetting, remembering; possibility/impossibility; capability/incapability; local conclusion; uncertainty; obligation, permission, and more (van Ek, 1976, pp. 45–47).

Emotional Attitudes. Included in this area: expressing pleasure/displeasure, interest/lack of interest, surprise, hope, satisfaction/dissatisfaction, disappointment, fear and worry, preference, gratitude, sympathy, intention, wants and desires, and more (van Ek, 1976, pp. 47–48).

Moral Attitudes. This area includes apologizing, expressing approval/disapproval, appreciation, regret, indifference, and more (van Ek, 1976, p. 48). (For additional information see Munby, 1978; Wilkins, 1976).

This short section on attitudes has been included here in order to emphasize the fact that aurally received information is not truly understood unless listeners interpret the features of affect transmitted by speakers in *what they say, how they say it,* and *what they do* as they are talking.

DEVELOPING LISTENING COMPREHENSION ACTIVITIES AND MATERIALS

This part focuses on instructional considerations, while keeping in mind these three important points about listening as a language act: 1. Listening comprehension is an act of information processing in which the listener is involved in *two-way* communication, or *one-way* communication, and/or *self-dialog* communication. 2. Broadly speaking, real-world spoken communication can be viewed as serving two linguistic functions: an *interactional* (or interpersonal) function and a *transactional* (or ideational) function. 3. The cognitive processing of spoken language appears to involve simultaneous activation of both *top-down* and *bottom-up* en-

gagement in order for listeners to construct what they believe to be the "intended meaning" of the spoken message (i.e., in order to arrive at "understanding" of the aural text).

With these features of listening as a language act in mind, this section begins with a discussion of three important principles of materials development. Then, six kinds of communicative outcomes are outlined, with lesson suggestions provided for each. A final section presents some suggestions for creating a self-access, self-study listening center. Central to the underlying "belief system" reflected in this chapter is a communicative language teaching perspective, one which values meaningful tasks and communicative activities.

Principles

In order to get learners' attention, in order to keep them actively and purposefully engaged in the task at hand, and in order to maximize the effectiveness of listening/ language learning experiences, three materials development principles are suggested: *relevance, transferability/applicability,* and *task-orientation.* These three principles are important in making choices about both *language content* (i.e., the "information" presented) and *language outcome(s)* (i.e., the way the information is put to use).

Relevance

Both the listening lesson *content* (i.e., the "information") and the *outcome* (i.e., the nature or objective of the "information use") need to be as relevant as possible to the learner's life and life-style. This is essential for getting and holding learner attention—and provides genuine (not fake) motivational elements. Lessons need to feature content and outcomes that have "face validity" to students. The more lessons feature things that are relevant, the more they can appeal to students, and the better the changes of having learners' ears *really* tuned in. And if students really want to listen, we have accomplished at least part of the task which Strevens (1988) has called "encouraging the intention to learn."

Relevance is easy to control in your own specially prepared classroom listening activities. However, in using published materials, it will be necessary to choose only those lessons with topics that are relevant to your students, and it may be necessary to modify the way the material is presented and the way students are asked to "use" the information. Richards (1983, pp. 237–238) suggests some ways to adapt materials in areas such as modifying objectives, adding prelistening activities, changing the teaching procedures for class presentation and devising postlistening activities.

Transferability/Applicability

Whatever is relevant is also likely to have potential for transferability. Insofar as possible, at either the *content* level or the *outcome* level (or both), listening lessons need to have transferability/applicability value, either internally (i.e., to other classes) or externally (i.e., to out-of-school situations) (or both). In a "transfer of training" sense, if teachers can mount rather specific in-class activities that mirror real-world *content* and/or *outcome* patterns, the better the potential for outside application, consciously or unconsciously, now or in the future.

Here are some examples, ones that make use of audio or video listening and analysis. (Note: The "outcomes" included here are listed on p. 93 and discussed in detail under "Communicative Outcomes.")

1. For teen and preteen students music videos, such as *"We Are the World": The Video Event,* can be used with outcome 4 (i.e., listening and evaluating information) as well as 6 (i.e., listening for enjoyment and pleasure) and can be applicable to out-of-class music concerts or video viewing, and related peer talk.
2. For elementary school students class story-listening (and storytelling), either

live or on an audiotape such as *The Day it Snowed Tortillas* or a videotape such as *Goldilocks and the Three Bears* can be used with outcome 2 (i.e., listening and transferring information, in either speaking or writing) as well as 6 (i.e., listening for enjoyment and pleasure) and can be applicable to similar activities in daily classwork.
3. For adult students (e.g., immigrant and new resident students, foreign or second language students in college or university, international businesspeople) radio or television news broadcasts, using either live or permitted off-air recordings, can be used with outcomes 2 (i.e., listening and transferring information into notes or summary form) and 3 (i.e., listening and problem solving) and can be applicable outside of class as a regular daily structured listening practice with media, and as a source of conversation topics with friends and neighbors.

Task Orientation

In formal classes with teenage and adult students, and with children in carefully selected ways, it is important to combine two major types of work: (1) language use tasks and (2) language analysis activities.

Notions of "task" have developed out of communicative teaching and materials production. In Johnson's sense (Brumfit & Johnson, 1979, p. 200) task-oriented teaching is defined as teaching which provides "actual meaning" by focusing on tasks to be mediated through language, and where success or failure is seen to be judged in terms of whether or not the tasks are performed. Maley and Moulding (1979, p. 102) focus on instruction which is *task-oriented* not *question-oriented,* where their aim is to provide learners with tasks which *use the information* in the aural text, rather than asking them to prove their understanding of the text by requiring them to answer questions. Candlin and Murphy (1987, p. 1) note: "The central process we are concerned with is language learning, and tasks present this in the form of a problem-solving negotiation between knowledge that the learner holds and new knowledge. This activity is conducted through language in use, which may itself be seen as a negotiation of meaning."

Language Use Tasks. The purpose here is to give students practice in listening to get information and specifically, to do something with it immediately. This encompasses *specific* Listen-and-do communicative outcomes such as the following:

1. Listening and performing actions (e.g., command games and songs such as "Do the Hokey Pokey," "May I?" "Simon Says").
2. Listening and performing operations (e.g., listening and constructing a figure, drawing a map).
3. Listening and solving problems (e.g., riddles, "intellectual" or "logic" puzzles, real-life numerical, spatial, or chronological problems).
4. Listening and transcribing (e.g., taking telephone messages, writing notes).
5. Listening and summarizing information (e.g., outlining, giving the gist of a message in either speaking or writing).
6. Interactive listening and negotiating meaning through questioning/answering routines (e.g., questions to get repetition of information, questions to get verification, questions to get clarification, questions to get elaboration).

(Note: More detailed information on outcomes follows.)

These listening and language use tasks help students to build two things: (a) a base of content experiences that helps to develop expectancies and, gradually, a repertoire of familiar top-down networks of background knowledge in the second language. This in turn increases predictive power for future communicative interludes, including *schemata* (i.e., the larger order mental frameworks of knowledge) and *scripts* (i.e., the situation-specific mental frameworks that allow us to predict actors, events, action sequences, and alternative outcomes). These include formulaic speech routines and assumed elements in the physical setting; (b) a base of outcomes experiences that helps to build a repertoire of familiar information-handling operations in the second language, ones that are applicable to future communicative encounters in the second language. (See "Communicative Outcomes" for information on outcomes.)

Language Analysis Tasks. The purpose here is to give students opportunities to analyze selected aspects of both language structure and language use (i.e., forms and functions) and to develop some personal strategies to facilitate learning. (See Peterson in this volume for more information.) The goal is one of consciousness raising about language, what Wenden and Rubin (1987) discuss as "awareness-raising" tasks, with some that focus on how language works. Activities can focus on one or two points at a time and can include attention to a variety of features of grammar, pronunciation, and vocabulary, discourse markers, sociolinguistic features, and strategic features (Canale & Swain, 1980). Specific activities can include these:

1. Analysis of some of the features of "fast speech," through the use of tasks that will help students work at learning to cope with rapid, natural, contextualized speech.
2. Analysis of phrasing and pausing points; attention to the ways the grouping of words into functional units (ones that "follow" grammar) can be used to facilitate listening, and "chunking" the input into units for interpretation.
3. Analysis of both monolog "speeches" and dialog exchanges with attention to discourse organizational structures.
4. Describing and analyzing sociolinguistic dimensions, including participants and their roles and relationships, settings, purpose of the communicative episodes, expected outcomes.

5. Describing and analyzing communicative strategies used by speakers to deal with miscommunication, communication breakdowns, distractions.

(*Note:* Real-life recordings of conversations, telephone conversations, talks, discussions can be used to introduce listening analysis tasks. See Morley 1984, 1985.)

Texts by Lynch (1983), Ur (1984), and Davis and Rinvolucri (1988) all give a variety of language analysis tasks.

Communicative Outcomes: An Organizing Framework

It is clear by now that a Listen-and-Do format—that is, information gathering and information using—is recommended for listening instructional activities in the second language curriculum. Listening comprehension in today's language curriculum must go far beyond a 20-minute tape a day (or a paragraph or two read aloud), followed by a series of "test" questions about the factual content.

Listen-and-Do in the listening comprehension context implies an "outcome" objective. The purpose of oral communication in the real world is to achieve a genuine outcome; it may be very simple (e.g., enjoying sociable conversation) or it may be very complex (e.g., understanding intricate instructions), but an outcome is achieved. And so it must be in any listening comprehension activity planned for use in the second language learning context.

Minimum requirements for two-way oral communication are two active participants and an outcome. Participants alternate roles of speaker-sender and listener-receiver. One-way communication requires one active participant (a listener-receiver), one long-distance participant, either 'live' or recorded (who functions as speaker-sender), and an outcome.

What is an *outcome*? An outcome, in Sinclair's words (1984), is a "real job where people can actually see themselves doing something and getting somewhere. . . ." "Outcome" is an essential component in both two-way and one-way communication listening comprehension activities.

Six broad categories of outcome are discussed below. Each, of course, can be subdivided into more narrowly focused specific outcomes. A specific outcome can be modified to suit a given student group. Lesson outcomes can be graded toward gradual expansion of difficulty, complexity, and increasing performance expectations for students.

A lesson may contain more than one outcome although too many outcomes for a given activity may be overwhelming. Any outcome can be used at any age, as long as it is a part of a task that is appropriate to the age, interests, and language proficiency level of the learners.

There is overlap between some outcome categories, and no attempt is made here to make them mutually exclusive. They are presented here as an organizing framework for consideration by teachers in developing class or listening library materials. The six outcome categories are as follows:

1. listening and performing actions and operations
2. listening and transferring information
3. listening and solving problems
4. listening, evaluating, and manipulating information
5. interactive listening and negotiating meaning through questioning/answering routines
6. listening for enjoyment, pleasure, sociability

Listening and Performing Actions and Operations

Included in this category are responses to directions, instructions, descriptions in a variety of contexts. Examples include listening and

1. drawing a picture, figure, or design
2. locating routes of specific points on a map

3. selecting a picture of a person, place, or thing from description
4. identifying a person, place, or thing from description
5. performing hand or body movements as in songs and games such as "Simon Says" or "Hokey Pokey"
6. operating a piece of equipment, such as a camera, a recorder, a microwave oven, a pencil sharpener
7. carrying out steps in a process, such as steps solving a math problem, a science experiment, a cooking sequence

---

SAMPLE LESSON ACTIVITIES

Sample 1. Picture Dictation
(from Ur, 1984, pp. 73–74)

The following picture description task is suggested for upper elementary school children.

There's a table in the middle of the picture and a cat is under the table. He's a white cat. Near the table is a chair. There's a very fat boy sitting on it. He's very fat indeed, and very happy, because there's a big cake on the table and he's going to eat it in a minute. The cat is happy too; he's going to eat the mouse which is under the fat boy's chair.

Ur suggests an even easier picture dictation that can be based on simple items dictated as a series, such as "Draw a chair. Next, draw a boy. Now draw a house, etc."

Sample 2. Following Instructions in Order to Identify a Sport
(from Schechter, 1984, pp. 6–9)

The task shown in Figure 1 asks students to listen and identify the appropriate picture. Additional tasks are also suggested. Six small pictures of different sports are provided in the students' book. The excerpt shown in figure 1 is from the teachers' book.

Listening task Tell students their task is to identify the sport being taught by putting a check below the appropriate photograph. Play the tape again and have students make a list of the key words and phrases that brought them to their conclusions. Let them check their answers with each other and then with you. If it is appropriate in your teaching situation, you could ask students to get up and try to act out the instructions as the tape is played for the second time. Then, as they listen again, they can identify the sport being taught. If you want to make the task more challenging, ask students to select one of the other pictures and to give each other instructions in pairs. The student receiving the instructions could act out the instructions (if possible) and should identify the picture being described.

Listening and Transferring Information

One kind of information transfer is from *spoken* to *written*—that is, hearing information and writing it, in order to achieve outcomes such as the following:

1. Listening and taking a telephone or in-person message by either transcribing the entire message word-for-word or by writing down notes on the important items (in order to give the message to a third person).

2. Listening and filling in blanks in a gapped story game (in order to complete the story).

3. Listening and completing a form or chart (in order to use the information for some further purpose, such as making a decision or solving a problem).

4. Listening and summarizing the gist of a short story, report, or talk (in order to report it to a third person).

5. Listening to a "how to" talk and writing an outline of the steps in the sequence (e.g.,

COMPLETED LISTENING TASK
2 Following instructions about a sport

Which sport is being taught? Put a check (√) in the box below the correct photo. Make a list of the important words that helped you reach this conclusion.

Gymnastics ☐

Tennis ☐

water
head first
legs follow
jump
arms forward
straighten legs
point toes

Jogging ☐

Diving ✓

Surfing ☐

Swimming ☐

Morley: Listening Comprehension in Second/Foreign Language Instruction

how to cook something, how to run a piece of equipment, how to play a game) (in order to carry out the action).

6. Listening to a talk or lecture and taking notes (in order to use the information later for some further purpose).

A popular activity called "jigsaw listening" is suggested by Geddes and Sturtridge (1979). In one form of jigsaw listening, small separate groups of students listen to different parts of a total set of information and write down the important points of their portion. Then they share their information with other groups in order to complete a story or a sequence of actions, or some form of larger-level outcome such as making a decision or solving a problem.

Jigsaw listening also can be used with a second kind of transfer of information—*verbal transfer* (i.e., aural to oral) from person to person, or group to group. Other aural-oral activities are these:

1. listening to directions, then passing them along to a third party (in order to use the information to carry out a task)
2. listening to part of a story and repeating it to others

SAMPLE LESSON ACTIVITIES

Sample 1. Taking a Message
(from Davis & Rinvolucri, 1988, pp. 29–30)

The authors suggest that each of the students in a class call the teacher one evening at a prescribed time, and write a sentence that is dictated to them over the telephone. Next day students share their sentences and put them in proper order to tell a story.

A man and his son had been to a party.
They were driving back together.
They had had a very good time.
It was raining and the road was wet.
A cat was crossing the road.
The man swerved to avoid the cat.
The car skidded on the wet road.
It crashed into a tree.
The man was killed.
His son was seriously injured.
Someone called for an ambulance.
It rushed the son to hospital.
He was immediately taken to the operating theatre.
The surgeon washed and went into the theatre.
The surgeon saw the boy and shouted, 'My son! My son!'
Can you explain?

© Cambridge University Press 1988

The authors suggest that by combining sentences or adding new ones, you can make it suitable for the size of the group. Further, they suggest that if you have around 30 students, the story construction can take place in two parallel groups. They note that this activity is a confidence builder for students who have never used English over the phone.

Sample 2. Using Recorded Messages
(from Morley, 1984, pp. 68–69)

Morley suggests that students practice with the following kind of real telephone recorded message from a movie theater. Then each student is given the telephone number of a local theater and asked to call, to write down all pertinent information, and to report to class next day. A listing of current movies can then be compiled and posted for all classes.

EXAMPLE 2. THEATRE MESSAGE

A. *INTRODUCTION (recorded on the tape preceding the telephone message)*

You will hear a voice say, "This is a recorded message from your Northgate Movies located next to J.C. Penney's in the Northgate Shopping Center. Our feature today in Theatre 1 and Theatre 3 is a re-run of Cleopatra." The voice then gives six show times and other information.

B. *LISTENING TASK (recorded on the tape preceding the telephone message)*

Listen and get the location, the show times and prices, and the names of the movie stars. Replay the tape as many times as you wish to get the information. Ask the teacher for help if you have any questions. Check your answer key as you finish each section.

C. *INFORMATION QUESTIONS*
   1. Where is the Northgate movie theatre located? (two prepositional phrases of place)

   _____

   _____

   2. What are the six show times?

   _____

   3. What is the price for adults?

   _____

   4. Write the names of the two movie stars.

   _____

D. *ANALYSIS QUESTIONS*
   1. What information is given in the first five words?

   _____

   2. Do you think the voice was that of a young person or an older person?

   _____

   3. Was the voice clear and easy to understand?

   _____

   4. Was the voice friendly?

   _____

   5. Write one additional question that you might ask; write the answer.

   _____

Script. *This is a recorded message from your Northgate Movies located next to J.C. Penney's in the Northgate Shopping Center. Our feature today in Theatre 1 and Theatre 3 is a re-run of Cleopatra, starring Elizabeth Taylor and Richard Burton. Show times are at 1:20, 3:20, 4:45, 6:45, 9:15, and 11:15. All seats are $4.50 for adults and $2.00 for children under twelve. If you have any further questions, please call 568-7878. Thank you for calling your United Artists.*

Listening and Solving Problems

Many kinds of activities for either groups or individuals can be developed in this category. One is games and puzzles:

1. Word games in which the answers must be derived from verbal clues.
2. Number games and oral story arithmetic problems.
3. Asking questions in order to identify something, as in Twenty Questions or Animal, Vegetable, or Mineral.
4. Classroom versions of Password, Jeopardy, Twenty Questions in which careful listening is critical to questions and answers or answers and questions.
5. "Minute mysteries" in which a paragraph-length mystery story is given by the teacher (or a tape), followed by small group work in which students formulate solutions.
6. A jigsaw mystery in which each group listens to a tape with some of the clues, then shares information in order to solve the mystery.

Another more demanding variety of activity in this category involves:

1. riddles
2. logic puzzles
3. intellectual problem-solving

Real-world problems can include these:

1. Comparison shopping tasks using recorded conversations for practice (a customer asking for prices from several rent-a-car dealers, or several florist shops, or several barber shops, then choosing the best bargain), followed by similar kinds of field trips.
2. Short descriptions of court cases, with lis-

SAMPLE LESSON ACTIVITIES

Sample 1. Picture Dictation and Problem Solving
(from Davis & Rinvolucri, 1988, pp. 56–57)

In this activity students listen and perform an action—that is, drawing a picture. Then, on the basis of the drawing, students are asked to solve a problem.

Ask the students to take a sheet of paper and lay it lengthways. Check that they understand all the spatial terms in the dictation that follows. Dictate sentence by sentence—they draw what they hear.

The Quickest Way

Draw a line across your page from left to right—draw the line across the middle of the page.
Above the line there are waves.
In the top left-hand corner there is a sailing boat.
Draw a man lying on the sand in the bottom left-hand corner.
Top right-hand corner—there is a swimmer in the water.
The swimmer is shouting, 'Help! Help!'
Make a dotted line from the swimmer to the nearest point on the shore.
Draw a dotted line from the man on the sand to the swimmer.
What's the quickest way for the man on the beach to reach the swimmer?

Ask the students to work in pairs and answer the above question.

Sample 2. Filling in an Informational Grid and Solving Problems
(from Morley, 1972, pp. 137–138)

In this activity students listen and fill in the items on a grid. Then they are asked to solve three problems: Who plays the guitar? Who is going to San Francisco? Who is studying Business?

Directions in the Student's Book:

Listen carefully. First practice the vocabulary. Then listen to each statement. Find the correct square. Write the correct word from the list below.

Instruction in the Teacher's Book:

This is difficult lesson. It is a test of memory, logic and spatial relationships. Students must concentrate very hard. Read slowly and repeat as is necessary. Give adequate writing time.

Tapes: (A recording of everything in both student workbook and teacher book of readings.)

Workbook Page 137:

SPACE PUZZLE: WHO PLAYS THE GUITAR?

Five students from five different countries were studying English in the United States. They lived in adjoining houses. They planned to study in five different cities. Each of the five had a different hobby.

	Red House	Blue House	Green House	White House	Purple House
Country					
Field					
City					
Hobby					

Country	City	Field	Hobby
Turkey	San Francisco	Engineering	dancing
Peru	Miami	Law	soccer
Korea	Chicago	Business	swimming
Spain	New York	Chemistry	travel
India	Boston	Psychology	playing the guitar

Teacher's Book Page 76:

1. The student from the country of Turkey lives in the middle house.
   Write *Turkey* in the correct square.
2. The student in the field of Engineering lives on the far right.
   Write *Engineering* in the correct square.
3. The student who's going to New York to study lives next to the red house.
   (continue . . .).

teners asked to make a decision and defend it.

Field trips can be assigned in which pairs of students go out to do comparison shopping for products or services, then report back to the entire class. This activity is suitable for both adults and children.

Listening, Evaluating, and Manipulating Information

These outcomes are intellectually challenging ones in which the listener evaluates and/or manipulates the information received in some manner. Tasks which focus on this outcome are important both for children and adult second language learners. Lesson activities for individuals, pairs, or small groups can take many directions, including the following:

1. Writing information received and reviewing it in order to answer questions or to solve a problem.
2. Evaluating information in order to make a decision or construct a plan of action.
3. Evaluating arguments in order to develop a position for or against.
4. Evaluating cause-and-effect information.

5. Projecting from information received and making predictions.
6. Summarizing or "gistizing" information received.
7. Evaluating and combining information.
8. Evaluating and condensing information.
9. Evaluating and elaborating or extending information.
10. Organizing unordered information received into a pattern of orderly relationships—chronological sequencing, spatial relationships, cause-and-effect, problem-solution.

Field trips in which students are assigned fact-finding, information-gathering tasks for panel presentations or use in a project are very challenging and useful for intermediate and advanced learners. At more advanced levels, preparing for and carrying out a debate or discussion assignment on current local, national, or international issues can make use of a number of kinds of aural and written information evaluation and manipulation. A jigsaw listening format in which two separate groups receive a portion of information on the topic, summarize it, and share it with the other group is a useful activity for learners of all ages.

Tasks that are planned around outcomes

SAMPLE LESSON ACTIVITIES

Sample 1. Film Analysis and Evaluation
(from Morley, 1981, pp. 10–11)

The following activity is one of six assignments suggested for the development of a listening workbook for documentary films of 18 to 25 minutes, for use in an intermediate to advanced teen or adult class. *Prelistening, during-listening,* and *post-listening* assignments are suggested. The following assignment is one of two *during-listening* activities. The instructional material is from *Films for EFL Practice: Listening/Speaking/Vocabulary Building* (a workbook of materials for 12 documentary films), Joan Morley, The University of Michigan English Language Institute, 1973. The film is *Food for Life,* a 22-minute color film produced by the National Dairy Council of America and distributed by Wexler Corporation.

The following two assignments are designed to provide the focus during a showing of the film. As noted before, many teachers stop the film from time to time during a showing for questions or for discussion. They may rewind a segment and show it again. Students are encouraged to relisten. It may take 40 minutes to show a 20 minute film.

1. Assignment #3—Analysis of the Structure of the Film.

 The purpose of this assignment is to focus student attention on the overall structure of the film. It is designed to develop identification of form of presentation and identification of central issues of the film. Working in groups of three, students are asked to answer each question immediately after the first showing. The questions involve the PURPOSES of the film, the SUBJECT MATTER of the film and the MOST IMPORTANT MESSAGE. Students are asked to consider the following: Why was the film made? What was the central content area? What was the main issue of the film? How did the film attempt to deliver its most important message? Students are asked to be prepared to present and to defend their answers in class discussion. Students are encouraged to express any opinion as long as they are willing to try to defend it with reasonable argument; no answer is ruled as "wrong" if the student can give good reasoning. Answers may be written on the chalkboard and examined for clarity and precision of answer. The give-and-take of the situation can enable even shy students to be drawn into the discussion. Sometimes a student leader can be chosen to guide the discussion and to encourage participation from all. The length of the discussion may vary from a few minutes to half an hour depending upon the interest value of the film and the disparity of student answers; some answers may be too broad and some too narrow; some may lack precision; others may not answer the question at all. Through the series of films the intent is to sharpen the students' ability to focus on key ideas and to enhance their ability to formulate precise and explicit answers. Figure 3 presents an abridged sample of this assignment.

FIGURE 3—Analysis of the structure of the film (abridged sample)

Assignment # 3

FOOD FOR LIFE

Directions:

Please answer each question. Be prepared to present and defend your answers during class discussion.

1. What were the PURPOSES of the film in your opinion? Choose one, two, three, or any number you believe appropriate. (Put them in rank order and number them accordingly.)

   _____ (1) to inform (general information)

   _____ (2) to instruct (specific method)

   _____ (3) to entertain

   _____ (4) to present a problem and propose solutions

   _____ (5) to convince

   _____ (6) to arouse to action

2. What was the SUBJECT MATTER of the film? (4 or 5 words) The subject matter of the film was this:

3. What was the most important MESSAGE of *Food for Life*? (one sentence) The most important message of the film was this:

4. The TITLE of the film is Food for Life. Is that a good title? Why?

5. Think up a new title for the film and defend your choice. (i.e., tell why you chose it.)

Sample 2. Radio Broadcast Analysis and Evaluation

(from Numrich, 1987, p. 61)

The following excerpt is from one of 12 National Public Broadcast recordings included in this collection. The topic is What's Happening to the American Family? with interviewer Susan Stamberg, from "All Things Considered," April 24, 1983. The two assignments given here focus students' attention on listening, evaluating, and manipulating information.

UNIT 7   WHAT'S HAPPENING TO THE AMERICAN FAMILY?

Task Listening Listen to the interview. Find the answer to the following question.

> What word came up over and over as people responded to the survey?

Listening for Main Ideas Listen to the interview again. The interview has been divided into four parts, each expressing a main idea. You will hear a beep at the end of each part. Answer the question for each part in complete sentences. You should have four statements that make a summary of the interview. Compare your summary with that of another student.

Part 1 What are the readers of *Better Homes and Gardens* feeling about family life?

_____

Part 2 What type of person reads this magazine and responded to the questionnaire?

_____

Part 3 How has the attitude toward divorce changed?

_____

Part 4 Based on the survey's responses, how are teenagers different today?

_____

that focus on information evaluation and manipulation are especially useful in the learner's development of the base of operational experiences discussed earlier, and contribute to building a repertoire of familiar information-handling routines.

Interactive Listening and Negotiating Meaning Through Questioning/ Answering Routines

Here the focus of the outcome is on both the *product* of transmitting information and the *process* of negotiating meaning in interactive reciprocal listener/speaker exchanges. To introduce and practice this kind of listening skill-building, the following kind of work can be undertaken. Initially, in small group activities (i.e., 4 to 10 students), one "speaker" can give a brief presentation, such as a short set of locally relevant "announcements," a 5-minute "how-to" talk (i.e., giving a sequence of steps in a process), storytelling (i.e., telling a personal anecdote), an explanatory "visuals" talk (i.e., expressly calling for the use of visually presented information as the focal point of the talk). Either during or immediately after the presentation, each of the "listeners" is required to participate by asking at least one question in a questioning/answering routine. At first each listener can be given a card with a question-type listed and assigned the responsibility for asking that kind of question. The listener-questioner must continue with follow-up questions, as necessary, until both speaker and listener are satisfied that clear meaning has been "negotiated." This means that the speaker is also a listener and must keep questioning the listener to make sure of the nature and intent of the listener's question. Students quickly become involved in this negotiating process and hone their interactive listener/ speaker skills (Morley, in press). Video- or audiotape recording of these class sessions with subsequent class viewing and discussion of selected segments quickly demonstrates how important "negotiation of meaning" really is, how much "work" and energy must be expended in arriving at meaning. Students

soon come to realize that meaning is not a magic entity, but something that must be created by speaker–listener interaction.

A wide variety of question types can be used in this kind of activity but for each lesson it is useful to have only a limited number of question types being used. Some question types are the following:

> *Repetition*—questions asking only for verbatim repetition of information ("Could you repeat the part about xx?")
>
> *Paraphrase*—questions asking only for restatement in different words, often words that are simple and easier to understand ("Could you say that again?" "I don't understand what you mean by xx.")
>
> *Verification*—questions seeking confirmation that the information was understood correctly by the listener ("Did I understand you to say that xx?" "In other words you mean that xx." "Do you mean xx?")
>
> *Clarification*—questions seeking more details, an explanation of an item, examples ("Could you tell me what you mean by xx?" "Could you explain xx?" "Could you give us an example of xx?")
>
> *Elaboration*—questions that ask for additional information on a point introduced in the presentation ("Could you tell us more about xx?")
>
> *Extension*—questions that ask for information on a new point, one that was not introduced in the presentation ("What about xx?" "How is this related to xx?")
>
> *Challenge*—questions that challenge points given or conclusions drawn ("What did you base xx on?" "How did you reach xx?" "How did you xx?" "Why did you xx?")

Listening for Enjoyment, Pleasure, and Sociability

Tasks with this outcome can include listening to songs, stories, plays, poems, jokes, anecdotes, or, as suggested by Ur (1984, p. 29), "general interesting chat improvised by the teacher." Some of the activities in this category come under the heading of "interactional" talk/listening, different from the previous outcome categories, which by and large are "transactional" outcomes.

In regard to setting tasks for this kind of outcome, Ur (1984) notes that setting any more of an outcome other than "enjoying," in this case, may become superfluous or even harmful to the completion of the outcome of "enjoying."

Ur makes an especially good case for informal "teacher-chat" as an excellent source of listening "material," and observes that it serves as a relaxing break from more intensive work. She suggests teacher-talk on personal topics (e.g., a member of your family, a friend, something you like doing, your favorite hobby, some plans for the future, your opinions on topical or local issues and much much more (Ur, 1984, pp. 62–63). She notes that this, in turn, may lead naturally to student-talk on similar subjects for loosely structured and comfortable communicative classroom interludes, ones that afford student "practice" opportunities in both listening and speaking.

Self-Access Self-Study Listening and Language Learning

The purpose of a self-access self-study resource is to create an inviting "nouveau" style listening language center, *not* the old "ho-hum" language laboratory but a facility that offers a wide choice of appealing topicalized audio and video materials with carefully designed accompanying worksheet materials setting listening tasks for self-study, pair-study, or small-group study both on the school premises and for check-out and home use.

Materials can include "fun" listening for free listening time (like free reading time), in which students can choose from an inventory which includes stories and poems, talks and lectures, plays and literary classics, participatory games, puzzles, riddles, and read-along or sing-along stories, songs, and games. Commercial audio- and videotapes can easily be adapted for listening library use. And, more innovatively, your own school or personal amateur audio or video recordings of local situational scenes, conversations, songs, music events, lectures, or panel discussions (home videos) can be exciting additions to a listening library. Such locally produced auditory materials have a special *relevance* and *applicability* potential that commercial materials lack.

Setting Up a Self-Access Self-Study Listening Resource Center

A self-access self-study listening resource center can be started with a modest library of audio (and video) recorded material and the teacher-time to structure materials into self-study packets or modules.

Ideally, listening materials can be made available to students in a special language learning center or multipurpose study room that also features reading and writing materials and has a teacher (or monitor) present at all times to guide students in the selection and use of materials and equipment.

Alternatively, self-access self-study materials can be used in a more conventional language laboratory setting, but only if the individual student has complete control of the playing of the materials. It is essential that students be able to control the source of input so that they can pace it—stop it, start it, replay it—at will. Such control allows students to regulate their own schedules of study, rather than having a rate and volume of auditory input imposed on them. This helps reduce the anxiety and pressure that many students, particularly beginners, seem to experience when listening in their second language. Some materials might even be made available for checkout and home study. However, a study facility often has fewer distractions than a home or dormitory environment, and the atmosphere is usually more conducive to the self-discipline often necessary for concentrated listening in a second language.

The procedure for using self-access self-study materials might go something like this:

1. Students check out a listening packet (or module) that contains the audio (or video) tape, prelistening introductory material, worksheets (and perhaps some visuals), answer key (and perhaps a script), and instructions.
2. Students play the tape on their own schedule of starting, stopping, and replaying.
3. Students check their work themselves for verification of comprehension.
4. Students consult the teacher or monitor when necessary.

Self-access listening materials can be organized into self-study packets or modules of manageable lengths. They can be cross-referenced in a variety of ways to meet the needs of individual students or groups of students (i.e., categories such as content or topical groups, notional categories, functional categories, situational or activity categories, level-of-difficulty groupings, specific listening-task groupings.)

Modules that feature up-to-date, locally relevant, authentic aural texts are especially effective and are recommended wherever possible. In addition, segments from selected commercially prepared listening materials can be adapted to fit into a self-access self-study format.

Guidelines for Developing Self-Access Self-Study Listening Materials

In addition to the principles of relevance, transferability, task orientation, and the communicative outcomes framework, the following guidelines are suggested as a planning reference in preparing self-access self-study aural comprehension practice materials:

(1) a focus on listening as an active process with instant or only slightly delayed manipulation of the information received;

(2) a focus on purposeful listening:
   (a) in order to process information and do something with the information immediately, by performing a task of some nature;
   (b) in order to analyze particular features of the message (i.e., linguistic features, sociolinguistic features, discourse features, strategic features);
   (c) in order to build a base of content experiences and outcomes experiences.

(3) a focus on a variety of practice materials that includes a mix of authentic, semi-authentic and simulated language activities;

(4) a focus on internal communicative "interaction," as the listener receives language data aurally and visually, restructures it and makes a response that is either a reformulation of some of the data or an analysis of some features of the data;

(5) a focus on providing learners with verification of comprehension (i.e., immediate or only slightly delayed feedback with self-check answer keys or scripts provided as necessary);

(6) a focus on encouraging guessing and following "hunches" when in doubt;

(7) a focus on selective listening, ignoring irrelevant material and learning to tolerate less than total understanding;

(8) a focus on self-involvement, with an emphasis on self-study and taking both responsibility for one's work and pride in one's accomplishments;

(9) a focus on providing learners with less threatening listening experiences by giving them self-controlled, self-regulated schedules of study, and reducing the high-anxiety levels created by externally imposed rates and volumes of auditory input, allowing students to experience self-paced instruction without interruption/interference from the teacher;

(10) a focus on integrating auditory and visual language by combining listening, reading and writing, and observing relationships between spoken forms and written forms;

(11) a focus on gradually increasing expectations for levels of comprehension (i.e., encouraging students to challenge themselves and to move themselves along toward increasingly demanding expectations);

(12) a focus on the fun of listening! (Morley, 1985)

FINAL COMMENTS

The importance of listening comprehension in language learning and language teaching has moved from a status of incidental and peripheral importance to a status of significance and central importance over the last two decades. Whereas only a few instructional materials were available 20 years ago, today there are many texts and tape programs to choose from, and, in general, materials are becoming more carefully principled, with serious attention to theoretical considerations. Each year more diverse materials are developed, and many now focus on narrowly specified listening needs of particular groups of learners.

But the listening curriculum in a second language program cannot be equated with "buying the right books and tapes." Skill building in listening comprehension is not something that can be accomplished in a half-hour lesson three times a week, nor can attention to listening be limited to language laboratory tapes. Listening, the language skill used most in life, needs to be a central focus, all day, every day, limited only by the availability of the target language—in the school, in the community, in the media. Listening instructional activities need to include both *two-way* interactive listening activities and tasks and *one-way* reactive Listen-and-Do activities and tasks. Materials development should be done with careful attention to principles of design, communicative outcomes, language functions, language processes, and affective considerations.

DISCUSSION QUESTIONS

1. Discuss the concepts of two-way, one-way, and self-dialog communication. Give some personal examples of each of these three kinds of communication.

2. Listening has been the "neglected" skill area of language teaching. Give some reasons for this curious circumstance.

3. In your own experience how much time do you feel you spend in each of the four areas of listening, speaking, reading, writing? Compare your estimates with other members of the class.

4. Discuss the differences between "language experience" tasks and "language analysis" tasks. How does the distinction relate to listening activities?

5. Examine the three principles of materials development. Consider how they can be implemented in listening activities.

6. Contrast interactional language use and transactional language use. Give examples from your own personal experience and compare them with others in your class.

SUGGESTED ACTIVITIES

1. Observe and note the amount of time in which there is "teacher-listen" and the amount of time there is "student-listen" in two or three second language classes. Observe the teacher/student roles in these same classes.

2. Working with others, draw up some suggestions for "enriching" the listening opportunities in one or two classes where the central focus is on some other aspect of learning.

3. Working with others, use Richards' matrix and draw up a collection of one or two examples in each cell.

SUGGESTIONS FOR FURTHER READING

Anderson, A., and **T. Lynch (1988)**
Listening. Oxford: Oxford University Press.

The purpose of this book is to stand back from the surface detail of comprehension materials and to provide an overall perspective on listening as a communicative activity and as a language learning activity. It includes a research design focus.

Brown, G. (1977)
Listening to Spoken English. London: Longman.

Describes how normal conversational English differs from the "slow colloquial" form usually described and taught, and offers a positive methodological approach to teaching the comprehension of spoken English.

Brown, G., and G. Yule (1983)
Teaching the Spoken Language. Cambridge: Cambridge University Press.

In an approach based on the analysis of conversational English, examines the nature of spoken language and presents principles and techniques for teaching spoken production and listening comprehension.

Richards, J. C. (1983)
Listening Comprehension: Approach, Design, Procedure. *TESOL Quarterly, 17* (2), 219–240.

Examines *approach* and the processes involved in comprehending spoken discourse, *design* and listening needs, microskills, and learning objectives, and *procedure* with classroom activities and exercise types.

Richards, J. C. (1990)
The Language Teaching Matrix. Cambridge: Cambridge University Press.

In Chapter 3, "Designing Instructional Materials for Teaching Listening Comprehension," Richards pro-

poses a new model of materials design for teaching second language listening comprehension. It combines insights from current perspectives on language purposes and language processes.

Ur, P. (1984)
Teaching Listening Comprehension. Cambridge: Cambridge University Press.

Analyzes real-life listening characteristics and the problems encountered by language learners and presents a wide range of exercise types, ranging from elementary to advanced, and with material appropriate for both adults and children.

Special periodical issues devoted to listening comprehension include

Applied Linguistics, 7 (2), Summer 1986.

ELT Documents Special, The Teaching of Listening Comprehension, 1981.

Foreign Language Annals, 17 (4), September 1984.

JALT *Newsletter, 6* (4), 1982.

Language Teaching, 17 (4), October 1984 (Part I), and *18* (1), January 1985 (Part II).

TESOL Newsletter, 19 (6), December 1985.

A Synthesis of Methods for Interactive Listening

Pat Wilcox Peterson

THE IMPORTANCE OF LISTENING IN LANGUAGE LEARNING

Teachers who want to provide the most effective classroom experience for their second language students should consider this: No other type of language input is as easy to process as spoken language, received through listening. At the beginning stages of language study, before students have learned to read well, it is by listening that they can

have the most direct connection to the meaning of the new language. They can use spoken language to build an awareness of the interworkings of language systems at various levels and thus establish a base for productive skills.

At the intermediate level, when students are refining the grammatical system of the language, listening can be used to stimulate awareness of detail and to promote accuracy. At advanced levels, when written language becomes a viable source of input, a regular program of listening can extend the limits of learners' vocabulary and use of idioms, and build their appreciation for cultural nuances.

There is such a wide range of listening tasks for different purposes and for every proficiency level, that teachers can find listening activities to promote learning at every stage. This chapter will present a brief developmental view of listening skills: how people learn to listen, and how listening promotes learning. Sample exercises will be given to facilitate listening at beginning, intermediate, and advanced stages of language development.

"Oh, but the last thing I need to do is talk more in class!" This is a common response from teachers who are asked to include more effective listening activities. "There is already too much teacher talk in class. I must have the floor over half the time already, so I'm really looking for ways for the students to be more active."

True, it is easy to lapse into a teacher-dominated style in the second language classroom, particularly at beginning levels. However, a simple increase in the amount of student talk does not guarantee more learning. In fact, an increase in the right kinds of listening activities can work to make the students more active. In the attempt to find the right proportion of listening to speaking for students at each proficiency level, the following questions may help:

What Is the Purpose of the Teacher Talk in the Class?

Is the teacher talk focused on the lesson? Does it function to set up the context for a new situation, to provide practice with familiar material in new combinations, and to highlight key structural differences? Or do the teachers spend a great deal of time explaining grammar, defining vocabulary, setting up complicated exercises, and managing the paper flow—all activities which have less language value for the students?

Is The Teacher Talk at a Level That Is Accessible to the Students?

Do the teachers support their monologs so that new vocabulary is comprehensible in the context of their presentation? Do they use structures within or only slightly beyond the students' receptive control? Or do they ramble on about abstractions that are outside of the students' realm of experience in any language?

Whose Voice Do the Students Hear?

In the listening input to the students, do the teachers provide a number of voices, songs, radio clips, taped dialogs, and video programs? Or, does teacher talk always come from the same person, following rather familiar routines set up by the textbook?

Does the Student Talk Spring Naturally from a Readiness to Speak?

Do students reach easily for the words they need, and are the necessary structures already part of their competence? Are vowels and consonants well formed, and are stress and intonation patterns nativelike? Or is student talk laborious, stilted, painful, and mostly incorrect? Does the production of each sentence take a long time? Does speaking follow a process of translation from the native language?

The point should be clear: A strict accounting of minutes spent in teacher talk and student talk does not begin to assess the quality of the learning in the classroom. More important than an abstract time ratio are the following issues: the type and purpose of the aural input; the sequence of activities for global comprehension, structured practice, and review; and the natural readiness of the student for language production activities. Fortunately, psychological researchers and language theorists can offer some guidelines for these issues.

THEORIES OF LANGUAGE COMPREHENSION

The following ideas about the listening process have gained wide acceptance in the last 30 years.

Listening Is the Primary Channel for Language Input and Acquisition in the Beginning Stages of Learning

Nida (1957b) recounts his observations of the way in which Africans easily learn the many tribal languages in their environment. They go to a place to live, they listen without attempting to speak, and quite soon they find that they can "hear" the language. Only after internalizing some part of the language do they try to speak. The similarity to first language learning is striking; this is the same progression that infants follow in learning a language.

The natural route to language learning depends on two qualitatively distinct subprocesses, which Nida terms "passive listening" and "selective listening." (The term "passive" tends to misrepresent the process as Nida describes it, and the term "global" will be used here instead.) Global listening is actually a very active process. Nida points out that the mind operates on incoming language input even when we are not making a conscious effort to learn; the mind assimilates, sorts, and stores the many features of the input in order to gain a total impression of its form and meaning.

In the tradition of Nida's global listening are the several variations of comprehension approaches to learning: total physical response, delayed oral production, and the natural approach. (See Blair, in this volume, for a more detailed description.) The leading theorist for the natural approach, Krashen (1982), suggests that acquisition of a second language depends primarily on students' receiving plenty of comprehensible input. The input must be interesting and must include language slightly beyond the current level of the students. Krashen points out that a good lan-guage classroom is designed to make input comprehensible, through extralinguistic support (use of visuals, gestures, and context) and by use of textual features (repetition, redundancy, and simplification.)

In selective listening, attention is directed towards specific language features. Nida recommends a program of selective listening in immersion situations but also when contact with the second language is limited to the classroom. Selective listening is particularly recommended when first language production habits might otherwise interfere with accurate perception of the second language. The learner listens to one feature at a time, in this order: (1) tone of voice, (2) strange (new L2) sounds, (3) similar sounds (to determine which sounds are allophones under a single phonemic grouping), (4) words and phrases, and (5) grammatical forms. Selective listening raises one's awareness of important linguistic distinctions, and also promotes self-monitoring in production. Nida concludes, "Learning to speak a language is very largely a task of learning to hear it."

Bottom-Up Processing: Language Learning Depends on the Movement from Controlled to Automatic Processing

When a skill is first being developed, learners must focus a great portion of their limited attention on the various subcomponents of that skill. Later, after the skill has been rehearsed many times, it can be performed automatically, and the learners' attention can be freed up for learning other new skills (McLaughlin, Rossman, & McLeod, 1983). This principle is easily illustrated with nonverbal tasks such as riding a bicycle, driving a car, or serving a tennis ball.

A controversial issue in second language acquisition research has been the debate on the role of controlled and automatic processing in language learning. On one extreme, Krashen (1982) maintains that material which has been consciously learned through attention to form will never transfer to the learner's store of acquired competence. However, there is evidence that focus on form and conscious attention to accuracy do transfer into students' productive use of the language (Long, 1983a). Moreover, proponents of the proficiency movement in foreign language education warn that unmonitored practice of inaccurate language forms may cause acquisition to fossilize at a certain developmental stage and may prevent the learner from ever attaining nativelike proficiency (Clifford & Higgs, 1982). Thus, current theory supports the inclusion of activities which focus the learner's attention on form and build toward automaticity in decoding skills.

Top-Down Processing: Schemata Use Promotes Restructuring of Language Data So That Greater Segments of Text Can Be Grasped as a Whole

Educational psychologists have discovered that verbal learning proceeds more easily when information can be chunked into meaningful patterns and then be related to existing meaning structures in the mind (Ausubel, 1963, 1968). McLeod and McLaughlin (1986) found that as learners become more proficient, they are able to restructure incoming linguistic data into a larger pattern and understand the pattern as a whole. There are many terms for the meaning structures in the mind; they been called "frames" (Minsky, 1975), "scripts" (Schank, 1975), and "schemata" (Rumelhart, 1980). Rumelhart defines a schema as "a data structure for representing generic concepts stored in memory" (p. 34).

Carrell and Eisterhold (1983) point out that background information in the listener's mind is of two kinds: content schemata and formal schemata. Content schemata include cultural knowledge, topic familiarity, and previous experience with a field. Formal schemata have to do with people's knowledge of discourse forms: text types, rhetorical conventions, and the structural organization of prose. Both content and formal schemata

can aid the listener in comprehending text (Floyd & Carrell, 1987).

Interactive Processing: Comprehension Is a Combination of Meaning-Driven and Form-Driven Operations

By accounting for both global and selective listening, Nida was able to integrate both fluency and accuracy in his approach. He avoided the split which occurred later between learning theories which recommended one kind of language activity at the expense of the other. In audiolingualism, the emphasis was on selective listening. Input was controlled carefully in accordance with a structural syllabus, and listening was used as a preparation for pattern drills. Class activities were based on decoding and bottom-up processing with attention to accuracy through constant monitor use. In the later communicative approaches, listening experiences were much more global in nature as input was freed from the structural syllabus. Emphasis was on listening for meaning, use of background knowledge, and top-down processing with relatively little monitor use.

Recent advances in understanding the dual nature of language processing have prepared the way for a return to a synthesis of methods. Proficient listening is described as a multilevel, interactive, compensatory process (Kintsch & vanDijk, 1978). This model of listening as an interactive process suggests a new integration of both global and selective listening in the classroom.

When good listeners involve themselves with any type of spoken discourse, a number of processes work on various levels simultaneously to produce an understanding of the incoming speech. The higher level processes (top-down) are driven by listeners' expectations and understandings of the nature of text and the nature of the world. The lower level processes (bottom-up) are triggered by the sounds, words, and phrases which listeners hear as they attempt to decode speech and assign meaning.

Top-down and bottom-up processes interact, so that lack of information on one level can be compensated for by checking against information on the other level. For example, proficient listeners use their knowledge of lexis and topic to interpret the confusing sounds in the speech stream and to aid them in word recognition. On the other hand, they also use their basic decoding skills to check the progress of the argument and to determine whether the discourse is going in the direction they had predicted. Listening in their native language, people never hear all the information in the message, and they do not need to; proficiency in comprehension is the ability to fill in the gaps.

Listening Comprehension Can Best Be Understood Through an Information-Processing Model

Language comprehension in reading and listening have been described as a series of steps of information processing which take advantage of both top-down and bottom-up operations (Kintsch & vanDijk, 1978). Comprehension of a message is essentially the internal production of that message. When raw speech enters the mind as acoustic data, it first enters the sensory stores and is taken into short-term memory (STM.) Processing of the information is necessarily cyclical, due to the capacity limitations of the STM. No more than 7 to 12 bits of information can be held in short-term memory at a time. These bits must be analyzed into syntactic constituents, converted into semantic units (propositions), and related to other propositions in the long-term memory (LTM) store. If there is no proposition in the short-term memory to which the incoming proposition can be related, then an LTM search must be initiated. A suitable proposition is recalled and rehearsed with the new information.

Capacity limitations apply to the top-level controlled processes of attention, deci-

A Model of Listening Comprehension Processing in the Adult Language Learner

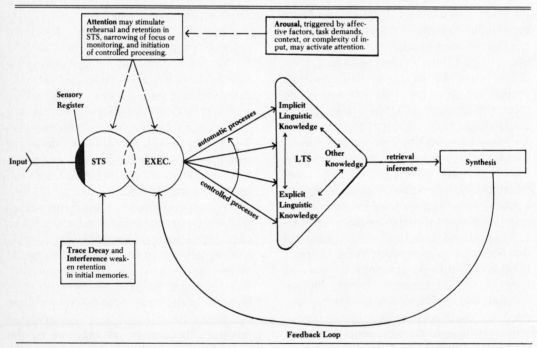

Note: STS = short-term storage; LTS = long-term storage.

FIGURE 1. *A model of listening comprehension processing in the adult language learner. (This figure is reprinted from "Comprehension theory and second language pedagogy" by S. Nagle and S. Sanders, 1986, TESOL QUARTERLY 20, p. 19, by permission of TESOL and the authors.)*

sion making, memory, storage of information, inferencing, and response production. On the other hand, the bottom-up processes are largely automatic (in proficient language users), unlimited in capacity, and out of conscious control.

Nagle and Sanders (1986) offer an information-processing model of comprehension which incorporates the distinction between controlled and automatic processing as well as the effects of attention and monitoring. They propose an executive decision-maker which decides how to deal with input, and a feedback loop to allow the listener to monitor ongoing comprehension. Their model is specifically intended to describe comprehension in a second language. They make the point that while comprehension is not exactly the same thing as learning, successful comprehension makes material available for learning see Figure 1, p. 110.

In a review of information processing in bilinguals, Dornic (1979) points out that L2 processing takes more time at every stage: decoding, rehearsal in STM, organization of information for storage, and retrieval of information from the long-term store. Memory capacity is less in the second language, so the input is available for processing for a shorter time in the working memory store (Lado, 1965; Miller, 1956). Thus, one goal of L2 processing is greater speed; Dornic claims that greater speed is largely a product of habit formation as decoding processes become automatic.

Another goal in L2 processing is the activation of students' background knowledge and use of their schemata in predicting what will come next. Some studies have found that use of top-level schemata can actually compensate for deficiencies in low-level processing (Adams, 1982; Cummins, 1980a; P. Johnson, 1981, 1982). Teaching schemata use has been found to increase second language comprehension (Floyd & Carrell, 1987; Hudson, 1982). However, instruction in schemata use is not enough in itself. Unless students have a strategy for checking the accuracy of their assumptions, schemata use may actually interfere with comprehension (Block, 1986; Kasper, 1984).

There are also important studies which suggest that learners below a certain threshold of language proficiency are unable to activate their top-down processing skills (Clarke, 1979, 1980). However, even if the threshold effect is a limiting factor for low-level students, the pedagogical value of practicing top-level skills is well established.

It would be a mistake to wait with lessons which activate background knowledge until students have reached advanced levels of language use. It would also be a mistake to discontinue lessons which build automaticity in bottom-up processing as soon as students have left beginning-level classes. In fact, students at all levels can benefit from direct instruction in three different kinds of listening exercises: top-down, bottom-up, and interactive.

PRINCIPLES FOR LISTENING COMPREHENSION IN THE CLASSROOM

The research findings above suggest a set of principles for conducting listening activities in the second language classroom.

1. *Increase the Amount of Listening Time in the Second Language Class.* Make listening the primary channel for learning new material. Input must be interesting, comprehensible, supported by extralinguistic materials, and keyed to the language lesson.

2. *Use Listening Before Other Activities.* Have students listen to the material before they are required to speak, read, or write about it.

3. *Include Both Global and Selective Listening.* Global listening encourages students to get the gist, the main idea, the topic, situation, or setting. Selective listening points student attention to details of form and encourages accuracy in generating the language system.

4. *Activate Top-Level Skills.* Give advance organizers, script activators, or discussions which call up students' background knowledge. Do this before students listen. Encourage top-down processing at every proficiency level.

5. *Work Towards Automaticity in Processing.* Include exercises which build both recognition and retention of the material. Use familiar material in recombinations. Encourage overlearning through focus on selected formal features. Practice bottom-up processing at every proficiency level.

6. *Develop Conscious Listening Strategies.* Raise students' awareness of text features and of their own comprehension processes. Encourage them to notice how their processing operations interact with the text. Promote flexibility in the many ways that they can use to understand the language. Practice interactive listening, so that they can use their bottom-up and their top-down processes to check one against the other.

A DEVELOPMENTAL VIEW OF LISTENING SKILLS

Profile of the Beginning Level Student in Listening

True beginners in a second language are lacking in bottom-up processing skills because they have not yet developed the cognitive categories against which the language must be heard. They perceive the new language as undifferentiated noise. They are not yet able to segment the speech stream into word units, to tell where one word begins and another ends. The new phonemic system is an unbroken code: Sounds which native speakers consider similar may be perceived and classified as different; sounds which native speakers consider different may be perceived and classified as the same. Learners have no idea about phonological rules which change sounds in certain environments, or cause reductions of sound. To decode the sensory data as a native speaker would, learners must first build a cognitive structure of important sound distinctions and categories. Clearly, breaking the code demands an interaction of bottom-up and top-down skills.

The structural competence of beginners also places limitations on their bottom-up processing skills. They are not familiar with rules for word formation, inflections, or word-order rules. Their vocabulary store is nonexistent. The redundancy that is built into a language is lost on them, since there is no area of grammatical understanding that they could use to unlock the meaning of the whole.

The true novice stage is of very short duration. Almost immediately upon hearing the new language, learners begin to sift and sort the acoustic information, to form categories, and to build a representation of the L2 system. If teachers follow principles of comprehension training, learners will have plenty of opportunity to work with a limited amount of language that is focused on clearly illustrated subjects. The simplified code that is used in the classroom at this point helps learners direct their attention to the important features of the message. After a few hours of instruction, most learners know a tiny bit of the language very well, and can use their emerging understanding of linguistic categories to decode new utterances.

Despite its brevity, the novice stage is important for the development of positive attitudes toward listening. Learners should be encouraged to tolerate uncertainty, to venture informed guesses, to use their real-world knowledge and analytical skills, and to enjoy their success in comprehension. The world outside the classroom asks, "Do you speak English?" and ignores the very formidable accomplishment of skilled comprehension. Rarely does anyone ask, "Do you understand English?" Teachers can help correct this situation by attaching value to students' progress in listening skills.

True beginners are found in beginning classes for immigrants to English-speaking countries, and in EFL classes abroad. Many of the teachers in the second category are not native speakers themselves, and some may lack the confidence to provide students with the kind of global listening experiences they need. Yet, considering the great value of exposure to spoken English, teachers should attempt to provide this important input. The following suggestions are meant to encourage such teachers:

1. Global listening selections can be short, one to three minutes in duration.

2. You don't have to speak as if you were addressing colleagues at a professional meeting. Teachers' monologs are most effective at beginning levels if they are delivered in a simplified code. Such language involves short, basic sentences, clear pronunciation, repetition of ideas, limited vocabulary, and visual or situational support for new words.

3. It is best to add new material (vocabulary and structures) gradually. Experience with recombinations of familiar material builds learners' confidence and lessens the amount of totally new texts the teacher must prepare.

4. Global listening exercises such as short teacher monologs can be given to large classes, which are often found in the EFL setting, whereas speaking activities for the same number of students are more difficult to manage. Students can be kept active with a task to perform while listening, so you can be sure that you are using class time wisely.

5. Selective listening exercises, which focus on structures or sounds in contrast, are relatively easy to prepare. Most EFL teachers have come through educational systems where grammar was emphasized, and are quite comfortable with this kind of task. Listening discrimination tasks can focus on tenses, singular/plural differences, word order, or new vocabulary; there are many possibilities.

Techniques for Global Listening. One important usage of global listening is the presentation of new material. Until the students are skilled readers, it is best to present new material aurally. Teachers may select any part of the lesson for a global listen-

ing experience, or they may write their own short text based on the lesson. Introduction of new material through global listening is common to many of the newer comprehension approaches, yet the technique is not given in language textbooks. Once teachers have mastered a few simple principles and routines, they can use the technique daily.

Texts for global listening should be short, and preceded by a prelistening activity. Wherever possible, the theme and situation of the story should be presented visually by drawing on the chalkboard, overhead projector, or a large poster. If the new material is a dialog, draw the participants and tell their ages and relationships to each other. Setting the scene in this way arouses the learners' background knowledge and encourages them to make predictions about the text. New vocabulary can be used in short, illustrative sentences before learners hear it as part of the lesson. If possible, use new vocabulary in a personal way, supported by the context of the classroom, so its meaning is clear. Descriptive words, colors, numbers, sizes, shapes, action verbs, and spatial relations are easy to model and to support with a tangible example.

The prelistening stage should develop learners' curiosity about how all the phrases and words they have heard will fit together in a context. The new text should be modeled at normal speed, but with pauses between natural phrase groups. The teachers should not slow their speech, because the students' STM capacity is too short to remember sentences when they are extended by slow speech. The psycholinguistic processing model described above indicates that short phrases can be held in working memory until the next pause; during the pause, the phrase is analyzed, interpreted, related to the rest of the message, and comprehended.

A true beginner first hears the speech stream as undifferentiated noise. However, if objects and actions are demonstrated clearly, and if the message contains a clear dramatic structure, even beginners will soon begin to perceive patterns of sound. Vocabulary from the prelistening phase will stand out especially clearly from the rest of the speech stream, providing listeners a pleasant shock of recognition.

Working with a few content words, learners can use top-down processing to fill the gaps and guess the general meaning of the text. Comprehension of every function word and grammatical marker is really not necessary when the goal is to find the gist.

It should be clear from this description of global listening that comprehension at the beginning stage is not total, but neither does comprehension depend on understanding every word. Students on the first day of class can understand some words of the story through use of these techniques. They will not remember the words or be able to use them, but they will quite likely recognize the words when they hear them again in a familiar context. At the least, they have been exposed to three to five minutes of the new language with its own distinctive sound system, intonation patterns, pause system, and word order. Comprehension theorists like Nida point out that during this time, a great deal of active processing has been going on just under the students' level of conscious awareness.

Selective Listening Techniques. The other half of the listening plan is to bring some of the new contrasts and patterns into conscious awareness through selective listening exercises. Nida's suggested progression began with intonation, followed with sounds, and built to words, phrases, and grammar points. Listening goals for beginners are listed below, with exercise types to promote them.

The classification of exercises as bottom-up or top-down does not indicate that only one kind of cognitive activity can occur during each exercise, but rather that some exercises foster predominantly bottom-up responses, and some exercises promote predominantly top-down activity. An exercise is classified as bottom-up if focus is on form and the exercise deals with one of the structural systems of English. Alternatively, this designation may indicate selection of specific discrete items from the listening text, such as listening for details. An exercise is classified as top-down if the focus is on meaning and the listener uses global listening strategies. Alternatively, this designation may indicate a reliance on extralinguistic skills which the learner brings to the listening task.

All listening is to some degree interactive, due to the nature of the processing mechanism. An exercise is classified as interactive if the listeners must use information gained by processing at one level to check the accuracy of their processing on another level.

Exercise Types for Beginning-Level Listeners

Bottom-Up Processing Goals and Exercise Types

Goal: Discriminating Between Intonation Contours in Sentences

• Listen to a sequence of sentence patterns with either rising or falling intonation. Place a check in column 1 (rising) or column 2 (falling), depending on the pattern you hear (Abraham & Mackey, 1986, p. 29).

Goal: Discriminating Between Phonemes

• Listen to pairs of words. Some pairs differ in their final consonant (stay/steak), and some pairs are the same (laid/laid). Circle the word "same" or "different," depending on what you hear (Hagen, 1988, p. 2).

Goal: Selective Listening for Morphological Endings

• Listen to a series of sentences. Circle "yes" if the verb has an -ed ending, and circle "no" if it does not (Hagen, p. 77).
• Listen to a series of sentences. On your answer sheet are three verb forms. Circle the verb form that is contained in the sentence that you hear (Hagen, p. 78).

Goal: Selecting Details from the Text (Word Recognition)

• Match a word that you hear with its picture (Boyd & Boyd, 1982, p. 27).

- Listen to a weather report. Look at a list of words and circle the words that you hear (Abraham & Mackey, p. 111).
- Listen to a sentence that contains clock time. Circle the clock time that you hear, among three choices (5:30, 5:45, 6:15) (Abraham & Mackey, p. 124).
- Listen to an advertisement, select out the price of an item, and write the amount on a price tag (Abraham & Mackey, p. 31).
- Listen to a series of recorded telephone messages from an answering machine. Fill in a chart with the following information from each caller: name, number, time, and message (Fassman & Tavares, 1985, p. 21).

Goal: Listening for Normal Sentence Word Order

- Listen to a short dialog and fill in the missing words that have been deleted in a partial transcript (Griffee & Hough, 1986, pp. 86–87).

Top-Down Processing Goals and Exercise Types

Goal: Discriminating Between Emotional Reactions

- Listen to a sequence of utterances. Place a check in the column which describes the emotional reaction that you hear: interested, happy, surprised, or unhappy (Abraham & Mackey, p. 102).

Goal: Getting the Gist of a Sentence

- Listen to a sentence describing a picture and select the correct picture (Huizenga, 1987, pp. 30–31).

Goal: Recognize the Topic

- Listen to a dialog and decide where the conversation occurred. Circle the correct location among three multiple choice items (Abraham & Mackey, pp. 46–47).
- Listen to a conversation and look at a number of greeting cards that are pictured. Decide which of the greeting cards was sent.

Write the greeting under the appropriate card (Fassman & Tavares, p. 18).
- Listen to a conversation and decide what the people are talking about. Choose the picture that shows the topic (Abraham & Mackey, pp. 74–75).

Interactive Processing Goals and Exercise Types

Goal: Build a Semantic Network of Word Associations

- Listen to a word and associate all the related words that come to mind (B. H. Foley, 1984, p. 62).

Goal: Recognize a Familiar Word and Relate It to a Category

- Listen to words from a shopping list and match the words to the store that sells it (English Language Center, 1990, pp. 104–106).

Goal: Following Directions

- Listen to a description of a route and trace in on a map (Abraham & Mackey, p. 53).

Profile of the Intermediate-Level Learner

Intermediate-level learners continue to use listening as an important source of language input to increase their vocabulary and structural understanding. Although they have internalized the phonemic system of the language fairly well, they may have little understanding of the complexities of phonological rules which govern fast speech: reductions, elisions, and so forth. They need practice in word recognition and in discriminating fine differences in word order and grammatical form, registers of speaking, and emotional overtones.

Intermediate-level learners have moved beyond the limits of words and phrases; their memory can retain longer phrases and sentences. They can listen to short conversations or narratives that are one or two paragraphs in length. They are able to get the gist, finding the main idea and some supporting detail (ACTFL Proficiency Guidelines, reprinted in Omaggio, 1986). They are ready to practice more discourse level skills: predicting what will happen next, and explaining relations between events and ideas.

Techniques for Global Listening. At the intermediate level, it is no longer necessary to provide learners with simplified codes and modified speech. Indeed, learners need to hear authentic texts with reduced forms, fast speech features, false starts, hesitations, errors, some nonstandard dialects, and a variety of different voices.

There are several definitions of authenticity in materials. Porter and Roberts (1987) state that authentic texts are those "instances of spoken language which were not initiated for the purpose of teaching . . . not intended for non-native learners" (p. 176). In contrast, teacher-made texts are easily identified by their slower pace, limited vocabulary, complete sentences, repetition of target structures, exaggerated intonation, clear enunciation, and lack of background noise—all features that we noted as desirable at the beginning level when comprehension is expedited by a simplified code!

The need to introduce authentic material into students' listening repertoire by the end of the beginning level is supported by the fact that most listening in the world outside the classroom does not conform to simplified codes. At every level, students are able to understand much more than they can produce, and that principle also holds for the practice of listening to authentic texts. With some practice, learners can cope quite well with authentic material, given the following features of authentic texts:

1. The background noise, interruptions and overlapping in turn-taking, the nonverbal gestures and tone of voice in authentic speech actually provide clues to understanding the setting, the relationship of the partici-

pants, their motivations and purpose for speaking. Rather than working to complicate the decoding process, these features may actually aid comprehension because they facilitate access to learners' understanding of cultural and formal schemata.

2. Authentic texts are actually more redundant and repetitious than many scripted texts, and so are easier to understand (Ure, 1969).

3. Authentic texts bear an informational structure which conforms to their communicative purpose (Porter & Roberts, 1987). The proper use of these texts is to identify the key points of information and to let the rest of the information go. Thus, the learner's task load is actually rather limited. Learners should not be asked to retain every point of information, but only those details which the text was originally constructed to convey.

Refinements in the use of authentic texts are also possible. For learners who are not yet ready to listen to unedited authentic material, Geddes and White (1978) suggest the use of semiscripted simulated authentic speech (SSAS.) This is "language produced for a pedagogical purpose, but exhibiting features which have a high probability of occurrence in genuine acts of communication" (p. 137). Finger (1985) works with unedited excerpts from the evening television news, but has developed a framework of linguistic support which includes (1) prelistening exercises, (2) listening to the unedited excerpt, (3) listening to a modifed version of the text in which the content is maintained but the language is simplified, and (4) a second listening to the original, unedited version.

Techniques for Selective Listening. At the intermediate level, students need a well-organized program of selective listening to focus their attention on the systematic features of the language code. At this level, accuracy in discriminating grammatical features is very important. If learners cannot hear certain unstressed endings, articles, inflections, and function words, they are less likely to incorporate them into their grammatical competence. Intermediate-level students who were trained with simplified codes and with clearly pronounced models may not recognize the same words and phrases in normal fast speech.

Finally, the intermediate level is an appropriate time to teach explicitly some strategies of interactive listening: how to use one's knowledge of formal grammar to check the general meaning of a speaker's statement. Listeners can be presented with sentences which vary slightly in structure and wording, and they can be asked to identify whether the meanings are the same or different.

Exercise Types for Intermediate-Level Listeners

Bottom-Up Processing Goals and Exercise Types

Goal: Recognizing Fast Speech Forms

- Unstressed function words. Listen to a series of sentences that contain unstressed function words. Circle your choice among three words on the answer sheet—for example: "up," "a," "of" (Hagen, p. 10).

Goal: Finding the Stressed Syllable

- Listen to words of two (or three) syllables. Mark them for word stress and predict the pronunciation of the unstressed syllable (Hagen, p. 4).

Goal: Recognizing Words with Reduced Syllables

- Read a list of polysyllabic words and predict which syllabic vowel will be dropped. Listen to the words read in fast speech and confirm your prediction (Hagen, p. 6).

Goal: Recognize Words as They Are Linked in the Speech Stream

- Listen to a series of short sentences with consonant/vowel linking between words. Mark the linkages on your answer sheet (Hagen, p. 13).

Goal: Recognizing Pertinent Details in the Speech Stream

- Listen to a short dialog between a boss and a secretary regarding changes in the daily schedule. Use an appointment calendar. Cross out appointments that are being changed and write in new ones (Schechter, 1984, p. 36).
- Listen to announcements of airline arrivals and departures. With a model of an airline information board in front of you, fill in the flight numbers, destinations, gate numbers, and departure times (Tansey & Blatchford, p. 33).
- Listen to a series of short dialogs. Before listening, read the questions that apply to the dialogs. While listening, find the answers to questions about prices, places, names, and numbers. Example: "Where are the shoppers? How much is whole wheat bread?" (Tansey & Blatchford, 1987, p. 40).
- Listen to a short telephone conversation between a customer and a service station manager. Fill in a chart which lists the car repairs that must be done. Check the part of the car that needs repair, the reason, and the approximate cost (Schechter, p. 26).

Top-Down Processing Goals and Exercise Types

Goal: Analyze Discourse Structure to Suggest Effective Listening Strategies

- Listen to six radio commercials with attention to the use of music, repetition of key words, and number of speakers. Talk about the effect these techniques have on the listeners (Fassman & Tavares, p. 4).

Goal: Listen to Identify the Speaker or the Topic

- Listen to a series of radio commercials. On your answer sheet, choose among four types of sponsors or products and identify the picture which goes with the commercial (Fassman & Tavares, p. 4).

Goal: Listen to Evaluate Themes and Motives

- Listen to a series of radio commercials. On your answer sheet are listed four possible motives which the companies use to appeal to their customers. Circle all the motives which you feel each commercial promotes: escape from reality, family security, snob appeal, sex appeal (Fassman & Tavares, p. 5).

Goal: Finding Main Ideas and Supporting Details

- Listen to a short conversation between two friends. On your answer sheet are scenes from television programs. Find and write the name of the program and the channel. Decide which speaker watched the program (Schechter, p. 22).

Goal: Making Inferences

- Listen to a series of sentences, which may be either statements or questions. After each sentence, answer inferential questions, such as: Where might the speaker be? How might the speaker be feeling? What might the speaker be referring to? (Hagen, p. 18).
- Listen to a series of sentences. After each sentence, suggest a possible context for the sentence (place, situation, time, participants) (Hagen, p. 19).

Goal: Discriminating Between Registers of Speech and Tones of Voice

- Listen to a series of sentences. On your answer sheet, mark whether the sentence is polite or impolite (Tansey & Blatchford, p. 57).

Interactive Processing Goals and Exercise Types

Goal: Recognize Missing Grammar Markers in Colloquial Speech

- Listen to a series of short questions in which the auxiliary verb and subject have been deleted. Use grammatical knowledge to fill in the missing words: ("Have you) got some extra?" (Hagen, p. 9).
- Listen to a series of questions with reduced verb auxiliary and subject, and identify the missing verb (does it/is it) by checking the form of the main verb. Example: " 'Zit come with anything else? 'Zit arriving on time?" (Hagen, pp. 14–15).

Goal: Use Knowledge of Reduced Forms to Clarify the Meaning of an Utterance

- Listen to a short sentence containing a reduced form. Decide what the sentence means. On your answer sheet, read three alternatives and choose the alternative that is the best paraphrase of the sentence you heard. Example: You hear, "You can't be happy with that." You read: "(a) Why can't you be happy? (b) That will make you happy. (c) I don't think you are happy" (Hagen, p. 69).

Goal: Use Context to Build Listening Expectations

- Read a short want-ad describing job qualifications in the employment section of a newspaper. Brainstorm additional qualifications which would be important for that type of job (Fassman & Tavares, p. 10).

Goal: Listen to Confirm Your Expectations

- Listen to short radio advertisements for jobs that are available. Check the job qualifications against your expectations (Fassman & Tavares, p. 11).

Goal: Use Context to Build Expectations. Use Bottom-Up Processing to Recognize Missing Words. Compare Your Predictions to What You Actually Heard

- Read some telephone messages with missing words. Decide what kinds of information are missing, so you know what to listen for. Listen to the information and fill in the blanks. Finally, discuss with the class what strategies you used for your predictions (Fassman & Tavares, p. 21).

Goal: Use Incomplete Sensory Data and Cultural Background Information to Construct a More Complete Understanding of a Text

- Listen to one side of a telephone conversation. Decide what the topic of the conversation might be, and create a title for it (Tansey & Blatchford, p. 77).
- Listen to the beginning of a conversation between two people and answer questions about the number of participants, their ages, gender, and social roles. Guess the time of day, location, temperature, season, and topic. Choose among some statements to guess what might come next (Lougheed, 1985, p. 1).

Profile of the Advanced-Level Learner

There is evidence that in the learning contiuum, somewhere between high intermediate and advanced levels, a qualitative shift occurs in the learner's processing style (Cummins, 1980a). Cummins notes that truly proficient bilingual subjects are able to use their second language skill fully to acquire knowledge: They have cognitive and academic language proficiency (CALP). Advanced students are no longer simply learning to listen, or listening to learn the language. They are listening in the language to learn about the content of other areas. To build toward this level, curriculum and program planners establish courses in English for Specific Purposes (ESP) (see Johns in this volume), English for Academic Purposes (EAP), and adjunct courses where language support is offered in mainstream content classes (see Snow in this volume).

The descriptions of the advanced listener in the ACTFL Proficiency Guidelines (reprinted in Omaggio, 1986) list the following competencies. Advanced learners can listen to longer texts, such as radio and television programs, and academic lectures. Their vocabulary includes topics in current events, history, and culture; they can deal with a

certain degree of abstraction. Listeners begin to fill in gaps and can make inferences when the text is incomplete or their background knowledge is lacking. However, their understanding of the language remains on a fairly literal plane, so that they may miss jokes, slang, and cultural references.

Many advanced learners are more skilled at reading by this time than they are at listening. This is particularly true of students who have learned their English in a foreign language context and whose training has emphasized grammar, vocabulary, and reading. Such students may comprehend spoken discourse better if they can activate their knowledge first with a related reading selection.

For many international students, the informal tone of lectures and the reductions in normal speech present a major comprehension problem. Listening classes at the advanced level may need to include a systematic program of listening to reduced speech as well as a strategic listening component to distinguish important from unimportant discourse features. A review of stress, pause, pitch, and intonation patterns can serve to unlock mysteries of discourse structure, and point students toward recognition of organizational markers, cohesive devices, and definitions in context. As students learn to identify the important content words through knowledge of sentence stress, they will find that their note-taking skills improve.

A useful technique for helping advanced students make the transition from written to spoken language is suggested by Lebauer (1984): use of lecture transcripts in the initial stages of listening shows students that cohesive devices, discourse markers, and important definitions do appear in the text, and shows students how to recognize these features.

The second language teaching profession has generally come to recognize the value of top-level processing, and the last decade has produced a number of articles that prove the efficacy of schemata use in both lecture listening and reading (Carrell & Eisterhold, 1983; P. Johnson, 1981, 1982). However,

Eskey (1988) points to the need for continued concern with bottom-up skills, even at advanced levels. What differentiates good readers from poor readers is not really their ability to draw on background knowledge, but their automaticity in decoding (Stanovich, 1980). For listening or reading to fit the interactive model of the skilled native speaker, both top-down and bottom-up processes must be learned.

Peterson (1989) studied the written lecture summaries of native speakers and nonnatives at two proficiency levels to determine which propositions were retained from the lecture: main ideas or low-level information. All three groups recorded the same top-level information, which indicates that less proficient listeners are as likely to use their formal and content schemata in processing lecture text as are proficient listeners. However, every index of completeness of recall within propositions and within the lecture as a whole indicated that the less proficient nonnatives simply were not retaining as much information on the propositional level. Consequently, they also were less skilled at drawing inferences or filling in missing information in the lecture. Without proficient bottom-up skills, the interactive nature of listening is not realized.

The following recommendations for advanced listeners assume an international student population which needs to develop cognitive and academic language proficiency for effective study in English.

Exercise Types for Advanced-Level Learners

Bottom-Up Processing Goals and Exercise Types

Goal: Use Features of Sentence Stress and Volume to Identify Important Information for Note Taking

- Listen to a number of sentences and extract the content words, which are read with greater stress. Write the content words as notes (Ruetten, 1986, pp. 78–79).

Goal: Become Aware of Sentence Level Features in Lecture Text

- Listen to a segment of a lecture while reading a transcript of the material. Notice the incomplete sentences, pauses, and verbal fillers (Lebauer, 1984, pp. 7–15).

Goal: Become Aware of Organizational Cues in Lecture Text

- Look at a lecture transcript and circle all the cue words used to enumerate the main points. Then listen to the lecture segment and note the organizational cues (Lebauer, p. 11).

Goal: Become Aware of Lexical and Supersegmental Markers for Definitions

- Read a list of lexical cues that signal a definition; listen to signals of the speaker's intent such as rhetorical questions; listen to special intonation patterns and pause patterns used with appositives (Lebauer, p. 54).
- Listen to short lecture segments which contain new terms and their definitions in context. Use knowledge of lexical and intonational cues to identify the definition of the word (Lebauer, p. 55).

Goal: Identify Specific Points of Information

- Read a skeleton outline of a lecture, in which the main categories are given but the specific examples are left blank. Listen to the lecture, and find the information which belongs in the blanks (Ruetten, p. 36).

Top-Down Processing Goals and Exercise Types

Goal: Use the Introduction to the Lecture to Predict Its Focus and Direction

- Listen to the introductory section of a lecture. Then read a number of topics on your answer sheet and choose the topic that best expresses what the lecture will discuss (Lebauer, p. 50).

Goal: Use the Lecture Transcript to Predict the Content of the Next Section

- Read a section of a lecture transcript. Stop reading at a juncture point and predict what will come next. Then read on to confirm your prediction (Lebauer, p. 21).

Goal: Find the Main Idea of a Lecture Segment

- Listen to a section of a lecture which describes a statistical trend. While you listen, look at three graphs that show a change over time and select the graph that best illustrates the lecture (Lebauer, p. 48).

Interactive Processing Goals and Exercise Types

Goal: Use Incoming Details to Determine the Accuracy of Predictions about Content

- Listen to the introductory sentences to predict some of the main ideas you expect to hear in the lecture. Then listen to the lecture as it is played. Note whether or not the instructor talks about the points you predicted. If s/he does, note a detail about the point (Aebersold, Kowitz, Schwarte, & Smith, 1985, p. 12).

Goal: Determine the Main Ideas of a Section of a Lecture by Analysis of the Details in That Section

- Listen to a section of a lecture and take notes on the important details. Then relate the details to form an understanding of the main point of that section. Choose from a list of possible controlling ideas (Aebersold, et al., pp. 37–42).

Goal: Make Inferences by Identifying Ideas on the Sentence Level Which Lead to Evaluative Statements

- Listen to a statement and take notes on the important words. Indicate what further meaning can be inferred from the statement. Indicate the words in the original statement that serve to cue the inference (Aebersold, et al., p. 94).

Goal: Use Knowledge of the Text and the Lecture Content to Fill In Missing Information

- Listen to a lecture segment to get the gist. Then listen to a statement from which words have been omitted. Using your knowledge of the text and of the general content, fill in the missing information. Check your understanding by listening to the entire segment (Aebersold et al., p. 109).

Goal: Use Knowledge of the Text and the Lecture Content to Discover the Lecturer's Misstatements and to Supply the Ideas That He Meant to Say

- Listen to a lecture segment that contains an incorrect term. Write the incorrect term and the term which the lecturer should have used. Finally, indicate what clues helped you find the misstatement (Aebersold et al., p. 113).

SUMMARY

ESL/EFL teachers have several responsibilities with respect to the listening skill. First, they must understand the pivotal role that listening plays in the language learning process to utilize listening in ways that facilitate rather than thwart this process. Second, they must understand the complex interactive nature of the listening process and the different kinds of listening that learners must do in order to provide their students with an appropriate variety and range of listening experiences. Finally, teachers must understand how listening skills typically develop in second language learners—and be able to assess the stage of listening at which their students are—so that each student can engage in the most beneficial types of listening activities given his/her level of proficiency.

DISCUSSION QUESTIONS

1. In a group discussion, recall the stages that you went through when you learned a second language. What elements did you hear first? What elements took a long time to hear? What part did memory play in your listening at each stage?

2. In your opinion and based on your experience, what is the most effective relationship between teacher talk and student talk in the L2 classroom?

3. Relate the word pairs below and show how the two sets form different views of language processing:

top-down / bottom-up
restructuring / automaticity
global / selective
fluency / accuracy

4. Describe the differences in texts with simplified codes, semiscripted simulated authentic speech, and authentic language. What purpose does each text type have in the L2 classroom?

5. The learner proficiency profiles given in the chapter are loosely based on the ACTFL Proficiency Guidelines for listening. The profiles assume a certain learning context, one where the target language is not spoken outside the classroom (similar to a TEFL context). Discuss ways in which context variables might lead to a different learner proficiency profile at each level. (Consider class size, age of learners, amount of exposure to the language, length of instruction, and similar factors.)

SUGGESTED ACTIVITIES

1. Prepare a presentation of new material from an ESL/EFL text. Choose a short dialog or narrative passage. Plan a prelistening phase in which you use visual and situational support to teach the new words and concepts. Then present the text aurally. Your presentation should last no longer than three to five minutes.

2. Prepare a selective listening exercise which focuses on language form and which guides students to discriminate aurally between structural forms.

3. Choose a listening comprehension text that has been published in the last five years. Select a typical chapter of the book and analyze the cognitive processing demands of the exercises. How many are top-down? How many are bottom-up? Interactive? What is the plan for sequencing the exercises?

4. Choose an older listening comprehension text and evaluate the exercise types using the questions in number 3 above. Can you draw a generalization about shifts in teaching methods that are reflected in the principles behind materials design?

5. Record one or two minutes of authentic text from the radio or television. Develop a framework of language support for the text and show how you could use it in an intermediate-level class.

SUGGESTIONS FOR FURTHER READING

Beile, W. (1978)
Towards a classification of listening comprehension exercises. *Audio-visual Language Journal, 16,* 147–153.

> Outlines a sequence of activities that can be used with any text. Beile's steps in listening include exercises which make use of both top-down and bottom-up processes.

Blair, R., (ed. (1982)
Innovative approaches to language teaching. New York: Newbury House.

> "Learning to Listen," the third chapter of Nida's book, is reprinted in Blair, pp. 42–53. Also, this anthology includes representative articles by Asher, Postovsky, Nord, and Krashen.

Dirven, R., & J. Oakeshott-Taylor (1984)
Listening comprehension (Part I). State of the art article. *Language Teaching, 17,* 326–343.

Dirven, R., & J. Oakeshott-Taylor (1985)
Listening comprehension (Part II). State of the art article. *Language Teaching, 18,* 2–20.

> Review developments in research into the psychological processes involved in various levels of listening, and suggest pedagogical strategies for teaching the skill.

Nagle, S., & S. Sanders (1986)
Comprehension theory and second language pedagogy. *TESOL Quarterly, 20,* 9–26.

> Presents the information-processing model of listening comprehension, with suggestions for classroom applications.

Porter, D., & J. Roberts (1987)
Authentic listening activities. In M. Long & J. Richards, *Methodology in TESOL,* pp. 177–187. New York: Newbury House.

> After listing the ways in which teacher-made texts differ formally from authentic texts, the authors present a variety of exercise types that can be used for authentic listening practice. They emphasize the various purposes for listening, and show how the listening task should reflect the text type.

II
Language Skills
B. Speaking

This section of the text focuses on how ESL/EFL teachers can facilitate the acquisition of oral skills by their students. The chapter by Riggenbach and Lazaraton focuses on fluency in oral communication and ways of helping students attain facility in this area, while the chapter by Celce-Murcia and Goodwin examines the teaching of pronunciation, recognizing that pronunciation constitutes a very important aspect of oral communication. Finally, the chapter by Olshtain and Cohen introduces the teacher to speech act theory, research, and teaching applications so that teachers can be alert to the possibility of teaching social appropriacy as well as fluency and accuracy while teaching speaking skills to their students.

Promoting Oral Communication Skills

Heidi Riggenbach and Anne Lazaraton

INTRODUCTION

It has become apparent in recent years that there have been marked changes in the goals of language education programs (Morley, 1987; Richards & Rodgers, 1987b). Today, language students are considered successful if they can communicate effectively in their second or foreign language, whereas two decades ago the accuracy of the language produced would most likely be the major criterion contributing to the judgment of a student's success or lack of success. There is little doubt now that these developments in language teaching—called the "proficiency movement" by some and the promotion of "functional" or "communicative" ability by others (Higgs, 1984; Mohan, 1986)—have moved us away from the goal of accurate form toward a focus on fluency and communicative effectiveness. Thus, the teaching of the speaking skill has become increasingly important.

Central to these changes has been the recognition by educators and researchers that "communicative competence" entails not solely grammatical accuracy but also a knowledge of sociocultural rules of appropriateness, discourse norms, and strategies for ensuring that a communication is understood. In fact, some applied linguists (e.g., Canale, 1986a; Canale & Swain, 1980) define communicative competence as comprising these very components: (1) grammatical, or linguistic, competence, (2) sociocultural competence, (3) discourse competence—the ability to sustain coherent discourse with another speaker, and (4) strategic competence—the means by which learners deal with potential breakdowns in communication.

Accordingly, rather than implementing activities and exercises which focus strictly on accuracy (such as those using memorization, repetition, and uncontextualized drills), many classroom teachers have concentrated on promoting communicative competence in language learners by using "communicative activities"—those which rely more on the students' ability to understand and communicate real information. The aim of such "fluency activities", as Brumfit (1984, p.69) calls them, is to "develop a pattern of language interaction within the classroom which is as close as possible to that used by competent performers in normal life." Informal,

125

unrehearsed use of language is encouraged, along with a relaxed classroom environment, the natural negotiation of turns, and the exchange of "new" information—all of which occur in ordinary conversation. In other words, some believe that communication in the classroom should mirror the authentic communication that occurs in the real world.

However, this does not mean that a focus on accuracy has no place in the communicative classroom. Some research (e.g., Higgs & Clifford, 1982) suggests that forcing communication too early without any regard for accuracy can result in early fossilization. Since a linguistic or grammatical base may be necessary before fluency can be attained, some instructors and researchers believe that grammar should be explicitly taught, and that this is possible through communicative means (e.g., Celce-Murcia & Hilles, 1988).

When using communicative activities, it is important to strive for a classroom in which students feel comfortable and confident, feel free to take risks, and have sufficient opportunities to speak. In a study on interaction in the classroom, Pica, Young, and Doughty (1987) suggest that there are two different kinds of linguistic environments available to second language learners: (a) one characterized mainly by input that has been modified or simplified—such as that found in the more traditional "teacher-fronted" classroom, and (b) the other characterized by student-to-student interaction, which emphasizes authentic rather than simplified input. This study lends support to the assertion that the second kind of linguistic environment provides more opportunities for learning, since, in this setting, speakers focus on the immediate task of communication itself in "real time," and collaborate to achieve mutual understanding, modifying their language according to the demands of the situation. In addition, interactive-type activities seem to address the issue of student "comfort" as a factor in second language learning. Some research suggests that interactive group work lessens many students' anxiety about performing and lowers their "affective filters",

thereby facilitating learning (Doughty & Pica, 1986; Gaies, 1985; Long & Porter, 1985; Pica & Doughty, 1985).

GOALS

Simply put, the goal of a speaking component in a language class should be to encourage the acquisition of communication skills and to foster real communication in and out of the classroom. Taylor (1987, p. 47) suggests that the teacher present "activities which are meaningful to students and which will motivate them to become committed to sustaining that communication to accomplish a specific goal." It follows then that the objectives for developing oral fluency will address this goal by setting forth specific content, activities, and methods which foster communication.

Often objectives for speaking (and other skills as well) are mandated by the particular program in which a teacher must work, and the guidelines established by that program. That is, the ESL/EFL teacher is often presented with a syllabus and is expected to teach from it. In some cases, the syllabus will consist of a list of grammatical structures to be taught, perhaps as part of a multiskills class; specific goals for speaking may not be explicitly given. It is then up to the teacher to decide how to integrate speaking with other skills to form a coherent curriculum. More problematic are those cases where the only explicit objectives given to the teacher do not seem to encourage fluency or communication (i.e., a list of grammar points to be covered). Here the teacher needs to improvise and to be flexible in making best use of what is available for teaching purposes.

In other teaching situations, the instructor may have some leeway in deciding what objectives to meet, what content to cover, and what activities to use. In this case the teacher can go beyond the more specific goals and objectives of the particular program to the speaking needs the students have in the "real world." For instance, the needs of EST (English for Science and Technology) students in China may have little in common with those of Indochinese refugees in Seattle.

Accordingly, a necessary first step in implementing a course in speaking is a needs analysis which identifies the requirements of the learners involved. Specifically, the instructor can determine the kinds of situations in which the students will find themselves, the linguistic information they will need to possess, and the resources they have available. While university-level students may be required to lead discussions, explain ideas, or present opinions, adult learners have more pragmatic needs that concern survival skills in everyday life, such as using the telephone, going to the bank, and riding the bus. With the overall goal of authentic oral communication in mind, it is perhaps simpler and more beneficial to state these objectives in terms of speech functions (e.g., making requests) as opposed to grammatical categories (e.g., the correct use of modals).

Once speech functions have been identified, it can then be determined which linguistic structures are most naturally related to these particular speech functions and tasks. The teacher may want to list the specific structures that can be used to fulfill a language function: for requests these may be such structures as "Can I please have . . ." "I would like to have . . ." "Give me . . .", for example. Alternatively, and fortunately, there are many commercially available texts which are organized according to speech functions (e.g., Keller & Warner, 1979; Sharpe, 1984; Tillit & Bruder, 1985); this eliminates a step for the teacher.

Whether the objectives for a course are organized in terms of language functions, grammatical structures, or situational episodes, several factors must be considered in choosing both the specific material to be covered and the methodology with which to cover it. The first is the level of the students. While beginners require a recycling of material, from controlled practice and drills to more "free expression" activities, relatively advanced learners may instead need to polish already-developed skills and can be trusted to carry out less-structured activities on their own.

Another factor to consider is the cultural makeup of the group. A culturally and linguistically homogeneous class is common in EFL contexts and may allow culture-specific materials to be used (such as discussions of national current events or the presentation of folk tales). In an ESL context there will more likely be a mixed group and thus a more pressing need to use the common second language for communication. However, in this context sensitivity must be shown toward differing cultural values and cultural "styles": A group of Middle Eastern students discussing women's rights may appear very heated in contrast to a group of Asians discussing the same topic, although both groups can have opinions that differ widely from North American views for cultural reasons.

ACTIVITIES

For use in the ESL/EFL classroom, there are as many speaking activities and materials available as there are creative teachers. For the purposes of this discussion, we have organized oral skills activities into distinct types: (1) drills, or linguistically structured activities, (2) performance activities, (3) participation activities, and (4) observation activities. Evaluation techniques, which allow students to focus on the structures which occur in their utterances and to analyze their own and their classmates' performances, will also be discussed in conjunction with other activities. Each kind of activity will be described, and examples will be given of some of the more successful and interesting choices available to the teacher from each type.

Linguistically Structured Activities

Prator (1972) classifies classroom activities for ESL learners by means of a continuum, with "manipulative" activities at one extreme and communicative activities at the other extreme. Although today, in ESL/EFL classrooms throughout the world, communicative activities tend to more effectively meet the goals of the curriculum, also useful are "manipulative" activities, or those which provide the student with a "prepackaged" structure by means of teacher, tape, or book.

Such activities need not be void of meaning, as were some of the more classic manipulative techniques associated with the audio-lingual approach, with its repetition drills and pattern practices. Rather, it is possible to contextualize such activities so that they are predominately rather than wholly manipulative and thus meet some of the requirements of a communicatively oriented design.

In controlled practice the teacher can model the forms to be produced, providing necessary linguistically correct input. The students are then allowed to practice the material, and the teacher follows up by reinforcing the forms practiced. What is important is that students are allowed to speak about what is true, real, and interesting. The *structured interview* is an example of this, where students question each other and answer factually, thus exchanging "real" information, while at the same time repeating and reinforcing specific structures (e.g., yes-no, or wh- questions). A variation on this requires students to take on assigned roles while asking and answering questions, prompted, perhaps, through the use of pictures (see, e.g., Molinsky & Bliss, 1980).

Some *language games* can also provide opportunities for controlled practice. Again, it is important to model the structures for beginning students, either verbally or by writing the forms on the board. Picture games which require students to match texts with pictures are ideal for beginning students who need to practice manipulating certain structures (e.g., the word "cup" with a picture of a cup; or, for more advanced students, a sentence which describes one step in a process, with its corresponding diagram).

Psychology games also offer many possibilities for beginning students: descriptions of "ink blots" or unidentifiable forms (or objects); speculations about the age and character of people in pictures or photographs; the game of Twenty Questions, where a group of students has 20 chances to "intuit" what object the "leader" is thinking about; or memory games such as Story Building, where one person, usually the instructor, starts with a sentence or clause (e.g., "I had a friend named Mary"), and the students take turns building upon this clause, turn by turn (e.g., Person 2: "I had a friend named Mary who cheated whenever she took tests." Person 3: "I had a friend named Mary who cheated whenever she took tests by writing notes on her shirtsleeve"). For a good source of games for language learners, see Wright, Betteridge, and Buckby (1984).

From a more theoretical perspective, Gatbonton and Segalowitz (1988) suggest general principles for designing classroom activities which are naturally "automatized" yet communicatively oriented—which offer students the chance to focus on and repeat specific structures, while at the same time performing natural, "authentic" tasks. One such activity, the "Class Photo," requires students to arrange other class members into poses for photographs. Such an activity is designed to elicit formulaic utterances such as "Please move to the back," or "Mei, stand in front of Juan," in the context of a task where such utterances would naturally occur.

Performance Activities

"Performance" activities are those in which the student prepares beforehand and delivers a message to a group. A good example of such an activity is the student *speech*, which could be made as specific in content as necessary. An EST course, for example, might require students to explain a process or experiment; a course in conversational or "social" English might assign students to simply tell a story from their own experience in a casual, social setting.

In the usual classroom setting, students deliver a speech and the teacher gives feedback, often using an evaluation form.

However, to capitalize more fully on the possibilities for language-learning activities, more is required than one-time student performance and teacher evaluation of errors and other features. Peer evaluation can be a useful component of oral performance activities since (1) the "audience" becomes involved in such a way that students, as members of the audience, become more than simply passive listeners; (2) the evaluation process helps students to gain confidence in their own ability to evaluate language; and (3) the evaluation activity itself becomes an opportunity for real, spontaneous interaction since the "message" (the evaluation) is important to the student performer.

One technique in peer evaluation of oral performance is for the teacher to select beforehand two students to formally evaluate another student's peformance. They then outline the main points of the presentation in order to demonstrate their ability (or lack of ability) to follow the student's speech; they orally sum up, before the rest of the class, their reactions to the performance; and, finally, they fill out the evaluation sheet in some detail for the presenter to read and consider. Other students in the class also fill out the evaluation form (but need not give an oral summation) and ask the presenter follow-up questions.

The evaluation sheet, drawn up by the teacher beforehand, can be the same as the teacher's. Its purpose is to structure the evaluation so that it meets the goals of the activity, with categories for such criteria as *content* (Is it focused? clear? original? Has enough detail been provided?), *organization* (Is it logical? Are there appropriate transitions?), and *delivery* (Is eye contact maintained? Are notes relied on too much? Is the volume adequate?). Other comments would relate to the focus of the particular assignment, and could include specific grammar or vocabulary points.

Another follow-up activity involves audiotaping or videotaping students during their initial performances and allowing them to evaluate themselves. With self-evaluation, students listen to or watch their recorded speeches and evaluate themselves according to the same criteria that the teacher and peer evaluators use. This can be especially illuminating for the students, who are usually unaccustomed to hearing themselves (or seeing themselves on videotape). Next, the student performers select a portion of their talk and transcribe it in detail (complete with hesitations, filled pauses—"uh"s—and grammatical errors). Where in their initial performance they focused on communication, in the follow-up they focus on their problems and nonnativelike features, considering ways to restructure the piece so that it would be more effective. This is an excellent opportunity for the teacher to combine concerns for fluency with accuracy. A useful option for this follow-up task would be for students to look at their transcription and rewrite it, correcting the grammar and vocabulary errors.

A variation on the speech given by one person is assigning two or more people to deliver a talk. Not only does this allow more content to be conveyed, but it gives students needed practice in negotiating tasks, sharing information, and providing assistance when needed. An additional benefit is that students are less likely to feel nervous or pressured when the responsibility for giving a good speech is shared among a group.

Role-plays and *dramas*, if performed in front of the class, can also function as "performance activities." In some cases, students could write the role-plays or dramas themselves; this would be especially appropriate in a course that is organized around speech functions or conversational strategies (e.g., complimenting and thanking behavior, greetings and closings). More guidance can be provided for beginning learners if they are allowed to perform their role-plays from scripts they have at hand. While reading from the script is not encouraged, as long as the teacher ensures that the content of the role-play is authentic, the activity can be approached as another variation on the contextualized drill. All such structured performance activities can use the techniques of peer evaluation, audiotaping, transcription, and self-evaluation.

Finally, *debates* can serve as an opportunity for a classroom performance activity for intermediate and advanced learners. Class time can be used for students to select a topic, plan their research and information-gathering strategies, pool the results of this research, and plan their presentations, making sure to anticipate questions from the other team. Thus, a class debate not only becomes a format for a final performance-style activity but also provides a preplanning stage rich in group interaction.

Participation Activities

"Participation" activities can be some of the most diverse and interesting in the oral communication repertoire. These are activities where the student participates in some communicative activity in a "natural setting." One of the most commonly used participation activities is the *guided discussion*, where the instructor provides a brief orientation to some problem or controversial topic, usually by means of a short reading. Students in small groups discuss the topic, suggesting possible solutions, resolutions, or complications. There are currently many prepared discussion books available commercially, such as *React Interact—Situations for Communication* (Byrd & Clemente-Cabetas, 1980), or *The Non-Stop Discussion Workbook* (Rooks, 1981).

Alternatively, students themselves can be assigned the responsibility of a *discussion-leading activity* in more advanced classes. In this situation, they (1) select a topic, (2) find a short background article or write a summary of the topic, (3) draw up a list of questions for consideration by the rest of the class, and finally, (4) lead a semiformal class discussion on the topic, with a prepared introduction and a spontaneous summing-up conclusion. Some of the same evaluation techniques discussed above can be used for this activity (peer evaluation, audiotaping or videotaping, and detailed self-evaluation with the aid of

the student transcription). Certainly this activity also provides an excellent opportunity to look at the dynamics of turn-taking and topic control, with a good opportunity to check on accuracy of grammar and pronunciation as well.

Another more innovative participation activity requires students to audiotape a spontaneous *conversation* that they have with a native speaker of their choice. (If access to a native speaker is difficult, the alternative is to find a partner who is considered "fluent"— someone who has studied or spent time in English-speaking countries, for example. If even this is difficult, students can converse with the most advanced language students.) The goal of these conversations is for the student to obtain "data" that are as natural and spontaneous as possible given the constraints of the recording procedure.

Once the conversation is recorded, the students transcribe, on their own, an excerpt of the conversation that they find interesting. Transcription, an important element of many student-generated materials and activities, allows the transcriber to focus on details—a valuable exercise in listening comprehension, as well as an opportunity to heighten awareness of the students' own difficulties of expression. In the process of transcribing, students discover much about natural language that is difficult to teach—that native speakers also make "mistakes": They hesitate, rephrase, pause, mispronounce words. Finally, the transcription process makes materials available in a written form for the class to use as a basis for many further activities.

After the initial conversation data are audiotaped, transcribed, and checked by the instructor for faithfulness to the tape, there are many options for activities based on them. One use of the material is for vocabulary-building: the students note down unfamiliar words or idioms in the native or fluent speaker's language, and also target areas in their own speech where there was some difficulty in achieving clear communication. Another possibility is for the students to concentrate on the native speaker's speech and to note effective or interesting usage. With the aid of a transcript and the heightened awareness of detail brought about by the transcription process, students can focus on details which are difficult or impossible to catch during the actual conversation itself. Finally, this procedure can be used as an exercise in discovering regularities of conversation strategies, such as topic control, feedback markers (interactive listening), or specific "gambits" (such as how to appropriately disagree, register surprise or sympathy). For some students it is also useful—as a final step—to look at the accuracy of what they have produced (in terms of grammar and vocabulary) and to edit the transcript to render it more accurate.

All of these topics can be independently pursued by the students in the form of language learning journals (e.g., Bailey, 1980), small-group discussions, or student-created role-plays. Alternatively, the teacher may listen to the tapes or read the transcripts, select a particularly successful example of the feature under study, and, with the student's consent, use the sample as a focus for discussion.

Another participation activity that elicits enthusiastic student response is the *interview*. In it, the students become their own oral historians, interviewing their native-speaker acquaintances about some meaningful or memorable aspect of their lives (see Spradley, 1979; Terkel, 1974). The most successful of these projects seems to involve subjects whose experiences are different in some important way from the student (e.g., interview the oldest person you know, interview someone you know who has had unusual experiences). Another variation is to have students interview native speakers for their opinions on a given subject. As a class the students can generate questions relating to the topic and practice interviewing techniques. After the interviews have taken place, the students organize their information and present it to the rest of the class. This can be particularly interesting when native speakers express conflicting views (as they usually do) when responding to the topic, and the class can then

come up with reasons for the different responses native speakers gave.

In the interview exercise, follow-up activities can be similar to those used for the student-gathered conversations, but here other alternatives are available: students can be asked to retell or report the story or opinion in their own words, or use the activity as a basis for a writing assignment. If the interview is summed up orally and in writing, students can begin thinking about the difference between spoken and written discourse. This offers another opportunity for the teacher to merge concerns of fluency with accuracy, since the rules for writing are much more strict and allow fewer of the "errors" that naturally occur in speaking.

A final participation activity that has been used successfully is the *oral dialog journal*, where students speak spontaneously on an audiotape on a given topic, such as a response to an assigned article or essay, or on anything of interest, much like a written journal. With this activity it is the teacher who is the other "participant," and who responds to the student orally, via audiotape. This teacher response would primarily focus on content, thus creating a real dialog, but it could also touch on linguistic factors of the student's speech, such as fluency, pronunciation, and grammar. When there is limited access to native speakers, this activity can be particularly effective as an opportunity for students to interact with and obtain exposure to native or fluent speakers.

Observation Activities

These are activities in which a student observes and/or records verbal and nonverbal interactions between two or more native or fluent speakers of the target language. This technique is useful for building student appreciation and awareness of language as it is actually used in the real world, and since the student is taking the role of nonparticipant observer, he or she is free to concentrate on the subject without fear of performance errors, a problem for beginners, whose productive skills usually lag behind their receptive capabilities.

A typical *observation* assignment, in an area where native speakers are plentiful, might be to assign two students, as a team, the responsibility for exploring how native speakers negotiate a certain social situation. For example, in a unit dealing with conversation strategies, the focus of an assignment might be on greeting behavior. There are many such possibilities which can also serve as the focus for this assignment; almost any communicative task that is addressed in a language classroom can be observed in its "native habitat"—whether it be how or when people greet each other, make requests, interrupt each other, thank each other, compliment one another, disagree, or receive compliments.

After a brief in-class discussion or reading on field observation techniques (Spradley, 1980), the students select a site, carry out their observations, and take detailed field notes in the manner of an ethnographic researcher or anthropologist. After observing a certain number of cases, the students write a brief summary and present these findings to the class. Alternatively, a follow-up activity could be a performance, in which the students create a role-play which demonstrates the nonverbal and verbal behavior appropriate to the particular conversational strategy under analysis. For less advanced students the procedures can be less formal, while still serving to inform students about what native speakers actually do.

As in the conversation task described above, observation activities have the drawback of assuming access to a pool of native speakers. For purposes of observation, this problem may be partially alleviated by making use of native English speakers on radio and television, especially in "natural" settings, such as unrehearsed interviews. Also, if native speakers are not available in large numbers, some of the same results may be achieved through the use of *elicitation* techniques, in which students ask native or fluent speakers to draw upon their intuitions about

acceptable nativelike behavior in a given circumstance (e.g., Hawkins, 1985). In this case, the students and/or teacher would propose a hypothetical situation. For example, in the study of "compliments," a basis for elicitation might be the following:

Let's say you were invited to an acquaintance's house for the first time. When you arrive, your hostess shows you around the house. What would you say?

or:

You just found out that your advisor, a respected professor in your department, just heard the news that her recent book has received an award for "Best Original Research of the Year." What would you say?

The students would "collect the data"—the native or fluent speakers' responses—either by recording them on a tape recorder or by taking detailed notes.

The same type of follow-up activity could be assigned here as well: Students could simply list the conversation strategies (or "gambits") most often used (e.g., "This is a lovely . . . ," "I really like your . . . ," or, in the second case, "Congratulations. I'm so pleased that . . . ," "I would like to compliment you on/congratulate you for . . . ," "You are very deserving of . . ."). As with the first observation activity, students often become interested in the sociolinguistic variance they observe in the different responses. For example, if they present their results in the form of role-play before the rest of the class, discussions are likely to arise concerning which conversation strategies appear to be most "nativelike," which ones might be effective with certain age groups, which ones would be used only in (a) very formal situations, versus (b) very informal situations, and so on.

METHODS OF EVALUATION

We have discussed some of the methods for evaluating specific speaking activities in the language classroom, including self-evaluation and peer evaluation. Some instructors might be required to test students in terms of general oral proficiency, in addition to or in place of rating performance on specific tasks. Considering the changes in language learning theory and language teaching practice, it is interesting to note that many established tests of oral proficiency (e.g., those by the American Council on the Teaching of Foreign Languages and the Educational Testing Service) continue to evaluate a student's performance primarily in terms of accuracy or grammatical competence. These and many other tests (see Table 1) look at orally produced language as something which can be broken down into separate categories, such as grammar, vocabulary, pronunciation, and fluency (e.g., see the rating sheets in Henning, 1987; alternate rating schemes are presented in Underhill, 1987). Although certainly these discrete components contribute to what is called "oral proficiency," it is questionable whether the

elusive quality called "communicative ability" can be evaluated in this manner.

We have found that an instrument which focuses more on the *message* conveyed by the learner is more useful for both the student and the teacher. One such approach (Lazaraton & Riggenbach, 1987) uses a test constructed with specific course objectives in mind. The test asks students to respond to six "tasks" related to functional units addressed in their coursework: opinion, comparison-contrast, narrative, description, process, and short question-and-answer. A more holistic approach to scoring was used; one rating scale was designed to ascertain "functional ability" to complete the task, while another scale addressed the more linguistically oriented aspects of oral proficiency: fluency, pronunciation, grammar, and vocabulary. Furthermore, these linguistic aspects were evaluated in terms of comprehensibility rather than accuracy; in other words, how well did control or lack of control of the spe-

Table 1
Some Established Oral Proficiency Tests

Name of test	Agency doing testing	Format/criteria for evaluation
Bilingual Syntax Measure (BSM)*	Psychological Corp., New York, NY	pictures/focus on syntax (errors in pronunciation and vocabulary ignored)
Cambridge Oral Exam	Univ. of Cambridge Local Examinations Syndicate (UCLES), Cambridge, England	theme-directed conversation/ fluency, grammar, interactive communication, vocabulary, pronunciation
Foreign Service Institute/Interagency Language Roundtable Oral Interview (FSI/ILR)	Interagency Language Roundtable, Arlington, VA	interview/functional skills on an overall proficiency scale
Ilyin Oral Interview*	Newbury House, New York, NY	pictures/judged on content appropriateness and structural accuracy
Second Language Oral Production Examination (SLOPE)*	Alemany Press, San Francisco, CA	pictures/performance on specific grammatical structures
Speaking Proficiency in English Assessment Kit (SPEAK)*	Educational Testing Service, Princeton, NJ	pictures and written material/ comprehensibility in terms of fluency, pronunciation, vocabulary, grammar
Test of Spoken English (TSE)*	Educational Testing Service, Princeton, NJ	written and recorded material/ comprehensibility in terms of pronunciation, fluency, and grammar

*Test is commercially available.

cific linguistic skill contribute to or detract from the ability to accomplish the task?

Again, it is necessary for the instructor to think in terms of the objectives for a particular course and a particular activity, and to gear methods of evaluation to these objectives. For example, a course for international teaching assistants with the goal of improving English in academic contexts would probably evaluate the student's performance in simulated activities (delivering a lecture, leading a discussion), whereas a more general oral skills course in conversation might choose to focus on the learner's progress in interactive skills and participation. Once the appropriate tasks for evaluation have been chosen, suitable rating scales can be designed or selected. We urge the teacher to consider alternative methods of assessing oral performance before resorting to the more traditional and perhaps less communicative approaches to measuring oral proficiency (discussed above), where specific linguistic "skills" such as grammar and vocabulary are measured as discrete components. For a thorough discussion of methods for testing spoken language, see Underhill (1987).

CONCLUSION

In this chapter we have mentioned some of the important features of a communicative component in a language class, and we have discussed various communicative activities that work toward the goal of oral fluency in ESL learners. At various points we have mentioned using other skill-based activities as a preliminary for, or as a follow-up to, oral activities. However, since multiskills classes appear to be more common than courses whose sole focus is the speaking skill, it should be emphasized that speaking can be easily and usefully taught in conjunction with the other traditional skills of listening, reading, and writing.

None of us speaks in a vacuum; we speak with the purpose of conveying information to our listeners. While an activity such as a speech is a speaking opportunity for one, it is a listening activity for the rest of the class. Peer evaluation is one possibility which exploits this dual communication situation.

Speaking can be easily integrated into reading and writing assignments as well by having students do the following: collaborate in brainstorming about composition topics, discuss reading comprehension questions, assist each other in guessing vocabulary items in the context of a reading passage, pool information on readings in order to write summaries or prepare for a composition, evaluate each other's compositions in a peer-evaluation format.

We have also found that spoken and written versions of a text provide a starting point for many interesting activities. Since one of the important components of communicative competence is an awareness of the differences between formal and informal language, and when one is preferred over the other, such texts provide ideal material for authentic language analysis. Students can produce an oral text, transcribe it, and then modify it appropriately to produce an acceptable written version of the text. It would also be possible to approach this activity in reverse: students would write a text and then give a speech on that topic, noting how the language changes in the spoken context. It is advisable, of course, to practice the modification process on some prepared texts or, again, to model the activity with spoken and written texts prepared by a native speaker.

Finally, it should be emphasized that the effective teacher will pick and choose activities with many criteria in mind. The movement toward the communicatively oriented syllabus in the ESL classroom has been so complete and, at times, unquestioned that some teachers and methodologists now are concerned that language skills associated with accuracy (such as pronunciation and grammar) are being unprofitably overlooked, and are deserving of more attention. There may, then, be a place in the future curriculum for more structured speaking tasks or for oral communication activities which focus on form, such as those which require transcription of orally produced language and follow-up accuracy activities. It is up to the instructor to decide, using the needs and career or educational objectives of the students as a guide.

DISCUSSION QUESTIONS

1. Do you agree with the argument that ignoring accuracy in the early stages of language acquisition can lead to fossilization? Why do some teachers and researchers say that a linguistic base is necessary?

2. Consider the Doughty and Pica study on teacher-centered versus learner-centered classrooms. What are specific features that you would expect to find in each environment? How can teachers take the focus off themselves and shift it to the students?

3. Why do most speaking tests evaluate language in discrete areas rather than holistically?

4. What are some ways that beginning ESL students, new to an English-speaking country, might differ from advanced students who have been living in the English-speaking country for several years? What would the considerations be in designing syllabi for two such different groups?

5. Reflect on a foreign language course that you have taken. Was the speaking skill addressed at all, or did you concentrate on other skills? Were communicative activities used? What activities might have improved the course in terms of your speaking skills?

6. In what ways might drills, or "manipulative" activities, be beneficial for beginning learners?

7. For the teacher of a speaking course, what are the advantages and disadvantages of using group activities rather than individual activities?

SUGGESTED ACTIVITIES

1. Record a short conversation and transcribe a small section (one to two minutes) of it. Note all the disfluencies, repetitions, etc. Use the transcript to develop a lesson on the nature of unrehearsed speech.

2. The students in your beginning-level university ESL class, composed entirely of Asians, are having trouble interrupting, asking for clarification, and requesting repetition in their other university classes. What are some possible activities that could help alleviate these problems? For each of these activities, decide how you would evaluate students' performance.

3. Using questionnaires, interviews, and/or observations, carry out an analysis of the speaking needs of an ESL class to which you have access. Consider the makeup of the class, the level, the needs of the students outside of the classroom, etc. Develop a syllabus based on these needs.

4. Imagine that you are teaching a multiskills course where one of the stated objectives is "to assist students in exploring the difference between spoken and written discourse." Keeping the goals of a communicative classroom in mind, design an activity to address this objective.

5. You are assigned to teach "survival English" to a group of refugees who reportedly don't speak a word of English. How would you begin? Give some examples of objectives and lessons for the first three or four classes.

SUGGESTIONS FOR FURTHER READING

Brumfit, C. (1984)
Communicative Methodology in Language Teaching—The Roles of Fluency and Accuracy. Cambridge: Cambridge University Press.

An overview of language teaching methodology, which attempts to lay out the communicative paradigm in practical terms and explores the fluency-accuracy distinction.

Canale, M., and M. Swain (1980)
Theoretical bases of communicative approaches to second language teaching and testing. *Applied Linguistics*, *1*, 1–47.

One of the early "classic" articles on communicative competence, on which so many goals, methods, and activities are based.

Celce-Murcia, M., and S. Hilles (1988)
Techniques and Resources in Teaching Grammar. New York: Oxford University Press.

For a multitude of techniques and activities, many using oral skills, that encourage communicative teaching of grammar.

Keller, E., and S. T. Warner (1979)
Gambits 1–3. Hull, Canada: Canadian Government Publishing Centre.

One of the earlier texts organized by means of speaking strategies; also a good example of a text and activities which could be used as a basis for a course.

Underhill, N. (1987)
Testing Spoken Language. Cambridge: Cambridge University Press.

A practical, easy-to-read guide which presents over 50 test techniques that can easily be adapted for classroom use.

Teaching Pronunciation[1]

Marianne Celce-Murcia and Janet M. Goodwin

INTRODUCTION

There have been many differences of opinion over the years in the language teaching profession about the value of teaching pronunciation and about how best to teach it. Teachers using grammar-translation and reading-based approaches have considered pronunciation irrelevant. In direct approaches pronunciation is very important, but the methodology is primitive: The teacher is ideally a native or near-native speaker of the target language who presents pronunciation inductively and corrects via modeling (listen and imitate me as best you can). For practitioners of the audiolingual approach, pronunciation is also very important. In fact, correct pronunciation is seen as a prerequisite to developing the speaking skill. As in direct approaches, the teacher models (listen and repeat); however, the teacher now has, as an additional tool, the structurally based minimal pair drill, in which lists such as the following are used in many different ways to practice sound discrimination as well as oral production:

/i/	vs.	/iy/
hit		heat
bin		bean
list		least

/l/	vs.	/r/	
lice		rice	
low		row	
lack		rack	etc.

This tool reached its most sophisticated and usable form in the contextualized minimal pair drills of Bowen (1972, 1975), which we discuss below in the section called Practice.

The cognitive code approach de-emphasized pronunciation in favor of grammar and vocabulary because the conventional wisdom of the late 1960s and early 1970s (see Scovel, 1969) held that nativelike pronunciation could not be taught. And, by extension, many practitioners argued that pronunciation should not be taught at all because there were many other more learnable objectives.

More recently, however, the widespread adoption of communicative approaches to language teaching has brought renewed urgency to the teaching of pronunciation, since at least one empirical study suggests that there is a threshold level of pronunciation in English such that if a given nonnative speaker's pronunciation falls below this level, he or she will not be able to communicate orally no matter how good his or her control of English grammar and vocabulary might be (Hinofotis & Bailey, 1980).

As Morley points out (1987b, Preface, p. 2), there are at least four groups of learners who need assistance with pronunciation to improve their oral communication:

1. *Foreign teaching assistants—and sometimes even foreign faculty—in colleges and universities in English-speaking countries;*
2. *Foreign-born technical, business, and professional employees in business and industry in English-speaking countries;*
3. *Refugees (adult and adolescent) in resettlement and vocational training programs wishing to relocate in English-speaking countries;*
4. *International business people who need to use English as their working lingua franca.*

The goal of teaching pronunciation to such learners is not necessarily to make them sound like native speakers of English. With the exception of a few highly gifted and motivated individuals, such a goal is quite unrealistic. The more modest and realistic goal that we have in mind is that of enabling learners to get above the threshold level so that the quality of their pronunciation will not detract significantly from their ability to communicate.

What are the variables that seem to impede or enhance the acquisition of a reasonable pronunciation in English? Kenworthy (1987, pp. 4–8) provides a useful inventory. For each of her six factors we offer our own brief elaboration:

1. *The learner's native language.* Mother-tongue transfer is generally more systematic, pervasive, and persistent in the area of pronunciation (the foreign accent) than it is in grammar or lexicon. This makes it important for teachers to know something about the sound system of the language(s) that their learners speak in order to anticipate problems and understand the source of errors. This information, in turn, can be made available to the learner, if appropriate. Fortunately, there are several sources, such as Avery and Ehrlich (1987), Kenworthy (1987), and Swan and Smith (1987), where such information is available—at least on the better known languages.

2. *The learner's age.* The younger the age when the learner begins to acquire English, the better the learner's pronunciation. In fact, complete mastery of English before age 12 generally results in accent-free speech, whereas acquisition after age 15 virtually guarantees some degree of accentedness in speech.

3. *The learner's exposure.* Exposure to the target language can refer to both the length of time and the intensity of the exposure over time. Generally speaking, the more time spent on learning the spoken language, the better the pronunciation. Exposure can also refer to quality; learners exposed to better English-speaking models and/or better explanations of the English sound system generally make more progress than learners with poor-quality models and inadequate information.

4. *The learner's innate phonetic ability.* Some people simply have more skill at or aptitude for imitating and producing sounds and sound patterns that are new to them. All other things equal, such learners will achieve a better pronunciation than will those learners with lesser aptitude.

5. *The learner's attitude and sense of identity.* The attitude the learner has toward the target language and its speakers may affect his or her pronunciation (the more favorable the attitude, the better the pronunciation, for the highly motivated learner is not opposed to sounding like the target speakers). Likewise, the learners' personality and sense of their own identity will also play a role; for example, extremely authoritarian, chauvinistic learners may (perhaps unconsciously) refuse to modify their pronunciation at all when speaking English.

6. *The learner's motivation and concern for good pronunciation.* This factor is of greatest importance in pronunciation instruction; if the learner's motivation to improve is strong and if the investment of time and effort (genuine not feigned) is great, there will be improvement.

CONTENT[2]

What exactly are the pronunciation features that the ESL teacher should cover? First, you should consider what type of ESL/EFL course you are teaching. Is it four skills, oral communication, exclusively pronunciation, or something else? The extent of pronunciation instruction will vary according to the time available and the focus of the course.

The attention paid to structured learning of pronunciation rules depends both on the level of the student and on the amount of time available for pronunciation in the course. It should be stressed that pronunciation can and should be taught at *every* level of ESL instruction. The applicability and simplicity of certain general rules offers the beginning learner in particular a welcome pattern and aid. Moreover, pronunciation instruction lends itself to integration with almost any type of activity.

For a course focusing on pronunciation at a more advanced level, it is useful to present a diagram of the organs of speech, the phonetic alphabet, the consonant chart, and the vowel chart (see Appendix). It would be quite difficult to teach pronunciation very thoroughly without a common system of transcription. As students are often so much more influenced by spelling than by actual aural input, they are typically amazed at phonetic transcriptions ("You mean, *that's* how it's pronounced?"). The organs of speech diagram illustrates the place of articulation for both consonants and vowels, and although not all students or sounds respond well to such articulatory explanations, it can be quite productive for others. In addition to place of articulation, the consonant chart allows us to address the manner of articulation and voicing. Vowels, on the other hand, are elusive for several reasons: the articulation is generally not visible, the sound/spelling correspondence for vowels is so much more varied than for consonants, and vowel quality varies a great deal from dialect to dialect. Nonetheless, the vowel chart is an aid in differentiating the sounds, and the use of colors to represent the vowels (as in the Silent Way) can bypass the sound/spelling difficulties.

What rules are relatively simple yet productive, and how can we integrate these into the syllabus? The importance of -*ed* and -*s* endings certainly comes to mind, especially at the early stages when habits are being formed. The teacher may elicit the rules for the three phonemic representations of -*ed* and of -*s* by providing numerous examples of each, but it is necessary for the students to have a clear understanding of the voiced/voiceless distinction beforehand. Just as the discussion of these endings naturally combines with structural practice in regular past tense, possessives, plurals, and third-person singular present, a discussion of intonation patterns would ideally accompany exercises in question-formation: wh- questions, yes/no questions, tag questions, alternative questions, among others.

Similarly, the rules for stress placement when adding suffixes could be integrated with vocabulary study of word families (e.g., hístory-histórical). When teaching phrasal verbs, the frequency of voiced intervocalic (or flapped) /t/ suggests an opportunity to explain the rules for its use in American English (e.g., put it on, set it up, cut it out).

Listening comprehension exercises which involve rapid speech will be incomprehensible to learners who have no understanding of the rules for reduced speech and blending. In fact, better listening comprehension is a good reason for teaching pronunciation rules to our students right from the start.

As an additional note, students often find it quite beneficial to read a brief summary of phonological contrasts between their native language and English. This often sparks an awareness of where potential difficulties lie and which rules will ultimately be most productive to them personally.

In determining pronunciation objectives for an ESL/EFL course, the teacher must be well acquainted with the English sound system. This system consists of the English vowel and consonant sounds (see Appendix) and their possible combinations, as well as the modifications the sounds can undergo in various contexts. It also consists of the rhythms of English words and phrases—English is a stress-timed language (many languages are syllable-timed)—and the use of pitch to reinforce or signal meaning, i.e., intonation. The appendix gives only the briefest overview of the English sound system. For further information, the ESL professional should consult sources such as Bowen (1975), Catford (1987), and Prator and Robinett (1985), or better yet, take a course in English phonetics as preparation for teaching pronunciation.

PRACTICE

Before making our own suggestions about teaching pronunciation to nonnative learners, it would perhaps be useful to review the specific techniques that have been proposed and used in earlier approaches and in most of the materials currently on the market.

First, there is the "listen and imitate/ repeat" technique, which was used in direct approaches and also the audiolingual approach. Second, there are tongue-twisters like "She sells sea shells by the seashore," which are a feature of the speech correction literature designed for improving the articulation or enunciation of native English speakers. Third, there are the minimal pairs we have already mentioned and illustrated above. Somewhere between the technique of using lists of words as minimal pairs and Bowen's contextualization technique, there are two kinds of widely used sentence-based drills for practicing minimal pairs:

> syntagmatic: Don't *sit* on that *seat*.
> (within the same sentence)
> paradigmatic: Don't (slip/sleep) on the floor. (in two contrasting sentences)

A fourth technique that is suggested by first language acquisition research is the developmental approximation drill, where the developmental sequence followed by most L1 children becomes a way to get nonnative

speakers to produce a problematic sound or sound quality:

> /w/---------->/r/   /y/--------->/l/
> wed--------->red   yet--------->let

The fifth technique that is widespread is the drilling of vowel shifts and stress shifts, something that was given impetus by the early work in generative phonology (Chomsky & Halle, 1968) and exemplified in the work of Dickerson (1975) and Dickerson and Finney (1978):

> *vowel shift:*   /ay/   /ɪ/
>   bible------------->biblical
> *stress shift:* phótograph------>photógraphy

While useful on a limited, individual basis for purposes of correction and drill, none of these exercise types is truly compatible with the communicative approach to language teaching or will directly meet the needs of the groups of learners we specified in the introduction. What we have had to do, therefore, is to apply the most useful and usable of the old techniques along with some new and innovative exercises suggested in some of the recent work on teaching pronunciation. In addition, we have developed some of our own ideas from our experiences with teaching pronunciation to nonnative speakers of English.

Contextualized Exercises and Drills

Bowen's Technique

Bowen was one of the first to stress the importance of teaching pronunciation in meaningful contexts. His argument that learners may control a feature when focusing on form but lose it once they focus on the meaning of the message is clear in all aspects of language instruction. The type of exercises he devised set up a contextualized situation in which the learner must *distinguish* the correct form aurally in order to provide the correct response or *produce* the correct form in order to elicit the correct response. The exercise may involve a sound contrast:

This pen leaks.
  Then don't write with it.
This pan leaks.
  Then don't cook with it.

or even a stress or intonation contrast:

Where can I buy còld créam?
  At the dairy.
Where can I buy cóld crèam?
  At the drugstore.
              (Bowen, 1972)

In this type of activity, the teacher may provide the stimulus, with the class or individual students giving the rejoinder. Bowen offers another variation, however, which lets the students play both parts. The following example contrasts voiced and voiceless final consonants. The teacher (or a student) first draws a picture of a cab on one side of the board and a cap on the other. Standing in the center, the teacher recites the following sentences in varying order with students pointing to which they hear:

He's gone to get a cab.   He's gone to get a cap.

It is evident by how quickly and how uniformly the students point whether or not they can hear the difference easily. Once students are generally able to differentiate, the class should agree on two gestures to represent the two sentences (often this particular example elicits a touching of the head and the steering of a wheel). The teacher then moves to the back of the room and calls a volunteer to the front. Using two cards with the simple drawings, the teacher cues the volunteer to produce one of the two sentences. The class then signals comprehension by performing one of the agreed-upon gestures. Thus, it is clear to the speakers whether or not they are being understood. Large classes may be divided into two or three groups to perform the same activity. Easily sketchable contrasts of this type include: eyes/ice, sang/sank, mob/mop, five/fife, bag/back. Bowen (1975) offers a

wealth of contrasting sentences to choose from.

Another example which conveys to students how much pronunciation affects meaning involves intonation and stress. Students receive a handout with multiple choice items such as the following:

What do you think?
  a. *I already know what he thinks.*
  b. *Should we do it or not?*
  c. *I'm sorry, I didn't hear what you said.*
Depending on intonation and stress, the sentence elicits a different communicative response:

a. <u>What do</u> you think?
b. <u>What do you think?</u>
c. <u>What do you think?</u>

As a variation on this exercise, the teacher might write a sentence on the board such as *Mary's dress was blue.* Dividing the class into four groups, the teacher assigns the first group the task of interpreting this sentence when the stress is on *Mary's*, the second group with the stress on *dress*, and so on. Students may either describe the situation in which such an utterance makes sense or create a question which would elicit that particular response, e.g.:

Q: *Was Mary's prom dress blue?*
A: *Mary's dress wás blue . . . (but now she's dyed it purple)*

The basic principle of creating contextualized exercises is to find a context in which the linguistic feature (in this case, phonetic feature) occurs frequently and to use it as the basis of the exercise. Take, for example, the syllabic /n̩/; it occurs frequently in the negative modal perfect (e.g., couldn't have, shouldn't have,). Thus, a pair exercise was devised in which one partner reads a situation aloud and the other partner responds using "shouldn't have" /šʊdn̩əv/ or "couldn't have" /kʊdn̩əv/ (the negative modal perfect also illustrates reduced speech where the /t/ of *not* and the /h/ of *have* are dropped). The following are examples which should be modified to reflect information about your students:

Partner A reads: Bob ate ten hot dogs at the baseball game and now he's sick.
Partner B responds: ("He shouldn't have eaten so many.")
Partner B reads: My birthday's today and I haven't received a card from my mother. Did she forget?
Partner A responds: ("She couldn't have forgotten.")

Chain Drills

Memory chain drills can be used for a variety of pronunciation objectives. A class introduction chain drill for practicing *-s* endings is:

{My/His/Her} name's _____
and {I/he/she} like (s) to _____.

The teacher or a selected student begins the drill and then each subsequent student repeats all the introductions that came before him and adds a personal one for himself. If the class is too large, this activity can be done in smaller circles.

A step beyond the chain drill is the chain story. For this activity, each group of four or five students receives 8 to 12 words on separate cards which are used to create a story to tell to the rest of the class. The choice of words depends on the pronunciation focus: regular verbs in past tense, plurals, minimal pairs with r/l (e.g., "long," "pirate," "deal," "collect"), vowel contrasts, stress differences (e.g., appropriate-*adjective*, record-*verb*, permit-*noun*, graduate-*verb*, suspect-*noun*). As a listening task for the other groups, distribute a complete list of all possible words for all the stories in scrambled order and have each student mark the words that come up in a particular group's story (they can also note whether they were pronounced correctly!). Have groups compare what words they checked and ask one group to use the words checked to retell the story (further practice of

the pronunciation feature being focused on). The original storytellers can judge if it is accurate or not.

Recitation

For practicing rhythm, stress, intonation, reduced speech, and blending, nothing seems to motivate ESL students quite like Carolyn Graham's *Jazz Chants* (1978). They can even be personalized to fit the students in the class, e.g.:

What's your name and where are you from?
What's your name and where are you from?
    My name is Mei and I'm from Taiwan.
    My name is Mei and I'm from Taiwan.
Been here long?
Been here long?
    Not too long. Just a few months.
    Not too long. Just a few months.

Some teachers may hesitate to snap their fingers and recite these catchy verses, yet these chants work successfully with all ages, backgrounds, and proficiency levels. The original *Jazz Chants*, as well as Graham's *Small Talk* (1986), also provide useful structures and idioms.

Dialogs are a natural source for pronunciation practice since they are used frequently for reading aloud or drill. However, since they often highlight a function, situation, or structure, the essential elements of intonation and stress are often overlooked. Clifford Prator shared the following dialogue as an illustration of the importance of intonation:

A. I've just read a book.
B: What?

Ask students to read it aloud as many different ways as they can think of. Depending on the intonation, B's "What?" might mean:

What did you say? OR
What book was it? OR
What! You actually read a book?

This variety of interpretation will not occur in every dialog, but it serves to remind both teacher and student that intonation needs to be brought to conscious awareness. Below are some steps the teacher can follow when working with a dialog:

1. Have students listen and mark stressed words (as an additional clue, you may want to tell students how many words are stressed in each line).
2. Have students mark each line with an intonation contour (e.g., rise, fall, rise-fall).
3. Read certain lines with various intonations and ask the students to decide which mood is being expressed (e.g., anger, sadness, amazement).
4. Ask students to read or act out the entire dialog in one particular mood and to note the variations in intonation patterns.

Poems, such as Tennyson's "Break, Break, Break," highlight the stress-timed quality of English rhythm. Vowel reduction, which does not occur in syllable-timed languages, such as Spanish, can also be exploited through poetry. Limericks, because of their humor and brevity, are enjoyable as well.

For some learners a very effective individual strategy is silent (or vocalized) shadowing, whereby the learners move their mouths and "visualize" themselves speaking simultaneously with a recorded native speaker. The learner produces all sounds in imitation of the native speaker—often with a script to read—including stress, intonation, and even voice quality. Students should be encouraged to try this, and if it seems productive, the teacher should make arrangements for such practice in the language lab or with a cassette recorder in or out of class. For all pronunciation students such an activity can help focus attention on important cues.

Pictures/Diagrams/Slides

Many kinds of drawings can be used for pronunciation practice. Stick figures can easily be drawn to elicit a story about "Peter's Day." This focuses on blending and voiced intervocalic (flapped) /t/ (not to mention phrasal verbs and past tense):

Peter shut off the alarm, got up, lit a cigarette, put on his hat, got on the bus, and got off downtown where he works.

Don't worry if the drawings are less than artistic. Students seem to have as much fun trying to figure out what we have drawn as they do trying to find the words to describe it.

Pictures or drawings of objects that begin with a vowel sound can be used to practice vowel-to-vowel or consonant-to-vowel blending (as well as recycling the -s endings):

two ⁀ʷ apples
three ⁀ʸ elephants
four ⁀ʳ eggs
six ⁀ˢ oranges

As Celce-Murcia (1987) points out, charts and diagrams can be very useful for establishing context for certain groups of sounds. A body-parts diagram offers lots of /r/ and /l/ practice: hair, elbow, lips, finger, shoulder, arms, legs, heel, throat, ear, forehead, knuckle. A family tree can contain a great deal of practice with words containing /θ/, /ð/, /s/, and /z/, as well as words with these sounds in consonant clusters:

Who is Martha's brother? Jonathan.
Beth's mother's name is Catherine.

An appointment calendar can elicit all kinds of contexts for /θ/ and /r/ (particularly in ordinals):

What's Janet going to do on Friday, the thirteenth?
Where will she be on Saturday, April 24th?

This works well as an information-gap exercise in which each partner has different information to share. For university students, a map of the campus, or—even better—slides, is informative and will help them learn to pronounce difficult names that they need to use frequently—e.g., University Research Library (URL), Career Placement Center, Engineering Library, the Graduate Dormitory. For nonuniversity students, a map of the neighborhood or city they are in will provide practice both in giving directions and in pronouncing useful street or building names.

Classification Activities

One type of problem-solving group activity is that of classification. This is one way of introducing a concept and having students generate the rules for categorization or simply a way for them to process and organize what they already know. The teacher provides a classification system, usually consisting of one example or model for each category. Then, different packets of cards with additional words or phrases are distributed to each group and they must decide in which category each card belongs. For example, for regular past -*ed* endings, the teacher writes at the top of three columns on the blackboard:

/əd/	/d/	/t/
added	moved	baked

The teacher first elicits how the -*ed* ending is pronounced in each case (/əd/, /d/, /t/) and writes this above the underlined endings. Then, cards with regular past-tense verbs are distributed evenly among the groups (e.g., laughed, studied, acted, cared). Each group is then responsible for classifying each word and then copying it into the proper columns on the board. (Don't have them write on the cards; save them for future classes!) The class as a whole then looks at each column, first checking to see that all are in agreement about the placement of each word and then trying to generate a rule ("What do all these verbs have in common?") for each ending. As stated previously, understanding these rules depends on an understanding of the voiced/voiceless consonant distinction.

This type of classification activity can also work for vowels using one key word for each stressed vowel. We have used the following words to teach vowel recognition in a color-coding system; these color words each contain the vowel they represent):

/iy/	/ɪ/	/ey/	/ɛ/	/æ/	/a/	/ɔ/	/ow/
green	pink	gray	red	black	aqua	mauve	gold

/ʊ/	/uw/	/ʌ/	/ɜʳ/	/ay/	/aw/	/oy/
soot	blue	rust	purple	white	brown	oil

For example, we have used flash cards with words or phrases where the stressed vowels are replaced by a colored box (only consonants and unstressed vowels are written out) and the students guess and practice the word or phrase, e.g.:

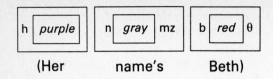

(Her   name's   Beth)

The teacher can build up such vowel recognition and production exercises beginning with single words, then phrases or sentences, then dialogs.

Students can also classify multisyllabic words according to stress patterns:

ópen   upón   éducàte   spaghétti   ùnderstánd

Dictation

It is also possible to employ a dictation with gaps as a means of making students aware of reduced speech. In the following dialog (read on tape or by the teacher), the underlined word or words are omitted from the student text and must be filled in:

A: Have *you* seen Tom?
B: *He's* not here.
A: Where *did he* go?
B: I *don't* know.
A: Where *do you* think *he* went?
B: How *would* I know?
    He's *been* gone *for a* week.

Donna Brinton shared the following dictation exercise in which students receive a text with some word endings and unstressed words left out for them to provide, e.g.:

Students see:

Even though kinesic is a relative young science, anthropologist are able offer variety of observation about human gesture and other body movement.

Teacher reads:

Even though kinesics is a relatively young science, anthropologists are able to offer a variety of observations about human gestures and other body movements.

In addition to practicing listening comprehension, the above activity helps learners to edit their compositions more effectively since they are now focusing on features that they often leave out in their writing.

Communicative Activities

Activities which are performance-oriented—such as interviews, speeches, role plays, drama scenes, and debates—lend themselves to either audiotaping or videotaping. Although this is not feasible for every activity done in class, it is often the only means we have for promoting self-correction. It gives the learner an opportunity to focus on *meaning* during the communicative activity and to focus on *form* during the replay. The kind of feedback students regularly receive on their written competence is sometimes nonexistent with regard to their spoken English. The following activities are useful for any kind of oral practice, not just for pronunciation alone.

Interviews

Students often interview each other the first day of class as an introductory activity. The following variation was developed to include some personal choice and to provide a note-taking task for the rest of the class.

One pair at a time comes up front to interview each other about four class-chosen topics (e.g., family, hobbies, future) while the remainder of the class writes abbreviated notes about each reply. If students have any gaps at the end of the activity, they can ask one another for the information. However, it's more stimulating if Yong doesn't ask Maria about her own answers; rather Yong should ask Mohamed about Maria's answer, which she can then verify. This allows for a great deal of question formation and is an interesting and informative way to practice the intonation patterns for questions. This personal information, which students now have in written form, can also be useful for many other language activities. In an advanced pronunciation course where the phonetic alphabet is taught, the teacher can devise a sentence description of each student (without the name) using the information from this grid, e.g.:

/ðɪsmæθstuwdn̩tpleyztɛnɪs/

Each group then tries to "guess the student" in each description, referring back to their own notes. The individualized, personal, and problem-solving aspects of this activity make even the potential drudgery of learning the phonetic alphabet highly motivating to the students.

Speeches

Many ESL texts give topics for oral presentations. Anything related to the current unit of your course will do as long as the speaker feels comfortable and knowledgeable, and the listeners are interested. The class may wish to negotiate topics; e.g., each student brings in three topics he or she would be willing to talk about and the class votes on which one they would most like to hear about. Each individual should try to monitor for one particular phonetic feature in each speech—whatever they need to work on most: blending, intonation, stress, individual sounds. As will be discussed in the next section on feedback, the class should ideally fill out a brief form on their reaction to the speaker *with particular attention to the feature the speaker has chosen to focus on* so that he or she receives input from the audience as a whole, not just the "teacher-audience."

Role-Playing and Dramatization

Role plays and drama scenes are always fun and are an ideal vehicle for practicing pronunciation. They are fully contextualized, include gestures and body language, and provide a multitude of opportunities for practicing natural speech. It seems that the taking on of a new identity releases certain students from their inhibitions and allows them to overcome constraints that might affect their pronunciation.

Individualized practice

The above activities take place during classroom instruction. In addition to these, there are a number of out-of-class activities which can help students improve their pronunciation in a more individualized way.

Audiotaped Dialog Journals

The value of written dialogue journals in ESL classrooms is well documented (Kreeft-Peyton, 1987; Staton, 1983). The same benefits can be applied to pronunciation using audiotape as the medium of communication. Both student production and teacher feedback is individualized. The conversation partner in most cases is the teacher—or a native English-speaking aide or tutor; however, it can be challenging and effective to have students converse with a native speaker on tape with whom they have no face-to-face contact. The weekly entries can combine both guided practice (e.g., exercises read on tape) and free conversation. In this context, students may redo class exercises, choose field-specific texts or terminology to practice, ask questions about class material, or request specific correction or advice. Since nothing should be erased as these conversations progress, they provide a record of problems as well as improvement. The value of audiotaped dialog journals for pronunciation is to be found in the areas of self-correction, reviewing correction, locating systematic errors, student-directed learning, and measuring progress over time (Goodwin, 1988).

Language Laboratory

Another important source of individualized pronunciation practice is the language laboratory. Either in class with the teacher monitoring or out of class as homework, lab exercises are beneficial. The rationale for language lab use in teaching pronunciation is evident; although students have no external feedback if working on their own, the use of the lab promotes autonomy in our students as they learn to monitor their *own* errors by comparing their performance against that of the model. Thus, laboratory practice is as important for the ear as it is for the mouth.

An ideal situation is to have copies of pronunciation/listening texts in the lab which can be checked out by the student along with the corresponding tapes. Several of the current texts have answer keys in the back which allow students to check their work independently. Teachers should be aware of the lab possibilities at their school or institution and encourage the school's purchase of one copy of the textbook to accompany each tape series. Most tapes are useless without the book, and there are many useful textbooks beyond the one the teacher may have chosen as the class text.

Tutoring

Tutoring services for individual students are a luxury not every institution can offer. If, however, there is an academic tutoring center or willing native speakers available, students have an opportunity for individual tutoring. Sources include ESL teachers-in-training, international clubs, conversational exchange programs, undergraduate work-study students in linguistics, education or foreign languages, etc.

How to tutor someone in pronunciation is not self-evident, and without training by the class instructor, tutors will not be maximally effective. Ideally, tutors should have experience using phonetic transcription and working with nonnative speakers. The teacher should brief the tutor(s) on diagnosed student difficulties and offer suggestions for activities and exercises. One of the most successful techniques is for the tutor and tutee to record a short conversation or exercise at the beginning of the session and then to re-play it, allowing the tutee to self-monitor to the extent possible before the tutor adds some additional comments about areas of difficulty. These sessions also allow students to follow their own agenda, whether it be to practice for next week's oral report in history class, a job interview, an important phone call, or small talk at parties. Students should be en-

couraged to make notes of instances when their speech was misunderstood and to try to figure out with their tutors what was wrong with the way they said it.

IMPLEMENTATION

Needs Assessment

As Wong (1987) points out, at the beginning of a pronunciation class, multidimensional assessment of each learner is highly desirable if the teacher wishes to establish relevant priorities. To this end, the following tools may be useful:

1. *Questionnaire.* What are the learner's attitudes about pronunciation? What are his motivations for improvement, if any? Does the learner have any background in phonetics? Does the learner know what some of his/her major problems are? When and how does the learner prefer to be corrected? (in class? privately?)

2. *Listening discrimination/comprehension tests.* Which sounds can the learner distinguish easily? Which are problematic? Contextualized multiple-choice items such as the following can help answer these questions (choices can be textual, pictorial, or both, depending on the level and background of the learner):

1. The _____ leaks.
   a. *pen*   b. *pan*
2. There's something wrong with my
   _____.
   a. *bag*   b. *back*

A good source of such discrimination exercises is Bowen (1975). How good is the learner's overall listening comprehension? Some multiple-choice items such as the following might be useful; however, a dictation would probably provide a better holistic measure if the learners are literate.

1. *John has _____ cassettes.*
   a. *14*   b. *40*
2. *The _____ beautifully.*
   a. *girls sing*   b. *girl sings*
3. *I wonder why they _____ do that.*
   a. *can*   b. *can't*

3. *Production sample.* On a tape recording, what aspects of the learner's English sounds, stress, intonation, and linking are most in need of improvement? To answer these questions, a tool such as Prator and Robinett's (1985) Diagnostic Passage and Accent Inventory, which are part of the book, can be very useful. Students read the specially constructed diagnostic passage aloud while it is recorded, and teachers later analyze the recording using the Accent Inventory (i.e., a checklist). We recommend that in addition to the diagnostic passage, teachers also elicit a spontaneous speech sample from each student to double-check problematic areas and to be certain that problems noted in analyzing the recorded passage are not artifacts of reading aloud.

Information from these three sources will allow the teacher to develop a systematic program for the class as a whole (class time for common problems and common background training—e.g., the phonetic alphabet), as well as for groups (exercises for three to five students with the same problems) and for each individual student (problems for practice in tutorials or in the lab). Information from these three sources also constitute the baseline data that allow the teacher to assess the progress of the class as a whole and to evaluate the progress of each student both informally and formally (e.g., for grading).

Feedback and Correction

One of the most important issues in pronunciation instruction is how to give effective feedback. Some of the techniques discussed under "Practice" provide opportunities for feedback by the teacher, tutor, peers, and the students themselves. The question is what aspects of a student's pronunciation to correct and how to do this successfully.

Who is to provide the feedback students need? Self-correction is the most valuable since it encourages the student to be autonomous. Yet how can we guide students to self-correct? Using audio-or videotape, we can have them both locate and correct errors. This is done most effectively with a self-evaluation form to be filled out when relistening to the tape.

As mentioned earlier, it is also useful to have students read a brief contrastive analysis of their language and English to make them aware of potential difficulties and to let them know that the kinds of errors they make are not unusual for native speakers of their language. If this contrastive information is not available, ask them to imitate an American speaking their native language. This can be a humorous ice-breaker and usually exposes phonetic differences between the two languages.

Peer feedback is also important because students listening for other students' errors will be developing their own monitor and listening awareness. Students may be grouped with peers who have similar difficulties and are tuned into the same errors in their own speech or with peers who have different problems. However, the most successful peer teaching often occurs between students of the same language background, one of whom has mastered the particular feature. Peers may be used as providers of feedback for any oral performance, especially speeches, interviews, debates, or roleplays. The type of evaluation sheet may differ from activity to activity, but students can be quite adept at giving constructive feedback, even if it consists only of naming one area that needs improvement (with examples).

As the final step, teacher feedback is indispensable in making students aware of errors that they are as yet unable to distinguish. Teachers may want to keep a checklist for each student of the various kinds of errors he or she makes and then make decisions about what to work on.

Selecting which pronunciation errors to correct involves the same decisions which apply to other language skills:

1. Does the error cause a breakdown in communication?

2. Is this a recurring pattern or an isolated mistake?
3. Does this error stigmatize the student?
4. Can it be corrected easily?

It is better to focus on a single pattern or error rather than overload the learner with excessive correction. This might include only the feature currently being dealt with in class or that student's specific difficulty, which might be rhythm, word and sentence stress, blending, intonation patterns, final voiced consonants, or similar elements.

After discussing what to correct, the natural question is: how to correct? First, it should be noted that feedback can be quite positive and we should offer encouragment and praise when students are able to distinguish sounds and patterns aurally as well as produce them orally.

One simple technique for students who are unable to hear how their pronunciation differs from the native speaker model is to mimic the student's pronunciation and to contrast it immediately with one's own. In order not to embarrass the student, this technique is suggested for individual conferences or the above-mentioned audiotaped dialog journals.

During class, the teacher may provide either on-the-spot correction or note errors on a sheet for later correction. It is best not to interrupt the speaker but rather to use silent correction techniques for immediate correction. The teacher may have signs or symbols posted in the classroom to point to such as the following:

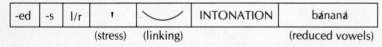

-ed	-s	l/r	'	⌣	INTONATION	bánaná
			(stress)	(linking)		(reduced vowels)

to alert the student to the type of error being made (without pinpointing the error). If the student is unable to locate the error, the teacher may write the student's utterance on the board, e.g.:

I wrote_it yesterday. OR
She hánded it in.

The teacher might also repeat the student's utterance and pause just before the error occurred to give the student an opportunity to complete the utterance and correct the error. If a student is still unable to correct the error, peers should be invited to try. If one repeats the utterance with the correct pronunciation, he or she should be used as the model for the original speaker. Correcting by simply repeating the student's utterance without error is distracting and gives little clue about where the error occurred. For these reasons, explicit nonverbal correction can often be more effective.

Two points should be noted about student performance with regard to pronunciation correction. First, students will more likely be able to correct themselves when they are actively monitoring rather than in free speech. In practical terms, this means that students may still find themselves misunderstood when speaking, but after learning about the English sound system, they will be better equipped to restate themselves intelligibly. The second point to remember is that many pronunciation students, particularly advanced fluent speakers, report that at first their pronunciation seems to get worse rather than better. Since this happens frequently, it is possibly a stage of development that occurs with some learners as they become more self-conscious about the accuracy of their speech.

Evaluation of Classroom Instruction and Materials

The teacher's role in pronunciation instruction can be described—and thus also evaluated—with reference to three phases[3]:

Phase One: *Planning and Preparation*

Phase Two: *Classroom Tasks*
Phase Three: *Assessment*

Each of these phases consists of two or more tasks (or steps) involved in the process of teaching pronunciation. Phase One, *Planning and Preparation,* includes at least five steps:

1. Assess needs of students (as described above under "Needs Assessment," for example).
2. Set priorities (for whole class, groups, individuals).
3. Develop a syllabus or course outline. For teachers doing a multiskills course, the task is one of integrating pronunciation objectives into the overall syllabus or curriculum.
4. Select and/or adapt appropriate existing materials that will address the students' needs (including selection of a textbook, if appropriate).
5. Devise materials for those areas where nothing suitable exists.

During Phase Two, *Classroom Tasks,* the teacher has at least seven objectives to accomplish:

1. Help students recognize and distinguish important features of the English sound system.
2. Help students produce the sounds and rhythms of English that are problematic for them.
3. Where applicable, make students aware of critical features of the English sound system and especially how these features can affect meaning.
4. Provide feedback, i.e., make students aware of what their major problems are, giving contrastive information on English and their native language(s) where applicable and possible.
5. Ensure that sufficient practice is provided in each of the following:
   a. Recognizing the sound or feature in context.
   b. Producing the sound or feature when attention is focused on pronunciation.
   c. Producing the sound or feature when attention is not focused on pronunciation.
6. Provide a logical progression of activities for practice: structured, contextualized, communicative.
7. Provide opportunities for correction in a variety of forms: peer, teacher, and, especially, self-correction.

Phase Three, *Assessment,* includes both *formative* (or ongoing) and *summative* (or final) assessment. In formative assessment the teacher judges student progress and reevaluates needs and priorities, making changes in the syllabus and in planning and preparation whenever new evidence emerges to suggest that change is needed. In summative assessment the teacher rates (or grades) each student in terms of the amount of individual improvement made as well as overall accuracy of pronunciation at the end of the instruction period. Any standards or measures used in grading should have been clearly understood by the students at the beginning of the course.

Teachers of pronunciation can continuously evaluate themselves and their courses in terms of how well these three phases (and each phase's discrete tasks) are being accomplished. Likewise, pronunciation courses and materials (textbooks, tapes, visuals) must be judged, in part, by how easily, and how well, they enable teachers to carry out the three phases discussed above.

NOTES

1. We are most grateful to Clifford Prator, Donna Brinton, and Barbara Baptista for their comments on an earlier version of this chapter. We accept total responsibility, however, for any errors or omissions.

2. The dialect of English represented in the description offered in this chapter is General American English.

3. Kenworthy (1987, pp. 1–2) also offers a list of tasks the ESL/EFL teacher must carry out when teaching pronunciation.

DISCUSSION QUESTIONS

1. Identify three ESL/EFL teaching contexts in which pronunciation is critical (thus requiring some instruction in pronunciation) and three contexts in which pronunciation is irrelevant. Are there teaching contexts where it is difficult to come to a clear-cut decision concerning the teaching of pronunciation?

2. Some teachers of pronunciation feel that suprasegmental phenomena (i.e., stress and intonation) are more important than segmentals (i.e., sounds, combinations of sounds, syllable structure) and should thus receive primary, if not exclusive, attention in a pronunciation class for ESL/EFL students. Do you agree?

3. Not every ESL/EFL learner is motivated to acquire good pronunciation in English. In fact, some learners "resist" making any changes in their speech. What are some explanations for this?

4. Do you agree that a student cannot be said to have mastered a second or foreign language unless s/he controls its spoken form? Why?

5. Think about a foreign language you have learned. Did you find the sound system difficult or easy to master? What techniques did you use as a learner to acquire the pronunciation of this new language?

6. Do you think it is easier to teach pronunciation at the beginning when learners are forming new habits or at a more advanced level when learners have more vocabulary and syntax?

7. Do teachers of pronunciation need to be native speakers? What are the relative merits of having native versus nonnative teachers of pronunciation?

SUGGESTED ACTIVITIES

1. Develop a pronunciation lesson using communicative activities to teach a contrast that may be problematic for the students you are likely to teach (e.g., ɪ/iy, b/v, s/z)

2. Interview and record a nonnative speaker of English in order to identify his/her major pronunciation problems. What will you ask the learner to do so that you will be able to perform a reasonable analysis? How will you determine the degree to which sounds in his/her mother tongue transfer to English?

3. Interview a nonnative speaker of English who has a good accent. Try to find out what strategies s/he used to acquire it.

4. Examine a multiskills ESL/EFL textbook currently on the market. If it has a pronunciation component, analyze it (see chapter by Skierso in this volume). If it doesn't, choose one lesson and integrate one or more pronunciation exercises into it.

5. Discuss three activities or techniques for teaching pronunciation that are discussed in this chapter and give the advantages and disadvantages of each. Can you think of at least one good technique or activity that was not mentioned?

SUGGESTIONS FOR FURTHER READING

The following references are for teachers who seek more background and guidance on the teaching of pronunciation:

Avery, P., and S. Ehrlich, eds. (1987)
The Teaching of Pronunciation: An Introduction for Teachers of English as a Second Language. TESL Talk, 17(1). Ontario, Canada: Ministry of Citizenship and Culture.

Kenworthy, J. (1987)
Teaching English Pronunciation. London: Longman.

Morley, J., ed. (1987)
Current Perspectives on Pronunciation. Washington, DC: TESOL.

Wong, R. (1987)
Teaching Pronunciation: Focus on English Rhythm and Intonation. Englewood Cliffs, NJ: Prentice-Hall Regents.

The following are texts that we suggest you examine if you are looking for a pronunciation textbook to use with a specific group of students. (Teachers may well want to have some of these texts as reference books even if they decide not to use them as textbooks.)

Bowen, J. D. (1975)
Patterns of English Pronunciation. New York: Newbury House.

Gilbert, J. B. (1983)
Clear Speech. New York: Cambridge University Press.

Hecht, E., and G. Ryan (1979)
Survival Pronunciation: Vowel Contrasts. Hayward, CA: Alemany Press.

Morley, J. (1976)
Improving Spoken English. Ann Arbor: University of Michigan Press.

Prator, C. H., and B. W. Robinett (1985)
Manual of American English Pronunciation, 4th ed. New York: Holt, Rinehart & Winston.

The following are additional textbooks with good and complete accompanying tapes that can be used in the language lab to supplement or individualize pronunciation instruction:

Chan, M. (1987)
Phrase by Phrase. Englewood Cliffs, NJ: Prentice-Hall.

English, S. L. (1988)
Say It Clearly. New York: Collier Macmillan.

Graham, C. (1978)
Jazz Chants. New York: Oxford University Press.

Hagen, S. (1988)
Sound Advice. Englewood Cliffs, NJ: Prentice-Hall.

Orion, G. (1988)
Pronouncing American English. New York: Newbury House.

Weinstein, N. (1982)
Whaddaya say? Englewood Cliffs, NJ: Prentice-Hall.

APPENDIX

The English Sound System (General American English)

The English Sound System

English has 24 distinct consonant sounds that we can describe in terms of their place and manner of articulation and in terms of voicing—i.e., whether the vocal cords are vibrating (voiced) or not (voiceless).

In order to represent each distinct consonant and vowel sound unambiguously, we will introduce a few special symbols. Sounds will appear between slanted lines, i.e., / /, to distinguish them from conventional spellings.

Before we present the inventory of English consonant sounds, we would like to elaborate a bit on the phenomenon of voicing

as well as the place and manner of articulation.

One of the best ways to appreciate the difference between voiced and voiceless sounds is to put your fingertips on your Adam's apple and alternate hissing like a snake /sssssssss/ and then buzzing like a bee /zzzzzzzz/. When you buzz like a bee, you can feel the vocal cords vibrate: /z/ is a voiced sound. But when you hiss like a snake, you feel nothing because the vocal cords are still: /s/ is a voiceless sound.

To demonstrate the place of articulation of a consonant sound, teachers use a variety of visual aids. A saggital section diagram of the human speech organs can be a useful aid in describing the points of articulation.

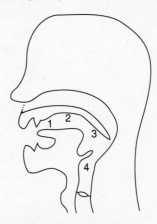

POINTS OF ARTICULATION
BILABIAL-the two lips, e.g., /b/
LABIODENTAL-lower lip, upper teeth, e.g., /v/
DENTAL-inner edges of the teeth, e.g., /θ/
ALVEOLAR-tongue on tooth ridge, e.g., /d/ (1)
PALATAL-tongue on hard palate, e.g., /j/ (2)
VELAR-tongue on soft palate, e.g., /k/ (3)
GLOTTAL-throat passage, e.g., /h/ (4)

The manner of articulation describes what happens to the air stream as the sound is articulated. If the air stream gets blocked completely, we refer to the sound as a *stop* (e.g., /p/, /g/). If the air stream is compressed and passes through a small opening, we call it a *fricative* (e.g., /f/, /z/). If the sound begins like a *stop* and then is released like a *fricative,* we call it an *affricate* (/č/ and /ǰ/). If the air passes through the nose instead of the mouth, we call the sound a *nasal* (e.g., /m/, /n/). If the airstream moves around the tongue in a relatively unobstructed manner, we call the sound a *liquid* (/l/ and /r/). And if the sound is very close to being a vowel, we call it a *glide* (/w/ and /y/).

The English consonant sounds are as follows:

SOUND	EXAMPLES
1. /b/	boy, ca*b*
2. /p/	pie, li*p*
3. /d/	dog, bed
4. /t/	toe, cat
5. /g/	go, beg
6. /k/	cat, back
7. /v/	view, love
8. /f/	fill, life
9. /ð/	the, lathe
10. /θ/	thin, bath
11. /z/	zoo, goes
12. /s/	see, bus
13. /ž/	leisure, beige
14. /š/	shy, dish
15. /h/	his, ahead
16. /č/	cheek, watch
17. /ǰ/	joy, budge
18. /m/	me, seem
19. /n/	no, sun
20. /ŋ/	sing(er)
21. /l/	long, full
22. /r/	run, car
23. /w/	win, away
24. /y/	you, soya

Some teachers of pronunciation like to summarize all of this information in a chart as shown below.

A major problem that learners have with English consonant sounds is the fact that they cluster both initially and finally. In initial position there are many clusters of two consonants and even some with three. With clusters of two, either the first sound is /s/ or the second one is /l/, /r/, /w/, or /y/; in some instances both conditions hold:

TWO: /sn/ snake; /sp/ speak; /sk/ sky; /pl/ play; /pr/ pray; /kw/ quite; /hy/ hue; /py/ pure; etc.

With initial clusters of three, the first sound is always /s/, the second sound is /p/, /t/, or /k/, and the third sound is /l/, /r/, /w/, or /y/:

THREE: /str/ strong; /spl/ splash; /skw/ square; /sky/ skew; etc.

In final position there are even more consonant clusters than in initial position, and these clusters can consist of two, three, or four consonants (clusters of four are generally the result of adding a plural (/s/, /z/) or past tense (/t/, /d/) inflection to a stem):

TWO: /lb/ bulb; /md/ seemed; /rv/ serve; /vz/ loves; etc.
THREE: /rts/ hearts; /ldz/ builds; /sks/ asks; /mpt/ tempt, etc.
FOUR: /mpts/ tempts; /ksts/ texts; /ltst/ waltzed; etc.

Classification of Consonants

Manner of Articulation	Place of Articulation						
	Bi-labial	Labio-dental	Dental	Alveolar	Palatal	Velar	Glottal
Stop	p b			t d		k g	
Fricative		f v	θ ð	s z	š ž		h
Affricate					č ǰ		
Nasal	m			n		ŋ	
Liquid				l	r		
Glide	w				y		

(Voiceless sounds in upper parts of box, voiced sounds in lower.)

The English vowel system—all vowels are voiced—has 14 distinct vowel sounds that occur in stressed one-syllable words. Eleven of these sounds are simple vowels or vowels plus related glides and 3 of these vowels are diphthongs (i.e., vowels consisting of two distinct sounds). These sounds can be distinguished from each other by their position in the mouth along two dimensions: how far front or back? how high or low? For some of the vowels, lip and jaw position are also factors.

The eleven simple vowels and vowels plus related glides are as follows:

SOUND	EXAMPLES
1. /iy/	beat, he
2. /ɪ/	bit, kin
3. /ey/	rain, hay
4. /E/	bet, hen
5. /æ/	bat, can
6. /a/	ma, pot
7. /ʌ/	cut, son
8. /ɔ/	bought, saw
9. /ow/	sew, goat
10. /ʊ/	book, wool
11. /uw/	glue, boot

The three vowel diphthongs, all of which move from a lower vowel sound to a higher glide, are as follows:

SOUND	MOVEMENT	EXAMPLES
12. /ay/	low-central to high-front	sky, nine
13. /aw/	low-central to high-back	house, cow
14. /oy/	mid-back to high-front	joy, voice

Some pronunciation teachers like to summarize all 11 basic vowel sounds and the 3 diphthongs in one stylized diagram of the mouth as follows:

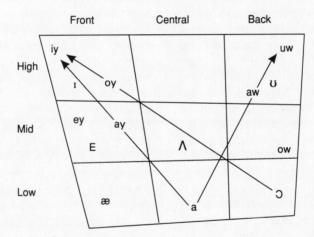

This appendix is simply an inventory of segmental features. The ESL/EFL teachers also needs to know about suprasegmental features such as word and utterance stress, intonation, linking phenomena, and reduced speech.

Teaching Speech Act Behavior to Nonnative Speakers

Elite Olshtain and Andrew Cohen

INTRODUCTION

The stewardess on a European airline walked down the aisle with a coffeepot and some cups. "Coffee, please!" she said smilingly to the passengers. A young American smiled back at her and said, "You're the one who is serving the coffee, ma'am, not me." The stewardess blushed and seemed somewhat bewildered. What happened here? In reaction to an inappropriate offer the American tried to explain to the stewardess that the expression which she used would be more suitable for a request than an offer. This is an example of pragmatic failure caused by the woman's translating a function from the mother tongue to the target language, and the result is an inappropriate utterance. Although the woman's mastery of the structure of English was excellent, she did not have the same mastery of the sociolinguistic rules of appropriacy.

If we wish to master another language we need to become communicatively competent in that language. Linguistic accuracy is important for this communicative competence but is not sufficient. In acquiring the new language one needs to assimilate, in addition to the structural rules, a set of sociocultural rules that will guide the learner in the choice of appropriate forms. In other words, successful speaking is not just a matter of using grammatically correct words and forms but also knowing *when* to use them and under what circumstances.

Canale and Swain (1980) suggest a model of communicative competence which incorporates grammatical competence, discourse competence, and sociolinguistic competence. In other words, if the goal of the language course is to enable students to reach a level of communicative competence, then all three components are necessary. Discourse competence relates to features of text, whether it is spoken or written. Thus, cohesion (the grammatical "glue" that holds sentences together within a large piece of discourse) and coherence (the organizational rules which make the sequence of the text meaningful) need to be acquired by learners of a second language. Although cohesion and coherence operate in all languages, their actual realization might take different forms in different languages. In English, for instance, the pronoun system is the most important means of signaling reference of nouns within paragraphs, while in another language gender might be more significant.

The sociolinguistic component of Canale and Swain's model of communication refers to rules of speaking which depend on social, pragmatic, and cultural elements. Thus, which linguistic realization we choose for making an apology or a request in any language might depend on the social status of the speaker and/or hearer, and on age, sex, or any other social factor. Furthermore, certain pragmatic, situational conditions might call for the performance of a certain speech act in one culture but not in another. Thus, it may be appropriate to compliment someone on wearing a new garment in one language and not in another.

In addition to the mastery of these components of communicative competence, Canale and Swain suggest that successful learners also develop effective communication strategies which will enable them to overcome their deficiencies in any particular area. It is the aim of this chapter to present a framework and suggestions for the teaching of speech acts in an integrative manner, thus enabling students to become aware of the sociolinguistic rules of the target language and of the cultural differences involving what constitutes appropriate use in their new language as opposed to their first language.

WHAT ARE SPEECH ACTS?

It seems that every language develops a set of patterned, routinized utterances that speakers use regularly to perform a variety of functions, such as apologies, requests, complaints, refusals, compliments, and others. By using a routinized utterance of this kind, the speaker carries out an act with respect to the hearer. In formal terms, the routinized utterance carries both a basic, propositional meaning ("I'm hot" = the speaker is feeling hot) and an intended effect or illocutionary meaning (e.g., "I'm hot" = under the given circumstances the speaker is requesting someone else to open the window). Speakers of the language recognize the illocutionary force of an utterance by pairing up the situational information within which the utterance has been produced with the content of that utterance. When such utterances become conventionalized we recognize their function as speech acts.

A speaker of a language who has knowledge of the speech act realization patterns in that language usually knows the rules of appropriateness for choosing certain specific utterances to fit defined social situations. Some of these utterances have come to be recognized as routines or highly conventional

forms, while others are available in the language as part of a wider repertoire with options of politeness, face saving, solidarity, self-humiliation, and others. When a learner is faced with familiar social situations in the new language, the first natural step is to try and translate the most conventional routine in the first language verbatim into the new language. Very often this attempt, even if grammatically correct, may result in a communicative failure. How can language teachers guide their students so as to avoid such pitfalls?

In recent years, teachers have been encouraged to give attention in their instruction to speech acts, but even mature and effective native speakers cannot rely entirely on their intuition with respect to speech acts. Research in the area of speech act analysis needs to come to the teacher's rescue with better insights concerning the rules of appropriateness in both the target and the first language of the students. One of the major concerns of such discourse studies across languages is that of setting up comparable units of analysis. We have proposed the notion of a "speech act set" (Olshtain & Cohen, 1983) to encompass the major linguistic and pragmatic strategies, any one of which would suffice as a minimal element to represent the particular speech act. A speech act set consists of the explicit and conventional patterns as well as the more implicit or indirect strategies (Searle, 1975). It provides the researcher with a framework for defining the relationships holding between illocutionary intent and linguistic repertoire in a specific language and with the possibility of comparing speech act sets across languages.

EXAMPLES OF SPEECH ACT SETS

Speech act sets encompass the routinized realization patterns of a speech act related to the semantic criteria and the illocutionary intent. These patterns need to be further matched to sets of pragmatic and situational features according to which any one of these patterns might be more appropriate than others. Such considerations entail both social and situational factors. In the case of an apology, for instance, the perfomance of an apology aims to provide support for and placate the hearer who was actually or potentially adversely affected by a violation for which the speaker is at least partially responsible. When apologizing, the speaker is willing to humiliate him/herself to some extent and to admit to fault and responsibility for the offense. Therefore, the semantic criteria that need to be met by the act of apologizing are an expression of regret and an acknowledgment of responsibility on the part of the offender/speaker. Accordingly, the apology speech act set needs to include patterns or formulas that meet such semantic criteria. We have reason to believe that these criteria hold true across cultures, but cultures may allocate the need to apologize and the degree of apology differently in different situations. Thus, in one culture "coming late to a meeting" might be considered a much graver offense than in another, and therefore the type of apology used in each might be quite different. Furthermore, cultures may attach different degrees of status to the participants interacting in the situation and vary strategy selection accordingly. Thus, in some cultures age might play a significant role while in others social status.

Apologies

The apology speech act set consists of five strategies or realization patterns (Olshtain & Cohen, 1983), two of which are general and depend less on contextual constraints, and three of which are situation-specific. The two general strategies are the explicit expression of an apology, which consists of formulaic, routinized expression containing some explicit performative verb (e.g., "I'm sorry," "Excuse me," "I regret," "I apologize"), and the expression of responsibility, which reflects the speaker's degree of willingness to admit to fault for the offense.

The other three strategies, an expla-

nation, an offer of repair, and a promise of nonrecurrence, are situation-specific and semantically reflect the content of the situation. An explanation is an account of the situation which indirectly caused the apologizer to commit the offense (e.g., "The bus was late" as a statement intended to set things right). An offer of repair is a bid by the apologizer to carry out an action or provide payment for some kind of damage which resulted from the offense. In a promise of nonrecurrence, the apologizer commits him/herself to not allowing the offense to happen again. The preference for any one of the five apology strategies, or for a combination of them, will depend on the specific situation within the given language and cultural group.

In addition to the main strategies which make up the speech act set, there are ways in which the speaker can modify the apology either by intensifying it or by downgrading it. An intensification would make the apology stronger, creating even more support for the hearer and more humiliation for the speaker. The routinized intensification usually consists of internal modification within the apology expression—in the form of a conventional intensifier such as "really," "very," "terribly." External modification can take the form of a comment signaling added concern for the hearer. Such comments intensify the apology since they express stronger interest on the part of the speaker to placate the hearer. External modification which downgrades the apology can take the form of a comment which minimizes either the offense or the harm it may have caused.

Putting all of these components together, we could have the following apology in response to forgetting a meeting with the boss: "I'm really very sorry (intensified expression of apology). I completely forgot about it (expression of responsibility). The alarm on my watch didn't go off as it was supposed to (explanation). Is it possible for me to make another appointment? Can we meet now? (offer of repair). This won't ever happen again (promise of nonreoccurrence).

Requests

The speech act of requesting is realized when the speaker verbalizes a wish which can be carried out by the hearer. Thus a request, if it is complied with, requires the hearer to carry out an act or to provide some information or goods for the speaker's sake. The speech act set for requests consists of three major categories of strategies: the explicit impositives, the conventionalized routines, and the indirect hints. Indirect hints are individual, nonconventional utterances, which under given circumstances can act as requests. According to Blum-Kulka, Danet and Gherson (1985) and Blum-Kulka and Olshtain (1984), the explicit, most direct strategies are usually realized by syntactic requests such as imperatives or other performatives (Austin, 1962); the conventionalized requests are polite realizations through conventional forms such as yes-no questions, with *modals* in English ("Could you help me?" "Would you open the window?"), and the nonconventional indirect requests form an open-ended group of hints which could be interpreted as requests under certain given situational circumstances. Thus, the expression "It is rather hot in here" could be interpreted as a request in a room where the windows are closed and where the hearer is in a position to open the windows.

The speech act of requesting is viewed by Brown and Levinson (1978) as an inherently face-threatening act for the hearer since by uttering the request the speaker imposes some action on the hearer. All languages exhibit, therefore, some well-recognized, conventionalized forms that signal a polite or acceptable manner in which to make a request. While learning a second language, there is a good chance that learners will tend to translate the conventional forms of their first language into the second one and come up with something which is not quite appropriate. Thus, for instance, a learner in whose first language imperatives followed by the expression "please" is one of the conventionalized types of requests may produce a similar request in English and sound too direct or patronizing, without intending to do so.

Every language has its syntactic and lexical ways in which to downgrade a request and make it less threatening and ways in which to upgrade it and create more urgency of compliance. If we want to soften the request, we may choose to justify our need to make the request and/or we may lessen the imposition, as in the following example: "I missed my bus; if you are going downtown could I hitch a ride with you?" If, on the other hand, we need to impress the urgency of the request upon the hearer, we might choose a more direct strategy and add an "aggravator," such as the word "immediately." A policeman might say, for instance, to a driver stopping in a no-parking zone: "You can't park your car here. Move your car right away."

Complaints

The speech act of complaining is a hearer face-threatening act by definition. When complaining, the speaker verbally expresses displeasure or annoyance as a reaction to a past or ongoing action (Olshtain & Weinbach, 1987). Such a complaint may be addressed to the hearer as the person responsible for the act which caused the annoyance, or it may concern a third or unavailable party. Thus, for example, if someone pushes in front of the speaker in a line at the post office, the speaker may say, "Excuse me, I am the last person in line," while if the service at the post office is slow, one person may say to the other, "Lately the service here has become terribly inefficient." The latter is often referred to as a "gripe."

The speech act of complaining has two major goals: One is to point out the violation in behavior and thus relieve one's own frustration and anger, and the second, when such possibility exists, is to request some repair. However, since this is a face-threatening act toward the hearer, some speakers may prefer to avoid the potential confrontation and never seek the goal of the complaint. In the latter case the speaker opts out of performing the speech act of complaining.

The speech act of complaining consists of at least three types of strategies: a mild complaint which refers indirectly to the consequences of the violation from the speaker's perspective, an explicit complaint which mentions the responsibility of the hearer and the act which caused the violation, and a more severe complaint which embeds a threat or warning. Some cultures might prefer the less direct realization while others may be tolerant toward directness and severity of complaining. Such differences can result in rather serious breakdowns in communication when nonnative speakers transfer norms from their first language to the second. Previous work (Beebe & Takahashi, 1987; Blum-Kulka, 1982; Cohen & Olshtain, 1981; DeCapua, 1989; Wolfson, 1983) establishes the fact that pragmatic competence entails the knowledge of the rules of speaking which are sociocultural in nature. When learning a new language speakers are likely to transfer such sociocultural rules from their first language to the second language and often bring about unwarranted stereotyping.

Compliments

The speech act of complimenting is intrinsically courteous and enables the speaker to make use of available opportunities to express politeness and interest in the hearer. The goal of complimenting is usually to express solidarity between speaker and hearer and to enhance the feeling of common interests. A number of studies on compliments in American English (Manes & Wolfson, 1981, Wolfson 1981; Wolfson & Manes, 1980) have pointed to the fact that this speech act fulfills an important role in maintaining social harmony. However, for a compliment to work, the speaker needs to know when it is appropriate and to what extent it requires a truth value. In American English, half of the time an adjective is used in a compliment, it is either "nice" or "good" (e.g., "That's a nice shirt you are wearing," "It was a good talk

you gave"), with "beautiful," "pretty," and "great" making up another 15 percent (Wolfson & Manes, 1981). This is further reinforcement of the fact that compliments in American English are intended for solidarity and not necessarily for truth value. In another culture, where compliments are less common and where the hearer expects the speaker to commit him/herself to the content of the compliment, such adjectives may sound "empty" and "meaningless." It is therefore important for the language learner to develop some sensitivity to rules of appropriacy in the target language, even in the case of compliments.

THE TEACHING OF SPEECH ACTS: THE CASE OF APOLOGIES

Teaching materials dealing with speech acts have for the most part been constructed largely in the absence of empirical studies to draw upon. They have relied on the curriculum writer's intuition and can best be characterized as reflecting a high level of simplicity and generality. Most of the currently popular English/foreign language textbooks treat speech acts such as "apologies" rather simplistically. For example, emphasis is almost exclusively on the expression of an apology: "sorry," "I'm sorry," "I'm very sorry." Brief reference is made to other apology strategies, but without underlying principles for when to use what. No effort is made to analyze the apology speech act set into its semantic formulas (see, e.g., Berry & Bailey, 1983; Blundell, Higgens, & Middlemass, 1982; Jolly, 1984; Swan & Walter, 1985).

Studies concerning the nature of apologies in a variety of languages and cultures have been steadily accumulating over the last few years (e.g., Blum-Kulka & Olshtain, 1984; Cohen & Olshtain, 1981; Cohen, Olshtain, & Rosenstein, 1986; Olshtain, 1983; Olshtain & Cohen, 1983, 1988; Owen, 1983). As a result, there is a growing source of empirical data on strategies for apologizing. Hence, there is now an opportunity to move from general, intuitively based materials to more specific, empirically based ones.

One such textbook series that has two books based on empirical findings from speech act studies is the ESL series developed by Bodman and Lanzano (1981 and 1984). Their coverage of apologies includes reference to the semantic formulas of responsibility and offer of repair, as well as the overt expression of an apology. They also deal with modifications on apologies, such as through using comments as softeners. This series was developed before the most recent empirical findings, but it definitely takes the learner beyond simplistic coverage of the speech act set.

As an example of what is involved in the learning of speech acts, one speech act in one pair of language/cultural groups will now be used to illustrate the kinds of information it would be useful to have in order to realize the speech act effectively. We will focus on the speech act of apologizing, and the two groups will be American English speakers and Israeli Hebrew speakers. For the purposes of this example, we will assume that the learners are native Hebrew speakers in Israel learning American English as a foreign language.

Below are the strategies for apologizing which were mentioned above and which apply universally to apologies in any language (Cohen & Olshtain 1981, Cohen et al., 1986). The trick is knowing which one or ones to use in a given apology situation in a given language—as well as knowing which language forms are appropriate for realizing that strategy.

1. *An expression of an apology*: The speaker uses a word, expression, or sentence containing a verb such as "sorry," "excuse," "forgive," or "apologize." Languages have certain words that are used to express an oral apology more than others. For example, in American English, "I apologize" is found more in writing than it is in oral language. An expression of an apology can be intensified whenever the apologizer feels the need to do so. Such intensification is usually accomplished by adding intensifiers such as "really" or "very"—e.g., "I'm really sorry."

2. *Acknowledgment of responsibility*: The offender recognizes his/her fault in causing the infraction. The degrees of such recognition on the part of the apologizer can be placed on a scale. The highest level of intensity is an acceptance of the blame: "It's my fault." At a somewhat lower level would be an expression of self-deficiency: "I was confused/I didn't see/You are right." At a still lower level would be the expression of lack of intent: "I didn't mean to." Lower still would be an implicit expression of responsibility: "I was sure I had given you the right directions." Finally, the apologizer may not accept the blame at all, in which case there may be a denial of responsibility: "It wasn't my fault," or even blaming of the hearer: "It's your own fault."

3. *An explanation or account*: The speaker describes the situation which caused him/her to commit the offense and which is used by this speaker as an indirect way of apologizing. The explanation is intended to set things right. In some cultures this may be a more acceptable way of apologizing than in others. Thus, in cultures where public transportation is unreliable, coming late to a meeting and giving an explanation like "The bus was late" might be perfectly acceptable.

4. *An offer of repair*: The apologizer makes a bid to carry out an action or provide payment for some kind of damage which resulted from his/her infraction. This strategy is situation-specific and is only appropriate when actual damage has occurred.

5. *A promise of nonrecurrence*: The apologizer commits him/herself to not having the offense happen again. This strategy is situation-specific and less frequent than the others.

These five major strategies which make up the apology speech act are available to speakers across languages, yet preference for any one of them or for a combination of them will depend on the specific situation within the given language and culture group. Let us take a situation, for example:

You completely forget a crucial meeting at the office with your boss. An hour later you call him/her to apologize. Your boss gets on the line and asks, "What happened to you?"

If the learners are Israeli Hebrew speakers, their culture may support two types of behavior in their reply. First, in this and similar situations they would emphasize the strategy of explanation—more than an American would: e.g., "Well, I had to take a sick child to the doctor and then there was a problem with the plumbing . . ." On the other hand, they would underplay the strategy of repair, because in Israeli culture, it would be for the boss to determine the next step. It would be presumptuous for the employee to suggest what happens next.

Perhaps just as important as knowing which strategies to use when, is knowing how to modify these strategies in a given situation. Factors that may affect how interlocutors would deliver an apology (intensified with added explanation and personal justification or in its most brief and direct form) in their native language or target language may depend on social and situational factors. When the offense is more severe it may be necessary to greatly intensify the apology, but which offense is considered a severe offense would depend on the specific culture. Thus, forgetting a meeting with a friend may be considered a less severe offense in one culture and a very grave offense in another. Learners need to become sensitive to specific situations that call for certain speech acts and for appropriate intensification of these speech acts. When teaching apologies in English to Hebrew speakers we might draw up a number of specific goals and develop materials and teaching techniques to fit these goals.

Goals for Teaching the Apology Speech Act

Before we can set up specific goals for the teaching of the apology speech act, we have to identify our student population. If the students are beginner ESL/EFL learners, we may want to limit the goals to an awareness of the linguistic features of the two main strategies: the expression of an apology and the acknowledgment of responsibility. The teaching of the expression of an apology will require students to learn to recognize the most common form of an apology in English—namely, the "sorry," "I'm sorry" realizations. Some learners might be tempted to translate the form from their own language and choose "forgive" or "pardon" instead of the more common form "sorry." Furthermore, students might be confused as to the difference between "I'm sorry" and "excuse me." These two items could therefore constitute the goals for a beginner level. On the other hand, if the student population is advanced, it may be more appropriate to focus on appropriate ways of intensifying the apology in various social situations.

Teaching Techniques

Whatever the goals of teaching, there are various ways to present and practice the use of speech acts. What all these different ways should have in common is the specification of situational and social factors matched with the most common realizations of the speech act. It is important for learners to realize, for instance, that in English an expression of apology with no intensification would not be considered a very sincere apology and is therefore not appropriate for interaction with friends or interlocutors who are at a higher status than the speaker. Such unintensified apologies are most common with strangers and in cases where the infraction is not severe. Furthermore, students need to become aware of the fact that intensification with the word "very" is not always perceived as true intensification, since "terribly" and "really" are more common intensifiers in colloquial American English. In order to help students become aware of such variation in apology use, they need to be given the chance to compare apologies in a variety of contexts, carefully considering the differences and similarities.

In this section we will briefly discuss five different ways in which to present and practice the apology speech act.

1. *The diagnostic assessment* is often the first step which helps the teacher to establish the students' level of awareness of speech acts in general and of the particular speech act to be taught. Such assessment can be carried out in writing or in an oral interaction with the teacher. If it is done in writing, the student is usually given a situation followed by a number of possible choices. For example, you have accidentally bumped into an older lady at the supermarket and caused her to drop some packages. Which of the following apologies would be most appropriate: (a) Forgive me, please. (b) I'm terribly sorry. Are you okay? (c) Lady, such things may happen.

If the students tend to choose (a) we may conclude that they tend to translate from their first language. If they choose (c) they do not recognize the situation as one calling for an intensified apology, and if they choose (b) they have a good grasp of appropriate apology realization patterns. According to the results received on such an assessment questionnaire, it would be easier for the teacher to plan teaching goals and procedures.

2. *The model dialog* is a useful way to present students with examples of the speech act in use. These dialogs should be short and natural. Telephone conversations are often very suitable. At the first stage of using dialogs students just listen and identify the apology. Then they are given the dialogs without the information concerning the particular situation, and they have to try and guess if the people speaking know each other, if they are of the same age, and whether they are apolo-gizing for some serious offense. These considerations, which can be discussed in groups, help students become sensitive to the social and pragmatic factors that affect speech acts. Such model dialogs could focus on the distinction between "I'm sorry" and "Excuse me" or on the appropriate choice of a strategy or any other element of the apology act.

3. *The evaluation of a situation* is a useful technique to further reinforce the students' awareness of the factors affecting the choice of strategies. In this activity they are given a set of apology situations, and for each they have to decide, in pairs or small groups, whether the violation requiring the apology is severe or mild, whether the speaker/apologizer needs to intensify his/her apology, whether the hearer is likely to accept an apology without further ado, whether a certain situation specific strategy is called for, and similar factors.

4. *Role-play activities* are particularly suitable for practicing the use of speech acts. Here it is important to supply the learners with ample information about the interlocutors who are going to interact in the conversation and about the situation. It is a good idea to present students with sets of cards depicting these interlocutors and giving detailed information about them. Thus, for an apology situation the students may receive a card showing Julia Wynne, who is a young secretary working for a well-known travel agency, and Mr. Milton Stowe, who comes into the agency for some information. The students are directed to think of a potential violation that might have occurred where first Julia is the offender/apologizer and then Milton is in the same role. They provide their own details of the violation and then act out, in role-play fashion, the conversation which is likely to take place between the two interlocutors.

5. *Feedback and discussion* are useful activities for speech act teaching since students need to talk about their perceptions, expectations, and awareness of similarities

and differences between speech act behavior in the target language and in their first culture. Such feedback related to the role-plays, for instance, and further discussion with a larger group of learners helps all participants become more aware of speech act behavior and helps them recognize areas of interference where pragmatic failure may occur.

The five techniques discussed above are but a few examples of the kind of activities that might be suitable for speech act teaching, but they indicate the need to expose students first to the most common realization patterns and then gradually make them understand some of the factors involved and finally enable them to practice the use of the speech act. Even if, as a result of such carefully planned activities, students do not necessarily begin to behave like native speakers, they have a good chance of becoming better listeners and of reacting more appropriately to what native speakers say to them.

THE ROLE OF RESEARCH IN THE DESIGN OF SPEECH ACT MATERIAL

With the increasing demand for evidence and reliable information on speech act behavior which is needed to guide both the materials developer and the teacher in the preparation of ways in which to teach speech acts, research in this area has attempted to provide better insights into speech act performance. Many of the studies are intracultural, attempting to describe the range of usage within the same society with respect to social and pragmatic variation, while other studies are cross-cultural, attempting to establish universal versus language-specific speech act behavior. In this section of the chapter we would like to report on a number of studies that the authors have been directly involved with, in an effort to determine what speech forms need to be taught to nonnative learners. Again for purposes of illustration, we will confine the discussion to apologies.

Our first apology study (Cohen & Olshtain, 1981) involved eight apology situa-

tions selected to assess sociocultural competence in the target language among speakers of Hebrew learning English. The research questions were the following: (1) How does learners' apology behavior differ from native performance? (2) Can one identify negative transfer from the first language to the second language? (3) Are there situations for which there is a clear difference between native and nonnative speech act behavior? (4) Does lack of grammatical proficiency affect the learners' speech act performance?

Eight apology situations were selected as the instrument of data collection—four of the situations were especially set up to present a range in the severity of offense requiring the apology: hitting a car, bumping into a lady just startling her as opposed to hurting her, and bumping into a lady because she was in the way. The other four situations were meant to assess the effect of status of the hearer on the formality of the apology: insulting someone at a meeting, forgetting a meeting with a boss/a friend/a son.

The subjects were 44 college students around 20 years of age; 12 were native speakers of English, who provided the data on how English speakers apologize in their native language. The remaining 32 were native Hebrew speakers, 12 of whom provided Hebrew responses and 20 who were enrolled in an intermediate-level English class and constituted the learner population. The situations were given to the subjects on cards, in random order. Each respondent read the situation silently from the card, and then the investigator role-played by the person who had been offended, with the respondent providing the apology.

Findings. The results revealed situations in which the EFL deviations from cultural patterns appeared to be a result of negative transfer from the first language. Such transfer related to the need for apologizing in certain situations, the selection of the appropriate strategy, and the degree of intensification. Transfer was established on the basis of a comparison of the native responses in the two languages (English and Hebrew) and a comparison with the learners' responses in English. Furthermore, we found that in some cases the EFL respondents lacked linguistic proficiency in English and as a result avoided the use of intensification and some of the apology strategies.

On the basis of this study we suggested that ESL/EFL teachers include speech acts in their intermediate courses of study with emphasis on the following: the use of the different strategies of apologizing; special focus on intensification both in terms of the form such intensification might take and the situational features that might call for intensification. We further encouraged teachers to make their students aware of cultural differences in speech act behavior and become better listeners so that they develop sensitivity to such behavior.

The second study which we would like to report in this chapter is a follow-up study with advanced learners. The study (Cohen et al., 1986) sought to determine the nature and extent of gaps between native and advanced nonnative apology. The study asked two questions: (1) What differences do we find between advanced nonnative learners and native speakers in apology behavior with respect to the five main strategies and as regards modifications of these strategies? (2) Are there differences in apology behavior resulting from the severity of the offense and/or from the familiarity of the hearer?

The 180 respondents for this study included 96 native speakers of American English, studying at one of six U.S. universities, and 84 advanced learners of English, who were native Hebrew-speakers, studying at one of five Israeli universities. The data-collection instrument was a discourse-completion questionnaire which has been used in a large number of cross-cultural studies (Blum-Kulka & Olshtain, 1984).

Findings. From the data collected in this study it appeared that natives and advanced learners did not seem to differ markedly in the use of main strategies for apologizing. Yet striking differences emerged in the various modifications of such apologies, especially in the use of intensifiers such as "very" and "really." Furthermore, nonnatives lacked sensitivity to certain distinctions that natives made, such as between forms for realizing the strategy of expressing apology such as "excuse me" and "sorry." Nonnatives tended to use "excuse me" more often and sometimes in contexts where this realization was not appropriate.

Following the above study on advanced learners' speech act behavior with respect to apologies, we felt the need to develop teaching materials and find out to what extent it is possible to teach such fine points of apologizing to advanced learners. Hence, we undertook a study which involved the teaching of such forms (Olshtain & Cohen, 1988). Our findings showed that after instruction, advanced learners were somewhat more likely to select apology strategies similar to those that native speakers use in similar situations and that they were more likely to use intensifiers appropriately.

In addition to teaching materials used for the teaching of apologies, the students were given evaluation sheets in order to tell the teachers and the course designer what types of activities they preferred. It turned out that the students, who were adults studying in a private language school, preferred above all else that the teacher give an explanation of the main points concerning speech act behavior. They also welcomed information sheets describing the points and saw some value in role-play activities to help reinforce the points. They indicated that they got less out of listening to dialogs which incorporated the forms. Such an evaluation might, however, be quite different if carried out with younger learners.

CONCLUSION

This chapter intended to present teachers with some insights into speech act behavior and to encourage them to incorporate such work into their courses of study. It may, at this stage, be difficult to find sufficient material on the various speech acts and on the cross-cultural differences that exist between languages. However, we believe that sensitivity to this area of language acquisition will often help teachers make suitable choices and teaching decisions. Perhaps the most important point made in this chapter is the fact that this is a language area in which performance is not absolute and therefore we cannot expect all learners ever to acquire perfect nativelike behavior. What we are after is the development of an awareness of sociocultural and sociolinguistic differences that might exist between one's first language and the target language. Such awareness will often help explain to both teachers and learners why sometimes there is unintended pragmatic failure and breakdown in communication. If we are aware of it, it might be easier to find the appropriate remedy.

DISCUSSION QUESTIONS

1. How would you teach requests in English? Develop a number of activities to teach requests with a well-defined student population of your choice.

2. To what extent is it important to include speech acts such as complaints and compliments in (a) an EFL course for beginners, (b) an advanced ESL course for adults, and (c) any course of your choice?

3. Write five short dialogs or brief exchanges which incorporate apologies in natural interaction. Try to incorporate all five strategies in your dialogs. (More than one strategy is often used in the same interchange.)

4. With a partner, discuss the value of research for teaching in general and for speech act teaching in particular.

5. Set up a sequence for teaching any speech act of your choice specifying goals for (a) beginners, (b) intermediate-level students, and (c) advanced learners.

SUGGESTED ACTIVITIES

1. If you are a native speaker of English who teaches or intends to teach ESL/EFL courses:

(a) You may want to develop your own sensitivity to the kind of speech act behavior that you carry out naturally. Think of a number of everyday situations for apologies, requests, complaints, and compliments and start noticing and writing down your own behavior. Develop a set of such situations which you can later analyze. For instance, if one of your situations is: "You open a door into an office and accidentally bump into a strange person. You say: 'sorry'/'I'm sorry,' 'excuse me,' 'forgive me,' etc." Write down your own, most typical responses and some other responses spoken by native speakers.

(b) Work out a discourse-completion questionnaire for your students based on your finding in (a) above. Your questionnaire should have 10 to 12 situations presented as follows:

"You open a door into an office and accidentally bump into an elderly man/woman; a young person holding some packages; a child who is quite startled. You say _____."

Give the questionnaire to a group of nonnative speakers or to your own students and find out what realization patterns you get and how similar or different they are from the native patterns that you collected in (a) above.

(c) On the basis of the findings of (b) above, design a number of teaching activities to help students become more sensitive users of speech acts.

2. If you are a nonnative speaker of English teaching ESL/EFL courses:

(a) You may want to become more aware of your own speech act behavior in English and compare it with the performance of native speakers. Develop a discourse completion questionnaire with about 20 different situations depicting suitable contexts for apologies, requests, complaints, and compliments. The following are three examples of such discourse completion items:

Apologies: You promised you'd buy your neighbor medicine for a sick child in town, but you forgot. Your neighbor: "Did you get the medicine?"
You: "_____"
Requests: You are completely out of cash and you

want to buy a cold drink in the school cafeteria. You see a friend and you approach him/her in order to borrow some money.
You say: "_____"
Complaints: You have made an appointment with the dentist for three o'clock in the afternoon. You have been waiting for over an hour. The nurse comes out of the office and invites another patient to go in. You say to the nurse: "_____"

(b) Answer your questionnaire in the way you are most likely to react in a real-life situation.

(c) Prepare a number of questionnaires which you can give to native speakers. These questionnaires should contain all the items that you answered, but the native speakers should not be aware of your responses. Compare the native responses with your own and evaluate your own performance.

(d) Together with a native speaker (if possible), develop some teaching materials to deal with the deviations you found in your own performance.

SUGGESTIONS FOR FURTHER READING

Wolfson, N. (1989)
Perspectives: Sociolinguistics and TESOL. New York: Newbury House.

> Provides a critical overview of those aspects of sociolinguistics most relevant to members of the TESOL profession. The book deals with face-to-face interaction, cross-cultural differences in speech behavior, problems in the analysis of sociolinguistic rules, descriptions of speech behavior in native English-speaking communities, miscommunication, language contact/choice/use/maintenance/ change at the societal level.

Wolfson, N., and E. Judd, (1983)
Sociolinguistics and Language Acquisition. New York: Newbury House.

> Constitutes a pioneering volume wherein for the first time one was able to find articles describing refusals, apologies, requests, complaints, compliments, disapprovals, and invitations. The book contains useful information for teachers and researchers.

II
Language Skills
C. Reading

Teaching the reading skill to nonnative speakers of English involves unique problems and challenges at all conceivable levels of instruction. ESL teachers working with young children will be greatly assisted by Hawkins' chapter with its overview of theoretical considerations and practical suggestions. The chapter by Haverson is addressed to adult ESL teachers who must simultaneously cope with the issue of literacy; his prescriptions and teaching suggestions provide a good starting point. Dubin and Bycina take us into the realm of reading for academic purposes; those teaching intermediate- and advanced-level students who still need to improve their reading skills and strategies will find this chapter useful. Finally, the chapter by Lynch and Hudson introduces the reader to contexts where students of science and technology require nothing more than an ability to read technical literature in English. Not only are the issues addressed but the type of materials and activities used in such reading-based language programs are presented in a comprehensive manner.

Teaching Children to Read in a Second Language[1]

Barbara Hawkins

In discussing how to teach children (grades K–6) to read in a second language, there are various points of view that can be considered. Several of them have to do with the various facets involved in teaching reading, whether it be in a first or second language, and are colored by our definitions of reading in general. Others have to do with how reading in a second language is the same as, or different from, reading in one's first language, and are colored by our beliefs about the influence of native language competencies and strategies on the second language. In this chapter, we will discuss some of the information that has to do with both areas; i.e., we will examine various facets that have been regarded as essential in teaching children to read in general, and then we will examine various facets that have spoken specifically to the issue of learning to read in a second language as distinct from (or the same as) reading in one's mother tongue. Finally, we will review several current approaches/methodologies used in teaching reading to children in a second language, with the aim of showing the connection between the approaches and underlying beliefs about reading.

READING AS A MULTIFACETED ACTIVITY

Although researchers may dwell on a single facet of the reading process at any given time, most agree that reading is not limited to the facet which they are examining. In fact, most researchers are convinced that reading is a multifaceted process that goes beyond the description of any single facet (e.g., Duran, 1987; McLaughlin, 1987b; Rumelhart, 1977; Schank, 1982; Swaffar, 1988; Weaver, 1980). "Of all the skills that the child must acquire in school, reading is the most complex and difficult. The child who accurately and efficiently translates a string of printed letters into meaningful communication may appear to be accomplishing that task with little mental effort. In fact, however, the child is engaging in complex interactive processes that are dependent on multiple subskills and an enormous amount of coded information" (McLaughlin, 1987b, p. 59). Not only are there various facets which go into the reading process, but the process becomes even harder to untangle and understand as we realize that these various facets are operating *in parallel time frames*. "Viewed in the past as either a top-down or bottom-up process, we now think reading comprehension results from interactive variables that operate simultaneously rather than sequentially" (Swaffar, 1988, p. 123). Even though we may speak, therefore, of a single facet that we think is important to remember that all facets com-important to remember that all of them combine together to produce the activity that we call reading. Keeping this in mind, let us review briefly some of the various facets that are seen to play a role in the reading process.

Reading and Decoding

Perhaps because the letters on the page are the most obvious distinguishing characteristic of the written word, many teachers turn to the interpretation of the letters as "making specific sounds" as an obvious place to begin reading instruction. The emphasis here is on word-decoding operations, and usually involves the phonics of written language. A phonics approach teaches the learner to "sound out" the squiggles on the page, or more specifically teaches the phoneme–grapheme correspondences. Emphasis is on the letter-to-sound correspondence rather than on meaning. The thought is that once learners are able to sound out the letters, they will be able to read the words, and then, once they are able to read the words, they will be able to make meaning of the text. This is an example of a "bottom-up" strategy, whereby it is assumed that understanding the individual sounds will eventually lead to the understanding of text. In the basal readers used in elementary schools, the sounds encountered in English are sequenced such that all of the various sound–symbol correspondences are "covered," usually by the end of third grade. Throughout the readers

in the basal series, the vocabulary is controlled so that the students are not asked to read words for which they have not yet been taught the sounds.

Guidelines for phonics instruction usually suggest that teaching begin with consonants for which there is a single sound (b, d, f, j, k, l, m, n, p, r, s, t, v, z) and move to consonants for which there exist more than one sound, depending on the environment (c, g, h, w)—for example, the "c" in "cat" versus the "c" in "cent," or the "g" in "gallop" versus the "g" in "gentleman." This is to be followed by introduction of consonant blends, in which two or more consonants are joined together to make another sound which retains some of each of the original consonant sounds making up the blend. For example, the blend "sl" retains the sound of both the "s" and the "l" when it is pronounced in the word "slow." Some other blends are bl, cl, fl, gl, pl, br, cr, dr, fr, gr, pr, tr, st, and sk. Following consonant blends come consonant digraphs, which are combinations of two consonants which together are pronounced as one sound. Included among the consonant digraphs are ch, sh, ph, th, and gh. With respect to all of the consonant sounds, it is recommended that they be taught first as beginning sounds, then as ending sounds, and finally as middle sounds. Vowel sounds are usually introduced in relation to their syllable environments, and various consonant/vowel patterns are taught. Three major types of vowel patterns or clusters that are usually taught in a phonics approach are as follows: consonant-vowel-consonant (CVC) clusters, in which the vowel sound is "short" (e.g., "cat", "pet"); consonant-vowel (CV) or consonant-vowel-consonant-silent e (CVCe) clusters, in which the vowel has a "long" sound (e.g., "me", "go", "made", "time"); consonant-vowel-vowel-consonant (CVVC) clusters, in which the first vowel is usually pronounced "long" and the second vowel is silent. Sight words also become part of the phonics program, since some high-frequency words in English all but defy a sound–symbol correspondence. For example, the following words would be sight words since "sounding them out" is next to impossible and since they are probably frequent enough in written language to warrant attention: "tough," "thought," "though," "through." The idea is that the letters "ough" do not "say" the same sounds and have to be learned, therefore, by sight on a word-by-word basis. (For a comprehensive presentation of instructional guidelines for teaching phonics "word identification skills," see Mason and Au, 1986, pp. 58–96.)

A decoding or phonics approach presupposes that the learner knows the sounds of the language to start with. For example, if students hear no difference between /r/ and /l/—and many speakers of Asian languages don't—we can expect them to have difficulty in learning the correspondence of letters to sounds they cannot distinguish. If they hear no difference between /iy/ and /i/—and many nonnative English speakers don't—it may be difficult to teach them the letter symbols for these sounds. And when the task is complicated by a variety of spelling patterns for these same sounds, the situation becomes exceedingly difficult for the students.

The research (Serpell, 1968) does show, in fact, that students misread and misinterpret words containing sounds which they cannot discriminate. That is, if they cannot hear the difference between /r/ and /l/, they may read "light" for "right," "cloud" for "crowd." The sound discrimination problem may cause a temporary slowdown in comprehension, but it does not always mean that misunderstanding will take place. One of the reasons is that there is more going on than merely decoding sounds, and the context surrounding the reading selection is thought to have a major influence on reading comprehension. For example, if readers are asked to read the following sentence, more than likely they will understand that the word in question is "ship" and not "sheep," even if they do mispronounce the word. "The (ship/sheep) docked at the harbor after a long and ardous cross-Atlantic journey." The issue of context is very important and will receive attention later on in the chapter.

Although no one would argue that phonetic interpretation of the written symbol is not a part of reading, there are not too many people who believe that it constitutes the whole, or even the most important part, of the reading process. Along these lines, McLaughlin (1987b) examines reading from the point of view of information processing. The sequential implications of the phonics approach are clear as we read his summary of the assumptions behind the learning of the sound–symbol correspondences as skills "built up via controlled processes" which "gradually, through practice, become automatic. In reading, the assumption is that learners acquire sound–symbol correspondences; then, once decoding skills have been mastered, direct controlled attention to deriving meaning from text" (p. 60). McLaughlin proposes that "the more the reader has automatized the mechanical decoding skills, the more attention is freed up to grasp the overall meaning of a phrase or sentence" (p. 61). If this is true, it would mean that as automaticity in decoding develops, the learner would also improve in terms of comprehension, since there would be more "freed-up" processing capacity for comprehension as decoding skills became automatic. In fact, however, McLeod and McLaughlin (1986) did not find this sequence of events to be true in their research comparing the reading errors of beginning ESL, advanced ESL, and native English-speaking adults. The researchers tested the reading ability of the three groups, keeping track of their errors and classifying them according to error type. That is, they kept track of whether or not the errors were *meaningful*. A meaningful error (or miscue) is one which shows that the reader is using implicit knowledge of sentence structure (syntactic cues) in order to predict a word that is grammatically acceptable in context, or is using meaning (semantic cues) to predict a word that is meaningful in context (see the "ship/sheep" sample sentence above). A miscue that is not meaningful is one which uses solely phonological cues as a predictor to text interpretation, whether the result makes syntactic or semantic sense or not.

At the same time that the researchers tested the reading ability of their subjects according to how they read a passage, they also gave a cloze test to the three groups in order to find out if the learners were able to make semantic and syntactic predictions about the text. It was expected that as the learners became *more proficient at decoding* graphic cues from text, any *errors* that they would make *would be more meaningful,* since they had automated the decoding aspects of reading and freed up the controlled processing for drawing meaning from text. This, in turn, would mean that they would be expected to show differences in their performances on the cloze test which would mirror their proficiency on the reading passage. While the proportion of meaningful errors made by the native English-speaking students was significantly higher than that of the ESL students, there was no significant difference between the proportion of meaningful errors made by the two groups of ESL students. This occurred in spite of the fact that the advanced ESL students did make significantly fewer errors in reading than did the beginning ESL students, *and* indicated that they had a greater control of semantic and syntactic text prediction as measured by the cloze test. The reading miscue analysis indicated, however, that the advanced ESL students did *not* make use of their greater ability for syntactic and semantic prediction, and proportionately made just as frequent meaningless errors as did the beginning ESL students; i.e., there was no significant difference between the advanced and beginning ESL students in terms of meaningful errors, even though one would expect that there would be a greater proportion of meaningful errors on the part of the advanced ESL students, given both the greater automaticity that the advanced ESL students demonstrated over the decoding process and their greater ability for syntactic and semantic prediction as demonstrated in the cloze test. These results have led McLaughlin to explore

the notion in contemporary cognitive psychology of "restructuring" as it applies to reading. Restructuring consists of the addition of new structures for the interpretation of facts, and involves the addition of a new organization or schema. His assumption is that restructuring may be helpful in explaining discontinuities in the reading process.

The main point for our discussion here, however, is that the research of McLaughlin (1987b) and McLeod and McLaughlin (1986) reiterates that phonics, although it plays a role in reading competency, is not the whole story; there are obviously other facets that enter the picture, since greater automatic control over the phonics of reading did not necessarily mean that their subjects were able to read more accurately for meaning.

An obvious question for a teacher is to determine more exactly the role that phonics does play. May and Eliot (1978) suggest that there are really only seven phonics rules worth spending time on in teaching English reading. They are referring to instruction for native speakers of English, but it is interesting to look at what they have chosen. Weaver (1980, pp. 57–58) lists the seven rules May and Eliot refer to as follows:

1. The "c rule," distinguishing "hard c" from "soft c": "cat" as opposed to "city."
2. The "g rule," distinguishing "hard g" from "soft g": "game" as opposed to "gem."
3. The VC pattern in which a single vowel letter followed by a consonant letter, digraph, or blend usually represents a short vowel sound: "bat," "bath," "bask."
4. The V V (vowel digraph) pattern in which a word or syllable containing a vowel digraph, the first letter in the digraph usually represents the long vowel sound and the second letter is usually silent: "fee," "coat," "seat."
5. The VCe (final e) pattern in which one-syllable words, containing two vowel letters, one of which is a final e, the first vowel letter usually represents a long vowel sound and the final e is silent: "nice," "plate," "vote."

6. The CV pattern, which indicates that when there is only one vowel letter in a word or syllable, and it comes at the end of the word or syllable, it usually represents the long vowel sound: "he," "go," "my."
7. The "r rule," in which the letter r modifies the short or long sound of the preceding vowel letter, thus modifying the VC, VV and VCE patterns mentioned above: VC: "cat"/"car"; VV: "feat"/"fear"; VCE: "cape"/"care."

Mason and Au (1986) consider phonics and other "linguistic" approaches (e.g., syllabaries, word patterns) to teaching reading as important in terms of word identification skills. There are other means of word identification, however, and the authors are clear in their belief that the curriculum must be broad-based in this regard. They indicate that one of the dangers inherent in a program that relies too heavily on phonics-only instruction is that children, especially those with reading problems, come to identify reading as unraveling the sound–symbol relationships that confront them every time they look at the printed page. This gives the students a misleading picture of what reading is all about and they rarely have the opportunity to develop and practice the idea that reading is a process of constructing meaning from text.

"Phonics-only instruction is not generally beneficial and may actually slow learning to read, instead of speeding it. . . . A sound reading program with children with special needs (e.g., ESL students) will always include many comprehension activities in addition to those in word identification. (p. 274, parentheses added)

The question of how to teach children to construct meaning from text beyond the level of phonics is an important question, and has received the attention of researchers and teachers alike. In addition to phonics, then, another area of importance that has been cited is that of the ability of the reader to make good predictions about the text they are reading, based on knowledge of, for example, syntax, semantics, and discourse.

Reading and Prediction

One characteristic of good readers that has been noted in the literature on reading is that they are able to make predictions about the text they are reading while they are reading it (Cohen & Hosenfeld, 1981; Goodman, 1967; Hochberg, 1970; Hosenfeld, 1977, 1979; Weaver, 1980). As we read, our eyes do not sweep in a steady movement across the print. Rather, we move our eyes in jumps called eye fixation movements. We scan a line, fixate at a point to permit eye focus. We pick up graphic cues and make a guess, a prediction about what appears on the printed page. While the guess is partly based on graphic cues, it is also subject to our knowledge about the language and what we have read up to that point. If the guess makes semantic and syntactic sense, we continue to read. If it does not—especially if it doesn't make semantic sense—we recheck and make an amended guess. Neisser (1967) has even suggested that at each focus point, the reader must be able to recognize which features seen in peripheral vision are uninformative in order to move effectively to the next fixation point. Cloze tests often provide us with an example of a good reader's ability to make ongoing predictions about text since the reader is called upon to make both syntactic and semantic predictions about what goes in the blanks.

One discovers a great deal about the reading ability of children by examining the miscues that they make while reading aloud (Goodman, 1965; Goodman & Goodman, 1977). Even though two children may have roughly the same *number* of miscues in a screening test, the *type* of miscues that they make is perhaps a more important indicator of their reading ability. Nonproficient readers will tend to make many more local errors, fixating on the pronunciation of specific words; their reading will often lose track of the overall meaning of the passage as it becomes an exercise in decoding. Likewise, they will often neglect syntactic, semantic, and/or punctuation cues, dwelling instead on each and every word of the text, as if each one were equally weighted in terms of meaning. (See Stafford, 1976, for a case study of the reading skills of a Spanish-speaking ESL student.) Proficient readers, on the other hand, will tend to make mistakes that do not affect meaning; that is, the mistakes do not change the essential meaning of the passage, or they anticipate the author's intent at a macro level. Also, proficient readers will often *correct* mistakes as they become apparent during continued reading of the text; they more often pay attention to syntactic, semantic, and punctuation cues in the text, using these cues as meaning indicators.

The guessing process model (Goodman, 1967) that underlies the discussion above assumes readers can identify important words in reading, and *can* in fact make semantic predictions about their relationship to one another. It assumes they have acquired enough language to predict syntactic relationships and that somehow these two systems (semantic and syntactic) allow them to hold passage content in memory for further guesses.

In fact, second language learners are not able to predict at all in the beginning stage of reading with much accuracy, since their experience with the language, in terms of both syntax and semantics, is so limited. This seems to be particularly true for children who not only are learning a second language but also are learning to read at the same time. The inclusion of teaching learners to make predictions about what they are reading as a formal part of reading instruction has been shown to be helpful to second language learners. In a series of studies using a "think aloud" protocol, Hosenfeld (1977) asked her high school subjects to introspect about their reading as they read in a foreign language they were studying. She compared the reading strategies of previously identified successful and nonsuccessful readers, and was able to make "reading maps" outlining the strategies used by each group. In general, she found that the successful readers kept the context of the passage in mind, translated in broad phrases, skipped words viewed as un-

important to the total meaning, used context to discover the meaning of unknown words, looked up words in the dictionary only as a last resort, and remained faithful to proposed solutions to problems. Using this information, Hosenfeld (1979) then worked with a particular student, Cindy, who was a nonsuccessful reader in the foreign language she was studying. During an eight-week period, Hosenfeld had Cindy introspect aloud about her reading and then had her compare her strategies with those of a successful reader. Cindy's main deficiency was that she was not a contextual guesser, and Hosenfeld was able to devise a list of things Cindy could do to help develop this skill. At the end of the eight-week period, Cindy had improved her reading a great deal by employing the methods on her list. There were still some weak areas, but the overall results were dramatic. Hosenfeld offers Cindy as an example showing where methodology can lead to an understanding of a student's individual learning style while enabling the teacher to deal with the particular needs of the student.

As learners become more proficient in the second language, they seem to use semantic cues to make guesses; i.e., they seem much more skilled at making guesses using the semantic system. For many students, the syntactic system seems to be "noise" that gets in their way. Schlesinger, in a series of impressive studies (1968), found this to be true even for native speakers of English. That is, in reading very complex syntactic structures we use a lexical strategy to understand what we read rather than a syntactic one. For example, in the following sentence from Schlesinger's work—"This is the hole that the rat, which our cat, that the dog bit, made, caught"— most people, reading such a sentence, would claim something made a hole, and it was probably the rat. If they used syntactic processing, they would discover they were wrong. The conclusion is that we can, and do, read without attending to the syntax when syntax becomes extremely complex. This accounts for the lack of difference found in experiment after experiment where syntactic complexity is varied in an attempt to show that syntactic complexity equals reading difficulty. If we can identify content words, and if we use our knowledge of the real world, we can make fairly successful guesses about what we read without always paying attention to syntax.

We know that ESL students do this, at least those students at beginning levels. They may recognize words in sentences and try to figure out some logical connection between them. The sentence structure is probably ignored in many instances. Once the learners discover that the first noun is usually the subject, they can make fairly accurate (if slow) predictions about the rest of the content words. Hatch, Polin, and Part (1974) approached the effect of syntax somewhat differently. If you turned to the beginning of this chapter and crossed out as quickly as possible every letter "e" on the first page, you would miss a large number of "e"'s if you were a native speaker of English. They found that ESL university students were highly successful at the task, much more so than native speakers of English. Once they started looking at where letters went unnoticed for the two groups, an interesting pattern appeared. First, native English speakers marked letters when they appeared in content words but not in function words. The ESL students marked them everywhere; they paid as much attention to letters in words which show grammatical relationships (prepositions, articles, conjunctions) as they did to letters in content words. Second, native speakers crossed out letters which appeared in strongly stressed syllables. That is, asked to cross out the letter "a," they marked the first "a" but not the second in "vocabulary"; they marked the second but not the first in "apparently." ESL students showed no pattern for stressed or unstressed syllables. Since ESL students marked letters in function words, we might suppose that they were paying attention to grammatical relationships expressed by them. This, once the researchers looked at their responses on comprehension questions, did not seem to be the case. Their answers were based, for the most part, on semantically based interpretations which did not always turn out to be correct.

Perhaps a clearer example occurs in a study reported by Johnston (1972). In the pilot study for her project, Johnston found that university ESL students did not attend to graphic cues which signal stress and intonation information. This allowed them to misread sentences in a variety of ways. For example, after reading a sentence from a passage on the San Diego Zoo about Monkey Mesa and the Great Ape Grotto, students ignored the capital letters in "Great Ape Grotto" and changed "grotto" from a noun to a verb; they thought the great ape was grottoing (even though "grotto" was mentioned earlier in the passage as the place where apes live). Having read about the Children's Zoo where one can pet friendly little deer, camels, and backyard animals, they responded that you could pet dear little camels. They ignored periods, thus assigning time clauses from one sentence to another. They misinterpreted pronoun reference and word group boundaries, and misread clause groups.

In summary, although it is recognized that "good readers" constantly make predictions about what they are reading while they are reading, and that these predictions are based on semantic, syntactic, and punctuation cues, the same behavior is not easily accessible for ESL readers, especially in the beginning stages of reading. One problem is that they have very little to go on in terms of their understanding of syntax and semantics in the second language, which forms the basis of their ability to make good predictions. This is not to suggest that they cannot be taught to make reasonable predictions, as in the case of Hosenfeld's subject Cindy, but that the ability to predict improves as the learner's second language proficiency improves. One could also make the argument that increased ESL reading skills reciprocally contribute to increased general ESL proficiency, since the analysis that attends instruction on prediction heightens awareness of syntax and semantics in the second language.

Reading and Schema/ Script Building

One of the major areas of research that is connected to the issue of prediction in reading is that of schema building as it relates to one's ability to interpret text meaningfully. Rumelhart (1977) presents the concepts of schema and similar notions (such as scripts, plans, goals) and relates them to the process of reading as the cognitive structure underlying the process. Although the author is careful to point out that not all of the terms used to refer to a set of interrelated concepts are synonymous, he states that they are "closely enough related that a discussion of one will serve as an introduction to the others" (p. 33).

Schemata (the plural of "schema") are the fundamental elements upon which all information processing depends, and in this sense, Rumelhart (1977) calls them the "building blocks of cognition." As such, they are used in the process of "interpreting sensory data, in retrieving information from memory, in organizing actions, in determining goals and subgoals, in allocating resources, and generally, in guiding the flow of processing in the system" (p. 34). Schemata are "packets" or "units of knowledge" that represent our beliefs about "objects, situations, events, sequences of events, actions and sequences of actions" (p. 34).

Referring to scripts, Schank and Abelson (1977) also speak of "knowledge structures" that serve to organize the events of one's world such that they become understandable. A script is "a structure that describes appropriate sequences of events in a particular context" (p. 41). As such, it is the interconnected whole of its parts and is capable of handling standardized, everyday situations. An example might be the "restaurant script," which would include at least the following:

1. Be seated at a table by a host or by yourself if there is a sign directing you to do so.
2. Read a menu in order to find out what food you would like to order.
3. Order your food from a waiter, who will take your order to the kitchen and then bring it to you when it is prepared.
4. Pay the bill and leave a tip for the waiter when you are finished eating.

In reality, the script would be much more detailed, but the example suffices to show that we all know pretty much what to expect when we enter a restaurant. We know, for example, that we are not going to buy a new pair of shoes, or have our teeth cleaned. These events belong to other scripts. We have built up a reservoir of scripts to deal with everyday life based on expectations we have because our experiences have given us these expectations. That is, in trying to understand the experiences in our lives, our internal mental systems attempt to see the connections between events that make up our experience. It is through this structure of scripts, or schemata, that we come to comprehend the events in our lives. If there is a good match between our current schemata and the events or situation happening in front of us, then we have no trouble comprehending those events. If, on the other hand, there is not a good match, or the events happening in front of us are so entirely new to us that we don't have a script or schema for them, then we will have some trouble comprehending the new events.

Rumelhart (1977) argues that "the total set of schemata instantiated at a particular moment in time constitutes our internal model of the situation we face at that moment in time, or, in the case of reading a text, a model of the situation depicted by the text" (p. 37). As mentioned above, if our schemata or scripts are incomplete in the sense that they do not provide an understanding of the incoming data from the text, then we will have difficulty understanding the text, and must do something to achieve a level of comprehension that satisfies the cognitive dissonance brought about by the mismatch between the text presentation and our own schemata.

In terms of reading instruction, the idea of schemata or scripts has an important role to play. Weaver (1980) and Mason and Au (1986) speak about the meaning that the reader brings *to* the text in order to get meaning *from* the text. As we sit down to read, we have a background of experiences that has given us a repertoire of scripts/schemata through which we understand our world. We interpret the text we read in light of these knowledge structures. We have all experienced reading passages written about topics for which we do not have any—or only a very limited—expertise. Sometimes we reread the passage several times, or we might struggle with looking up every other word written, figuring our problem is merely a question of vocabulary. We do all of the things that "good readers" are supposed to do, and yet we still do not understand the text. At some point we might give up, blaming the author for an inability to write clearly. If we absolutely need to understand the text, we might not give up so easily, and decide to talk to someone else who knows a little more than we do about the subject area. Gradually, we might come to understand the new text, and even eventually be able to read it and talk about it as if it were "second nature." Maybe we will realize that the text presented us with entirely new ideas about which we had never thought before (we had no schemata or scripts to handle the new ideas), or maybe we were viewing the text through inadequate or misleading ideas that we had; i.e., we had previous ideas that actually caused us to misunderstand the new text, and it was not until we adjusted our old ideas that we were able to understand and include the new ones (our old schemata/scripts needed expansion or adjustment or rejection).

With respect to teaching children to read, schemata/scripts play an obvious role. It is not only because children are faced with possibly new schemata every time they approach a text, but also because they need to develop a schema for what reading is in the first place. This is to say that children do not always understand what it means to read, let alone what it is that they are reading. They are sometimes led to think that it is "sounding out letters," or filling in phonics worksheets, but the real connection between the spoken word and the written word often eludes them. The first job for the teacher is, of course, to try to help their students develop a script that lets them in on the nature of reading as the interpretation of the written word.

Vygotsky (1978) speaks directly to the issue of the written word and its interpretation. He sees written words as signs or symbols needing interpretation, but he goes beyond the mechanical decoding of the signs as the only, or even principal, way of interpreting the written language. He states that a feature of the written system is that it starts out as a second-order symbolism that will gradually become direct symbolism. By this he means that written language consists of a system of signs that "designate the sounds and words of spoken language, which, in turn are signs for real entities and relations. Gradually this intermediate link, spoken language, disappears, and written language is converted into a system of signs that directly symbolize the entities and relations between them" (p. 106).

Vygotsky argues that this conversion of the written language into a first-order symbolism cannot be accomplished in a purely mechanical and external manner, but rather that it is "the culmination of a long process of development of complex behavioral functions in the child" (p. 106). He regards learning to interpret written symbols as learning to read, and that there are at least two stages in the development of this ability. The first is when the child regards the written word as a symbol of the spoken, and the second is when the child is able to disregard the spoken word as the intermediary. "Understanding of written language is first effected through spoken language, but gradually this path is curtailed and spoken language disappears as the intermediate link. . . . Written language becomes direct symbolism that is perceived in the same way as spoken language" (p. 116).

In comparing the child's learning to interpret written language with the child's learning to speak, Vygotsky notes that children "are taught to trace out letters and make words out of them, but they are not taught written language. The mechanics of reading what is written are so emphasized that they overshadow written language as such" (p. 105).

The work of Heath (1983) has taught us much about students who are disenfranchised from the interpretation of the written word. In her study of two rural communities, she examined the language habits of a black working-class community (Trackton) and a white working-class community (Roadville). She suggests that, in order for literacy to "catch on," students need to engage in interaction that allows them to do event-casts (i.e., planning of future actions) and accounts, and that also provides them with opportunities to talk about language, to talk about text (i.e., develop a sense of metalanguage about the tasks that they are trying to perform). The preparation that children receive for literacy during this interaction allows them entrance into "literate behavior" (Heath, 1984). Literacy, however, only happens when the learners are actively engaged in interaction that gives meaning to the symbols with which they are working. That is, they need to understand how the symbols with which they are working are manipulated, and can be manipulated, in order for them to use them effectively to mediate both their own behavior and that of others. It is the *interaction* about text, however, that facilitates entrance into understanding text. In this sense, it is interaction that provides the necessary link about which Vygotsky (1978) speaks when he talks about the child's gradual movement to comprehension of the written language as first-order symbolism. So also, it is through interaction about text that we can help children develop their schemata such that they can deal with new schemata/scripts with which the reading presents them. At first, this interaction allows them to understand the new schemata/scripts introduced in the text, but eventually it will help them discover how they can use the text

itself to mediate their understanding of the new ideas presented therein.

In summary, the child learning to read needs to understand, first, that print is meaningful and, second, that reading may require developing or changing or discovering new knowledge structures. People involved in teaching children to read may need to spend a great deal of time helping them understand these two things; and talk about text, especially talk that allows the child to explore the meaning of the text and how the meaning can be discovered within the text itself, is essential. Children will need help with decoding and semantic and/or syntactic prediction, but even more importantly, they will need time spent on interaction about what it is they are reading.

VARIOUS APPROACHES USED TO TEACH READING

In discussing various approaches or strategies that are used in teaching children to read, bear in mind that the list is not exhaustive. Those presented will be related to the foregoing discussion of the various elements involved in the reading process. We will examine the basal reader approach, the language experience approach, and the literature-based approach. At the same time, different methodologies will be mentioned as they apply. Particular attention will be given to the concerns of the ESL teacher who is faced with teaching children to read.

Using the Basal Reader

The use of the basal reader has been outlined above. The main assumption behind the basal reader approach is that reading is a bottom-up process whereby one begins reading instruction with the phonics of the language and works up to increasingly more difficult reading passages. All of the readers are controlled such that the students are not responsible for reading passages that include sounds/sight words to which they have not yet been introduced. Clearly, mastery of sound/symbol correspondences is at the heart of the approach in that they are considered the fundamentals that are necessary for reading instruction. In short, basal series are well-controlled systems which provide detailed scope and sequence charts outlining the "chunks" to be learned.

There are basal reading series that are broader than others in terms of the ancillary skills that they also include in their series. That is, in addition to phonics instruction, there are usually skill practice books that accompany a basal reading series and include drill in areas ranging from comprehension of text to various of the language arts objectives (e.g., punctuation, prefixes and suffixes, parts of speech). Teachers are also usually given instructions in the teacher's guide to question the students in various areas, especially in the area of comprehension. Sometimes the questions will reflect a very factual, literal level of comprehension, and sometimes they are more cognitively demanding, requiring recognition of such things as cause/effect relationships, inference, and character analysis. Nevertheless, the emphasis, especially in the primary grades, is on giving students control of the sound–symbol correspondences in written English.

The current research which emphasizes that reading is neither a bottom-up nor a top-down process, but rather a multifaceted phenomenon with various processes operating in parallel, is not well reflected in the traditional basal reading series. This is apparent in the changes in emphases in the new reading series being put out by the publishers. (For a good summary of the desired emphases, see the *California Framework on Language Arts, K-12,* which calls for an integrated, literature-based approach, not only with a greatly reduced amount of phonics instruction, but also phonics instruction which is limited almost exclusively to the first two years of reading instruction.)

With respect to ESL students, it seems clear that an approach that is based almost exclusively on phonics will not be adequate. Some reading publishers (e.g., Open Court) and reading teachers believe that ESL students are even more in need of a strong phonics approach than monolingual English speakers. The idea seems to be that the sound system in English is less familiar to ESL students, and therefore will require more attention. We would predict, however, that an approach based too exclusively on phonics will focus the student on decoding as reading, and will not encourage reading for meaning. It would seem that if our notions about schemata/scripts are correct, then ESL students are in special need of approaches that help them understand text as meaningful. If we rely solely on phonics, or use phonics as the main approach for reading instruction, ESL students will not focus mainly on meaning; rather, they will possibly learn to "sound out" words for which they may have little or no understanding. In this sense, a strict basal approach will need to be supplemented with other meaning-based activities if ESL students are to succeed.

Language Experience Approach

The emphasis in the Language Experience Approach (LEA) is on acquiring a reading vocabulary that is "personally meaningful and immediately useful" (Dixon & Nessel, 1983). The general idea is that the reading selections are generated from the life experiences of the students. The students dictate a "story" based on these experiences and the teacher writes their words down. The teacher then has the students read the story that they have told and s/he has written, helping out whenever the student needs assistance. This is done until the students are quite familiar with the story. Then individual words in the story are discussed and learned, and other reading skills are practiced and reinforced via specific activities designed by the teacher. These activities may introduce phonics patterns, punctuation, syntax, and semantics, among others. Finally, students are supposed to move from reading their own dictation to reading materials dictated or authored by others. (See Dixon & Nessel, 1983, for a more complete description of the steps followed in the LEA.)

There are several variations on the steps that are used in LEA. Sometimes the stories are recorded by a teacher and then transcribed later, especially if there are several students and the teacher wants each one to have his/her own story. At other times, the stories are group stories which the whole class participates in generating. Oftentimes, such a group story is the result of a common experience that the class has had together, such as a field trip to a museum. When this is the case, the teacher often moves into elements of writing as s/he asks the students to edit their group story, in terms of both organization and word choice. The teacher will often encourage the students to use new words they may have been exposed to during the field trip or experience that underlies the story.

Going back to the idea that the emphasis of LEA is on acquiring a reading vocabulary that is "personally meaningful and immediately useful" (Dixon & Nessel, 1983), one is able to see that the vocabulary used in the stories is "personally meaningful" in that it comes from the students who are telling the stories. The same vocabulary is "immediately useful" in that it enables the students to read their stories upon being written. In this sense, LEA has a built-in advantage that helps teach the student the connection between text and meaning. It allows for the "intermediate link" of spoken language en route to understanding written language as a first-order symbol— i.e., "a system of signs that directly symbolize the entities and relations between them" (Vygotsky, 1978, p. 106). By this is meant that LEA allows for the fact that the written language is still a second-order symbolism for students when they are first learning to read, and that in order for it to pass over to a first-order symbolism, the students will need experience of it first as reflecting oral language.

Other approaches ask the students to immediately begin using the written text as a first-order symbolism, without giving time for the conversion from second-order symbolism. LEA, on the other hand, is based on oral accounts of the students' experiences, which are then written down. This gives students the time to develop a bridge between oral and written language so that the conversion can eventually be made. It lets the students know that text is meaningful, that meaning can be derived from it.

LEA seems especially appropriate for ESL children who are beginning readers. As beginning readers, they need to engage in activities that help them know that text is meaningful. The dictated stories that result from LEA are evidence of this in that the student's own words form the text, showing very graphically the connection between spoken and written language. Second, as ESL students, LEA allows them to use what they know to begin to read. They do not spend an inordinate amount of time reading words which they might be able to sound out, but which have no meaning for them. Phonics can be taught through lessons that are based on the dictated text of the students. In this way, the phonics is related to the passage and is used as a way to facilitate reading for meaning. LEA also helps the ESL student with building the skills of prediction based on context. Since the context is perfectly clear, predictions based on semantics are easily made. The student brings meaning to the text and is therefore able to get meaning from the text. This is a tremendous advantage for beginning ESL students, since published texts often present them with passages for which they have very limited schemata and for which they therefore are able to make only very limited predictions. Syntactic prediction can also be encouraged by means of specific activities that the teacher develops related to the passage. Teachers can gear their lesson for the students to look at pronouns as cohesive markers, for example. Once the students realize the role of syntax in helping them create and understand text, they may well transfer this knowledge to other texts.

LEA encourages the use of literature and other content areas to move children beyond the confines of student-initiated texts. For example, a content area, such as social studies or science, can provide the experience that underlies student texts. Student texts can then be used as the bridge to published texts in the same areas. In this way, students are well prepared for what they read in the science textbook, and it is based on an experience that has been discussed and written about. The key for ESL students is that there be sufficient experience and discussion as preparation for understanding the text. Again, this reflects the idea that there are many schemata which the children need to build up before text will make sense to them.

In summary, LEA offers many advantages to ESL students who are beginning readers. Mainly, it provides opportunities for them to learn that text is meaningful and to make accurate predictions about text.

Literature-Based Approach

A literature-based approach to teaching reading is one in which children's literature is used as the starting point for teaching students reading and all of its subskills. The literature selected can include, but is not limited to, any of the following: picture books, folk tales, fables, myths, epics, modern fantasy, poetry, modern fiction, historical fiction, and biography. The methods usually begin with a clear reading of the selection of literature to be studied. Sometimes this can be done by the students on their own, and other times it is read by the teacher; e.g., when the students are nonreaders. During this phase, the emphasis is on the students' understanding the story, not only literally, but with all inferences intact. It is essential, therefore, that the reading of the literature be accompanied by scaffolded interaction that helps the children understand the text. This process is likely to be truncated in cases where the teacher usually thinks the students are clear about the

story before they actually are. In this sense, it is the art of scaffolded interaction to which the teacher must tend (Hawkins, 1988; Tharp & Gallimore, 1989). The time spent in discussion is time spent talking about text, which is necessary for entrance into new schemata that the text might introduce to the students. It will show the students how authors are able to communicate with their audience via written language.

For the beginning reader, the literature books are often story-picture books that have writing on one page and a picture on the opposite one. Vygotsky (1978, p. 114–115) believes that children first begin to write by drawing. That is, they realize that their drawings are not the real thing, but a symbol of the real thing, and as such, they are a first-order symbol of the real thing. Likewise, when children interpret pictures, they are engaged in symbol interpretation. They will, if allowed to do so, notice details in the pictures that require high-level cognitive skills in terms of the story interpretation. Among other things, they will check the information found in earlier pictures against that found in later pictures, make predictions about where the story is going, and compare one book with another, all based on interpretation of the pictures. This behavior often reflects what it is that good readers do, according to Hosenfeld's (1977, 1979) studies. This early talk about pictures in conjunction with talk about the text accompanying the pictures forms the basis of the interaction that will lead to understanding the story and building the necessary script for understanding story grammar. The children grow to learn that, just as the pictures represent events, writing represents speech. Pictures and the discussion of them, then, are an important part of the child's path to learning to read and write. (Oftentimes children will draw a series of pictures when asked to write a story. This series of pictures can then become the basis for a LEA story dictation. What is interesting is that teachers usually tell students that they have to write the story first, and that then, as a reward, they may draw a picture to go with the story. In fact, the reverse order may be more logical developmentally.)

Once children have read (or been read to) and understand a selection of literature, the teacher plans specific activities which help the students see how the author was able to accomplish the story, including such areas as character development, plot development, and point of view. There are several methodologies that lend themselves to these activities, ranging from story maps to sociograms to plot/tension graphs. (See Johnson & Louis, 1987; Mason and Au, 1986, for complete explanations and examples of these and other activities.) The students also study vocabulary, language arts skills, phonics, and other reading skills based on the literature selection; everything is related to the literature selection. In this way complete scripts are built up that allow the children to understand the literature selection, the author's viewpoint, how the author used language to accomplish his/her goals, and how we can read what the author had to say. Follow-up activities are also based on the literature selection and can include such things as story retelling, story modeling (in which the children write a story of their own, modeling it on the literature selection), plays, puppet shows, and similar activities. Again, all of these activities are to be accompanied by a good deal of discussion, so that children have time to do event casting and accounts (Dixon and Nessel, 1983), and so that they have the opportunity to move from informal, unplanned spoken/ written language to formal, planned spoken/ written language. (See Flashner, 1987, for a presentation of the linguistic abilities of a group of fourth-grade ESL children in this regard.)

A literature-based approach to teaching reading is helpful for ESL students in that it guides them to read for meaning. It helps them understand that writers use language to communicate, and that part of their task as readers is to try to understand what that author has written. If the context of the piece of literature is developed by means of scaffolded interaction with the students, then the approach provides the ESL student with optimum interactive and cognitive demands for learning English and learning how to read. The approach also allows students to develop their metalinguistic abilities in that it provides them with ample opportunities for examining language and experimenting with it.

Although one of the stages of LEA is to introduce the student to published texts, the emphasis is on student text. Using children's literature as a basis for reading instruction helps move the child to published texts easily. The illustrations that accompany text help to contextualize the literature for the student, and can often act as the student's entry into the literature. Because the literature will introduce vocabulary and schemata with which the child is not familiar, Heath's (1984) ideas of talk about text are very important. If this is true of monolingual English-speaking children, it is even more true for ESL children, since their familiarity with English literary language and themes will be more limited. Gradually, the children should build a new script, one for approaching new text with which they are not familiar.

SUMMARY

Although the discussion presented here does not include all of the work done on teaching children to read, it has included three basic areas of reading instruction that are generally considered when teaching children to read. Viewing reading as decoding, prediction, and schemata building offers different areas of emphasis, each with its own specifics. If we view reading as a multifaceted process with the various processes going on simultaneously, however, then no one point of view is complete. We have also introduced three approaches to teaching reading to ESL children: basal reader, LEA, and literature-based. Again, the approaches all need to include in their development the various facets that make up reading.

Most importantly, ESL children need to realize what reading is as an activity—that text is meaningful, and then how to parlay this knowledge into helping them to read in their second language. The various approaches all offer a part of the picture, but it is the teacher's challenge to see that each child gets what is needed in order to build up all of the skills that make up reading.

NOTE

1. I wish to acknowledge Evelyn Hatch for the inspiration and ideas used in this chapter that first appeared in her chapter in the first edition of this book.

DISCUSSION QUESTIONS

1. In your first-grade class there is a girl named Vanessa and another one named Veronica. Every day you choose a student to read off the names of students that are in various cooperative learning groups. Many of the children read Veronica's name for Vanessa's and vice versa when they are reading the names on the lists, seemingly no matter how many times you correct them. What do you think is happening? Are they decoding? Are they using context? Are they using scripts? Are they doing all three?

2. In testing a child for reading, you observe that s/he often pauses at places that are not indicated (i.e., in the middle of a sentence), and neglects to pause at indicated places (i.e., at the end of sentences, after commas). What do you make of this behavior and what are some of the things that you would do to try and remedy it?

3. You are introducing a piece of children's literature to your first-grade reading group of second language students. You have just begun reading *The Five Chinese Brothers* to them, and one student notices that the five brothers are all sitting on chairs that are exactly alike.

a. You notice that the five brothers are actually sitting on stools, not ordinary chairs. Do you bring this up and discuss it?
b. You decide to raise the issue, and a discussion ensues among the children as to why the stools are all the same. As it is

winding down, one little girl says quietly, to no one in particular, that her grandmother has stools/chairs like those in the picture in her house, except that her grandmother's are red. You have already spent about 5–10 minutes discussing the stools. Do you let her share more information about this with the rest of the class, or do you move on? What would be the advantages either way?

4. You have been working on *Where the Wild Things Are* with your second-grade reading group of second language students. The children have reached the point where they are anxious to try reading the book aloud with and for each other. You have them organized in groups of 6–8 for the purpose of doing so, and you notice two things as the children read. The first is that the child whose turn it is to read aloud often has trouble reading words that you know s/he knows from working with him/her earlier. The second is that the other children who are following along while the one child is reading aloud often break in when there is a problem, helping the first child out. Yet, when it is their turn to read, these same children stumble over the same words they were earlier helping out with, and the first child is now able to help *them* out. What do you think is going on?

5. Your first-graders have written a book, modeled on a literature book they worked on earlier. They first drew pictures of what they wanted to write about, and then did a group language experience in order to form the text that went with each of their pictures. They each copied the story for themselves, studied the vocabulary that resulted from the text they created, and understood the punctuation that they used in the story, and you are satisfied that they have a good grasp of the material. They are very proud of their story and are begging you to let them read it to you. You decide to do so, and find that several of the children almost seem to have memorized the text of the story. That is, they barely seem to look at the text, and yet they tell you exactly what is on the page. You try to watch their eye fixations, and it appears to confirm your suspicions. Are they reading the story? Should you be worried, or have you "succeeded"? Do you think you should insist that they read it more carefully to you, perhaps indicating the words while they are reading them? Do you think it would be a good idea to have them read their stories in front of an audience other than yourself?

SUGGESTED ACTIVITIES

1. Interview several ESL children about what they think reading is. If possible, vary the age groups and reading abilities of the children. Ask them if they know someone in their class who is a good reader and someone who is a poor reader. Ask them how they can tell the difference and if they think they are good readers or poor readers. Do their answers reflect any of the reading approaches discussed in this chapter?

2. Ask two first- or second-grade intermediate ESL children to write a story about something that they did with a good friend. If the children cannot do so on their own, tell them that they may begin by drawing their story. You may then turn this into a language experience exercise by writing down what they tell you about their pictures and then reading it back to them. Finally, see if they are able to read the story after you have read it to them.

3. Perform a miscue analysis on two fifth-grade students, one who is an intermediate ESL student and one who is a monolingual English speaker who reads well. Do they make the same kinds of miscues? How are they the same or different? Finally, do another miscue analysis on a fifth-grade monolingual English speaker who has reading problems. How do these miscues compare and contrast with those of both the other students?

SUGGESTIONS FOR FURTHER READING

Dixon, C. N., and D. Nessel (1983)
Language Experience Approach to Reading (and Writing): LEA for ESL. Hayward, CA: Alemany Press.

Introduces LEA to ESL teachers and includes a lot of detailed information about the actual classroom practices involved in this approach. What is unique about the book is that it includes information about how to deal with various levels of ESL students and reasonable levels of expectation from them as these issues apply to LEA.

Johnson, T. D., and D. R. Louis (1987)
Literacy Through Literature. Portsmouth, NH: Heineman Educational Books.

Contains a wealth of ideas for presenting literature to children, grades K–6. It also includes many actual samples of children's work, giving the reader a good idea of what to be able to expect from children at various grade levels.

Mason, J., and K. Au (1986)
Reading Instruction for Today. Glenview, IL: Scott, Foresman.

An excellent examination of current reading practices as well as an excellent source of information about reading theory. The bibliography included in the book makes it especially useful. It does not go into much detail about teaching reading to ESL students, but it does make broad suggestions to use as a guide for their reading instruction.

Schank, R. C. (1982)
Reading and Understanding: Teaching from the Perspective of Artificial Intelligence. Hillsdale, NJ: Erlbaum.

Offers an interesting approach to teaching reading that includes valuable information on script building as it relates to learning to read. It is very helpful in terms of the considerations that teachers need to keep in mind at the level of schemata/scripts.

Tharp, R., and R. Gallimore (1989)
Rousing Minds to Life. New York: Cambridge University Press.

Covers many topics of relevance to reading teachers, including an illuminating observational study of a teacher who is trying to learn to scaffold her classroom interaction with her primary grade reading students. Her students are native Hawaiian Pidgin speakers learning to read in English.

Adult Literacy Training

Wayne W. Haverson

In recent years the changing nature of immigration patterns and birthrates has presented adult English as a second language instructors with a student population that is much different from those of previous years (Barnes, 1982; Bliss, 1986; Chall et al., 1987). A decade or more ago adult immigrants were a more urban and educated group and fit more easily into the traditional classroom environment. Literacy was assumed and the focus of much instruction was print-dominated. At the present time, however, native language literacy rates are low, and many adults arrive in the United States having had little or no exposure to urban settings. Adults are entering classrooms with little formal education and development of the accompanying cognitive processing skills (Kozol, 1985).

Basic literacy, the need to read, write, and compute well enough to be able to function in the community or on the job, now constitutes a major part of most adult ESL programs (Bliss, 1986; Bright, Koch, Ruttenberg, & Terdy, 1982). Adult educators are faced with the task not only of providing training in communicative competence but also of providing these learners with the means to access basic literacy as a first step in self-sufficient, independent learning (Meyer, 1987).

Accordingly, teachers of English as a second language need to be given specific training in literacy instruction that will respond to the needs of this changing population (Haverson, 1986). This training begins with an understanding of the reading process and the relationship of this process to the acquisition of basic literacy.

APPROACHES TO THE TEACHING OF LITERACY

The literature identifies two approaches to the teaching of literacy: a skills-based model and a strategy-based model (Goodman, Smith, Meredith, & Goodman, 1987; Holdaway, 1985). The difference between skills and strategies is a crucial one. Most approaches to reading and reading instruction emphasize the development of reading skills (Smith, 1983). Although some of these are comprehension skills, a great deal of attention is paid to skills for pronouncing and/or identifying words. In contrast, most socio- or pyscholinguists emphasize the development of strategies for getting meaning from connected text (Newman, 1985; Smith, 1983; Weaver, 1988).

Specifically, the skills-based model focuses on pieces of language, building from the smallest units of language (i.e, sounds to larger units such as words and phrases), or on breaking down the larger segments of language into individual units (Smith, 1983). In the strategy-based model, the primary focus is on comprehension. Reading is defined as a language-thinking process involving an interrelationship of semantics, syntax, and graphophonics (Holdaway, 1985).

In a skills-based approach, on the other hand, great emphasis is placed on the mastery of sound–symbol relationships (Ekwall & Shanker, 1983). It is based on the assumption that once this mastery has been achieved, meaning will follow. Learners are taught that once they have mastered basic phonics and letter-word recognition, they can use these skills independently to glean meaning from print (Jones, 1981).

A variation of the skills model identifies four distinct areas of language: vocabulary, sound–symbol relationships, grammar, and comprehension. Each area is analyzed in isolation. The underlying assumption of this model is that meaning will follow if one can integrate the subskills that have been presented to the reader in the form of long lists of vocabulary words, grammar rules and exercises, comprehension questions relating to factual recall of predetermined material, and sound-mastery (Liberman & Shankweiler, 1979). Most basal readers follow this model (Chall, 1983).

Both of these models of skill building are essentially ineffectual for teaching reading to learners who are beginning readers in English (Haverson & Haynes, 1982; Vorhaus, 1984). Such readers need to internalize strategies to unlock meaning from print, rather than to spend time attempting to make sense of isolated letters, words, and rules (Jones, 1981; Smith, 1983).

Moreover, the human brain is limited in the amount of information it can absorb, process, and commit to memory at one time (Hart, 1983). This means that reading must be a selective process which is necessarily rapid and which cannot proceed word by word (Smith, 1983). The application and integration of rules in the teaching of reading can only result in an overload of short-term memory. In a building block or decoding approach the meaning of one word can be forgotten before the next word is built, and thus, no meaningful message will emerge from print (Holdaway, 1985).

Furthermore, decoding does not allow the adult language-minority reader to take an active role in the reading process—that is, to bring his or her knowledge of the world and of a particular topic to the text (Amoroso, 1985; Carbo, 1987). For an adult, it denies the very nature of adultness and places that person in a childlike environment, as though the mind were a blank page in a book waiting to be written (Maring, 1978). Frank Smith

suggests that reading is only incidentally visual. Understanding print is far more dependent on what the reader already knows, on what is already in his or her head than what is printed on the page. For reading to make sense, it must respect the worldview of the reader so that the reader can actively, yet unconsciously, participate in construction of meaning from the printed page (Goodman, 1970; Pearson and Johnson, 1978; Smith, 1973, 1978a, 1983).

A strategy-based, or a whole language reading model, as it has come to be identified (Newman, 1985; Watson, 1987), incorporates a psycholinguistic perspective on reading based on insights from contemporary linguistics and cognitive psychology. Reading is viewed as a successful interaction of conceptual abilities, background knowledge, and processing strategies (Rigg & Kazemek, 1983, 1985). The target is comprehension, not the decoding of subvocal utterances. Reading, writing, and oral language are not learned in isolation. Rather, they are the components of a mutually supporting communication system and should, therefore, be presented together (C. Goodman, 1967; K. Goodman, 1973, 1979).

In this interdependent system, the focus is always on meaning. It is only after meaning is in place that the reader incidentally discovers the distinctive features in letters and words (Haverson & Haynes, 1982). In a whole language instructional environment, the reader learns to take chances, to risk errors, in order to learn about printed texts and to predict meaning. It places the primary focus on reading and not on vocabulary building, rule mastery, or sound–symbol relationships in isolation (Smith, 1983). The beginning reader develops the strategies of sampling, predicting, confirming or revising (Newman, 1985).

In summary, whole language literacy training programs are based on the following eight principles:

1. Learning in the classroom and out of the classroom are not different. Classroom

learning needs to be viewed as a continuation of the real world. Instructors must accept and respect the language and experiences the learner brings to the classroom. The instructor starts with what the learner knows and builds from there. This is building from the learner's strengths and expanding what the learner already knows. Learning should be personalized; that is, the learner must be involved in language activities which are meaningful, purposeful, and relevant.

2. The belief that language learning is a social event permeates the literacy classroom. These classrooms have a workshop atmosphere where learners interact and share. Some language learning is done with the support of others in a small group setting. Language learning is viewed as a transactional event whereby the construction of meaning is brought about as the result of the ongoing interaction among language users. Learning is risky business. The classroom environment must be one that encourages learners to take risks. They and the instructor learn from their errors because errors are viewed as information that tells where the learner is, developmentally, in the reading process.

3. The emphasis is on process in the literacy classroom. Instructors observe where in the process the learner is and how he/she uses it. These classrooms are organized to support individual growth. Although every learner may be involved in the same activity, individualization occurs at the level of response.

4. Language, both oral and written, is the primary means of creating new knowledge as well as the means for communicating that knowledge to others. Language is verbal thinking.

5. The four language processes (listening, reading, speaking, writing) are interrelated and interdependent. Deficiency or growth in one may cause deficiency or growth in another. Language is balanced between the two receptive processes of listening and reading and the two productive processes of speaking and writing.

6. Authentic reading materials—i.e., newspapers, menus, signs—provide the best models of language. Learners learn language in a way superior to direct instruction by internalizing literacy models through listening, reading, retelling, discussing, dramatizing, and writing.

7. The purpose of language is to create meaning. Skills are important in that they aid meaning. Skills are part of, and never separate from, purposeful communication.

8. Learners must be involved in real language activities. They must be reading meaningful materials every day. Learners also should be writing every day in a variety of ways and for a variety of purposes. There should be time for the sharing of what has been written. Throughout the writing activities, the learners will be listening and discussing ideas and messages with each other to facilitate the meaning-making process.

CHARACTERISTICS OF THE BEGINNING READER

In building a second language literacy training program, consideration must be given to the unique characteristics and needs of the nonliterate.

Being unfamiliar with a classroom and the tools of literacy, many learners will enter the program filled with anxiety and a lack of self-confidence. It is important to ensure that the environment for language learning is a safe and supportive one where the learners feel comfortable enough to take risks with learning (Bell & Burnaby, 1984).

In addition, instructors must be aware of additional factors that influence reading success of the nonliterate learner (Colvin & Root, 1981; Haverson, 1986; Haverson & Haynes, 1982; McGee, 1977; Thonis, 1970). Among those factors are the following:

- The ability to concentrate for a minimal period of time.
- The ability to follow directions.
- The ability to work both independently and with others.

- The ability to accept peer relationships.
- The ability to name things in pictures.
- The ability to follow left-to-right and top-to-bottom progression.
- The ability to categorize (same, different).
- The ability to perform fine and gross motor skill functions.
- The ability to follow along a line of print.
- The ability to distinguish left-to-right and top-to-bottom progression.
- The ability to understand and form symbols.
- The ability to follow proxemic signals (hand, facial, body).
- Recognition of the idea that a picture represents a real thing.
- Recognition of visual/auditory symbols.
- Recognition that oral speech may be written.
- Recognition of auditory statements and questions.
- Recognition and production of intonation patterns.
- Recognition of the idea that a two-dimensional object—i.e., a picture, a book, a piece of paper with text—may be used to convey meaning.

Most nonliterate learners will acquire these abilities as a result of involvement in real reading and writing activities. The process is accelerated if initial literacy instruction occurs in the learner's first language and if the learner has general good health and good visual and auditory acuity.

At any rate, the acquisition of second language literacy will be further influenced by the following eight factors (Colvin & Root, 1982; Gudchinsky, 1973; Haverson & Haynes, 1982; Thonis, 1970).

1. Learners without formal schooling have difficulty with transfer and generalization of knowledge and will require extensive orientation to the printed page in order to develop print awareness.
2. Learners respond negatively to long and numerous pages of dense print.
3. Learners tend to concentrate efforts on decoding words in the new language while limiting attention to the comprehension of meaning.
4. Special difficulty can be expected in comprehending texts if the learner lacks familiarity with the content.
5. Oral experience with the language which learners can use to help them decode text varies with their age and life experiences in the target language.
6. The ability to reflect on and talk about language and the lack of an understanding of concepts such as words, phrases, sentences, sounds, and other concepts relate to initial reading success.
7. The kinds of texts which are understandable vary with the age of learners and their experience in the culture of the target language.
8. The need for cultural information and explanations for figurative and idiomatic language is greater for second language than first language literacy learners.

It is important to remember that beginning second language learners who read in their first language already know what reading is all about. They have print awareness and many reading skills that are transferable to English, such as use of context clues, reading for the main idea, sequencing events, making predictions, and some decoding skills, depending on the orthography of the first language of the students. Learners who were taught to read in their first language before being introduced to English reading have a head start over learners whose first encounter with reading is in English, a language that is still a struggle for them to acquire.

THE CLASS AND THE CLASSROOM

Being unfamiliar with a classroom and the tools of literacy, most learners enter into the classroom with great fear and anxiety. Instructors must create a secure, nonthreatening learning environment. To do this, instructors must provide maximum opportunities for success with literacy. Oral directions used to facilitate the learning process should be simple and limited in number and should be accompanied by a clear set of hand signals. Remember, this may be the first time the learners have been exposed to a formal learning process. Consistently using the same words and signals and establishing a class routine can help make the class less stressful (Henderson, Portaro, & Wilensky, 1984). It is important, however, to be especially sensitive to, and aware of, cultural differences in order to avoid embarrassing or offending learners.

Mistakes are inevitable and, indeed, are part of the learning process. Too much correction can result in great frustration. It is wise not to correct every mistake but rather to attend only to those involving the items on which the lesson focuses. A good way to do this is to prepare learners thoroughly with a lot of class and group practice before calling on individuals (Bell & Burnaby, 1984).

Learners may lose their concentration if too much time is spent on any one item (Henderson et al., 1984). The teaching pace should be appropriate to the learners' rate of mastery. More advanced learners should be paired to do group or writing practice, thus freeing the instructor to review with the slower ones. Always save writing practice for the end of the lesson. This puts less pressure on learners who might otherwise feel as though they were holding up the rest of the class.

In language learning, recognition precedes production. Presenting all material in context facilitates the former. Learners need visual cues. The most successful cues are those closest to reality. Each step from the real item to an imitation (e.g., a miniature object, to a photograph, to a realistic drawing, to a sketch or diagram) is a further abstraction. Students may not connect the abstract with the concrete unless instructors point out the connections (Bright et al., 1982).

All new material must be reintroduced and practiced continuously. Presentation of the same material should be done in as many ways as possible because these nonliterate learners, as all learners, have different learning styles. Some will respond better to visual cues while others respond better to audio or to tactile/kinesthetic cues. Frequent review is a necessity for nonliterate learners (Bell & Burnaby, 1984; Haverson & Haverson, 1987).

MATERIALS AND TEXTS

Visual materials are a primary teaching tool for nonliterate learners. It is necessary for instructors to select and create materials relevant to the interests, capabilities, and needs of individual learners. Therefore, realia such as clocks, coins, calendars, and maps are essential. Whenever possible, the instructor should use real objects.

Symbolic representations may have to be taught. Matching real objects to pictures, and then to written symbols, such as a dollar sign, is one way to do this. Photographs are preferable to drawings because they are less abstract. Or, as an alternative, the instructor may select other visuals such as slides, film strips, and videos.

TEXTS

Many literacy instructors feel that presenting learners with a textbook can have a psychologically overwhelming effect, and thus they recommend only giving out material page by page rather than all at once in book form.

Most instructors find that they want to develop materials for each class based on the learners' particular needs and interests. Some instructors choose a beginning text and supplement it with their own specially developed materials and props, while others focus on their own special materials and supplement these with ideas or pages from textbooks (Bright et al., 1982).

As for any level of ESL, texts should be examined carefully before selection for classroom use. Many of the texts are inconsistent in level of difficulty. Some contain difficult material in between simpler sections. Therefore, many instructors prefer not to use a classroom text.

However, some learners can be confused and/or overwhelmed even by teacher-made material if too much is included. Simplicity is the key (Bell & Burnaby, 1984). Direction words used on materials should, whenever possible, be consistent with the oral directions used in class. Direction words written in a different color from the black-and-white text stand out and are helpful to the learners.

BEGINNING INSTRUCTION

A good way to begin to assess and teach initial literacy concepts is through variations of the language-experience approach (Dixon & Nessel, 1983; Haverson & Haynes, 1982). As in any type of instruction with nonliterates, it is useful to teach the concept of language experience. This can be done with picture stories, strip stories, and/or action-based activities.

Picture Story 1

1. Draw a picture of yourself on a small piece of newsprint.
2. Tell the class something about yourself (My name is _____, I have brown hair, I am wearing black shoes).
3. Distribute small pieces of newsprint and colored pencils or pens to the class.
4. Ask the class to draw pictures of themselves.
5. Ask class members to tell something about themselves.
6. Put the pictures on the bulletin board and ask individuals to "read" other class members' pictures at subsequent class meetings.

Variations of the above activity may be done with actual photographs of class members.

Picture Story 2

1. Select a picture from a magazine of inter-

est to you and tell the class about it (This is my house. It is white. There are three doors to my house).
2. Distribute magazines and ask class members to select pictures of interest to them.
3. Ask class members to "read" their pictures.
4. Put the pictures on the bulletin board and ask individuals to "read" other class members' pictures at subsequent class meetings.

Variations of this activity may be done as a progressive thematic collage (my house, my car, my living room).

Strip Story

1. Take a piece of newsprint and fold it into three sections (a beginning, a middle, an end).
2. Using simple stick figures, illustrate an event that has happened in the class (the class is in session, someone arrives late, the class continues). Make sure the illustration has a beginning, a middle, and an ending.
3. Tell the story to the class.
4. Divide the newsprint into three sections and distribute the sections to class members.
5. Ask the class members to come to the front and hold the story in the proper sequence.
6. Ask the class to "read" the story again as class members hold up segments of the story.
7. Put the strip story on the bulletin board and ask individuals to "read" the story at subsequent class meetings.

Action-Based Activity

1. Tell the class that you are going to teach them how to make pink lemonade from frozen concentrate. Show them a pitcher of lemonade and invite selected members to taste it.
2. Demonstrate the steps of making pink lemonade from concentrate.
3. Distribute the materials to small groups

and give them the instructions for making lemonade.

4. Make sentence strips with the directions (use pictures if the group has minimal letter-recognition skills).
5. Review the steps in the process with the sentence strips.
6. Distribute the sentence strips and invite the class members to come to the front of the room and sequence the directions.
7. Ask the class to read the sentence strips (large group, individuals).
8. Put the sentence strips on the bulletin board and ask class members to read them at subsequent meetings.

Group language-experience stories may be created from the strip story or action-based activities. When the class has completed the initial activity, ask the class questions about the sequence of events. Write their responses on a piece of newsprint. Remember to write the responses exactly as they are given. Expect errors of omission and incorrect grammar usage. Leave blanks where significant omissions occur, and ask the class to fill in the blanks at a subsequent class session. Put the completed language experience story on the bulletin board for future additions.

After the class has had success in several different variations of language experience activities, it is appropriate to begin individual language-experience activities.

Nonliterate learners need to develop "books" in order to help them see themselves as readers. Most learners can recognize some print words in their environment in the context of the logo or ad. They often do not read the words "Burger King" as much as they recognize some distinguishing feature. However, they do know that the words "Burger King" are a part of that logo. By separating these words, the nonreader can begin to build a sight vocabulary of environmental print words.

Word Books

The instructor assists the learners in the preparation of a book of words from the im-

mediate environment of the learner. The book may be made by the learners following an action-activity sequence, or they may use a spiral notebook, three-ring binder, or photo album.

1. Share with the learner a number of advertisements from the newspaper or a glossy magazine.
2. Ask the learner to cut out all the ads that he/she recognizes.
3. Ask the learner to read the ad. Circle the words and discuss them with the learner.
4. Write the circled word on a card in block print.
5. Place the ad on a page in the learner's book with the word card next to or below it.
6. Read these ad words with the learner until they are identified instantly.

Word Banks

A word bank consisting of words the learner has gathered is much more powerful than arbitrary lists of words. This sorting of words also gives the learner an opportunity to learn initial consonant phonic skills as well as other word-categorizing skills.

As the learner learns or encounters new words, the word is written on a 3 × 5 card. These words become a part of a word bank. Words from language-experience stories and environmental print books would be logical initial words in this word bank.

1. Write the new word on a word card. This word should be one that is familiar to the learner.
2. On the back of the card, put a picture or any other graphic that would help the learner identify the word on the other side.
3. Place this word card in an appropriate organizer (shoe box, recipe card holder).
4. Use the words as flashcards to build sight vocabulary.

When the learner has collected twenty or more cards, the cards can be sorted by categories.

1. Ask the learner to sort the words by the categories provided, e.g., initial consonants.
2. Ask the learner to sort into other categories, e.g., things, people.
3. Develop other categories of interest to the learner, e.g., food, cars, holidays.
4. Invite the learner to sort the cards into other categories. Put learners into groups of two and have them exchange their cards and guess each other's categories.

Sentence Stems

Sentence stems provide the learner with high-interest repetitive sentence structures guaranteeing reading success. The repeating stem makes that part of the sentence easy to read. The stem completing word is provided by the learner, thus building a positive "I can read" attitude.

The instructor creates a sentence stem of two or three words with a subject and a transitive verb. The learner provides the object word. The same stem is used over and over again with the learner providing different object words.

1. The instructor chooses a two or three word stem (I like _____).
2. The learner provides a word that makes sense with the stem, e.g., hamburgers.
3. The instructor writes in the word and reads the sentence. The instructor then asks for something else the learner likes and fills in another blank slot.
4. After the instructor and learner have done two or three sentence stems, the learner practices reading them. If desired, these object words may be added to the word bank.

An alternative to the single stem is to design two alternating, contrasting stems:
I like _____ .
I hate _____ .

Predictable Stories

The nonreader is helped by a predictable text. If the pattern in the story is repetitive, the learner can figure out the pattern and read with success. Predictability should be a strong criterion for selecting stories for use with nonliterates. These stories can provide many successful reading experiences.

The instructor should create predictable stories around the interests of the learners. If they are interested in cars, for example, the instructor makes up a predictable car story. It might read like this:

> I wanted to see how fast my car would go.
> By the end of the first block
> I was going 30 miles per hour.
> By the end of the second block
> I was going 40 miles per hour.
> By the end of the third block
> I was going 50 miles per hour.

Silly Sentences

The "silly sentence" strategy puts the emphasis on whole sentences rather than upon individual words. The entire sentence must be read with meaning to determine which word is silly. In addition, it forces the learner to read for meaning rather than individual word identification.

To start this activity the instructor makes up a sentence in which one word is silly and does not make sense (e.g., I ate my foot). Then the instructor asks the class to figure out which word is silly. The instructor presents additional sentences containing silly words, and then asks the learners to make up silly sentences. However, while this activity is carried out, the instructor stresses that good readers always try to make sense out of what they read.

Written Conversation

Written conversation connects reading and writing and helps develop fluency in both processes. It reduces the threat and increases the interest in both reading and writing. It helps to develop the initially useful concept that reading is the process of decoding written speech.

Instead of talking about something, a

conversation is written. Specific events that both the instructor and learner know about form the basis for the written conversation. The conversation is started by the instructor, who briefly writes down on a sheet of paper what he/she wants to say about the topic selected. The instructor then hands the sheet to the learner, who reads the comment and responds with a comment. The learner hands the paper back to the instructor. This process continues until they have no more to say during the allotted time. At this point, the instructor should take a few minutes to discuss what has been written.

In doing such an activity the learners are encouraged to write, even if it is little more than scribbling. The instructor needs to be aware of problems with writing and devote additional time to letter formation and/or different styles of writing. This can best be done by copying and recopying materials generated experientially.

If the learner cannot read the instructor's writing, the instructor will write first and then read aloud what was written, pointing to the words so the learner can follow the writing as it is read.

Flashcard Directions

Often beginning readers start at the beginning of a passage and slowly read every word no matter what the reading purpose. Also, they tend to start over no matter how many times the passage (sentence) has been read. The flashcard strategy requires learners to quickly read what is already known, and read carefully only that which they do not know.

The flashcard directions activity, a variation of a Total Physical Response activity, forces the beginning reader to read more than one word at a time.

1. On an index card or sentence strip the instructor writes a direction of 5 to 10 words. (Please put your hand on the desk.) The learners read and carry out the instruction.

2. Flash each card, asking the learners to do what the card says. (Put your hand on your head.) Encourage chunking of all words in one glance.
3. Flash the card again and explain to the learners that they must read ahead and look at all the words. (Put your pencil on your desk.)
4. Each time the card is flashed urge the learners to skip the words already read and read the new words. (Put your notebook on the floor.)

CONCLUSIONS

In conclusion, it is essential that prospective adult ESL instructors have a knowledge of the reading process. This knowledge will provide the basis for guidelines for the development of beginning literacy instruction. These guidelines, then, can be used to develop classrooms where learners are actively involved in literacy activities that have meaning and application to the real world; where learners achieve success in literacy tasks because the curriculum has been designed not only to accommodate, but also to capitalize on, their unique experiences; where learners become and remain literate in their first and second languages; and where learners are in an environment where success and achievement for all are not only attainable but taken for granted.

DISCUSSION QUESTIONS

1. What is ESL literacy? How does ESL literacy differ from native language literacy? How is it similar?

2. How do socio-psycholinguistic definitions of reading typically differ from other definitions?

3. What is the difference between reading skills and reading strategies?

4. What observations about how adults learn underlie a whole-language approach to ESL literacy?

5. What classroom accommodations must be made to meet the needs of the nonliterate limited-English-speaking learner?

6. What are some ways, other than testing, in which instructors can assess limited-English proficient learner's needs and progress in becoming literate?

SUGGESTED ACTIVITIES

1. Draw on paper how you might design the physical aspects of an ESL literacy classroom. How would you arrange the desks and/or tables? What other areas would you have in the classroom? Where is the instructor's desk? Would you have an area for learners to share their writings? A class library? Centers for writing, for other activities? These are only some of the major aspects that you might consider in designing your classroom.

2. Pretending you are a new part-time ESL instructor who has been assigned to an ESL literacy class at a remote site, write a letter to the program administrator explaining your approach for teaching literacy to limited-English-speaking adults. Explain how it reflects what we know about adult learning and the language acquisition process. Restrict your letter to two single-spaced pages or the equivalent. Avoid technical terms, since the administrator does not have an ESL or reading background.

3. Think further about the learners you want to teach and the situation and classroom in which you want to teach. Describe the first sessions/weeks in your classroom.

4. Select meaningful, adult texts—e.g., driver's manual, shopping list, grocery ads, rental agreements, bus schedules—for placement in your class library. Prepare three activities that could be used with these texts for student projects as prereading activities.

SUGGESTIONS FOR FURTHER READING

Teacher References

Bell, J., and B. Burnaby (1984)
A Handbook for ESL Literacy. Agincourt, Ontario: Dominie Press.

Dixon, C., and D. Nessel (1983)
Language Experience Approach to Reading (and Writing). Hayward, CA: Alemany Press.

Goodman, K. S., ed. (1968, 1973)
The Psycholinguistic Nature of the Reading Process. Detroit: Wayne State University Press.

Haverson, W. W., and J. Haynes (1982)
Literacy Training for ESL Adult Learners. Washington, DC: Center for Applied Linguistics.

Jones, E. V. (1981)
Reading Instruction for the Adult Illiterate Chicago: American Library Association.

Kozol, J. (1985)
Illiterate America. Garden City, NJ: Anchor Press/Doubleday.

Smith, F. (1985)
Reading Without Nonsense, 2nd ed. New York: Teachers College Press.

Vygotsky, L. (1962)
Thought and Language (Translated by E. Hanfmann and G. Vakar). Cambridge, MA: M.I.T. Press.

Weaver, C. (1988)
Reading Process and Practice: From Socio-psycholinguistics to Whole Language. Portsmouth, NH: Heinemann Educational Books.

Student Textbooks

Boyd, J., and M. A. Boyd (1982)
Before Book One. Englewood Cliffs, NJ: Prentice-Hall Regents.

Haverson, W. W., and S. H. Haverson (1987)
Celebration: Festivities for Reading! Hayward, CA: Alemany Press. (For young adults only)

Molinsky, S., and B. Bliss (1989)
Expressways Access. Englewood Cliffs, NJ: Prentice-Hall Regents.

Mrowicki, L., and P. Furnborough (1982)
A New Start Literacy Workbook I. Portsmouth, NH: Heinemann Educational Books.

Wigfield, J. (1989)
First Steps in Reading and Writing, 2nd ed. New York: Newbury House.

Academic Reading and the ESL/EFL Teacher

Fraida Dubin and David Bycina

APPROACHES TO ACADEMIC READING

Introduction

While it may seem to be another specialization altogether, modern language teachers often find that they must also serve as reading skills teachers since emphasis on reading has become one of the primary curricular concerns in second and foreign language programs. In fact, reading is often the chief goal of learners in countries where English is taught as a foreign language; while reading and writing together are the central activities in most intermediate and advanced ESL programs at the secondary and postsecondary levels. Attention to academic reading or reading-for-the-purpose-of-learning, therefore, has come to be one of the most important methodological topics in the field of teaching English to speakers of other languages.

Interest in reading within the context of second and foreign language instruction has evolved cyclically over the years. Some generations back, the prevailing approach was centered, often exclusively, on the reading of texts in the target language, thus the names "reading approach" or "grammar-translation method" were used. The focus was on matching words in the foreign language text with meanings in the student's native tongue. The process of gaining an understanding of large chunks of text tended to be obscured. While the approach had certain limited advantages—for example, it emphasized word knowledge and proved satisfactory for reading literary genres such as poetry—it

came to be thoroughly rejected because it overlooked the spoken characteristics and communicative purposes of language.

In the 1940s and 1950s, a new generation of experts called for more attention to matters of pronunciation. They held that speech was basically what mattered in language; writing (and, by implication, reading) was merely a secondary manifestation. The resulting audiolingual method used reading and writing simply to reinforce grammatical patterns and vocabulary items that had been introduced orally. But this narrow vision, too, receded in time as learners' purposes for being able to use second or foreign languages became the focus in planning instructional programs. Reading was again elevated to primacy when the main function of language instruction was to enable students to learn academic subject content, typically through reading textbooks and similar materials. Owing to this shift in emphasis, ESL/EFL teachers took on the additional responsibility of providing instruction in reading skills.

In today's ESL/EFL classrooms, academic subject content is frequently the context through which the target language is studied. Whether it is history, social science, or computer science, students are learning English by reading and studying the subjects that are part of their academic programs. But often in modern classrooms, teachers' and learners' attention is centered as much on the skills for deriving meaning from texts as it is on the meaning which resides in those texts. At the same time, the field of ESL/EFL recognizes that learners need to have control of basic patterns of the language in order to learn new subject content. In addition, they must possess well-developed word-stocks to cope with unedited materials.

Actually, academic reading is a cover term for a variety of strategies that bring together advanced reading, study skills, vocabulary building, and even writing activities such as note taking, summarizing, and underlining. In ESL/EFL-for-academic-purpose courses, teachers must be able to simultaneously juggle a variety of objectives: instruction in reading skills per se; language-culture concerns, or the element that makes working in an L2 classroom different from teaching native-born students; study skills, or instruction in how to learn content from texts.

The assignment to teach academic reading is challenging since it requires that the teacher has an understanding of the nature of reading and of learning through reading. In addition, teachers of academic-purpose courses must also have some familiarity with the subject content of the texts their students are using in their academic course work. Or, possibly equally important, they must be enthusiastic about learning new subject content even if it is outside their customary sphere of knowledge. They need not be technical specialists themselves, but they must be able to handle subjects that often demand close reading.

This chapter first surveys the specialization of academic reading: What theory knowledge about the reading process can help teachers understand their assignment? What are the chief differences involving academic reading programs for native-born as opposed to English as a second and foreign language contexts? What strategies for learning how to learn need to be incorporated in academic-purpose programs? What is the teacher's unique role in providing preparation in academic reading skills?

Models of the Process of Reading

Reading is one of those human capacities which tends to be taken for granted by those who do it effortlessly in their everyday lives. Yet, although it has been studied and scrutinized for generations by scholars from a variety of disciplines, the process of reading remains a mystery. Since it is an activity which takes place, at least in part, as a function of the brain—as does language itself—questions about its nature are answered through constructing theoretical models of what might take place when the mind gets meaning from what the eyes see on the page of print.

Bottom-Up-Reading

An older, and now considered outdated, view was that reading takes place by matching sounds and letters; or, stated in terms of more sophisticated terminology, reading was considered a process of manipulating phoneme–grapheme relationships, as described by a structural linguist (Bloomfield, 1933, pp. 500–501):

The person who learns to read, acquires the habit of responding to the sight of letters by the utterance of phonemes. This does not mean that he is learning to utter phonemes; he can be taught to read only after his phonemic habits are thoroughly established.

The approaches to reading which are part of some children's first-language experience in terms of recognizing letters, memorizing names of the letters in the alphabet, and sounding out simple words (i.e., the "phonics method") are part of the traditional, conventional view of what reading is all about. An aspect of this view was that reading is a passive activity, with writing as the active counterpart. Basically, the model fostered practices in reading instruction which built up learners' decoding abilities from the bottom up, starting with the smallest units, single letters, "letters blends," and building up to words and phrases.

Top-Down Reading

That more static view was upset over 20 years ago by reading specialists who offered a competing model, one which became known as a "psycholinguistic" theory about reading.

(Goodman, 1967; Smith, 1978b). According to this newer model, the role of readers was considered to be quite active: they predict meaning as they read, they take in large chunks of text at a time, they do not attend to separate letters, rather they match what they already know with the meaning they derive from the text. In this view, reading is more a matter of reconstructing meaning using only partly the graphophonic, syntactic, and semantic systems of the language. More salient to successful reading is being able to guess what the author will say next by confirming predictions related to one's past experience and knowledge of the language. Inevitably, this model took on the nickname of "top-down reading" since it stresses comprehension of larger units of meaning.

Second language reading specialists were early advocates of this dynamic view of the nature of reading, with the result that many of the materials produced for reading in English as a second or foreign language adopted instructional strategies which stressed activities such as guessing the meaning of words from the context, previewing an article before reading it in order to have an overall view of its theme, and actively engaging in predicting what the author might say next. In addition, materials have stressed reading strategies derived from top-down reading theory, such as reading for main ideas of whole sections and paragraphs, looking for details which offer supporting evidence, and reading as rapidly as possible in order to understand the overall theme of a passage.

Interactive Models

During the 1980s an alternative model of reading was proposed that puts together the two views, bottom-up and top-down. The result is called an "interactive" (Perfetti, 1985; Rumelhart, 1977; Stanovich, 1980) model of the process of reading. It stresses the interplay of all meaning-gathering activities which take place during reading. While the basic theoretical work has centered on native or first language readers, the interactive model has been adopted by many second language reading researchers as well (Eskey, 1986).

Interactive theory acknowledges the role of previous knowledge and prediction but, at the same time, reaffirms the importance of rapid and accurate processing of the actual words of the text. According to the interactive model, the reading process works like this: First, clues to meaning are taken up from the page by the eye and transmitted to the brain. The brain then tries to match existing knowledge to the incoming data in order to facilitate the further processing of new information. On the basis of this previous experience, predictions are made about the content of the text, which, upon further sampling of the data, are either confirmed or revised.

Essentially, then, the two processes, bottom-up and top-down, are complementary; one is not able to function properly without the other. Thus, interactive theory accounts for the ability which mature readers have when they read rapidly for main ideas as well as their ability to read closely when necessary—for example, in scanning for specific information or proofreading material after composing it.

Within second language reading theory, particular prominence has been given to the role that the reader's background information or previous knowledge plays in text comprehension (Carrell & Eisterhold, 1983; James, 1987). If it is the case that there is little understanding of what one reads if one does not already possess some information about the topic at hand, then the entire activity of reading for the purpose of learning must be viewed in a different way. For example, the importance of background information for comprehension makes the strategies which teachers present for the purpose of reading-to-learn even more significant.

What Needs to Be Taught

The implication of the interactive model for reading instruction is that practice in both bottom-up and top-down strategies must be provided. This is particularly necessary in the case of second language learners who often fail to comprehend written material. Some, because of their previous training in translation, plod through the text from beginning to end in a laborious word-by-word fashion, pausing often to consult a dictionary for lexical items that they do not know. Such students rely on bottom-up processing and fail to take advantage of previous knowledge and prediction. Contrary to their expectations, their slow pace and the frequent interruptions tend to short-circuit understanding rather than facilitate it. Other students, however, seem to employ just the opposite strategy; they often overlook textual clues and guess wildly at the meaning of a passage on the basis of incomplete or missapplied preconceptions. Clearly, overreliance on either type of processing to the neglect of the other is bound to cause difficulties.

The result of combining approaches to reading that embrace both top-down and bottom-up views is particularly apt in working with second language learners who do not have sufficiently well developed reading skills to cope with extensive academic reading assignments. For example, low-intermediate-level readers can benefit from working on perception tasks which require instantaneous recognition of lexical and syntactic forms through rapid recognition exercises (Stoller, 1986).

At the intermediate level of ESL instruction, learners can practice attack skills such as simple phrase perception, recognition of clues which signal phrases and link whole sentences. For example, students work on exercises which provide a list of letters, words, or phrases and several parallel lists of alternatives, one of which contains the target item. The task is to locate and circle the matching item as quickly as possible. Phrase-identification exercises based on this format are of particular value in that they reinforce the notion that texts should be attacked in meaningful chunks, rather than word by word.

Such identification exercises can be combined into a systematic rate-building or speed-reading component in an academic reading program. Too often overlooked in advanced ESL courses, the skill of reading rapidly may not be familiar or may even be intimidating to students from other language backgrounds. Typically, students even at advanced levels read English language textbooks at a ponderously slow pace. Contrary to their beliefs, a slow reading rate actually reduces rather than ensures their understanding of the text. It has been estimated that reading at a rate of 200 words per minute would appear to be the absolute minimum in order to read with full comprehension (Fry, 1975). Further, the demands of most academic programs pressure students to cover a vast amount of reading material. Certainly in ESL academic settings, helping students learn to cope with the quantity of their reading assignments is a high-priority objective (Mahon, 1986).

Being able to comprehend an unsimplified text accurately and at a relatively rapid rate presupposes a rather extensive knowledge of vocabulary and grammar; both of these aspects of language learning cannot be overlooked in a reading class. However, too often foreign or second language reading instruction has simply been used as a vehicle through which to teach structure and lexis of the language rather than the skill of reading. Although it can be assumed that intermediate and advanced students by definition have been introduced to the basic grammatical structures of the language, authentic texts frequently contain more complex constructions—for example, anaphoric reference and cohesive devices—which pose problems of the kind that result in second language readers' having trouble synthesizing information across sentences and paragraphs. Therefore, reading classes should include instruction of the grammatical elements which typically occur over large stretches of text. Ideally, such instruction would use the unedited passages which constitute the reading course syllabus as the core material.

At advanced levels, vocabulary building is an important aspect of the reading course since without well-developed vocabularies the process of reading completely breaks down. Often, students themselves are the first to recognize their own needs for vocabulary work. While vocabulary learning is entirely a topic by itself (see the chapter by Seal in this volume), reading and vocabulary have a symbiotic relationship: one really is not possible without the other. The reading teacher can help students by preparing them with a brief list of some of the most important terms in a passage, together with their meanings in the context of the material at hand, before they read it. In addition, the teacher can point out words in the text which are linked together thematically, and words which have previously appeared in the materials already covered in the course. ESL/EFL reading teachers should not overlook the need for their students to work on vocabulary, but at the same time new vocabulary should not overshadow reading. One rule of thumb the teacher can use is this question: what words in the text are vital to understand in order to read the text accurately and critically? For example, the exercise below illustrates one way to alert students to words that are keys to overall meaning of the passage and that have occurred in previous thematically related passages (Dubin & Olshtain, 1990, p. 147):

Vocabulary Preparation

These words and expressions are thematically related to each other. Which ones do you already know? Which are familiar from your reading of other selections?

> *ancestral, ancestor*
> *branches of descent*
> *descended, descendant*
> *diverge*
> *evolution*

Cultural Dimensions to Reading

Although our understanding of the nature of the reading process crucially influences the instructional practices which teachers provide, there is far more to reading than its psycholinguistic aspect alone. As with all literacy uses, there is a significant cultural side as well. Indeed, the cultural dimension to reading is central in second and foreign language classrooms (Parry, 1987; Steffensen & Joag-Dev, 1984).

Models of the reading process attempt to describe what all readers are able to do, usually without specific regard to the writing system involved. So, theory-building work generally assumes alphabetic writing and, in almost all cases, the Roman alphabet letters in which English is written. There is an absence of research regarding reading processes with other writing systems. But since the dimension that makes an ESL/EFL context unique lies in its cross-linguistic, cross-cultural elements, they must be taken into account in planning for academic reading courses as well.

Learners in ESL/EFL academic reading courses come with values, beliefs, and attitudes which reflect their own cultural patterns of living and thinking. At the same time, all of the reading/writing activities which are carried out in classrooms are themselves reflective of a distinct subculture, namely, the world of schooling. While teachers are usually sensitive to cultural differences—certainly an awareness of culture modes is the most basic requirement for ESL/EFL teachers—they may take for granted, or simply overlook, those cultural aspects which belong uniquely to the world of academics.

Some of the culture-based instruction that needs to take place in academic reading courses includes information about how particular text types are set out, arranged, and organized. Activities that deal with locating the parts of a book, for instance, can ease the demands of academic learning. Learners can discuss what information is found on the publication page, the title page, the table of contents, the preface, the introduction, the chapter abstracts, the index, the reference section, the appendix, and so on.

Another cultural dimension to reading involves one's purposes for reading and the attitudes one holds towards the book and its content. It may be appropriate for theorists to conjecture about the idealized dialog which takes place between the reader and the author, but if a reader has been culturally embued with the idea that texts are sacred, not to be doubted or discussed, then the ESL/EFL teacher needs to utilize techniques and instructional practices which take attitudes based on cultural backgrounds of learners into account. One effective technique is to give students ample opportunities to work in dyads and small groups in which they share with each other some of the details concerning the practices of reading—and literacy in general—in their own countries. Frequently, helping students bring some of these culture contrasts into conscious recognition helps them to learn to live in two worlds—their own native-born language/culture as well as the second language/culture.

A further cultural dimension lies in the nature of a subject matter content and the academic discipline from which it stems. Physical and biological sciences tend to have their own systems for presenting information; they are written in particular formats; they make use of specialized vocabularies; they contain a tone which is associated with the field. Similarly, the subfields of social science have their own ways of presenting knowledge in texts. Learners/readers must be made aware of these significant subcultural differences among disciplines since it can make academic reading and learning easier to cope with. (Bensoussan & Goland, 1985; J. A. Foley, 1985; Mustapha, Nelson, & Thomas, 1985; Szöllösy, 1985).

Reading to Learn and Learning by Doing

It may be true enough that people learn to read by reading and that good readers are people who read a lot (Smith, 1978b), but academic reading goes beyond the demands of recreational reading. Many ESL/EFL students need to be introduced to a variety of self-help strategies which can aid them with the specialized purpose of learning new subject content through reading. These learning-through-reading techniques (the term "study skills" is sometimes used) are often less well understood by students whose basic early education took place outside of the United States, particularly if memorization of texts was the key activity in the educational process.

In its broader structure, an ESL/EFL academic reading course should emphasize both reading to learn (activities that stress comprehension of subject matter content) and learning by doing (activities that call for utilization of the ideas in the text). The former deals with the text at hand exclusively; the latter takes the learner beyond the text and into some kind of reformulation of the facts, information, and concepts found in it. For example, in reading to learn, emphasis is given to close reading of texts, often paragraph by paragraph, in order to find the function which each paragraph fulfills in the passage. Does the paragraph contain the author's main thesis, supporting ideas, fuller expansion of supporting ideas, transition to another theme, or what else?

Reading to learn also involves complex thinking skills in which students must be able to make the material their own through activities which guide them into analyzing texts, such as summarizing passages and chapters, picking out main ideas and building them into an outline, finding comparison and contrast or cause and effect examples, following an argument in the text, deciding whether a piece of information is relevant to a topic under discussion.

A classic activity associated with reading to learn is the SQ3R technique (Robinson, 1962). The letters and number represent a formula for learning from textual material in which learners carry out the following self-discovery procedures: (1) Survey the text to discover its overall meaning, general outline, and main points; (2) ask questions based on the headings and topics discovered during the "survey" step; (3) read the text, often paragraph by paragraph or section by section, taking notes while reading; (4) recite by giving answers to the questions raised in step 2;

and (5) review the material by going back over the main points with the help of the brief notes, citing major subpoints and trying to memorize both the main points and supporting ideas.

A further objective in reading to learn is gained through introducing more cognitively complex tasks in which students read critically in order to understand the author's implied ideas, make inferences about the material at hand, and link the ideas in one text to those that have been introduced in another one.

Many of the reading-to-learn activities that have been outlined above lend themselves to thematic, or topic-centered, reading in which a set of materials is composed of a variety of passages, all with a common subject area focus. By reading in depth around a particular subject area, students experience marked growth in background knowledge (Dubin, 1986). While the initial reading may prove difficult, with each additional piece on a related topic the reading becomes easier. In addition, this technique frequently gives students opportunities to encounter the same words and expressions across materials, thus reducing the formidable vocabulary load problem which reading unedited texts, even textbooks designed for school use, presents to second and foreign language learners.

Learning-by-doing activities help students extract meaning from texts by using note-taking skills, following directions, following a sequence of ideas, solving problems set up in the text, and similar methods. Information in a text which is highly structured in nature often lends itself to being transferred to graphic forms, such as lists, diagrams, and flowcharts. By manipulating the data, learners gain more experience with the language as well as with the underlying organizational systems presented in the material.

A vital aspect of learning by doing goes beyond reading itself for it moves into peer discussion activities. The talking which follows reading is an important part of both language learning and content learning. Students should be encouraged to find a part-ner or a small group with whom they feel comfortable to express ideas in the new language which they have discovered through their reading. It is the teacher's responsibility to ensure that the small groups, or dyads, take form so that each individual has maximum opportunity to express him/herself. Structured questions which deal with the content of the texts at hand, as well as questions which give students opportunities to relate the information and ideas in the reading passages to elements in their own lives, can be introduced during the discussion periods.

The Role of the Teacher

In academic reading classes, teachers have responsibilities that are unique to the skill of reading itself, for it is the teacher who must provide a model—granted an implicit one—of how a good reader behaves. Unfortunately, too many teachers feel they are shirking their duties if they fail to "instruct" during each and every minute of a class session. But the experience of reading is essentially an individual one which requires that the reader be caught up with the text. Or, metaphorically speaking, that the reader be engaged in a dialog with the author. Teachers need to respect learners'/readers' rights to have a quiet reading environment. Actually, the teacher can impart the idea of the importance of reading by actually sitting at his/her desk for some part of the reading period, and reading.

It is up to the teacher to impart a positive attitude about the activity of reading. Many students need to be introduced to the idea that through reading there lies an entire world of new ideas, fantasy, and wonderment. Even though the materials for reading may relate to school topics, the reading teacher can play a pivotal role by showing students how the topics in textbooks are carried over into the real world outside of the classroom. By providing additional materials for reading—paperback books, popular magazines, newspapers, and other print materials, the teacher can help make academic subjects come alive.

PUTTING THEORY INTO PRACTICE: TEACHING A CONTENT-BASED READING LESSON

The teaching of reading has often involved little more than assigning the students a text and requiring them to answer a series of comprehension questions when they have finished. This procedure, however, is really a testing rather than a teaching strategy. It can determine whether the students are already able to extract certain kinds of information from the text, but it does nothing to provide them with the skills and strategies needed to become efficient, effective, and independent readers. Attempting to teach such skills and strategies is the main thrust of current approaches to reading instruction.

In contemporary practice, a reading lesson is usually divided into three parts, the prereading, while-reading, and postreading stages, each of which has its own particular aims and procedures. In this section, each of these stages will be discussed in turn.

The Prereading Phase

The goals of the prereading stage are to activate (or build, if necessary) the students' knowledge of the subject, to provide any language preparation that might be needed for coping with the passage, and, finally, to motivate the learners to want to read the text.

The first goal of the prereading stage is founded upon the notion, discussed earlier, that the students' previous knowledge and experience affect their comprehension of the material. What teachers do in the way of summoning up the proper frame of reference before the students confront the text, therefore, will influence their success.

Various techniques have been suggested to mobilize existing knowledge, including the use of pictures, movies, field trips, values clarification exercises, and even role-plays.

Research has not yet determined which, if any, of these is most effective, so teachers are free to experiment according to the nature of the reading material and the inclinations of their classes (Carrell & Eisterhold, 1983). In an academic setting, however, somewhat more formal techniques might be more appropriate. These could entail word-association activities, discussion, and text surveys, among others.

Word-association tasks generally involve eliciting from the students as many ideas as they can offer regarding the announced subject of the text. Normally, their suggestions are written on the board and sometimes arranged into a semantic map or "graphic organizer," which indicates how the concepts are related to each other. Because such brainstorming is a random process, it may sometimes be necessary for the teacher to supplement the students' contributions with new vocabulary and concepts critical to an understanding of the reading.

Discussions have also been found to activate what students know and, through the exchange of information, to enhance their knowledge of the subject. Discussions can be initiated by simply posing questions about the content of the text or by more elaborate means, such as "anticipation guides." The latter is a series of statements, often provocative in nature, which are intended to challenge students' knowledge and beliefs about the content of the passage. After the students have individually indicated their agreement or disagreement on the worksheet provided, they may be put in groups to justify and elaborate upon their responses.

The last of the prereading techniques, text surveying or previewing, is often, but not exclusively, used with longer stretches of discourse, such as a chapter from a textbook. The purpose of this activity is to quickly determine the structure of the piece and to identify the key ideas. Normally, this involves examining the title and subtitles, the summary and conclusion, and the visual support material, such as pictures, charts, maps, and the like. Along the way, questions are formulated which will provide the students with a reason for reading.

The While-Reading Phase

The aims of the second stage are to help students to understand the specific content and to perceive the rhetorical structure of the text.

This stage, too, requires the teacher's guidance to ensure that students assume an active, questioning approach to the material. Such guidance can be supplied by a number of while-reading tasks. The simplest technique for this purpose is to provide the students before they read with a list of questions that direct their attention to the major ideas of the text. For maximum benefit, the questions should address three levels of understanding: the explicit, the implicit, and the applied (see Figure 1). The first solicits literally stated information, the second asks for information that can be inferred, and the third necessitates relating new ideas to previous knowledge or experiences.

Also useful in guiding the students through the text, but considerably more work for the teacher, are "guide-o-ramas" and "pattern study guides," both of which were originally developed for secondary school content reading classes. A guide-o-rama is a series of statements, instructions, and/or questions that leads students through the assigned reading and indicates what information is important, how a paragraph or section is organized, and what is to be learned (see Figure 2, p. 204). Pattern study guides, which are somewhat more limited in scope, focus the students' attention on the ways that paragraphs, or even larger units of text, are typically structured to represent relationships between the main idea and subordinate detail, cause and effect, comparison and contrast, problem and solution, and so on. The most familiar form of pattern study guides is the traditional outline, but other graphic devices such as diagrams and flow charts have recently become fashionable (see Figure 3, p. 205). By having the students complete an outline or fill in a graphic, teachers can help students to perceive the relative importance of text concepts and how these ideas are re-

---

Directions: Look over the statements below before reading. While reading, indicate whether you think the statements in section 1 and 2 are true or false by circling "T" or "F." When finished, do section 3 in the same manner.

Explicit Level

T	F	1. Cultures never change.
T	F	2. Simple cultures focus on obtaining basic needs, complex cultures on fulfilling wants.
T	F	3. Culture is passed from parents to children.

Implicit Level

T	F	1. Today's English has evolved from the English of Shakespeare's time.
T	F	2. The Bushmen of Africa have a "complex" culture.
T	F	3. Most people today produce their own food.

Applied Level

T	F	1. The main reason for cultural change today is technological innovation.
T	F	2. A simple life is best.
T	F	3. Tools can be used for good or evil.

FIGURE 1. *A three-level guide.*

As you read pages 64 and 65 of your text, follow the instructions listed below:

Para #1   This paragraph provides a transition from the previous section and
                 a definition of culture. What is that definition. What is meant by
                 "ways"? Give some examples.
Para #2   This paragraph lists the main parts of the text. Convert the four
                 subtopics into questions.
Para #3   Paragraphs 3 and 4 deal with the first subtopic: cultural change. In
                 addition to language (given), what other cultural traits have
                 changed?
Para #4   Why do cultures change? (3 reasons)
Paras #5–#7   These paragraphs deal with the second topic: simple and complex
                 cultures.
                 What are the aims of simple and complex cultures?
                 How are they different in terms of food procurement and tool use?
                 Do you know any other simple cultures that still exist today?
Paras #8–#13   These paragraphs deal with the third point: cultures are learned.
                 Summarize the main point of paragraphs 8, 9, and 13. How many
                 inventions can you find mentioned in paragraphs 10–12?

FIGURE 2. *A guide-o-rama.*

lated to one another. (Note: the text for Figures 1, 2, and 3 is not provided.)

It should be noted that not all of these techniques are suitable for each and every text; the selection of any of them should depend on the nature of the material to be read. All, however, afford the same benefits in that they promote active engagement with the text instead of passive and purposeless reading and, at the same time, develop skills rather than merely test them.

The Postreading Phase

The last stage of the reading lesson is intended to review the content; work on bottom-up concerns such as grammar, vocabulary, and discourse features; and consolidate what has been read by relating the new information to the learners' knowledge, interests, and opinions.

Many of the devices introduced during the while-reading stage can be used for the purpose of review. At this point, it would be appropriate to put the students in pairs or small groups to compare and verify their responses to the questions or graphics and then check the results with the entire class.

Once the main ideas of the text have been reviewed, work on discrete elements of the passage can be undertaken. Exercises could focus on grammar points, vocabulary in context or word roots, or discourse markers. It should be obvious that not all of these exercises need be pursued with each reading, for there is a real danger of murdering the text by dissection. Judicious choices should therefore be made depending on the character of the text and the needs of the students.

The final segment of the postreading stage should be devoted to integrating the new information from the text with what the students already know. In the context of an academic ESL/EFL course, the usual means of doing this is through a writing assignment, but other techniques are available, including discussions, debates, role-plays, and project work. The choice in this case depends on the goals of the program, the inclinations of the class, and, to some degree, the need for variety.

The three-phase approach outlined above need not be carried out slavishly for every reading. Under certain circumstances, it might be appropriate to cut or curtail one or

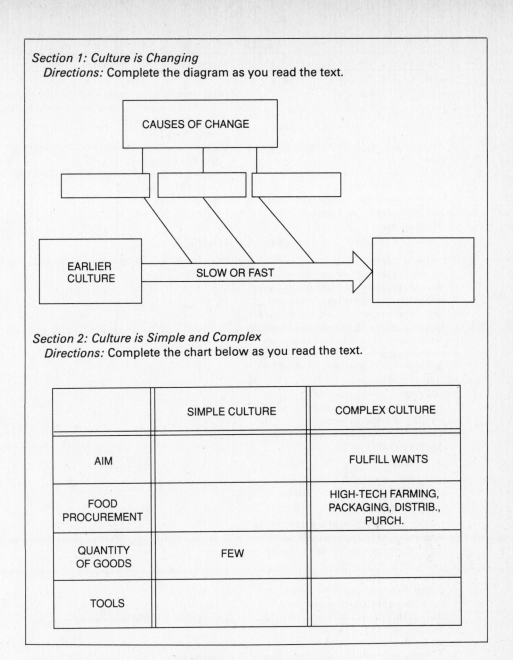

Section 1: Culture is Changing
    Directions: Complete the diagram as you read the text.

CAUSES OF CHANGE

EARLIER CULTURE

SLOW OR FAST

Section 2: Culture is Simple and Complex
    Directions: Complete the chart below as you read the text.

	SIMPLE CULTURE	COMPLEX CULTURE
AIM		FULFILL WANTS
FOOD PROCUREMENT		HIGH-TECH FARMING, PACKAGING, DISTRIB., PURCH.
QUANTITY OF GOODS	FEW	
TOOLS		

FIGURE 3. *A pattern study guide.*

more of the stages. For example, if the students have been reading a series of texts on the same topic, it might not be necessary to spend much time on the prereading stage insofar as they will have already activated their previous knowledge and become familiar with the vocabulary and concepts associated with the subject. Similarly, if further reading on the topic is planned, it might be better to delay work on consolidation until the entire sequence is complete. The key principle to observe is one of flexibility; teachers should avoid using the same exercise types or mechanically following the same lesson plan

TABLE 1

Time	Activity	Comments
05 m	1. *Preliminaries* (roll, warm-up)	
15	2. *Speed reading:* "Galaxies"	Object: rate building. (In general, rate-building texts should be simpler than texts for intensive reading. This one was taken from a children's encyclopedia.)
	a. Activate knowledge; elicit predictions about content.	The topic is already familiar to the students from previous reading.
	b. Review comprehension questions. Encourage, set to work, time.	Object: provide a reason for reading. (Questions focus on the main ideas.)
	c. When finished, have students check answers in pairs; let them scan to resolve discrepancies.	Object: Scanning practice.

(THE PREREADING STAGE)

	3. *Transition to new topic*	Object: Provide continuity and arouse anticipation.
	a. By way of transition, say something like this: What we have read thus far has given us an idea of how scientists view the universe today. Our ancestors have a very different picture of the world. During the next section of the course, we will be examining early conceptions of the universe and tracing the development of our modern world picture.	
	4. *Elicit what students know*	
	a. Have them give you examples of civilizations and individuals that have contributed to the development of astronomy. Arrange items in two categories: Ancient and Modern. Example:	

Ancient	Modern
the Greeks	Ptolemy
the Mayans	Galileo
the Celts	Hubble

	Indicate that we will be focusing first on the Babylonians and Greeks. A quick sketch of the Mediterranean and Middle East might be useful. Explain that even the early Babylonians were good observers. They plotted the movements of the planets and discovered a peculiar phenomenon, "retrograde motion." (Illustrate on board and indicate its significance.)	Object: preteach important concept.
	5. *Surveying the text*	
	a. Prefatory remarks: In our work on skimming, we have already used subheadings to get the general idea of the contents of an article. When using a college text, it is also useful to survey the table of contents and look over the introduction and conclusion before attacking the text. Reading these will help you to focus on what is important, predict what is coming, and see the relationship of subsections to the chapter as a whole.	Object: Provide a rationale for the activity and information about this study skill.

(continued)

TABLE 1 *Continued*

Time	Activity	Comments
	b. *Table of Contents*	
	(1) Distribute the packet and have students review the contents of Chapter 2. Elicit what subjects will be dealt with and handle any vocabulary problems (e.g., cosmos, geocentric).	Object: Arouse expectations; address new vocabulary and concepts.
	c. *The Introduction*	
	(1) Review the functions of an introduction: provide background and indicate structure.	Object: Remind students about text structure.
	(2) Have students skim and see if this was done.	Object: Provide purpose and practice skimming.
	(3) Ask:	
	(a) Where did you find an outline of the chapter?	Object: Work on paragraph functions.
	(b) What is the function of paragraph 1?	
	(c) What were ancient conceptions of the cosmos like?	Object: Identify main ideas.
	(d) What was different about Babylonian astronomy?	
	(e) What was the contribution of the Greeks?	
	Note: If they can't answer (c)–(e), send them back to the text. If they still can't answer, skip over. The summary might clarify things.	
	d. *The Summary*	
	(1) Tell the students to read for answers to the following questions:	Object: Provide a reason for reading.
	(a) What was the difference between Babylonian and Greek astronomy?	
	(b) What was the Greek model based on?	
	(c) Who were some of the major Greek astronomers?	
	After dealing with these questions, have the students formulate other questions about matters that are not fully explained in the introduction. E.g.:	Object: Develop the habit of asking questions of a text and providing their own reasons for reading.
	(a) What were the geometric and aesthetic notions of Pythagoras?	
	(b) What does "save the appearances" mean?	
	(c) What "mechanical devices" were used by the Greeks to explain planetary motion?	
	(d) Etc.	
	e. *The Subheadings*	
	(1) Direct the students to the body of the text and have them make a list of the subtopics.	Object: Scanning; clarifying the structure of the text; generating new questions.

(THE WHILE-READING STAGE)

| | 6. *Scientific Models* | (Note: The text and activities for this section are on pp. 210–214.) |

(continued)

TABLE 1 *Continued*

Time	Activity	Comments
	7. *Babylonian Skywatching* and *Greek Models*. . .	
	a. Divide the class into two teams: The Babylonians and the Greeks. Each will be responsible for reading its own section of the text and then explaining it to the other group.	
	b. Tell them to speed-read their section.	Object: practice speed-reading; get the general idea.
	c. When finished, have them follow the instructions and answer the questions of the "guide-o-rama."	Object: provide guidance while reading.
	(THE POSTREADING STAGE)	
	8. *Review*	
	a. Have the students check the results in their own groups. Help if necessary.	Object: confirm understanding.
	b. Create pairs or small groups representing both sections. Have the students explain the main points to the members of the other team. Listeners should take notes.	Object: set up an information-gap exercise; practice oral summaries; note taking.
	9. *Vocabulary* (optional)	
	a. Vocabulary in context exercise.	Object: practice in guessing meaning.
	(1) Review; have students explain how they decided on the meanings of the terms.	
	10. *Reference Words* (optional)	
	a. Anaphora/cataphora exercise.	Object: sensitize the students to textual cohesion.
	11. *Grammar* (optional)	
	a. Elicit grammatical difficulties from the students. Discuss.	Object: clear up grammatical problems
	12. *Writing*	
	a. Have the students take notes on their section and then write a summary.	Object: note taking; summarizing.
	(1) Put students in pairs to compare their summaries for completeness, accuracy.	
	b. Have the students write a comparison of Babylonian and Greek astronomy.	Object: practice in comparison/contrast.
	(1) Brainstorm content in groups.	
	(2) Write first draft.	
	(3) Peer feedback using guidelines provided.	
	13. *Research* (homework)	
	a. Have the students choose a topic related to the theme and find additional information on it in an encyclopedia or book. Have them report next time.	Object: practice library skills, note taking, summarizing, oral reporting.

each time, for to do so will only diminish students' interest and consequently their desire to learn.

A Sample Lesson

To illustrate how these various techniques can be brought together in a cohesive fashion, a lesson plan based on an introductory astronomy text will be discussed below. The text, which has been used in an intermediate course for students of science and technology at the University of Southern California, has been chosen for two reasons. First, although it is desirable to expose readers to a range of text types, it is perhaps most critical for academically involved students to learn to cope with the demands of a textbook, and, second, the material is sufficiently abstruse to require all the teacher's skills to make it interesting and intelligible.

The selection to be examined deals with the early history of astronomical investigation, just one of a series of subtopics in a unit that ran for approximately four weeks. In the sequence, this particular theme followed a consideration of our current knowledge about the solar system, the galaxy, and the creation of the universe. The objective, in terms of content learning, was to indicate to the students that conceptions of the cosmos had changed greatly over the course of time and to trace the emergence of the modern world view.

Although all texts are unique and require somewhat different treatment, the general principles and many of the procedures employed with this particular passage can be applied to most textbook material, and, for that matter, to most types of reading assignments.

Table 1 is the lesson plan provided to teachers of the course. The only change has been to add a column with comments addressed to the reader in order to relate the activities of the lesson to the content of this article.

CONTENTS

1   In the previous chapter we described what can be observed in the sky without optical aid, specifically the motions of the sun, moon, and planets. In this and the next three chapters we will discuss the historical development of models to explain these facts.

2   Most ancient cultures viewed the cosmos as finite and geocentric. Some boundary, usually a shell of stars, closed off the universe with the earth enthroned in the center. Usually ancient cosmologies paid little attention to the details of celestial motions, even if the cycles were carefully observed, as was done by the Babylonians.

3   The Greeks were the first to attempt to take their cosmological ideas beyond the skeleton of a finite, geocentric cosmos. Grappling with the problem of planetary motions, Greek philosophers fleshed out the bare cosmological structure with mechanical devices to account for the celestial cycle. These schemes marked the first earnest models: mental constructions that exhibited features like those observed in nature. Such systematic efforts to explain the natural world culminated in the geocentric model of Claudius Ptolemy. His

2.2 BABYLONIAN SKYWATCHING: THE SEEDS OF A SCIENCE

1 Washed by time and rivers, Mesopotamian civilizations came to flood and ebb in a succession of cultures, each enriched by its predecessors. The oldest was that of the Sumerians, a people who used clay tablets, bearing notations in the cuneiform alphabet, to preserve written records. When Hammurabi of Babylon (1725–1686 B.C.) rose to power, the fabled Babylonians adopted much of the culture, mythology, and technology of the Sumerians.

cosmological model marks the first careful effort to represent accurately the observed celestial motions. So well did Ptolemy succeed that his system was not seriously challenged for over fourteen centuries.

This chapter examines Babylonian and Greek cosmologies (1) to see how closely early cosmological ideas related to actual astronomical observation; (2) to see how these cultures tried to make sense of what they saw in the sky; (3) to contrast cosmic ideas grounded in myths to those grounded in aesthetic, physical, and geometrical ideas—those which are scientific models; (4) to investigate the birth of the first comprehensive model of the universe, one that eventually led to the models used today. **4**

SUMMARY

This scan of astronomy from Babylonian to Greek times has picked out one important aspect of cosmological ideas: the evolution of a mechanical model of the universe. The invention of a model was lacking in Babylonian astronomy, even though the Babylonians were excellent observers and developed arithmetical methods to predict planetary positions. The cosmos was explained in terms of myths, such as the *Enuma Elish*. **1**

Cosmological model making began in Greek times. The early cosmological model of the Pythagoreans included geometrical and aesthetic elements (spheres and the harmony of the spheres), but lacked physical ideas. In these attempts by Plato and Eudoxus to "save the appearances," mechanical devices, usually with a simple geometry, were used to explain the actual observed motions of the planets. Aristotle injected physics into his cosmological model, but knew that the correspondence of his model with some observations, especially retrograde motion, just wasn't terribly good. **2**

Ptolemy put together the first comprehensive cosmological model, one that incorporated all three key elements: geometry from the Greeks, aesthetics of his own, and physics from Aristotle. More important, his model conformed to observations within sufficient accuracy for his day (Table 2.1). The *Almagest* provided a conceptual framework for and a practical approach to the geocentric cosmos. So Ptolemy's model worked and was complete. That's why it survived for so long. **3**

Babylonian Skywatching

Directions: Fill in the diagrams as you read the related sections of the text a second time.

Para. 1 Introduction

  Mesopotamian Civilization ("meso" = in the middle of; "potamos" = river; therefore, "in the middle of the Tigris and Euphrates Rivers")

  a. *Cultural Influence*

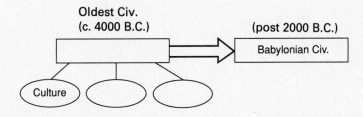

Babylonian Astronomy

2   About 1600 B.C. the Babylonians compiled the first star catalogs and began making crude records of planetary motions. By 800 B.C. the Babylonian astronomers were able to fix planetary locations with respect to the stars. They kept records of planetary positions that compared a planet's position with that of recognized constellations. Their early observations included the motions of Venus, Jupiter, and Mars. From the ninth century B.C. the Babylonians kept continuous astronomical records on clay tablets.

3   For what reasons did the Babylonians become careful observers? In part, the development of astronomy relied on state support as far back as the time of Hammurabi. Astronomical information was needed for both the calendar and the practice of astrology (Focus 2.1). These problems stimulated the development of arithmetical techniques that the Babylonians used to predict planetary positions. In addition, observations preserved on cuneiform tablets enabled the Babylonians to find the daily, monthly, and annual cycles— the main themes of celestial motions/

4   Such permanent records indicate that the Babylonian astronomers also knew of the variations in the celestial cycles. For example, the angular size of a planet's retrogradeloop and the duration of its retrograde motion vary from one time of opposition to the next. The Babylonian astronomers had lists of these cycles, with each major cycle represented by a table of consecutive numbers. The departures from the average cycle were also tabulated. A Babylonian astronomer could sum the set of numbers of all major and minor cycles to predict, for example, the next time of retrograde motion.

5   So Babylonian astronomers could predict future planetary motions from their tables of past cycles. This procedure did not require an explanation of the cycles, merely a knowledge of their existence over a long period of time.

Babylonian Cosmology

6   In Babylon, the priests were the astronomers. They occupied the holy ziggurats, towers that also served as observatories. The existence of the priest-astronomer fostered the continuity of astronomical knowledge, but it also divorced Babylonian cosmology from astronomy. In the cosmic picture the gods created, ordered, and controlled the world, and these divine functions were considered far beyond human comprehension. Consequently, the greatest store of observed knowledge was held by men who believed that it was not explicable except as religious myth.

Excerpts from *Astronomy: The Cosmic Perspective* by Michael Zeilik and John Gausted. Copyright © 1983 by Michael Zeilik and John Gausted. Reprinted by permission of HarperCollins Publishers Inc.

Para. 2 *Babylonian Astronomy*

a.

Date	Significant Event in Astronomy

Para. 3 and 4 b. Why did the Babylonians become careful observers?

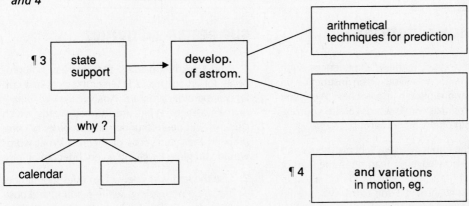

¶ 3 state support → develop. of astrom.

why ?

calendar

arithmetical techniques for prediction

¶ 4 and variations in motion, eg.

Para. 5 c. Did the Babylonians explain the planetary cycles that they carefully recorded?

(Circle one)   Yes   No

Para. 6 *Babylonian Cosmology*

a. Babylonian observatories = _____ = _____
b. Babylonian astronomers = _____

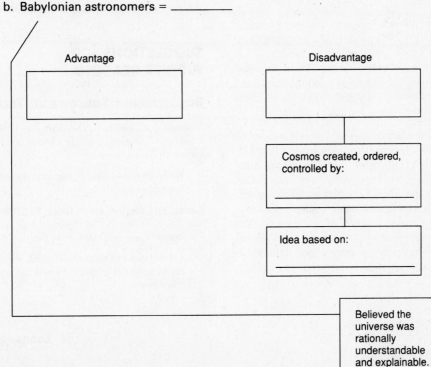

Advantage

Disadvantage

Cosmos created, ordered, controlled by:

_____

Idea based on:

_____

Believed the universe was rationally understandable and explainable. (Circle) Yes/No

7 The fantastic Babylonian tale of genesis, the *Enuma Elish* (literally, "when above"), carefully pictures the creation of space and the ordering of time by the god Marduk. The details of astronomical motions pale before the grand scheme. The actual predictions were purely arithmetical; no geometrical framework provided any skeletal support to the natural appearances. The Babylonian astronomers knew well the periods of the planets, sun, and moon through the zodiac and the occurrence of retrograde motion. They did not, however, attempt to account for the causes of these motions beyond a religious, mythical explanation. They were able to predict, but not to explain, in the modern sense of a scientific explanation. Their ideas lacked the notion of physical cause—a concept central to modern science. Instead, religious myths secured the structure of their world.

DISCUSSION QUESTIONS

1. What were your earliest experiences with learning to read? Were you given instruction in one of the various phonic approaches? Were you taught to recognize whole words? Share your experiences with others in your group.

2. Discuss the implications of schema theory and background knowledge for reading in the light of this statement: "It is very difficult to read a text in your native language if you don't already know the content." Do you agree with the statement? Can you offer any examples of it based on your own experiences in learning new subject matter content?

3. What have been your own experiences with reading-in-depth? What new subject areas have you encountered for which you used the strategy of reading a variety of texts that dealt with the same subject content?

4. You have been assigned an advanced reading class in a college preparatory ESL program. You are free to select a textbook from the list which appears at the end of this chapter. What are some features you would look for in making a selection? For what reasons would you decide to use teacher-prepared materials in a reading program?

5. Discuss the advantages and disadvantages of these two possible course designs for an ESL or EFL academic reading course: (1) The course uses reading passages and texts which are taken exclusively from the subject content textbooks which the students read in their other academic courses. (2) The course uses a variety of reading materials which are drawn from various types of genres ranging among nonfiction writing, popular science writing, journalists' reports, technical journal articles, etc.

SUGGESTED ACTIVITIES

1. Find a reading passage that you feel is appropriate for an advanced EFL reading class in a college preparatory program. Analyze the vocabulary in the passage: What are the key words which students will need to understand in order to comprehend the main ideas or themes? What words would you gloss by giving a very brief definition?

2. Use the text you selected for question number 1: Prepare a prereading, while-reading, and postreading plan. Follow the model set out in the second part of this chapter—"Putting Theory into Practice."

3. What follow-up discussion questions could be presented to learners after they have completed the postreading stage?

4. What writing assignment could be introduced during the postreading stage that would allow students to explore the content more thoroughly?

SUGGESTIONS FOR FURTHER READING

Background Sources for Teachers

Alderson, J. C., and A. H. Urquhart, eds. (1984)
Reading in a Foreign Language. London and New York: Oxford University Press.

> Research papers directly related to second language reading issues.

Carrell, P., J. Devine, and D. Eskey, eds. (1988)
Interactive Approaches to Second Language Reading. Cambridge: Cambridge University Press.

> Current views of models of reading; empirical studies with second language learners; pedagogical implications.

Para. 7 c. *An Evaluation of Babylonian Astronomy*

The Babylonian picture of the cosmos was based on: <u>Y</u>   <u>N</u>   <u>?</u>
1. aesthetic notions
2. geometrical ideas
3. physical laws

Devine, J., P. Carrell, and D. Eskey, eds. (1987)
Research in Reading English as a Second Language.
Washington, DC: TESOL.

> Papers presented at the Reading Colloquium held at the TESOL convention, April 1985.

Dubin, F., D. Eskey, and W. Grabe, eds. (1986)
Teaching Second Language Reading for Academic Purposes. Reading, MA: Addison-Wesley.

> Chapters on theoretical foundations for reading along with coverage of practical issues in teaching second language reading at low-intermediate through advanced levels.

Grellet, F. (1981)
Developing Reading Skills: A Practical Guide to Reading Comprehension. New York: Cambridge University Press.

> Emphasis is on reading in the context of foreign language instruction; includes a large section on a reading program in a British middle school.

Nuttall, C. (1982)
Teaching Reading Skills in a Foreign Language. London: Heinemann Educational Books.

> A very thorough compendium of theory and teaching issues covered from a British viewpoint.

Ulijn, J. M., and A. K. Pugh, eds. (1985)
Reading for Professional Purposes. Leuven/Amersfoort, Netherlands: ACCO.

> Research papers presented at an International Symposium on Language for Specific Purposes, Eindhoven, 1982.

Reading Textbooks for ESL/EFL Students

Baudoin, E. M., E. S. Bober, M. A. Clarke, B. K. Dobson, and S. Silbertstein (1988)
Reader's Choice, 2nd ed. Ann Arbor: University of Michigan Press.

Dubin, F., and E. Olshtain (1990)
Reading by All Means: All-New Edition. Reading, MA: Addison-Wesley.

Dubin, F., and E. Olshtain (1987)
Reading on Purpose. Reading, MA.: Addison-Wesley.

Latulippe, L. D. (1987)
Developing Academic Reading Skills. Englewood Cliffs, NJ: Prentice-Hall.

Lynch, E. S. (1988)
Reading for Academic Success: Selections from Across the Curriculum. New York: Collier Macmillan.

Romstedt, K., and J. T. McGory (1988)
Reading Strategies for University Students. New York: Collier Macmillan.

Rosenthal, L. and S. B. Rowland (1986)
Academic Reading and Study Skills for International Students. Englewood Cliffs, NJ: Prentice-Hall.

Salimbene, S. (1986)
Interactive Reading. New York: Newbury House.

Wegmann, B., and M. P. Knezevic (1985)
Mosaic: A Reading Skills Book. New York: Random House.

EST Reading

Brian K. Lynch and Thom Hudson

INTRODUCTION

Introduction to EST Reading

The identification of reading skills in English for science and technology (EST) as an area of pedagogical concern has been motivated by two factors. First, numerous surveys have indicated that reading may be the most important skill for academic success (Johns, 1981; Ostler, 1980; Robertson, 1983). This gives special importance to the development of reading skills in English as a second language (ESL) students who need English for academic purposes. Second, it is generally recognized that most scientific and technical writing is first published in English. This means that students and professionals in scientific and technological fields who are not native speakers or fluent users of English have an especially important need to be able to read relevant subject matter in English.

Given the fact that there is a large audience that needs to be able to read scientific and technical English, the three central concerns become the following: (1) an adequate description of what it means to read EST, (2) how best to teach that ability, and (3) how to accurately assess, or test, that ability. It will be the central thesis of this chapter that EST reading can be best described through the integration of methods, materials, and assessment techniques. The methods and materials used in EST reading instruction must obviously be sensitive to what is known about reading and English for specific purposes (ESP). It is also crucial that assessment, or testing, be sensitive to, and integrated with, an understanding of the reading process, EST, and the methods and materials developed for teaching EST reading.

A discussion of EST reading necessarily involves two major areas of teaching and research: English for specific purposes (ESP) and the nature of the reading process, in both the first language (L1) and the second language (L2). The following sections of the introduction, then, will present a discussion of ESP and reading in the L1 and L2. The introduction will be followed by sections on methods and materials focusing first on the requirements for an EST reading curriculum, and then on appropriate materials for such a curriculum. The third section will discuss the assessment of EST reading ability in the context of such an instructional curriculum. This section will focus on problems associated with the measurement of EST reading ability and examples of possible assessment techniques. The final section will present conclusions. Methods, materials, and assessment techniques for EST reading will be illustrated with examples taken from the Reading English for Science and Technology (REST) project at the Universidad de Guadalajara (UdeG), Mexico. This project was initiated and developed under a cooperative agreement between the UdeG and the University of California, Los Angeles (UCLA).[1]

ESP

While the history of teaching English for particular purposes goes back to the 1800s, the early 1960s is seen as the time when ESP first came into being, and it was in the early 1970s that it became a major influence on

ESL and EFL curriculum design. This was the result of the fact that more and more of the world's technical information was being written in English. As the developed and the developing nations of the world became more and more linked through the need for this information, English began to play an increasingly important role in international communication.

The new explosion of information, which Peter Strevens (1979) has called "the second industrial and scientific revolution," was coupled with an increasing number of nonnative speakers of English attending universities where English was the language of instruction. In addition, the general educational atmosphere of the 1970s demanded that all courses of instruction be "relevant" to the students' interests and to the events taking place in the world outside the classroom. These influences, then, contributed to the identification of specialized courses for ESL and EFL.

At the beginning of the 1970s, the general view was that there were different kinds of English being used in the world and that there were students who needed to learn these specific Englishes. This view had, at its core, the notion that ESP was a subject matter, to be described in terms of its distinctive features and taught through the use of carefully selected texts and practice exercises. This did not entail a change in how English was to be taught, just a change in the instructional content. The first set of distinctive features to be described was the lexis—vocabulary. Representative texts in a particular subject matter—nuclear physics or computer science, for example—were analyzed for the words that were specific to that subject. "The idea was that normal ESL materials would be used but that subject-specific lexical items would be substituted for more general terms (e.g., 'This a book' would be replaced by 'This is an Erlenmeyer flask')" (Master, 1985a, p. 15).

This work describing the various specific Englishes eventually included grammatical structures; this research was especially thorough in the subarea of EST. However, the 1970s also saw the concept of communicative competence emerge as an influence on language teaching methodology and curriculum design. This resulted in a focus on language as communication rather than linguistic structure, and it helped to move language teaching away from a sentence-level pattern practice focus. More and more, the emphasis was now on the discourse function of language—what people do with language in various communicative settings.

Responses to the communicative movement in English language teaching have included the functional approach, the notional approach, and the communication strategies approach. The functional approach emphasized the way in which English functions in social situations, using categories from discourse analysis, such as definition, explanation, apology, and invitation (see Allen & Widdowson, 1974). The notional approach organized the teaching syllabus around conceptual categories and notions, such as dimension and measurement (see Bates & Dudley-Evans, 1976). In the communication strategies approach, the activities and skills needed for one to perform in a particular occupation or field become the basis for teaching (see Candlin, Bruton, Leather, & Woods, 1981; for a more complete discussion of these three approaches, see Howatt, 1984).

These approaches tended to define ESP as a subject matter and did not, necessarily, define different teaching methodologies per se. The important focus of ESP was on content—what was to be taught, rather than how to teach it. The 1970s, in general, did not see much of a systematic development of teaching methodology. Rather, the trend was eclectic, with language teachers exploring a variety of pedagogical styles: some Silent Way, some Counseling Learning, some Total Physical Response, as well as the use of role-play, simulation, and problem-solving tasks. The unifying theme was, and continues to be, communication, and the focus was, and continues to be, on the learner. This is perhaps an oversimplification, but without a single teaching methodology that most people agreed upon, innovation in language teaching was encouraged, albeit in an unsystematic fashion. ESP, without a specific set of teaching techniques to guide it, demanded, and continues to demand, innovative teachers in order to be successful.

By the end of the 1970s, the focus in language teaching and research was, more strongly than ever, on the discourse level. Researchers presented evidence that certain rhetorical functions and discourse acts were the same across different languages. Mage (1978), for example, found that the formal definition and explicit classification in science were presented the same way in both English and Spanish texts. This and similar findings led to the realization that EST instruction could make use of the learner's background knowledge. In other words, students could use what they already knew in their native language about a topic to help them "crack the code" of English. This had remarkable potential for motivating students—English could become less abstract and more a part of their world and their specific interests.

In order to take advantage of this potential for motivation, ESP teachers, like many other English language teachers, began to search out real-world language materials, to be used for accomplishing authentic tasks by the students. That is, real-world materials were identified and exercises developed that required students to use the materials in ways which were similar, if not identical, to the ways in which they would be required to use such materials in the real world. The real world, in the case of ESP, was a specific concept with specific purposes identified.

The 1980s have not proven to be a period of innovation and growth for ESP. As Master (1985b, pp. 12, 15) has stated, "the honeymoon is over and self-analysis has set in." ESP is left, at the end of the 1980s, without a particular teaching methodology with which it is associated. Hutchinson and Waters (1987) have proposed that ESP place primary emphasis on the student processes of learning and have de-emphasized course materials as a product to be mastered. Materials in this view are selected less for the language they contain than for the language processes they encourage. The distinction between ESP and general ESL/EFL has become blurred. However, what continues to be distinctive about ESP programs is that they tend to have a more focused and specialized group of students to work with, and that there is a guiding focus on preparing them for the eventual use of English in a specific occupation or academic field of study. This concern means that, more and more, the ESP teacher is required to develop some familiarity with content areas outside the ones traditionally part of the ESL/EFL teacher's background, such as English literature, history, and culture. At the very least, the ESP teacher must acquire a taste for, or an interest in, the specific content area defined by the students' need for English.[2]

Reading

The literature on reading, both in L1 and in L2, tends to discuss the reading process in terms of top-down and bottom-up reading models. The top-down model refers to the selection of the fewest and most productive elements from a text in order to make sense of it. This has been characterized as a "psycholinguistic guessing game" (K. S. Goodman, 1967) in which the reader uses minimal language cues to make hypotheses about the meaning of a text. These hypotheses are then confirmed, rejected, or modified as the selection of minimal language cues from the text continues. The basic idea is that efficient reading is not word-by-word identification.

Related to this view of the reading process is the notion that people read for meaning and comprehension by relating new information to what they already know. The way in which what we already know—our background or world knowledge—is organized in the brain is characterized by research in Schema Theory as being organized into units called "schemata" (Rumelhart, 1980; Rumelhart & Ortony, 1977). Good readers make use of their existing schemata to make predictions about what is coming next in the text and about how some new, unfamiliar piece of information relates to what is already known. Making use of schemata allows readers to avoid word-by-word reading while extracting meaning from the text.

The bottom-up model describes reading as a process of exact identification of letters, words, and ultimately sentences by moving the eyes from left to right across the page while building comprehension from letter to word to phrase to sentence. The problem with limiting the notion of reading to this model lies in the relationship of memory to reading. This plodding, exact identification approach slows the reader down to the point that the information cannot be held in short-term memory long enough to make sense of whole sentences or larger pieces of discourse and makes the process of reading overly laborious and unenjoyable (Eskey, 1986).

Rather than continuing as mutually exclusive models, however, the two have combined into an interactive model of reading (Grabe, 1985; Rumelhart, 1977). In this model the bottom-up skills—recognition of lexical units and grammatical clues necessary to "decode" the text—are seen as playing an important role in reading, especially, perhaps, for the second language learner. A good reader, from this perspective, does not avoid bottom-up skills but becomes so proficient at them that they become automatic in their interaction with top-down skills. As Eskey (1987) notes, the fact that top-down processing skills which focus primarily on meaning, rather than on form, play a major role in reading does not do away with the reader's need for simple bottom-up language-processing skills. The reader must still decode the graphic forms of print and the grammatical structures which provide textual relationships.

METHODS AND MATERIALS

Curriculum and Materials

Issues involving methods and materials in ESP focus on two major areas. First, what is the role of needs analysis? What information does it cover? Second, what is the role of authentic materials in the curriculum?

Methods and materials should reflect an overall concern with the context of the ESP program. That is, the results of any needs analysis do not apply simply to the language content of the syllabus. They also apply to how the students will be taught and the organization of the materials to be used. As noted above, much recent work with EST has emerged to represent a "nonproduct" approach to the curriculum and materials. That is, more attention is being paid to the processes and strategies that the student must learn than to the mastery of particular language products, such as a particular rhetorical style or a particular grammatical structure. The curriculum needs to represent this in any EST reading program. Hence, there is a strong need to carry out needs analyses that adequately capture not only "what" the students will need to be able to read, but "why" they need to read it and "who" they are. Needs analysis will necessarily be an ongoing long-term project that will evolve over the first two or three generations of students. Any external model will have to be adapted to a particular setting before a complete curriculum can be in place. However, there are several constants which should be incorporated.

First, the EST reading curriculum should have topic-based content. This allows the students to utilize their background knowledge. Part of that background knowledge is the knowledge that when one reads in the real world, one reads materials on a given topic and for a particular reason. People do not normally read just because someone told them to read an odd collection of articles on eclectic topics. As Mohan (1986) notes, any educational approach that considers language learning alone, ignoring the learning of subject matter, is inadequate to the needs of language learners. This is particularly true of ESP courses and is perhaps most easily avoided in these programs. There are several methods of going about developing topic/content-based materials. If the reading program is an independent course, the curriculum content can project what types of materials the students will eventually be required to read. However, if the program exists within an existing course of study, such as engineering, chemistry, medicine, or architecture, the content of the ESP course can be determined by the course materials the students are studying in their content courses. This "modified adjunct model" works well since the students feel the material they are dealing with is relevant to their current studies.[3] One example of a "modified adjunct" EST reading program is the REST (Reading English for Science and Technology) Project at the Universidad de Guadalajara (UdeG), Mexico. The discussion which follows describes the ongoing process of development of the REST Project. Rather than claiming to present a model project, the description is intended to present some notion of how a team can proceed with an EST reading project, and to reflect the array of decisions that must be made in such a process.

The students of Chemical Engineering at UdeG have a five-year undergraduate course load. The REST Project identified 10 content-based themes by examining course descriptions of the students' degree courses. These themes are as follows:

Year One

1. General Science/Physics and Chemistry
2. The Field of Chemical Engineering
3. Energy
4. Materials and Properties
5. Environment: Technical Issues and Solutions

Year Two

6. Technology

7. Electronics
8. Computers
9. Equipment Design
10. Physical and Mechanical Processes

Although these themes evolved from a close examination of the required syllabus in the chemical engineering major, the first two units of Year One are very much schema-based. Since the REST course begins in the third year of a five-year content sequence, the students have a background in general science and have spent some time thinking about their future careers. Although they have all studied English for several years in secondary school, they are, for the most part, false beginners with little or no functional ability in English. Given their lack of ability in English, it is important to show the students at the start that they can already read a great deal in English. For example, a straightforward description in English on the method of science is relatively easy for the students to read given that they already know the material and that there are many cognates between Spanish and English.

The materials developed for each of the content-based themes constituting the REST curriculum are technical selections dealing with topics that could well be assigned in one of the required courses for the major. The initial materials tend to be content from courses that the students have already taken as part of their studies; throughout the two years of the REST course, they frequently read materials which cover known information. Thus, they have the "schemata" for the articles and have become confident about reading English. The later units in the second year of the course cover material that the students are currently—or will soon be—studying. The focus on course design thus shifts to relevance for their future professional preparation.

Materials

Materials selection emerges from a set of criteria developed for each of the units. An example of the text criteria for the fifth unit of year one is provided in Figure 1 (adapted from Smith, 1988).

The text criteria attempt to include information about the language content as well as information regarding the language processing and learning of the students. For example, the criteria require that there be "readables" in the materials selected.

These texts are selected to reinforce in the minds of the students that they can read English, perhaps not all English, but some English. Additionally, the text criteria provide information regarding the type and distribution of text content, length, and language characteristics.

A second concern of materials selection concerns the role of authentic materials in the curriculum. Justifications for the use of modified or simplified materials have focused on allowing the students access to the language form and thus to the content of the text. However, there appear to be five major arguments in favor of the use of authentic materials in EST programs.

First, when material is simplified or modified, it is often changed in ways that actually make the material more complex to process (Fillmore, 1981). That is, there are no clear guidelines for the simplification of material, and when material is simplified to reduce the length of sentences, frequently the cohesive elements of the text are reduced such that relationships between ideas are lost. Further, there are few content experts who are trained in how to simplify material, and most EST teachers have little training in the content area. Thus, most language materials developers use a seat-of-the-pants approach to "simplify" the material.

Second, processing simplified texts is not genuine reading. It may be learning grammar, or learning to read simplified text, or some other type of classroom-bound learning, but it is not a reading activity which exists in the real world. In the real world, people read for information or enjoyment, not to learn the medium through which the information is processed.

Environment: Technical Issues and Solutions

* • content should reflect student background knowledge
  • content relates to unit theme of technical solutions to environmental problems
  • content should be general in nature and avoid very specific discussion of any one solution
  • readings should be one to six pages in length
  • content differs in each text (e.g., problem/ solution to different environmental problems—try to avoid a "one-topic" unit
* • content discusses technology appropriate to Mexico
  • content is not so much issue-oriented as solution-oriented
* • content is of academic interest to the students
* • texts are no older than 1984–1985 or are of a nature that they are not liable to date too quickly
  • the first texts are "readables" (contain no idiomatic language, are related to main ideas or important details, the vocabulary is largely cognates, the information is already familiar to Ss in Spanish)
* • unit contains as little idiomatic language as possible throughout unit
* • articles make good use of graphs, charts, illustrations
* • articles exhibit good scientific writing (ideas and details clearly presented, easy-to-follow argument)

FIGURE 1. *Text criteria for unit five, year one of the REST project. (The criteria marked with an asterisk will be considered general content for each unit.)*

Third, if we assume that in no method of instruction from ALM to Counseling Learning do the students learn or understand everything presented to them, there is no reason to use simplified material. We can accept that they will not understand everything in any particular article presented to them. By reading carefully selected authentic materials, the students can see how much they understand. Furthermore, since students do not learn in a linear fashion, a grammatical sequence for "false beginners" will work no better than did the first grammatical syllabus these students were exposed to.

Fourth, there is adequate nonsimplified material available which the students can read. It is sometimes more work for the teacher or materials developer to find these "readables" than it is to simplify a particular article, but if the students' interests and prior knowledge, both of the content and of language, are taken into account, the appropriate material exists.

Fifth, simplified material is too frequently developed with no real-world task in mind. If students will eventually need to examine a catalog to find the most appropriate transistor for a particular use, then the best method of teaching the students that skill is to have them actually use a catalog for ordering transistors. In such text, the language is already simple, perhaps too simple, with too many deletions. However, when a materials developer adds more complex language to the passage to include all the verbs, nouns, and other parts of speech, and provides all the missing language to the student, the student is not learning a real-world task. An explanation of the conventional deletions can take place in the class as a learning activity. Here, the grammar and vocabulary to be taught emerge from the activity.

An example of how authentic materials can be selected and used is provided in Figure 2, as an extension of the text criteria mentioned in Figure 1. It should be mentioned that the articles were selected by the students from among those in a larger collection of passages regarding environmental issues and technical solutions. A general lesson guide for the teacher is also included.

Once the texts have been selected, they are then examined for the relevant strategies and grammatical points. The activity flowchart indicates the types of tasks the articles lend themselves to.

ASSESSMENT OF EST READING[4]

Measurement Problems

There is a direct and important parallel between assessment and teaching that is of-

UNIT VOCABULARY:
- Teacher gives out handout of key vocabulary for all texts in Unit Five
- Students add the Spanish equivalent to all the English terms
- Students exchange lists, compare words they do not know with other students
- Teachers and students agree on meanings of all words

TEXT ONE: "Reducing Equipment Cleaning Wastes" (4 pages) *Chemical Engineering*, July 18, 88 (117–122)
- Teacher gives students outline of main ideas
- Students add details
- Teacher and students discuss, agree on details
- Teacher gives students scrambled order comprehension question (CQ) sheet; students use outline and text to answer the questions
- Teacher and students go over the answers, discuss problems
- Teacher and students discuss the logical connectors in the reading.

TEXT TWO: "Air Pollution Control with a Bonus" (1.5 pages] *Chemical Engineering*, May 9, 88 (107–108)
- Teacher gives outline; students add details
- Students (in small groups) write CQs for other group, Ss exchange lists of CQs, answer, and then pass back to original group for correction and feedback
- Students discuss author's intention

TEXT THREE: "Soil Beds Weed Out Air Pollution" (4 pages) *Chemical Engineering*, Apr. 25, 88 (73–76)
- Students write outline of article
- Teacher gives list of scrambled order CQs; students answer, using outlines and texts
- Teacher and students discuss answers
- Students summarize use of soilbeds

TEXT FOUR: "Succeeding at Waste Minimization" (4 pages) *Chemical Engineering*, Sept. 14, 87 (91–94)
- Students read and underline main ideas and details on their texts
- Students write CQs for teacher's other group OR: Teacher write CQs as practice for the Unit One exam

SYNTHESIS WORKSHEETS: Students write a summary (in Spanish or English) of one technical issue and solution; students write a position paper comparing two solutions

GRAMMAR WORKSHEETS: All articles emphasize use of the following grammar points. These points are to be recycled through the articles.
- logical connectors
- WH- question words

FIGURE 2. *Unit Five, Year One flowchart.*

ten obscured or overlooked by teachers and researchers alike. The teacher attempts to operationalize the reading process in terms of tasks that will engage the students and reveal how they are approaching that process. The teacher then uses this information to modify the tasks or create new ones that will encourage development of their ability to read. The person responsible for developing reading assessment instruments is charged with very much the same job. The reading process must be operationalized in terms of tasks that will demonstrate what the student knows, and what the student can do in terms of that process. This information is then used to modify and create new instruments that will better reveal the students' ability to read. In the discussion that follows, then, it should be kept in mind that the process of developing an EST reading curriculum (or any curriculum) closely parallels the process of developing assessment instruments for that curriculum. Indeed, all the concerns mentioned here are also reflected in the process of developing classroom materials.

A central problem in the measurement of reading ability is the fact that the behavior of interest is an internal process. Since it is impossible to observe this internal process, measurement schemes must be developed that assess the ability indirectly. Most commonly, this assessment has been done by asking the test-taker to answer "comprehension questions." These questions can take various forms, from constructed response formats, such as short written answers, to selected response formats, such as multiple-choice test items.

Constructed response formats are useful in the assessment of reading ability in that they reveal the nature of the test-takers' understanding of the reading text in their own words. This can afford judgments concerning the degree and quality of reading comprehension. On the other hand, constructed response formats are measuring more than just reading. The test-takers' ability to express their ideas and understanding in writing en-

ters into the interpretation of their reading ability.

Selected response formats overcome, to a certain extent, the problem of measuring writing ability as well as reading in that the test-takers are not asked to produce anything but are merely asked to indicate their comprehension by selecting the correct answer to a question or a statement. These formats also have an obvious practical value by being easier to score than constructed responses. While selected response formats do not require the test-takers to use language skills other than reading, they do allow for the possibility of guessing or for selecting the correct answer without truly comprehending the reading text. For example, in a multiple-choice format designed to measure the ability to find the main idea of a paragraph, the test-taker may be able to pick out the answer that seems to have main idea characteristics (e.g., by eliminating the answers that appear too general or too specific) without having had a clear understanding of the text paragraph itself. Such "test wiseness" can give a distorted impression of the test-takers' true reading ability.

In addition to the difficulty of measuring reading in isolation from other language skills, there are other problems that occur when attempting to measure specific reading skills. Even with tests that are composed of "reading comprehension" questions, an examination of the individual questions will generally reveal that, for any particular question, a particular reading skill is being called for. The skills most often being tested are finding specific information, finding the main idea, drawing inferences, and understanding vocabulary in context. In addition, most comprehension questions will be measuring the test-takers' command of certain grammatical structures, discourse markers and elements such as pronominal reference, and vocabulary. If the test is being used to assess the test-takers' general reading ability, the degree to which one skill or another is being measured by any particular question may be of little concern. It is important, however, to know that the test is sampling across these skills and not focusing on only one or two of them for a general assessment of reading ability.

In the case of EST reading achievement testing, the concern will most often be for measuring specific curriculum objectives. When these objectives are specific reading skills, such as previewing, skimming, scanning, and understanding vocabulary through context, the problem becomes that of measuring the particular skill of interest in isolation from other skills. For example, a question designed to measure the ability to scan for specific information may contain vocabulary that is unfamiliar to some of the test-takers. As such, the question becomes more a measure of vocabulary knowledge than one of scanning for specific information.

Another problem when attempting to measure specific reading skills lies in being certain that the test-takers are actually using the skill of interest. For example, if the test-takers are asked to skim for the main idea of a paragraph, how can the test format ensure that they are actually skimming and not reading each sentence, word by word? Similarly, if the measurement goal is to identify the test-takers' ability to preview a text in order to determine the general idea and to formulate hypotheses, how can the test ensure that they are not making use of other reading skills such as skimming for main ideas or reading closely for details? If the test-takers are being asked to scan for specific information, how do we know that they are actually scanning?

The measurement of reading ability is obviously a complex task involving problems. Very often, in attempting to solve one measurement problem, another problem will be created. Thus, the development of reliable and valid tests of EST reading ability becomes an interesting, if sometimes frustrating, problem-solving process. This process is perhaps best described with actual examples from an EST reading project. The next section, then, will present some assessment techniques that were developed in the course of the UdeG/UCLA REST project.

Example Assessment Techniques

During the first two years of the UdeG/UCLA REST project the curriculum was focused on the teaching of reading skills and strategies. Under the guidance of the project coordinators, the teachers attempted to develop achievement measures for these skills using the principles of criterion-referenced measurement (CRM). With the CRM approach, specifications are first written for the skill or ability being measured. Then, test items are written from the specifications, sometimes leading to modification of the specifications, followed by more item writing and piloting of the test items. In the case of the REST project, test specifications for certain reading skills went through substantial revisions, reflecting changes in the teachers'/researchers' conceptualization of the skill as well as their ideas on how best to measure the skill.

In order to demonstrate this process of achievement test development, two reading skills from the REST curriculum will be used: previewing and predicting the overall meaning of a text, and using context clues to determine the meaning of unfamiliar vocabulary. The previewing/predicting skill, in particular, will demonstrate the extent to which assessment techniques can vary and change during the test development process.

Measuring the Skill of Previewing and Predicting

The first attempt at developing a measure for the ability to preview a text and predict what it will be about, in general, produced the test specification shown in Figure 3.

The reason for having so much of the test written or translated into Spanish was to ensure that the test was measuring the specific skill of previewing/predicting and not knowledge of English grammar and vocabulary. However, in the effort to focus the assessment

1. *General Description of the Criterion Being Tested:* The students will demonstrate their ability to use the reading skill of prediction. After being given a summary (in Spanish) of the introduction to a text, the title and subheadings (where present), and the first sentence (in English) of each paragraph that follows the introduction, the students will choose from four options the best statement of the general idea of each paragraph.
2. *Requirements for the Text:* The text should have a suitable introduction and title for prediction. The content of the text should be scientific in nature but may come from popular/nontechnical magazines or journals. There should be at least four paragraphs (other than the introduction) with organization around one general idea.
3. *Description of the Test Item:* The student will be presented with an introduction to a text, the title and any subheads (in Spanish), and the first sentence of a paragraph (in English). Any unusual or idiomatic vocabulary in the first sentence will be translated into Spanish. The students will then be instructed to choose from among four alternatives the best statement of the general idea of that paragraph (i.e., their *prediction* of that general idea). The four alternatives will be:
   a. correct statement of what the paragraph is about
   b. an overgeneralization
   c. a misinterpretation of some part of the first sentence
   d. a mention of information present in the introduction, summary, title, or subheads which is not present in the first sentence (= less likely than "a")
   In addition, the students will be asked to demonstrate their degree of understanding of the first sentence by writing a summary/translation (in Spanish).
4. *Description of the Answer Format:* The answer sheet will contain two blank lines for the summary/translation of the sentence followed by the letters "a," "b," "c," and "d" corresponding to the alternatives of the multiple-choice question format. The students will write short summary/translations in Spanish and circle the best response to the M-C question.
5. *Sample Item* (translated from the Spanish): Previewing/Prediction Test I ("Sulfites"): The title and summary of the first paragraph that follows comes from an article published in *Time* magazine, Health section. Read them carefully. Afterwards, answer the questions according to the instructions on your answer sheet.
   Title: Eliminating Sulfites from Salads: The Food and Drug Administration prohibits the preservatives used on fruits and vegetables.
   Paragraph 1 (summary): Salads and fruit are very attractive to the sight and touch and, to many, symbolize health. However, to maintain their freshness sulfites are employed which could cause allergic reactions, illness, and even death.
   Paragraph 2 (1st sentence): "This *fall (*otoño), after almost three years of study, the Food and Drug Administration (FDA) will impose a *ban (*prohibición) on the use of six sulfite preservatives in fresh *produce (*frutas y verduras)."
   The second paragraph will most likely be about (choose only one of the alternatives):
   a. The prohibition by the FDA of the use of six types of sulfite preservatives and its consequences.
   b. The duties of the FDA in the maintenance of public health.
   c. The studies completed over three years concerning the use of sulfite preservatives.
   d. The effects of the use of sulfites on fruits and vegetables.

FIGURE 3. *Test specification: Previewing/prediction.*

on a particular skill, the measurement task had become overly artificial. Ultimately, the students were not doing what they would normally do with an actual text. Furthermore, they were never allowed to read the complete text to confirm or disconfirm their predictions, and this lack of closure was eventually felt to be too frustrating for the students. The test also proved to be extremely difficult

for the teachers, in part because of the difficulty in writing "distractor" alternatives for the multiple-choice format that were plausible but somehow inaccurate predictions.

In the next version of the previewing/predicting test, it was decided to give the students a complete text but to limit the amount of time they would have to answer the test questions. The revised specification

conceptualized the skill more in terms of previewing and making use of the physical layout of the text than in terms of predicting. It
also included skimming for main ideas as a
part of previewing, as indicated below in Figure 4.

While somewhat more satisfying than the
previous assessment technique, this version
presented a new problem: It was difficult to
determine the appropriate time limit for answering the question. The specification originally set two to three minutes as the limit, but
this was changed to four minutes after pilot-

ing a form of the test with the students. Depending on the length and difficulty of the
text (in addition to the clarity of the illustrations and diagrams), four minutes might be
too short for previewing, or, if too long, it
might allow some of the students to do more
than just previewing.

In order to make sure that the students
were, in fact, using previewing skills, and at
the same time allow them to eventually see
the entire text, another version of the previewing test was developed. This technique
made use of what came to be called the "un-

---

1. *General Description of Criterion Being Tested:* The students will use some or all of the following "previewing" skills in order to determine the main idea of a reading text:
   1. reading the title and subtitles; looking at pictures, diagrams; observing the physical layout of the text
   2. recognizing cognates; reading numbers, names, and dates
   3. using prior/background knowledge
   4. skimming for the main idea of the text (quickly moving the eyes across the page, either across the first and last sentences of each paragraph, down the center of the page, or diagonally)

2. *Requirements for the Text:* The text should be a journal article or a textbook chapter or section from the field of Chemical Engineering. It should be from 1 to 3 pages in length and include a title and subtitles and/or illustrations, numbers, names, and dates.

3. *Description of Test Item:* The test item will consist of a set of directions followed by a multiple-choice item format. The directions will instruct the students to use any and all of the "previewing" skills taught in the course in order to determine the best statement of the main idea for the entire text and will inform them of the time limit for answering the question (2–3 minutes, depending on the length of the text). The multiple-choice format will be an incomplete statement: "The best statement of the main idea of this text is:" followed by four alternatives:
   a. the best statement of the main idea of the text
   b. an overgeneralization of the main idea

c. a detail from the text
d. a misinterpretation of some part of the text (this can include illustrations)
Directions, incomplete statement, and alter-
natives will all be written in Spanish.

4. *Description of Answer Format:* The directions and multiple-choice item will be printed on the answer sheet. Next to each alternative—a, b, c, and d—will be a pair of parentheses—( )— and the students will be instructed (in the directions) to indicate their choice for the best statement of the main idea by *filling in* the parentheses. The test item will be on a separate answer sheet that will be collected at the end of the allotted time.

5. *Sample Item* (translated from the Spanish):
   Previewing for the Main Idea of the Text
   (Text = "Solvent Recovery System Recycles Benzene Derivatives")
   Directions: Using the strategies taught in this course fill in the space between the parentheses to the side of the answer "a," "b," "c," or "d," that best represents the main idea of the text. You will have 3 minutes to answer this question.
   1. The main idea of the text is:
      (   ) a. A solution to the problem of benzene derivative pollution in a processing plant.
      (   ) b. The need for pollution control in industrial processing plants.
      (   ) c. The solvent recovery system uses a "cross-bore" heat ex-change to recover solvents.
      (   ) d. A system to produce benzene derivatives and recover sol-vents.

FIGURE 4. *Revised test specification: Previewing/prediction.*

folding text." The students were first presented with a page that contained the title and any pictures and diagrams present in the original text. This ensured that they were only making use of previewing skills. The students were asked to write three things they thought the text would tell them about and to answer a multiple-choice question concerning what the main idea of the entire text would be. With the next part of the test, the first sentence of each paragraph was presented along with main idea questions for each paragraph in which the students wrote out their prediction for the main ideas. Finally, the entire text was presented, and the students were again asked to write their understanding of the main idea for each paragraph.

In addition to controlling how much of the text was presented to the student (with the eventual unfolding of the entire text), this assessment technique differed from previous ones in that the responses were constructed, or written out, by the students. They were allowed to write their answers in Spanish or English (or both) but were advised not to copy word for word from the text. This approach solved the problem that the previous multiple-choice formats created—i.e., the problem of the students' being able to recognize the best statement of the main idea from four alternatives without having actually used the reading skills begin tested. By allowing them to write their answers in Spanish, we felt that their limited EFL writing ability would not interfere with an assessment of their reading ability. Finally, in terms of the authenticity of the test task, this technique allowed the students to check and reformulate their predictions and hypotheses as the text unfolded.

The obvious problem created by the unfolding text technique is the scoring procedure. What would be considered an acceptable/correct response for the question that asked them to predict three things that the article would tell the reader about? As the text unfolded and the students reformulated their hypotheses and predictions, would they be allowed to go back and change their answers to the first section of the test? These

kinds of questions led to yet another conceptualization of the reading skill being assessed. Perhaps previewing and predicting were not skills that could be isolated and tested with questions that assumed one correct answer. If this were true, then the best that could be done would be to present a reading text followed by a set of comprehension questions of various types (inference, main idea, specific information, perhaps with a time limit), and to assume that in order to efficiently approach the text and retrieve the necessary information the student would have to make use of previewing and predicting.

Measuring Vocabulary in Context

The first efforts at developing a test to measure student understanding of vocabulary in context produced the specification given in Figure 5 on the following page.

One obvious problem, regardless of the assessment technique, in attempting to measure the skill of using context clues to get at the meaning of unknown vocabulary is the possibility that the student already knows the vocabulary item in question, regardless of context. Having the students indicate the context clues they used to arrive at the correct meaning for the vocabulary item would give some information as to whether they could have made use of context even though they already knew the word. However, in practice it was very difficult to tell whether the students were reporting clues they actually used or were just mentioning the generic clues that had been presented in class.

Another problem was the scoring procedure. If the student mentioned the appropriate context clues, but selected (or produced) the wrong meaning for the vocabulary item, should the item be scored wrong or given half credit? If one student mentioned three appropriate context clues and another mentioned only one, should they be scored the same? Ultimately, it was decided that scoring the context clues portion of the test was too problematic, and the items were marked right or wrong depending on the

1. *General Description of the Criterion Being Tested:* The students will be able to guess the meaning of certain vocabulary words from context. The texts and words will be of both a scientific/technical and a general/nontechnical nature, to tap into the students' background knowledge of a variety of areas.
2. *Requirements for the Text:* The texts should be both scientific and general in nature. They should *not* be overly simplified and may be authentic texts that the students have already seen. Sources include: *Scientific American, Omni, Science Digest, Reading by All Means* (Dubin and Olshtain, 1981), and any other textbooks that contain 1–2 medium-length paragraphs containing words fitting the following requirements:

    The words should be examples of:
    a. cognates, both exactly matching with Spanish and not exactly matching
    b. words repeated in the text
    c. prefixes and suffixes
    d. technical and nontechnical words
    e. words set off by punctuation (appositives, relative clauses)
    f. words included with "typographical clues" (boldface, italics, parentheses)
    g. words the students have seen in class
    Each text should have its lines numbered.
3. *Description of the Test Item:* Each item will consist of four columns. The columns will be labeled: *Line Number, Vocabulary Item, Context Clues, Meaning.* There will be a total of 10 items from 2–3 texts. Five items will have a Multiple-Choice (M-C) format for the *Meaning* section, and five items will be fill-in-the-blank formats for the *Meaning* section. The students will be given the line number in which the word can be found, perhaps with the word underlined.

    The words will be listed in the second column. The third column (*Context Clues*) will have 2 subheadings: *Textual Clues* and *Other Info. Used* (other info., e.g., prior knowledge).

    The M-C format will consist of four alternatives corresponding to the following (in Spanish):
    a. the correct translation
    b. a synonym not appropriate in this context
    c. an antonym
    d. an "off-the-wall" word not fitting the context
4. *Description of the Answer Format:* The students will mark their answers on the question sheet, filling in the blank or circling the letter of the best alternative.
5. *Sample Item* (translated from the Spanish): General Instructions: This section is divided into two parts. Both parts ask you to indicate the context clues that helped you determine the meaning of the vocabulary item. The first two questions ask you to choose from four alternatives indicating the meaning of the vocabulary item, and the second two questions ask you to give the meaning of the vocabulary in Spanish.

VOCABULARY IN CONTEXT

Part 1.

1. LINE NUMBER	VOCABULARY ITEM	CONTEXT CLUES?	MEANING?
photo caption	SOOT	_____	a. partícula de oxígeno
25 (par. 3)		_____	b. flama
15 (par. 4)		_____	c. partícula de carbón
		_____	d. fósil

Part 2.

1. LINE NUMBER	VOCABULARY ITEM	CONTEXT CLUES?	MEANING?
8 (par. 1)	VENOMS	_____	_____
11 (par. 1)		_____	_____
		_____	_____
		_____	_____

FIGURE 5. *Test specification: Vocabulary in context.*

"meaning" selected or produced by the students.

Based on the experience with this first technique, the test specification was revised to have the students write out, in Spanish, their understanding of the meaning of words in particular contexts. Care was taken to find words whose meaning was clearly determined by the context, and the students were asked to indicate whether (a) they already knew the word and did not use the context to answer, (b) they did not know the word and used the context to answer, (c) they had a vague idea of the word and used the context to clarify their understanding and to answer.

Assuming the students were responding honestly, this technique allowed a judgment of their use of the vocabulary-in-context skill. However, the scoring procedure still remained somewhat problematic. One approach was to give one point for a correct answer and an indication of (a), above. A correct answer with an indication of (b) would receive an additional point, and a correct answer with an indication of (c) would receive an additional half point. This has the obvious disadvantage of penalizing students who have a well-developed vocabulary. Ultimately, the REST teachers/researchers elected to score the items based on the meaning response only, but to save the context-use information for guiding future item selection and test development.

An additional scoring problem occurred as a result of using a constructed response format instead of a selected response. This was the same problem that occurred with the previewing/predicting formats. Constructed response formats are more difficult to score, given that there will be many acceptable answers produced by the students. With selected response formats, the scoring becomes more straightforward, but the items become more difficult to write. One question is whether the alternatives to select from should be written in English or the native language of the students (assuming that you have a homogeneous L1 group). If the alternatives are to be in English, then they should consist of vocab-

ulary that the students can be expected to know. Otherwise, it ceases to be a test of the ability to understand vocabulary in context.

Whether the alternatives are in English or the L1, it becomes difficult to write the "distractors," or incorrect alternatives, and still measure the skill of interest—the ability to use context clues. In order to have alternatives that are plausible but incorrect in the given context, the test will often require the students to sort through various shades of meaning between the alternatives. This becomes a different task from using the contextual clues to get a sufficiently clear notion of the unfamiliar vocabulary to comprehend the overall meaning of the text.

In general, the problems that confront the measurement of reading skills revolve around the difficulty of specifying a test task that is authentic and valid, on the one hand, and is capable of being objectively and reliably scored, on the other. The examples offered from the experience of the REST team are not meant to be taken as ultimate answers to the questions that face the measurement of EST reading but, rather, as preliminary efforts that have framed these questions in interesting ways. The initial efforts were aimed at a precise specification of the reading skills taught in the REST curriculum. More often than not, it seemed impossible to measure these skills in isolation. As a result, the tests developed at REST tended to become more integrated in nature, using formats that involved the use of several reading skills simultaneously (e.g., previewing and skimming) without being able to distinguish them individually. While the test task appears more authentic in these integrated formats, it becomes difficult to make judgments concerning the relative strengths and weaknesses in the curriculum —that is, which instructional objectives are being mastered and which are not.

CONCLUSION AND COMMENTS ON FUTURE DEVELOPMENT

As may be seen from the above discussion, many of the considerations of ESP course design are the same as the concerns in general English course design. That is, just as ESP courses and materials are based on needs analysis, general English courses should also be based on an analysis of who the students are and why they need to learn English and what they need to learn. Additionally, regardless of the care with which a set of ESP materials is designed, the materials must fit into the context of the institution they are designed to service. For example, at one point the REST project attempted to offer an optional advanced course for the chemical engineering students during their final year in the university. The students had asked for such a course. However, it soon became clear that the students simply did not have the time to take on an additional course during their fifth year. Thus, the needs analysis should focus both on the students' needs and aspirations and on the total educational context in which they are learning.

To say that ESP courses must focus on the needs of the learner may seem almost banal. However, this now means that the definition of the learner's needs must be expanded. First, it means that while a target language and target situation analysis must be carried out, these analyses are not enough. The ESP syllabus and materials must also be based on the strategies that the learners have and will need to have. A successful ESP course is not based on mastering particular materials, it involves mastering learning skills and strategies, including the skill of knowing how to learn more on one's own.

The future development of EST reading curricula can also benefit from the use of reading labs, both traditional paper-and-pencil labs and computer-assisted reading labs. The traditional reading lab can include articles and activities much like those which the students are required to read in class. However, this is also an excellent venue for students to perform additional authentic reading tasks, such as using catalogs or technical dictionaries. Computer-assisted instruction can play a very valuable role in EST reading programs. This is particularly true with the more recent authoring systems such as Computer Assisted Language Instructional System (CALIS) (Duke University, 1987). In using such an authoring system the teacher may include any particular text and any particular questions or tasks he or she determines are important. This is a great deal more effective than typical programs which go little beyond pattern practice or isolated passages with situational dialogs. It allows the teacher to include schema activation, prediction, and feedback as well as traditional types of activities. Further, the teacher can cause the program to provide particular feedback if the student answers incorrectly. For example, if the student answers with the incorrect chemical name, the feedback can explicitly state that this is the problem and direct him or her to the appropriate section of the text. On the other hand, the materials developer may decide this error is unimportant and ignore it.

Other issues that should be addressed by future research and curriculum development are the role of translation in EST reading and a rationale for approaching vocabulary (or grammar) in an EST reading curriculum. While translation has usually been considered detrimental to development of communicative skills in the ESL/EFL classroom, it seems likely that it can have an important, positive role in the EST reading classroom. EST reading students will typically need to access material written in English and be able to translate that material quite accurately into their native language for purposes of discussion, application, and professional growth. Translation, in this context, becomes an important skill to be developed. In terms of vocabulary, the traditional notions that students need to learn how to guess at meanings through context in order to become successful readers must also be reexamined in the context of EST reading. Given that EST readers typically need to have a very accurate and precise sense of the content they are dealing with, simply guessing at the meaning of unfamiliar vocabulary could have potentially disastrous effects. There is research which suggests that the logical use of context by second language readers can lead them to very inaccurate conclusions that distort their overall comprehension of texts (Dubin & Olshtain, 1987). Vocabulary, then, may play a different and critical role in the context of EST reading. These and other issues will drive future research and curriculum development, which promises to result in ever-improving instructional programs for students of EST reading.

NOTES

1. The project received support from UCLA and UdeG. In addition, the United States Information Service provided support for five academic specialists to visit the project and for a Fulbright Professor appointment for four years.

2. For a more in-depth discussion of the ESP movement, see the chapter by Johns in this volume.

3. See the chapter by Snow in this volume for a discussion of the modified adjunct model.

4. Please see the chapter by Cohen in this volume for a discussion of the basic issues related to language testing.

DISCUSSION QUESTIONS

1. Why are needs analyses important in the design of an English for science and technology reading project? What are some areas that should be included in needs analyses?

2. How generalizable is the notion of thematic units in REST course design? What are the advantages of such an organization? What are some of the problems that are associated with this method of organization?

3. This article criticizes the need for and effectiveness of simplified reading material in EST programs. Look at the five arguments presented and discuss whether you think they are correct or not.

4. What is the relationship between classroom materials and testing instruments? The article indicates that the two are directly addressing the same issue. Do you agree?

5. What are some of the major problems involved in designing testing instruments to measure specific reading skills? Should the measurement of

specific skills be abandoned in favor of more global measurement of reading comprehension?

SUGGESTED ACTIVITIES

1. Develop a flowchart such as the one in Figure 2 for some other context—e.g., a faculty of medicine, biology, electronics.

2. Find a coursebook for an ESP reading course. Compare its approach with that used at the REST project discussed here.

3. Identify a reading curriculum objective in a teaching context you are familiar with and write a test specification for it, following the examples in Figures 3, 4, and 5. Does this format and approach help you to become clearer about the teaching objective as well as how to measure it?

4. Take the specifications in Figures 3, 4, and 5. Write a sample test section and administer it. How well do the test items work in your context?

SUGGESTIONS FOR FURTHER READING

Carrell, P., J. Devine, and D. Eskey, eds. (1988)
Interactive Approaches to Second Language Reading. Cambridge: Cambridge University Press.

> Provides a comprehensive set of articles on the interactive approach to second language reading. Includes a description of the model in both L1 and L2, provides the results of several empirical studies, and discusses the implications and applications for reading pedagogy.

Dubin, F., D. E., Eskey, and W. Grabe, eds. (1986)
Teaching Second Language Reading for Academic Purposes. Reading, MA: Addison-Wesley.

> While the focus of this book is EAP rather than EST, it presents an important discussion of reading theory, instruction, and materials in the context of particular environments. Also explores the areas of reading laboratories and computer-assisted reading instruction.

Hutchinson, T., and A. Waters (1987)
English for Specific Purposes: A Learning-Centered Approach. Cambridge: Cambridge University Press.

> Discusses the history of ESP development and examines it in terms of current learning theory. This some-

what controversial book questions many of the assumptions of traditional ESP, such as the need for subject-specific materials and whether the best way to train subject-specific students is with subject-specific materials. Follows this through with discussions of needs analysis, course design, and curriculum development.

Swales, J. (1985)
Episodes in ESP. Oxford: Pergamon Press.

Presents 15 articles on ESP which date from 1962 through 1981 and precedes each with a discussion which attempts to place the article in its historical context. Swales's goal is to explain and illustrate the major lines of development in ESP. This is a valuable source for anyone attempting to follow the history of ESP concerns.

II
Language Skills
D. Writing

The ability to express one's ideas in written form in a second or foreign language and to do so with reasonable accuracy and coherence is a major achievement; many native speakers of English never truly master this skill. Olshtain's chapter shows how the teacher of even beginning-level ESL/EFL students can provide practice in writing which reinforces the language the students have learned and which teaches valuable mechanics of writing (e.g., penmanship, spelling, punctuation, format) right from the start. Kroll's chapter gives the reader a comprehensive overview of current theory and method in teaching writing to nonnative speakers of English, especially with reference to teaching ESL students in courses devoted exclusively to the writing skill. Finally, Frodesen's chapter explores the problematic area of grammar (i.e., accuracy) in writing which plagues so many nonnative speakers even after they have more or less mastered the more global features of written English, such as organization and coherence.

Functional Tasks for Mastering the Mechanics of Writing and Going Just Beyond

Elite Olshtain

INTRODUCTION

Within the communicative framework of language teaching, the skill of writing enjoys special status—it is via writing that a person can communicate a variety of messages to a close or distant, known or unknown reader or readers. Such communication is extremely important in the modern world, whether the interaction takes the form of traditional paper-and-pencil writing or the most advanced electronic mail. Writing as a communicative activity needs to be encouraged and nurtured during the language learner's course of study, and this chapter will attempt to deal with the early stages of ESL/EFL writing.

The view of writing as an act of communication suggests an interactive process which takes place between the writer and the reader via the text. Such an approach places value on the goal of writing as well as on the perceived reader audience. Even if we are concerned with writing at the beginning level, these two aspects of the act of writing are of vital importance; in setting writing tasks the teacher should encourage students to define, for themselves, the message they want to send and the audience who will receive it.

The writing process, in comparison to spoken interaction, imposes greater demands on the text, since written interaction lacks immediate feedback as a guide. The writer has to anticipate the reader's reactions and produce a text which will adhere to Grice's (1975) cooperative principle. According to this principle, the writer is obligated (by mutual cooperation) to try to write a clear, relevant, truthful, informative, interesting, and memorable text. The reader, on the other hand, will interpret the text with due regard to the writer's presumed intention if the necessary clues are available in the text. Linguistic accuracy, clarity of presentation, organization of ideas are all crucial in the efficacy of the communicative act, since they supply the clues for interpretation. Accordingly, while the global perspective of content organization needs to be focused on and given appropriate attention, it is also most important to present a product which does not suffer from illegible handwriting, heavy spelling errors, faulty punctuation, or inaccurate structure, any of which may render the message unintelligible.

The present chapter focuses on the gradual development of the mechanics of writing, which is a necessary instrumental skill without which meaningful writing cannot take place; the chapter then moves on to early functional writing, which can be carried out with a limited level of proficiency in the target language. It is important to remember that in the ESL/EFL context, writing, like the other language skills, needs to be dealt with at the particular level of linguistic and discourse proficiency which the intended students have reached (Raimes, 1985). The proposed sequence of activities will start with more focus on the mechanical aspects of writing, as the basic instrumental skill, and gradually move on to a combination of "purpose for writing" and language focus.

EARLY WRITING TASKS: COPING WITH THE MECHANICS

What Do We Teach?

The first steps in teaching reading and writing skills in a foreign or second language classroom center around the mechanics of these two skills. By "mechanics" we usually refer to letter recognition, letter discrimination, word recognition, basic rules of spelling, punctuation, and capitalization, as well as recognition of whole sentences and paragraphs. As such, these activities are cognitively undemanding unless the learners happen to come from a first language with a different writing system.

The interaction between reading and writing has often been a focus in the methodology of language teaching, yet it deserves even stronger emphasis at the early stages in the acquisition of the various component mechanics. In order to learn how to discriminate one letter from another while reading, learners need to practice writing these letters; in

order to facilitate their perception of words and sentences during the reading process, they might need to practice writing them first. It is therefore the case that writing plays an important role in early reading—facilitating the development of both the reading and the writing skills.

Sound–Spelling Correspondences. English presents the learner with a number of unique problems related to its orthographic rules, even in cases where the learner comes from a first language that uses a version of the Roman alphabet. Students and teachers alike often throw their arms up in despair, ready to give up on finding reliable rules for English orthography; yet the English writing system is much more rule-governed than many realize. In fact, English has a very systematic set of sound–spelling correspondences (Chomsky & Halle, 1968; Schane, 1970; Venezky, 1970). These sound–spelling correspondences enable the second or foreign language teacher to combine the teaching of phonetic units with graphemic units and to give students practice in pronunciation along with practice in spelling.

The English Consonants. The first rule to remember about English orthography is that students may tend to look for a one-to-one letter–sound correspondence and then discover that they get into a lot of trouble by doing this. For most of the 21 consonant letters, this type of rule works fairly well (if we disregard allophonic differences in pronunciation, such as an aspirated initial /t/ as opposed to a nonaspirated, unreleased final /t/ for monosyllabic words in English). Yet there are consonant letters whose sound depends on the environment in which they occur: Thus, the letter c can have the sound /k/ when followed by the vowel letters a, o, or u or by the consonant letters l or r, but it has the sound /s/ when followed by the vowel letters e or i. Although these rules may appear confusing to a learner coming from a first language with a simpler grapheme–sound correspondence system, they work quite consistently in English and need to be practiced from the very start. The story of the letter *c* is not finished, however, and now we come to the part that is less consistent. This is the case when *c* is followed by the letter *h* and can have the sound of /č/ (*chocolate*) or /k/ (*choir*). There is no help we can give our students in this respect but to tell them to pay special attention to such words and try to remember their sound according to the meaning of the word. The letter *c* also occurs in quite a number of common words followed by the letter *k* (not initially, but in the middle or at the end of words—such as *chicken* or *lock*). The sound in this case is /k/ and the correspondence should create no difficulty.

The letter *c* in English demonstrates the fact that even for some of the consonants (*g*, too) we need to alert students to the fact that the correspondence in English is not between letter and sound but between the letter and its immediate environment and the most appropriate sound. In many cases such correspondences are quite predictable, while in others the rules do not work as well.

A helpful generalization for English consonants is related to the letter *h*, which is very powerful in changing the sound of the consonant which it follows. Thus, the letter combinations *ch*, *sh*, and *th* represent distinct consonant sounds, and learners need to recognize these graphic clusters as such.

To summarize, when teaching consonant letters and their sound correspondences, it seems that for students whose own alphabet is similar to that of English, we need to focus only on the differences. Yet for students coming from a completely different writing system, such as Arabic, Hebrew, Chinese, Japanese, or Korean, it will be necessary to work carefully on the recognition of every consonant letter. Here learners might have difficulties similar to the ones encountered by young children who learn to read and write in English as their mother tongue, and we might need some special exercises for this purpose (see Appendix A).

The English Vowels.   The vowel letters in English present more complex sound–spelling correspondences, but again there is much more consistency and predictability than many learners realize. Thus, learners need to be made aware of two basic types of environments that are very productive in English orthography: C(consonant)V(vowel)C(consonant) (CVC) (often known as the environment for short vowels) and CV and CVCe (the latter ending in a silent letter *e*) (known as the environments for long vowels). The terms "short" and "long" vowels are rather unfortunate, since for the second or foreign language learner it might, erroneously, become associated with vowel length rather than vowel quality. Thus, the difference between the vowel sounds in the words *pin* and *pine* is not one of length (or production time) but one of phonetic quality. A difference in vowel length can be observed in the words *pit* and *pin*, where the quality of the two vowel sounds is the same but the one preceding the voiceless stop is shorter than the one preceding the voiced nasal.

Although we often say that the five vowel letters of the English alphabet result in at least 11 or more vowel sounds (depending on the particular English dialect), these sound–spelling correspondences are, at least in part, consistent and predictable. What teachers and learners need to take into account is the fact that in English we must consider both the vowel letter and the environment in which it occurs. The term "environment" might be delimited here to those features which may influence the quality of the vowel sound. Thus, the environment CVC is quite productive, and all five vowel letters *a*, *i*, *e*, *o*, and *u* will occur as lax (with relatively relaxed muscles) and simple, nondiphthonged vowel sounds, as in the words *pan*, *pin*, *pen*, *pot*, and *but*. However, the same five vowel letters occurring in the CVCe environment will all become tense and diphthongized, as in the words *pane*, *pine*, *Pete*, *rope*, and *cute*. Similarly, those vowels that can occur in the CV or V environment are also tense and usually diphthongized: *go*, *be*, *ma*, *I*, *Lu* (as in *Lulu*). Here again we have a very productive set of sound–spelling correspondence rules, yet not all of these patterns are equally frequent in English orthography. Thus, the letter e does not usually occur as the vowel in the CVCe environment, and learners have to encounter the more common spellings as in *meet* and *meat* for the sound /iy/. In other words, there are some basic sound–spelling correspondences in English, knowledge of which can greatly facilitate the acquisition of these correspondences, but there are also quite a number of exceptions or expansions of these rules that need to be learned individually.

In teaching the basic sound-spelling correspondences in English, it is important to emphasize the rules which provide the learners with useful generalizations and which therefore help them become effective readers. Once students have assimilated and internalized the basic features of such correspondences—namely, the distinction between CVC and CV or CVCe syllables—this will work well not only for all monosyllabic words but also for polysyllabic ones, where the stressed syllable can act as a monosyllabic environment for letter–sound vowel correspondences (e.g., *dispóse*).

Furthermore, some of the more advanced spelling rules related to English morphology can be facilitated by this knowledge. In polysyllabic verbs if the final syllable is stressed, the spelling rules for adding the inflection -*ing* works in the same manner as for monosyllabic ones. Thus, learners who know the rule for consonant letter doubling when changing *sit* to *sitting* will be able to apply the same rule to any polysyllabic verb that ends with a stressed syllable having the form CVC. Therefore, the verb *begin*, since its final syllable is stressed, will undergo doubling of the last consonant *beginning*, as opposed to the verb *open*, where the final syllable is not stressed and therefore is spelled *opening*.

However, in spite of all that has been said so far, English orthography has a notorious reputation because, in addition to all these helpful and relatively reliable rules, we must account for various less productive rules. Some of these are quite predictable, such as

the occurrence of the letter *a* in front of *l* or *ll*, which quite consistently is realized as the sound /ɔ/ as in *call*, and *a* in front of the letter *r*, which has the sound /a/ as in *car*. In general, the letter *r* affects the sound of the vowel preceding it, and causes it to become more centralized, as in the words *world, bird, curd*. Furthermore, the vowel diphthongs have a variety of spellings, such as the following letter combinations, which all correspond to the same vowel diphthong /ow/: *rope, boat, low, foe*. So, while it is true that there are quite a few cases in English which need to be remembered as individual words, there are far fewer than people imagine (for good sources of rules on sound–spelling correspondences, see Schane, 1970; Venezky, 1970).

In summing up this section dealing with the teaching elements relevant to the mechanics of reading and writing, we should emphasize the fact that it is important for learners of English as a second or foreign language to realize from the start that English orthography is by no means a one-to-one letter–sound correspondence system; it has its own consistency embedded in the combination of letters with their immediate environments, resulting in what we tend to call sound–spelling correspondences. By practicing the proper pronunciation of sounds in relation to given spelling patterns, we can provide learners with a good basis for pronunciation as well as for the skills of reading and writing.

How Do We Teach Them?

The stage devoted to the teaching of the mechanics of reading and writing aims at three different goals: (a) to enhance letter recognition—especially when learners come from a different writing system, (b) to practice sound–spelling correspondences via all four language skills, and (c) to help the learner move from letters and words to meaningful sentences and larger units of discourse.

Recognition and writing drills constitute the first steps in the development of effective reading and writing habits. However, in order to acquire active mastery of the sound–spelling correspondences, it is necessary for the learners to arrive at relevant generalizations concerning these correspondences. Such generalizations will lead to a better understanding of the systematic representation of sounds in English orthography, and will require the learners to master some basic phonological rules in English and to develop an ability to recognize the distinctive features of each letter within a spelling pattern.

Three major types of recognition tasks are used at this early stage of reading and writing, each type incorporating a great variety of drills:

a. matching tasks
b. writing tasks
c. meaningful sound–spelling correspondence practice

Examples of different *matching tasks* are given in Appendix A. These tasks enable the learners to develop effective recognition habits based on distinctive graphic features. Many of these have the form of games, puzzles, and other "fun" activities. Examples of different *writing tasks* are given in Appendix B, starting with basic letter formation and leading to meaningful writing of words and sentences. Examples of *sound–spelling correspondence* tasks are given in Appendix C. The common feature of all the tasks in Appendix C is that they require the learner to focus on the pronunciation as well as the written shape of the spelling patterns.

An important feature of this early stage of writing is the need to get learners accustomed to correct capitalization in English and to basic punctuation rules. While practicing sound–spelling correspondences, students can be writing meaningful sentences (accompanied by pictures) with proper capitalization and punctuation, such as the following:

1. There is a cat on the mat and a cake on the plate.
2. The ball is near the tall boy next to the wall.

These sentences contain words which exemplify sound–spelling correspondences, and, at the same time, they are words that students have probably just learned. They may not work out too well as a story or an interesting piece of discourse since our focus in this case is first and foremost on the sound–spelling correspondence. But eventually, discourse units will grow and incorporate more meaningful and interesting texts. The language knowledge the students gain can be the basis for developing further more sophisticated and interesting texts, however.

More Advanced Writing Tasks: Developing Basic Communication Tools

More advanced writing activities which start shifting their goal from the focus on the mechanics of writing to basic process-oriented tasks will need to incorporate some language work at the morphological and discourse level. Thus, these activities will enable a combination of focus on accuracy and content of the message. In this chapter, since we are concerned with the beginning level, we will work with categories of practical writing tasks, emotive writing tasks, and school-oriented tasks (Nevo, Weinbach, & Mark, 1987).

In order to develop and use these more demanding writing activities in the ESL/EFL classroom, we need to develop a detailed set of specifications which will enable both teachers and students to cope successfully with these tasks. Such a set of specifications should include the following:

Task Description: to present students with the goal of the task and its importance.
Content Description: to present students with possible content areas that might be relevant to the task.
Audience Description: to guide students in developing an understanding of the

intended audience, their background, needs, and expectations.

Format Cues: to help students in planning the overall organizational structure of the written product.

Linguistic Cues: to help students make use of certain grammatical structures and vocabulary selections.

Spelling and Punctuation Cues: to help students focus their attention on spelling rules which they have learned and eventually on the need to use the dictionary for checking accuracy of spelling, and to guide students to use acceptable punctuation and capitalization conventions.

Practical Writing Tasks

These are writing tasks which are procedural in nature and therefore have a predictable format. This makes them particularly suitable for writing activities that focus primarily on spelling and morphology. Lists of various types, notes, short messages, simple instructions, and other such writing tasks are particularly useful in reinforcing classroom work.

Lists can be of many types: "things to do" lists, "things completed" lists, shopping lists. Each of these list types provides us with an opportunity to combine some spelling rules with morphological rules and with the logical creation of a meaningful message. "Things to do" lists are useful for practicing verb bases and reinforcing various sound–spelling correspondences. When assigning such an activity, the teacher will have to indicate whether the list is personal or intended for a team. The content specification will have to indicate whether this is a list of things to do in preparation for some event or more a plan for someone's daily routine. For example, a list for a group of students who are preparing a surprise birthday party might look like this:

Things to Do

1. Buy a present for Donna (Sharon).

2. Call Donna's friends (Gail).
3. Write invitations (Dan) . . . etc.

Following up this type of list, we can easily move on to the "things completed" list, which specifies the things that have already been taken care of and is therefore useful for practicing past forms of verbs. As part of this activity students will need to review the regular past formation of verbs where *-ed* is added and its exceptions in spelling are taught, such as the deletion of a final *e* before adding *-ed*, as in *lived*; the doubling of the last consonant in monosyllabic bases of the form CVC, as in *planned*, and the same doubling rule when the final syllable of a polysyllabic verb is stressed, such as in *occurred* but not in *opened*; the replacement of *y* with *i* when the base ends in C + *y*, as in *tried*. Such an activity also enables students to practice the spelling of irregular past-tense formations. For example, the above list might look like this when partially completed:

Things Completed

1. Planned the games for the party.
2. Wrote the invitations.
3. Bought the present.
4. Called the friends.
5. Tried to call mother.

Shopping lists provide us with a very good opportunity to practice the spelling of the plural ending of countable nouns and the use of quantifiers. The sound–spelling correspondences here consist of the plural inflection with two of its three phonetic variants—/s/, /z/—which can be combined with the spelling pattern *s* as in *pens*, *pencils*, whereas in words like *brushes* or *oranges* the plural takes the phonetic form /əz/, an additional syllable, with such words ending in the spelling pattern *-es*.

Another type of practical writing task is notes and messages that are left for another person. These allow students to practice brief and simple sentences with proper punctuation and a meaningful message. To make the activity more interesting, students can design their own message headings and then fill them in. Here is an example:

Messages for My Little Sister

> Wash the dishes in the sink.
> Feed the dog.
> Watch your favorite program on TV and have a good time.

Other types of practical writing activities might include the filling-in of forms and the preparation of invitations, "greetings" and "thank you" notes, and other such written communications. All of these activities, when carried out in class, will require the set of specifications mentioned above, with appropriate focus on orthographic, mechanical, and linguistic accuracy. (For various examples of such tasks see the appendices.)

Emotive Writing Tasks

Emotive writing tasks are concerned with personal writing. Such personal writing includes primarily letters to friends and narratives describing personal experiences, as well as personal journals and diaries. When dealing with letter writing, emphasis can be placed on format, punctuation, and spelling of appropriate phrases and expressions. When writing about personal experiences—usually done in a narrative format—spelling of past-tense forms can be reviewed and practiced. Diaries and journals can take the form of personal letters and serve as a review of letter writing in general.

It seems that emotive writing, to serve the personal needs of the learners, has to be quite fluent. How can this be done in the early stages of the ESL/EFL course of study? The different emotive types of writing activities are, of course, suitable for the more advanced stages of the course, but they can be carried out, in a more limited manner, even at the initial stages. Thus, letters can be limited to the level of structural and vocabulary knowledge of the students at each point in time. Similarly, journal and personal writing activities can reflect the learner's proficiency level.

It is important, however, in all cases, to provide students with the specifications of the task, limiting it to their level of knowledge.

School-Oriented Tasks

One of the most important functions of writing in a student's life is the function it plays in school. It is still the case that much individual learning goes on while students are writing assignments, summaries, answers to questions, or a variety of essay-type passages. In most cases, the audience for these writing tasks is the teacher, but gradually students must learn to write to an unknown audience who needs to get the information being imparted exclusively via writing. Here again, at the early stages of ESL/EFL learning, the assignments might be short and limited. Answers might be single phrases or sentences, summaries (a listing of main ideas), and similar elements. However, all of these writing activities should be given attention both at the linguistic-accuracy level and at the message-transmission level. It is the combination of content and organization with accepted formal features that will lead learners to better utilization of the writing skill in their future use of English.

CONCLUSION

It has been the objective of this chapter to encourage teachers to use a variety of writing tasks at all levels and particularly at the beginning level. Writing, in addition to being a communicative skill of vital importance, is a skill which enables the learner to plan and rethink the communication process. It therefore provides the learner with the opportunity to focus on both linguistic accuracy and content organization. It has been the major aim of this chapter to emphasize the fact that the mechanics of writing are particularly important at the initial stage of the course since they help students establish a good basis in sound–spelling correspondences, which are important for effective use of the reading and writing skills and also for good pronunciation. A carefully planned presentation which combines the mechanics of writing with the composing process can serve the learner well during the early stages of a language course. This is especially true for children, but also true for adults whose native language uses a completely different writing system. And for preliterate adults, the more advanced activities suggested in Haverson's chapter in this volume can be combined with some of the suggestions offered here to ensure that a proper foundation in writing is also established while such adults are learning to be better readers.

DISCUSSION QUESTIONS

1. How would we plan the early writing stage differently for students whose first language uses a Roman alphabet as compared to students whose first language has a completely different writing system?

2. Mention an important sound–spelling correspondence in English that was not mentioned in the article, and discuss how you might teach it.

3. How should we sequence the teaching of the various sound–spelling correspondences?

4. How can writing be used to ensure the interaction of all skills at the early stages of the ESL/EFL course of study? Give an example.

5. Give an example of how the teacher of beginning-level ESL/EFL students can combine elements of the composing process with elements of the mechanics of writing.

SUGGESTED ACTIVITIES

1. Prepare a game or a set of cards to practice the difference between the vowel sounds in the environment CVC and CVCe. Example: /hat/, /kit/, etc., versus /hate/, /kite/. Incorporate as many words as might be meaningful for the intended student population, but you may have to use some new words that serve the sound–spelling correspondence and are not known to your students. What will you do to present the new words to your students before you practice the spelling patterns?

2. Design a lesson to focus on the different sounds associated with the letter c. First present the various environments, and then develop some challenging activities to practice the relevant sound–spelling correspondences.

3. Find a picture or a number of pictures that depict various words with unusual spelling patterns. All of these should be useful words. Play a memory game with your students: They are allowed to look at the picture for two whole minutes, then the picture is taken away, and the students are supposed to write on a piece of paper all the words which they remember. How did this activity work?

4. Find pictures which can be used for simple descriptions. Develop a number of activities that will enable pairs and small groups to answer a set of questions about each picture. The questions should lead to a concise description of what can be seen in the picture.

SUGGESTIONS FOR FURTHER READING

Sources for an Overall Approach to Writing

Hedge, T. (1988)
Writing. Oxford: Oxford University Press.

Raimes, A. (1983)
Techniques in Teaching Writing. New York: Oxford University Press.

White, R. V. (1980)
Teaching Written English. London: Heinemann Educational Books.

Sources for Teaching Prereading and Early Writing Exercises

Crittenden, J. (1978)
English with Solo. Oxford: Oxford University Press.

Herman, M., and P. Sacks (1977)
Tell Me How to Spell. Tel Aviv: University Publishing Projects.

Johnson, K. (1983)
Now for English, Course and Activity Books 1, 2, 3. Surrey: Thomas Nelson.

Llanas, A., and E. Taylor (1983)
Sunrise 1. Surrey: Thomas Nelson.

Olshtain, E., et al. (1970)
English for Speakers of Hebrew, Pre-reader Workbook. Tel Aviv: University Publishing Projects.

Prince, E. (1990)
Write Soon! A Beginning Text for ESL Writers. New York: Maxwell Macmillan.

APPENDIX A

1. Letter recognition activities:
   a. Find the ODD MAN OUT.
      h h (k) n h n f j j p b b d b d
   b. Find the same letter.
      b: n d (b) c k
      k: j f k h i
      d: b p l d h
   c. Find all the **d**'s.
      f k s n (d) j
      s j d d b p
      h f k s z m
      f d k j n m

      Find all the **h**'s.
      s k j h n d
      z k n b s d
      m h n h s s
      f g h k h b

   d. Underline the words that have **n**.
      n net
          ben
          bed
          ten
   e. Underline the words ending in **ed**.
      ed ned
          bed
          dip
          net

2. Match capital letters with lower case. *Example:* Connect the words beginning with the same letter.
   Pin   tin
   bin   pin
   Tin   Bin
   net   Net

APPENDIX B

Writing Practice—tracing letters, words, and sentences

c C C C C C C C C

C c C C C c C c C c C c C c

c C C C C C C C C

Carl Carl Carl Carl Carl

There's a cup on the table.
There's a cup on the table.

APPENDIX C

Practicing sound–spelling correspondences

1. The letter **a** in **all** and **al**

   a. Read the following words out loud.

all	also
ball	always
call	almost
fall	although
wall	
tall	
hall	
small	

   but *not in the word*—**shall**

   b. Write the missing letters and then read the sentence.

   ll the sm _ _ _
   _ _lls f_ _ _ _.

2. Underline the word your teacher says.

tin	tam	mit
tine	tame	mite
tan	time	mat
bad	hide	can
bade	hid	cane
bid	had	cap

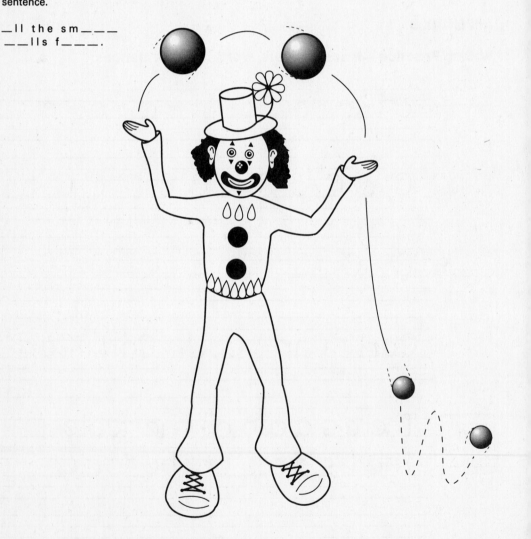

3. Use the first sound of the word in the picture to write a sentence.

Example:

I'm hot.

Teaching Writing in the ESL Context[1]

Barbara Kroll

The teaching of writing has undergone a tremendous metamorphosis in the past quarter century, and this has been true for both the teaching of native speakers and the teaching of nonnative speakers. While a college or high school composition teacher from the 1940s might have comfortably stepped into a classroom of the 1960s and conducted a lesson similar to what he or she had always done, the 1960s teacher would barely have recognized many writing classrooms of the 1980s. Similarly, an ESL teacher from the 1960s would find little in today's ESL writing class that resembled his or her teaching approaches of the past, since it is hard to even imagine that an entire class would have been devoted to ESL writing 25 years ago. To understand current attitudes and practices, though, it is helpful first to understand the evolution of the teaching of writing.

Prior to the mid-1960s, teaching writing to native speakers at the college level was primarily conducted within a framework focused on responding in writing to literary texts. Students read works of literature (including poems, short stories, plays, novels, and essays), wrote "themes," and submitted them for a grade. Indeed, the teachers of such courses were (and, in countless institutions today, remain) trained in techniques of literary analysis, and were certainly not trained to consider how one might approach the teaching of writing. Things were no better at the high school level. Based on a survey of 158 high schools in 45 different states conducted in the mid-1960s, Squire and Applebee (1968) reported that high school English classes devoted only 15.7 percent of the total classroom time to the teaching of writing and that the bulk of that instructional time was spent *after* students' papers had been written. They concluded that for most high school teachers, "correcting papers [was] synonymous with teaching writing" (1968, p. 122).

245

Based on textbooks of the period, the model for teaching composition was clear and included the following four steps: (1) Instruct the students in fairly rigidly defined principles of rhetoric and organization which were presented as "rules" for writing; (2) provide a reading text for classroom discussion, analysis, and interpretation (preferably a work of literature); (3) require a writing assignment (accompanied by an outline) based on the text; and (4) read, comment on, and criticize student papers prior to beginning the next instance of this cycle. This approach has come to be known as "the traditional paradigm" (Hairston, 1982). Because teachers following this model tended to focus on evaluating student essays, the approach also merits the label the "product approach," since the primary concern with writing was really with the completed written product, not with the strategies and processes involved in its production.

Meanwhile, ESL composition teaching in the 1960s was dominated by a controlled composition model whose origins seem to lie in the oral approach promulgated in the 1940s by Charles Fries (1945). While the written *product* was also the focal point of evaluation and concern, as in L1, the ESL approach differed in that the stimulus for L2 student writing was rarely a genuine text, and written tasks were not meant to elicit interpretive commentary on texts. That is, whatever writing took place was meant to serve as reinforcement of language principles (and not, for example, for such other purposes as addressing a topic or communicating with an audience), and the writing task was tightly controlled in order to reduce the possibility for error. Silva (1990, p. 13) notes that controlled composition stems from the notion that language is habit formation, and the result of written practice is a text which "becomes a collection of sentence patterns and vocabulary items, a linguistic artifact, a vehicle for language practice." In fact, writing was "the handmaid" of the other skills, according to Rivers (1968), and did not have a separate place in the ESL curriculum.

There has, however, been a radical shift in how writing is viewed in the ESL curriculum, and a major factor contributing to the shift has been a change in first language composition methodologies motivated by a shifting paradigm in L1 composition teaching (Hairston, 1982). In his book detailing the emergence of first language "composition studies" as a discipline in its own right and the impact of the professionalization of the discipline on the teaching of writing, North (1987, p. 9) notes that "any date chosen to mark the beginning of 'modern' composition is bound to be arbitrary." But it does appear that a number of forces converged in the mid-1960s to change the way composition has come to be viewed and taught, starting with the call by Braddock, Lloyd-Jones, and Schoer (1963) for teachers or researchers to examine the ways in which writing is actually produced. Others, including Hairston (1982), cite the 1966 Anglo-American Seminar on the Teaching of English held at Dartmouth College as issuing a clarion call to de-emphasize the formal teaching of grammar and to emphasize the writing process in K–12 classrooms. In the late 1960s, Janet Emig pioneered the technique of the "think aloud" procedure[2] for collecting information about student writing processes, and she is usually cited as the first researcher to call wide attention to the fact that the ways in which student writers produce text do not necessarily match the model that had been traditionally promulgated (Emig, 1971). One of her watershed observations was the fact that writers do not, in general, produce text in a straightforward linear sequence that the traditional paradigm outlined, an observation which exposed the fact that much of what textbooks suggested in terms of a writing "process" was based on intuitions of textbook writers and not based on analysis of writers at work. Once the insights of process-based inquiry began to slowly but inexorably shift the teaching of first language writing, the field came to have a profound impact on the teaching of composition to ESL students as well, and insights from L1 pedagogy have gradually been imported into the second language classroom, often many years later.

The most significant single transformation in the teaching of composition has undoubtedly been the shift from a focus on product to a focus on process. That is, instead of conducting writing courses where the emphasis is on the teacher's evaluating examples of student written work, the conventional wisdom today asks writing teachers to offer courses which provide students a repertoire of strategies for composing texts and at the same time provide them an understanding of the goals and purposes of written communication. The process approach "provided a way to think about writing in terms of what the writer does (planning, revising, and the like) instead of in terms of what the final product looks like (patterns of organization, spelling, grammar)" (Applebee, 1986, p. 96). In contradiction to the traditional paradigm that dominated textbooks and teaching practices in the 1960s, research into writing processes has allowed us to find out that for many "writing is an act of discovery" in which writers may develop what they want to say *during* rather than *before* the process of writing (Hairston, 1982). Further:

usually the writing process is not linear, moving smoothly in one direction from start to finish. It is messy, recursive, convoluted, and uneven. Writers write, plan, revise, anticipate, and review throughout the writing process, moving back and forth among different operations involved in writing without any apparent plan. (Hairston 1982, p. 85)

Researchers in ESL writing have replicated many of the L1 research studies on the composing processes of student writers, often with a focus on the pedagogical implications of such studies. Krapels (1990) provides a thorough review of a large number of such studies, and concludes that research findings have been contradictory regarding the similarity of L1 and L2 composing processes. While some of the ESL findings echo the findings of L1 studies (see, e.g., Arndt, 1987; Edelsky, 1982; Zamel, 1983), Raimes (1985) also details some of the differences in L1 and L2 composing behavior on the part of un-

skilled students. For example, "unskilled ESL writers do not go back [in their texts] to edit as often as unskilled native speakers" (Raimes, 1985 p. 247). She concludes from her case study that "we should neither use the same pedagogical strategies for ESL students in writing classes as for native speakers nor should we treat our students simply as learners who need large doses of language instruction" (Raimes, 1985 p. 250). While Zamel (1987) and Raimes (1986) caution that much ESL writing instruction today is not informed by new research insights and too many textbooks continue to promote rigid and arbitrary rules, I feel we must also recognize that much ESL writing instruction *has* been informed by valuable research insights, and we should join with our colleagues to work toward continued improvement of ESL writing instruction at our various institutions.

If the ways in which ESL writing lessons are now often conducted and the goals to which they are dedicated further result from a shifting paradigm within the field of ESL itself and the attempt "to incorporate into our work much that is being discovered about language acquisition" (Raimes, 1983b, p. 543), then the teaching of ESL writing today has gone far beyond the "reinforcement" function of the audiolingual approach (Raimes, 1987). Thus, I believe that ESL writing teachers need to adapt a well-grounded philosophical stance to underpin their own approach to the teaching of writing, enabling them to choose methodologies and materials which arise from principled decisions. Without a stance toward how to promote student learning, teachers would be forced to make ad hoc choices which may or may not be the best possible ones for the student. They also run the risk of spending class time on counterproductive activities or evaluating student progress according to questionable criteria.

In the rest of this chapter, I will discuss several key components in the ESL writing curriculum and the ESL writing class which teachers must address as they develop their own philosophy of teaching, enabling them to structure programs and courses to facilitate improvement of student writing skill.

THE WRITING CURRICULUM

General Placement Concerns

Almost every institution that offers ESL writing courses sets up a number of different classes at various levels which are meant to reflect the range of skill levels of the students enrolled in that particular program. To facilitate establishing a writing curriculum (as opposed to a general ESL curriculum) which can target specific principles to address in any one course of a given program, it is essential that students be given a (direct) placement test in writing, and that means asking them to produce one or more writing samples. Without a placement instrument that can sort students into levels of writing proficiency, it is not possible to establish clear curricular goals, since there is no way of assuring that students are grouped in classes that are relatively homogeneous, a necessary prerequisite for curriculum planning. And it is the curriculum of the writing program that designates the goals for each course and helps to distinguish one course from another. Although scoring writing placement tests is a complex and time-consuming procedure, indirect measures of writing, such as a multiple-choice grammar test, have proven to be undesirable as indicators of productive skills. For example, Braddock et al. (1963) point to their lack of validity since they do not require the students to create texts; Troyka (1982) criticizes multiple-choice grammar tests for their very narrow focus and consequent lack of validity as a writing test. A good writing placement instrument can help to determine (1) how many different levels of writing courses are appropriate to offer within a program, and (2) how to place students into individual courses. Creating a placement instrument and scoring procedure appropriate to the goals of a particular program thus serves as a critical factor in providing teachers with principled reasons for selecting the materials and the methodologies they will use in the ESL writing classroom.

Placement Concerns for High-Intermediate and Advanced Students

Topics that are to be used for placement essays in academic-level programs should present tasks which students at a variety of skill levels can address but which are sufficiently complex to produce a range of responses representative of differing levels of writing skill. Research on the testing of writing has indicated that many factors in the presentation of a topic influence student performance, and that is why a two-sample test—in which the student produces two rather different styles of writing—is preferable for obtaining more reliable information about a student's writing skill. It should also be borne in mind that placement tests which are based on responding to reading passages may not yield reliable results regarding student writing skill, since reading skill is being indirectly measured with such an instrument as well. Further, Greenberg (1989) cautions that "a lengthy reading passage is likely to have adverse effects on the writing performance of weaker readers, particularly ESL students."

Once one or more placement essays have been collected, teachers in the program can score them using either a global holistic scale, such as the 6-point scale developed for the TOEFL Test of Written English, which awards the top score of 6 to an essay that "clearly demonstrates competence in writing on both the rhetorical and syntactic levels" and the bottom score of 1 to an essay that "demonstrates incompetence in writing" (*Test of Written English Guide*, 1989), or a more detailed set of scoring guidelines, such as the widely used 100-point ESL English Composition Profile (developed by Jacobs, Zingraf, Wormuth, Hartfiel, & Hughey, 1981), which has raters assign differentially weighted separate subscores in the five categories of content, organization, vocabulary, language use, and mechanics. Typical holistic scores are derived by asking readers to rate the essay as a "whole" for adherence to principles spelled out in a set of written guidelines, i.e., a rubric; many rubrics ask readers to consider such issues as content, organization, and language features at each of the points along the scale, so that no essay will receive the highest score that does not show at least a fair amount of control in all three of these areas.

There is, however, a significant problem with both these types of scoring procedures: the possibility that two essays with quite different characteristics may be assigned the same overall score because of the nature of the scoring system used. As pointed out in Kroll (1990, p. 42), it is perfectly possible, for example, for an essay with very weak syntactic control and reasonable competence in essay organization to receive the same midrange score as one with excellent syntactic control that fails to address the topic at hand in an appropriate manner. Thus, when such scoring procedures are used to assign students to classes, the result may be that classes at a specific level have students with very different writing strengths and weaknesses.

In fact, once ESL students are capable of producing a full piece of prose, they can (not unlike native-speaker writers) fall into one of four general categories based on the relative strength of their syntactical and rhetorical skills: (1) plus rhetoric/plus syntax, (2) plus rhetoric/minus syntax, (3) minus rhetoric/plus syntax, and (4) minus rhetoric/minus syntax (Kroll, (1990, p. 44), but the classes in which they enroll may not be so divided.

However, placement scoring instruments can be made sensitive to these distinctions in order to identify which students need to learn rhetoric and which students need to learn syntax, particularly in academic programs for fully matriculated college or university students. It is also possible to offer courses to address these needs separately.

For example, a class for students at the highest level, those who fall into the plus rhetoric/plus syntax category, can be offered as a parallel course for freshman composition, or ESL students can simply enroll in regular sections of freshman composition. ESL students and native speakers might also be placed together in a rhetoric course for students with excellent syntax but limited rhetorical control. The goal of this course would be learning to produce "reader-based" prose, "a deliberate attempt to communicate something to a reader" (Flower, 1979, p. 20), through a focus on how audience and purpose determines the shape of content.

However, for those ESL students whose rhetorical control is adequate but whose language skills are limited, a third class needs to be provided with enrollment limited to ESL students only. Such a course needs to focus on syntax in ways that contextualize language rather than presenting or reviewing rules of grammar.[3] Finally, students who have serious limitations in both syntax and organization should first focus on obtaining minimal mastery of rhetoric before being asked to improve their syntactic control so that the course can present syntax as a tool for controlling written language rather than as an object of study.

The divisions outlined above stem from a particular stance about how best to sequence courses within a writing curriculum. To argue for or against them, teachers must understand how their own philosophy of teaching motivates them to make choices and how what they choose relates to what they identify as the best interests of the student learner. If one is committed, for example, to the idea that learning to write takes place in incremental steps, each step building on and incorporating knowledge gained from a previous step and each new step involving ever more difficult or complex tasks, then one kind of curriculum might emerge. On the other hand, if one is committed to the idea that learning to write is a more global undertaking where sequencing of material is less important than engagement with material and the need to take the reader's expectations into account from the earliest stage, then another type of curriculum might emerge. A firm commitment to how the curriculum must be structured and sequenced to promote student learning is a prerequisite for determining specific methods and materials that will be introduced in the various classes.

Establishing Curriculum Principles: Controlled-Guided-Free

Once students are placed into classes, their particular skill levels will determine to a large extent the scope of any writing activities they are able to undertake. While the ultimate goal of a writing curriculum might be to have ESL students write essays that match the level of content and mastery of language skills required of native speakers in an academic environment, it is not possible for beginning- or even intermediate-level language learners to produce essays that exhibit such mastery. One approach that attempts to address the developmental path of learning to write characterizes writing tasks along a continuum from "controlled" to "guided" to "free," representing a category scheme for considering writing tasks ranging from those with maximal teacher control and minimal student input to tasks in which students have to supply content, organization, and language structure.

For students in earlier stages of language learning, it is probably helpful to present opportunities for writing which are absolutely or relatively "controlled." The "controlled composition" approach, as mentioned earlier, derived from the audiolingual approach; by asking students to "work on given material and perform strictly prescribed operations on it" (Raimes, 1983a, p.6), its main purpose was to allow students to produce relatively error-free writing. While this concept of "controlling" writing might seem quite dated given our concern today with student-centered learning and communicative approaches to language teaching, we still need to set do-able writing tasks for students with a limited range of vocabulary and an incomplete knowledge of English grammatical structures. For example, dictation can be viewed as a kind of controlled writing exercise which allows students to get the kinesthetic experience of writing in their own hand a well-structured text, which can then also serve as a model for the more difficult task of imitation in which students might use the passage dictated as a guideline for another passage they produce following either the content area and/or the sentence structure of the dictated text. (Frodesen, in this volume, provides more detailed discussion of the uses of dictation.) Another common kind of controlled writing is to present a paragraph in which the student is asked to change a given feature, such as verb tense, which often requires other concomitant changes to be made, such as time references. While potentially deadly dull for more proficient students, especially if such an exercise uses vapid material as its starting point, such a task can be made very useful for students with limited vocabulary and syntax by presenting a text that has value both as a model of good writing and for its interesting subject matter. Frodesen (this volume) also discusses how this kind of text conversion exercise can serve to improve a student's grammatical control as well.

An example of a guided writing task, which allows for a wider range of text construction than a controlled task, is to ask students to produce a short text by answering directed, yet open-ended questions which provide a rhetorical structure for a student-generated text. An illustration of this would be to elicit an autobiography by prompting the student with such questions as what his/her country of origin is, how big his/her family is, what his/her previous educational experiences have been, and so forth. By responding to the questions, the student of limited language proficiency would be able to produce a coherent, unified text. Another guided procedure is called a "dicto-comp," a combination of a dictation and a composition. Using this technique, the teacher first reads aloud a passage at normal speed—i.e., much too fast for ordinary dictation. Then the teacher puts some of the key vocabulary items from the text on the blackboard, and asks the students to write the text down from memory, using the key words and their knowledge of grammatical and text structure to guide them. A news article from the newspaper often serves as a good source for this type of exercise.

Finally, "free" writing tasks ask students to produce complete texts in response to a variety of writing stimuli, such as pictures, texts which have been read, or the more "traditional" type of writing assignments which provide some suggestions as to content and/or method of text organization. Free writing can also be encouraged without undue regard as to the correctness of grammar or of format by having students keep a journal.[4] Writing that forms part of the academic curriculum, which I will focus on in the rest of this chapter, falls at the "free" end of the continuum outlined here.

THE WRITING CLASS

The teacher's tasks in the writing class involve designing and/or implementing a syllabus, structuring individual lessons, providing students with opportunities for writing, and responding to the writing that students produce. While this listing of tasks may seem self-evident, how the tasks are actualized can serve to facilitate or inhibit improved student mastery of writing skills.

Syllabus Design

A syllabus should be designed to take into account curricular goals and the particular students the teacher will face.[5] The syllabus further reflects, whether intentionally or unintentionally, a direct representation of the philosophy of teaching writing that a teacher has adopted for that particular course in that particular institution.

One of the reasons why teaching writing is such a challenge is that most classes contain a mixture of students who have been placed directly into a particular level of course and students who have passed into that course as it follows in sequence from a previous course. J. D. Brown (1981) has reported that "placed" students have stronger skills than continuing students (i.e., those promoted from lower-level courses within a program), a fact that contributes to the heterogeneity of skill levels within a single class. While this might make it difficult to plan a rigidly outlined course in advance of the term, students do need to be given a syllabus which indicates at least the following information: (1) how many writing assignments students are expected to complete during the term, (2) what the timelines and deadlines are for working on and completing papers, (3) how many of the writing assignments will be done in class as "timed" pieces and how many will allow for the full drafting process including one or more rounds of revision, (4) what aspects of the composing process will be presented, (5) what aspects of English grammar and syntax, if any, will be directly addressed in class, (6) what will be seen to constitute "progress" in acquiring improved writing skills as the term moves along, (7) how much reading, if any (and possibly which specific readings) will be covered, and (8) how the student's grade or a decision of credit/no credit will be determined.

In general, then, the teachers use the syllabus to announce to their students what they see as important to the course as well as what is important to good writing. Without some informed sense of how they plan to use the class to foster individual growth in writing, teachers will find it most difficult to devise any syllabus at all.

Whether operating from a tightly organized or a fairly loose syllabus, the writing teacher needs to structure individual class sessions that will allow students to learn and practice principles of producing good writing. Good writing results from a time-consuming process which cannot be reduced to some formulaic rules, though many students, trained for years in English classes which emphasized rigidly controlled grammatical exercises, will come to the writing class with the belief that there are rules and exercises to be learned which will yield them fully conceived essays. Another fundamental guideline students must learn in an academic environment is what the expectations of the academic audience are in terms of content, form, and language of the academic assignments they will be required to submit (Reid, 1989). With those basic assumptions in place, the ESL writing class then becomes a workshop for students to learn to produce academic essays through mastering techniques for getting started and generating ideas (discussed in more detail below), drafting papers which they will anticipate revising, and learning to utilize feedback provided by the teacher and other students in the class to improve the writing assignment at hand. The goal of every course should be individual student progress in writing proficiency, and the goal of the total curriculum should be that student writers learn to become informed and independent readers of their own texts with the ability to create, revise, and reshape papers to meet the needs of the task at hand.

Techniques for Getting Started

Regardless of the type of writing tasks the teacher might favor assigning, a good place to begin classwork is to explore the prewriting stage, the stage prior to actual production of a working text. Because there isn't *one* composing process, the goal of the teacher should be to expose students to a variety of strategies for getting started with a writing task and to encourage each student to try to discover which strategies (in which circumstances) work best for him or her. Several heuristic devices[6] (or invention strategies) which can be explored in class for the purpose of providing students with a repertoire of techniques for generating ideas are the following:

1. *Brainstorming*: This is often a group exercise in which all of the students in the class are encouraged to participate by sharing their collective knowledge about a particular subject. One way to structure this is for the teacher to suggest a broad topic, such as reasons for choosing a particular academic major, and have students call out as many associations as possible which the teacher can then write on the board. The result would be far more material generated than any one student is likely to think of on his/her own, and then all students can utilize any or all of the information when turning to the preparation of their first drafts.

2. *Listing*: Unlike brainstorming, as described above, listing can be a quiet and essentially individual activity. Again, as a first step in finding an approach to a particular subject area (such as the use and abuse of power, to cite an example), the students are encouraged to produce as lengthy a list as possible of all the subcategories that come to mind as they think about the topic at hand. This is an especially useful activity for students who might be constrained by undue concern for expressing their thoughts in grammatically correct sentences, because lists do not require complete sentences.

3. *Free writing*: Suggested by Elbow (1973) for helping native speakers break through the difficulty of getting started, free writing is also known by various other terms, such as "wet ink" writing and "quick-writing." The main idea of this technique is for students to write for a specified period of time (usually about 5 minutes) without taking their pen from the page. As Elbow (1973, p. 3) puts it, "Don't stop for anything. . . . Never stop to look back, to cross something out, . . . to wonder what word or thought to use. . . . If you get stuck it's fine to write 'I can't think what to say' . . . as many times as you like." Freed from the necessity of worrying about grammar and format, students can often generate a great deal of prose which provides useful raw material to use in addressing the writing assignment at hand. For ESL students, this technique often works best if the teacher provides an opening clause or sen-

tence for the students to start with. So, for example, if the next assignment is to write a paper about one's personal philosophy of life, a short free writing session can begin with the words "Life is difficult but it is also worthwhile." The free writing generated after the students copy this sentence and continue to write down whatever comes into their heads can be kept private or shared with other students. It can also be used as the basis for one or more subsequent 5- to 10-minute free writing "loops" (Cowan & Cowan, 1980), which are additional free writing sessions starting with whatever key idea derives from material discovered through the process of the previous quick-writing step.

4. *Clustering*: Another technique for getting many ideas down quickly, clustering begins with a key word or central idea placed in the center of a page (or on the blackboard) around which the student (or teacher using student-generated suggestions) jots down in a few minutes all of the free associations triggered by the subject matter—using simply words or short phrases. Unlike listing, the words or phrases generated are put on the page or board in a pattern which takes shape from the connections the writer sees as each new thought emerges. Completed clusters can look like spokes on a wheel or any other pattern of connected lines, depending on how the individual associations are drawn to relate to each other. By having students share their cluster patterns with other students in the class, teachers allow students to be exposed to a wide variety of approaches to the subject matter, which might further generate material for writing. Rico (1986, p. 17) notes that clustering allows students to get in touch with the right-hemisphere part of the brain to which she attributes "holistic, image-making, and synthetic capabilities." She further notes that clustering makes "silent, invisible mental processes visible and manipulable" (Rico, 1986, p. 17).

It is very important that students experiment with each of these techniques in order to see how each one works to help generate text and shape a possible approach to a topic. The purpose, after all, of acquiring invention strategies is for students to feel that they have a variety of ways to begin an assigned writing task and that they do not always have to begin at the beginning and work through an evolving draft sequentially until they reach the end. Spack (1984) underscores the importance of having students practice a variety of strategies since she observed that none of her ESL students utilized invention strategies presented in the course textbook which they had read about but not practiced. She further notes that students may also devise their own invention strategies once they have learned the value of systematic exploration of a topic. But we must keep in mind the fact, as Reid (1984) asserts, that for some students, the strategy of choice may be to produce a text in a linear fashion, possibly generated by an outline prepared prior to writing a full first draft. For some people, she points out, brainstorming can be more difficult than, and not as successful as, outlining.

Using Readings in the Writing Class

The use of readings in the writing class is another topic that has generated a great deal of debate among those searching for methodologies which promote improvement in writing proficiency. Before awareness of how to address the writing process in class and of the importance to students of actually *doing* writing in class, the primary activity of so-called writing classes was actually reading. As mentioned earlier, the traditional paradigm for L1 writing classes was rooted in having students read and discuss texts which they would then go on to write about. When the process approach was first introduced, many writing instructors eliminated the use of readers, and used only texts written by the students themselves as the reading material for the course. The dominant philosophy seemed to be that one learns to write by writing, and that perhaps reading had very little to do with the acquisition of writing. ESL teachers following the developments in L1 writing classrooms also went through a period in which reading played almost no role in the writing classroom. But the pendulum has begun to swing in the opposite direction, and while readings have been reintroduced into the so-called modern process writing class—both L1 and L2—the nature of the readings and their function is viewed quite differently.

On one level, readings serve some very practical purposes in the writing class, particularly for ESL writers who have less fluency in the language. At the very least, readings provide models of what English texts look like, and even if not used for the purpose of imitation where students are asked to produce an English text to match the style of the model text, readings provide input which helps students develop awareness of English prose style. Krashen (1984, p. 20) makes the case even stronger by claiming, "It is reading that gives the writer the 'feel' for the look and texture of reader-based prose."

In class, close reading exercises can be done to draw students' attention to particular stylistic choices, grammatical features, methods of development, and so on. Such exercises help to raise student awareness of the choices writers make and the consequences of those choices for the achievement of their communicative goals. Spack (1985, p. 706) points out, "An active exploration of [the] writer/reader interaction can lead students to realize and internalize the idea that what they write becomes another person's reading and must therefore anticipate a reader's needs and meet a reader's expectations."

On another level, writing tasks assigned by many professors require students to do a great deal of reading in order to synthesize and analyze academic material in particular content areas (Horowitz, 1986). Thus, the ESL writing class can incorporate lessons which assist students in preparing academic writing assignments by using readings as a basis to practice such skills as summarizing, paraphrasing, interpreting, and synthesizing concepts.

Finally, many ESL students are not highly skilled readers, having had limited opportunities to read extensively in English; it is highly unlikely that anyone who is a nonproficient reader can develop into a highly proficient writer. For that reason alone, ESL writing teachers are well advised to include a reading component of one nature or another in their classes.

Writing Assignments

As the object of any writing class is to have students work on their writing, the topics students write about must be carefully designed, sequenced, and structured so that the teacher knows exactly what the learning goal of each paper is and so that the student gains something by working on the assignment. There are many factors to consider in selecting topics for student writing, but even if not consciously aware of it, the teacher will be primarily influenced by a particular philosophy about teaching writing which he or she (or the textbook being followed) adheres to and which significantly shapes the approach to topic design. In fact, even when topics are chosen in a random and ad hoc fashion, the teacher will probably select an assignment which seems appropriate on the basis of a felt inner sense of appropriateness, reflecting perhaps unconsciously how the teacher views the goals of the course, the ways in which writers learn, and what he or she values as good writing. For example, if the teacher wants the students to focus on standard organizational patterns common to English writing, it is usually because the teacher values essays which follow discernible patterns and/or believes that training students to recognize and produce those patterns is an important goal of the course. If the teacher believes that writers learn best by writing about topics of their own choosing and that text to be valued is that which reveals the most about the persona of the writer, then the assignments in that teacher's writing class will be presented to achieve those goals.

One very common approach to topic

generation may be referred to as the "rhetorical patterns" approach, in which ESL students are exposed to a variety of types of discourse structure common to English prose. This is done by presenting examples of professional writing or samples of prose written by textbook writers for the purposes of illustrating a particular pattern that forms the focus of a lesson or sequence of lessons. Some textbooks also offer edited or unedited essays written by ESL students as samples of the various prose patterns. Then, typical writing assignments which derive from this philosophy ask students to imitate the structural pattern of the prose model—be it a genuine piece of professional or student writing or an artificially constructed one—using different content.

These sorts of assignments will usually be presented so that the student has to either create or plug in particular content according to a specified manner of presentation. Examples of the "create" assignments are those which specify an organizational structure, such as comparison and contrast, but do not specify any content. Examples of the "plug in" assignments are those which specify an organizational structure, such as "cause and effect," and also specify the content area, such as "drugs and crime." The student's task in the former case is to identify two items which *can* be compared and contrasted and which lend themselves to presentation in that manner. The student's task in the latter case is to write about drugs and crime in such a way as to show the cause-and-effect relationship. Other patterns commonly included in the organizational approach to specifying writing assignments are chronological order, exemplification or illustration, classification, analysis, problem solution, and definition—all commonly referred to as patterns of exposition. Regardless of what else takes place in the class that shows concern for the process of writing, the "products" which result from this philosophy of assigning topics will invariably be judged primarily on how closely they follow discernible and traditional formats of the specified rhetorical pattern.

There is ample evidence that "real-world" writing does not get produced in this fashion, which is one of the major criticisms leveled at textbooks which encourage these approaches. Not only do real writing tasks *not* begin from a particular form which merely lacks content to be complete, but content itself usually does not get generated without the writer's first having a purpose for writing. Taylor (1981) also points out:

A major result of a writing program which focuses primarily on form is an insufficient emphasis on content which would create the opportunity for students to experience the process of discovering meaning and then of *struggling to give form through revision.* (Taylor, 1981, p. 9, italics added)

However, I caution against abandoning this "rhetorical patterns" approach altogether, for there is evidence that many academic writing tasks outside of English departments or ESL classes *do* ask students to prepare papers which follow a particular format (Horowitz, 1986), and the ability of ESL students to prepare papers which meet reader expectations has a definite value within an academic environment.

A completely different philosophy of teaching leads to viewing writing as a vehicle of self-revelation and self-discovery, and assignments are presented to students in which they must reflect on and analyze their own personal experiences. Some examples would be asking students to write about their experiences as second language learners or to reflect on a lesson learned in childhood. The content in either case would arise from their own personal biographies. This type of assignment has the potential of allowing the writer to feel invested in his or her work, not usually the case with the rhetorical pattern approach. Perhaps more centrally, the value of writing is seen in its role as a tool of discovery of both meaning and purpose. Proponents of the discovery approach claim that the writing skills learned in practicing personal writing will transfer to the skills required to produce academic papers.

Regardless of the underlying philosophy of teaching which motivates the types of assignments presented to students, teachers must also make a number of other decisions about assignments. They must decide *where* the writing is to be produced: in class or at home. When students are writing in class, teachers are often uncertain of what they themselves should be doing while the students are writing. Students also generally feel pressured by the limited amount of time available. When students write at home, teachers may be concerned that the student might receive outside input from another writer or from textual material, rendering the student's text unrepresentative of his/her own writing. For some students, writing at home will be completed in even less time than writing produced in class (Kroll, 1982). One way to resolve this is that some assignments should be considered "timed" writing, written in a given time framework, submitted, and responded to as final products, while other writing assignments can be prepared over a span of several class periods (either in class or at home) and feedback provided to assist in the revision process.

In fact, another decision teachers must make concerns the number of drafts for any given text that they want students to produce. Given the immense value to the student writer of learning to revise text and to work through a series of drafts before considering a paper "finished," new writing topics should not be assigned before the student has had a chance to work through a cycle of drafts on a prior assignment. If the teacher's goal is to foster student improvement, then providing a multiplicity of writing assignments on different topics (whether they be of the rhetorical pattern type or prompted by a more open-ended approach) will not allow students sufficient time to devote to working on writing in progress. That is, students working on a second or third draft of a given topic which is scheduled to be submitted the following week should not simultaneously be working on a first draft of yet another topic. But as Reid (1984) cautions us against dogmatism in presenting approaches to how students generate texts, Harris (1989) cautions us against dog-matism in applying an inflexible call for revision. In her research, Harris (1989) finds that writers range along a continuum from what she calls "one- to multi-drafters," and not everyone benefits from being asked to produce multiple revisions since the preferred strategy for some successful writers is to produce a single, polished draft. She notes, in fact, that "studies of revision do not provide the conclusive picture that we need in order to assert that we should continue coaxing our students into writing multiple drafts" (Harris, 1989, p. 175) because both efficient and inefficient writers are to be found who favor one or the other of these approaches to writing.

A final consideration regarding topic design is one of essay length, for in cases where teachers don't specify length, students often want to know how long their papers should be. Many ESL students are concerned with doing the bare minimum and will invariably submit very short papers; others may produce far too much text for the teacher to find time to respond to, or for the student to be able to process and benefit from the extensive feedback that the teacher might need to provide on a lengthy but highly problematic text. One must bear in mind the need for a relationship between what the topic calls for and the length of paper produced. For example, to ask students to write 250 words on an encyclopedic topic is to ensure superficiality of treatment; conversely, to ask them to produce a lengthy paper on a narrowly focused topic is to invite padding and digressions. Also, what a teacher believes a student will learn from preparing a particular assignment should not be out of proportion to the amount of time the student will need to invest in preparing it.

Finally, if one believes that students best learn to write by writing, then the design of writing tasks is perhaps the key component of curriculum design. It is in the engagement with, and the completion of, writing tasks that students will be most directly immersed in the development of their writing skills; thus, a great deal of thought must go into choosing such tasks.

Responding

Responding to student writing—once seen as the main task of the writing teacher and certainly the most time-consuming one—is a complex process which also requires the teacher to make a number of critical decisions. Key questions to address include these:

1. What are the general goals within the writing course of providing feedback to student writers?
2. What are the specific goals of providing feedback on a particular piece of writing?
3. At what stage in the writing process should feedback be offered?
4. What form should feedback take?
5. Who should provide the feedback?
6. What should students do with the feedback they receive?

Goal Setting

Responding to student writing has the general goal of fostering student improvement. While this may seem to be stating the obvious, teachers need to develop/adopt responding methodologies which *can* foster improvement; they need to know how to measure or recognize improvement when it does occur. Although the teaching of first language writing has come a long way since most response took the form of written *criticism* by the teacher detailing what the student had done wrong on a paper, and teaching ESL writing has ceased to be seen as a vehicle for monitoring student acquisition of grammar, there remains no easy answer to the question of what type of response will facilitate improved student mastery of writing. In reviewing dozens of research studies investigating various methodologies of responding, Hillocks (1986, p. 165) concluded, "The results of all these studies strongly suggest that teacher comment has little impact on student writing." Therefore, in setting goals, teachers should focus on implementing a variety of response types and on training students to maximize the insights of prior feedback on future writing occasions.

Shaping Feedback

Regardless of whatever repertoire of strategies teachers develop to provide feedback on student papers, students must also be trained to use the feedback in ways that will improve their writing—be it on the next draft of a particular paper or on another assignment. Without such training, it is quite likely that students will either ignore feedback or fail to use it constructively. In fact, research studies to date have shown a number of discouraging findings. Research on how L1 students process written response from teachers has indicated that (1) sometimes students fail to read the written comments on their papers, caring only about the grade (Burkland & Grimm, 1986); (2) sometimes they do not understand or indeed misinterpret the written comments, and find themselves unable to make appropriate changes in future drafts (Hayes & Daiker, 1984); (3) sometimes they use comments to psych out a particular teacher's personal agenda, only hoping "to make the teacher happy" in the future (Freedman, 1987; Sperling & Freedman, 1987); and (4) sometimes they become hostile at the teacher's appropriation of their text (Leki, 1990, p. 3). In research on student response to comments in an L2 environment, Leki (1986) found that students expressed a lack of interest in teacher reaction to the content of their papers, and instead indicated a desire to have every error marked on their papers. Cohen (1987) found that students had a very limited repertoire of strategies for processing feedback, and as such, Cohen and Cavalcanti (1990, p. 176) conclude, "Clear teacher-student agreements on feedback procedures and student training in strategies for handling feedback could lead to more productive and enjoyable composition writing in the classroom."

To address some of these issues, one step is to assure that the feedback on a particular piece of writing addresses that text in the context of how it was produced and with a clear agenda for what the student is expected to do with any feedback. In a process-oriented classroom, for example, students routinely produce more than one draft of an essay, reflecting the steps of producing real-world texts. Thus, feedback on a first draft should most appropriately provide guidelines and suggestions for how to produce a second draft which would show improvement at the level of content and organization. However, Zamel (1985, p. 81) reported that studies provide "overwhelming evidence that teachers attend to surface-level features in what should otherwise be considered first drafts," completely ignoring the philosophy of process which they claim to espouse. In examining the responding behaviors of 15 ESL teachers by reviewing their written comments on portfolios of student papers, Zamel (1985, p. 93) goes on to identify a host of "incongruous types of comments" in which "the major revisions suggested and the interlinear responses are at odds with one another." This use of "mixed signals" helps explain why many students find it difficult to decipher teacher commentary. Why, for example, should the student pay attention to problems in the sequence of tenses in a particular paragraph if a marginal or end note indicates that the whole paragraph is irrelevant to the development of the paper?

As with other issues we have discussed, the question of the teacher's philosophy is a key determinant of his or her approach to commenting. Zamel (1985, p. 86) notes of her 15 ESL teacher subjects:

. . . the teachers overwhelmingly view themselves as language teachers rather than writing teachers; they attend primarily to surface-level features of writing and seem to read and react to a text as a series of separate sentences or even clauses, rather than as a whole unit of discourse.

Unless the teacher adopts the stance of a *writing* teacher, he or she will be unable to provide feedback appropriate to that role.

Forms of Feedback

Up to now we have been discussing feedback that is provided in writing by the teacher on various drafts of a student paper, a fairly traditional and undoubtedly time-consuming method, even for those teachers who do not respond to every draft as a finished product. But there are other ways for students to receive feedback on their writing which can and should be considered in structuring a writing course. Writing teachers who view themselves as judges or repositories of certain truths about effectiveness in writing will want, of course, to be in charge of providing feedback to their students, believing that such feedback can play a vital role in the improvement of student writing. Those who view themselves as coaches or editorial advisors will also want to provide feedback, though not necessarily in the same way. Teachers should bear in mind that feedback can be oral as well as written, and they should consider the value of individual conferences[7] on student papers and/or the use of tape cassettes as two additional ways to structure teacher feedback. From another point of view, most writing teachers realize that they have many students in one class and they might also be teaching two or more writing classes, so the teacher has a very limited amount of time to provide feedback to any one student. Teachers whose philosophies embrace the value of collaborative learning[8] therefore turn to the other students in the class to assist in the feedback process. Other students in the writing class can be taught to provide valuable feedback in the form of peer response, which serves to sharpen their critical skills in analyzing written work as well as to increase their ability to analyze their own drafts critically.

Oral Teacher Feedback. Because of potential communication problems, ESL students in a writing class need to have individual conferences with their teacher even more than native-speaking students do. Conferences of about 15 minutes seem to work best, and can provide the teacher an opportunity to directly question the student about intended messages which are often difficult to decipher by simply reading a working draft.

Further, conferences allow the teacher to uncover potential misunderstandings the student might have about prior written feedback or issues in writing that have been discussed in class. Another benefit is that students can usually learn more in the one-to-one exchange than they can when attempting to decipher teacher-written commentary on their own.

Some teachers provide all their feedback orally by asking students to submit a cassette tape with each draft. This method probably works best when the teacher silently reads a student's paper and makes comments directly into the tape recorder while marking some accompanying numbers or symbols on the student's text. For ESL students, this method has the advantage of providing more extensive feedback than that likely to be made in writing, as well as allowing the student to replay the tape as many times as necessary to understand and benefit from the teacher's comments. Once the teacher has learned to use this technique, it probably takes less time to complete taped remarks about a paper than it would to put them in writing.

Peer Response.[9] Because the use of peer response is a key component of classrooms teaching writing as a process in the L1 environment, many ESL teachers embraced the idea of having students read and/or listen to each other's papers for the purpose of providing feedback and input to each other as well as helping each other gain a sense of audience. But embracing a philosophy without understanding how to translate it to the L2 environment can often lead to rather disappointing results. That is, simply putting students together in groups of four or five, each with rough draft in hand, and then having each student in turn read his or her paper aloud, followed by having the other members of the group react to the strengths and weaknesses of the paper in the role of interested audience member, indicating further reader needs that have not been addressed, is *not* a format likely to work with even the most sophisticated class of ESL students. Because ESL students lack the language competence of native speakers, who can often react intuitively to their classmates' papers, peer responding in the ESL classroom must be modeled, taught, and controlled in order for it to be a valuable activity.

One way to control peer response is for teachers to provide a short list of directed questions which students address as they read their own or other students' papers. A first exercise of this type can involve giving students a short checklist of attributes to look for in their own papers, such as to check for a particular grammatical feature that might have been discussed in class (e.g., subject–verb agreement) or to check to assure that no irrelevancies have been included. The checklist is submitted with the paper as a way for the student to assume responsibility for reading over his or her paper carefully. Next, students can be trained to read and respond to other students' papers by reviewing an essay written by a student in a previous class and working through, as a class, a peer editing sheet that asks a few specific questions that would elicit both a general reaction to the paper and suggestions for improvement. As the students gain practice in reading and analyzing each other's papers and their awareness of the conventions of writing increases, the questions can be made more complex and varied. Some typical questions to begin with might include these: "What is the main purpose of this paper?" "What have you found particularly effective in the paper?" "Do you think the writer has followed through on what the paper set out to do?" Some peer guideline sheets for students who have more practice in the technique might include the following steps: "Find at least three places in the essay where you can think of questions that have not been answered by the writer. Write those questions in the margins as areas for the writer to answer in the next draft." "Read only the introduction and then write what you predict the rest of the essay will discuss. Then read the essay and compare your predictions with the actual content of the essay."

In order to maximize the value of the feedback to the ESL student, responses should be written, incidentally providing practice in the valuable skill of text analysis for the student commentator. These written responses can be given to the student writer with or without the anonymity of the student reader preserved or used as the basis for oral discussion between reader(s) and writer. The teacher might also want to read the student feedback sheets to assess the analytical skills of the student readers.

Error Correction

Regardless of what agenda the writing teacher sets and the number of drafts that students produce, the papers that ESL students write are likely to exhibit problems in language control. However, it is very important that the teacher not be swayed by the presence or numbers of these problems into turning a writing course into a grammar course. Rather, error must be dealt with at an appropriate stage of the composing process, and is perhaps best considered part of the final editing phase. The role of editing, when seen as distinct from rewriting, is essentially working to eliminate grammatical problems and stylistic infelicities; this type of editing is certainly essential to the production of good prose, but it should be an activity that is probably best attended to when a text is considered complete in terms of having been shaped by content, organization, attention to the needs of the reader, and a consideration of its purpose. In fact, editing or correcting errors on first drafts can be a counterproductive activity, possibly exacerbating whatever insecurities students might have about their writing and drawing their attention away from the other kinds of revision work that must be attended to. Chenoweth (1987, p. 28) concedes, "It may be hard for teachers to give up their habit of correcting every grammatical mistake," but also believes that grammatical problems should only be dealt with "when

the meaning the student wants to express has been adequately dealt with (Chenoweth, 1987, p. 28).

In addition to deciding *when* to correct errors, teacher must also decide *who* will correct the errors, *which* errors to correct, and *how* to correct errors. Besides the obvious role the teacher plays as a corrector of errors, the student writer and other students in the class can also be called upon to provide feedback on errors as part of the peer feedback process. Again, the use of a checklist naming specific grammatical features often helps to focus student attention on areas the teacher feels the student should be able to monitor for and self-correct. (For a discussion of methods which can be used to train students in error detection procedures, see the chapter by Frodesen in this volume.)

The decision whether to address all or selected errors is a complex one and probably depends a great deal on the level of writing the student is capable of producing. However, correcting all of a student's errors is probably rarely called for, unless there are very few errors present in the text. Rather, the teacher should probably concentrate on calling the student's attention to those errors which are considered more serious and/or represent a pattern of errors in that particular student's writing. In a survey of 164 faculty members at Iowa State University asking about 12 typical ESL errors, Vann, Myer, and Lorenz (1984) noted a consensus among faculty in all disciplines regarding a hierarchy of error in terms of what were perceived to be more and less serious problems. Traditionally, we take "serious" to mean that which most interferes with communication, so errors of sentence structure are very important to deal with, while those errors which are unlikely to lead to faulty interpretation or to interfere with the reading process might be seen to be less significant. Unfortunately, some errors which are not serious by these standards tend to have an "irritation factor," and many faculty outside ESL programs, for example, find little tolerance for errors in ESL writing which seem like careless proofreading mistakes to them, most notably mistakes in article usage. Since mastery of the article system is actually a very difficult task, consciousness raising about typical ESL learner problems among non-ESL faculty might be just as important as attempts to improve proficiency in article usage among ESL students.

Finally, the "how" of calling students' attention to the errors they have committed is also a complex issue. Teachers can choose to (1) point out specific errors using a mark in the margin or an arrow or other symbolic system; (2) correct (or model) specific errors by writing in the corrected form; (3) label specific errors according to the feature they violate (e.g., subject–verb agreement), using either the complete term or a symbol system; (4) indicate the presence of error but not the precise location (e.g., noting that there are problems with word forms); or (5) ignore specific errors. Most teachers use a combination of two or more of the methods mentioned above, depending on what they perceive to be the needs of the student, and studies of teacher feedback are inconclusive as to what the best methodology might be. One study of feedback procedures by Robb, Ross and Shortreed (1986, p. 88), for example, concludes that "the more direct methods of feedback do not tend to produce results commensurate with the amount of effort required of the instructor to draw the student's attention to the surface error." However, another study by Fathman and Whalley (1990) involving feedback on content versus feedback on grammar reports that all students who received feedback on grammar improved the grammatical accuracy of their revised texts while only some students improved the content of their writing following feedback on content. The best approach to feedback on errors must undoubtedly derive from considering the circumstances of the individual student coupled with the goals of the course and the stage of the composing process a particular draft reflects.

CONCLUSION

Producing a successful written text is a complex task which requires simultaneous control over a number of language systems as well as an ability to factor in considerations of the ways the discourse must be shaped for a particular audience and a particular purpose. Teaching ESL students to become successful writers is no less a complex task. But it can be a tremendously rewarding one as well.

This chapter has presented some of the issues involved in establishing an ESL writing curriculum and in teaching the ESL writing class. As the ability to write well in a second language is no doubt even more difficult to achieve than the ability to read, speak, or understand the language, it is not surprising that many students take several years to achieve even a modicum of success. What must be emphasized to teachers in training is the importance of designing curriculum and shaping classes with a clear understanding of how the acquisition of written skills can be fostered. Our real goal is to gradually wean our students away from us, providing them with strategies and tools for their continued growth as writers and for the successful fulfillment of future writing tasks they might face once they have completed their last writing course with us. Earlier hopes to find the best method "were based on the faulty assumptions that there was a best method and one just had to find it, that teaching writing was a matter of prescribing a logically ordered set of written tasks and exercises, and that good writing conformed to a predetermined and ideal model" (Zamel, 1987, p. 697). There can be no "best" method when students' learning styles are so different; our hope now is rather to find methodologies which empower students rather than restrict them, and to create courses which arise from principled decisions derived from thorough research investigations.

The growth of composition studies as a discipline with its own independent body of research (apart from, say, literary studies or linguistic studies) has enormously influenced the formal training of writing teachers who teach native speakers of English. For ESL writing teachers to be able to provide courses which assist their students in learning to produce academic prose, their training should be no less rigorous, extending beyond the language acquisition concerns of applied linguistics and into the realm of writing theory as well.

NOTES

1. The final version of this paper benefited from comments made by Joy Reid.

2. In this procedure, the writer is asked to verbalize all of his or her thoughts while composing and to write down only those words and thoughts that form part of the task of text production. The event is either audiotaped or videotaped, and a transcript, referred to as a "protocol," is prepared for subsequent analysis, also known as "protocol analysis."

3. A number of detailed suggestions for teaching grammar through writing activities are provided by Frodesen (this volume).

4. Two different practical approaches to using journals in the ESL writing class are provided by Spack and Sadow (1983) and Blanton (1987).

5. A full-length discussion of issues in curriculum and syllabus design, particularly as they relate to materials selection and development, can be found in Dubin and Olshtain (1986). Some of the topics covered in their book include presentation of a framework for considering the interrelationship of curricula and syllabi, and examples of a variety of syllabus designs. Yalden (1983) also discusses syllabus design and curriculum issues at length.

6. A heuristic device refers to a specific set of steps one can follow in order to work through personal discoveries as a way of finding a solution, answer, or path to adopt in a given circumstance. While there are guidelines for utilizing heuristic devices, the important thing is that what they will yield are highly individual results; i.e. there are no "right" or "wrong" answers. In contrast, algorithmic devices are steps which are tightly controlled and invariable; they yield the same results for all those who follow a given algorithm, such as the process of addition. When followed correctly, an algorithm will yield the "right" answer, and if followed incorrectly, it will yield a "wrong" answer. A full discussion of a wide variety of heuristic devices useful in ESL teaching is presented in Hughey, Wormuth, Hartfiel, and Jacobs (1983, pp. 62–84).

7. An excellent introduction to ways of structuring conferences and the rationale for holding them is found in Carnicelli (1980). In another interesting paper, Newkirk (1989) reports on a study of how an agenda needs to be set in the first five minutes of a student–teacher writing conference. Both these papers are based on work with L1 students. Marshall (1986) provides a lengthy report on one ESL teacher's conference approach to teaching.

8. "Collaborative learning," a term that dates back to the 1950s, provides a social context for students to work together toward the achievement of some goal, such as completion of individual papers whose final forms are determined to a greater or lesser extent by advice and feedback provided by peers. Its role in the writing class is described fully by Bruffee (1984), a leading spokesperson for the collaborative learning approach and the effective utilization of peer tutors in the L1 setting. A handbook of guidelines and methods for setting up and maximizing collaborative learning in the classroom is provided by Kagan (1985), whose book is an excellent teacher resource for ESL teachers as well as L1 teachers.

9. A more complete discussion of the rationale behind peer response and its implementation in the ESL classroom is provided by Mittan (1989).

DISCUSSION QUESTIONS

1. What does the shift from a concern with product to a concern with process refer to?

2. What about the controlled-guided-free continuum for describing writing tasks is still valid today?

3. Explain how students whose writing might exhibit quite different strengths and weaknesses might be placed in the same class.

4. What would be the consequences of claiming that there is just one composing process?

5. In what ways can a syllabus for a writing course reflect the underlying teaching philosophy of a particular teacher?

6. What should a teacher do if a student can't seem to do any of the techniques for getting started that are identified in the text?

7. What do writing assignments for academic classes tend to look like when the teacher follows a "rhetorical pattern" approach?

8. Discuss some of the factors that the teacher should consider in preparing feedback for students.

SUGGESTED ACTIVITIES

1. Design a brief survey, say six to eight questions, aimed at identifying whether faculty outside of English departments have different expectations for writing assignments produced by native and nonnative students. Distribute your survey to a few faculty members in three or four departments at your school that have heavy enrollment of ESL students, and report on your results.

2. Collect about three or four ESL composition textbooks aimed at the same level of student, either high-intermediate or advanced. Examine several writing assignments suggested throughout each of the books you select. On the basis of the writing assignments you have reviewed in each book, what would you say the textbook author's philosophy is about what constitutes the best way to learn to write?

3. Prepare an exercise in which you pose five questions that would be appropriate for use on a peer feedback sheet for use with any writing assignment that students in a high-intermediate or advanced class might have to address. Then prepare a second peer feedback sheet specifically geared to one specific writing assignment you found interesting among those you examined in the suggested activity above. That is, ask questions which require the student reader to pay attention to particular features of that *one* writing assignment. Which type of peer feedback sheet might you prefer to use in teaching? Why?

4. Obtain a copy of an essay written by an ESL student that has a large number of grammatical errors. Make four photocopies of the essay. Correct each copy of the essay using four different methods, as outlined in the section on "Error Correction" in the reading. Time yourself to see how long it takes to correct each essay. Discuss with others in the class whether or not you think the method that took the most time to follow is the correction method that the student might find the most valuable form of feedback.

SUGGESTIONS FOR FURTHER READING

Hedge, T. (1988)
Writing. Oxford: Oxford University Press.

An excellent and up-to-date guide to examples and discussion of actual classroom materials and techniques useful in both the ESL and EFL context. Part of Oxford's Resource Books for Teachers series.

Johnson, D. M., and D. H. Roen, eds. (1989)
Richness in Writing: Empowering ESL Students. New York and London: Longman.

An anthology of 18 articles concerning the nature of writing instruction for ESL, offering both scholarly research and specific suggestions for classroom applications.

Kroll, B. ed. (1990)
Second Language Writing: Research Insights for the Classroom. New York and Cambridge: Cambridge University Press.

An anthology of 13 articles providing an overview covering the current state of thinking on several key issues in teaching writing and presenting several data-based research articles highlighting specific aspects of the writing situation or teacher evaluation of writing.

Raimes, A. (1983)
Techniques in Teaching Writing. New York: Oxford University Press.

A widely used and highly readable book addressed to beginning teachers of writing. Covers major issues to address in the classroom and provides numerous exercises both for teachers in training and for their ESL students.

Raimes, A. (1987)
Why write? From purpose to pedagogy. *English Teaching Forum, 25,* 36–41.

Raimes answers the question posed by identifying six pedagogical purposes for writing, reviewing the history and approach of each purpose and concluding that "writing to learn" creates an integrating, comprehensive overview to all other purposes. Must reading in developing a philosophy of teaching.

Tucker, A. (in press)
Decoding ESL: International Students in the American College Classroom. New York: McGraw-Hill.

A case history study of a number of nonnative students from different linguistic backgrounds, describing their progress through a sequence of writing and literature courses.

Grammar in Writing

Jan Frodesen

INTRODUCTION

Developments in composition theory and research during the past few decades have certainly contributed to our understanding of writing processes and have helped us to design and implement more effective composition programs and teaching materials. Unfortunately, the paradigm shift in composition theory from a focus on writing products to that of writing processes has also resulted in confusion about the role of grammar in ESL/EFL writing instruction. Adding to the uncertainty about whether grammar has a place in the teaching of writing are the results of a considerable body of native English speaker writing research which indicates that formal grammar instruction has little or no effect on writing improvement (Hillocks, 1986).

At the same time, ESL writing teachers know from experience that their students often have difficulties with both sentence- and discourse-level English grammar, ones that cannot be ignored. Moreover, research has provided evidence that ESL writers' errors may negatively affect assessments of overall writing quality. A study by McGirt (1984) showed a statistically significant difference between holistic ratings of ESL essays with morphosyntactic and mechanical errors intact and ratings of the same essays in which errors had been corrected; in contrast, the difference in ratings for a control group of native English speaker essays with and without errors was not significant.

It would appear that much of the confusion and, in some cases, misconceptions about the role of grammar in writing stem from a narrowly defined view of "grammatical instruction" as traditional, decontextualized grammar lessons with a focus on formal analysis of sentence-level syntax (e.g., types of clauses) and/or a preoccupation with correcting errors. In contrast to this view, as Widdowson (1988) discusses in his article "Grammar, Nonsense, and Learning," is one of grammar as a *resource* for communication, or what Widdowson terms "the adaptation of lexis" (p. 154). In other words, grammar is regarded as an aid to language users in accurately communicating their messages, not as some isolated body of knowledge that must be studied for its own sake. Widdowson states that "language learning *is* essentially grammar learning and it is a mistake to think otherwise" (p. 154). This claim might at first seem to reflect a long outdated language teaching methodology, concerned with forms rather than functions of language, and with discrete sentence-level units rather than connected discourse. However, Widdowson, who is known for his work in communicative language teaching (e.g., Widdowson, 1978), is simply stressing that grammar as a component of language enables us to make our meanings clear and precise. For example, in English, word order is an essential determinant or meaning. The sentences "John loves Mary" and "Mary loves John" obviously convey two different messages.

This positive orientation toward grammar points to a solution to the problem discussed above. If grammar is seen as an essential resource for writers in the process of shaping accurate and effective communication, ESL writing teachers can use knowledge of grammatical forms and functions to address specific needs of students and to guide instructional materials development for learners at all stages of the writing process. In this way, grammar instruction is integrated with various writing goals; it is presented to learners not just as a prescriptive model for error correction but rather as an aid to conveying meaning appropriately to intended readers.

SOME GENERAL GUIDELINES FOR INTEGRATING GRAMMAR INTO WRITING INSTRUCTION

In deciding what kinds of grammar-based activities are most relevant to a particular writing context, the ESL/EFL instructor will need to assess both learner and instructional variables.

Celce-Murcia (1985b) suggests that the following learner variables be considered in making choices about grammar instruction: age, proficiency level, and educational background. According to Celce-Murcia's schema of variables influencing grammar teaching, a focus on formal aspects of language is increasingly useful as writers become older, more advanced in English proficiency, and more highly educated/literate.

Another learner variable to consider is students' backgrounds in grammatical instruction, particularly with reference to knowledge of grammatical terminology. One of the frequent criticisms of traditional grammar instruction in writing has been its overemphasis on teaching terminology to students; it is argued that such instruction is time-consuming and often results in confusing students rather than helping them. In the field of basic writing for native English speakers, the prevailing recommendation to teachers is to use as little terminology as possible and to keep it as simple as possible (e.g., D'Eloia, 1975; Neuleib & Brosnahan, 1987). While this is certainly good advice for teachers in many ESL/EFL contexts, it should be noted that some learners of English as a second or foreign language enter the writing classroom with a sophisticated knowledge of traditional grammar. For example, in American colleges and universities, writing instructors often find that foreign students have a strong background in formal grammar, whereas long-term immigrant students tend to be less familiar with grammatical terms. Since terminology can be useful in providing teacher feedback on syntactic and morphological error patterns in students' writing, an awareness of individual learners' knowledge of grammatical terms is important. This can be achieved at the beginning of a course by giving students a list of terms and asking them to check ones with which they are familiar.

Of course, there will be some basic terms, depending on the writing context, which the writing teacher will want to familiarize all students with in order to help them edit their writing. For these, the advice to keep terminology as simple as possible seems wise. For example, progressive verbs, gerunds, and present participles in adjective/adverb phrases might be distinguished as -*ing* main verbs, -*ing* modifiers and -*ing* nouns, respectively. Relative clauses could be referred to as *which/who/that*-clauses used as adjectives. Such designations link grammatical functions with actual morphemes or words that student will see in writing so that there is less of a requirement to memorize terms. Along with learner variables, instructional variables must be considered in developing grammar-oriented writing activities. Celce-Murcia's schema, which was referred to earlier, points out that the more formal the register and the more professional the use of language, the greater the need for focus on form. In most types of academic writing, conformity to standard English conventions of grammar and mechanics is assumed; therefore, writing instructors in secondary and higher education will need to help students become aware of the expectations of academic discourse communities in this regard.

The specific objectives of a writing class will of course influence greatly the ways in which grammar will be integrated with writing. In ESL/EFL writing programs where students are placed on the basis of diagnostic tests which evaluate syntactic and rhetorical fluency, some courses may focus particularly on helping students to reduce error frequency, while those for advanced writers may be more concerned with the grammatical choices writers make to achieve certain stylistic effects. Thus, courses designed for writers with numerous morphosyntactic problems might include considerable work on editing and on guided writing practice, with a focus on common grammatical problems such as verb forms, word classes, or articles. Courses for advanced ESL/EFL writers with few grammatical problems could offer extensive practice in such activities as contextualized sentence combining and discourse analysis/evaluation to help students achieve greater stylistic sophistication and to heighten awareness of the ways in which grammatical choices serve various discourse-pragmatic considerations, such as topic emphasis and reader expectations.

Whatever the instructional objectives, in keeping with a positive approach toward the role of grammar in writing, it seems beneficial to include grammar-oriented activities not only to help students edit errors in their writing but also to provide them with a variety of syntactic strategies for effective communication and to help them understand how grammar contributes to meaning. In the sections which follow, specific activities and techniques for achieving these goals will be suggested.

TEXT ANALYSIS

The study of text models is emphasized less in the process-oriented, student-centered writing class than it was in the past when presentational modes of instruction predominated (see Hillocks, 1986, for an overview of instructional modes). However, exercises based on text analysis can help ESL/EFL writers to see how particular grammatical/syntactic features are used in authentic discourse contexts—that is, in texts written for actual communicative purposes and not just to illustrate grammatical points. Text analysis can be especially useful as an inductive approach for helping learners who are already familiar with prescriptive grammar rules but who still have problems understanding and using appropriately grammatical oppositions such as definite and indefinite articles, restrictive and nonrestrictive clauses, and present perfect and past- or present-tense verb forms.

In selecting authentic texts for inductive exercises, the writing teacher should keep in mind the proficiency level of students, avoiding writing that might be too complex or lengthy, and should look for texts with ample instances of the grammatical feature to be analyzed. Since finding an appropriate text when needed for a lesson is often difficult, it is useful to create files beforehand of short texts (e.g., magazine and newspaper articles, advertisements) that would be good for examining grammatical features most often problematic for ESL writers. At least some texts should represent the kinds of writing that students will be expected to produce; however, a variety of writing samples can help to keep interest levels high. Especially for less advanced students, advertisements can be excellent sources for illustrating grammatical features; they often incorporate grammatical repetition as a rhetorical device.

The following are a few examples of lessons that focus on grammatical features in texts. For each, it is assumed that the text used has sufficient instances of the particular grammatical item or items. Since text analysis in the writing class should be subordinate to actual writing activities, exercises should usually be kept brief. If the instructor decides to incorporate text analysis routinely into classroom or out-of-class activities, students could be asked to purchase differently colored pens or pencils to highlight contrasting functions of different grammatical features.

1. To help students distinguish restrictive and nonrestrictive relative clauses,

ask them to underline restrictive clauses in a text with one color pen and nonrestrictive relative clauses with another color. Have them circle commas to locate nonrestrictive clauses. Ask them to identify which type of relative clause is more frequent. Elicit functions of clauses (e.g., nonrestrictives used for definition, restrictives which provide cohesion by repeating information previously given) to point out salient differences in usage.

2. Select a text that illustrates several functions of the definite article "the" (e.g., second mention, shared knowledge between writer and reader, uniqueness through postmodification). Underline and number only those uses of "the" on which you want students to focus. Present function classifications and ask students to classify each numbered use. A variation of this would be to focus only on function. For example, students who are familiar with abstract nouns but unsure as to when no article or "the" is appropriate with them could be asked to highlight with different colors abstract noun phrases preceded by "the" (including any postmodification) and those with no article. In discussion or writing elicit the principles that account for use of the no article or "the."

3. To help students understand how the present perfect contrasts with past and present tenses, find a passage that uses all three. Ask students to mark instances of the three verb types in different ways (using different pen colors or circling, boxing, and underlining). On a blackboard, overhead projector, or handout, present students with a time chart including the following categories: completed events in the past, events that started in the past and continue to the present, repeated events in the past, events in the present (from the writers' perspective), and any other categories relevant to the text. Have students complete the chart by writing verbs from the text under each appropriate category; then ask them to summarize the uses of the present perfect.

For advanced ESL writers, grammatical analysis can be used for lessons concerned with stylistic options and methods of rhetorical focus such as passive voice. In addition, this approach can be used to demonstrate exceptions to prescriptive rules. For example, advanced ESL students who have been taught to avoid sentence fragments are often confused when they encounter them in authentic texts. Text analysis can help to clarify the contexts in which some types of fragments are acceptable and to point out how they differ from fragment "errors" that would be inappropriate in almost any context. As an illustration, the following passage about developments in running shoes, taken from Burfoot (1988), uses repeated noun phrase fragments as a stylistic device:

Over the last two decades, we have seen shoes that were light and firm. Shoes with high heels or low heels, wide heels or narrow heels. Shoes that promised motion control and stability. Schizophrenic shoes: firm on one side, soft on the other.

After discussing rhetorical functions of examples such as in the above text, students could then examine sentence fragments in their own writing to see whether they serve a rhetorical purpose or need to be revised.

In all types of text-analysis exercises, students can develop greater understanding of how grammar contributes to communication by identifying and explaining the meanings or functions of grammatical structures in discourse contexts. These exercises should help students to develop not only their writing but also their reading skills. As follow-up activities either writing or editing practice related to the grammatical focus can be assigned.

GUIDED WRITING PRACTICE

Perhaps the most obvious purpose for guided writing with focus on a particular grammatical structure is to address grammar problems of learners as diagnosed in their writing. In fact, some discussions of the role of grammar in writing for native English speakers suggest that grammar study be limited to the elimination of error (D'Eloia, 1975; Kean, 1981). However, for ESL/EFL students, at least, another benefit of guided writing exercises requiring the use of certain grammatical constructions is that such practice can build writers' confidence in their ability to use English grammar and syntax and thus encourage them to develop syntactic complexity in their writing. Schachter and Celce-Murcia (1977) point out that ESL learners may avoid using constructions they find difficult; they cite evidence from Schachter (1974) that Chinese and Japanese learners avoid producing English relative clauses and from Kleinmann (1977) that native speakers of Arabic avoid using passives in English. Avoidance strategies may be especially common in writing contexts where students' work is graded; these students may avoid constructions they think will produce errors affecting their grades on writing assignments. As a result, the learners may end up using less effective or less appropriate ways of communicating their ideas as well as failing to make much progress in developing syntactic maturity.

Many of the guided writing activities described below were used long before process-centered approaches to writing became widespread (e.g., see Paulston, 1972; Ross, 1968). However, in the past these exercises were sometimes presented either in no contextual framework or in the context of a grammatically organized syllabus. Here they are suggested as components of prewriting, revising, or editing stages in the writing process. In other words, the activities should have a purpose other than simply grammar practice; the grammatical focus should be subordinated to a communicative goal. Decisions as to what types of exercises will be most helpful should be based on the parameters of the learning context, including the demands of major writing tasks and learner needs assessment.

Dictation

Mention of dictation as a teaching technique may evoke memories of elementary school spelling quizzes, but dictation can be an effective way to address grammatical errors in writing that may be the result of erroneous aural perception of English. American high school and college teachers of ESL immigrants who have lived in the United States for a number of years are finding that some of their students have nativelike fluency but that their writing exhibits frequent omissions of bound morphemes such as -s plural, -'s possessive, -s third person singular, and -ed for regular past participles. These errors are very common to native speaker basic writers also (Shaughnessy, 1977). Omissions of some articles and prepositions may also result to some extent from the fact that these words are generally unstressed in spoken English. In addition, the writing of these students may include words or phrases that are incorrect or unidiomatic but phonologically similar to correct forms (e.g., "firsteval" for "first of all," "would of" for "would have," "under contrary" for "on the contrary"). Dictations can help students to diagnose and correct these kinds of errors as well as others. Their usefulness is not, however, limited to error detection and correction; they may also provide practice in syntactic constructions that appear to be infrequently used by students but are appropriate for writing tasks and proficiency levels of the class.

In the most common procedure for dictation, the instructor reads aloud a short text several times. If the class is working on a composition unit, the text should be related to the theme of the unit. The first time, the text is read at a normal pace with the students just listening. For the second reading, the teacher pauses after each phrase to allow students to write. During this reading, care should be taken not to put undue emphasis on word endings or function words that are not normally stressed. The third reading, done at a normal pace, gives students the opportunity to read over their texts and make corrections. The instructor then shows students the passage visually so that they can check their version with the original and edit it. If the activity's main objective is error detection/correction, the instructor could give more specific directions, such as to circle all missed -*s* third person singular or -*ed* endings. If the goal is to familiarize writers with a particular grammatical feature, such as participial clauses or past perfect verbs, the students could be asked to underline them; discussion of their meanings and/or functions could follow.

Text Elicitation

In text elicitation with a grammatical focus, the instructor specifies both a topic or writing objective *and* a grammatical construction (or constructions) to be used. D'Eloia (1975, p. 9) advises that the study of the grammatical concept be integrated as much as possible into the process of writing so that the student's understanding of a grammatical principle is transfered to correct production. One of her suggestions is to have students develop a topic sentence that establishes a time frame. An example is the following sentence with a present perfect frame: "My parents have (not) had a lot of influence on my beliefs and values." As Celce-Murcia and Hilles (1988, p. 160) note, teachers can take advantage of the fact that "certain writing topics or tasks seem naturally to elicit certain structures." They give as an example a writing task in which students are instructed to use the hypothetical conditional (i.e., the subjunctive) in explaining what they would do if they won a million dollars in the lottery. Surveys and graphs/charts on various topics are good sources for eliciting summaries that employ comparison/contrast transitions; even advanced ESL writers often have difficulty using sentence connectors and clause connectors in appropriate syntactic contexts. For example, they may not understand how "in contrast," a sentence connector, is used differently from "whereas," a clause connector. Summaries of surveys, graphs, and charts can also provide good text-based practice of passive verbs and, depending on the time frame, verb tenses such as simple past or present perfect.

Prewriting exercises such as brainstorming or outlining could involve lists that use parallel structures such as noun phrases or infinitives. For example, as a brainstorming exercise to begin a composition unit on education issues, students in a university writing class were asked to list all the purposes of higher education they could think of, using infinitive of purpose phrases (e.g., "to prepare for a career"). The grammatical objective here was not so much on practicing infinitive phrases as it was on using parallelism as a systematic way of organizing information in prewriting. Students then read an article on the purposes of education, after which they compared the purposes on their lists with those in the article.

In summary, text elicitation which includes the use of certain grammatical structures can serve a number of purposes: to develop syntactic maturity, to familiarize students with grammatically based discourse conventions (e.g., the use of passive in survey reports), to provide strategies for organizing and displaying information, and to focus on diagnosed structural problems.

Text Conversion

In text conversion exercises, students are given paragraphs or short texts which they must rewrite, changing some feature of the grammatical structure, such as present tense to past tense or direct speech to indirect speech. Exercises of this type were commonly used as "controlled composition" techniques in audiolingual methodologies; they were also used to apply principles of transformational generative grammar in ESL writing instruction (e.g., Arapoff, 1969).

As with text elicitation, text conversion exercises for the composition class should reflect learner needs, including diagnosed grammar/syntax problems and writing objectives. Since, as Celce-Murcia and Hilles (1988, p. 156) point out, these exercises do not involve actual composing but rather provide practice in making structure-discourse matches, they should be as relevant as possible to writing problems and/or actual writing assignments. For example, if students have frequent subject–verb agreement errors in their writing, as a pre-editing exercise they could be instructed to change all third person present plural forms in a text to singular and to make necessary verb changes. To give students practice using the appropriate register of English for science and technology or research reports, they could be asked to rewrite sentences in a text, changing all sentences with first-person subject pronouns to the passive voice, deleting the agent. The following is a brief example:

I analyzed the results of the values survey as follows. First I totaled the responses for each of the four categories. I then ranked the ten values in order of importance.

Rewritten:
The results of the values survey were analyzed as follows. First, the responses for each of the four categories were totaled. The ten values were then ranked in order of importance.

If an actual text is used, the teacher may find that not all parts of it can be transformed. Even in texts created for exercises, rewriting every sentence might produce an awkward or very artificial text. For example, science texts do not usually have all sentences in passive voice. To solve this problem, the instructor can simply mark the sentences to be rewritten, using numbers or underlining. Afterwards, the class might be asked to identify contextual factors that influence use of the passive.

One type of text conversion that has been the focus of much research and discussion in the field of composition for over 20 years is sentence combining. In its early stages, this technique, developed by John Mellon (1969), often involved exercises in combining a set of kernel sentences such as the following:

The man was old.
The man had gray hair.
The man walked down the street.
The man walked slowly.

Combined:
The old, gray-haired man walked slowly down the street.

Sentence combining can be very useful for practice of a particular grammatical structure, such as relative clauses or prepositional phrases, to help writers become aware of and develop a range of strategies for highlighting key information, subordinating less important information, and improving syntactic fluency. However, recent discussions of this technique caution against using unnatural examples such as the one above. De Beaugrande (1985) recommends that writing samples used for sentence combining should resemble naturally occurring language; otherwise, as he so aptly puts it, "the whole exercise will be treated as some gratuitous venture into a bizarre domain of communication where people regale each other with inane kernal sentences" (p. 72). De Beaugrande further cautions that students should be taught to avoid "excessive, muddled complexity" (p. 74). Most teachers who have used sentence combining with ESL students are probably aware that this technique sometimes results in students' producing confusing or even incomprehensible sentences.

Perhaps the most useful application of sentence combining theory for advanced ESL writers involves actual revision or editing of their drafts. Students, with help from peers and the instructor, can identify passages in their writing where sentence combining could achieve a better flow of information or greater clarity. Combining could include adding transitions to express logical relationships. Another technique based on sentence combining theory, although it may result in shortening rather than lengthening sentences, is proposed by Elbow (1985): First, the students identify a passage in their writing that is problematic. They then "decombine" the sentence, breaking it into simpler sentences. (Elbow stresses that the sentences "needn't be pulverized into pure Chomskyan kernels" [p. 237]). In recombining, the students attempt to solve whatever the problem was. Although Elbow's technique is not limited to grammar problems, it provides a good approach to rephrasing ideas that are difficult to understand because of sentence structure errors without having to resort to grammatical terminology. This technique could also be used for small group revision tasks, with writing samples selected by the instructor from student drafts. The teacher could then focus on grammatical problems common to a number of students or could even divide the class into groups according to particular problems and give each group different samples of texts to revise.

Text Completion

Two of the most common types of text completion are the cloze passage and the gapped text. Whereas in the cloze passage each blank represents a single word to fill in, in the gapped text the blanks may require one or more words. In a third type of text completion, sentences with similar meanings coded in different ways are presented and the student uses the discourse context to select the most appropriate grammatical coding of the information.

Cloze passages can be created either by random deletion of words (e.g., every seventh word is deleted) or by deletion of a specific item (e.g., articles). The second kind of cloze passage is most suitable for grammatical focus (Celce-Murcia & Hilles, 1988, p. 152). An example of this type is given below; it requires students to select appropriate prepositions. (The text is from Ross, 1984.)

Every Superbowl played _____ the 1970s
(1)
rates _____ the top television draws
(2)
_____ the decade—pro football's champi-
(3)
onship is right up there _____ the charts
(4)
_____ blockbusters _____ Rocky,
(5)   (6)
Jaws, *and* Gone with the Wind.

Although the sources for cloze passages are usually texts written by proficient native speakers, student writing could also be used, providing that the samples have no serious grammatical problems which might distract or confuse students. The following is part of a student essay which has been made into a cloze passage by deleting articles. (Blanks have also been put before nouns with no article.)

____(1)____ pollution may be defined as ____(2)____ deterioration of ____(3)____ everyday life's natural resources. ____(4)____ pollution is ____(5)____ global problem that has affected ____(6)____ quality of ____(7)____ water we drink. ____(8)____ air we breathe and ____(9)____ land we use. ____(10)____ scientific solutions to overcome ____(11)____ problem have increased ____(12)____ destruction.

The text above illustrates the advantage of presenting a passage for practice in article usage rather than a group of unrelated sentences. In the last sentence, the definite article "the" is needed before both nouns because of second mention; "problem" is a partial repetition of "global problem," and "destruction" may be interpreted as either a synonym for "deterioration" or a superordinate term for the effects mentioned in the second sentence.

Students usually enjoy exercises that involve their own writing; also, cloze passages based on student texts can serve as an error correction technique if the writer has produced errors in the grammatical item deleted. Whatever the source, this type of cloze passage can provide an excellent context for discussing extrasentential syntactic, semantic, or pragmatic features that may influence writers' selections of such grammatical items as articles and pronouns.

Since gapped text completion exercises do not specify the number of words required for each blank, they can be used to elicit deleted verbs that include forms with more than one word, such as passives, progressive aspect, and present perfect. Other grammatical items that could be deleted for gapped exercises are comparatives and superlatives, phrasal verbs, and logical connectors.

The third type of text completion, as described by Rutherford (1988), asks the student to consider several syntactic arrangements that realize essentially the same propositional content and to choose the most appropriate rendering of the information based on the preceding discourse context. The following exercise, modeled after Rutherford's (p. 240) and based on information from Filosa (1988), is an example. The appropriate choices have been indicated.

Climatologists have predicted that the continual warming of the earth's surface, known as the "greenhouse effect," could have dramatic consequences.

(a)	(b)
1 The melting of the polar polar ice caps could be one result.	One result could be the melting of the polar ice caps.

(a)	(b)
2 This melting would, in turn, cause a rise of the sea level.	A rise of the sea level would, in turn, be caused by this melting.

(a)	(b)
3 Coastal flooding would occur as the sea level rises.	As the sea level rises, coastal flooding would occur.

(a)	(b)
4 Such disastrous effects might be lessened to some degree by cloud reactions.	Cloud reactions might lessen to some degree such disastrous effects.

As the example shows, this activity emphasizes the importance of context in making grammatical choices and also demonstrates the significant role of word order in presenting "given" and "new" information in English (Chafe, 1976). This type of exercise can help advanced ESL students to gain nativelike competency in written English. Such writers employ a sophisticated range of syntactic structures but need to develop greater awareness of how grammar is used to focus information and to achieve cohesion across sentence boundaries. Also, in courses concerned with writing for academic purposes, this technique can familiarize students with grammatically based discourse conventions such as the use of passive voice in describing research procedures.

EDITING

Many of the guided writing activities described above can, of course, be incorporated into the editing process of writing. However, the techniques discussed here, unlike the guided writing exercises, have a single focus: to develop student's abilities to detect and correct errors so that they will become effective self-editors of their writing.

Error Detection/ Correction Exercises

Text-based exercises which involve identifying and correcting the kinds of errors students frequently make in their writing can help intermediate and advanced writers to develop systematic strategies for editing. It is, of course, important for the instructor to analyze students' errors, at least informally, so that the exercises are relevant to their writing problems. Obviously not all students in a class will produce the same errors. Thus, whenever possible and appropriate, the writing of students in the class should be used for exercises; in this way, if a few students do not have the particular error problem, they can contribute via peer correction.

The following are some variations of error detection/correction techniques, with an example given for each; it should be assumed that the examples are excerpted from a text (a paragraph or composition). Usually an authentic text must be adapted in some way to make it appropriate for instructional purposes.

1. A text is constructed with one error in each sentence, and with the errors representing a range of types. Each sentence is divided into three or four parts. The student must identify the section with the error and correct it. Although this task could involve identification only, the teacher should keep in mind that students might choose the section with the error for the wrong reason; therefore, when possible it is best to have them correct the perceived error also.

Example: Many people worry about the
                a   b

numerous effect of TV on children.
        c   d

TV is a very common form
a   b

of entertainments for families.
        c   d

2. In a text with different types of errors, students are told the total number of each kind of error to identify and correct. (Fox, 1983, uses a number of these exercises in his writing textbook.)

Example: *The text below has the following errors: 1 incorrect preposition, 1 verb tense, 1 subject–verb agreement, 1 missing article.*

This paper report on survey about values. Our English class take the survey last week in UCLA.

3. To focus on just one error type, students are given a text with numbered lines. They are told all of the line numbers which have a certain type of error.

Example: *Identify and correct all of the verb form errors in the following text. Use the guide below to find the errors.*

   1 *The Olympics were hold in Seoul, Korea in 1988. Athletes from all over*
   3 *the world participated. The Olympics have inspire many young people to excel in athletics.*

   Guide: Errors—lines 1, 4

For less advanced students, the teacher could locate errors more specifically by underlining instead of giving line numbers.

For any editing exercise, the teacher should consider carefully how much guidance students may need to complete the task successfully. All of the variations above provide some direction either by identifying to some extent error location or by indicating numbers of errors and error types. Editing tasks which are not guided in any way can overwhelm students, unless they are quite advanced, especially if the text is a composition; they are also difficult for students or the teacher to correct.

Read-Aloud Technique

In this procedure, the students simply read their papers aloud, listening for errors and correcting as they proceed. A variation of this is to have students work in pairs, with each student reading aloud his/her partner's paper; the writer can ask the reader to stop at any time to make corrections. The rationale for this technique is that some students are better able to hear their errors than to see them; this can be a helpful activity for editing the last draft before the final version of a composition.

Algorithms

Flow charts, or algorithms, to guide students in editing their grammatical choices have been developed by Raimes (1988) and Sharwood Smith (1988). In this procedure, the student responds to a series of questions about a grammatical item; each answer leads to a narrowing of choices, until at the end a single choice remains. The following example, from Raimes' (1988, p. 54) textbook, *Grammar Troublespots: An Editing Guide for ESL Students,* is the first part of an algorithm for editing article usage:

Is the noun a common noun?

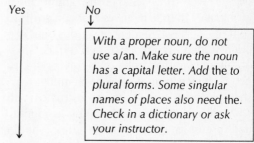

Yes   No

With a proper noun, do not use a/an. Make sure the noun has a capital letter. Add the to plural forms. Some singular names of places also need the. Check in a dictionary or ask your instructor.

Does the common noun have a specific, unique referent for the writer and the reader?

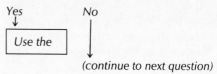

Yes   No

Use the

(continue to next question)

Raimes' chart continues with features of countability and number to guide correct selection of an article in context. As can be seen from the example, the algorithmic procedure may be best for more advanced writers who are familiar with grammatical terminology. It provides a step-by-step process for self-editing, which makes it more effective than simply a list of grammatical rules.

TEACHER CORRECTION AND FEEDBACK ON ERRORS

Recent research suggests that direct correction of surface errors does not produce significantly better results in EFL student writing than less time-consuming correction measures such as underlining or highlighting errors (Robb et al., 1986).

Since students often do not pay much attention to corrections on their final, graded compositions, instructor feedback on error seems most helpful in the editing stages of composing. Even before this, however, the teacher should help individuals identify frequent error patterns and discuss goals for reducing error frequency. In this way, a writer, with instructor guidance, can set reasonable objectives for improvement. A frequent complaint of students during short courses (e.g., a 10-week term) is that they don't notice their writing getting any better. Especially for writers who have numerous grammatical problems, limiting intensive work on errors to some of the most frequent or serious ones can build students' confidence and reduce anxiety about grammar problems by giving them a better chance to observe improvement over a short period of time. Although instructors will want to refer to students' writing to identify and discuss grammar problems, they should be careful that grammar focus does not contradict other types of teacher feedback. When teachers point out errors to be edited on drafts at the same time that they suggest meaning-level changes, such as further developing a topic, students may be confused as to how they should revise (Zamel, 1985).

One method of charting progress in reducing error frequency during a course is for each student to keep a chronological record of the errors being focused on, with the teacher helping by either coding or underlining them on selected writing assignments, such as final drafts before a paper is due.

Another method of individualizing error correction, recommended by Celce-Murcia and Hilles (1988), is the "blue sheet." In this technique, the teacher attaches a blue sheet to each student's paragraph or essay, on which two obvious structural errors are listed. Again, this could be done with drafts preceding final revision. The teacher also refers each writer to exercises in the class grammar text or provides handouts relevant to these errors. (Some ESL textbooks, such as Graham & Curtis, 1986; Raimes, 1988, include text-based exercises.) The teacher then corrects the practice exercises before the writing assignment is revised by the student.

If the teaching environment permits conferencing with students outside of class, conferences can provide opportunities for more individualized help with grammar problems in writing. Even if this is not possible, the teacher may be able to hold "miniconferences" with individuals or small groups of students in the classroom. In conferences, teachers can demonstrate directly the difficulties a reader might have as a result of grammatical errors in the student's writing. This setting allows the teacher to act as a collaborator rather than as an error detector or corrector; he/she can help students to identify errors that create reader confusion or misinterpretation of ideas, to develop strategies for systematic editing of frequent errors, to set goals for improvement, and to assess progress in these goals. In conferences teachers and students can also discuss possible reasons for errors. The Cohen and Robbins (1976) case studies of writers based on this technique indicate that writers' attitudes about the importance of grammatical accuracy may affect error frequency. Although, as Cohen and Robbins note, students may lack metalanguage to describe reasons for structural problems, they can often provide insight into sources of error that a teacher might not have considered. For example, in one of my recent conferences, a native speaker of Korean revealed a pervasive problem with verb forms in English to be the result of applying a grammatical rule from her third language, French, concerning use of the imperfect rather than the simple past for past description. When students are able to analyze their error sources, the teacher can suggest effective correction strategies.

CONCLUSION

This discussion of grammar in writing has argued that grammar is indeed an essential aspect of written communication and that students in the ESL/EFL classroom should be taught to view grammar as an aid to shaping effective and appropriate messages. As Ponsot and Deen (1982, p. 133) put it, "grammar is clearly not remedial. Like baking powder, it can't be stirred into the cake after the batter has been poured into pans." Thus, while concern for grammatical correctness should be integrated with editing processes, grammar in its broader meaning—i.e., the structural patterns of language—plays a role in all phases of composing. In selecting and developing grammar-oriented activities for the classroom, the teacher should always bear in mind the students' needs and background as well as the demands of writing tasks.

DISCUSSION QUESTIONS

1. Is grammar instruction compatible with a process approach to writing? In explaining your opinion, include a definition of "grammar."

2. Discuss how learner variables of age, proficiency level, educational background, and/or course objectives might influence the role of grammar instruction in writing for each of the following groups of students. Can you think of other variables not mentioned that might also be relevant?

a. Seventh-grade ESL students with limited English proficiency; most are immigrants who have been in an English-speaking country for less than two years and have little knowledge of formal grammar.
b. EFL graduate science students with advanced English proficiency and a strong background in formal grammar; they are enrolled in a writing course intended to prepare them for writing journal articles in their fields of specialization.
c. Adult ESL immigrants enrolled in an intermediate-level, adult education writing class; knowledge of formal grammar varies among individuals; most hope to attend college in the future.

3. Why is it important for grammar exercises to be (a) text-based rather than a series of unrelated sentences, (b) developed from authentic discourse, and (c) presented in a communicative context rather than only as practice in grammatical structures?

4. You are teaching a class of advanced ESL/EFL students whose writing generally has only minor grammatical errors. What types of grammatically focused writing activities might be most appropriate to help them further develop their writing abilities?

5. If one of your students expressed disappointment that you did not correct all of the errors in her final drafts, how would you respond?

6. What are some of the advantages of teacher–student conferences in helping students with grammatical problems in writing?

SUGGESTED ACTIVITIES

1. Evaluate one or more grammar-oriented exercises in an ESL composition textbook or workbook according to the following criteria: (a) What appears to be the purpose of the exercise? Do you think it is pedagogically sound? (b) Is the exercise text-based? If not, do you think it is still appropriate for its purpose? (c) Does the language seem authentic? (d) If the exercise is included in a content-based or rhetorical framework (e.g., as part of a unit on cause/effect), is it clearly and appropriately related to the larger context? (e) If the exercise is not part of a larger context, for what aspect of writing instruction do you think it would be appropriate? (f) Does the level of difficulty seem appropriate for the intended learners?

2. Select a text that you think illustrates well the use of a particular grammatical structure (e.g., agentless passives, present perfect verbs, presentative "there" to introduce information). Develop an exercise to accompany the text that students could complete in small groups as a classroom assignment or individually for homework. Explain the objective of the exercise and the writing context in which it might be used.

3. Examine several ESL/EFL compositions that have numerous and varied grammatical errors. For each, identify two of the most frequent or serious errors. Develop sets of exercises or activities that would help the writer to address these grammatical problems.

4. Make a list of grammatical errors you observe in your students' writing that seem to be influenced by spoken English patterns. Create short dictation exercises to focus on these errors or find authentic texts that would be appropriate for dictation.

5. Interview ESL writing teachers about the techniques, both oral and written, that they have used to provide feedback on grammatical errors in their students' writing. During what stages of composing processes do they address errors? Which error feedback and/or correction techniques have they found to be most effective? What student variables have affected the success of techniques used? Compare your findings with those of recent research on the effectiveness of error correction and feedback methods.

SUGGESTIONS FOR FURTHER READING

Bardovi-Harlig, K. (1990)
Pragmatic Word Order in English Composition. In U. Connor and A. M. Johns (eds.), *Coherence: Research and Pedagogical Perspectives*. Washington, DC: TESOL.

> The pragmatic functions of five syntactic constructions in English written discourse are discussed, followed by sample exercises and activities intended to help writers understand how grammar is used to organize and focus information.

Daiker, D., A. Kerek, and M. Morenberg, eds. (1985)
Sentence Combining: A Rhetorical Perspective. Carbondale, IL: Southern Illinois University Press.

> This anthology of articles on sentence combining discusses both theoretical issues and practical applications of a widely used technique for developing syntactic fluency.

Hartwell, P. (1985)
Grammar, Grammars, and the Teaching of Grammar. *College English, 47,* 105–127.

> To explore the issue of grammar's role in composition instruction, five meanings of grammar are outlined and discussed; the author suggests redefining error as a problem of metacognition and metalinguistic awareness.

Shaughnessy, M. (1977)
Errors and Expectations: A Guide for the Teacher of Basic Writing. New York: Oxford University Press.

> A systematic analysis of types and sources of error is presented, as well as numerous practical suggestions for addressing students' grammatical problems. Although analysis is based on native English speaker data, much of the discussion is relevant to ESL writing also.

II
Language Skills
E. Grammar and Vocabulary

Grammar and vocabulary have often been viewed as incompatible elements in language teaching. The Reading Approach, for example, elevated vocabulary but treated grammar only selectively, with the result that language learners could not produce coherent sentences even after several years of language study. The Audiolingual Approach did the reverse: it elevated grammar but suppressed vocabulary. The result was that ESL learners had generally poor comprehension of natural, unedited speech or written materials even after a year or more of intensive language instruction. In any multiskill language program, both grammar and vocabulary are important and both can and should be taught without sacrificing one for the other. In this section of the book, Larsen-Freeman's chapter presents a view of grammar that relates it to other aspects of language as well as to a psychological model of learning. Seal's chapter explores the many issues involved in the teaching of vocabulary and gives the teacher a number of practical suggestions and useful resources.

Teaching Grammar

Diane Larsen-Freeman

INTRODUCTION

Over the centuries, second language educators have alternated between favoring teaching approaches which focus on having students analyze language in order to learn it and those which encourage students' using language in order to acquire it. Earlier this century, this distinctive pattern was observable in the shift from the analytic grammar-translation approach to the use-oriented direct method (Celce-Murcia, 1979). Although the character of the field is somewhat more heterogeneous today, a recent example of the shift, this time in the opposite direction, is the loss of popularity of the Chomsky-inspired cognitive code approach, in which analyzing structures and applying rules were common practices, and the rise in popularity of more communicative approaches which emphasize language use over rules of language usage (Widdowson, 1978). In fact, no fewer than three language teaching methods or approaches, Community Language Learning, Suggestopedia, and the Communicative Approach, devote a significant amount of classroom time to promoting communication among students (Larsen-Freeman, 1986). Moreover, one current approach, the Natural Approach, explicitly eschews any class time for grammatical analysis, relegating any which does occur to homework exercises. Proponents of this approach believe that the only sufficient and necessary conditions for successful second language learning are that learners receive comprehensible input somewhat beyond their current stage of development and that the learners' affective state make them receptive to the input (Krashen and Terrell, 1983).

Despite the popularity such approaches now enjoy, if the pattern alluded to earlier is perpetuated, then one would expect them to be challenged. Indeed, there are already signs that this is happening. As Eskey (1983) points out with exasperation: "We used to believe that if students learned the form, communication would somehow take care of itself. Now we seem to believe that if students somehow learn to communicate, mastery of the forms will take care of itself" (p. 319).

The problem, as Eskey suggests, is that form does *not* take care of itself, at least not for many learners and not in the most efficacious manner possible. Indeed, researcher Pienemann (1984) concludes that "giving up the instruction of syntax is to allow for the fossilization of interlanguage in simplified form" (1984, p. 209). Thus, while comprehensible input may be necessary and sufficient for untutored second language acquisition, it does not necessarily follow that instruction should be limited to what is necessary and sufficient. Surely the motivation for language instruction is not simply to supply what is minimally necessary for learning to take place, but rather to create the optimal conditions for effective and efficient L2 pedagogy (Larsen-Freeman & Long, 1990).

Although some educators are frankly relieved that grammar, which has received short shrift for a decade or so, is once again receiving its due, an unfortunate consequence of this shift will result if the pendulum is allowed to swing beyond its point of equilibrium. Must it be the fate of the field to vacillate forever, or is there a way in which a synergy may be realized between language analysis and language use? It would be too ambitious to think that this chapter might achieve such a reconciliation, but perhaps we can take a modest step in the direction of maintaining balance. To do so, it seems we must come to a broader understanding of what it means to teach grammar than has usually been entertained. Whereas opponents of a language-analytic approach have usually equated the teaching of grammar with the teaching of explicit linguistic rules, we submit that whether or not the students are provided with explicit rules is really irrelevant to what it means to teach grammar. Neither should the teaching of grammar require a focus on form or structure alone. Nonetheless, a concession by those who would zealously abandon language analysis must also be made: communicative competence should be seen to subsume linguistic competence, not to replace it. We claim that linguistic accuracy is as much a part of communicative competence as being able to get one's meaning across or to communicate in a sociolinguistically appropriate manner. Thus, a more satisfactory characterization of teaching grammar, harmonious with the above assumptions, is that teaching grammar means enabling language students to use linguistic forms accurately, meaningfully and appropriately.[1]

A THREE-DIMENSIONAL GRAMMAR FRAMEWORK

In order to guide us in constructing an approach to teaching grammar which strives to meet the above definition, it would be helpful to have a frame of reference. Our framework takes the form of a pie chart. Its shape helps us to make salient the fact that in dealing with the complexity of grammar there are three dimensions of language that must be dealt with: the form or structures themselves, their semantics or meaning, and the pragmatic conditions governing their use.[2] Moreover, as they are wedges of a single pie, we note that a further assumption is that the dimensions are not hierarchically arranged as many traditional characterizations of linguistic strata depict.[3] Finally, the arrows connecting one wedge of the pie with another illustrate the interconnectedness of the three dimensions, thus a change in any one wedge will have repercussions for the other two.

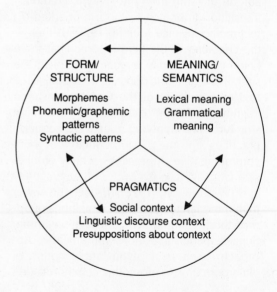

In the wedge of our pie having to do with structure, we have those overt forms that tell us how a particular grammar structure is constructed. In the semantic wedge we deal with what a grammar structure means. Note that the meaning can be lexical (a dictionary definition for a preposition like *down* for instance) or it can be grammatical (e.g., the conditional states both a condition and outcome or result). It is very difficult to arrive at a definition of pragmatics distinct from semantics, and thus we are sympathetic to Levinson's suggestion that pragmatics deals with all aspects of meaning not dealt with by semantic theory! Since this definition is too circular and too broad for our purposes here, however, we will limit pragmatics to mean "the study of those relations between language and context that are grammaticalized, or encoded in the structure of a language" (Levinson 1983, p. 9). We will leave the term "context" broad enough though, so that context can be social (i.e., a context created by interlocutors, their relationship to one another, the setting), or it can be a linguistic discourse context (i.e., the language that precedes or follows a particular structure in the discourse or how a particular genre or register of discourse affects the use of a structure), or context can even mean the presuppositions one has about the context. The influence of pragmatics may be ascertained by asking two questions:

1. When or why does a speaker/writer choose a particular grammar structure over another? For example, what factors in the social context might explain a paradigmatic choice such as why a speaker chooses a yes-no question rather than an imperative to serve as a request for information (e.g., *Do you have the time?* vs. *Please tell me the time*). Or what presupposition about the context would a speaker hold who used a negative yes-no question, rather than an affirmative one?
2. When or why does a speaker/writer vary the form of a particular linguistic structure? For instance, what linguistic discourse factors would result in a syntagmatic choice such as the indirect object being placed to create *Jenny gave Hank a brand-new comb* versus *Jenny gave a brand-new comb to Hank?*

Despite the permeable boundaries between the dimensions, we have found it useful to view grammar from these three perspectives. We trust that the utility of this approach will become clearer as we proceed. A teacher of grammar might begin by asking the questions posed in the three wedges of our pie for any given grammar point.

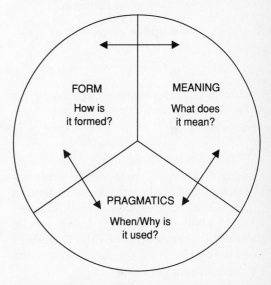

Let us take an example. A common structure to be taught at a high beginning level of English proficiency is the *'s* possessive form. If we analyze this possessive form as answers to our questions, we would fill in the wedges as shown at the top of p. 282 (analysis based on Celce-Murcia & Larsen-Freeman, 1983).

Form of Possessive. This way of forming possessives in English requires inflecting regular singular nouns and irregular plural nouns not ending in *s* with *'s* or by adding an apostrophe after the *s* ending of regular plural nouns and singular nouns ending in the sound *s*. This form of the possessive has three allomorphs: /z/, /s/, and /əz/ which are phonetically conditioned: /z/ is used when it oc-

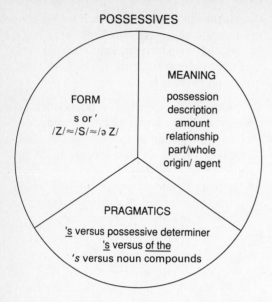

POSSESSIVES

FORM
s or '
/Z/ ≈ /S/ ≈ /ə Z/

MEANING
possession
description
amount
relationship
part/whole
origin/ agent

PRAGMATICS
's versus possessive determiner
's versus of the
's versus noun compounds

speakers often prefer to use the 's even with inanimate head nouns if the head nouns are performing some action (e.g., *the train's arrival was delayed*).[4] Finally, students will have to learn to distinguish contexts in which a noun compound (*table leg*) is more appropriate than either the 's form or the *of the* form.

Thus, by using our ternary scheme, we can classify the facts that affect the form, meaning, and use of the possessive structure. The articulation and classification of the facts is, of course, only a first step. Teachers would not necessarily present all these facts to students, and they certainly would not do so at a single time.[5] Before continuing, however, it might be worthwhile to apply our approach to another grammar structure. Let us analyze phrasal verbs this time. By considering the three questions posed earlier, we can state the following about phrasal verbs (analysis based upon Celce-Murcia & Larsen-Freeman, 1983):

curs after voiced consonants and vowels, /s/ following voiceless consonants, and /əz/ after sibilants.

Meaning of Possessive. Although all languages have a way of signaling possession, they do not all regard the same items as possessable. For example, Spanish speakers refer to a body part using the definite article, instead of a possessive form. ESL/EFL students will have to learn the semantic scope of the possessive form in English.

Besides possession, the possessive form can indicate description (*a debtor's prison*), amount (*a month's holiday*), relationship (*Jack's wife*), part/whole (*my brother's hand*), and origin/agent (*Shakespeare's tragedies*).

Pragmatics of Possessive. Possession in English can be expressed in other ways—for example, with a possessive determiner or with the *of the* form (e.g., *the legs of the table*). Possessive determiners (e.g., *his, her,* and *their*) are presumably used when the referent of the possessor is clear from the context. As for the *of the* form, while ESL/EFL books will often offer the rule that says that the *of the* possessive is used with nonhuman head nouns and 's with human head nouns, we are aware of certain pragmatic conditions where this rule does not apply. For example, native

PHRASAL VERBS

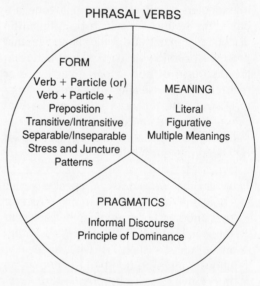

FORM
Verb + Particle (or)
Verb + Particle +
Preposition
Transitive/Intransitive
Separable/Inseparable
Stress and Juncture
Patterns

MEANING
Literal
Figurative
Multiple Meanings

PRAGMATICS
Informal Discourse
Principle of Dominance

Form of Phrasal Verbs. Phrasal verbs are two-part verbs comprising a verb and a particle (e.g., *to look up*). Sometimes, they can be constructed with three parts, in that a preposition can follow the particle (e.g., *to keep up with*). As with all other verbs, phrasal verbs are transitive or intransitive. A distinctive feature of phrasal verbs is that in many of them the particle can be separated from its verb by an intervening object (e.g., *Alicia looked the word up in the dictionary*). Phrasal verbs also have distinctive stress and juncture patterns, which distinguishes them from verb plus preposition combinations:

Alicia lóoked up̀#the word.
Alicia wálked#ŭp the street.

Meaning of Phrasal Verbs. There are literal phrasal verbs, such as to *hang up,* where if one knows the meaning of the verb or the particle or both, it is not difficult to figure out the meaning of the verb-particle combination. Unfortunately, for the ESL/EFL student there are far more instances of figurative phrasal verbs (e.g., *to run into,* meaning "meet by chance") where a knowledge of the meaning of the verb and of the particle is of little help in discerning the meaning of the phrasal verb. Moreover, as with single-word verbs, phrasal verbs can have more than one meaning (e.g., *to come across,* meaning "to discover by chance" or "to make an impression"), the latter meaning occurring when the phrasal verb is used intransitively.

Pragmatics of Phrasal Verbs. When is a phrasal verb preferred to a single-word verb? For the most part, phrasal verbs seem to be more common in informal spoken discourse as opposed to more formal written discourse. When is one form of a phrasal verb preferred to another; i.e., when should the particle be separated from its verb? Erteschik-Shir's (1979) principle of dominance seems to work well to define the circumstances favoring particle movement: If an NP object is dominant (i.e., a long, elaborate NP representing new information), it is likely to occur after the particle; if the direct object is short, old information (e.g., a pronoun), it would naturally occur before the particle.

Identifying the Challenge. Again, we would like to underscore the fact that it would not be reasonable for the ESL/EFL teacher to present all of this information to students at once. The framework does, however, help to organize the facts. Furthermore, by organizing the facts in this manner, teachers can more easily identify where the challenge(s) will lie for their students. Identifying the challenging dimension or dimensions is a key step which should be taken prior to lesson preparation. Teachers should, therefore, ask themselves for each structure they teach which of the three dimensions of language is likely to offer the greatest challenge for their students.

All three dimensions will have to be mastered by the learner (although not necessarily consciously). For phrasal verbs, however, it has been our experience that it is the meaning dimension which ESL/EFL students struggle with most. It is often the fact that there is no systematic way of associating the verb and the particle. To make matters worse, new phrasal verbs are constantly being coined, adding to the students' woes. By recognizing where students will likely struggle, an important clue is given the teacher as to where to focus work on phrasal verbs. We will amplify on this point below. For now, however, it is worth noting that although it is grammar structures with which we are dealing, it is not always the form of the structures which creates the most significant learning challenge for students (Larsen-Freeman & Celce-Murcia, 1985).

THE LEARNING PROCESS

We should pause here to acknowledge that as important as it is to develop our understanding of the grammatical facts of the language we are teaching, it is not these facts that we wish our students to learn. We are not interested in filling our students with grammatical paradigms and syntactic rules. What we do hope to do is to cultivate linguistic performance in our students which is consistent with the facts. In other words, grammar teaching is not so much knowledge transmission as it is skill development. By recognizing this, we can take advantage of several insights from second language acquisition (SLA) research concerning how students naturally develop their ability to interpret and produce grammatical utterances. Three particular insights are germane to our topic:

1. Learners do not learn structures one at a time. It is not the case that a learner masters the definite article, and when that is mastered, moves on to the simple past. From their first encounter with the definite article, learners might master one of its pragmatic functions—e.g., to signal the uniqueness of the following noun phrase. But even if they are able to do this pragmatically appropriately, it is not likely that learners will always produce the definite article when needed, because learners typically take a long time before they are able to do this consistently. Thus, learning is a gradual process involving the mapping of form, meaning, and pragmatics; structures do not emerge in learners' interlanguage fully developed and error-free. To expect that they will do so in an instructional setting is therefore unrealistic. Recycling various aspects of structures over time seems a much more reasonable alternative.

2. Even when learners appear to have mastered a particular structure, it is not uncommon to find backsliding occurring with the introduction of new forms to the learners' interlanguage. For example, the learner who has finally mastered the third person singular marker on present-tense verbs is likely to overgeneralize the rule and apply it to newly emerging modal verbs. Thus, teachers should not despair at similar regressive behavior on the part of their students. Well-formedness is usually restored once the new additions have been incorporated and the system reanalyzed.

3. Second language learners rely on the knowledge and the experience they have. If they are beginners, they will rely on their L1 as a source of hypotheses about how the L2 works; when they are more advanced, they will rely increasingly on the L2. In understanding this, the teacher realizes that there is no need to teach everything about a structure to a group of students; rather, the teacher can build upon what the students already know. It also follows that the challenging dimension for a given grammatical structure will shift from class to class depending on the students' L1 backgrounds and level of L2 proficiency. Successful teaching involves identifying the relevant challenge for a particular group of students.

To these three observations, we will add a fourth one that is not to our knowledge treated in the SLA research literature, but rather one based upon our observations and supported by learning theorists:

4. Different learning processes are responsible for different aspects of language. Indeed, given that language is as complicated as it is, one would not expect the learning process to be any simpler. In reviewing a learning taxonomy from Gagne (1965),[6] it becomes clear that a variety of types of learning contribute to mastery of a second language (see Table 1 on p. 285).

Despite its decidedly behaviorist leaning, then, we could readily imagine language learning examples for the types of learning in Gagne's taxonomy. More importantly, being aware of the fact that different learning processes contribute to SLA suggests a need for the teaching process to respect the differences. How the nature of the language challenge and the learning process affect teaching decisions is the issue to which we next turn.

DESIGNING ACTIVITIES TO PRACTICE GRAMMAR STRUCTURES

Grammar lessons are usually composed of three phases: presentation, practice, and communication (although all three may not be conducted within one class period). Rather than illustrating a single lesson plan from start to finish, it seemed more beneficial to concentrate on characterizing and exemplifying activities which could be used during the practice phase. It used to be that the practice phase of a lesson was devoted almost

TABLE 1
Gagne's Taxonomy of Learning Types Applied to the Acquisition of English

Types of Learning	Aspects of English Addressed
1. Signal Learning: A connection is learned between a signal (conditioned stimulus) and an involuntary response (e.g., Pavlov's experiment where a dog "learned" to salivate upon hearing a bell).	No apparent connection with the acquisition of language.
2. Stimulus–Response Learning: Learning to make a voluntary response to very specific stimuli through a process involving shaping and reinforcement.	A student learns how to pronounce an unfamiliar English word in response to a teacher's cue.
3. Chaining: The connecting of two or more previously learned stimulus–response connections.	Students learn to produce formulaic utterances, e.g., "How are you?" following "Hello."
4. Verbal Association (verbal chains).	Students learn a vocabulary item (e.g., *house*) or a function (e.g., *That's right*, for agreement) through associating it with either an L1 translation or a real-world referent.
5. Multiple Discrimination: Being able to distinguish among various verbal chains.	A student learns to discriminate *house* from *home*, *habitat*, *dwelling*, *residence*, *domicile*, etc., or to distinguish one exponent for a particular function from another (e.g., *That's right* versus *I agree, of course, why not?*) for expressing agreement.
6. Concept Learning: Placing items into a particular class and then generalizing about the class.	A student learns that preverbal adverbs in English deal with frequency.
7. Principle Learning: Learning chains of concepts and the relationship between/among them.	Students learn that fronted negative preverbal adverbs of frequency trigger subject–auxiliary inversion (e.g., *Never before have I seen such a sight*).
8. Problem Solving: Combining old principles into new ones to solve problems. What emerges is a higher-order principle established through an "inductive leap."	A student learns that the principle that new information tends to occur toward the end of the sentence in English and old information toward the beginning of a sentence explaining a lot of previously unaccounted-for structures in English (e.g., existential *there*) or word-order phenomena (e.g., indirect object alternation).

exclusively to grammar drills. Ever since the ineffectiveness of using drills which do not engage students' attention was acknowledged, there has been little by way of guidance offered on what to do during the practice phase of a lesson. What follows, therefore, is an attempt to fill this void. During the course of our discussion, however, we will also illustrate what transpires in the presentation and communicative phases of a grammar lesson. Practice activities will be addressed in terms of which dimension of language they relate to.

Form

Once a particular grammar structure has been analyzed, a challenging teaching point for the particular class of students should be chosen. The learning process associated with the teaching point should also be identified, to the extent possible. The nature of the learning process and of the learning challenge give important clues as to activity characteristics. For example, when dealing with the formal dimension of grammar, it would appear that the *major* learning processes involved would be stimulus–response learning for phonemic patterns and verbal chaining or principle learning for morphemes or syntactic patterns. Recall that stimulus–response learning would be the type of learning required for learning to pronounce an unfamiliar word. Chaining and principle learning seem the applicable learning processes for morphology and syntax since what we are attempting to have our students learn is to comprehend and produce either verbal chains between morphemes/words or rule-governed syntactic patterns.

Identifying the type of learning involved helps us to think about the desirable characteristics of any practice activity. For instance, for a verbal chain to be learned or a principle to be acquired would seem to require a great deal of meaningful repetition. Learners would have to receive feedback on the accuracy with which they produced the target form. Students would have to be restricted to using just the particular target form; in other words, structural diversity would not be permitted.[7] Finally, for a chain to be acquired or a principle inferred/applied, it would seem important to concentrate on only one form at a time,[8] although, of course, the target form could be introduced in contrast to forms that the student already controls.

Let us take an example and see how these characteristics are applied. If we were to teach yes-no question formation to ESL students, we might determine the immediate challenge to be linguistic form, based on our analysis of the three dimensions and what our students know how to do. The first step in the lesson is the presentation of the linguistic rule (or some portion of it, say, involving the be verb and modals). We have several options regarding the presentation phase: The rule could be presented inductively or deductively. Also, the rule could be made explicit or not. We will discuss these options for the presentation phase later in this chapter.

We next need to use the characteristics enumerated above to plan the second or practice phase of the lesson. We will need to select an activity that encourages *meaningful repetition of the pattern,* not verbatim repetition.[9] We want the students to concentrate on producing only yes-no questions. A game like Twenty Questions would appear to meet the criteria. Students get to ask 20 yes-no questions about an object or person in an attempt to guess the identity; hence, they receive abundant practice in forming the questions, and the questions they produce are meaning-

ful. The teacher would work with each student to enable the student to produce the pattern accurately. The game can be repeated for as long as students remain interested.

Questions can also be used to elicit other structures when it is the formal dimension with which the lesson is dealing. For example, a variation on the same game might be to have students guess "Whose _____ is it?" Their responses (e.g., *It's Maria's, It's Sumet's, It's Grace's*) would provide an opportunity to practice the three allomorphs of the possessive. Then, too, the responses to the guesses would offer a good deal of practice with short forms (e.g., *No, it isn't, Yes, it is*).

Another example of a game which appears to meet the above criteria is the Telephone Game, which can be used to practice the forms of reported speech. One student would whisper something to another student (e.g., *"I'm happy it's Friday"*). The second student would whisper to a third student what he or she heard from the first student (*Ahmed said that he was happy it was Friday*). Ahmed's message would be passed from one student to the next, with the last student reporting the message out loud. What usually happens, of course, is that the original message has changed considerably during its passage along the telephone. In order for the teacher to provide feedback on accuracy to the students on their reported speech afterwards, it would be desirable for each student to write down the message that she or he passes on.

In sum, certain games are good devices for practicing grammar points where the identified challenge resides in the formal dimension. While not an activity, in and of itself, another useful device for working on the formal dimension is the use of cuisenaire rods. The rods are ideal for focusing student attention on some syntactic property under scrutiny. One example that comes to mind is an adaptation of Stevick's (1980) Islamabad technique. After having been presented with how to form OS[10] relative clauses during the presentation phase of the lesson, students might use the rods to construct a view of some spot in their hometown. The students would be encouraged to use OS relative clauses where appropriate (e.g., *There is a fountain which is located in the center of my town; Around the fountain there are many vendors who sell fruits, vegetables and flowers, etc.*).

One final example of a type of activity which is useful for working on the formal dimension is a problem-solving activity. The problem to be solved could be most anything, but if we are dealing with the formal dimension, then we would want it to conform to the characteristics delineated above. An example might be an activity where the students are given a class information sheet with certain items missing.

Name	Age	Country
Beatriz	18	Bolivia
Mohammed	19	Algeria
Jean Claude	_____	France
_____	18	Brazil
Werner	17	_____

etc.

Students could circulate, asking one another Wh-questions to complete the chart. Another example might be a sentence-unscrambling task. This is a useful problem-solving activity when the challenge is getting students to produce correct word order, such as when the objective is to have students use auxiliary verbs in the proper sequence.

It is important to take note that there is nothing inherent in the three examples we have provided (games, use of rods, problem-solving activities) which make them useful for addressing the formal dimension; i.e., we could easily use rods to work on some aspects of the semantic or pragmatic dimensions. What is significant to remember is that the activity should be structured in such a way that it is compatible with the characteristics presented earlier. We will review these here in tabular form, at the same time proposing the characteristics for the other two dimensions (see Table 2 on p. 288).

Meaning

If the teacher has decided that the challenge of a particular structure lies in the semantic dimension for the class, then a different sort of practice activity should be planned. It would seem that verbal association, multiple discrimination, and concept learning would all come into play when working on the meaning of a particular grammar structure. The major procedures would call for the student to learn to bond the form with its meaning and also to distinguish the meaning of one particular form from another. Repeated opportunities to associate the form and the meaning may be desirable, but it has

Language	Major	Hobby
Spanish	Dentistry	_____
	Accounting	Going to movies
French		Painting
	Education	Hiking
Swiss German	Business	_____

been our experience that repetition is not needed to the same extent as it is when teaching some aspect of the formal dimension. Sometimes a single pairing of form and meaning suffices for a student to make the bond. Due to memory constraints, it seems prudent to restrict the number of new items being practiced at any one time (see note 8 for a definition of one time) to between two and six. The students would receive feedback on their ability to demonstrate that they had acquired the form-meaning bond.

Celce-Murcia and Hilles (1988) mention that when dealing with the semantic dimension, realia and pictures are very useful. An example taken from their work is to use pictures to teach the semantics of comparatives. After a presentation phase in which students have been presented with various forms for making comparisons in English (e.g., _____er than, as _____ as, more_____ than, less_____

TABLE 2
Characteristics of Activities That Focus on the Three Dimensions

	Formal	Semantic	Pragmatic
Major learning processes	Stimulus–response	Verbal association	Principle learning
	Verbal chaining	Multiple discrimination	Problem solving
	Principle learning	Concept learning	Multiple discrimination
Major type of practice activity	Meaningful repetition	Associate form with meaning	Choose one form over others
		Discriminate one form from another	
Type of feedback given	Accuracy	Form—meaning match	Appropriateness
Number of forms worked on at one time	1	2–6	2–?

than), students can be shown a pair of pictures for which they make meaningful statements of comparison.

Actions, too, can make meaning salient. The initial challenge for ESL/EFL students grappling with prepositions is to associate the "core" meaning with each. Thus, a good strategy is to work with students on having them make an association between a preposition and its use in locating objects in space. One way of doing this is to conduct a Total Physical Response sequence where students act out a series of commands along with the teacher involving the placement of objects in various parts of the room; e.g., *Put the book under the desk, Put the pen on the shelf, Put the pencil near the door.* Once students have appeared to have made the connection between form and meaning, the teacher can assess their ability to discriminate one form from the other by having them carry out commands on their own and by issuing novel commands—e.g., *Put the pen on the desk*—and assessing the students' ability to comply.

We said earlier that a persistent challenge for students' learning phrasal verbs was the fact that the meaning is not often detectable from combining the meaning of the verb with the meaning of the particle. One final example of an activity that would address this semantic challenge is an operation (Nelson & Winters, 1980). In an operation, a series of separate actions are performed to accomplish some task. The teacher might issue commands, or mime the actions with the students as she or he describes them.

I want to call up my friend. First, I look up the phone number. Then I write it down. I pick up the receiver and dial the number. The number is busy. I hang up and decide to call back later.

By practicing this operation several times, the students can learn to associate the form and meaning of certain phrasal verbs. If students are given an operation with which to associate phrasal verbs, recall at a later time will be enhanced. To determine if students can distinguish among the various phrasal verbs, students might be given phrasal verbs out of sequence and asked to mime the appropriate action. Feedback on their ability to match form and meaning can be given.

Pragmatics

When teaching pragmatics, we want our students to be able to select the right structure or form of a structure for a particular context. It stands to reason, then, that students will be learning principles (e.g., phrasal verbs tend to occur in informal contexts) and will be involved with problem solving (e.g., sorting out an ambiguous social context to select an appropriate form of greeting). Working on pragmatics will also involve the type of learning known as multiple discrimination; i.e., students will have to select, from among the repertoire of exponents that they control, the one which best suits the pragmatic conditions of a given context.

Thus, relevant practice activities will provide students with an opportunity to choose from two or more forms the one most suitable for the context. Students would receive feedback on the appropriateness of their choice. In some cases, their choice might involve selecting between two options (e.g., when to use the passive versus the active voice). Other times, their choice would be from among an array of options (e.g., which modal verb to use when giving advice); hence, we noted in Table 2 that the number of forms being worked on at one time would be at least two, but could involve many more.

Celce-Murcia and Hilles (1988) recommend that teachers use skits and role plays when working on the pragmatic dimension. Their recommendation makes sense because when dealing with the factors present in social contexts, it would be advantageous for the teacher to be able to systematically manipulate social variables (e.g., increase or decrease the social distance between interlocutors) to have students practice how the changes in the social variables affect the choice of form they make.

One example of this is the role-play "dilemma." In this role-play, one person has a problem; e.g., the keys to the car have been lost. The car is locked and the person wants to get in. Students are asked to use modal verbs to give advice to the person with the problem; e.g., *you might try breaking the window, you could try calling the police*. The teacher could next alter a salient feature of the context, thus creating a new social context in which a different modal verb would be more appropriate. For example, the teacher might ask, "What if it were a young child that had this dilemma?" A more appropriate form and content for the advice, then, might be *you had better wait for your mother to come!*

Role-plays are useful for highlighting other structural choices as well. Often we find that it is neither the form nor the meaning of the English tenses that presents the greatest

long-term challenge to ESL/EFL students; rather it is when/why to use one tense and not the other. In other words, it is the pragmatic usage of the tenses that is the major obstacle to their mastery. Giving students practice with situations in which a contrast between two tenses is likely to arise may sensitize students to the usage differences. For instance, a notorious problem for ESL/EFL students is to know when to use the present perfect versus when to use the past tense. A situation where a contrast between them would occur might be a job interview. In such a context, the perfect of experience is likely to be invoked (e.g., *Have you ever done any computer programming?*). An affirmative answer is likely to contain the past tense (e.g., *Yes, I have. I once worked on . . .* or simply, *Yes. When I worked at . . .*). Students can take turns role-playing the interviewer and interviewee.

As we mentioned earlier, it is not only the social context that will be involved in the choice of which forms to use, but also it is often the linguistic discourse context that will make a difference. Such is the case with the passive voice. Its use is not particularly sensitive to social factors; i.e., whether one is using the active or passive voice does not depend upon with whom one is conversing. What usually does cause students considerable difficulty with the passive voice, however, is determining when to use it. The fact that the focus of a particular discourse is on some noun that is not the agent motivates the use of the passive. Furthermore, if the agent has already been established in the linguistic discourse, it would likely not even be mentioned in subsequent discourse. Thus, most passive sentences are agentless.

Challenges of this nature call for text-generation or text-manipulation-type exercises. As the passive is used more often in written than in spoken English, teachers might give their students a text-completion exercise in which the first few lines of the text are provided. From these first few lines, it should be clear to the students that the focus of discourse is on the "issues" not the agents (i.e., participants) at the town meeting.

Town meetings were held throughout New England yesterday. Many issues were discussed, although the big one for most citizens was the issue of growth. Many changes have been made recently. For example,

Students then are asked to complete the text using the appropriate voice. As not all the sentences should be in the passive voice, students will be making choices, in keeping with a characteristic of practice activities designed to work on the pragmatic dimension. Later the teacher will give feedback to the students on the appropriateness of their choices.

Before leaving our discussion of the passive voice, it would be useful illustrating why we feel that identifying the challenging dimension is a worthwhile step to take before teaching any grammar structure. By being clear where the challenge lies, the challenge can shape our lessons, even when the lessons themselves do not directly address the challenge. For instance, as we stated earlier, it has been our experience that the greatest long-term challenge for students working on the passive voice is for them to figure out the pragmatics or when to use the passive. With the first lesson on the passive, however, we are likely to be concerned with presenting the form. If, while we plan our lesson on how to form the passive, we keep the challenge in mind, we are likely to avoid a common practice of ESL/EFL teachers, which is to introduce the passive as a transformed version of the active (e.g., "Switch the subject with the direct object . . ."). Presenting the passive in this way is misleading because it gives the impression that the passive is simply a variation of the active. Moreover, it suggests that most passive sentences contain agents. What we know in fact to be the case is that one voice is not a variant of the other, but rather the two are in complementary distribution, with their foci completely different. We also know that relatively few passive sentences contain explicit agents. Thus, from the first

introductory lesson, the passive should be taught as a distinct structure which occurs in a different context from the active. (See Celce-Murcia & Larsen-Freeman, 1983, for several examples of how to do this.)

This brings us to the close of our discussion on how to design practice activities for grammar points.[11] As was mentioned earlier, the practice phase is usually considered the second phase of a lesson. Most approaches to second language pedagogy involve a third, or more communicative phase, as well.

Communicative Phase

In the communicative phase, less control over grammatical structure is exercised than during the practice phase. The aim during this phase is to have students use the structures they have been practicing in as natural and fluid a way as possible. In many cases, this may result in students' finding ways to communicate which the teacher had not anticipated and in which the target structures are not always used. The teacher should accept this outcome.

- An example of a communicative activity which would follow the presentation phase of a lesson on the semantics of prepositions is a direction-giving exercise. One student traces a particular route on a street map while guided by the directions of a partner. (*Walk to the corner. Turn right at the corner. The cinema is near the corner, next to the bank.*)

- Another example of an activity appropriate to this phase, which would complete a three-phase lesson on the semantics of comparatives, might be to have students write a composition discussing their preference for living either in a big city or in a small town.

- A communicative activity which would fit with the lesson on the pragmatics of using modals for giving advice would be having students write a reply to a letter addressed to a newspaper columnist whose advice was being sought for some personal problem.

- Finally, a communicative activity which would be relevant to a lesson on reported speech might be to have students report what transpired at a press conference they had been assigned to listen to or to watch.

We hope these examples will suffice to illustrate activities which would be appropriate for the communicative phase of the lesson. Since the rise of the Communicative Approach, there are many sources a teacher can consult for more examples of this type of activity (see, for example, Prabhu, 1987, Appendix V).

Another feature of the communicative phase of grammar lessons has to do with the role of feedback or error correction. While feedback was considered a vitally important part of the practice phase, it has a much more circumscribed role during the communicative phase. As what we are trying to promote during the latter phase is our students' fluency, error correction during oral activities, at least, should be postponed. Perhaps at a later time a remedial lesson could be prepared to address common errors that a teacher notes.

We will have more to say about error correction below. At this point we will turn to several pedagogical issues we have yet to treat.

RELATED PEDAGOGICAL ISSUES

Sequencing

Earlier we noted that grammar structures are not acquired one at a time through a process of "agglutination" (Rutherford, 1987). Rather, different aspects of form, meaning, and pragmatics of a given structure may be acquired at different stages of interlanguage development. As we suggested earlier, this observation confirms the need for recycling—i.e., introducing one aspect of a form and then returning to the form from time to time for reinforcement and elaboration. Even when recycling, however, one must begin somewhere.

Many teachers, of course, have little control over where they start a grammar sequence. They must adhere to prescribed syllabi or textbooks. But for those who have a choice, there are few clear-cut answers. The usual advice is to begin with the simple structures and work up to the more complex. What constitutes simplicity and complexity has not ever been operationally defined with any success, although some relevant research is currently being conducted which suggests that learnability, and thus teachability, is determined by the complexity of speech-processing strategies required for particular structures. Thus, all structures processable by a particular strategy or cluster of strategies should be acquired at roughly the same developmental stage. This approach has been shown to account for certain developmental sequences in German as a second language (Clahsen, 1984) and ESL (Pienemann & Johnston, 1987).

A corollary to this research finding is that learners should not be able to omit a stage in a developmental sequence, since each new stage depends upon the availability of processing strategies acquired earlier. This prediction has also been supported by evidence in a study conducted by Pienemann (1984). He demonstrated that items will be successfully taught only when students are psycholinguistically "ready" to learn them; i.e. they have mastered the prerequisite strategies.

Despite these compelling findings and their enormous implications for grammatical structure sequencing, we have yet to see any definitive developmental sequence established, and thus teachers are still left to their own resources for judgments on how to proceed. We should also note that even if a developmental sequence were to be fully specified for English, there might be justification for preempting the developmental sequence when students' communicative needs were not being met and when, therefore, certain structures would need to be taught, at least formulaically (David Nunan, personal communication).

Inductive Versus Deductive Presentation

An additional choice teachers face is whether to work inductively or deductively during the presentation phase. An inductive activity is one in which the students infer the rule or generalization from a set of examples. For instance, students might induce the subject-auxiliary inversion rule in forming yes-no questions, after having been exposed to a number of such questions. In a deductive activity, on the other hand, the students are given the rule and they apply it to examples.

If one has chosen an inductive approach in a given lesson, a further option exists—whether or not to have students explicitly state the rule. Earlier, we said that the use of explicit rules was irrelevant. What we meant by this is that one certainly can teach grammar without stating any explicit rules. Recall that what we are trying to bring about in the learner is linguistic behavior that conforms to the rules, not knowledge of the rules themselves. Having said this, we have seen no a priori reason to avoid giving explicit rules, except perhaps if one is working with young children. Usually students request rules and report that they find them helpful. Moreover, stating a rule explicitly can often bring about linguistic insights in a more efficacious manner, as long as the rule is not oversimplified or so metalinguistically obtuse that students must struggle harder to understand the rule than to apply it implicitly.

Returning now to the inductive versus deductive question, we again find that the choice is not one resolvable with an *either/or* approach. There are many times when an inductive approach in presenting a grammar point is desirable because by using such an approach one is nurturing within the students a learning process through which they can arrive at their own generalizations. Other times, when one's students have a particular cognitive style that is not well suited for language analysis or when a particular linguistic rule is rather convoluted, it may make more sense to present a grammar structure deduc-

tively. Indeed, one takes comfort from Corder's sensible observations:

What little we know about the psychological process of second language learning, either from theory or from practical experience, suggests that a combination of induction and deduction produces the best result. . . . Learning is seen as fundamentally an inductive process but one which can be controlled and facilitated by descriptions and explanations given at the appropriate moment and formulated in a way which is appropriate to the maturity, knowledge, and sophistication of the learner. In a sense, teaching is a matter of providing the learner with the right data at the right time and teaching him how to learn, that is, developing in him appropriate learning strategies and means of testing his hypotheses. The old controversy about whether one should provide the rule first and then the examples, or vice versa, is now seen to be merely a matter of tactics to which no categorical answer can be given. (Corder, 1973, in Rutherford & Sharwood Smith, 1988, p. 133)

Presenting a Structure

Now that we have discussed the inductive/deductive and implicit/explicit issues, we can briefly illustrate options for presenting a structure during the initial phase of a lesson. A necessary ingredient for this phase is having some language sample/examples which illustrate the teaching point. In the audiolingual method, grammar points are introduced via a dialog which students listen to, and subsequently memorize. While dialogs are useful for introducing points of grammar, there are a variety of other formats which can be used:

- songs and poems
- authentic texts (e.g., newspaper articles)
- realia (e.g., clothes)
- segments of taped radio/television broadcasts

Moreover, who selects these samples can be varied, too. For example, if the grammar point had to do with the distinction between mass and count nouns,

- *The teacher* could bring in an advertising circular from a local supermarket.
  or

- *The students* might be invited to bring in their favorite recipes.

or

- *The teacher and students* might generate a language sample together which contained count and mass nouns (e.g., "I went to the supermarket" game).

When practicing an inductive approach, students would be presented with the language sample, let's say the advertising circular. They then would be encouraged to make their own observations about the form of mass and count nouns. The teacher would listen to their observations, and then might summarize by generalizing about the two categories of nouns in English. If practicing a deductive approach, the teacher would present the generalization and then ask students to apply it to the language sample. This approach would be suitable for our example of teacher–student-generated language since students might be aided in playing the game by having a knowledge of the mass/count distinction.

One advantage of using an inductive approach during the presentation phase is that it allows teachers to assess what the students already know about a particular structure and to make any necessary modifications in their lesson plan. Clearly, one's prior expectation about where the challenge lies may not be borne out in the course of the lesson. Assessment during this phase and throughout the lesson is crucial to determining what needs to be taught and to what extent learning has taken place, respectively.

Error Correction

In his delineation of the function of a language teacher, Corder (1973) writes, "the function of the teacher is to provide data and examples and where necessary, to offer explanations and descriptions and, more important, verification of the learner's hypotheses (i.e., corrections)" (in Rutherford & Sharwood Smith, 1988, p. 134). Thus, Corder considers error correction a necessary element of peda-gogical practice, and we would certainly concur. There are, however, those who would proscribe it, believing that error correction will inhibit students from freely expressing themselves. While there are clearly times that error correction can be intrusive and therefore unwarranted (e.g., during communicative phase activities), at other times focused error correction is highly desirable. It provides the negative evidence students often need to reject or modify their hypotheses about how the target language is formed or functions. Students understand this, which explains why they often deliberately seek error correction to assist them with their language learning task.

The same pie chart upon which we relied when preparing lessons can be a useful aid in diagnosing errors. When an error is committed by a student, a teacher can mentally hold it up to the pie chart to determine if it is an error in form, meaning, or pragmatics. Of course, sometimes the cause of an error is ambiguous. Still, the pie chart does provide a frame of reference, and if the diagnosis is accurate, the remedy may be more effective. More than once we have observed a teacher give an explanation of linguistic form to a student when consulting the pie chart would have suggested that the student's confusion lay with the area of pragmatics instead.

A FINAL CHALLENGE

As long as we find ourselves back affirming the utility of the pie chart, we should perhaps point out one further way in which it can be employed. The pie chart is useful in helping teachers to assess where there are gaps in their own knowledge of the subject matter. For instance, teachers can ask themselves what are the formal properties of conditionals, the meaning of logical connectors, the pragmatics of relative clauses. Where lacunae exist, teachers can work to educate themselves. Of course, there are many gaps in what is known about the three dimensions. In particular, there is a great deal of investigation necessary before we satisfactorily understand the pragmatic conditions governing the use of particular structures. For this reason, the pie chart can also serve as a means by which items for a common research agenda can be generated.[12]

In any event, teachers should not feel discouraged by the fact that they are unable to fully articulate the contents of the three wedges of the pie for each structure. Teachers can only consciously teach what they know. By continuing to work with the pie chart, over the course of time, teachers will be able to make more observations about the respective wedges. This is the final challenge: for teachers to use the pie chart, the observations about learning, and the characteristics of the practice activities to stimulate their own professional growth, as well as contribute to the development of their students.

NOTES

1. We acknowledge that by equating the teaching of grammar with the teaching of linguistic structures, we have not addressed Rutherford's (1987) objection to "the learning of language as the accumulation of separate entities" position. While his objection is well taken, we would be concerned if teaching grammar becomes solely a matter of teaching *process*. We have learned from our colleagues who have investigated the area of writing of the need for balance between *process* and *product* (Larsen-Freeman, 1990).

2. Some time after we had begun to view grammar in this way, the work of Charles Morris (1939) was brought to our attention. Although he uses the terms in a somewhat different manner, Morris applies the ternary scheme of syntactics, semantics, and pragmatics in portraying the field of semiotics or the study of signs. The ternary scheme we are adopting here may also sound reminiscent of Kenneth Pike's "particle, wave and field" (1959). However, although there is some overlap, there is not an isomorphism between the models.

3. For example, the model of language that descriptive linguists prefer is one in which various areas of language are depicted as strata in a linguistic hierarchy beginning with the sounds of language as the lowest level from which all else is composed and following in turn with morphemes, lexicon, syntax, and discourse.

4. For more exceptions to this rule, consult Celce-Murcia and Larsen-Freeman (1983).

5. Indeed, the teacher might *never* present some of the information. We recognize, and can take advantage of, the fact that our students will learn much without it receiving explicit pedagogical focus.

6. We were introduced to this taxonomy in H. Douglas Brown's (1987) book *Principles of Language Learning and Teaching*. It should be further acknowledged that we have taken certain liberties with Gagne's taxonomy. His taxonomy was intended to reflect a hierarchial view of learning with the types of learning listed high on the hierarchy being subsumed by later types. Since we have done away with this hierarchial treatment of language in our pie chart, we have also treated the types of learning as being associated with different aspects of language in a nonhierarchial manner. Moreover, Gagne's taxonomy is decidedly behavioristic in character, although this orientation has been somewhat modified in the fourth edition of his work, which appeared in 1985. Although we believe behaviorism can account for certain aspects of SLA (e.g., production of a new L2 sound, acquisition of formulaic utterances), it does not, by any means, account for all aspects. The use of Gagne's taxonomy here is simply intended to illustrate the complexity of the learning/acquisition process. If language is as complex as it is, why should we expect the learning process to be less complicated?

7. Such a restriction might seem uncharacteristically autocratic in today's climate, where one of the features of the Communicative Approach is that students be given a choice of how they wish to express themselves. It is our contention, however, that students have a true choice only if they have a variety of linguistic forms at their disposal which they can produce accurately. Without being restricted to using a particular target form during a structure-focused activity, students will often avoid producing the structure and, hence, never have an opportunity to learn it so that it can be included in their repertoire.

8. One form at a time does not mean one form per class period. Teaching one form could take more than one class or it might be possible to introduce several different items in one class. The point is, only one form at a time should be worked on.

9. We recognize that for many second language teachers, the word "repetition" conjures up an image of students' being run through a series of ALM repetition drills. We are certainly not advocating that here, which is why we underscore the word "meaningful." We do believe that repetition is helpful for mastering syntactic patterns given this caveat, and the meaningfulness is necessary to keep students attentive. Without their attention, there is little gain to be made.

10. An OS relative clause is one in which the subject of the embedded sentence is replaced by a relative pronoun because the subject is identical to an object or objectlike noun in the predicate of the main clause.

11. It should be acknowledged that the pie chart, the observations about learning, and the characteristics of practice activities enumerated here may not significantly alter the way grammar is taught today. Indeed, many of the activities recommended here are tried and true. What these tools do offer, however, is principled means for dealing with grammar. They should help teachers to be clear about the reasons they make the decisions they do when teaching grammar.

12. The working hypothesis for such an agenda is that each wedge of the pie chart should contain information pertinent to any given structure.

DISCUSSION QUESTIONS

1. Think of all the language teaching approaches with which you are familiar. Can you categorize them according to whether they favor language analysis or language use?

2. In explaining the pragmatics of phrasal verbs, the principle of dominance was invoked. Explain why the principle of dominance falls in the pragmatic dimension.

3. The effect of the mother tongue on second language learning has traditionally been seen to be one of *interference*. How does observation 3 on the learning process differ in its perception of L1 influence?

4. Can you explain why the major learning processes responsible for the semantic dimension are claimed to be verbal association, multiple discrimination, and concept learning?

5. Why was it stressed that the repetition in a practice activity working on form should be meaningful?

6. Why is it important to identify the challenge in a particular grammar structure for a particular group of students, even if the aspect of structure you are planning to teach lies in a different wedge of the pie from where the challenge lies?

7. What are some differences between the practice and communicative phases of a lesson when teaching a grammar structure?

8. When would a teacher want to present a grammar structure deductively? Inductively?

SUGGESTED ACTIVITIES

1. Think of a language teaching approach which tends to favor language use over language analysis. How could the approach incorporate more language analysis? Now think of an approach that favors language analysis over language use. Assuming that it was desirable to have both approaches worked on in a class, how could more of a balance be achieved?

2. Analyze restrictive relative clauses in terms of the three dimensions of the pie chart. What has been the most challenging dimension for the students with whom you have worked?

3. Think of something you have learned in a foreign language. To what type of learning in Gagne's hierarchy can you attribute the result?

4. Design practice activities for dealing with the pragmatics of the following:

a. falling versus rising intonation in tag questions
b. indirect object alternation
c. infinitives versus gerunds
d. presence or absence of existential *there*
e. restrictive versus nonrestrictive relative clauses

SUGGESTIONS FOR FURTHER READING

Celce-Murcia, M., and S. Hilles (1988)
Techniques and Resources in Teaching Grammar. New York: Oxford University Press.

Discusses issues germane to teaching grammar and provides abundant examples of techniques and materials applied to teaching English structures.

Celce-Murcia, M., and D. Larsen-Freeman (1983)
The Grammar Book: An ESL/EFL Teacher's Course. New York: Newbury House.

Seeks to guide teachers to an understanding of the grammar of those structures they will have to teach (their form, meaning, and use in context) and offers relevant teaching suggestions for those same structures.

McKay, S. (1985)
Teaching Grammar: Form, Function and Technique. New York: Pergamon Press.

A useful compendium of techniques/materials for teaching language forms and functions.

Prahbu, N. S. (1987)
Second Language Pedagogy. New York: Oxford University Press

> Reports on a five-year project in Bangalore, India, in which meaning-focused activity was favored over the practice of particular parts of language structure in order to enhance students' grammatical competence.

Rutherford, W. (1987)
Second Language Grammar: Learning and Teaching. London: Longman.

> An interesting and provocative treatment which challenges the view that learning grammar is an "accumulation of entities."

Rutherford, W., and M. Sharwood Smith, eds. (1988)
Grammar and Second Language Teaching. New York: Newbury House.

> An anthology which deals with both theoretical issues and pedagogic grammars.

Ur, P. (1988)
Grammar Practice Activities: A Practical Guide for Teachers. Cambridge: Cambridge University Press

> A discussion of pedagogical issues followed by a number of grammar teaching activities grouped according to the grammar structure they work best for.

Vocabulary Learning and Teaching

Bernard D. Seal

A HISTORICAL PERSPECTIVE

To the non-language specialist, the common sense view of how languages are learned is that you substitute the words in your first language for the corresponding words in the second language. "Words"[1] are perceived as the building blocks upon which a knowledge of the second language can be built. Armed with this common-sense but naive view, non-specialists would therefore be surprised if they were to survey the history of language teaching. For, far from being regarded as of pivotal importance in language learning, the status of vocabulary in the last 50 years has, on the whole, been relatively low. Indeed, there was a period not so long ago when too much vocabulary learning was regarded as a positively dangerous thing. We are, however, emerging from this period, and there are signs that a new era is upon us in which the place of vocabulary in the language learning process and as an area of research is being restored to respectability and prominence.

In the early decades of this century, in fact, vocabulary teaching and research were eminently respectable. At that time the leading language teaching methodologies were the Grammar Translation Method and the Reading Approach. Both these approaches involved a great deal of direct vocabulary teaching and learning. In the same period, EFL lexicography flourished, and much research was undertaken to establish which words were most useful to be taught at different stages in the learning process. This research culminated in the appearance of Michael West's *A General Service List* in 1936, and Thorndike and Lorge's *The Teacher's Wordbook of 30,000 Words* in

1944, two reference works that for many years played a major role in determining the lexical content of commercial coursebooks and ESL/EFL readers.

Unfortunately, the more or less exclusive focus on grammar, vocabulary, and reading in this pre-World War II era of language teaching frequently produced learners who could read and write a foreign language but were unable to understand or produce natural conversational speech. In part, this explains why, when the Audio Lingual Method (ALM) was being advanced in the late 1940s and early 1950s, it was so readily embraced. ALM was perceived (erroneously, as it turned out) as a methodology that would produce language "users," not just language "learners." However, the emergence of ALM as the dominant teaching methodology had an immediate and devastating effect on further development in vocabulary teaching and research, for it was an established tenet of audiolingualism that vocabulary learning should be kept to a minimum. The argument was that too much vocabulary learning, especially at the early stages, would overtax the learner's learning capacity and get in the way of the main purpose of language teaching, which was to establish through habit formation the basic phonological and grammatical patterns of the language.

By the 1970s, ALM had fallen into disrepute; nevertheless, the notion that vocabulary learning was somehow of secondary importance in second language pedagogy had not passed with it. It was during this period that several voices could be heard challenging the status quo (Celce-Murcia & Rosensweig, 1979; Judd, 1978; Meara, 1981; Richards, 1976). For example, Judd observed disparagingly that "vocabulary has been relegated to secondary status in favor of syntax" and "vocabulary knowledge is not taught as a skill in itself." In the area of second language research, too, Meara (1981) noted the same neglect, "Vocabulary acquisition is part of the psychology of second-language learning that has received short shrift from applied linguists, and has been very largely neglected by recent developments in research."

The 1980s, however, have seen a resurgence of interest and activity in lexical matters. One can point as indirect evidence to several significant publishing events. There has been the publication of several innovative lexical reference works: the Longman Lexicon (McArthur, 1981), which lists items according to their semantic fields; the BBI Combinatory Dictionary (Benson, Benson, & Ilson, 1986), which lists items together with their most frequent collocates; and the Collins COBUILD Dictionary (Sinclair, 1987), which uses as its citation source a computer corpus of 7.3 million running words. A number of handbooks for teachers devoted entirely to the teaching of vocabulary have been published (Allen, 1983; Gairns & Redman, 1986; Morgan & Rinvolucri, 1986; Wallace, 1982). Some theory-based vocabulary textbooks for ESL students have come onto the market (Rudzka, Channell, Ostyn, & Putseys, 1981, 1985; Seal, 1987, 1988).[2] An anthology of vocabulary-based research has been published (Carter & McCarthy, 1988). By contrast with other areas in language learning such a record in publishing may not seem overly impressive; however, in contrast with the amount of attention given to vocabulary over the previous two decades such activity may be considered a veritable flood.

No comprehensive language learning theory has emerged that would account for this renewal of interest in vocabulary. However, three recent developments in the theory and practice of language teaching may explain why a reassessment of the role that vocabulary can play in second language learning has occurred at this time. First, the notion that second language learners develop their own internal grammar in predetermined stages that cannot be disturbed by grammar instruction has led some to propose that the traditional teaching of structure should be de-emphasized. At the same time, there has been a shift toward communicative methodologies that emphasize the use of language rather than the formal study of it. These two forces together have led to a view of language teaching as empowering students to communicate, and clearly, one effective way to increase students' facility in communicating is to increase their vocabularies. Finally, within the domain of teaching English for Academic Purposes (EAP), teachers have become increasingly aware that nonnative students are significantly disadvantaged in their academic studies on account of the small size of their second language vocabularies. Thus, the de-emphasis on grammar, the newly placed emphasis on communication, and the perceived needs of EAP students have had the effect of elevating the importance of vocabulary in recent years.

RESEARCH ISSUES IN VOCABULARY TEACHING AND LEARNING

Descriptive Studies

A number of linguists in recent years have pondered some seemingly basic questions: What is a word? What is an idiom? How is a word best defined? (Lyons, 1977a). Other areas of inquiry involve observing how words are actually used in discourse. In this pursuit, the computer is proving a new and valuable resource (Sinclair, 1966; Sinclair & Renouf, 1988). Another important area of research involves investigating the underlying relations that may be said to exist between words. There are attempts to construct systems that would place individual lexical items within the complex web of the lexicon as a whole (Lehrer, 1974).

The results of such lexical studies have not traditionally trickled down to the practicing language teacher. Whereas teacher-training programs for language teachers often require trainees to study grammar and phonology, study of the lexicon is not usually a significant part of the program. However, as we attribute more importance to the teaching of vocabulary, so it will become necessary for teachers to become better informed as to its structure and organization.

Acquisition Studies

The second set of questions is concerned with the acquisition of second language vocabulary. Are some words more difficult to learn than others, and, if so, what are the properties of those words that make them more difficult? What role does the learner's first language play in facilitating or interfering with successful vocabulary learning? What factors affect the ability of learners to retain words? What are the relative merits of learning words through translation pairs, word lists, dictionary use, word–image associations, contextualization? Indeed, one question is: Should learners be taught vocabulary directly at all or should acquisition take place through exposure alone?

The answers to these questions will eventually prove critical to the methods that teachers apply in the second language classroom. However, at this time, it must be stated that we have no absolute answers to any of the questions. The following sections, then, on vocabulary teaching practices is based on a received body of strong intuitions based on experience and some promising directions provided by research.

TECHNIQUES IN THE TEACHING OF VOCABULARY PART 1: UNPLANNED VOCABULARY TEACHING

This discussion of the teaching of vocabulary is divided into two parts. This first part deals with "unplanned vocabulary teaching" —that is, the extemporaneous teaching of problem vocabulary items that come up without warning in the course of a lesson. The second part deals with "planned vocabulary teaching"—that is, where the teacher goes into the classroom with an item or a set of vocabulary items that s/he has decided beforehand will be taught during the course of the lesson. Comments made about the teaching of unplanned and planned vocabulary teaching are not exclusive. Clearly, what is said about one may well apply to the other.

Nevertheless the distinction is a useful one and should help teachers think about their own vocabulary teaching in the classroom.

However "neglected" vocabulary has been in theory, there is little doubt that a great deal of vocabulary teaching is currently going on, and has always been going on, in the second language classroom. Walk into almost any ESL class and you will doubtless find the board covered with words that have arisen during the lesson. Listen in to the lesson for a while and you will hear the students and teacher discussing the meanings of words. Look on the students' desks and you will see papers filled with new words to be learned. Vocabulary, then, is being taught in the ESL classroom, albeit for the most part unsystematically.

Much of this teaching is unplanned. It may arise because one student has a problem with a word that has come up in the lesson. Alternatively, it may be that in the course of the lesson the teacher suddenly realizes that an important vocabulary item that s/he has just introduced or is about to introduce is unknown to the majority of the students. At such points the teacher has to improvise an explanation and do some unplanned teaching.

Being able to deal with unanticipated vocabulary problems is a key skill in the art of second language teaching, although it is not a topic that has received much attention from teacher educators. Some teachers can think quickly on their feet and are very adept at providing ad hoc explanations. However, others flounder and make an encounter with an unanticipated problem word an interlude of little value to the students in the lesson. There are, however, steps that can be taken to help teachers prepare for such moments.

There are two great dangers in unplanned vocabulary teaching. One is that the teacher may not go far enough in dealing with the new word, and after the teacher's efforts, the students still don't understand the meaning of the word. The other is that the teacher may go too far and get carried away, devoting an excessive amount of time to the word and other related words.

The first decision to be made by the teacher when a word comes up in a lesson is: Should I take time out to deal with this word at all? Naturally a language teacher is reluctant to tell a student who asks about a word, "Forget it. You don't have to worry about this word. It's not that important." Students tend to believe that it is the duty of the teacher to clarify everything that they don't understand. However, it is clear that there are some words that students would be better off ignoring. For example, some words and expressions are too low-frequency, too colloquial, or too specialized for students at certain levels. The best strategy is to reach an understanding with your class so that they accept that it is not necessary for them to understand every word that they encounter with the same degree of depth. Then when such a word arises in the lesson, the teacher can warn the student that it is not important and give either a very perfunctory explanation or possibly none at all.

However, if the teacher believes that the word is worth explaining and learning, then it is important that this is done efficiently, and a set of procedures should be automatically set into operation. Let us call this a 3 C's approach. First, the teacher should *convey meaning*. This is done by drawing from a wide range of possibilities: a mime, a synonym, an anecdote (see next section on planned vocabulary teaching). Second, the teacher *checks* that the student has understood properly. This can be done by a rapid-fire series of questions, often providing the opportunity for a hint of humor. If the students consistently answer these questions correctly, the teacher can judge that they have an understanding of the word. Third, the teacher should *consolidate* and try to get the students to relate the word to their personal experience, preferably using it in a personally meaningful context.

Let us see these three steps in operation in an example. Imagine that a student at a preintermediate level has asked the teacher to explain the word "boring."

Step 1: Convey meaning

Teacher: *(To class) When you go to the movies sometimes the movie is not very interesting, it makes you want to go to sleep. (The teacher puts a hand to his/her mouth and yawns.) The movie is very boring. Or sometimes you have a teacher who speaks very slowly and who never makes you laugh and whose lessons make you go to sleep. The teacher is so boring.*

Step 2: Check understanding

Teacher: *(To student 1) Do you like boring teachers? (To student 2) Is this lesson boring? (To student 3) Is this book boring? (To student 4) Are you a boring person? (To student 5) Am I a boring teacher?*

Step 3: Consolidate

Teacher: *(To class) Turn to the person next to you and ask them if they had a boring weekend. If they say "yes," find out why. (A general hubbub) Now ask the person next to you what shows on television they think are boring. (Murmuring)*

It may seem as though this approach could be too time-consuming. It need not be. Talk through the above example, imagining the students' answers, and time it. You should find that it takes only about two or three minutes.

Many teachers stop at step 1. They think that they have explained the word, but don't check to make sure. In fact, a teacher's impromptu explanation is often confusing and inadequate, and this can only be discovered by direct "check" questions to the students. It is never a good idea to simply ask the class, "Does everyone understand?" since the ensuing silence or sporadic head nods should never be interpreted as assent. With the 3 C's approach, students demonstrate that they understand and can use the word, and you can feel confident that they may retain enough to be able to understand it on a future encounter, and maybe even use it appropriately themselves.

TECHNIQUES IN THE TEACHING OF VOCABULARY PART 2: PLANNED VOCABULARY TEACHING

There are two types of planned vocabulary teaching. The first is similar to unplanned vocabulary teaching in that the words taught are incidental to the objective of the lesson. The teacher has predicted that certain key words are going to cause difficulty for the students and has devised an approach to deal with them in order for the rest of the lesson to proceed smoothly. The second type of planned vocabulary teaching we can describe as "the vocabulary lesson," since the primary objective of the teaching activities is the presentation and practice of the lexical items themselves. It is with this latter type that the rest of this section will deal.

Many language students are concerned that they are not learning enough words. True, they are learning words incidentally in almost every activity that takes place in the second language classroom. However, students still need a time set aside for vocabulary study when words can be presented to them thoroughly and systematically. Students need a sense of measurable growth in their vocabulary knowledge and this is what the vocabulary lesson can achieve.

This does not mean that the vocabulary lesson should occur in isolation. On the contrary, a set of vocabulary items can be taught as the precursor or the follow-up to any number of activities: discussions, situational dialogs, readings, listening tasks.

In teaching vocabulary it is suggested that the items selected for the lesson come from the same lexical domain—e.g., words relating to marriage, words of size and shape, adjectives of happiness and sadness, verbs describing ways of looking. There are several advantages to this. First, by learning items in sets, the learning of one item can reinforce the learning of another. Second, items that are similar in meaning can be differentiated. Third, students may more likely feel a sense of tangible progress in having mastered a circumscribed lexical domain. Finally, follow-up activities can be more easily designed that incorporate the items. Comments below assume that the vocabulary lesson being taught involves the teaching of such a lexical set.

The vocabulary lesson needs to be staged in the same sequence as unplanned vocabulary teaching, except that each stage can be more elaborately developed. In Stage 1 (conveying meaning), the items are presented to the students. In Stage 2 (checking for comprehension), exercises test how far the students have grasped the meaning of the items. In Stage 3 (consolidation), students deepen their understanding of the items through use and creative problem-solving activities.

Stage 1: Conveying Meaning

There are a multitude of ways to present a new lexical item to learners so that they can grasp its meaning. The number is limited only by the creativity of the teacher. The following list is therefore not intended to be all inclusive. Neither are the various suggested modes of presentation meant to be used in isolation. It is quite clear that often a combination of several different presentation modes will be most effective.

Visual Aids. ESL professionals frequently have their own personal stock of pictures, everyday objects, models, and plastic replicas which are ideal for teaching the names of concrete objects at the lower levels. However, a stock of high-quality, impactful, situational pictures cut from magazines, brochures, and catalogs may also be useful in presenting more abstract, conceptual, and complex vocabulary at higher levels.

Frustrated artists and actors will find a release for their talents while teaching vocabulary. A quick mime can easily convey an action or a concept, as can a drawing or a five-second sketch on the board. One needs no special talent for drawing; in fact, it may be a handicap, since a good artist may be tempted to be too meticulous. Clumsy efforts will amuse the class and will probably be as effective as a well-drawn picture. The trick is to use only a couple of strokes and avoid time-consuming elaborate drawing.

Word Relations. A common way for a teacher to elucidate the meaning of a target word is to relate it to another word that the students already know. The two most common types of word relation are synonymy (a word similar in meaning) and antonymy (a word opposite in meaning). Another useful word relation is that of the lexical set. One can facilitate the identification of an item by showing to what superordinate class of items it belongs; for example, a "rose" belongs to the class of items "flowers." Additionally, one can place the item against other items that are in the same set; for example, "gray" belongs with "black," "blue," "green," since it is also a color. The main caution about using word relations is, of course, that any words used to explain the meaning of the target word should not be more difficult than the target word itself.

Pictorial Schemata. Explaining the relations that exist between words can be greatly enhanced by the use of some form of visual display or diagram. Lindstromberg (1985) calls such instruments "pictorial schemata," which may include Venn diagrams, grids, tree diagrams, or stepped scales. Such diagrams that show the relations between a number of words can be simply created. Students can be taught the basic schemata, and thus when new words are presented within the schematic frame they can be readily interpreted. A good example is adjective intensification. Once students have been taught the significance of the simple step diagram, items that have the same relationship can be taught.

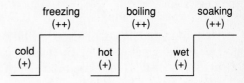

Definition, Explanation, Examples, and Anecdotes. In some sense the ESL teacher can be considered a walking dictionary. The teacher's definition may not be as precise as that of the dictionary, but the teacher has the advantage of being able to give multiple examples of usage and of being able to discuss the target word at length. Some words that are difficult to define can be brought to life by relating a short story or by having the students imagine a set of circumstances from which it becomes possible to deduce the meaning of the item. For example, if the teacher is explaining the item "a guided tour," s/he may ask the class to imagine a museum or an art gallery in which there is a group of people listening to a man explaining a picture. The man goes from this picture to the next picture and the people follow him. The teacher explains that the man is called a guide and the group is on a guided tour. If this is not clear, the teacher can illustrate with another example, perhaps of a guided tour of a city.

Context. A challenging way to present a new item is by embedding the word in a sentence or couple of sentences in such a way that it may be possible for the students to guess the meaning of the item. For example, if the target word is "beg," the teacher may say, "The little boy begged the man to follow him. He pulled on his arm and said, 'Please, please, please come with me.' " This is a good technique for helping students to use context to guess meanings; however, there is the danger that your example may be followed by confused silence when students fail to understand the item either because the context chosen by the teacher is unclear to the students or because the student has a listening problem. It is probably advisable to use this technique with sentences that the students can read, thus having adequate time to process them.

Word Roots and Affixes. Some teachers claim to have great success by teaching students some of the more common Greek and Latin roots to be found in English. When

these are combined with a knowledge of the most common prefixes and suffixes it may be possible to work out the meanings of a large number of derived words. For example, having been taught the meaning of the prefix "contra" (against), the stem "dict" (say/speak), and the suffix "-tion" (the state/act of), students might be able to work out in context that the word "contradiction" has something to do with speaking against, disagreeing, or not being consistent in meaning.

Stage 2: Exercises That Check Understanding

Fill in the Blank. A traditional and effective way of checking students' vocabulary comprehension is to have them fill in the blanks in a passage with an appropriate word. It encourages students to consider the context of the sentence to work out the probable missing word. At the same time, students are being exposed to the typical linguistic environment for an item. They perceive other words that can co-occur with the target word and the grammatical context in which the item can occur.

The most common type of fill-in-the-blank exercise is the forced-choice exercise, where the student is given the words to fit into the passage or sentences and has to find the appropriate gaps for each. The blanked-out word need not always be the newly presented word. For example, in the sentence "I'm so thirsty. I need a drink," one could blank out either "drink" or "thirsty" to test the student's understanding of the word "thirsty."

Matching Pair. Most exercise types, in fact, involve some sort of matching. The matching-pair exercise is the easiest to set up for checking vocabulary comprehension. In one place are listed the target words; in the other can be a set of synonyms, antonyms, definitions, or pictures. More creative matching can be done by matching the items to some associational characteristics. For example, if the target words are ways of walking, the matching items could be people who might walk in that way (stagger—a drunk; stroll—an elderly couple in the park; march—a soldier).

Sorting Exercises. In this exercise type, the teacher gives the students a large group of words and asks them to sort the words into different categories according to different characteristics. For example, a group of animal words can be sorted into mammals, fish, or reptiles. Or foods can be sorted into vegetables, meats, and fruit. More creative sorting can be done by selecting less predictable shared characteristics; for example, articles of clothing can be sorted into clothes worn above the waist and clothes worn below the waist.

A variation on the sorting exercise is the game Odd Man Out. This exercise is very easy to construct. The teacher gives the students four words, one of which does not belong, and has the students work out which represents the odd man.

Pictorial Schemata. Students can complete grids that have the target items along one axis and characteristics along another. Students then check off whether a characteristic belongs to a particular item. An example

of this exercise type, from Seal (1988), is given in Figure 1.

As previously stated, pictorial schemata can be used to present items and the relations that exist between them. This technique may also be adapted for checking that students have understood newly presented lexical items. Students who have been presented with the weather words below and who understand the meaning of the step diagram should be able to complete it.

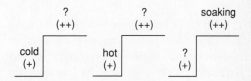

Stage 3: Consolidation

Problem-Solving Tasks. Problem solving must perforce remain a rather vague category, for the type of activity that the teacher designs will be determined by the lexical items that are in the set. There are numerous types of problem-solving activities. The best should be challenging and fun and should involve the pooling of students' ideas in order to complete the task. In designing them for

Exercise 3

Complete this chart by putting a cross (X) next to the characteristics of each type of music.

	pop	punk	folk	reggae	jazz	classical
1 often played by a big orchestra in a concert hall						
2 often played by young people with guitars in a group						
3 often played by young people with brightly colored hair						
4 often simple tunes which are popular for a short time						
5 music coming originally from black American musicians						
6 music of a specific region, popular for a very long time						
7 music with a strong regular rhythm, originally from Jamaica						
8 music which is popular for dancing in discos						
9 often played freely, not following written music						

FIGURE 1. *Pictorial schemata exercise.*

vocabulary use, the trick is to design activities that repeatedly require the students to use the items when they are trying to solve the problem. One example may serve as an illustration. The target vocabulary is different types of television programs: news, documentaries, game shows. Students are asked to design a weekend's television schedule for a TV station, which must involve each type. They write out a schedule of programs and have to justify why certain programs are scheduled at certain times.

Values Clarification. Many values-clarification exercises make excellent vocabulary-consolidation exercises. Take, for example, a ranking activity where the students are asked to put into an order the qualities that they consider most to least important for the ideal spouse. In the exercise are included such words as "tidy," "faithful," and "sociable." The students create their orders, defend them, and reach consensus in a group. Such an activity cannot be done unless the students have a thorough understanding of the items that are being ranked. Another typical values-clarification activity has students assign punishments to certain crimes. Students work with two set of items: the punishments (go to prison, go on probation, pay a fine) and the crimes (steal a car, rob a bank, drunk driving). As the students do the exercise in their groups, they continuously have to use the items as they decide on the most appropriate punishment.

Write a Story or a Dialog. The teacher gives the students a number of words (10 to 15 is usually an appropriate number) and tells them to write a story or compose a dialog in which the words occur. For more advanced students, this can be made more challenging and more fun, too, if the students are also told to use the words in the order that they have been written on the board.

Discussion and Role-Play. Some sets of items lend themselves to discussion work. Students are given a set of questions and

asked to share their opinions, their experience, or their knowledge. The questions may contain the target words or be designed to elicit them in discussion. For example, if the vocabulary set contains different symptoms of illness (e.g., cough, sore throat, headache, insomnia), the students are asked to exchange opinions on what they consider to be effective treatments for each.

Role-plays can also be designed so that a given set of items will predictably have to be used by the role-play participants. For example, the set of items above (symptoms of illness) could be activated by a visit-to-the-doctor role-play. Vocabulary relating to the law (e.g., crimes and punishments) could be activated by a role-play trial scene.

The emphasis in this section has been on the presentation of "new" lexical items to the learner. However, vocabulary teaching involves more than the presentation of new items. Students also need to review and practice words with which they are already familiar. As Richards (1976) points out, there is great deal involved in being able to say that one "knows" a word. One's knowledge of a word may be hazy, and well-designed vocabulary activities are needed to clear some of the fog that exists around one's knowledge of an item. In fact, many textbooks that claim to "teach" vocabulary actually contain exercises that can only be done if the students already know the items presented. Such activities are, of course, worthwhile provided teachers are aware that they are suitable for reinforcing student's knowledge of an item, rather than for initial presentation.

VOCABULARY AND READING

The most traditional vehicle for vocabulary study is a text—in particular, a reading passage. The main reason for reading the text may not be to study the vocabulary in it, but at some point the teacher will inevitably have to deal with lexical problems. One commonplace practice is for the teacher to prepare students for reading by selecting a number of "difficult" or key items and preteaching them. Sometimes these words have been selected by the textbook writer and appear listed or glossed at the head of the reading. This practice of preteaching vocabulary makes intuitive sense, but may in fact be unsound.

Several pieces of research strongly suggest that preteaching vocabulary may have a negative effect on reading comprehension. Hudson (1982), for example, found that, except for beginning-level students, preteaching of vocabulary was less effective at promoting reading comprehension than no prereading activity at all. Taglieber, Johnson, and Yarborough (1988) report similar findings.

At first sight this seems to run counter to common sense, although some reading theorists would predict that this should happen. Providing glosses and preteaching vocabulary "may encourage word-by-word reading and consequently prevent the ESL reader from the development of the skill of processing syntax and context in sampling and confirming meaning" (P. Johnson, 1982).

Rather than preteach vocabulary, research seems to suggest that a more effective approach is to provide prereading activities that build the student's general background knowledge of the topic of the text (Carrell & Eisterhold, 1983). Following these activities, the students should be allowed to read the text and confront the difficult vocabulary in context, searching for clues, using guessing strategies, and thereby working out meaning for themselves. It is argued that such a process aids retention, since "any meanings the pupils work out for themselves will be better remembered than any one they are given" (Madden, 1980).

Once students have been given an opportunity to tackle the text on their own, then it is appropriate to have postreading vocabulary activities. The students' guesses can be confirmed or disconfirmed, and activities that check and consolidate meaning can be done, as described in the section above on planned vocabulary teaching.

Besides intensive study of shorter texts, language students may also need to read extensively. Literate native speakers build up massive vocabularies, mostly through reading, with little or no conscious effort. Therefore, Twaddell (1973) and, more recently, Krashen (1986) both argue that nonnative speakers will also most efficiently increase their vocabulary through reading programs, rather than through direct vocabulary teaching.

Both Twaddell and Krashen advocate approaches that involve massive amounts of reading. Twaddell suggests that at the intermediate level and above, learners read 50 or so pages in an hour with the task of having to understand five simple questions after such reading. Such a task, he believes, would encourage learners to skim text and to tolerate a large degree of imprecise understanding without getting frustrated. Krashen would have students "get hooked on books" and be guided toward "a massive program of pleasure reading."

The notion that second language learners can effortlessly acquire large amounts of vocabulary in context is intuitively attractive. It is, however, largely untested. One study by Ferris, Kiyochi, and Kowal (1988) does provide some empirical evidence. They tested students' knowledge of 50 of the "difficult" vocabulary items occurring in the novel *Animal Farm* (Orwell, 1946) eight weeks before and two weeks after reading the novel. The students read the novel as homework, and discussion in class focused only on the themes of the novel and not on vocabulary difficulties. A control group did not read the novel and also took both tests. Vocabulary gains by the experimental group in the posttest were significantly greater than those made by the control group.

One factor that appears to affect the ease with which a learner can acquire words in context is the proportion of known to unknown words in a text. Liu and Nation (1985) investigated the effect of unknown-to-known word density on the learner's ability to guess the meaning of an unknown word. Their research suggests that the higher the percentage of known words in a text, the easier it is for the learner to interpret the unknown words. This finding is corroborated in a way by Ferris and Kowal, who found in their *Animal Farm* experiment that learners who started with the highest scores on the pretest had the greatest gains in the posttest.

Another factor affecting the learner's ability to use context to guess the meaning of an unknown item is learner training. A study by Clarke and Nation (1980) demonstrated that learners can improve their guessing skills by being trained to search for context clues within a text.

Students may, then, be able to greatly increase their vocabularies by reading extensively at an appropriate level of difficulty, after having been trained in effective guessing strategies. Thus, it would seem ESL programs and teachers should make efforts to have appropriate books available for their students to read (see Brown, 1986, for examples). Language schools and institutions could set up lending libraries containing a wide variety of simplified and unsimplified readers. Students could then be encouraged to check out and read outside class at least one book a week.

In conclusion, our current state of knowledge would suggest that reading in a second language is an excellent way to increase a second language learner's vocabulary. Learners should be trained in using appropriate guessing strategies when encountering difficult words, direct vocabulary teaching should occur after the student has grappled with the text, and the "reading habit" should be encouraged by motivating students to do a large amount of outside-class pleasure reading at an appropriate level of difficulty.

COLLOCATION

So far in this discussion of vocabulary teaching and learning, the notion of what constitutes vocabulary knowledge has not been examined. There is a commonplace assumption that the more words a learner knows, the larger is the learner's vocabulary knowledge. However, there is another dimension to vocabulary knowledge that should be considered—namely, how far a learner knows the combinatory possibilities of a word. For any given word, a native speaker also knows a range of other words which can cooccur or collocate with it. This is an aspect of vocabulary knowledge that has until very recently been largely ignored.

The term that is most commonly used to describe the cooccurrence of lexical items is "collocation."[3] Words can collocate with different degrees of frequency and acceptability. Where two words frequently collocate one may speak of high-frequency or habitual collocation. For example, a high-frequency verb collocate of "story" would be "tell," as in "tell a story." When two words cannot cooccur, one speaks of unacceptable collocation. For example, whereas it is possible to talk of "strong tea," one cannot speak of "powerful tea." "Strong" is an acceptable collocate of "tea," but "powerful" is not.

Benson (1985) points out two types of collocation. The first is grammatical collocation; that is where a lexical item frequently cooccurs with a grammatical item. In many cases the grammatical item is a preposition—for example, reason + for; worried + about; believe + in. Lexical collocation, on the other hand, involves the combination of two full lexical items.

The three main categories of lexical collocation are (1) noun (as subject) + verb, (2) verb + noun (as object), (3) adjective + noun. Thus, if we were to examine the collocates of the lexical item "noise," we would ask ourselves: What verbs tend to collocate with "noise" when it is in subject position? What verbs tend to collocate with "noise" when it is in object position? and What adjectives collocate with noise? If we then were to compare how a native speaker might answer those questions with how a nonnative speaker might answer them, we might possibly find the following differences.

	NS	NNS
1. Verb collocate (noun as subj.)	DIMINISH INCREASE	SOFTEN GET BIGGER
2. Verb collocate (noun as obj.)	MAKE	CAUSE/HAVE
3. Adjective collocate	LOUD SOFT	BIG/STRONG SMALL/QUIET

As we see from the above, and as ESL instructors and researchers know from experience, the way items combine can represent a major source of difficulty for nonnative speakers.

Part of what a second language learner needs to know, then, in order to combine individual lexical items is whether they collocate and with what degree of frequency. Such knowledge would clearly facilitate the learner's ability to encode language, since when selecting items to cooccur with other items, the learner would be aware of the restricted range of possibilities. Moreover, even in decoding language, knowledge of collocation would be useful, since it is easier to decode a message when we are able to anticipate part of the message.

How can this knowledge be imparted to the learner? Brown (1980) and Seal (1981) believe that collocational information should be presented to learners. Brown states, "When learning a new word a student needs to learn at the same time the common collocates." She acknowledges that textbooks persist in presenting word lists of single items, but argues that the teacher can always find ways to improve a textbook. In this case, the teacher can simply have the students add the frequent collocates to the list. Thus, given the item "bitter" on a word list, students can be told to add "taste" or "experience" depending on the way the word is used in the text that follows.

A more discovery-based methodology is suggested by McKay (1980). She has students analyze a number of authentic sentences, each of which contain the target lexical item. From these, students are led to discover what the different collocates are for the item. McKay's methodology ideally requires a computer-based corpus of several million running words from which the target items in their sentence contexts can be called up. The computer is particularly well suited for working on collocation, and conceivably McKay's methodology could be adapted for use with much smaller texts and still give students insight into how items collocate.

Sinclair (1988) reports that in an innovative course series (Willis & Willis, 1990), the data that McKay would have students discover is in fact displayed. For each lexical item the percentage of co-occurences (taken from the COBUILD computer-based corpus) with other items is presented in tabular fashion so that students can see which are the most frequent collocates.

A number of collocation exercise types are suggested in Brown (1974). These are mostly matching exercises and are particularly suitable for reviewing a student's knowledge of collocation rather than for initially teaching the collocations. For example, from two lists, one of adjectives and one of nouns, students are asked to decide which items could come together to form the most likely collocations. A large number of exercises which operate on the same principle can also be found in Rudzka et al. (1981, 1985).

In this section we have seen that there is more to learning vocabulary than simply learning individual lexical items. Learners must also learn the collocational range of an item and its high-frequency collocations. Some ways that this might be achieved have been suggested. Clearly, however, this area has not received much attention from second language professionals, and more needs to be done to promote this important area of second language learning.

A NOTE ON DICTIONARIES

There are three broad categories of dictionary available for the second language learner. First, there is the bilingual dictionary (BD), sometimes referred to as a translation dictionary, which contains words in the target language translated into the learner's first language and vice versa. Second, there is the learner's monolingual dictionary (LMD). This is a dictionary that is written only in the second language and has been designed for all learners of the second language, regardless of their first language. It contains a number of features specifically for the second language learner, including a simplified defining vocabulary. Third, there is the standard monolingual dictionary (SMD), which has been written with native speakers in mind.

A few years ago the conventional wisdom about dictionaries for second language learners was that, despite the student's preference to have and use a BD (see Baxter, 1980), students should be discouraged from using BDs and encouraged to use only a good LMD. Students were generally upbraided for looking for equivalents in their first language to second language words. However, according to Rossner (1985), there has been a pendulum swing in recent years, and a much more permissive attitude toward first language use may be discovered in many second language classrooms. Rossner, while recognizing the dangers of BDs, regards the BD as particularly useful to both the very basic learner and the very advanced learner, especially in first encounters with a word. As Rossner says, "the whole point of the dictionary is that very often it can do little more than provide a clue, a starting point. . . ." Even Underhill (1985), who enumerates seven advantages of having students work with an LMD, recognizes that there is a role for the BD. Underhill suggests that as students become more proficient in a language they should progress from using a BD alone to using an LMD alone. The stages of this progression he appropriately calls "a weaning process"

and is as follows: (1) BD, (2) BD + LMD, (3) LMD + BD, (4) LMD.

Many writers on second language dictionary use warn against taking for granted the student's ability to use the dictionary efficiently (Celce-Murcia & Rosensweig, 1979; Rossner, 1985; Scholfield, 1982; Underhill, 1985). They call for the promotion of activities that give students insight into how the dictionary should be used and for having students practice the art of using a dictionary. Whitcut (1979) and Underhill (1980) have written books for students to practice using the *Longman Dictionary of Contemporary English* (Procter, 1978 edition, 1987 edition) and the *Oxford Advanced Learner's Dictionary of Current English* (Hornby, 1974 edition, 1980 edition), respectively. Some study skill textbooks (e.g., Yorkey, 1982) contain exercises that can be used with any SMD or LMD. However, as Underhill (1985) points out, not only do teachers need to have their students learn how to use the dictionary but "teachers should keep an eye open for ways of integrating the dictionary with classwork."

THE RECORDING OF WORDS

Teaching activities, dictionary activities, and extensive reading, which are all aimed at teaching new words, or at increasing a student's knowledge of familiar words, may be ineffective if the student makes no effort to retain the words. Learners, therefore, need to be trained to record words and be presented with strategies for reviewing them.

Anyone who has ever taught a foreign language knows that students usually do one of two things with a new word. Either they make no attempt to record it, or they write the word down on a scrap of paper or in a notebook. Sometimes the word is accompanied by a translation; occasionally there is a definition in the second language. That these words are ever referred to again is doubtful.

Yorkey (1982) recommends as ideal that learners should enter new words onto index cards, with the word's part of speech, the sentence in which the word was first encountered, its pronunciation, its definition, and similar elements. Such an elaborate and time-consuming activity may be unrealistic. Yorkey's second and alternative suggestion actually seems more realistic. He would have students enter the words in special vocabulary notebooks that are organized either alphabetically or, better still, thematically.

A somewhat less elaborate method, using 3 × 5 cards is suggested by Brown (1980). She recommends that lower-level learners put the new word on one side, together with a phrase in which it occurs, and a translation on the back of the card. More advanced learners can put a definition in English on the back. She suggests learners make up packs of 30 cards that can be carried around for perusal at any odd moment. Nation (1980) advocates the same method, arguing that this has an advantage over notebooks in that the cards can be shuffled so that the order of words in the list is not being used to help remember them, and more difficult words can be brought to the top of the pile.

Cohen and Aphek (1980) claim to have had some success with what is known as the keyword technique. In this, students are trained to associate words imagistically. Students are asked to think of a word in their first language that sounds similar to the second language word. The two words are then pictured in some way together. Thus, in trying to recall the second language word the student recalls the image, and thereby the sound of the target word. An example from Nation (1982) may serve as an illustration:

. . . if a learner wants to master the Indonesian word *pintu,* which means *door,* he would think of an English word (the keyword) which sounds like pintu, or a part of *pintu* for example, *pin.* Then he would form a mental image of a pin and a door interacting with each other. pp. 25–26

Students' word-recording strategies is an area that has received very little attention. This could, however, prove to be a worthwhile area of research. We need to know what learners actually do, which strategies are more or less effective, and whether different strategies may be effective for learners with different learning styles. Until such research has been done, however, we should still encourage our students to adopt some sort of system for recording and reviewing vocabulary, at the very least familiarizing them with some of the strategies listed above.

CONCLUSIONS

For years learners have been telling us that they need to increase their vocabularies. For years this has not been a priority in most curricula. Now, after a period of relative neglect, language teachers and researchers are waking up to the realization that vocabulary is an important area worthy of effort and investigation. We are still in need of empirical studies that can shed light on how the second language learner's lexicon is organized and what the most effective means are to enlarge and solidify that lexicon. The most promising directions at the moment seem to be using intensive and extensive reading programs as a means of exposing learners to large amounts of vocabulary in context. Time should also be set aside for vocabulary study, showing lexical items within their semantic fields, illustrating the sense relations between items, using pictorial schemata, and creative problem-solving exercises to deepen an awareness of how the lexical items operate and fixing the items within the second language learners' lexicon. Students also need to be made aware of how items combine with other items in collocations. Finally, in increasing their vocabularies, students also need to be trained to become independent learners, by becoming both effective dictionary users and effective word recorders.

NOTES

1. In this chapter, no attempt has been made to differentiate the following: "words," "lexical items," and vocabulary." For the sake of convenience, these items are used more or less interchangeably, although the author recognizes that significant technical differences can be identified. For a full discussion see Carter (1987).

2. Several other vocabulary textbooks have come out in the last 10 years; however, the majority of these essentially "test" students' knowledge of the vocabulary that they may or may not have acquired rather than presenting new vocabulary in a systematic and theoretically grounded manner.

3. The term "collocation" is not used in the same way by all writers. Seal (1981) contains a thorough discussion of the different ways in which this term has been variously applied.

DISCUSSION QUESTIONS

1. How has the relative importance of vocabulary learning fluctuated in the last 90 years and why?

2. One area of vocabulary acquisition research is to discover what makes some words more difficult to learn than others. What do you think might be some of the variables involved?

3. When, if ever, do you think a teacher might be justified in not pausing to explain a word to a student who has asked for an explanation in class?

4. What advantages can you see in teaching a group of related vocabulary items in a vocabulary lesson (a lexical set or topic-related vocabulary) as opposed to a group of unrelated items? What disadvantages might there be also?

5. What factors might affect a student's ability to guess vocabulary from context? What sort of training activities would you have students do to improve their ability to guess vocabulary from context?

6. What problems can you see if a learner relies heavily on a bilingual dictionary? What advantages do you see in learners using a good learner's monolingual dictionary?

7. Explain the notion of collocation. How could students be sensitized to the collocational range an item has?

8. What role, if any, do you see for the learner's mother tongue in the learning of second language vocabulary?

9. What are some recommendations you would

make to students who ask you how they might improve their vocabulary?

SUGGESTED ACTIVITIES

1. A student in your low-intermediate-level class interrupts you in the middle of the lesson and asks you to explain the following words. For each word explain what you would do.

a. turkey   d. exaggerate   g. cure (v)
b. opaque   e. expert   h. ambitious
c. fastidious f. status quo   i. shabby

2. Read four essays written by four students from different first language backgrounds. What was the proportion of lexical to grammatical errors? Hypothesize as to the source of the lexical errors.

3. You have decided that it is important for your advanced level class to study the following lexical sets:

• ways of looking (gaze, glance)
• types of building (house, castle)
• bodies of water (lake, river)
• adjectives denoting largeness (huge, vast)
• adjectives denoting price (cheap, expensive)
• kinship terms (brother, sister)

a. Which items in the sets would you choose to teach? How would you present them? What checking exercises would you create?

b. Create a problem-solving activity, a role-play, or a discussion question which you think might get the students to produce the items in these sets.

4. Select two reading texts at two different levels of difficulty, each of about 500 words in length. Anticipate which lexical items might give students problems, and describe in detail how you would treat the teaching of the vocabulary in these texts.

5. Which collocations would you select for your intermediate-level students to be aware of for the following items?

a. opportunity   d. ride   g. priceless
b. experiment   e. reduce   h. narrow
c. train (n)   f. deny   i. hostile

6. Select a few words and compare the treatment of these words in a good learner's monolingual dictionary to a good standard monolingual dictionary. If you know another language, look at the treatment of these same words in a bilingual dictionary and consider how a learner might be misled or confused.

SUGGESTIONS FOR FURTHER READING

Carter, R. (1987)
Vocabulary. London: Allen and Unwin.

Provides an excellent overview of the different ways linguists have described the structure of the lexicon. Written from the perspective of an applied linguist, also contains a useful chapter on learning and teaching vocabulary.

Carter, R., and M. McCarthy, eds. (1988)
Vocabulary and Language Teaching. London: Longman.

A collection of essays that cover every aspect of issues surrounding the teaching and learning of vocabulary: historical background, memorization strategies, reading, dictionary use, collocation.

Gairns, R., and S. Redman (1986)
Working with Words. Cambridge: Cambridge University Press.

The later chapters present a wide variety of classroom activities that may be done to promote the learning of vocabulary. The activities are based on principles of vocabulary teaching and learning that are presented in the earlier chapters of the book.

Nation, I. S. P. (1990)
Teaching and Learning Vocabulary. New York: Newbury House.

One author provides a unified, research-based account of vocabulary teaching and learning, with applications to listening, speaking, reading, and writing skills. There is coverage of related issues such as acquisition, course design, translation, and word lists.

III
Integrated Approaches

This section represents a major innovation in this second edition. In the past decade we have seen a movement away from narrow methods to broader integrated approaches in language teaching, approaches that encourage the teaching of all four skills within the general framework of using language for learning as well as for communication. The first such approach is content-based language teaching, which is treated in Snow's chapter. This approach holds that a language is best learned when it is used as a means to accomplish some other purpose; Snow suggests when and how such an approach can be implemented. Stern's chapter offers us a new slant on literature, i.e., using well-selected pieces of literature in the target language as content for language learning and language practice. In this approach, the literature is not only read for comprehension and appreciation but is also used in a variety of related activities that promote language development. Finally, Eyring's chapter on using the learner's experience as a basis for language learning shows the reader how both the experiences the learner already has and the experiences the language class initiates can offer the learner a basis for meaningful language practice and language development. All three of these approaches promote all four language skills as well as language development in grammar and vocabulary— and potentially even pronunciation. They indicate both the cutting edge and future directions in the profession.

313

Teaching Language Through Content

Marguerite Ann Snow

Throughout the history of second language teaching, the word "content" has had many different interpretations. Historically, in methods such as grammar-translation, content was defined as the grammatical structures of the target language. In the audiolingual method, content consisted of grammatical structures, vocabulary, or sound patterns presented in dialog form. More recently, communicative approaches to the teaching of second languages define content in an altogether different way. Generally, content in these approaches is defined as the communicative purposes for which speakers use the second language. Thus, in a class following a notional/functional orientation, the content of a unit might be invitations, and individual lessons might cover question types, polite versus informal invitation forms, and ways to accept or decline invitations. Similarly, the content of a Natural Approach lesson might be a game in which students must locate the person who matches a certain description by asking each other questions, thereby using language for problem solving.

More recently, another definition of content has emerged in an approach which is the focus of this chapter. Content, in this interpretation, is the use of subject matter for second language teaching purposes. Subject matter may consist of topics or themes selected for student interest or need, or it may be very specific, such as the content course material which students are currently studying. This approach is in keeping with the English for Specific Purposes (ESP) tradition, discussed in the chapter by Johns in this volume, where the vocational or occupational needs of the learner are identified and used as the basis for curriculum and materials development. Content-based second language instruction generally has a strong English for Academic Purposes (EAP) orientation. The main instructional goal is to prepare second language students for the types of academic tasks they will encounter in school, college, or university.

This chapter begins with a rationale for content-based instruction followed by a description of several different types of content-based models. In the following sections, sample activities and instructional techniques for integrating language and content are presented. The chapter concludes with a discussion of key issues which must be considered in content-based instruction.

CONTENT-BASED INSTRUCTION: A RATIONALE

Content-based instruction fulfills a number of the conditions which have been posited as necessary for successful second language acquisition. According to Krashen, second language acquisition occurs when the learner receives comprehensible input, not when the learner is memorizing vocabulary or completing grammar exercises. He reasons, therefore, that methods which provide students with more comprehensible input will be more successful. Krashen (1984) states that "comprehensible subject-matter teaching *is* language teaching" (p. 62) since we acquire language when we understand messages in that language. In content-based instruction, the focus is on the subject matter and not on the form or, as Krashen says, on "*what* is being said rather than *how*" (p. 62).

Content-based instruction also provides students with opportunities for meaningful use of the academic language needed for current or future study. Swain (1985) suggests that in order to develop communicative competence, learners must have extended opportunities to use the second language productively. Thus, in addition to receiving comprehensible input, they must produce comprehensible output. She maintains that learners need to be "pushed toward the delivery of a message that is . . . conveyed precisely, coherently, and appropriately" (p. 249). Content-based instruction can provide this push since students learn to produce language which is appropriate from the point of view of both content and language.

Further theoretical support for content-based instruction is provided by Cummins (1980b, 1981b). He notes that child second language learners master social-interpersonal language quite quickly and easily because it generally occurs in a situation that is cognitively undemanding and context-embedded —i.e., there are multiple cues to meaning through gestures, shared background knowledge, or real objects. Second language learners, however, often have great difficulty with academic language (both written and oral), which tends to be cognitively demanding and context-reduced. Content-based instruction recognizes the inherent difficulty of academic language learning and provides learners access to and practice with the types of cognitively demanding, decontextualized language tasks that academic learning entails.

Snow, Met, and Genesee (1989) provide a framework for the integration of content and language teaching which assumes that second language learners must be exposed to academic learning through systematic, planned instruction. In their model, language and content teachers work collaboratively to define two types of language teaching objectives. These objectives derive from consideration of the content curriculum, the second/foreign language curriculum, and needs assessment and ongoing evaluation of student progress. The first type of objective is content-obligatory language. Content-obligatory language is the language (e.g., vocabulary, functions, structures) which is required for students to master concepts or material in any given content class. Without content-obligatory language, students will not be able to handle the demands of academic tasks which are cognitively demanding and context-reduced. The second objective is content-compatible language. This includes specification of the types of language which pair naturally with content material. Content-compatible language instruction allows teachers to provide students with extended practice with a troublesome grammar point, such as irregular past-tense forms, for example, through contextualized academic tasks.

Content-based instruction offers a viable approach to meeting the academic needs of second language learners. It satisfies several important conditions for second language acquisition and provides teachers with the means to create an instructional environment that prepares second language students for the academic tasks they will encounter in school. It also provides a necessary reorientation to teachers, both language and content teachers. Mohan (1986) reminds us of this important point: "In subject matter learning we overlook the role of language as a medium of learning. In language learning we overlook the fact that content is being communicated" (p. 1).

MODELS OF CONTENT-BASED INSTRUCTION

Content-based models can be found in both the foreign and second language settings. In this section, five models are described. The first two examples illustrate models designed to teach foreign languages to English-speaking children at the elementary school level. They are included here since they provide well-developed examples of integrating language and content teaching at the elementary school level. The last three models have been implemented in the secondary and postsecondary second language settings. Each of the models described differs somewhat in implementation due to such factors as educational setting, program objectives, and target population. All share, however, a common point of departure—the integration of language teaching aims with subject matter instruction.

Immersion Education

The immersion model of foreign language education is perhaps the prototype content-based approach. First established in 1965 in a suburb of Montreal, Canada, immersion programs can now be found across Canada and the United States, providing education in such diverse foreign languages as French, Spanish, German, Chinese, and Japanese. In the total immersion model, English-speaking elementary school students receive the majority of their schooling through the medium of their second language. Immersion

students, for instance, in Culver City, California, learn to read, do mathematics problems, and conduct science experiments all in Spanish; in fact, they go about the business of school like all other children, albeit in their second language. The immersion model is one of the most carefully researched second language programs. Consistently, immersion children perform at or above grade level scholastically, they are on par with the monolingual peers in English language development, and by the end of the sixth grade, they become functional bilinguals.

Content Enriched Foreign Language in the Elementary School

During the 1950s and 1960s, Foreign Language in the Elementary School (FLES) programs were widespread across the United States. In this model, "traveling" language teachers met with elementary school children for approximately 20 to 30 minutes, several times per week, for instruction in the foreign language. These classes tended to focus on formal study of the foreign language and were often criticized for their failure to produce functional users of the foreign language. More recently, there has been growing interest in a new approach to the traditional FLES curriculum. "Content-enriched" FLES curricula are being developed which select subjects from the standard school curriculum for introduction or reinforcement in the FLES class (Curtain & Martinez, 1989). In this content-based approach to the teaching of FLES, foreign language teachers find points of coincidence, or content-compatible language, from the standard school curriculum which pair with the objectives of the foreign language curriculum. So, for example, terms and structures for describing weather are not presented in isolation but rather are coordinated with a science unit on meteorology. There are a number of advantages that the "content-enriched" approach has over traditional FLES. First, FLES students have a more relevant, meaningful context for language learning. They use the foreign language to talk about the content of the unit—the "what" in Krashen's terms, not the "how" of language, such as verb conjugations, which was typical of the former version of FLES. Second, since students have already been exposed to the content under study in English, there is a richer context for use of the foreign language for meaningful communication (which is especially important given the limited exposure to the foreign language in the FLES class period). The foreign language class thus takes on the new role of providing reinforcement of content. Finally, the foreign language teacher does not have to search for material for the language class because the school curriculum provides a wealth of ideas which can be incorporated into FLES instruction.

There are at least three distinct models of content-based instruction that have been developed in the second language instructional setting (Brinton, Snow, & Wesche, 1989). They tend to be found most often in postsecondary school settings; however, some variations have been implemented in the secondary school setting as well.

Theme-Based Model

The theme-based model is a type of content-based instruction in which selected topics or themes provide the content for the ESL/EFL class. From these topics, the ESL/EFL teacher extracts language activities which follow naturally from the content material. Thus, a unit on "advertising" might engage the students in a variety of activities such as designing and administering a marketing survey, plotting a graph of the results of the survey, and comparing and contrasting consumer attitudes. This model is particularly suitable in a language institute or in the college or university setting, where ESL/EFL classes are often composed of students of diverse language backgrounds and interests whose common goal is to attend college or university in an English-speaking country.

Sheltered Model

Sheltered courses currently exist in a variety of secondary and postsecondary settings in both Canada and the United States. The term "sheltered" derives from the model's deliberate separation of second language students from native speakers of the target language for the purpose of content instruction. The sheltered model in the postsecondary setting was developed at the University of Ottawa as an alternative to the traditional university foreign language class (Edwards, Wesche, Krashen, Clement, & Kruidenier, 1984). At the University of Ottawa, students can opt to take a content course such as Introduction to Psychology or Introductory Linguistics conducted in their second language in lieu of taking a traditional second language class. All instruction in the sheltered class is given in the second language by content faculty members who gauge their instruction to an audience made up of second language students.[1] In the past, French sections have been offered for native English speakers and English sections for native French-speaking students. At the beginning of each content lecture, the ESL/FSL instructors hold short sessions of about 15 minutes in which they go over key terms or provide students with useful expressions, such as polite ways to interrupt the professor to request clarification; however, there is no separate language class per se.

Comparisons of sheltered psychology students with students attending more traditional ESL and FSL classes have found no significant differences in the gains of the two groups in second language proficiency despite the fact that the sheltered students did not "study" the second language. In addition to their gains in second language proficiency, the sheltered students demonstrated mastery of the content course material at the same levels as comparison students enrolled in regular native-speaker sections of psychology. Furthermore, the sheltered students reported greater self-confidence in their abilities to use their second language as a result of participation in the sheltered class.

In the secondary school setting in the United States, ESL students are often placed in sheltered content courses such as "ESL Math" or "ESL Social Studies." These courses are frequently an alternative to content courses taught in the students' native languages in settings where trained bilingual teachers are not available or the student population is so heterogeneous as to preclude primary language instruction. Sheltered courses offer language minority students an alternative to traditional ESL classes, which are often taught in isolation from the rest of the school curriculum, giving them access to school subjects from which they might otherwise be barred on the basis of their limited English proficiency. Students in sheltered classes follow the regular course curriculum; however, instruction is geared to their developing levels of second language proficiency through the use of various instructional strategies and materials, which will be discussed in more detail later in this chapter. When properly conducted, sheltered courses can offer an effective approach to integrating language and content instruction for intermediate ESL students whose language skills may not yet be developed enough for them to be mainstreamed with native English speakers in demanding content courses.

Adjunct Model

The adjunct model is a content-based approach in which students are concurrently enrolled in a language class and a content course. This model is typically implemented in postsecondary settings where such linking or "adjuncting" between language and content departments is feasible. A key feature of the adjunct model is the coordination of objectives and assignments between language and content instructors. The language class becomes content-based in the sense that the students' needs in the content class dictate the activities of the language class.

In the Freshman Summer Program (FSP) at UCLA, for example, native and nonnative English speakers enroll in one of six undergraduate survey courses and the corresponding English composition/ESL classes. The material of the content courses becomes a springboard for activities and assignments in the English/ESL classes as students' immediate academic needs are treated as well as exposing them to more general academic skills that can be transferred to other content courses. Comparison of the ESL students who had participated in FSP with students who followed a more typical EAP curriculum revealed that, despite having significantly lower ESL placement scores, the FSP students performed as well as the ESL students on a task requiring them to use lecture and reading material in the composition of an essay (Snow & Brinton, 1988).

In the EFL setting, a modified adjunct model has been implemented in the People's Republic of China at the Social Science English Language Center (SSELC) in Beijing. In the SSELC program, Chinese students attend English lectures in selected social science topics given by visiting American professors. The EFL classes focus on general academic skills development before the professor's arrival and then coordinate with the content course once it is under way.[2]

INTEGRATING THE "FIVE" SKILLS IN CONTENT-BASED INSTRUCTION

As mentioned, all the programs described in the preceding section have the common goal of teaching language through content. More specifically, they also provide a rich context for teaching the traditional four skills—listening, speaking, reading, and writing. In addition, since the focus of most content-based ESL/EFL courses is on academic language learning, the teaching of a fifth skill—study skills—is essential. To be successful academically, all students must, for example, be able to take good lecture notes. They must develop strategies for condensing large amounts of reading material into reading notes or preparing study guides. Clearly, students need to learn to manage their time wisely and to develop effective test-taking strategies. These and other study skills are perhaps even more critical for the ESL/EFL student, who may need more time to read and master content material and who may lack familiarity with the American educational system and/or experience with common Western modes of critical thinking and writing.

Since the four skills have been treated individually in other chapters of this volume, they will not be discussed further. Rather, the purpose of this section is to illustrate how the four skills, plus study skills, can be integrated effectively in content-based instruction. Three sample units are presented which integrate the teaching of the five skills within an instructional unit. The units were developed for use in the adjunct program at UCLA for a high-intermediate ESL course paired with introductory psychology.[3] The units reflect a "receptive to productive" teaching cycle. Each unit begins with a recognition or exposure activity. Students are presented models which illustrate the teaching point of the unit. These models may be in the form of a passage taken from the content textbook and used for a dictation, as in Unit 1; alternatively, the model may take the form of an example text to introduce the notion of coherence, which is the focus of Unit 2. The second activity of each unit engages the students in a directed exercise with the teaching point. So, for example, in Unit 1, students underline the logical connectors of classification, or, in Unit 3, they complete a cloze passage constructed from the ESL instructor's model lecture notes in which key terms or information have been deleted. Subsequent activities provide extended practice; for instance, in Unit 2, students reconstruct a paragraph (i.e., dictocomp) after listening to the instructor read it aloud. The culminating activity of each unit requires the students to put their newly acquired knowledge to work in the production of a text, such as a composition or a summary. In some cases, there are immediate follow-up activities, such as analysis of common error patterns found in the compositions, as in Unit 1. In other cases, persistent problems such as essay organization, documenting source material, or punctuation become the focus of future peer-editing groups or are recycled into other types of practice activities throughout the term.

UNIT 1: FOCUS—CLASSIFICATION

Skill:	Activity 1:
Listening	Dictation—Model paragraph of classification on the topic "Personality"
Skill:	Activity 2:
Prewriting	Using their dictations, students underline the nouns describing categories (e.g., types, kinds, stages) and the logical connectors of classification; discussion of the rhetorical organization of classification
Skill:	Activity 3:
Prewriting	From a list of characteristics of individuals, students classify the information into the appropriate categories and label the categories (e.g., shyness, assertiveness, aggressiveness)

Skill:	Activity 4:
Reading	Students reread their content text to check their categories and the accuracy of their classifications
Skill:	Activity 5:
Speaking	In groups, students compare/defend their categories and classifications
Skill:	Activity 6:
Writing	Students are given the following prompt: "Grace Ursini, a junior high school student, has an IQ of 140. She does well in school, especially in English, Spanish, and music." They are also given several explanations, such as "Grace's mother is president of the local Parent Teacher's Association," to use as supporting data for their claims. Using this fact situation, the students take the example of Grace Ursini and compose a classification essay on the topic "Environment verus Heredity"
Skill:	Activity 8:
Grammar	Group work—Students examine sentences taken from their compositions, determine the error patterns, and make the appropriate corrections; review of passive voice based on error analysis of compositions

---

UNIT 2: FOCUS—TEXT COHERENCE

Skill:	Activity 1:
Reading/ Speaking	Instructor introduces notion of text coherence; students read passage from content text on "The Development of Language" and underline elements of cohesion (e.g., pronouns, logical connectors, lexical chains; discussion of different ways in which ideas can be joined (includes a review of articles/pronouns and a review of synonyms/word forms)
Skill:	Activity 2:
Listening/ Prewriting	Dictocomp—Teacher reads a short passage on "Piaget's Stages of Cognitive Development" two times; the students listen the first time, take notes during the second reading, then recreate the passage in their own words; students compare their reformulations with the original passage from the content text, noting the different types of cohesive devices used
Skill:	Activity 3:
Writing	Students compose an essay comparing Bruner's and Piaget's theories of child development
Skill:	Activity 4:
Speaking/ Writing	Students critique each other's essays in peer edit groups and discuss ways to improve their papers; students revise their papers based on the feedback

UNIT 3: FOCUS—UNDERSTANDING LECTURES

Skill: *Activity 1:*

Listening   Lecture on "Altered States of Consciousness" (simulated by the ESL instructor or presented on video); students take notes

Skill: *Activity 2:*

Study skills   Students complete a cloze passage constructed from instructor's model lecture notes

Skill: *Activity 3:*

Speaking   Group work—Students compare their notes with the model notes and discuss ways to determine relevant/extraneous material, use of abbreviations, organization of notes

Skill: *Activity 4:*

Writing   Students prepare one-page summaries of the main points contained in their lecture notes

STRATEGIES AND TECHNIQUES FOR CONTENT INSTRUCTION

In the previous section, sample activities which the ESL/EFL instructor can use to teach language skills through content were presented. In this case, the instructor is using the content as a vehicle to present and practice language in the ESL/EFL class; the primary objective is the teaching of language skills, although the content is clearly reinforced in the process. In content classes, on the other hand, the instructor is primarily concerned with delivering subject-matter instruction. Immersion and sheltered instructors, for example, are responsible for presenting cognitively demanding subject matter in a manner that is comprehensible to second language students. The same is true for regular classroom teachers who have ESL students in their classes. The challenge to content teachers lies in modifying or "packaging" instruction in ways appropriate to the second language learner's developing language system. To do this, teachers must utilize a variety of techniques and strategies for making content instruction comprehensible. These instructional techniques fall into four general categories:

Modifying Input. Recalling that second language learners have difficulty with the cognitively demanding, context-reduced language of academic texts, it is critical that content teachers adapt the delivery of instruction to the second language learners' level of proficiency. The following techniques are useful ways to modify input:

1. Slower (yet natural) rate of speech.
2. Clear enunciation.
3. Controlled vocabulary/limited initial use of idioms.

Use of Contextual Cues. Content teachers must provide second language learners with multiple cues to meaning so that they do not have to rely solely on the spoken or written word to understand difficult material. These contextual cues include the following:

1. Gestures.
2. Dramatization of meaning through facial expressions, pantomine, role-play.

3. Visuals, including pictures, photographs, slides, maps, graphs, diagrams.
4. Realia (i.e., actual physical objects).
5. Bulletin boards.
6. Word banks (e.g., charts which associate math vocabulary with their corresponding symbols).
7. Building predictability into instructional routines such as opening and closing activities, directions, and homework assignments so that students can figure out what to do from the context even if they do not understand the spoken instructions.
8. Building redundancy into lessons through repetition, restatement, and exemplification.

Checking for Understanding. There are a variety of techniques which can be used to ensure that students understand both the language used in instruction and the concepts being imparted. Among these checks of comprehension are the following:

1. Asking students to decide if information is true or false.
2. Asking students to provide examples.
3. Having students paraphrase important terms in their own words.
4. Having students summarize key information.
5. Asking students both factual questions (e.g., "who?", "what?") and referential questions ("why?" and "what would you do if . . . ?").
6. Having students ask each other questions.

Designing Appropriate Lessons. All effective instruction requires adequate pacing, attention to students' developmental levels, specification of appropriate objectives, a variety of activity types, and ongoing, formative evaluation. In addition to these basic considerations, content teachers working with second language learners must take extra measures in lesson planning in the following areas:.

1. *Vocabulary instruction:* Systematic activities for vocabulary instruction must be devised since second language learners often lack the basic and specialized vocabulary which characterizes academic texts.
2. *Prioritizing objectives:* The content teacher must decide what key concepts should receive the most attention since it may not always be possible to cover all of the material.
3. *Providing schema-building activities:* Techniques should be employed such as reviewing previously covered materials, relating ideas to the students' own experiences, using brainstorming or clustering activities help students develop a frame of reference for cognitively demanding content material. Advance organizers such as outlines, charts, and study guides also help students see the inherent structure of academic material.
4. *Learner grouping strategies:* A variety of grouping arrangements should be employed. Students can work in pairs, in small groups, and in structured cooperative learning groups to maximize several different sources of input and output and to increase interaction.

SAMPLE SCIENCE LESSON PLAN

The following lesson plan developed at the Center for Applied Linguistics incorporates many of the strategies and techniques just discussed.[4] The lesson illustrates how instruction can be planned to create an environment conducive to both content learning and language learning at beginning, intermediate, and advanced proficiency levels and across grade levels.

Purpose

This strategy can be used to integrate language and content instruction in science classes with a laboratory focus. The approach takes standard laboratory experiments and integrates language learning. The following activity illustrates the implementation of the strategy at the primary school level for the specific scientific concept: "Air has pressure because it weighs something."

Materials

The materials necessary for this experiment are:

water	pencils and paper
towels	medium size glasses (glass or plastic—styrofoam doesn't
pans or sinks	work)
	stiff cards of various sizes, e.g., index cards

The Basic Approach

For students at *beginning proficiency levels*, conduct the following experiment (Steps 1–7). The steps for the basic experiment are appropriate at the elementary school level. The primary cognitive focus is observation, which can be expressed linguistically through simple unstructured discussion and/or note-taking activities, and by asking yes-no questions or giving imperatives.

Step 1: Write on the board and state orally: Air has pressure because it weighs something.

Step 2: Put water in the glass until it comes to the top.

Step 3: Push the card over the top of the glass.

Step 4: Hold your hand over the card. Turn the glass of water upside down. Be sure to leave your hand on the card.

Step 5: Remove hand and ask students to comment on what they have observed, eliciting relevant vocabulary and concepts.

Step 6: Divide class into small groups (2–3 students each). Each group is asked to reenact the experiment, keeping a record of when it does and doesn't work.

Step 7: Reconvene class and have group members relate results.

Extensions

The instructor may want to incorporate some higher level cognitive foci at the *intermediate proficiency level*. In that case, the following steps may be added to the basic experiment.

4b. Ask them to predict what will happen.

6b. Tell groups to record results on a prepared form which classifies what happens under different conditions. For example:

- glass not filled to the top with water _____

- card not large enough to fit over rim _____

- hand removed too quickly _____

- card not stiff enough _____

- glass made of styrofoam _____

7b. Ask students to relate what happened under the varying conditions and to provide an explanation.

At the *advanced proficiency level*, the experiment can be expanded to include the following steps:

6c. Have each student write his/her own conclusion(s)

6d. Assign a group recorder the task of collecting all the conclusions, writing down, and reporting to the group the various conclusions. Students in each group then add hypotheses and conclusions.

7c. Have each group make a report to the class. This may be structured according to a standard report form.

7d. Collect written group reports and return them at a later date with comments and perhaps allow for further discussion.

Variations

A related activity would be to take an empty clear glass, turn it upside down, and push it down into a pan of water. Demonstrate that the water doesn't go into the glass (or only slightly), because air pressure prevents it. Use similar steps as above, eliciting verbal responses and explanations from the students at the appropriate level of proficiency. Variations will, of course, depend upon whether the class is an ESL class or a mainstream class, as well as upon the nature of the specific experiment being used.

Other Uses

This same strategy can be used for the secondary and tertiary levels (see Table below). The *language foci* may be altered to include more sophisticated activities such as library work, science reports and projects, mastering technical vocabulary, and so on. The same experiment can also include additional *cognitive foci* to develop more complex or higher order thinking skills, such as hypothesizing, synthesizing, and experimenting.

The following table summarizes how lessons can be created for different grades and proficiency levels through the implementation of language foci (lf) and cognitive foci (cf) for each grade/proficiency slot.

TABLE: TEACHING SCIENTIFIC CONCEPTS

	Low	Intermediate	Advanced
Primary (4th–5th)	cf: observation lf: unstructured discussion, note taking, yes-no questions, listening for main ideas	cf: explaining, inferring, predicting lf: structured discussion, structured note taking, if-then (real), future tense, passives, adjective clauses	cf: hypothesizing, synthesizing, experimenting lf: structured group work, structured reports, if-then (real, unreal), quantifiers, modal verb phrases, noun clauses
Secondary (9th–10th)	cf: observation lf: unstructured vocabulary recognition, library work, illustrating conclusions	cf: explaining, inferring, predicting lf: pre-reading, guided reading, writing informal conclusions	cf: hypothesizing, synthesizing, experimenting lf: writing/expressing complete conclusions, completing standard reports, doing science projects
Tertiary	cf: observation lf: mastery of key vocabulary	cf: explaining, inferring, predicting lf: mastery of technical vocabulary, technical reading, lecture and note taking skills	cf: hypothesizing, synthesizing, experimenting lf: synthesizing lectures in writing, using science journals, writing technical reports

KEY ISSUES IN TEACHING LANGUAGE THROUGH CONTENT

As is clear (one hopes) from the description of programs and instructional activities, content-based instruction differs conceptually from more traditional second language teaching methods in a number of ways. First, the roles of the language teacher and the content teacher are necessarily expanded. Since the content dictates the selection and sequence of teaching points, the language teacher must learn to exploit the content material for its language teaching potential. This means that the language teacher must select the content material judiciously, or in the case where the materials are already selected (such as in adjunct classes), the teacher needs to pull out material which is most suitable for language teaching aims. It also means that the language teacher must become familiar enough with the content material to put it to meaningful use. This is one of the most difficult, yet indispensable, requirements of content-based teaching. By the same token, the content teacher, in this approach, becomes sensitized to the language needs of second language students. This entails systematic planning of instruction through a variety of strategies and techniques. In a content-based approach, a reciprocal relationship develops in which all instructors share responsibility for the academic growth of second language students.

A second key issue in content-based instruction is the need to develop appropriate curricula and materials which reflect the assumptions of the approach. Thus, while commercial language texts may be appropriate for some activities and are certainly useful references, content-based instruction necessarily requires extensive development of curricula and materials which integrate the teaching of language skills with content. The sample lessons presented earlier reflect many hours of preparation and planning for effective content-based instruction.

Content-based instruction is a student-centered approach. Choice of content should revolve around considerations of students' current proficiency levels, academic objectives, interests, and needs. When selecting an instructional model, these considerations must be taken into account. Assessment, therefore, plays an important role on a number of levels. First, the academic needs of the learner must be determined. These may be very general, as in the case of students who are enrolled in college preparatory programs in intensive language institutes, or very specific, as is the case of ESL students in the public schools who will be mainstreamed quickly into regular content classes. Second, the students' language proficiency levels must be assessed carefully in determining the type of content which will be most appropriate to select for instruction. Finally, once a content-based approach is implemented, assessment must be carefully planned to take into consideration both language development and content mastery.

CONCLUSION

The teaching of language through content is not so much a method as a reorientation to what is meant by "content" in language teaching. In fact, many of the more innovative methods such as TPR or Suggestopedia (see the chapter by Blair in this volume) could be used effectively within a content-based approach. There is theoretical support in the literature for a content-based approach and abundant existing programs in both the foreign and second language settings which effectively teach language through content. As we have seen, content-based instruction crosses over age groups and settings—providing access to the standard school curriculum for linguistic minority students in secondary schools or preparing EFL students for university work in English-speaking countries—and is very much in keeping with the communicative approach to second language teaching.

NOTES

1. For an interesting discussion of the strategies used by a French-speaking professor and an English-speaking professor lecturing in psychology, see Wesche and Ready (1985).

2. For more information on SSELC, see Brinton et al. (1989).

3. These units were jointly developed by the author and Donna Brinton for use in the Freshman Summer Program.

4. This strategy sheet was developed by Patricia Chamberlain, Mary Ellen Quinn, and George Spanos at a seminar on Methods of Integrating Language and Content Instruction held at the Center for Applied Linguistics.

DISCUSSION QUESTIONS

1. In the chapter, the distinction is made between context-embedded language and context-reduced language. Can you think of classroom situations which would elicit these different kinds of language? Which of the techniques and strategies listed do you think would be particularly helpful in making context-embedded language more comprehensible?

2. The author states that the immersion model might be considered the prototype content-based program. Immersion students upon completion of elementary school have acquired nativelike reading and listening skills, but typically are not nativelike in the productive skills of speaking and writing. How might these findings be explained in terms of the notions of comprehensible input and comprehensible output?

3. Analyze the sample science lesson. In what ways does it differ in terms of content demands for beginning, intermediate, and advanced students? How are the language demands different across proficiency levels?

4. Several points were raised at the end of the chapter about ways in which content-based instruction differs from more traditional methods. Can you think of any other differences to add?

SUGGESTED ACTIVITIES

1. Consider the framework suggested by Snow, Met, and Genesee. Imagine that you are a fourth-grade teacher who has limited-English-proficient students in your class. You are planning a unit on Explorers of the New World. What content-obligatory language skills should you anticipate? What content-compatible language could you reinforce in your lesson?

2. In the chapter, the author describes five different models currently in use which integrate language and content instruction. Compare and contrast them in terms of:

a. the degree of content integration
b. the degree of explicit language teaching
c. the types of curriculum and materials used
d. the role of the language and/or content teacher

3. Ellis (1985) stated: "Different features may aid development at different times. For instance, in [his study] teacher self-repetitions were more frequent at an early stage of development, and teacher expansions at a later stage. . . . Both the learner and the native speaker adjust their behavior in the light of the continuous feedback about the success of the discourse with which they provide each other" (p. 82). Consider these findings in terms of the list of techniques and strategies for content instruction. Consider the four categories (modifying input, use of contextual cues, checking for understanding, and designing appropriate lessons) and decide which techniques might be most appropriate for:

a. beginning students
b. intermediate students
c. advanced students
d. teaching mathematics
e. teaching history
f. immigrant students
g. foreign students

4. Using the receptive to productive cycle illustrated in the sample ESL/Psychology units, design an integrated content-based unit for teaching:

a. comparison/contrast
b. conditionals
c. guessing the meaning of words from context

SUGGESTIONS FOR FURTHER READING

Brinton, D., M. A. Snow, & M. B. Wesche (1989)
Content-based second language instruction. New York: Newbury House.

 A comprehensive treatment of content-based instruction at the postsecondary level, including discussion of materials development and evaluation.

Crandall, J, ed. (1987)
ESL through content-area instruction: Mathematics, science, social studies. Englewood Cliffs. NJ: Prentice-Hall Regents.

 In-depth treatment of three content areas and the language teaching implications.

Edwards, H. P., M. B. Wesche, S. Krashen, R. Clement, & B. Kruidenier (1984)
Second language acquisition through subject matter learning: A study of sheltered psychology classes at the University of Ottawa. *Canadian Modern Language Review, 41,* 268–282.

A detailed discussion of the research findings on sheltered courses at the University of Ottawa.

Genesee, F. (1987)
Learning through two languages. New York: Newbury House.

A thorough discussion of the history of the immer-

sion model and research findings in Canada and the United States.

Mohan, B. A. (1986)
Language and content. Reading, MA: Addison-Wesley.

A theoretical justification for teaching language and content simultaneously.

An Integrated Approach to Literature in ESL/EFL[1]

Susan L. Stern

Editor's note: It would be very helpful to read John Collier's short story "The Chaser" and Robert Frost's poem "Mending Wall" prior to reading this chapter, since both are discussed in detail to illustrate the integrated approach.[2]

Literature offers potential benefits of a high order for English as a second or foreign language (ESL/EFL). Linguistically, literature can help students master the vocabulary and grammar of the language as well as the four language skills: reading, writing, listening, and speaking. Numerous activities involving the students' application of these skills can be developed around the reading of a literary work.

Culturally, literature enables the reader to examine universal human experience within the context of a specific setting and the consciousness of a particular people.

Aesthetically, benefits include the teaching of literature for its own sake, for the perceptive insight it provides into man's existence within the artistic and intellectual boundaries of a literary framework.

All the elements of literature—plot, character, setting, and theme—help promote reading comprehension by presenting special challenges to readers which demand that they learn to put into practice specific reading strategies, and by helping carry students along in their reading. Moreover, they provide the subject matter, the context, and the inspiration for numerous written and oral activities so that a single literary work becomes the central focus of a classroom study unit. Literature, as opposed to materials written especially for ESL/EFL, can motivate students to want to read and help them develop the habit of reading both in and out of class.

Literature has often been described as a window, mirror, or key to a culture, for it can help the reader understand and empathize with another culture. Reading a literary work vicariously immerses students in the world it depicts, involving them with its characters, plot, and themes, its setting and language (Arthur, 1970). Literature can also help second language learners gain deeper insights into their own cultures in the same way that the study of another language helps us perceive the structure of our own (Newton, 1985).

Beyond the linguistic and cultural benefits literature provides, it fosters cognitive and aesthetic maturation (Gregg & Pacheco, 1981), develops the ability to make critical and mature judgments (Hargreaves, 1969), develops a feeling and appreciation for the language (Shumaker, 1975), and has the capacity to move the reader (Slager & Marckwardt, 1975).

Moreover, literature offers a special depth to language learning. As Newton (1985) suggests, one of the needs which is felt in the English-teaching profession at this time is what Stevick (1976) describes as the "dimension of depth"—implying a deeper dimension to language learning than does the current emphasis on communication, or communicative competence. It refers to the learner's mental involvement in what he is hearing or saying, leading to a kind of communication that is more than superficial. Newton explains that one possible source of depth in language learning is literature. The potentials of literature are only now achieving fuller realization.

BRIEF HISTORICAL OVERVIEW OF THE TEACHING OF LITERATURE IN ESL/EFL

British literature has been taught in non-English-speaking countries for over 125 years, playing a major role in the English syllabus. Two traditions have dominated the teaching of literature abroad—the British and the Continental.

In the British tradition, literature is assumed to have a special educational function as a logical development of literacy. Being able to read and appreciate the major British writers is the ultimate expression of literacy in English, and thus, the ultimate goal of English language instruction. In the Continental tradition, English literature is studied as evidence of a distinctly foreign civilization or culture and is integrally related to civilization studies.

Both traditions are dominated by academic, teacher-oriented instruction. The curriculum generally consists of a survey of classic literature in English. Teaching features lecture and examination, with occasional discussion and/or grammar translation (Press, 1963).

By the 1960s, English language educators were beginning to question what they saw as a blatant overemphasis on literature in the EFL curriculum and the way in which it was being taught. They expressed concern with the concomitant lack of interest in developing much-needed linguistic skills (Topping, 1968).

Based on the emerging recognition that literature study had to be adapted to new dimensions of EFL work and new, less elitist educational objectives, the British Council held a conference at King's College, Cambridge, in 1962 (see Press, 1963) to discuss the issues and make recommendations for change. This conference was the first and only major, organized attempt ever undertaken to evaluate the teaching of literature in EFL to make it more relevant to the goals of modern EFL instruction. No similar attempts to assess the role of literature have been reported. Thus, focal research on the teaching of literature in ESL/EFL has largely been ignored (Allen, 1965).

THE ROLE AND TEACHING OF LITERATURE IN ESL/EFL TODAY

Literature continues to play a prominent role in the English curricula of many non-English-speaking countries, and many ESL teachers throughout North America include literature in their classes even though it is not generally a curricular requirement (Stern, 1977, 1985). Literature teaching research, however, has receded even further into the background of ESL/EFL specialists during the past 25 years. The lack of interest is reflected in three major areas.

First, there is a paucity of resources and materials. Although many readers are on the market, most are merely simplified texts.

While there are many literature anthologies, few resources exist to aid teachers in presenting the material they contain. Second, there is a lack of preparation in the area of literature teaching in TESL/TEFL programs, at least in the United States. Third is the absence of clear-cut objectives defining the role of literature in ESL/EFL.

Consequently, literature still tends to be taught in the traditional way in most non-English-speaking countries. In ESL situations, instructors would like to enhance their teaching of literature with new approaches and techniques, but lack the resources to do so, and many more instructors would like to include literature, but lack the background and training.

Hence, the full array of values literature offers English instruction has yet to be fully realized. As ESL/EFL professionals we must ask ourselves how to translate these potentials into classroom practice.

One way, as described throughout this chapter, entails an integrated approach to literature, one which integrates literature study with mastery of the language (vocabulary and grammar), with further development of the language skills (reading, writing, listening, and speaking), and with increased awareness and understanding of British, American, and other English-speaking cultures.

The approach is also integrated in that study of a single literary work can combine all the language skills with one another, with exposure to American or British culture, and with increased literary understanding and appreciation. Activities focusing on each area can build upon and complement one another, contextualizing all aspects of language learning.

The chapter includes detailed examples of strategies and activities for the poem "Mending Wall," by Robert Frost and the short story "The Chaser," by John Collier, and a few examples for plays.[3] I chose these works because of my success using them, and because they are included in ESL anthologies,[4] implying that others have achieved similar results.

The integrated approach can be adapted to any age and level of ESL/EFL student. The techniques succeed with fairy tales, folk tales, simplified texts, and children's stories as well as short stories, plays, and poems. The idea is for instructors to select those activities which are most appropriate for their particular classes and the works being read, and to sequence them so that they build upon and complement one another.

LITERATURE AND LANGUAGE

In dealing with vocabulary and grammar as part of literature study in ESL/EFL, instruction should help students understand the work being read *and* help them further master English. Thus, vocabulary and grammar study should (1) occur within the context of the literary work; (2) consider the level of the students; (3) reflect course focus and objectives for including the particular work being taught.

Vocabulary

Research to identify second language (L2) reading difficulties, and self-reports of L2 students identify vocabulary as the main reading problem for second/foreign language learners (McKinley, 1974; Walsleben, 1975; Yorio, 1971). This is not surprising, considering the extensive English lexicon. Vocabulary acquisition by native and nonnative speakers depends largely upon the speaker's education, degree of sophistication, and personal experience.

Moreover, many words and phrases are culture-tied, such as *spring mending time* and *elves* in "Mending Wall," or the mythological reference to *sirens* in "The Chaser." Even when vocabulary items have similar denotative meanings in one language, they may have different connotations in another, such as *hunter* or *neighbor* in "Mending Wall," or *divorce* in "The Chaser." Nonnative speakers therefore require adequate preparation for culture-tied items, along with idioms, slang, and colloquial or dialectal words and expressions.

To prepare students for a selection, the instructor can define vocabulary items critical to understanding the text as a whole. This can be incorporated in a general introduction. For example, explanations of *frozen ground-swell* and *spring mending time* ("Mending Wall") fit naturally into a description of the poem's New England setting and the springtime wall-mending ritual. Before reading "The Chaser," students should know that a chaser is a beverage taken to mask the unpleasant taste of some preceding alcohol. An explanation will facilitate recognition and understanding that the "love potion" will ultimately require something to reverse it.

Only the most critical items need be defined beforehand. Student self-reliance should be encouraged, using context clues to derive meaning where possible, and a dictionary or glossary for the rest. The teacher can give a lesson on guessing meaning through context, illustrating it with examples from the work.

The meanings of *peered, obscurely,* and *imperceptible,* in "The Chaser," for example, can be guessed (underlining added):

Alan Austen, as nervous as a kitten, went up certain dark and creaky stairs in the neighborhood of Pell Street, and peered about for a long time on the dim hallway before he found the name written obscurely on one of the doors. (paragraph 2)

"Here is a liquid as colourless as water, almost tasteless, quite imperceptible in coffee, wine, or any beverage. It is quite imperceptible to any known method of autopsy." (paragraph 5)

(See Baudoin, Bober, Clarke, Dobson, & Silverstein, 1977, for specially prepared context exercises for "The Chaser.")

Neither the context nor the dictionary, however, will clarify all previously undefined items. Students should note such items for later discussion.

The instructor may also devise an in-class exercise consisting of one or more passages of text with selected words underlined. Passages would reflect difficulty and importance to the story in terms of setting and atmosphere, characters, symbolism, and theme. Students would explicate the passage(s) and define the vocabulary items, leading to discussion of the work and to observations about how language reflects meaning—e.g., how connotations set the tone and advance the theme.

Additional exercises can include writing original sentences for new lexical items; paraphrasing informal expressions or slang; identifying and analyzing connotations, imagery, tone, register, word choice. (See McConochie, 1975, for vocabulary exercises for "The Chaser.")

Grammar

Grammatical complexity does not seem to present the major reading difficulties to nonnative speakers that vocabulary does. As the previously described reading research suggests, syntactical complexity is not as formidable a problem as is often believed. Depending on the students' proficiency, they will at least recognize a certain number of grammatical structures (Yorio, 1971). Due to the systematic nature of language, students will ultimately master grammatical structures in almost the same way that a native speaker does.

This does not imply that syntax should be ignored as an aspect of reading instruction. Rather, the students' attention *should* be drawn to complex grammatical structures. They should be analyzed within the reading to facilitate and thereby deepen their understanding of the material, and to enhance their awareness of the grammatical and rhetorical structures of the target language (Arthur, 1968; Berman, 1975; Gebhard, 1973; Norris, 1970; Rivers, 1968; Walsleben, 1975; Whelan, 1977).

The key to dealing with problematic grammatical structures is to clarify them when encountered. The instructor might forewarn students when numerous grammatical irregularities occur, as with poetry. Even then, students should initially encounter the work on their own to see what they can make of it.

Discussion and assistance can always follow. The object is not for students to attempt to use irregular structures or "poetic" word order in their own writing, but to understand the work and strengthen their mastery of grammar and syntax.

Simplifying and restructuring, along with paraphrase and restatement, clarify grammatical difficulties. They help students master unfamiliar structures by analyzing them at the grammatical level and by manipulating the phrases and sentences in which they appear. Moreover, students can speculate on why the writer chose to use grammatical irregularities. This can help them understand how subtle shifts in structure can emphasize meaning. The following lines from "Mending Wall" illustrate several such procedures.

Simplification

a. "But they [hunters] would have the rabbit out of hiding, To please the yelping dogs." (lines 8–9)

> But the hunters were determined to get the rabbit out of its hiding place to please their barking dogs.

Restructuring

b. "Something there is that doesn't love a wall," (line 1)

> The unusual fronting of the noun before "there is" places emphasis on that mysterious "something."

Restatement

c. "To each the boulders that have fallen to each." (line 16)

> Placement of "to each" both at beginning and end of line, emphasizing the divisive nature of the wall, (his side and my side, his boulders and mine).

Paraphrase

d. "He is all pine and I am apple orchard." (line 24)

> The unusual usage of "he" and "I" in place of the expected "his land" and "my land," or the unusual usage of the verb "to be" in lieu of "to have," gives insight into what the wall actually divides and keeps in or out—much more than trees.

Finally, there is Frost's omission of an article in the poem's title, a deliberate ungrammaticality. It either calls for the definite article ("Mending the Wall"), the indefinite article ("Mending a Wall") or the plural ("Mending Walls"). The definite article would make the title specific to the wall in the poem, while the indefinite article or the plural would make the title very general. The poem, however, is both specific and general, and the title reflects this in a very striking and ingenious way.

A few exercises to provide further manipulation of the grammar point(s) being studied can assist students, since a literary selection can do no more than illustrate a specific grammar construction. The instructor can write short exercises typical of the kinds used in ESL/EFL texts (e.g., substitution, fill in the blanks, rewrites, transformations, restructuring), the context being, whenever possible, the literary selection.

LITERATURE AND READING

ESL/EFL instructors should strive for an active, student-centered approach toward comprehension of a literary work, anchored on questions posed by the instructor which lead into and become the basis for discussing the text. Discussion begins at the literal level with direct questions of fact regarding setting, characters, and plot which can be answered by specific reference to the text. With lower-level students, thorough discussion ensures that they absorb all the important details. In "The Chaser," for example, questions would include the following:

1. Who is Alan Austen and where is he going?
2. What has Alan come to buy? Does the old man have it? How much does it cost?

For "Mending Wall," the instructor might ask these questions:

1. What kind of wall is the poet speaking about in the first four lines?
2. Who makes the large gaps in the wall? When are they discovered, and by whom?

Once students achieve literal understanding, they progress to the inferential level, where they must make speculations and interpretations about character motivation, setting, and theme, and where they deduce the author's point of view. Lower-level students will require guidance in referring to specific passages in the text upon which interpretations and inferences may be based. Inferential questions for "The Chaser" would include these:

1. Will the love potion work well? Explain.
2. How can the old man make enough money to live if he sells the love potion for only $1.00?

Inferential questions for "Mending Wall" could include the following:

1. What exactly does the neighbor mean when he says "Good fences make good neighbors?" Why won't he go beyond this saying, and why do you think he likes it so well?
2. The specific wall described in the poem is the wall of boulders that marks the dividing line between the land belonging to the speaker and that belonging to his neighbor. But could Frost be saying something about other kinds of walls as well? Explain.

Once students understand a literary selection at the literal and inferential levels, they are ready to share their evaluations of the work and their personal reactions to it—to its characters, its theme(s), and the author's point of view. This is also the appropriate time for them to share their reactions to the work's inherent cultural issues and themes. This third stratum of comprehension, the personal/evaluative level, inspires students to think imaginatively about the work and challenges their problem-solving abilities, e.g., for "The Chaser":

1. If you were in love with someone who didn't have any interest in you, and a love potion were available, would *you* use it to make this person fall in love with you? Why or why not?
2. It is said, "Love is blind." How can this saying be applied to this story?

For "Mending Wall," personal/evaluative questions could include these:

1. Do you agree with the speaker that "something there is that doesn't love a wall?" Why or why not?
2. What kinds of walls have you personally experienced or lived with in your own life, that have walled you in or out? How have they affected your life?

Discussion evolving from such questions can be the basis and inspiration for oral, written, and culture-related activities.

LITERATURE AND WRITING

Literature can be a rich and inspiring source for writing in ESL/EFL, both as a model and as subject matter. Literature as a model occurs when student writing closely resembles the original work or clearly imitates its content, theme, organization, and/or style. It serves as subject matter when student writing demonstrates original thinking, such as interpretation or analysis, or when it evolves from, or is creatively inspired by, the reading.

Literature as a Model for Writing

The broad range of model-based activities includes everything from paragraph writing to compositions and stories, from controlled to independent assignments.

Controlled Writing. Used mostly in beginning-level writing, controlled model-based exercises typically entail rewriting passages in arbitrary ways to practice specific grammatical structures. Thus, literature passages are usually inappropriate for this activity because writings that derive from a litera-ture model should always be meaningful within the context of the particular work.

When a controlled model-based exercise can lead into discussion of the work, however, it can be a valuable early experi-ence in literature-based writing. For example, students can be reporters doing a live news-cast (of a past-tense narrative), or they can rewrite a third person passage into first person from a character's point of view (e.g., rewrite the first three paragraphs of "The Chaser" from Alan's point of view).

Guided Writing. Guided model-based writing consists of completion exercises based on advice and counsel rather than con-trol, usually corresponding to intermediate-level ESL/EFL. Students answer a series of questions or complete sentences which, when put together, retell or summarize the model, thereafter rewriting the sentences into one or more cohesive paragraphs. Alterna-tively, students complete the exercise after receiving the first few sentences or the topic sentence of a summary, paraphrase, or de-scription. Guided writing exercises help students understand the work, especially at the literal level.

Reproducing the Model. As a staple in literature classes for native speakers, re-producing the model has traditionally in-cluded such techniques as paraphrase, sum-mary, adaptation, precis, and parody. The first three are very valuable ESL/EFL writing exercises. The precis and parody, however, are highly sophisticated, requiring a strong background in literature and an even stronger grasp of the language. Hence, they are not discussed further here.

Paraphrase demands that students use their own words to rephrase what they see in print or hear aloud. It's an especially useful tool with poetry, because it coincides with the students' trying to make sense of the poem.

Summary works well with realistic short stories and plays, where events generally fol-low a chronological sequence and have con-crete elements such as plot, setting, and char-acter to guide student writing. Expository nonfiction provides more challenging mate-rial since it deals with abstract concepts and ideas that are harder to summarize.

Adaptation entails rewriting prose fiction into dialog or, conversely, rewriting a play or a scene into narrative. This activity helps make students aware of the differences be-tween written and spoken English, and lends itself to skits and student presentations. As prose, it compels the students to consider the voice from which they are writing. Since "The Chaser" consists almost entirely of dialog, for example, students can rewrite it in narrative from either Alan's point of view or the old man's. Since the whole story centers upon the contrast between what the old man knows and what Alan *doesn't* know about the love potion, the two narratives should be very different. A comparison of the con-trasting versions would be an interesting follow-up.

Imitation. This is the most advanced stage of model-based writing. Following the principle of analogy, a new but closely re-lated topic is suggested. Students can follow the model in overall organization and syn-tactic patterning, but must relate both to the new theme. Short stories and plays are espe-cially good for imitation because they gener-ally contain a concrete and linear plot upon which students can model their writing. Such works also present easily imitated characters, topics, themes, and distinctive styles.

At the paragraph level, descriptive pas-sages work especially well. The instructor se-lects a description of a character and students write a similar description of another charac-ter in the same work, a character from a differ-ent work, a real person, or an imaginary per-son. Beyond the paragraph level, situations presented in scenes from plays, short stories, or novels may be the inspiration and basis for student skits or narratives.

Literature as Subject Matter for Writing

There are essentially two kinds of writing that can be based on literature as subject matter: writing "on or about" literature, and writing "out of" literature. These categories, suggested by Knapton and Evans (1967) in their description of a literature-centered program designed for American high school students, are equally appropriate and valuable for ESL/EFL.

Writing "On or About" Literature

Writing on or about literature includes the traditional assignments—written responses to questions, paragraph writing, in-class essays, and take-home compositions—in which students analyze the work or in which they comment on literary devices and style. Depending on the presentation, such assignments may be appropriate for all student composition levels, ranging from guided to independent in nature.

As with reading, questions and topics for writing can be found at all three levels of literary understanding. The *literal level* can be the basis for short writings dealing with comprehension of the work. Questions at the *inferential level* can be turned into writing topics requiring analysis. Questions at the *personal/evaluative level* can be the basis for essays in which students express their personal reactions to and comments about the work and the issues it raises. (See section on reading for sample questions for "The Chaser" and "Mending Wall.")

Writing on or about literature can occur before students begin to read a work. The instructor generally discusses its theme or an issue it raises, and the students write about it in terms of their own life experience. This helps interest them in the work and prepares them for reading and writing about it. When reading a longer work, students can write the answers to comprehension questions presented after each assigned segment.

Once students have finished reading and discussing a literary selection, they may write fully developed and polished compositions on the work as a whole. Most writing assignments done during as well as after the reading, however, evolve from class discussion. They take many forms, such as questions to be answered, assertions to be debated, or topics to be expanded.

Practice in using the various discourse modes, or patterns of organization, can be integrated into all the described writing types. The following questions for "Mending Wall" illustrate writing topics patterned on selected discourse modes:

Analysis:
What is the "something" to which the speaker refers that doesn't love a wall? Explain.

Argument:
Defend or attack the neighbor's statement: "Good fences make good neighbors."

Description:
Describe the speaker's image of the neighbor (the simile in lines 38–42), and elaborate on it.

Comparison/Contrast:
Compare/contrast the neighbor's attitude toward the wall with that of the speaker.

"The Chaser" works equally well:

Narration:
"The Chaser" consists almost entirely of a conversation between Alan Austen and the old man. Rewrite the story as a narrative from the point of view of an omniscient (third person) narrator.

Cause/Effect:
The old man tells Alan: "Please a customer with one article, and he will come back when he needs another. Even if it is more costly. He will save up for it if necessary" (paragraph 9). Later in the conversation (paragraph 19), he tells Alan: "I like to oblige. Then customers come back, later in life, when they are better off, and want more expensive things."
Explain what the old man means by this. What is the article with which he pleases people? What is

the expensive thing for which they return later in life? How are they related?

Writing "Out of" Literature

Writing out of literature means using a literary work as a springboard for composition—creative assignments developed around plot, characters, setting, theme, and figurative language. Literature provides the impetus and inspiration; the students' ideas and experience provide the material.

"Adding" to the Work. This includes writing imaginary episodes or sequels, or, in the case of drama, "filling in" scenes for off-stage actions which are only referred to in the dialog. Writing a sequel would be ideal with "The Chaser," since the story only implies the eventual outcome. Logically interpreting the implications, students would follow events to the end, sharing their sequels as a subsequent exercise.

"Changing" the Work. Students can create their own endings, comparing the author's to their own. With plays, they can select an important scene that in some way determines the outcome of the dramatic conflict, and rewrite it to make a different ending inevitable. In Miller's *Death of a Salesman,* for example, students might rewrite the scene in which Willy Loman is fired so that he is given the home-based salaried position he has been wanting rather than being fired. A student essay might detail the play's new ending.

Short stories may be rewritten in whole or in part from the perspective of a character versus a third person narrator or of a different character. This would work well with "The Chaser" because of the contrast between the bliss which Alan expects the love potion to bring and the misery the old man knows it will cause.

Drama-Inspired Writing. Drama-inspired writing activities may be derived from plays, short stories, novels, and sometimes poetry. The student steps into the consciousness of a character and writes about that character's attitudes and feelings. Each activity can be coordinated with an oral presentation.

In the *dramatic monolog,* the students adopt a character's persona. Assuming the character's feelings, emotions, ideas, and style of speech, they write about a particular situation, issue, or other character depicted in the work. In "Mending Wall," for instance, students can portray either the speaker or the neighbor, and express his attitude toward the wall in the poem and walls in general. In "The Chaser," they can be the old man and talk about his business, or they can be Alan and write about his hopes for the love potion and his impressions of the old man.

The *dramatic dialog* is similar. Two characters conduct a conversation about a situation or an issue raised in the work, or the dialog could be between a character and the student.

For "Mending Wall," students could write a dialog in which the speaker pays a surprise visit to his neighbor to convince him that the wall is unnecessary. Rather than spending their energy mending the wall, they should take it down once and for all.

With "The Chaser," students can imagine that Alan and Diana were married soon after she was given the love potion, and she has become unbearably possessive and jealous. Alan must therefore persuade her to give him a divorce, or he will have to resort to more desperate measures (i.e., the "life-cleaner").

Writing *character histories,* an activity suggested by Via (1976), represents a variation of the dramatic monolog. The student applies his/her imagination to what is actually presented about one of the characters, and writes a first person account about the past history of that character.

In a *letter addressed to another character,* the student portrays one character and tries to persuade another to change his/her opinion on an issue and/or follow an alternative course of action. In "Mending Wall," for instance, the speaker might try by letter to convince his neighbor that they no longer need the wall and should take it down. For "The Chaser," the following could be presented:

It is one and a half years since you married Diana, and you must get rid of her. You have tried everything you can to get her to divorce you, but she absolutely refuses. There is only one thing left for you to try, for you are desperate—the "life-cleaner." You do not, however, have the $5,000 the old man charges for it. Anyway, you realize now that he has tricked you. So you must write a letter to the old man, persuading him to sell it to you for whatever amount you are willing to pay. Begin the letter by reminding him who you are, and explaining what has happened since he last saw you (how the potion worked on Diana, and what life with her has been like since).

As a variation, the student could write a letter to one of the characters, in which he/she gives the character personal advice about how to handle a particular problem or situation.

Original Writing Based on a Literary Work. Each of the "out of" literature writing activities described thus far is closely related to the work's plot, characters, and theme. The student is therefore guided by the work itself in terms of content and structure. Writing assignments may also be derived from a story, play, or poem—yet be completely original on the part of the student. The instructor might select a line of poetry or quote a line of drama dialog and have students write an appropriate paragraph or essay based upon their own life experience—e.g., "Good fences make good neighbors" ("Mending Wall"). A theme from the work or an issue it raises can be treated in the same way. Students might be asked to describe "walls" they've personally encountered, how they've been hemmed in or locked out.

LITERATURE AND THE ORAL SKILLS

Although the study of literature in a language class is traditionally associated with reading and writing, both speaking and listen-

ing can play an equally meaningful role. Oral reading, dramatization, improvisation, role-playing, discussion, and group activities may center on a work of literature. By participating in literature-based oral activities, the students are immersed in contextualized language learning situations which provide strong motivation for communication, where every utterance is relevant.

This is an especially valuable asset to pronunciation instruction, which is too often treated with isolated drills. Once teachers recognize literature as a source and inspiration for listening and speaking as well as reading and writing, the development of oral activities will flow easily and naturally.

Oral Reading

Instructors are often at a loss for ways to make listening comprehension and pronunciation interesting and contextualized, especially at the upper levels. Playing a recording or video of a literary work, or reading literature aloud themselves, can be an ideal solution. Listening to literature read aloud requires deciphering words and sentences as well as interpreting stress, intonation, and inflection.

Dialog, whether in plays or prose fiction, lends itself particularly well to this kind of analysis because these distinctions are much more pronounced and variable in conversation than in prose. Depending upon how one interprets the intent of the speaker, a line can be read very differently. What the nonnative speaker perceives as merely a subtle shift in inflection can be the difference between sincerity and sarcasm, thereby determining whether the speaker's attitude is supportive, critical, sympathetic, or annoyed.

In Neil Simon's play *Chapter Two*, for instance, Leo has been very concerned about his brother, George, ever since George's wife died, often worrying much more than necessary—like an overprotective mother. Leo's concern, genuine and loving as it is, therefore begins to annoy George, and his annoyance is reflected in his intonation. When George says "*Leo!* I'm *fine!* Everything is *wonderful!*" with the emphasis suggested by italics, he expresses a definite annoyance and irritation at his brother's constant worrying. His real meaning is: "I'm *fine,* so stop badgering me and treating me like a child. Leave me alone!" If the line were spoken without this emphasis, the words *fine* and *wonderful* would still be stressed—although much more gently—but the meaning would be: "I'm fine, really. I appreciate your concern, but you really needn't worry so much." Nonnative speakers must be able to recognize subtleties of intonation such as these in order to understand the speaker's intent, and they must be able to produce similar patterns in their own speech.

Class discussion and/or written listening-comprehension exercises immediately after a videotape or audio recording can tell the instructor how well the students understood it. Such listening activities also help attune students to the rhythms of the language and help them sense its poetry. Moreover, they serve as models for students' oral reading of the same work.

Having students read literature aloud helps develop speaking as well as listening ability; it also lends itself to improving pronunciation. In courses focusing on pronunciation, it can be a stimulating supplemental activity to analytical explanations and exercises, integrating pronunciation study with authentic materials. Where pronunciation is not an instructional highlight, reading literature aloud is an easy, unobtrusive, and relevant way to include at least some aspects of pronunciation.

In either situation, pronunciation may be the focus before, during, and/or after the reading. Before they read, students can be taught to pronounce difficult words and perhaps be advised to concentrate on a few selected sounds as they read. Prator and Robinett (1985) suggest that focusing on one type of difficulty (e.g., final -*ed* or the stress on nominal compounds) may enable students to progress from avoiding a given "error" by conscious effort to making the correct sound

automatically as they become increasingly engrossed in the meaning of what they are reading. The text can be prepared by marking all words in which the particular problem occurs. During the reading, students should be alert to these words and sounds, whether or not their oral readings imitate the teacher. Afterward, students can be advised of errors during discussion with the instructor.

Drama

Literature-based dramatic activities are invaluable for ESL/EFL. They facilitate and encourage development of the oral skills as they help students achieve a clearer understanding of a work's plot and a deeper understanding and awareness of its characters (Stern, 1980, 1983). Probably more than any other activity, they enliven classroom study of a literary work both for the participants, who are immersed in the consciousness and situations of the characters, and the spectators. Although drama in the classroom can assume many forms, there are three main types: dramatization, role-playing, and improvisation.

Dramatization

Dramatization entails classroom performance of scripted materials. While most scripted materials come from plays, some short stories include large portions of dialog that can easily be dramatized. Examples include "The Chaser" by Collier, "The Lottery" by Jackson, "The Killers" and "Hills Like White Elephants" by Hemingway. Certain verse, such as dialog poetry or monologs, can be dramatized as well. Examples include "For Anne Gregory" by Yeats, "La Belle Dame Sans Merci" by Keats, "The Witch of Koos" or "Home Burial" by Frost, "My Last Duchess" by Browning.

Students can write their own scripts for short stories or sections of novels, conforming them as closely as possible to the actual text. They must imagine what the characters would say and how they would say it, based on the story. Student-written scripts are also possible with plays, covering offstage situations or actions only implied by the characters. Poems containing one or more personae may also be scripted by students.

The nature of the course will determine the selection of dramatization materials. If the focus is on literature or reading, the instructor may choose a few key scenes or situations from the work being read. If the focus is on oral skills, one play can be divided into scenes for each student's participation, or scenes from different plays can be selected. An entire play can be dramatized as a culminating classroom activity (Via, 1976).

Students should carefully read assigned sections of dialog in advance and be able to answer questions about characters and plot. They should note vocabulary, idioms, or dialog they don't understand and words they cannot pronounce. These issues, especially pronunciation, are then resolved in pairs, small groups, or as a class with the help of the teacher or an aide. Students next rehearse the scene with their partner(s). They don't memorize it, but learn it well enough (script in hand) to make eye contact and say their lines with meaning and feeling. They also discuss facial expressions, gestures, and the physical aspects of staging the scene. Finally, the dramatization is presented before the class.

Improvisation and Role-Playing

Both improvisation and role-playing may be developed around the characters, plot, and themes of a literary work. Although these terms are often used interchangeably, they have distinct meanings here. Improvisation is a more structured activity, i.e., a dramatization without a script. It has an identifiable plot with a beginning, middle, and end. The plot may be presented to the students beforehand, or developed by them as they go along. Either way, it performs like a scene from a play. In role-playing, on the other hand, students portray characters from the work being read and participate in a speaking activity other than a dramatization, such as an interview or panel discussion.

Role-Playing. Role-playing interviews with the characters are an enjoyable and novel way for students to discuss and analyze the characters and their interrelationships. They adapt easily to any play, short story, or novel and are possible with some poems as well. A student assumes the role of a character and the class interviews him/her, focusing on such issues as how that character feels about an event or another character, the character's value judgments regarding an issue raised in the work, why the character thinks something happened or someone acted in a specific fashion, what the character hopes will happen, or how he/she hopes a dramatic conflict will be resolved. To successfully address these issues, the student must literally step into the consciousness of the character and view the world through that character's eyes.

Interview questions for the speaker and his neighbor in "Mending Wall" might include the following:

To Speaker:

1. Have you always felt negatively about the wall, or is this feeling fairly new?
2. If your neighbor insists on maintaining the wall, will you continue to help him mend it year after year?

To Neighbor:

1. What do you mean exactly by "Good fences make good neighbors?"
2. Your neighbor regards mending the wall as just another kind of outdoor game. Is that how you regard it too?

Interview questions for "The Chaser" might include these:

To Alan:

1. Why were you so apprehensive about going to see the old man, and so nervous during the visit?
2. Why don't you just find a girl who will fall in love with you rather than pick someone who isn't at all interested in you?

To the Old Man:

1. *Why do you keep such a dirty-looking place? Aren't you afraid it will turn customers away?*
2. *Don't you think $5,000 is too much for the "life-cleaner," or poison? Do you really mean it when you say you won't accept a penny less?*

Role-playing interviews work best directly after dramatizing a scene. The student actors maintain their roles, and the rest of the class questions them about what they did and said. The technique works because psychologically, the actors haven't yet shed their personae; the class still perceives them as characters. Because the scene remains fresh in mind, thought-provoking interview questions come easily and spontaneously.

Variations include an interview with the author, where one or more students portray the author and answer questions about the work. Another is the dramatic monolog, in which a student plays a character and discusses his/her feelings and thoughts about a particular situation, character, or issue.

Improvisation. Each work's theme, plot, and characters will suggest unique situations for improvisation. These situations should be meaningful to the selection as a whole in that they depict something significant about its characters, the plot, or the theme, or they depict a particular aspect of culture that is significant to an understanding of the work.

Each of the characters should be given a specific purpose or goal to accomplish in the improvisation, and these purposes or goals should conflict in some way. This guarantees that the students will have something specific to accomplish in the improvisation so that the problem of what to discuss or what to say never becomes an issue. Basing the improvisation on a conflict also helps establish a framework for the improvisation; i.e., it begins as the characters state their goals, and ends when the conflict is resolved in some way.

It is essential that the improvisation's "givens" be made clear to the students so that they know what is expected. The improvisational situation is initially explained to the entire class. The students who will enact it step outside the classroom for five minutes to plot the scene before performing.

For both "Mending Wall" and "The Chaser," the situations suggested for written dialogs (in the section on writing) work equally well as improvisations, as does the situation described for writing a letter to another character. As an improvisation, the latter becomes a personal confrontation. Alan returns to the old man determined to get the "life-cleaner" for *his* price.

Improvisations work particularly well when they immediately follow dramatization of the scene on which they are based, for both students and audience are already emotionally and psychologically involved with the characters and the dramatic situation. The ideal situation for oral communication practice, when possible, is a dramatic presentation followed by character interviews, concluding with an improvisation. In this sequence, each activity builds on and complements the previous one.

Although the spontaneous nature of improvisation and role-play precludes anticipation of pronunciation errors during a performance, problems can be noted as they occur or be evaluated via classroom recording. The results are individually discussed with the students.

Group Activities

Group activities encourage total participation by making each student responsible for facts and ideas to be contributed and discussed. All students are involved and the participation is multidirectional. Moreover, the students' attention focuses on what they wish to say rather than on how they wish to say it. For that reason, they concentrate on communicating a message and on the response they receive rather than on themselves, thereby losing their self-consciousness at speaking in English.

General Class Discussion. In-class study of any literary work should include as much class discussion as possible. Through the use of well-selected questions the instructor draws students into discussion and encourages them to describe, analyze, and explain the literature.

Small-Group Work. Small-group work on the characters, theme(s), and cultural issues a literary work presents allows each student the maximum opportunity to speak in class. In addition to facilitating the development of oral skills, small-group work encourages student interaction through the sharing of ideas and teamwork. By collaborating on a project and reporting their findings to the class, they become "authorities" in their individual areas of investigation. They discover that they are capable of interpreting and expressing complex ideas in English, and that they can learn from one another as well as from the teacher.

The key to the success of this activity is to give each group a specific task to accomplish, such as answering questions, solving a problem, or describing/analyzing a character. With "Mending Wall," for instance, after the class has discussed the speaker's and neighbor's attitudes toward the wall in the poem, students are ready to explore the work at a more symbolic level. Groups can be assigned to come up with other kinds of walls— political, personal, psychological—that hem people in or lock them out. They can divide them into walls that serve a positive purpose (protection, privacy), that serve a negative purpose (to alienate or persecute), or that serve no purpose at all.

Panel Discussions. Panels consist of four to eight students who conduct their discussion before the entire class. They prepare for the topic beforehand—usually a significant theme or issue raised in the work. The teacher serves as moderator, allowing the students to carry the discussion themselves.

In "The Chaser," the question might be: If scientists could produce a love potion that really worked (in the sense of romantic love, as opposed to Diana's smothering love), should it be made available to the public?

A variation of this activity is the role-playing panel discussion, in which each panelist portrays a character, discussing the issues from the character's point of view. Then the question might be: Should the old man go to jail for (1) selling the love potion (knowing the user will become impossible to live with, and/or (2) selling the "life-cleaner" (poison) to the same people later on in life essentially to commit murder?

Debates. Literature-based debates focus on controversial issues related to the work's theme or characters. The debate topic can be stated as a resolution: "Willy Loman (Miller's *Death of a Salesman*) was a good husband and father." Alternatively, the two sides can receive opposing interpretations of the work in the form of contradictory statements: "Willy Loman was the cause of his own destruction." "Willy Loman was the tragic victim of circumstance."

All of these group activities lend themselves to pronunciation practice in the same manner as suggested for drama. Instructors note errors as they observe or listen to recordings of the activities, discussing them one to one at a later time.

CULTURE

Cultural assumptions, beliefs, or materials embedded in a literary work often cause more comprehension problems than language, sometimes to the degree that the whole idea or theme of the story is misunderstood. Thus, the instructor should attempt to predict what might cause problems, and monitor students' reactions as they discuss the work in order to identify other areas that might cause difficulty. Likewise, the instructor might select a work precisely because it illustrates a particular attitude, belief, or practice. Cultural aspects of a literary work can be handled in one or more of the following ways.

Introduction to Cultural Context. The study of most literature will benefit from, or be enhanced by, an introduction to its cultural context. This may be unnecessary, however, where the content is universal in theme and/or free of culture-specific references, as is often the case with poetry, or when the embedded culture-specific references or assumptions become clear to nonnative readers through context.

In the introduction, the teacher should comment on the cultural material necessary to understand the work or make it more meaningful. It should be brief, with issues presented in the abstract, so that discussion of cultural themes may be postponed until the students are immersed in the work and can talk about them in relation to the work itself.

In an introduction to the musical *West Side Story* by Laurents, Bernstein, and Sondheim, the teacher might briefly explain the gang situation in New York and the racial tension between Caucasian and Puerto Rican teenagers. Photographs or slides of New York tenements would help the students visualize the streets where the "Sharks" and the "Jets" ruled and fought. To understand "Mending Wall," a brief introduction to Robert Frost's New England environment would be very helpful—its farmlands, orchards, seasons. On the other hand, "The Chaser" requires little introduction because the theme is relatively free of cultural elements.

Culture Aside. Another technique for handling cultural context is the culture aside (Chastain, 1976). As adapted here to literature, the aside is a brief cultural comment describing an issue as it arises during reading or discussion of a literary work. It can be planned or spontaneous, and be integrated into class reading or discussion as needed

(e.g., the references in "Mending Wall" to *hunters* in lines 5–9, and to *elves* in lines 36 and 37; the reference in "The Chaser" to *sirens* in paragraph 16).

Culture Capsule. The culture capsule and group work on culture enable the students to focus on a particular aspect of culture in greater depth, to examine it and compare it with their own cultures.

The culture capsule (Chastain, 1976) refers to a brief description of a single aspect of American culture followed by a discussion of the contrasts with the students' culture(s). As adapted to literature, the brief cultural description is replaced by the oral reading or dramatization of a portion of the literary work depicting a particular cultural theme. In Miller's *Death of a Salesman,* for example, Linda tries to convince her son Biff that he must respect his father. Biff rebels. Although we later learn Biff's reasons, this scene (Act I) still reflects the attitude that respect for one's parents is not automatic—it must be earned. This situation would be unheard of in cultures where children unquestioningly respect their parents.

Group Work on Culture. The instructor divides the class into small groups, with each assigned a cultural topic depicted in the literary work. Group members must collaborate to determine what the work reveals about American or British attitudes toward these themes, based upon the actions and reactions of the characters and clues the narrator might give. Another important theme in *Death of a Salesman,* for example, would be the cultural attitude toward marital infidelity. Biff's horrified reaction to his father's casual "affair" changes the course of both their lives. In some cultures, such behavior is tolerated and even considered usual. A father would therefore not feel Willy's guilt and shame.

Regardless which approach(es) an instructor takes in handling the cultural aspects of a literary work, two important factors should always be kept in mind to avoid having students form stereotypes or other misconceptions about Anglo-American culture based on what they read.

The first is that foreign students may not be able to distinguish between that which is characteristically American or British and that which is not—especially if what would be considered unusual or inappropriate behavior to Americans or the British would be considered usual or appropriate in the students' culture(s). The reverse is equally true. Thus, a distinction should be made among (1) customs, actions, attitudes, and values that are typically American or British, (2) those that are characteristic of a specific geographical, social, ethnic, religious, or age group, and (3) those that are based on individual differences.

The second consideration is that the instructor may focus on cultural similarities as well as differences. Recognizing and explaining cultural differences has been the focus herein because differences may be misunderstood. As has been discussed, nonnative readers must understand the cultural assumptions, attitudes, and activities that are foreign to them in order to appreciate the work as the author intended and in order to form the correct impressions about the target culture. Similarities, however, should often be noted as well to avoid the students' forming the impression that their culture is so very different from American or British culture—or, if it is in fact quite different, that the two cultures share no common ground.

SELECTION OF LITERATURE

The teacher must consider a number of factors in selecting literature for ESL/EFL students: the students' English proficiency, age, and literary sophistication; the course focus; and the time available for literature study, among other issues. The following are some basic guidelines:

Age of the Work. Prose fiction and drama should generally be contemporary, written during and related to the 20th century. However, some 19th-century writers are appropriate where their attitudes and language do not create barriers between them and the modern reader (Rivers, 1968).

Although it is also desirable to include 20th-century poems, the instructor must exercise care in selecting them. As Povey (1979) observes, much contemporary poetry, with its convoluted structures and highly esoteric metaphors, can be more difficult than traditional verse, while many earlier works are well received. Thus, comprehensibility, rather than age, should be the key selection criterion.

Theme. Themes should be universal to enable all students to relate to the work on a personal level. Examples are emotions (love, hate, jealousy, pride), interpersonal relations (husband–wife, parent–child), and activities (work, education, celebrations).

Language Proficiency. At the lower levels, simplified or specially written stories for ESL/EFL can be the students' first exposure to literature. Although written within certain structural and lexical limits, they still provide the subject matter and inspiration for a variety of the literature-based activities that have been described. Once students can read literature in its original form, however, the transition should be made, for there is no substitute for the original.

Much literature in its original form is accessible to intermediate-level students. An initial selection might be a contemporary drama, such as Gore Vidal's *Visit to a Small Planet* or one of Neil Simon's plays, or a short poem such as Frost's "Stopping by Woods on a Snowy Evening." Short stories could include authors known for their linguistic simplicity, such as Hemingway. For less advanced students, McKay (1982) recommends texts written for young adults, which are likely to be relatively short and stylistically less complex.

Genre-Specific Recommendations.   Brevity is desirable with short stories to facilitate class activities over one or two sessions. Students should be able to complete a short story in a single sitting. When time permits an entire novel or play, students should be able to read a chapter or an act in one sitting.

Students appear to prefer stories with clearly identifiable plots which move them through a set of sequential events to an unanticipated or dramatic climax (Bengur, 1973; Van Doorslaer, 1972)—a story whose action can be traced with relative ease.

Plays should include contemporary, spoken English, with all the contractions, cliches, and repetitions that occur in daily conversation. Instructors should avoid works consisting largely of highly colloquial or dialectal language.

Poems should be understandable to students on a literal level, and students should be able to feel a poem by connecting it to their own personal experience (Chesler, 1976).

The Personal Aspects of Literature Selection.   Two final criteria must be met to ensure the success of a literary work as a class activity: student interest in the selection, and instructor interest in teaching it. Students are simply more motivated to read works they find enjoyable, and the teacher's enthusiasm for a work can be contagious. Thus, instructors should take into consideration relevant personal information about their students, and consider their own tastes in literature as well.

CONCLUSION

The last few years have witnessed an emerging interest in literature in ESL—not in its traditional EFL role as the ultimate aim of English instruction but as an integral and integrated component of the language curriculum. An increasing number of presentations and articles on the teaching of literature are appearing in TESOL-related conferences and journals. In-service teacher workshops are now offered, and some of the first teacher-reference texts on the subject have recently been published (see Suggestions for Further Reading).

Some of the strategies and activities that have been presented for literature appear to be generally widespread, whereas others are as unique and individual as the teachers who devise them and the literary works for which they are designed. Those who are actively involved in developing and defining or, in the case of many EFL situations, redefining the role of literature in ESL/EFL today, however, appear to share the key assumptions presented here about the potentials literature offers second language learning—linguistically, culturally, and aesthetically. All seem to be in harmony with the idea of integrating literature with language teaching in ESL/EFL.

NOTES

1. An earlier version of this chapter appeared in the *English Teaching Forum* (Special Anniversary Issue), Vol. XXV:4, October, 1987, pp. 47–55. The version appears here with the kind permission of Anne C. Newton, editor of *English Teaching Forum.*

2. Both "The Chaser" and "Mending Wall" appear in regular anthologies as well as several ESL texts. "The Chaser" is included in *Twentieth Century American Short Stories,* Jean McConochie, ed., New York: Collier Macmillan International, Inc. 1975; and in *Reader's Choice,* E. M. Baudoin, E. S. Bober, M. A. Clarke, B. K. Dobson, & S. Silverstein, Ann Arbor: University of Michigan Press, 1977. "Mending Wall" may be found in *English for Today, Book Six: Literature in English* (1st ed., 1964, and 2nd ed., 1975), New York: McGraw-Hill, 1975.

3. For a complete integrated unit of study for "Mending Wall," see S. Stern (1985). Also included are complete integrated units for the short story "The Lottery" by Shirley Jackson and the play *Death of a Salesman* by Arthur Miller.

4. See note 2.

DISCUSSION QUESTIONS

1. As this chapter has demonstrated, literature can serve as the basis for many of the same language activities that are traditionally used with other kinds of reading materials, such as magazine articles, editorials, essays, and materials written especially for ESL/EFL. What *unique* values does literature offer ESL/EFL not offered by other reading sources? What aspects of ESL instruction should literature *not* be used to teach?

2. How can literature be integrated into the curricula of various types of ESL courses (reading, writing-composition, listening-speaking, pronunciation, and general skills)? What kinds of literature and types of activities would you use in each of these kinds of classes?

3. Why do you think literature has generally been ignored in ESL teaching and in TESL teacher-training programs in the United States? Why is it finally beginning to attract the interest of both researchers and teachers now?

4. How should literature teaching change as the students' level of English proficiency increases, both in terms of the selection of materials and the strategies and activities used with them?

5. How can literature be integrated with other types of reading and writing materials and activities into a module or unit based upon a particular theme (e.g., stereotypes, the role of women, the Old West, technology, animals)?

SUGGESTED ACTIVITIES

1. Develop an integrated unit of study for a short story, poem, or play based upon activities described here. Include reading, writing, listening, and speaking activities. Try using "Mending Wall" or "The Chaser," adding to items presented in this chapter.

2. Design an ESL or EFL literature course (using the integrated approach) for a particular group of students (e.g., high school advanced-level ESL, intermediate-level Japanese university). Write a proposal, explain its rationale, and design the syllabus.

3. Try some of the student activities presented in this chapter for "Mending Wall" and/or "The Chaser" yourself to experience the linguistic and creative processes ESL students must go through to perform them. Answer the questions and write some of the essays, monologs, or dialogs. Perform some of the dramatic activities with a colleague.

4. If you are familiar with or are using "modules" or units as part of the ESL curriculum, add some thematically related literary selections to one of them. Develop writing and speaking activities that integrate your selections with the other texts.

5. Survey or interview ESL teachers about literary works they have successfully used; generate a list of titles. Add to these works which you personally enjoy and think might work well.

SUGGESTIONS FOR FURTHER READING

Teacher References and Resources

Collie, J., and S. Slater (1987)
Literature in the Language Classroom: A Resource Book of Ideas and Activities. Cambridge: Cambridge University Press.

> Presents a "resource bank" of student-centered activities appropriate to each stage of the study of a literary work, offering a wealth of practical and innovative ideas. Includes sample units for complete texts.

English Teaching Forum—A Journal for the Teacher of English Outside the United States. Published by the United States Information Agency. Subscriptions available from the Superintendent of Documents, U.S. Government Printing Office, Washington, DC 20402.

> Includes international articles on the role and teaching of literature in EFL/ESL; many with direct classroom application.

Moffett, J. (1968)
A Student-Centered Language Arts Curriculum, Grades K–13: A Handbook for Teachers. Boston: Houghton Mifflin.

> Moffett was one of the first to advocate an integrated approach to language teaching, in which reading, speech, literature, drama, composition, and language are interrelated and learned by each other. Much is adaptable to ESL/EFL.

Sage, H. (1987)
Incorporating Literature in ESL Instruction. Englewood Cliffs, NJ: Prentice-Hall.

> Summarizes the role of literature in ESL and its cultural, linguistic, and educational values. Presents excellent practical strategies for teaching poetry and short stories, and offers helpful guidelines for the selection of materials.

Theory

Brumfit, C. J., and R. A. Carter (1986)
Literature and Language Teaching. Oxford: Oxford University Press.

> An important anthology examining the relationship between the teaching of language and the teaching of literature to nonnative students.

Marckwardt, A. H. (1978)
The Place of Literature in the Teaching of English as a Second or Foreign Language. Hawaii: East-West Center —University of Hawaii Press.

> Focusing on English teaching in Asian countries, illuminates fundamental questions concerning the relationship of literature to ESL/EFL teaching.

ESL/EFL Literature Anthologies

The following are three of the best available to offer unadapted and unabridged works. Each includes teaching suggestions, comprehension questions, writing topics, and additional activities.

McConochie, J. A., ed. (1975)
Twentieth Century American Short Stories. New York: Collier Macmillan International.

Povey, J. F. (1984)
Literature for Discussion. New York: Holt, Rinehart & Winston.

Slager, W. R., & A. H. Marckwardt, eds. (1975)
English for Today (2nd ed.). Book Six: Literature in English. New York: McGraw-Hill.

Experiential Language Learning

Janet L. Eyring

If you are new to the second language teaching profession, it will not take long before you hear the term "experiential learning." It has become one of the latest buzzwords in ESL/EFL pedagogy. Yet it is also one of the least understood terms. In this chapter, a definition of, and a rationale for, experiential language learning will be provided, followed by a brief discussion of two options for structuring the learning process experientially. Finally, an overview of the types of "experiences" that could be or have been used in language teaching will be given.

BACKGROUND

What most ESL/EFL teachers mean when they speak of experiential learning is learning derived from activities which are somewhat natural—activities where both the left (analytic) side and right (holistic) side of the brain are engaged (Danesi, 1988), where content is contextualized (Omaggio, 1986), where skills are integrated (Moustafa & Penrose, 1985), and where purposes are real (Cray, 1988). With only these features highlighted, any of the following methods and approaches could be called experiential: counseling learning, cooperative learning, task-based learning, content-based learning, whole-language approach, the natural approach, language experience approach, and English for Specific Purposes (ESP).[1] However, this definition only accounts for the "experiential" part of the term. It does not account for the intended process of "learning."

While language teachers may have seen the "experiential" part of the term as more salient, general educators and psychologists have focused on the main idea, which is "learning": how one moves from a concrete experience and is finally able to apply experientially acquired generalizations to new situations (Kolb, 1984). For great educators like Socrates, Dewey, and Freire, this knowledge did not come to students by teachers' simply presenting information to them, but rather by students' grappling with information and learning to relate it to their own life experiences. Socrates' approach to learning involved dialogic reasoning between teacher and student (Weathersby & Henault, 1976), Dewey's focused on teaching the process of inquiry (Dewey, 1938), and Freire's dwelt on empowering the learner to help himself (Freire, 1973).

Psychologists have also promoted "experiential learning" for other but perhaps related purposes. From the 1960s onward, participants in T-groups shared experiences (i.e., visualization, role-playing) which provided opportunities for individuals to work toward goals, learn through feedback, and ultimately gain "consciousness" or "self-recognition" (Torbert, 1972, pp. 42, 56–61). Thus, experiential learning, besides being a means of acquiring cognitive knowledge, has become a route to social and moral development as well (Erdynast, 1981).

Applying these definitions of experiential learning to the language learning field broadens the use which was mentioned in the first paragraph. Experiential language learning is more than providing natural experiences so that learners acquire the language; it also deliberately teaches learners, as whole people, about how to learn.

How has empirical research on second language acquisition begun to support these educational, psychological, and language learning theories? Notions of "comprehensible input" and "meaningful negotiated interaction" and "learner strategies" are currently being investigated in terms of their value for second language acquisition (see Barker & Canale, 1986; Kramsch, 1985; Long, 1985; Pica, Holliday, Lewis, & Morgenthaler, 1988; Swain, 1985; Wenden & Rubin, 1987). Based on empirical studies of phenomena such as slips of the tongue, repair, language switching, hesitation, and extemporaneous talk, Hatch and Hawkins (1987, p. 249) conclude that the only acceptable model of second language acquisition is a "messy" one involving the reciprocal development of cognition, socialization, and language. Interestingly, they call their model "The Language Experience Model of Second Language Acquisition."

Thus, language research and theory support experiential learning as a viable approach. Providing real or quasi-real life *experiences* allows more opportunities for language learners to receive input. Interacting and cooperating with others allows opportunities for feedback on one's own language *learning* and humanizes the learning process.

In the following two sections, two models of how one might include experiential activities in the learning process will be discussed briefly, followed by an overview of the types and examples of experiential activities which have proved successful at various levels.

TEACHING MODELS

Hatch and Hawkins (1987, p. 248) propose that because of how language is acquired, a teaching model which trains the learner to develop a "language researcher" attitude is most consistent with research findings. Language learners need opportunities to learn by trial and error, get feedback, build hypotheses about language, and revise these assumptions in order to become fluent. The following two teaching models (the 4MAT system and Project Work) are two ways of organizing instruction so that students get maximal practice in the various learning processes mentioned above. The first approach might be best suited for teachers who desire more structure in their planning, the second for more experienced teachers who feel comfortable with its open-ended nature.

The 4MAT System

One systematic option for planning experiential language learning lessons is McCarthy's (1980) 4MAT System, which has been adapted for elementary and secondary ESL learners by a collaborative research group consisting of the Arlington Public Schools, ESOL/HILT Program and the Center for Applied Linguistics (1987). This type of lesson planning reflects the four phases of learning: (1) concrete experience, (2) observation and reflection, (3) formation of abstract concepts, and (4) generalization and testing implications of concepts in new situations (Kolb, 1984); each of these phases corresponds, respectively, to students' different learning styles: (1) the innovative learner, (2) the analytical learner, (3) the common-sense learner, and (4) the active experimentation learner.

One sample unit, "How to Write an Autobiography," illustrates how learner styles (holistic versus analytic) are acknowledged in a highly participatory, integrated way and how language experiences are supported by other reflective, cognitive activities in an ordered fashion (see Appendix).

Project Work

Unlike the more structured 4MAT System, where a lesson plan format is provided, Fried-Booth (1982, 1986) suggests a series of stages that a short- or long-term project may or may not go through, depending on the topic. At each stage "a layered approach" is used where one skill or a combination of skills is used depending on the task. (For example, during the Stimulus stage, students may watch an interesting TV program, take notes on it, and discuss it among themselves, reinforcing the skills of listening, writing, and speaking. On the other hand, during the Group Activities stage, reading skills might be emphasized.) The possible stages that Fried-Booth has outlined are discussed below in more detail.

During the Stimulus stage, students will initially discuss an idea for a project. During the Definition of the Project Objective stage, students will discuss, negotiate, suggest, and argue the focus of their project. Next, during the Practice of Language Skills stage, students will practice, with teacher guidance, the language they will need to gather data. During the Design of Written Materials stage, students will plan the types of written materials they will need for data collection. In Group Activities, students will work in groups or individually inside or outside the classroom, conducting interviews or surveys and gathering facts. During the Collating Information stage, students will review notes, assemble graphs, discuss information, and perform similar activities. In the Organization of Materials stage, students will discuss and negotiate the type of end product they will produce.

Last, in the Final Presentation, students will demonstrate what they have learned through such things as a chart, booklet, video display, or oral presentation. (Carter, Legutke, & Thomas, 1987, also suggest adding Evaluation and Follow-up stages at the conclusion of this process.) Project Work is another highly integrated approach which flexibly organizes language learning units for a few weeks or an entire school term.

This section offers two methods (i.e., the 4MAT System and Project Work) which provide a means of systematically incorporating experiential activities into the language learning curriculum.[2] Although the first method is more rigid than the second, both systems have two major features in common. First, activities are sensitive to individual needs and interests of students. Second, skills are integrated into the curriculum not as ends in themselves but as means to the accomplishment of more significant goals.

DIMENSIONS OF EXPERIENTIAL LANGUAGE LEARNING ACTIVITIES

Although it is not known how often experiential activities are used in second language learning classes, Coleman (1976, pp.

58–59) suggests that experiential learning in education, in general, is used in varying proportions at different levels: at a high level in elementary school, gradually decreasing through college, then increasing again in graduate school. This may also be the case in ESL and EFL classes.

Morgan (1983) proposes a two-axis model defining the ways in which projects in higher education may vary; this model has been adapted here for distinguishing between the different types of experiential language learning activities found in the second language learning literature.[3] In Figure 1, the vertical axis, labeled the "control" axis, represents the amount of control the teacher exerts versus the student in planning and directing the project. This axis is intersected horizontally by the "project location" axis, which relates to how classroom-centered versus real-world-centered the activities are. Thus, theoretically, those activities falling in quadrant C would independently be most able to develop the whole learner in the sense described earlier as a goal of experiential learning. Activities in the other quadrants could also do this, but to a lesser degree.

The remainder of this chapter will provide an overview of some successful experiential language learning activities described in the literature and taken from the author's own experience. Although, the authors of these published activities have not used the categories explained in this section, it is hoped that such a classification will be useful in clarifying how some activities are independently more experiential than others. Several activities/projects which have been used in foreign language classrooms in the United States will also be discussed because of their possible relevance and application to settings where English is taught as a foreign language. Where possible, notes on which activities are most successful with a particular age or proficiency level are included.

AN OVERVIEW OF EXPERIENTIAL ACTIVITIES

Teacher-Controlled Classroom Activities

Teacher-controlled classroom activities could be considered "less experiential" than the other three types of activities discussed here. Their main purpose is to provide multi-sensory stimuli for more interactive types of activities. They do not necessarily require any student input and they are usually the easiest for teachers to implement. They may be used at all levels, in ESL and EFL situations, even when the teacher is not a native speaker of the language.

Props, Realia, Visuals. Props, realia, and visuals can make any discussion/demonstration come alive. The use of flashcards, magazine pictures, or diagrams at any level help students visualize important concepts. Students in elementary school can become more focused through show-and-tell activities where discussion is reinforced with the showing of a favorite or unusual object. Tomlinson and Eastwick (1980) describe a successful "pet show" activity used in an elementary French class where students brought in their stuffed animals and the teacher awarded grand prix ribbons to the handsomest toy.

At the secondary level, there is no limit to objects and realia that might interest adolescents. A teacher gently tossing a baseball into the hands of class members could "start the

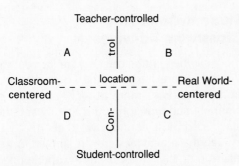

FIGURE 1. *Dimensions of experiential language learning activities. (Adapted from Morgan, 1983.)*

ball rolling" on a sports discussion. Bringing in such items of clothing and accessories as fishnet stockings, a poodle skirt, bell-bottom trousers, love beads, a bomber jacket, and a skull-and-crossbones earring could stimulate a historical discussion of fashion fads in the United States. Likewise, demonstrating how to juggle three balls is an unforgettable way to introduce hobbies.

In adult education where survival skills are often emphasized, utilizing real objects to supplement discussions can aid students in remembering important items related to tasks they may need to accomplish. For example, in a transportation lesson, the teacher could actually bring in real subway tokens and bus schedules. A measurement lesson could greatly be enlivened by the use of scales and measuring cups and spoons. A real telephone (or teletrainer) will authenticate a lesson on how to dial a telephone and make phone calls.

At the higher proficiency levels in tertiary education, perhaps the use of real objects may not seem necessary. But the use of diagrams, charts, and graphs obviously is, as a prompt for teaching students to detail processes, compare and contrast, or show cause and effect (Weissberg, 1987).

Games. In one sense, a discussion of games might seem out of place in a discussion of experiential learning because of their artificial or imaginary nature. Yet there is an independent place for games in the experiential learning literature (see Horn & Cleaves, 1980) as well as in the recreational life of native speakers.

Tomlinson and Eastwick (1980) mention the successful use of counting games and jump rope rhymes when teaching French to elementary students. It is easy to relate this idea to the teaching of English at this and other levels in the United States. Counting rhymes such as "One, two, buckle my shoe" and nursery rhymes such as "Jack and Jill" and "Mary had a little lamb" could supplement other kinds of experiential activities. For older children and at the secondary level,

board games like Monopoly and Clue could be taught. For adults, Trivial Pursuit and card games like Hearts and Crazy Eight could be motivating.

Songs. Songs, like games, selected for popularity at particular age levels can be very appropriate. For elementary students, songs with accompanying body movements can be especially fun. For example, the "Farmer in the Dell" or the "Hokey Pokey," both played in a circle, can be used. Adolescents, who are generally more sensitive to the idea that music be current, would especially enjoy learning the lyrics of songs in the Top Ten. Adults may enjoy learning some of the popular folk songs like "Oh, My Darling Clementine" or "Michael Row the Boat Ashore" or popular songs from a more recent, but bygone era (i.e., Frank Sinatra songs like "I Did It My Way").

Media. Showing movies, watching TV, and listening to the radio can all support classroom learning and bring the real world a little closer to students. Young children may enjoy Walt Disney movies and TV programs like "Sesame Street" and "Mr. Rogers' Neighborhood." Older children and adolescents may respond well to the latest action movie or mystery thriller. TV nature programs and news on the radio (especially news programs on National Public Radio in the United States) can be very informative to students. Finally, adults may enjoy more serious movies and TV soap operas, plays, and talk shows.

Student-Controlled Classroom Activities

Activities in this category might be considered more experiential because the student becomes more actively involved in planning and monitoring the activity and the teacher has less control over outcomes. Although these activities are still limited to the classroom, they may be more open-ended and challenging in nature than the previous activities discussed.

Role-Plays. Role-plays can be used at all proficiency levels. However, the types of situations presented should reflect the age and maturity level of the students. Karlin and Berger (1971, p. 52) give examples of scenes that children in regular elementary classrooms can act out—these could easily be applied to the second language classroom as well (e.g., child bringing home a poor report card, two siblings arguing about borrowing each others' things, son caught smoking by his father). Similar types of scenes could easily be extended for older secondary students (e.g., a first date or a first car accident). And for adults learning to survive in the community, role-playing how to buy stamps at a post office, return a purchase, or get directions are all very useful. Specialized groups of ESL students at the tertiary level might especially benefit from role-play. Fragiadakis (1988) describes a course where foreign TAs practice intensively how to explain a concept to a class, handle the first five minutes of class, explain a problem while involving the class in the explanation, explain confusing points from past or future lectures, and repeat presentations which have already been given.

Simulations. Simulations are somewhat like role-plays except they take place over an extended period of time (see Jones, 1974, for examples of already published simulation activities). Simulations have been successfully used at all levels. Tomlinson and Eastwick (1980) describe how elementary school students learning French take an imaginary trip to Paris. The target language is used as students pretend to buy their plane tickets, pack their clothes, enjoy dinner on board the plane, see a French film, and have a tour of Paris.

Canute (1988) describes a similar type of simulation activity used with Canadian secondary students called ESL Helicopter. Students role-play taking a trip somewhere. They first talk about the weather and directions. During their visit to various places they imagine restaurants they will dine at, super-markets they will go to, and zoos and farms they will see. Following or during the trip they may engage in rescues or talk about traffic conditions. They also may imagine trips into the future or to the place where E.T.—the lovable little science fiction creature—lives.

Adults may also enjoy simulations of travels and voyages; however, they generally can simulate more complex and sophisticated life situations. For example, they may be able to simulate Congress passing a law (in the United States) or an international committee finding solutions to various world problems such as hunger, pollution, and overpopulation (see Jones, 1982; Longman, 1973; Sturtridge & Herbert, 1979, for more ideas).

Hands-On Projects. Teachers need only think back to their own elementary school experiences to discover classroom projects that can be exciting for young people. Students can grow mung or soybeans, develop photographs, or make yoghurt to learn about scientific processes. Tomlinson and Eastwick (1980) discuss how their all-female French learners made doll houses and filmstrips about fairy tales as class projects. For older students, Fried-Booth (1986) mentions that students can demonstrate how to cook native dishes for each other, especially when the class consists of students from many different countries. Claassen (1984), a classics teacher, allowed his students to design their own individualized projects. Students became very creative with this task, making posters illustrating the Greek and Roman alphabet, writing a computer program for a Roman history-based computer game, making a model of a Roman house, and creating a tape slide show of Julius Caesar. Similar types of results could be expected from ESL and EFL students given the freedom to choose their own topics.

Computer Activities. Computer-assisted language learning programs can appropriately be identified as student-controlled classroom activities. However, some of the computer programs come close to being real-world experiences. Branvold, Chang, Pribst, and Bennion (1986), in an evaluation study, mention the use of interactive videodisk workstations using Raiders of the Lost Ark. Wilson and McCullough (1986) describe two MicroTICCIT programs which approximate real experience for students learning Spanish. In the first, the students see a map with four paths. They listen to directions which coincide with one of the paths. If they get lost, they can push keys to help with directions, repeat directions, or get the meaning and pronunciation of vocabulary words. Another program has students "dress" characters by selecting clothes which instantly disappear from the closet and appear on the person. Other activities briefly mentioned include getting through a customs inspection, filling in a calendar, and manipulating colors.

Culley, Mulford, and Milbury-Steen (1986) describe how computerized adventure games (such as the Infocom series) can be adapted for language teaching purposes. They resemble real experience because context must be understood in order to select appropriate choices (e.g., the program describes a scene where there is a small mailbox. The player, having understood the text, will type in a command such as "open the small mailbox" which reveals the next piece of information the player is to respond to).[4]

Teacher-Controlled Real-World Activities

Teacher-controlled real-world activities are more experiential than the previous two types because the classroom is extended to the outside world, where contacts with native speakers cause more uncertainty in the learning process (or information gaps, K. Johnson, 1979, p. 201). Because students can be outside the classroom, there are more opportunities for natural and varied encounters where students must take responsibility for their own learning. Consequently, these sorts of activities should be used with more advanced and more mature students. Although they may be applicable in EFL situations, they

are probably most suitable where there is a large surrounding target language population. This section will focus on the discussion of two types of activities: field trips and observation/collection activities.

Field Trips. There are several purposes for field trips in ESL/EFL settings—for general educational, recreational, or survival value. Each kind of field trip will be described in more detail below.

General educational field trips enliven course content and increase student knowledge about some topic. Visits to such public places as the library, newspaper office, atomic energy plant, control tower of the airport, or a courtroom will give students a broader view of public works. Tours of the newspaper office, a radio station, or a factory may give students an idea of how businesses operate. (Related to this, see Montgomery & Eisenstein's detailed discussion of community college students touring a bank, 1985.) Trips to a farm, an aquarium, a zoo, or a natural history museum will introduce or reinforce knowledge of the animal world.

Field trips might also serve recreational purposes. A trip to a movie or play may engender cultural appreciation. Observation of sports events such as baseball or football or actual participation in social and physical activities such as bowling or croquet can provide opportunities for group interaction and communication. Finally, trips where students can watch or participate in art, craft, dance, or cooking demonstrations can be enjoyable for students.

More practical types of field trips can also be arranged, especially for students who may be new to a community. Whole classes can practice ordering meals by going out to a restaurant, riding different bus routes, or going to a supermarket. Jerald and Clark (1983) suggest another unusual idea, having students go to various parts of a city to run the teacher's errands—this would be a way of helping the teacher as well as giving the students real opportunities to communicate. Students could, for instance, take shoes to be repaired, pick up a few items at the drugstore, return books to the library, or pay a parking ticket.

Getting oriented and learning how to ask for directions is a major task when someone first moves to a new place. Jerald and Clark (1983) mention a series of drop-off activities which can help teach these skills. In each case, students are dropped off by the teacher in a school van in various parts of the city. One activity has students dropped off in one part of the city, with a set of questions to answer. Another has each student direct the teacher to a particular location which has been marked on his/her map; another has students fill in an incomplete map of the area where they have been dropped off. In the last, students are dropped off to investigate a particular area of their city or an adjoining town to learn about its history or to familiarize themselves with what is there.

Observation/Collection. Another type of activity that can be assigned is observation or collection tasks. Some teachers have students take note of signs or T-shirt slogans that they see. Wiesendanger and Birlen (1979) describe an experience where French children learning English survey license plates in the school parking lot. Jerald and Clark (1983) suggest that students can also go on a scavenger hunt provided with a list of items which must be brought back to class, such as a twig, some moss, three pebbles, something red, something crooked, and something brittle.

An activity which Fried-Booth (1986) describes has students collect bottles, food labels, and wrappings on cartons, tins, packets, jars, or bottles to learn about the various sources of food products throughout the world.

Student-Controlled Real-World Activities

Student-controlled real-world activities are the most experiential of all the activities. Students plan and direct what they are going to do; thus, there is less predictability and less opportunity for the teacher to serve as sole knowledge source. These activities are usually large-scale and require the application of more than one language skill at a time. They also work best if students are intermediate or advanced and live within a community of target language speakers, although this is not always necessary. The types of activities discussed here include projects (informational, recreational, social-welfare), work study experiences, and cross-cultural exchanges.

Projects. Although most projects could be considered as having informational purposes, the projects described first are those which require extensive amounts of interpersonal contact (through interviews or surveys) or extensive amounts of library research.

Beginning at the elementary level, students can interview teachers and peers at school in order to create a school magazine or newspaper. Fried-Booth (1986, p. 10) mentions that small children may also engage in surveys of other students, asking questions like "How much pocket money do you get and what do you spend it on?" They can also learn to use the library to research different topics (e.g., other countries in order to have a school travel fair).

Students of all ages can also interview target-language speakers about their jobs, hobbies, and places they have traveled, or about controversial social issues like AIDS prevention, U.S. intervention in Central America, or raising the minimum wage. Legutke (1987) describes how German students interviewed and videotaped foreign travelers in English at Frankfurt airport. Students could also interview famous people or people in similar professions, or people with special talents. For example, Markee (1988, personal communication) describes students in the Bell School in Bath, England, who interviewed members of a circus and of the Theater Royale about their crafts.

Experiential activities can also be used to teach writing. Buckingham and Peck (1976) describe how Saudi Arabian hospital administrators studying at an American university used an interview with a hospital official as a catalyst for more extensive writing about their profession. Eyring (1988) had intermediate composition students at UCLA form groups to research and report on topics of their own choice. A range of topics was chosen, including Chinese gangs in Los Angeles, surrogate motherhood, foreign student adjustment, UCLA student attitudes about homosexuality, and the Ku Klux Klan. Fried-Booth (1986) discusses Italian EFL students who followed an important news event (like the American presidential election) in order to write up an article for a local newspaper.

Besides being informative, projects can also serve to orient someone to a new place. Hanson (in Candlin, Carter, Legutke, Samuda, & Hanson, 1988) guided students in an investigation of cultural and recreational opportunities in Edmonds, Washington. Students summarized their results in a slide show and oral presentation for the local Rotary Club and old folks homes. A similar project by Cushing (Eyring, 1989) outlined how a group of students at UCLA investigated beaches, parks, amusement parks, restaurants, and night spots around Los Angeles in order to compile a *Guide to Los Angeles for Foreign Students*.

Finally, Cray (1988) reported about students who investigated free-of-charge activities for women in Ottawa and then produced an orientation handbook for newcomers.

Social welfare projects epitomize the most experiential activities discussed in this chapter. Elementary students, although lacking in sophistication, can still participate in social welfare projects. Karlin and Berger (1971) suggest that young students can collect for charity organizations (e.g., Trick or Treat for UNICEF in the United States) or help organize food drives for older people.

Jerald and Clark (1983) suggest having students do extensive interviews with older people in order to obtain oral histories, which are later bound and presented to elderly inter-viewees. Students can also hold a lunch or a school activity for their new friends.

Fried-Booth (1986) describes several other social welfare projects which have been successful. In one, a group of students investigated access routes for a wheelchair in various parts of the city of Bath. Students made a wheelchair guide for the handicapped and shared their results with tourist offices and the media. A "Third World Display" was another successful activity described. Around World Food Day (October 16), students did wall displays, made posters, and built a shanty house to attract passersby and inform them of the issues affecting people in developing countries. Another group regularly visited a hospital and a spastic unit in order to make a videotape on the work of the unit which could be shown to prospective patients' parents. In another project, ESL students taught English-speaking elementary school students about some aspect of their home cultures: e.g., Danish students made a Viking helmet out of papier mache, Brunei students taught how to make and fly a Bruneian kite. Thai students taught the children the Thai alphabet and how to write their names in Thai. (A similar project is reported by Carter & Thomas, 1986, where upper intermediate ESL learners taught 8- to 11-year-olds for four days.) Finally, a collaborative project was organized between German and Danish teachers where students worked on "Mini-Project Peace." They did extensive research for a display and then also produced a Disarmament Calendar.

Victoria Markee (1988, personal communication) reports of another research project at the Bell School in Bath, England, where students interviewed homeless people and people on the street about the homeless situation.

Work Study. Work study can be short- or long-term. Markee (1988, personal communication) mentions students at the Bell School in England who sponsored and organized a jumble sale (rummage sale) on a weekend. Ebel (1985) describes a more permanent work site, the SPECTRA School in the Blue Ridge Mountains in Virginia, where native and nonnative speakers learn language while cooperatively building something and living together. Chamberlain (1985) describes a federally funded project in New York where ESL students worked on renovations. Besides learning English, they learned to operate a power saw, read blueprints, make phone calls, and earn a salary.

Cross-Cultural Activities. Cross-cultural activities generally relate to activities done by second language learners not living in the target language community. Either students create or participate in a second language cultural event or they travel to live in the target langauge culture for a limited period of time.

Pouwels (1988) describes a foreign language camp for gifted and talented students during two summers, 1986 and 1987, in Arkansas. Students with limited or no experience with foreign language were given two weeks of exposure to four different languages (French, Spanish, German, and Japanese) through a variety of instructional experiences: language classes, crafts workshops, ethnic discussions, folk dance classes, singing workshops, and foreign-food sampling. Perhaps this kind of activity could be used in EFL settings to motivate talented students to learn English or other foreign languages.

Semke (1980) describes a Cafe-Theater Evening organized by German students at a college in Iowa. Guests exchanged American money for German money at the border, purchased tickets, checked their wraps at a *Gardrobe,* entered the cafe where a polka band was playing, ate real German food, and enjoyed a program done entirely in German. Fried-Booth (1986) notes a similar type of "English Evening" activity that was done in Yugoslavia.

Craig (1985) documents a youth exchange between the French as a Second Language students at a college in Ontario and Francophone military personnel, where the native English speakers hosted the French speakers for a "Getting to Know You" evening in English.

Blackburn (1974) describes a month-long program directed by SEE (School of Experiential Education within the Board of Education for the Borough of Etobicoke, Ontario). Students received intensive instruction in French for two weeks and then spent two weeks in Quebec, living with French-speaking families. The mornings were spent in intensive language study and the afternoons were spent in cultural and recreational activities with the French-speaking people.

Stitsworth (1988) mentions one-month homestays in Japan for American students. Similar sorts of study-abroad experiences could be arranged for EFL students to English-speaking countries for shorter or longer periods of time.

CONCLUSION

The possibility for using experiential activities on a small or grand scale, in ESL or EFL settings, for beginning or advanced students is limited only by the teacher's and the students' imaginations. However, for experiential activities to be experiential *learning* activities, the students cannot passively "experience" them but must use them to take language risks, get feedback on errors, evaluate current linguistic knowledge, and the like. Students must use the activities to build their own language systems in meaningful ways. Experiential language learning activities thus constructed will encourage not only fluency but consciousness about language as well.

NOTES

1. Please see Blair, Hawkins, Johns, and Snow in this volume for further discussion of these approaches.

2. The Language Experience Approach (especially as described by Dixon and Nessel, 1983) might be considered a third experiential language learning model. However, because its focus is on the teaching of reading (with the development of writing, listening, and speaking as incidental), it will not be discussed here with approaches which seek to encourage the development of all skills equally. See Hawkins, in this volume, for a more detailed description of how the Language Experience Approach (LEA) is implemented in the elementary grades.

3. My thanks to the late Michael Canale, Visiting Professor in the TESOL/Applied Linguistics Program at UCLA Winter Quarter 1987, for directing my attention to the Morgan (1983) framework.

4. See Schreck and Schreck, this volume, for further discussion of computer-assisted language learning.

DISCUSSION QUESTIONS

1. How has the interpretation of "experiential learning" varied in the fields of education, psychology, and applied linguistics?

2. Is experiential language learning a viable approach for fostering second language acquisition? Why or why not?

3. How do the 4MAT System and Project Work differ in terms of organizing the instructional process?

4. What relationship does "control" have to experiential language learning?

5. Why is an oral history project more experiential than a simulation activity?

6. Why can computer-assisted language learning be considered experiential?

SUGGESTED ACTIVITIES

1. Following the lesson plan format developed by the Arlington Public Schools et al. (1987), develop an experiential language learning unit on a topic of your choice for a class of intermediate secondary students. Be sure to detail right and left brain activities for each of the four phases of learning.

2. Brainstorm various topics for large-scale, relevant projects which could be conducted in your community. Choose one of these topics and outline how library research, observation, interviews, questionnaires, and field trips could be incorporated into the learning process.

3. Imagine you are teaching a group of beginning ESL students at an adult school in your community. Your objective is to teach your students how to shop effectively at the supermarket. Outline experiential activities which could help reinforce the following skills: reading, writing, speaking, and listening.

4. Fried-Booth (1986) defines the Definition of the Project Objective stage as a time for project work group members to negotiate a topic. With a group of three or four other teacher trainees, spend one hour negotiating a topic and a plan for a 10-week social-welfare project in your community. Write a short report on (1) the roles that group members assumed (e.g., secretary, leader, passive observer) during the discussion and (2) the problems or surprises which occurred during the negotiation process.

SUGGESTIONS FOR FURTHER READING

Arlington Public Schools. ESOL/HILT Program and Center for Applied Linguistics (1987)
Integrating Styles and Skills: An Approach to Lesson Planning for the ESL Classroom. (ERIC Reproduction Services No. ED 292 292)

> A discussion of how Kolb's (1984) four learning phases and notions of analytic versus holistic learning can be applied in the writing of ESL lesson plans.

Dewey, J. (1938)
Experience and Education. New York: Macmillan.

> A pivotal work emphasizing the need to vitalize the learning of content through the process of experiential interaction.

Fried-Booth, D. (1986)
Project Work. Oxford: Oxford University Press.

> A comprehensive discussion of how experiential projects at all levels have been organized and implemented.

Hatch, E., and B. Hawkins (1987)
Second Language Acquisition: An Experiential Approach. In S. Rosenberg, ed., *Advances in Applied Psycholinguistics, Vol. 2 Reading, Writing and Language Learning* (pp. 241–283). Cambridge: Cambridge University Press.

> A convincing argument for incorporating social and cognitive components into any theory of the second language acquisition process.

Jerald, M., and R. Clark (1983)
Experiential Language Teaching Techniques: Resources Handbook Number 3. Brattleboro, VT: Pro Lingua Associates.

A variety of experiential language activities described and organized according to the degree of risk involved for the students.

APPENDIX

Lesson Plan taken from Arlington Public Schools, ESOL/HILT Program and Center for Applied Linguistics (1987)

LESSON PLAN I

Concept: Learning about Yourself
Topic: How To Write An Autobiography
Skill Emphasis: Writing
Audience: Beginning/intermediate/advanced-elementary and secondary students
Time Frame: Approximately 5 classes (50 minute periods). Primary students may need 10 days to complete the unit
Materials: Teacher's autobiography on newsprint
Submitted by: Shirley Porter

I. Motivation
   A. Teacher displays own autobiography on newsprint. Students make guesses as to what pictures/symbols might mean about teacher's life.
   B. Teacher shares autobiography with students. Students compare prior predictions with what they have learned about the teacher.

II. Information
   A. 1. Students compare autobiographical visual inventory.
      2. They also complete a web giving more details about the inventory.
   B. 1. Teacher uses a web of own name to extend thinking.
      2. Teacher models writing a descriptive composition about self.

III. Practice
   A. Each student uses own autobiographical visual inventory and personal verb to write a descriptive composition, "The Important Things About Me."
   B. Each child takes a turn in role of an author, reporter, and critic (Peer Conferencing).

IV. Application
   A. Students revise and edit stories. Copy stories in hand made books and illustrate.
   B. Students share books with reading partners. Contribute books to classroom library.

I. MOTIVATION

A. Create the Experience (Right Mode Strategies)

The teacher has a prepared autobiography done on newsprint. The paper can be divided into several sections, and a visual symbol or drawing relating to an important event in the teacher's life is represented in each section. After the students have looked over the pictures on the newsprint, they make guesses as to what the pictures might mean. This activity engages the students' attention immediately and helps to give focus to the lesson.

B. Reflect on the Experience (Left Mode Strategies)

The teacher now tells his/her own autobiography by explaining each picture. The students can talk about their prior predictions or what they now have learned about the teacher.

II. INFORMATION

A. Integrate Reflections Into Concepts (Right Mode Strategies)

Each student will relate the important parts of the teacher's autobiography to himself/herself. Each student will make a visual autobiographical inventory of himself/herself. Students will also make their own personal webs which are extensions of the visual autobiographical inventory. The visual imagery of the inventory will help students find appropriate vocabulary to put in their personal webs. The teacher will also use directed questioning to expand students' thinking about themselves. Both the visual inventory and personal web are excellent pre-writing activities. Ideally the information gathering process will help each student reflect on what makes each of them unique.

Autobiographical Visual Inventory

me	family
friends	house
pet	food
activities	things I like

B. Present and Develop Theories and Concepts (Left Mode Strategies)

As a group, the students will make a personal web of their teacher. Using his/her own web as created by the student, the teacher will model writing a composition, "The Important Things About Me." The teacher will ask the students' help in constructing the sentences. The students will be able to see how thoughts can be transferred into writing.

Personal Web

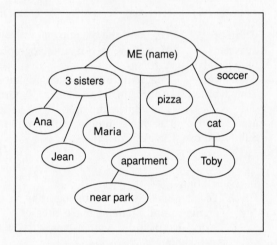

III. PRACTICE

A. Practice and Reinforce New Information (Left Mode Strategies)

Students will begin the writing process by transferring their ideas from their autobiographical inventories and personal webs into a descriptive composition about themselves. Prior thinking about themselves can now be extended into personal anecdotes.

B. Personalize the Experience (Right Mode Strategies)

Students meet in groups of three to share their compositions. The peer group conference gives the students a chance to interact with each other and share thinking about each other's writing.

IV. APPLICATION

A. Develop A Plan for Applying New Concepts (Left Mode Strategies)

Each student will now, with the teacher, go through the process of editing for capitalization, punctuation, and spelling. When the composition is completed, the student is ready to copy it into a book, illustrating each important event.

B. Do It and Share It With Others (Right
       Mode Strategies)
  The books will be read aloud and the reading
partner will have the opportunity to interact with
the author.

IV
Focus on the Learner

Many of the preceding chapters have focused on what the ESL teacher should know or what the teacher can do to facilitate student practice (and, one hopes, improvement) in a language skill, or in all four skills. However, unless the teacher is tutoring an individual, s/he must deal with a class—a group of individuals with different needs often growing out of their different linguistic and cultural backgrounds. The chapter by Peck recognizes classroom diversity and provides many constructive ways to meet learner needs. The three other chapters focus on special groups with special problems and needs. McGroarty's chapter on English instruction for minority students covers important issues for a variety of groups and provides useful teaching models and suggestions. Enright's chapter on ESL for children sensitizes the reader to the fact that the learners in this group offer teachers some of the biggest challenges yet also the greatest potential rewards and successes, provided that appropriate learning environments and materials are created. Hilles' chapter on the adult ESL learner offers an insightful overview of this population's dominant characteristics and needs.

Recognizing and Meeting the Needs of ESL Students

Sabrina Peck

INTRODUCTION

ESL students have widely different needs, because of differences in cultural background, age, and previous education. Even if the students in one class are all from the same language group, they inevitably have different learning styles and needs. And if teachers become sensitive to the needs of one group—for instance, nonacademic adults from many language backgrounds—they may still feel at a loss when their students are Eastern European senior citizens, or Navajo children, or Japanese businessmen, or highly motivated Taiwanese and Korean electrical engineering students. The goal of this article, then, is to offer some suggestions on how to find out the needs of one's students, and how to adapt oneself, the management of the class, and the curriculum to meet those needs. All the examples represent classes in North America; most of them are adult classes.

THE HOMOGENEOUS CLASS

Let's consider first classes that are homogenous according to age and cultural background. Later, because it is more complicated, we can consider heterogeneous classes. The students in homogeneous classes—Arabic-speaking graduate students, or Cantonese-speaking nonacademic adults, or Japanese high school students, or Puerto Rican first-graders, or Russian and Yiddish-speaking people in their 60s and 70s—are supposedly similar. But there are differences. Students have varied learning styles. And the teacher needs to be aware of the difficulties involved in teaching students with a common native language. Their social needs, their assumptions about the United States and about school, and the academic needs peculiar to each group also need to be taken into account. One way to deal with these differences—perhaps the only way

363

to do so creatively—is through individualized instruction.

Individualizing Instruction for Different Learning Styles

Handscombe and others (1974) suggest that teachers should individualize ESL instruction so that they teach in the ways in which students learn. They should assess each student's needs, recording a profile with such items as age, previous education and attitude toward education, preferred learning style, previous language learning, personality, occupation, and home environment. The teacher can assess student needs through observation, class discussions, individual talks with students, and assigned essays or questionnaires. Then, ideally, the teacher will have some notion about the students' needs, including these aspects of their learning style:

> preference for learning alone, in small groups, and in large groups
> ear/eye preference
> preference for observation vs. participation
> use of language analysis, rules, and explanations
> preference for immersion
> use of translation
> use of visuals
> uses of rote learning

Richterich (1983) cites many of the same methods of needs assessment, as well as surveys, polls, attitude scales, and tests. Richterich also argues that ongoing needs assessment is necessary. Schärer (1983) explains one format for ongoing assessment, a learner's logbook (with special pages supplying topics for the learner to respond to) and shows how the logbooks move teachers toward a more learner-centered approach.

Once teachers have some idea of their students' needs and learning styles, Handscombe et al. (1974) suggest a variety of individualized activities. Students could use the language lab alone during and outside of class. Even at the very beginning level, they could observe and note down the words they see on billboards and bring them to class for discussion. More advanced students could be assigned to find out prices and other information from restaurants or airlines, and later report back to the class. A variation of this would be to have students interview people in the community, such as personnel managers for a factory or a social worker at a clinic, and report back to the class on what they find out.

A teacher or an aide could form an interest group for students to learn vocabulary and structures relating to one specific area. For instance, a group could discuss how to describe a child's illness to a doctor, or their previous experience to a prospective employer. Another suggestion is for a group to discuss with the teacher appropriate clothes for a party or the beach, and then collectively make up dialogs for the occasion. Also, the teacher could introduce material for memorization, such as the language of weights and measures, and then supervise groups as they weighed and measured items in the classroom.

Pairs of adult students could teach simple material to each other, such as numbers or colors, and could do projects which they later presented to the group. They could discuss values clarification problems (Simon, Howe, & Kirschenbaum, 1972), or find out certain facts about each other, or make up a dialog to present to the teacher before they present it to the class. In addition, the teacher might work with one student on individual needs—the vocabulary for renting a house, or how to fill out a job application.

The article by Handscombe et al. (1974) gives a number of practical suggestions for individualizing ESL classes for adults, high school students, and elementary school children. Many of them could be adapted for use with any age group. For other accounts of individualized language instruction, see Pereyra-Suarez (1986) and Grossberg and Debenedetti (1984).

Increasing the Use of English Among Students Who Speak the Same Language: Teaching ESL to Children

With a homogeneous class of, for instance, all Puerto Rican children or all Korean children, the teacher can exploit the students' common cultural background as a natural source of subject matter, and plan interesting activities that are done in English. The children often enjoy studying aspects of life in their native country because they fondly remember their time there and because this material is something they can collectively explain to the teacher. Handscombe suggests role-plays such as acting out a day in a Korean school. Other ideas are to learn songs in the native language or in English, to make a mural or a model village, to cook native foods, and to talk about differences between life in the United States and life in the native country. Using culture as subject matter not only gives enjoyment and a clearer self-concept to the children; it also allows the teacher to learn about the children's culture through their eyes. The teacher can gain a general idea of their assumptions about school and teachers, home and family, which would be impossible to arrive at through library research or by asking children even the most expertly phrased questions.

If all the children speak the same language, how can the teacher encourage them to speak English to each other during the ESL class? One way is to use activities and materials that the children enjoy. If they are introduced to these materials in English, they will often continue to use English in connection with them, even to each other. For small children, the teacher could make flannelboard cutouts to represent the characters in a story such as "The Gingerbread Man." The teacher could encourage the children to learn the story, beginning with the parts that repeat (*Run, run, as fast as you can . . .*). Later steps could be for individual children or groups to tell the story, for the class to act it out, or for children to make their own paper-doll versions of the characters. The children could also learn some related songs, and of course, make some gingerbread men.

Some useful questions for planning lessons for ESL children of the same language background are these:

1. From what you know about the culture, and the individual children, what activities do they enjoy? (Example: Most Puerto Rican children in New England come from rural areas, and like animals.)
2. How could you plan activities that are keyed to the children's interests but presented in a slightly new way? (Example: The children may not have raised hamsters, built a hamster cage, or had a plastic, mazelike cage.)
3. How will you present the language of the activity? (Example: Take snapshots of the children building the hamster cage, and use the photos as the focus of a dialog, or as illustrations for a simple book.)

Teachers also need to respect the frequent desire of such children to do some work with reading and writing, even though they may feel that the pupils need oral work most of all. Second-graders and children in higher grades will probably expect and want reading and writing in English. They may have had some schooling in their native language and assume that school is where one reads and writes; at any rate, they will know that their American peers are reading and writing. There are ways to take advantage of ESL children's interest in written work while still giving them the oral work that they need. The teacher can give beginning students dittos for handwriting practice with the vocabulary and structures from the current oral lesson. Other exercises can involve more than copying. The teacher can use the language of classroom routines and activities for writing and sight-reading practice, and can label parts of the room (wall, window, desk, plants). It is useful to post the words for songs and poems the children are learning. Individual students or the entire group can dictate and then copy stories about the class hamster or the trip to the zoo. Polaroid pictures of the class are good material for the class to describe and write about.

When the children start to dictate stories to the teacher, s/he will have to decide whether correct English or the experience of copying or writing in English is more important. Some ESL teachers feel that they are fighting a battle twice by allowing children to dictate and copy such sentences as *Ms. Conlon, she coming down the stairs*. Others feel comfortable about transcribing the children's nonstandard English, and find that the language experience approach is a powerful tool for teaching reading and writing to nonnative speakers of English (see, e.g., Ashton-Warner, 1963).

These comments and suggestions on how to teach ESL classes for children of one language background, if stated in general terms, could be applied to classes for adolescents and adults as well. They are as follows:

1. Learn all you can about the students' culture, and use it as subject matter.
2. Plan activities that will be interesting, fun, and slightly novel.
3. Respect the students' attitudes about what "school" should be like, particularly the amount of reading and writing that should be involved.

The next three sections are examples of ESL classes in which teachers adapted their approach to meet the needs of a group. They give suggestions for meeting social needs (teaching ESL to older people), adjusting to students' assumptions about what school should be like (teaching ESL to Chinese nonacademic adults), and meeting academic needs that are common to one native language group (teaching Arabic-speaking university students).

Meeting Social Needs: Teaching ESL to Older People

Buzan (1972) describes a successful ESL program for senior citizens in British Colum-

bia. This group was heterogeneous in terms of language backgrounds, but homogeneous in the sense that all the students were older people. Many of them were lonely, and attending the ESL class was one of the few reasons for which they left their homes. Because of this, the teachers paid more attention than usual to the students' social needs. There was a coffee break at the halfway point of every evening. Students brought homemade cookies and breads, and the students from all levels gathered in one place. Friendships developed between people of different language backgrounds. Because the teachers allowed the students to socialize in a way in which they were comfortable, attendance was excellent, and students made new friends with whom they could practice their English. The teachers, the students, and their relatives thought that the coffee breaks and the friendships that developed out of them were vital in motivating the students, and giving them opportunities to practice English.

Adjusting to Students' Assumptions About School: Teaching ESL to Chinese Nonacademic Adults

Asian assumptions about the United States, the student–teacher relationship, school, and finding a job are very different from those of Anglo-Americans (Asian Project Materials, 1972). Teachers working with Asians for the first time can find that they need to adapt to attitudes which at first seem inexplicable. Such teachers might benefit from an explanation of the kinds of stresses that Asian refugees face, and some suggestions for crisis intervention (Quan, 1986).

Asians often think of the United States as a country that is rich in resources and opportunities for making money, but spiritually poor. Because they think of the United States as a young country without a mature culture, it is important to show them how our culture is derived from European cultures. Holidays would be good opportunities for the teacher to present lessons that make this point.

Asians have great respect for teachers and do not want to lose face with them. They are accustomed to rote recitation in the classroom, and may be reluctant to speak out or ask questions in class. Some suggestions for the teacher (Asian Project Materials, 1972) are as follows:

1. Explain the American customs concerning calling someone by a first or last name. Give the students a choice to be called "Ji Kim" or "Mrs. Kim," for example.
2. Be friendly.
3. Be nonthreatening in oral activities. For instance, ask students to repeat or to answer yes-no questions. Give them conversations to memorize.

Asians may feel that the teacher does not respect their maturity if the emphasis is on oral work with pictures. The teacher could explain the importance of oral skills. Oral drills should be contextualized, and each lesson could end with real communication utilizing the structures. With more advanced groups, the teacher should choose conversation topics with discretion. Many students may be uncomfortable discussing personal topics. The Chinese are particularly reluctant to talk about death, illness, or accidents (Asian Project Materials).

Handouts can relate oral and written work. To keep the students from being distracted, handouts could be distributed after the oral practice. Terrell (1971) suggests including Chinese translations of the English vocabulary, since students want translation and will otherwise waste time by noting the phonetic transcription in characters, or searching for the meaning in a bilingual dictionary.

Reading and writing should be included in the classwork and homework, even for beginners. Terrell notes that Chinese students can handle sight-reading (or word recognition) without phonics for a long time, since their system of writing with characters requires them to sight-read. The teacher could have students practice writing the new words of each lesson with the model provided on dittos. The handwriting dittos make good homework assignments, as do review drills, narratives to read with new words translated, and comprehension questions to answer. Terrell feels that Chinese students want and expect homework. However, since adult school students probably have jobs, it is best not to plan class time around completed homework assignments.

In a job interview, Chinese adults often do not stress their talents and past experience. While respecting the students' humble attitude, the teacher could help them to see that such an attitude is harmful when seeking employment in North America. The teacher could explain that the job applicant in the United States or Canada mentions relevant work experience, and tries to prove that s/he is the best qualified applicant. The teacher could help Chinese students by having them role-play job interviews, and write up their résumés. In general, teachers should be alert to the influence of cultural and social factors on their students' learning; see *Beyond Language: Social and Cultural Factors in Schooling Language Minority Students* (California State Department of Education, 1986).

Meeting the Academic Needs of Students from One Language Group: Teaching ESL to Arabic-Speaking University Students

The Chinese example gives pedagogical suggestions arising from a sort of cultural contrastive analysis. In the next case, Yorkey (1974) predicts areas or rhetorical and grammatical difficulty for Arabic-speaking students. In Arabic there is use of coordination, not subordination, in written paragraphs. A tightly organized English paragraph, with its topic sentence, controlling idea, and supporting ideas, is a manner of expression which is foreign to Arabic-speaking students, and one which they often interpret as "cold and calculating." Modifying the Arabic student's rhetoric, however, could be as sensitive a task for the teacher as explaining the need for oral work to Chinese adults. Sometimes students feel that the way in which they organize their ideas is a cherished part of their personality. They resent being told to write according to English rhetoric; it is as if the teacher had told them to think and feel differently.

Yorkey suggests that the teacher give Arabic-speaking students practice in writing and identifying different paragraph components. They need practice with subordinate clauses (particularly adverb clauses of time and place, result, concession, cause, purpose, and condition). They need practice in identifying the topic sentence and other components of a paragraph.

The correction of bad grammatical habits is usually not such an emotional process. Scott and Tucker (1974) state that most grammatical problems for Arabic-speaking students are in the areas of verbs, prepositions, articles, and relative clauses. An almost universal problem is the presence of redundant object pronouns in relative clauses, resulting in clauses which are grammatical in Arabic but ungrammatical in English:

The teacher is the woman that you know her.
The book which I am looking for it is sold out.

THE HETEROGENEOUS CLASS

The preceding sections have given some examples of how to take individual needs and learning styles into account, and how to meet some needs of a seemingly homogeneous group. But the more usual kind of adult ESL class in North America is composed of a wide variety of students, all with their own needs reflecting the amount of education they have had in their native languages, the types of previous instruction in English, their ages and emotional needs. When a teacher first meets with a heterogeneous class, it is easy to feel at a loss about what to do because the students seem to have nothing in common.

Amount of Education in the Native Language

The same class may include students from 10 different countries, ranging from some who are illiterate in their native languages to some with Ph.D.'s. The teacher will need some access to materials on basic literacy (see the chapter by Hawkins and the one by Haverson in this volume, and Eley & Lewis, 1976). The teacher may want to use the backgrounds of the students as a resource in the class. A doctor from Iran and a mechanic from Cuba each have access to a special vocabulary and a specialized body of knowledge. Each could explain some of this vocabulary, or present a dialog that would get results if someone needed a physical exam or a tune-up for a car.

Type of Prior ESL Instruction

Some differences in instructional needs are rooted in differences in the kind of ESL instruction students have had in their native countries. Many Japanese students, for example, have had rigorous instruction in grammar, but need listening and speaking practice. Arabic-speaking students often need extra help with spelling, handwriting, and the mechanics of writing. And people who have been exposed to spoken English more than written English (some Latino immigrants fall into this category) may need reading and writing more than the other skills. All of these statements are simplistic and overgeneralized, but together they give some idea of the range of differences the ESL teacher may encounter.

Age

High-school-age or adolescent students may have vastly different needs from those of adults with more defined personal goals. Adolescents are usually exploring goals and identities, while adults are more settled in their goals. How can the teacher accommodate the needs of both groups in one class?

In night schools, some of the younger students register for an ESL class because they want to make friends, especially of the opposite sex. Assigning papers to be written as a group, or skits to be made up and presented in class by groups may satisfy some of their social as well as academic needs. Values clarification discussions and other activities in which students examine and express their own feelings are effective with adolescents (Maureen Schmid, personal communication).

These young students may also need some counseling about America culture. One teacher gives the example of an 18-year-old woman from an Arabic-speaking country. In her native country the woman had not been allowed to go out by herself or with friends. In the United States, however, she had her own car and was drinking and driving with her high school friends. She thought that she was acting like an American teenager. There are many ways to explore the myths and realities of American teenage culture, and still teach ESL. Students could discuss advice columns such as Ann Landers or Dear Abby, and make up their own responses to the questions people have written in, or view and discuss movies such as *Rebel Without a Cause*.

The problem is, however, that there are not only adolescents in the class, but adults who are studying English in order to reach a specific goal: to get into a university, or become a dental technician, or join a construction workers' union. Generally, because their personal goals are definite, adults are less interested in group work and discussion activities, and intent on being taught and tested on specific points of English: grammar, vocabulary, spelling, reading, and writing. What many adult students want from the teacher are grammar explanations, assignments, and feedback. They have often had very little oral work, and may not feel that an ESL class is a place for them to practice speaking. Hurst (1985) found that adult school teachers and students, by and large, agreed on the students' needs. For example, the top-ranked need in every demographic category was for improved reading skills. Just the same, while students may report similar academic needs, the teacher can still have difficulty in teaching different kinds of students.

Obviously, the teacher cannot please all the students all the time. The adolescents need some grammar work, and group work can be an effective way of giving adult students more chances to talk in class. The teacher might be able to motivate some adolescents by discussing with them American attitudes toward people with foreign accents or grammatical mistakes in their speech. The teacher could give these students some information about sociolinguistic experiments (Lambert & Tucker, 1969) and ask the students to anticipate and interpret the results. Adults might show more interest in group discussions if the topics were relevant to their goals (how to act at a job interview, how to fill out an income tax form) or if they could use their own experiences as adults (what makes a good father, what makes people feel young or old). So in dealing with adolescents and adults in the same class, teachers can try to make each group see why traditional activities and nontraditional activities are important, and they can sometimes gear the subject matter of the activity to the group that has less interest in the educational purpose of the activity. Other ways of dealing with this problem are to individualize as many activities as possible (the teacher will need to make or buy materials) or to assign different tasks to different groups of students (if there is a teacher's aide or volunteer working in the class).

Emotional Needs

Teachers of young children have to be concerned with the different emotional needs of their pupils and the importance of meeting these needs. ESL teachers need to be concerned, too. Unfortunately, texts for ESL teachers may not discuss emotional needs, even though many writers compare the task of learning a language with becoming a child again. This discussion is limited to two common issues: students who are too loud or too quiet, and class reactions to a teaching style that seems too authoritarian or too free.

In one university-level class, students complained that one student talked too much and was wasting the class time. They appealed to the teacher to control the student. Sometimes loud students need to feel more important. One suggestion is to give such students extra responsibility in the class, such as coordinating the transportation to a party or collecting money for extra materials. In group work, it may be best to put all the loud students together. In addition, the teacher might chat with a loud student outside of class and, by listening to his or her comments and questions, make the student feel that it is unnecessary to bring up these points in class. The teacher could tell the loud student what the other students had said, and how the student might avoid annoying them. In classes where students seem to be too quiet, some of the comments in the section on teaching Chinese adults may apply.

Even adult students may have a strong need for an authoritarian classroom atmosphere. Because of personality, cultural background, or age, some students want to be told exactly what to do. They feel that a class is a place not for learning but for being taught. Other students want a democratic atmosphere; they want to contribute to discussions, give presentations, and make suggestions about what activities should go on in class. One way for the teacher to deal with this situation is to make his or her own objectives and standards clear to the students (e.g., by stating them in the course description and by discussing them with the class at the beginning of the course or unit) and accomplish some of these objectives through "democratic" teaching methods. For instance, if one goal of the course is that all students will write well-organized paragraphs, the teacher can lead a discussion in which the students are asked to come up with a set of defining qualities for a well-organized paragraph. The students will know, of course, that the teacher has his or her own ideas about what a well-organized paragraph is. Thus, the teacher has control over the content (and probably the outcome) of the discussion, but the students have a chance to consider, evaluate, and discuss the problem before the teacher gives any input.

SUMMARY

Because of (and in spite of) his or her background, every ESL student is unique. Some factors which combine to make students unique are native language, cultural background, age, emotional and social needs, learning style, level of education, and previous instruction in English. One goal of this article has been to make new teachers aware of some of the differing needs that ESL students have. These needs form a continuum from the purely academic (e.g., poor reading ability) to the social or personal (e.g., fear of talking to native speakers). Another goal has been to give examples of some ways that teachers can adapt their curriculum and their classroom management style, in order to meet the needs of more of the students more of the time.

Some ways to find out the students' needs are through individual and group discussions, forms or questionnaires, compositions, and an examination of their oral and written work. With children, asking them to make up skits or puppet shows can be an effective way for the teacher to find out about the child's culture and attitudes toward school. To have some idea about a student's social needs, emotional needs, and learning style, observation and intuition may be more productive tools than assigning questionnaires or essays to the students. Contrastive analyses may be very helpful for the teacher, not just in pointing out phonological, syntactic, and semantic problems, but sometimes in describing areas of cultural differences (Asian attitudes toward school) or discourse differences (Arabic rhetoric).

In adapting the curriculum to meet students' needs, teachers can use different types of commercial materials, and make use of the interests and talents of their students. They can design units around a particular culture (e.g., a unit on the Taino Indians for a class of Puerto Rican children) or allow each student to teach the class something about his or her own culture in a heterogeneous adult class. Teachers can take social and emotional needs into consideration when they pick topics for discussion and assign students to groups. They can plan lessons, choose commercial materials, and decide on groupings in order to meet students' varied academic needs.

In adapting their system of classroom management, teachers will want to be aware of whether the students, as a group, can handle an authoritarian or democratic style of teaching. They will need to be aware of which students like to participate orally and which do not. They may want to individualize some or all of the class instruction. Because older adult students and adolescent students have their own social needs, they may want to allow extra time for a coffee break during the class.

ESL teachers are, in one sense, jugglers, juggling the needs of an astonishing variety of students—a computer scientist from Korea, a Taiwanese dental student, the wife of a Latin American diplomat, and a young high school dropout from El Salvador. Even the students in a "homogeneous" class may seem to have little in common. While teachers cannot satisfy all of the students all of the time, they can strive to identify and to meet, as far as possible, their differing needs.

DISCUSSION QUESTIONS

1. What can a teacher do to help ESL students to make friends with other learners and with native speakers?

2. How would you balance your preferences and those of your students for a class that is "authoritarian" or "democratic"?

3. Schärer (1983) thinks that the training of language teachers should be planned around the identification of learner needs. If your teacher training program were reorganized in this way, how might it change? Would the changes be desirable?

4. When working with immigrant ESL students, is it more important for the teacher to adapt to the students or for the teacher to help students adapt to their new country? Give reasons for your position.

5. Is ongoing needs assessment essential (as Richterich suggests)? Why or why not?

SUGGESTED ACTIVITIES

1. Observe an ESL class for several days and focus on one student. Watch the student's expression and body language, and also note what s/he says. From your observations, make some hypotheses about what you think his/her needs are in the ESL class. If possible, discuss your ideas with the teacher or another observer.

2. If you are not studying a foreign language, take a minicourse at the beginning level of a language, or ask a teacher for permission to sit in during the first two weeks of class. Keep a journal of your reactions. As a learner, how do you feel in the class? Do you like the way the teacher treats you? What kind of teaching is helpful to you? What do you want from the other students? What are your needs?

3. Interview an ESL student about his/her needs in the ESL class. Use questions that you have prepared. With the student's permission, tape-record the interview. In listening to it later, ask yourself which of your questions received informative responses. Would other ways of phrasing them have been more effective? Would other questions have been more productive?

4. Interview ESL teachers to find out in what ways their students are different. Ask them how they deal with having a variety of students in the same class.

SUGGESTIONS FOR FURTHER READING

Ashton-Warner, S. (1963)
Teacher. New York: Simon & Schuster.

An account of how the writer taught Maori primary school children in New Zealand. Especially interesting is her individualized method of teaching reading and writing.

Holt, J. (1964)
How Children Fail. New York: Pitman.

Holt, J. (1969)
How Children Learn. New York: Pitman.

Holt describes children's individual learning styles and needs. A good example of what a sensitive observer can find out about students by watching and listening.

Logan, G. E. (1973)
Individualized Foreign Language Learning: Organic Process. New York: Newbury House.

A detailed description of the author's system for individualizing the teaching of German at the high school level.

Schmidt, R., and S. Frota (1986)
Developing basic conversational ability in a second language: A case study of an adult learner of Portuguese. In R. Day, ed., *Talking to Learn: Conversation in Second Language Acquisition*. New York: Newbury House.

This case study by the learner (Schmidt) and a linguist and native speaker of Portuguese (Frota) will stimulate your thinking about what kinds of questions need to be included in a needs assessment.

Simon, S. B., L. W. Howe, and H. Kirschenbaum (1972)
Values Clarification: A Handbook of Practical Strategies for Teachers and Students. New York: Hart.

Includes topics for groupwork and discussion.

Wolfram, W. (1969)
Sociolinguistic Implications for Educational Sequencing. In R. W. Fasold and R. W. Shuy, *Teaching English to Black Children*. Washington, DC: Center for Applied Linguistics.

Points out that grammatical features are a stronger sign of social class than are other language features.

English Instruction for Linguistic Minority Groups
Different Structures, Different Styles

Mary McGroarty

INTRODUCTION: STRUCTURES AND STYLES

It is a truism that one needs to know English to live and work in an English-speaking country like the United States. Yet for many social groups, both immigrant and indigenous, the questions related to acquisition of English are complicated. When standard English is either a second language or a second dialect for students from these groups, both the methods and curricula used to teach English may well differ to some degree from those used with native speakers who have already mastered the standard language. In this chapter, I discuss some of the issues to consider when planning instruction for second language or second dialect speakers faced with the task of mastering English within the U.S. school system.

Differences between the language a group uses and the language of mainstream classrooms and workplaces may be dramatic and easily noticeable or subtle and hard to identify. To speak of linguistic difference is to speak of differences in both the *structures* of language, the differences in pronunciation, morphology, vocabulary, and syntax, that may exist, and the styles, or *ways of using language,* i.e., the discourse patterns, conventions for taking turns, providing narrative accounts, and indicating agreement or disagreement; these go beyond surface level features into the way language is used in social interaction. Since 1980, scholarly work in sociolinguistics, discourse analysis, and anthropology has expanded our awareness of the different ways of using language that characterize different speech communities and social settings. While the types of differences described in Arthur (1979)— differences in the forms or structures of English which signal the influence of another language or a dialect—remain relevant to English instruction, we now seek to address other sorts of differences as well. Even where the forms of language are similar to those used in the mainstream, the ways of using language for communicative purposes may differ (Heath, 1983). Accustomed to looking for differences in the forms of language that may impede communication or comprehensibility, teachers and researchers have become increasingly aware of the need to include consideration of different approaches to style, or ways of using language, as factors that shape the language repertoire students bring to school. In this discussion, then, we will be concerned with both the formal and the pragmatic differences in language use evidenced in various linguistic minority groups, for both kinds of differences bear on the choice of appropriate educational programs.

DEFINITIONS: WHAT IS "STANDARD," AND WHO NEEDS IT?

First, some definitions. The term "linguistic minority group" is used here to refer to any person who uses a language or dialect other than standard English as the usual means of communication in everyday life. The nature of "standard English" in the American context is subject to some debate, for the boundaries and features of standardness are variable; I use it here to refer to the forms of language used on national communications networks, in newspapers and textbooks, and by most college-educated speakers. Hence, the term "standard English" refers to a set of related language varieties, not to an invariant norm. This definition of "standardness" is based on conformity to the norms of social acceptability more than accuracy in communication (see Williams, 1987, p. 161 ff.; Willinsky, 1984; Wolfram & Christian, 1989, pp. 9–14). However, since speakers communicate in a social world and students and teachers interact in social settings, it is reasonable to use such a definition.

Who are the linguistic minority groups of concern with respect to the teaching of English? There are many. Even a short overview serves to indicate the great diversity included in the term.

Most obvious, perhaps, are the groups of recently arrived immigrants for whom English is clearly a second language. They still use other languages as the typical means of communication in their neighborhoods, in churches, in business, at home. Whether the language in question is Spanish, a Chinese dialect, Haitian Creole, Korean, or Vietnamese, it is the common means of communication. For persons from such groups, techniques derived from English as a second language methods that build from the ground up in all four skill areas make up the clearly indicated course of action.

However, there is a caveat: Language use in immigrant communities is not static, any more than language in any community stands still. Cross-generational language shift away from the native language toward English is a common occurrence, with the first generation relying on the native language, the second generation usually understanding the native language but speaking English to age peers, and the third generation relying on English (Lopez, 1978, 1982; Veltman, 1983). Thus, in immigrant communities including more than one generation, as all eventually do, the matter of language use is a dynamic one. The same community may include persons with little usable knowledge of English all the way to those who are fluent English speakers, able to use English as well as native speakers. Indeed, in long-term second language communities, speakers of the non-English language may be far outnumbered by those who use English most often, although the English-dominant community members may retain some skills in the other tongue.

In such mixed communities, one often finds speakers with very different skill profiles in English. For example, children exposed informally to English speakers on the playground and in school often show very high degrees of listening comprehension in English and oral skills appropriate to the informal settings in which they have been exposed to English. Hence, they often sound entirely native-like in certain situations. Put into different settings, though, they continue to use informal forms of English even where these might not be appropriate. Furthermore, their control of standard grammar and reading and writing skills may well not be equivalent to those of native speakers. Cummins's work in Canada (1981a, 1984) as well as investigations by U.S. scholars (Collier, 1987) show that it takes five to seven years for immigrant children to approximate age norms of native-speaker peers on most academic tests. The English of immigrant students may thus sound native-like long before their school-related literacy skills permit native-like performance.

Other linguistic minority groups are not immigrants at all. The United States displays a rich history of indigenous languages and other languages which pre-exist widespread use of English (Ferguson & Heath, 1981). All of these languages, as well as the developments in present-day English, have contributed to the diversity of language used in American classrooms today.

Before discussing this diversity further, some general observations are in order. Dialect differences exist in all communities; their salience to educational programs is a matter of degree. Historically, one of the great motivators of dialect differences is the urban-rural split that generally led rural speakers to use forms of language that were often more conservative than their urban counterparts (Trudgill, 1983, chap. 2). With the migration of rural dwellers to the cities, regional dialects have taken on social significance (Labov, 1972b, pp. 299–304), so that speech patterns once indicative of place of origin now have social connotations which may be unfavorable for the speakers with rural origins or family connections. This phenomenon is not limited to communities of people of color: many whites with rural origins also use forms of language different from those of city dwellers. Thus, in the large cities of the North and Midwest to which many Appalachian natives migrated since World War II because of availability of jobs, there are often perceptibly different dialects spoken and different pragmatic conventions for language use evident in white communities also. This is one reason why many mid-Atlantic and Midwest states, whose cities include many former rural Southerners now employed in manufacturing or other large industrial concerns, have shown continuing interest in the questions of diversity of dialect and its impact on education (Underwood, 1983; Wolfram & Christian, 1976).

Native Americans preceded English speakers on this continent by millenia. The language situation of these indigenous Americans is unusually diverse, for they belong to some 235 different tribes (Deloria, 1988) which currently use, maintain, or are in the process of reviving 206 different languages (Leap, 1981, p. 116), many of which represent entirely disparate, nonmutually intelligible language families. The voluntary and forced movements of native American nations across the continent have dispersed speakers of different native languages widely and created small pockets of isolated speakers of native languages (Leap, 1981, p. 125). Tribes have shown different degrees of success in conserving their own languages while using English; some, such as the Navajo, still use the native language for many community purposes, while for others, such as the Piscataway or Miami, English has become the only means of communication (Leap, 1981). Even when English has become the usual medium of communication, though, it is often influenced by the substrate language in ways that lead speakers of other varieties to consider the English spoken by native Americans as nonstandard. Even when native Americans speak only English, they may grow up in a community where they have contact mainly with other speakers who learned English as a second language; thus, their use of language may reflect the nativized structures and styles of English similar to those that emerge in well-established creole situations (Beck & Foster, 1989). In native American communities, then, the range of language issues includes matters of both second language and second dialect.

Other indigenous communities also include speakers whose ancestral language, even if they are no longer fluent in it, has shaped the kind of English they use. Native Hawaiians who rely on Hawaiian Creole English (HCE) for all communication at home and in their neighborhoods often find some of the forms and the usage patterns of mainstream English foreign on school entry (Gallimore, Boggs, & Jordan, 1974). Among the styles of note in educational settings are the use of cooperative narratives, or talk-stories, which may be constructed by many speakers using overlapping speech and informal, rapid-fire turn-taking to create a mutually satisfying group conversation (Jordan, 1983; Tharp & Gallimore, 1989, pp. 151–53).

Black Americans, too, face language issues that derive from other languages as well as those motivated by dialectal development. Speakers of Gullah, a long-established creole found on the Sea Islands of South Carolina and Georgia, demonstrate notable influences from the languages of West Africa as well as features such as copula deletion and reduced past-tense marking and expanded aspectual systems typical of other English-based creoles (Nichols, 1981, pp. 73–77). Although the precise nature of the influence of African languages on Black English has long been debated (see Labov, 1983, p. 30; Williams, 1987, pp. 162–67), there is enough evidence to indicate that at least some features of the languages spoken by many of the original slaves have carried over into Black English.

Of far greater impact on Black Vernacular English, though, are the circumstances of geographical and social isolation which have often meant that black speakers of English interact mainly with other users of dialect and only rarely with other speakers, black or white, who use standard English. Furthermore, the use of Black Vernacular English as an in-group medium of communication also dictates change: as terms from Black English are absorbed into mainstream white usage, black speakers often develop new terms to convey the meanings "lost" to general use in the nonblack community (Smitherman, 1986, p. 49). Like the term "standard English," which denotes a whole set of related language varieties, the term "Black English" includes many varieties, not all of which could be called nonstandard. The black community includes a great range of speakers, all the way from those who are fully bidialectal and use the standard forms fluently, whenever appropriate, to those who rely mainly on dialectal forms and may have difficulty comprehending or, more often, using standard features of language. Lack of knowledge of the standard forms may be especially problematic for students who come to school knowing mainly dialect forms but must become literate in standard English (Labov, 1983; Underwood, 1983).

Hence, linguistic diversity is evident in communities of recent immigrants and long-term residents, in indigenous communities of native Americans and early creole speakers, in the black community, and indeed, in white communities that include speakers with rural origins or influences. Other language minority groups reflect yet other patterns of language use with respect to alternation between English and a different home language. Many of the Amish, for example, maintain use of varieties of Dutch and German in addition to English and have mastered appropriate literacy conventions for the use of each (A. Fishman, 1988). For groups like the Amish, whose participation in public education is generally limited, the persistence of bilingualism or bidialectalism is not perceived as a problem.[1] Nonetheless, these groups add to the language diversity that makes the United States linguistically "more interesting than it lets itself admit" (Hymes, 1981, p. v).

There is another linguistic minority deserving mention here: the deaf users of English for whom American Sign Language (ASL) is the principal means of intragroup communication. ASL, a system of visual sign language with its own conventions of syntax and expression, is not simply English translated into signs. Indeed, one of the current controversies in the deaf community is related to the appropriate use of language in instruction: should deaf students be instructed in ASL, in their native language, or in signed English, which is simply standard English transposed into sign (I. K. Jordan, 1989)? While the situation of deaf speakers will not be discussed further here, it is important to keep in mind that they too represent a linguistic minority community with particular communicative needs in the educational system. Questions related to the educational impact of the use of sign language are somewhat different from those related to differences in verbal languages. Nonetheless, some of the social and political questions related to appropriate education apply to the deaf as well as to other linguistic minority groups.

GOALS FOR ENGLISH LANGUAGE INSTRUCTION

The goals of English language instruction may well differ for each of the groups listed above. Furthermore, depending on age, first language background, and educational and occupational goals, differing emphases are in order. An examination of some of the needs within and across linguistic minority groups gives a sense of the range of different types of relevant language instruction.

For adults who are very recent immigrants (a group that will constitute 21 percent of all new workers between 1985 and 2000; see U.S. Department of Labor, 1988), comprehension of English sufficient to get a job and the ability to communicate orally in order to work are usually paramount (McGroarty, Delgado-Gaitan, Romero, & Hurst, 1989). For these individuals, English instruction needs to provide skills in basic forms of communication required to survive in the community and communicate with co-workers and the public. Related literacy instruction often includes reading work-related materials, filling out forms, and understanding materials related to parental assistance for school-age children.

However, mastery of simple oral English is not enough for any student, kindergarten through university, being educated in American schools. The questions of achievement of full academic literacy for second language or dialect students is the central question facing educators today. Students who come to school speaking other languages or divergent dialects of English need to develop the skills in reading and writing that allow them access to higher levels of education. For them, then, English instruction cannot be limited to oral skills, for such a limitation would constrain their ability to deal with the full range of curricular subjects in English. Even for relatively recent arrivals, oral skills in English do not always predict academic abilities well (Saville-Troike, 1984). In fact, many students who are second dialect users in the home or have been in American schools for more than three years have virtually no difficulties with comprehension of informal oral language and can speak fluent English. Difficulties arise, however, when they are asked to read and comprehend dense text materials or write academic prose that follows certain conventions. For these students, the issue of full communicative competence must include mastery of the range of uses of written language in academic settings.

Whether the goal of English language instruction is oral skills, written skills, or both, it must include attention to the socially appropriate forms of language that enable a speaker to interact successfully in relevant settings. This may include the awareness of the conventions of an American job interview, such as expressing interest in a particular job (even if none is felt) or stating one's qualifications and experiences in ways that are specific to the job in question (Akinnaso & Ajirotutu, 1982). For school-age students, it may be learning how to ask for help from the teacher or other students or managing to present a personal story so that it is accepted by teachers and peers as relevant (Kochman, 1981, chap. 2; Michaels, 1986). It must be emphasized that none of these forms or uses of language need supersede or replace the student's native language or dialect. There is no evidence to support the claim that extinguishing a native language or dialect leads to improved progress in the second language or standard dialect, a claim often made for both immigrant (discussed in Cummins, 1984) and indigenous (see Holm, 1989) linguistic minority groups. Instead, in all cases, English language instruction is to be directed at expansion of communicative resources, an increase in linguistic capital (Bourdieu & Passeron, 1977; Rossi-Landi, 1975), not replacement of one linguistic pattern by another.

Given, then, that English language instruction fulfills a function of expansion rather than contraction of resources, of additive rather than subtractive language use, how are teachers to begin to recognize the linguistic factors that bear on language instruction for their students? One way, as suggested above, is to conduct a needs analysis of communicative requirements. This is particularly suitable for older students whose occupational and academic goals are quite specific. The literature on English for Specific Purposes (see Johns, this volume) provides guidance here. Other questions related to general consideration in meeting learner needs are covered by Peck (this volume), and the needs specific to children who first encounter English in school and must develop the skill to succeed in English-medium classrooms are described by Enright (this volume). Whatever their age or goals, linguistic minority students have general instructional needs comparable to those of other students. Nevertheless, in addition to their many similarities to other students, individuals from linguistic minority groups bring with them communicative forms and patterns that may differ from those of other students. Often these differences are far less problematic for students than for mainstream teachers unacquainted with differing communicative styles (Kleifgen, 1988).

COMMUNITY LANGUAGE USE AS TEACHERS' KNOWLEDGE BASE

So that teachers can appreciate the skills of their students, it is useful for them to be able to recognize certain communicative events that form a part of students' experiences. Such events may include particular ways of combining English and another language in code switching, a form of language use very common in bilingual communities and often exploited for both communicative and expressive purposes (Attinasi, Pedraza, Poplack, & Pousada, 1982; Silva-Corvalán, 1983). Fluent intrasentential code switching indicates a high degree of proficiency in both languages (Poplack, 1979) and is thus a sign of communicative skill rather than deficit. Though code switching is comparatively rare in classrooms, teachers should recognize it as a natural part of the communication of bilinguals. Some methods of bilingual instruction (cf. Jacobson, 1981, 1989) even encourage teachers to code switch following certain cues in order to reach bilingual students effectively.

Some speech events are characteristic of certain dialect communities. The verbal skills displayed in rapping and sounding are often important indicators of status in the black community, particularly for adolescent male speakers (Kochman, 1981; Labov, 1972a). Again, while such events are rarely part of the "official" classroom discourse between students and teachers, teachers need to recognize them as important parts of a student's communicative repertoire.

In linguistic minority communities, students may be socialized to language in ways that differ from the patterns found in mainstream settings. In her study of black and white communication patterns in the Piedmont Carolinas, Heath (1983) found that the labeling and display questions so prominent in many early elementary school classrooms were not part of the socialization patterns of black children, while many questions related to general meanings or analysis of alternative interpretation of stories were not emphasized in either lower-class black or white childraising. Both groups of children were thus puzzled when asked to answer such questions in school. Differential orientations to language socialization have also been observed in communities of relatively recent immigrants. In northern California communities, Heath (1986) and her colleagues found that Chinese children were often in the care of an adult, frequently a grandparent, while young Mexican-American children spent relatively more time in the company of age peers. It is not surprising, then, that in bilingual classrooms there was a tendency for students' learning proclivities, particularly at the beginning level, to follow these cultural patterns, with Chinese children depending on teacher models and Hispanic children on peer models for English (Wong Fillmore, Ammon, McLaughlin, & Ammon, 1985). Moreover, because socialization to language is a lifelong process based on the continuing interaction of a speaker with members of his or her community (Ochs, 1988, p. 6), members of linguistic minority communities may continue to develop patterns of language use and norms different from those corresponding to the "invisible culture" (Philips, 1972, 1983) of mainstream classrooms. This again suggests that teachers need to take a replacive rather than a suppressive stance.

Teachers also need to be aware of competing norms for language use. As students move through elementary and junior high school years, they become increasingly sensitive to the influences of their peers in language use (Gardner, 1979; Labov, 1972a, 1982). The competition may be between the value system of the school and that of the street, or the larger community, as described in Labov (1982), or between the values attached to different ethnic styles of communication of students who must share a classroom, as noted by Kochman (1981, chap. 2). Whether students are second language or second dialect speakers, they will learn the kind of English used by their peers whom they hold in esteem; the basis for this esteem stems from the student's own values that may or may not match those of school authorities. Thus, in communities where second language learners have contact mainly with students who speak a dialectal variant of English, whether that dialect is Black Vernacular English or small-town Midwestern, they will acquire the dialect form of English because that is the form with which they have most frequent contact (Labov, Cohen, Robins, & Lewis, 1968). Teachers who work with such students need to be sure that, in terms of oral skills, they can understand the standard forms (usually not a problem, since receptive skills often reach native-like levels of development after two or three years' residence; in addition, students need to be able to use standard speech forms when appropriate.

Some of the differences in uses of language include uses of nonlinguistic aspects of communication, such as body language and management of silence. These are often crucially important in educational decision making, as Gilmore's (1985) work has shown. In the predominantly black junior high school she studied, having the proper "attitude" was just as important in determining entrance into the gifted program as scores on tests of academic skill. "Attitude" included demonstration of body postures that teachers interpreted as paying attention and not "sulking" or giving nonverbal signals of challenge to the teacher (at least not excessively). Many educators working with native American students have noted the relatively longer pause length which these students display in classroom interaction (Erickson & Mohatt, 1982; Greenbaum, 1985). This longer pause length does not indicate lack of knowledge but is simply consistent with turn-taking norms which govern other aspects of verbal behavior in many native American communities.

A final area for teacher awareness, and one that is critically important for teachers of young children, is that of the difference between the "normal" differences due to second language or dialect influence and any condition of language development or perception that indicates learning delay or difficulty. For too long, members of minority groups in American schools have been labeled as learning-disabled or even retarded based on testing done entirely in standard English (Mercer, 1973, 1983; Trueba, 1989); hence, members of such groups are, with reason, sensitive to any kind of testing for language delay or handicap. Nevertheless, it is important to be able to differentiate language patterns which are the result of the influence of another language or dialect from those that may indicate an idiosyncratic individual difficulty with production or comprehension of language. For aspects of oral language development, some tests now provide norms for other languages in addition to English. Many

testing batteries for young children (see, e.g., the SOMPA; Mercer, 1979) make explicit attempts to use tasks that are not bound to mainstream cultural contexts. Use of testing personnel who speak the language or dialect of the learners is also essential in the task of distinguishing the normal effects of community language patterns from those of individual developmental difficulties (Cummins, 1984; Mercer, 1983). The use of observational data contributed by parents, siblings, and others who know the child well is also another way to gauge the presence of any particular individual conditions that would call for the services of a speech therapist or a psychologist rather than (or along with) a teacher who could provide help in mastering standard English as a second language or dialect.

PEDAGOGICAL APPROACHES TO PROMOTING LANGUAGE MASTERY

Just as no single teaching approach is appropriate for all students whose native language is a mainstream form of English, so there is no one approach to providing English language instruction that is universally applicable for all linguistic minority groups. However, there is a growing body of research and practitioner experience that suggests a number of tools which have proven valuable in teaching English effectively in situations of linguistic and cultural diversity. These include use of the students' first language, use of culturally relevant language experience as the basis of classroom instruction, using students as informants regarding their own community language patterns, and finding ways to incorporate community norms of linguistic and cultural interaction into the participant structures of the classroom.

Use of the students' first language, or bilingual instruction, can enhance students' learning capabilities at no peril to achievement in English. Although bilingual education is controversial for many reasons besides language (see Crawford, 1989, chaps. 1–4;

MacDonald, Adelman, Kushner, & Walker, 1982; United States General Accounting Office, 1987), many English teachers and members of the public feel that using the native language in instruction may retard students' opportunities to learn English. In fact, English language instruction is always part of bilingual education programs in the United States, and research indicates that, where programs are consistently implemented so that students experience good instruction in both languages, their English language achievement levels match or exceed those of comparable second language children educated through the medium of English only from the first (Krashen & Biber, 1988; Willig, 1985). Full-scale bilingual programs demand cooperation of the entire administration and other teachers at a school (Tikunoff, 1983). A number of effective program models are further described in Crawford (1989).

For the English-speaking classroom teacher working outside a bilingual program, there are still some techniques that involve use of the first language. These may include special adaptations of a lesson plan, such as preview-review (where, in order to give the students an advance organizer, a lesson is previewed in the native language, perhaps by another teacher or aide who knows the language, then taught in English, then reviewed again in the first language), use of bilingual aides or peer tutors to provide first language support, or use of classroom materials in the first language to supplement the English language materials available. Students in the process of learning English may actually understand material quite well despite limited second language skill; discussions in their first language can confirm their level of comprehension and show that it is far more complete than teachers can tell by using questions only in English (Diaz, Moll, & Mehan, 1986). The students' first language is their basis for learning the second language, particularly in terms of academic skills (Cummins, 1979), so it should be viewed as a primary instructional resource.

Even where use of bilingual instructional techniques is not possible, students' own culture can be brought into the curriculum. Folk tales and stories, oral histories from the community, or accounts of current community problems or controversies can provide highly motivating language material for student discussion and analysis which could be done either in the native language or in English. Such techniques have been used successfully in areas of dialect diversity such as Appalachia, where the *Foxfire* collection of oral histories was collected by an enterprising teacher and his class, and in some native American communities, where materials based on, for example, Navajo or Ojibwe stories of origins and history, taught either in English or in the native language or in both, as circumstances dictate, become part of the academic curriculum (Fairbanks & Schmid, 1988; Rosier & Holm, 1980).

In English classes at all levels, teachers can draw on the rich English language literature of the American minority experience. By reading the novels and autobiographies of Richard Wright, Maya Angelou, James Baldwin, or Toni Morrison or the poetry of Langston Hughes or Ishmael Reed, students are exposed to part of the spectrum of Black English in some of its many manifestations. Puerto Rican students find their experience similar to, or in sharp contrast with, that of Piri Thomas. Mexican-American writers and poets such as Rodolfo Anaya, Gary Soto, Alurista, Alma Villanueva, or Miriam de Uriarte have contributed many kinds of texts in Spanish and English which provide provocative content as well as multiple models of language use. Students of Chinese background may find echoes of their own experience in the writings of Maxine Hong Kingston or the plays of David Huang. Native Americans find their contemporary experiences reflected in the novels and stories of Louise Erdrich, Simon Ortiz, Scott Momaday, and Leslie Silko. By using the literature that has come out of the historical experience of a group the same as or similar to the students in any one classroom, teachers provide evidence for the academic validity of the minority experience which may serve to stimulate students' interest and also demonstrate that, in literature, standard forms of English can be combined with usages characteristic of a minority community for powerful communicative ends.

Even when teachers cannot choose the material they will teach and must follow a standard curriculum, they can stimulate English language development by creating a "language-rich" environment in their classrooms (Enright, 1986; Enright & McCloskey, 1985). Such an environment includes many interesting materials to look at and talk about and many opportunities to use language in different ways with different people: students in the same classroom, students at other age levels, teachers, and any other adults who are a part of the school situation. Where children come to school with a set of language experiences different from those assumed by the curriculum, provision of a diversified language environment is an important way to build awareness and mastery of language skills (Enright, this volume; Hatch et al., 1987; Heath, 1986).

Teachers of English and language arts classes are not the only instructors who can help students build effective language skills. Growing interest in content-based language instruction (see Snow, this volume; Brinton et al., 1989), or instruction based on mastery of a content area such as math, psychology, or social studies taught through a second language, has led to the awareness that all teachers are language teachers when they teach through the medium of a second language. Furthermore, the emphasis on learning language through academic content is one now common to both bilingual and ESL instruction (Milk, 1985). Techniques for concentrating on aspects of the second language valuable for subject area instructors include study of specialized uses of everyday words (e.g., "set," "rational," or "acute") and preposition uses that occur in particular operations ("divided into" vs. "divided by") in mathematics; use of logical connectors ("because," "therefore," "consequently") in science and social studies texts; and uses of picture captions or subheadings within text for all written materials (Crandall, 1987). Content-based language instruction aims to promote conceptual mastery of a certain subject along with the language skills necessary to deal effectively with the subject (Chamot, 1985). Teachers with training in ESL may be in a good position to assist colleagues in other disciplines in working out ways to incorporate essential second language skills into subject matter instruction, either in mainstream or "sheltered" classes (that is, subject matter classes specially adapted to the needs of second language learners; see Parker, 1986), thus giving students additional opportunities for diversified uses of the second language in all of their school subjects.

An additional avenue for diversifying language skills is through the use of peer or cross-age tutoring, conducted either in person or through the medium of letters. Peer tutoring provides students an effective way to improve subject matter learning as well as to develop language skills in whatever language is used for the exchange (Sapiens, 1982). Working with a junior high school teacher of English, Heath set up a cross-age communication program run through exchange of letters which created a natural situation for students' attempts to get meanings across and stimulate reactions to the precision of written communication (Heath & Branscombe, 1985).

The advent of computer networks now allows such exchanges to take place all over the globe. Native American children in Arizona correspond with Athabaskan students in Alaska (Basham, 1989; Beck, Foster, & Selinker, 1989), and Chicano children in San Diego can send messages to students in Spain and Mexico (Diaz, 1987). While it is too early to tell what kinds of effects such innovations have over time, it is clear that, in creating another channel for meaningful use of language, they create settings in which mastery of language can be developed and refined both in composing messages to send and in learning to deal with the computer technology needed to send them, both tasks that stimulate a range of oral and written uses of the students' first and, where applicable, second languages (Sayers, 1989).

Allowing students' own experiences to become the basis of literacy instruction, a cornerstone of the language experience approach to reading, can be used with students of any age or any language background. One related technique is to have students keep dialog journals, journals which serve as an ongoing medium of communication between themselves and their teachers. Such journals can be incorporated into the classroom routine of students from first grade to university levels and can be written in the first or second language or a combination of the two; they have shown great promise in helping students develop fluency and confidence in writing (Staton, Shuy, Kreeft, & Reed, 1990). In these journals, students write something every day, and the teacher collects them at intervals of each week or two and then responds to the substance of the students' communication without making any overt correction. Useful even when students are beginners in a second language, this technique also creates a natural and low-risk learning situation where students can try out ways to express themselves without fear of corrections or ridicule.

Use of any of these techniques for language development in school settings raises the question about whether there is a role for teaching grammar and, if so, how grammar should be taught. If the purpose of any activity is simply development of fluency and confidence, an overt focus on grammatical form is not called for. However, success in certain activities and eventual ability to write acceptable English for advancement in employment and education call for good command of the conventions of standard written English. Indeed, a study of entrance essays written by second language learners at UCLA showed that, for one subgroup of advanced intermediate learners, correction of grammatical errors in their essays with no change in the substance or organization of ideas was enough to make a difference between being held for a remedial course and taking the usual composition class (McGirt, 1984). Hence, when students wish to master the forms of language relevant to academic advancement, they need good grammatical skills. The main question is how to make an awareness of grammatical forms and related instruction serve true communicative purposes so that they do not become ends in themselves. Creating natural communicative situations like the verbal or written exchanges described above is one way of doing this, for students must use language to make their meanings clear to others whom they do not know well. Other techniques for raising awareness of grammatical issues in the context of overall language mastery are presented in Celce-Murcia and Hilles (1988).

Adjusting the substance and the forms emphasized in the school language arts curriculum provide some ways to make language instruction more effective for language minority students. Other instructional innovations which promote language diversification in all subject areas, not only in language classes, offer additional promising ways to create a naturally rich linguistic environment.

One methodology currently receiving much attention is cooperative learning, a classroom arrangement wherein students are divided into smaller groups or teams that complete various curricular tasks (see Cohen, 1986 and Kagan, 1986, for further discussion of the variety of cooperative methods now in use). Cooperative learning models offer great promise for making effective language use accessible to many language learners (McGroarty, 1989). When implemented appropriately, cooperative learning is more than simply group work, for students have specified roles and individual responsibilities within each group; these roles and responsibilities create the need for particular kinds of communication to clarify tasks and solve problems. Second language learners can thus practice language in small groups without the fear of making errors in front of the whole class. Furthermore, because students operate as a team, it becomes important for other group members to provide input adapted to the individual comprehension skills of those in their group; moreover, because rewards depend on team achievements, individual learners are more likely to be motivated to accomplish the tasks using as much of the second language as they can muster. Hence, cooperative learning techniques put second language learning in the service of interesting tasks used to teach content. These techniques make all students natural language tutors for other students, and thus give learners many more sources of input and correction than they would get in a solely teacher-centered classroom. Also, there is some evidence to suggest that, when children come from backgrounds where cooperative rather than competitive activity is the norm in play and other daily activities, cooperative learning makes the classroom a more congenial learning atmosphere (Gonzalez, 1983; Tharp & Gallimore, 1989). While cooperative learning should certainly not be used to the exclusion of other methods, a situation that could result in the resegregation of minority students, it is a part of good instruction for all students, and particularly promising for language minorities.

Like other methods which encourage dialog as a basis of learning, cooperative methods offer a better chance for providing the cognitive and linguistic scaffolding that supports further language development (Hawkins 1988; Tharp & Gallimore, 1989). The scaffolding provided through interaction with the teacher and other students includes opportunities to hear the second language or standard dialect, ask questions, and test hypotheses about language. Because interaction is typically directed at academic subject matter, the language used generally includes the kind of discussion related to text types that might not be encountered outside the school environment. Thus, cooperative learning serves the dual goal of making academic content more accessible and giving students the chance to develop language skills that will help them accomplish academic tasks.

A final area for teachers of language minority students to consider is the nature of their relationships with the parents and community members concerned with students' progress. Although parents are eager for their children to succeed in school, they may not know of the kinds of assistance they can offer to enhance learning. Evidence from one study indicates that having children read aloud to parents, even when parents do not know English, improves reading achievement more than having a special reading teacher (Tizard, Schofield, & Hewison, 1982). It has also been found, however, that neither parents nor teachers generally take action to avert reading failure unless some aspect of the student's situation or behavior seems unusual enough to warrant direct intervention (Goldenberg, 1987). Hence, it is up to teachers, who see students deal with academic work daily, to take prompt action in communicating with parents at once if students are not making appropriate progress; parents, too, should be encouraged to share their concerns with teachers on a continuing rather than an occasional basis. Because language minority students are often enrolled in a variety of special programs, language teachers bear a particular responsibility to promote interaction among all the adults, parents, other teachers, and additional community members who have a stake in student success (Cazden, 1986).

FINAL THOUGHTS

There is no recipe for teachers to follow in all situations of language or dialect diversity. All language learners show individual variation in their learning patterns and preferences (Hudelson, 1989; Wong Fillmore, 1983, 1985). Moreover, each language community and each classroom is different, so teachers need to modify relevant techniques suggested here to suit their particular local contexts. Innovative materials and techniques for classroom instruction and organization are only part of the picture. Research indicates that both teacher training and teacher attitudes are important in providing successful instruction (Politzer, 1977), so teachers need to examine their own attitudes toward the students they instruct. The relative success of any new technique is premised both on the teachers' knowledge and on the teachers' belief that students can succeed and on their ability to communicate this belief to the students. In such a supportive environment, the instructional innovations in materials and techniques suggested here will help teachers provide better instruction for all students, not only those for whom standard English is a second language or dialect.

NOTE

1. Using a language other than the standard does not always signal educational difficulties. As the study of Amish literacy (A. Fishman, 1988) shows, groups may have highly developed literacy conventions which serve them well in all in-group interactions. When such groups make few or no demands on mainstream social institutions, the issue of control and use of standard forms of English and exclusion of other language varieties from education is not a major social concern. Furthermore, many ethnic communities continue to maintain social institutions such as newspapers, radio stations, or "Saturday schools" which promote the learning and use of languages other than English (J. Fishman, 1980). Because such operations are locally based and privately funded, they attract little notice from the larger educational community.

DISCUSSION QUESTIONS

1. What does the term "standard English" mean to you? List as many criteria as possible for identifying standard language, and explain which criteria, in your view, are most relevant in educational settings.

2. How many different dialects of English are spoken by people in your community and students in local schools? What is the history of each dialect group? Do you feel any of these speech varieties affects educational progress or social evaluation of the speakers? Why?

3. Speakers who use languages or language varieties other than standard English often have different conventions for both nonverbal and verbal communication. Have you observed any instances of differing communication patterns that proved problematic for participants in educational or occupational settings? What were they, and how did they reflect participants' ideas of appropriate communication?

4. It is sometimes said that differences in dialect, which may be rather subtle, cause more educational misunderstanding than differences between languages. Why might this be the case? Do you agree?

5. How could a teacher go about gathering information on the language varieties most relevant to his or her particular students? Identify as many sources of information as possible, and explain how each would contribute to pedagogical understanding of language varieties in the classroom.

SUGGESTED ACTIVITIES

1. Tape your own speech in an informal and a formal situation. Make a list of any differences in pronunciation, word choice, and sentence length or complexity that you notice. Could any of these differences be considered a dialect feature?

2. Interview a family member, friend, or peer who learned English as a second language after starting school. In this person's experience, what factors seemed to help or hinder the learning of English? Do these same factors affect students in U.S. schools today?

3. Visit a local elementary school, observe reading instruction, and talk to the teachers. What different first language or dialect groups are represented in the classrooms? Do teachers notice any influences of language or dialect diversity on their students' reading performance?

4. Examine the materials used for literacy instruction in any of the relevant languages used at the school you visit. Do these materials accurately reflect the language forms used in the students' community? Do the materials include dialect variants so that students are exposed to a range of vocabulary?

SUGGESTIONS FOR FURTHER READING

Those interested in the general area of English language education for linguistic minority groups should also consult these sources for more detailed information.

Beyond Language: Social and Cultural Factors in Schooling Language Minority Students **(1986).** Los Angeles: Evaluation, Dissemination, and Assessment Center, California State University, Los Angeles.

> Several social scientists and educators provide comprehensive articles describing the social and cultural factors which affect the educational progress of language minority students.

Cook-Gumperz, J., ed. (1986)
The Social Construction of Literacy. Cambridge: Cambridge University Press.

> Edited papers give several examples of the influence of social context on the acquisition of literacy skills in school.

Crawford, J. (1989)
Bilingual Education: History, Politics, Theory, and Practice. Trenton, NJ: Crane.

> Offers a very current and readable account of contemporary issues related to bilingual education. The last section includes detailed description of several types of bilingual programs implemented in various parts of the United States.

Ferguson, C. A., & S. B. Heath, eds. (1981)
Language in the USA. Cambridge: Cambridge University Press.

> A number of linguists and foreign language specialists give a panoramic view of the languages used in the territory of what is now the United States over the course of its history.

Gilmore, P., & A. A. Glatthorn, eds. (1982)
Children In and Out of School: Ethnography and Education. Washington, DC: Center for Applied Linguistics.

> Papers representing the perspectives of anthropologists, linguists, and educators who have worked to develop a broad understanding of children's language use both inside and outside the classroom.

Hakuta, K. (1985)
Mirror of Language: The Debate on Bilingualism. New York: Basic Books.

> Examines the linguistic and psycholinguistic questions related to bilingualism with reference to both historical and contemporary research.

McKay, S. L., & S.-L. Wong, eds. (1988)
Language Diversity: Problem or Resource? New York: Newbury House.

> Focuses on the specific language questions related to the largest and most recently arrived linguistic minority groups (i.e., Mexican, Cuban, Puerto Rican, Chinese, Filipino, Korean, and Vietnamese Americans) and also discusses general questions of relevant educational theory and practice.

Supporting Children's English Language Development in Grade-Level and Language Classrooms

D. Scott Enright

INTRODUCTION

The past two decades of research and instructional theory in the area of children's second language development have resulted in a dramatic shift in our overall conceptualization of how children go about developing a new language and about how we as teachers may support them in that endeavor. Today the theoretical consensus regarding the process of children's second language and literacy development is that they continuously and actively engage in purposeful interactions with speech and print in the second language environment in order to create and use new meanings in the new language. Much of the most recent research conducted in this area has focused on describing these interactions and creations in full detail and on attempting to embed them within an overall developmental picture. In addition, recent research has begun to uncover the full complexity of the multiple contexts (e.g., home, playground, reading group, bus) and materials (e.g., peer language, teacher language, environmental print, texts) that are used by children in constructing their new language both inside and outside the classroom.

In North America, this shift in the conceptualization of how children develop their new language and literacy capacities has been accompanied by a shift in the overall policy regarding educating exceptional children, from one in which these students are separated from their peers in order to receive specialized instruction to one of attempting to meet their specific needs within the ongoing academic program (this is often referred to as "mainstreaming"). With regard to children learning English as a second or additional language (henceforth referred to as "ESL" students), these twin developments in theory and policy, along with considerable increases in the size and linguistic and cultural diversity of the ESL student population, have resulted in an increasing reliance on using *all* teachers and classrooms to meet these students' needs. This includes those teachers and classrooms within the ongoing academic program, such as algebra and second-grade (henceforth referred to as "grade-level") teachers and classrooms, as well as those teachers and classrooms specifically allocated to instruct ESL students, such as bilingual education and "pullout" or "withdrawal" ESL (henceforth referred to as "language") teachers and classrooms.

Fortunately, the recent work in first and second language development theory and the numerous instructional programs that have been implemented in relation to it have also yielded many teaching insights which can be applied across both language and grade-level classroom settings in order to support ESL students' English language and literacy development. These insights come from research and theory in the fields of first language and literacy development and second language and literacy development. These insights also range from sources as diverse as anthropological studies of young ethnic minority children's oral and written language use at home and at school (Heath, 1983) to quantitative studies of the effects of peer interaction on ESL students' oral language development (D. M. Johnson, 1983) to longitudinal studies of the development of a young first language learner's composition abilities throughout her school experience (Calkins, 1983).

These insights can be synthesized into seven key instructional criteria for designing and conducting instruction to support ESL students' English language and literacy development (Enright & McCloskey, 1988):

1. Collaboration. Organize instruction so that students have many opportunities to interact and work cooperatively with each other and with teachers, family members, and community members. Collaborative activities are two-way activities in which learning takes place as teachers and students actively work together, as opposed to one-way lessons in which the teacher gives the instruction and the students receive it. Organizing for collaboration entails organizing learning activities which require communicating and sharing, such as discussion groups or lab-partner science experiments or student–teacher dialog journals. Organizing for collaboration also entails organizing learning activities that involve students in interacting with people outside of the classroom, such as interviewing the school secretary for the class newspaper or working with a parent or an elder to describe the origins of family members' names or a special family tradition.

2. Purpose. Organize instruction so that students have many opportunities to use authentic or "real" oral and written language to accomplish tasks that have authentic goals and purposes. Examples of purposeful composition and questioning activities would be students writing letters to city officials to invite them to a class election forum and then interviewing them about school issues at the forum. Examples of learning activities also designed to teach composition and questioning but without authentic purposes would be students writing "business" and "friendly" letters within a textbook format which are then read and graded by the teacher, and students practicing questioning forms in full group drill sequences in which the forms and not the content of the questions are the focus.

Four major kinds of purposeful discourse that can be embedded in learning activities across the curriculum are "share discourse," in which language is used socially to communicate and to share meanings and to accomplish social goals (such as playing a game or planning a skit); "fun discourse," in which language is used just for the fun of it (such as singing songs and writing riddles); "fact discourse," in which language is used to get new information and concepts (such as doing a research project and sharing the findings with the class); and "thought discourse," in which language is used to imagine and reflect and to create new ideas and experiences (such as writing poetry or reading about and deciding on the best theory for why the dinosaurs became extinct). ESL students are more likely to learn English in addition to content when they engage in activities centering on one or more of these kinds of authentic uses of speech and print.

3. Student Interest. Organize instruction to both promote and follow students' interests. Interesting learning activities either *build* on the interests that students bring to the classroom or *create* that interest as part of their design. Organizing for student interest in the curriculum does not mean giving up adult instructional goals, nor does it mean turning the classroom over to the students. What it does mean is organizing activities which combine student interests and purposes with the adult curriculum's topics and objectives. Thus, a class lesson and discussion concerned with King Henry VIII of England's divorce and the formation of the Anglican church might also include a discussion of U.S. divorce patterns and the students' own dating "customs."

4. Previous Experience. Organize instruction to incorporate students' previous experiences into their new learning. This includes tapping students' previous language and literacy experiences in their first language and/or in English (sometimes referred to as "linguistic schemata") as well as tapping their already developed knowledge and cultural experience (sometimes referred to as "content schemata" and "cultural schemata"; (Andersson & Barnitz, 1984; Carrell, 1984). Applying the previous experience criterion to instruction entails relating new concepts and materials to students' background experience, such as brainstorming ideas and anecdotes about a particular topic before reading an article about it or connecting previous class activities and learning to current ones. Applying the previous experience criterion to instruction also entails directly embedding students' knowledge and previous experience into the curriculum, such as including histories and folk tales from ESL students' families and native countries in reading group instruction and in the library corner or having students collect authentic speech and literacy data from their homes and neighborhoods to be studied in class (Heath, 1983; Wigginton, 1989). Finally, applying the previous experience criterion to instruction means finding places in the curriculum and in the daily schedule for ESL students to use their first language and literacy skills for learning and reflecting as well as for communicating and socializing with first language peers (Commins, 1989; Hudelson, 1987).

5. Support. Organize instruction so that students feel comfortable and able to take risks in using their new language. Creating a supportive classroom environment for ESL students entails providing challenging but safe opportunities for them to listen, speak, read, and write in English. Moreover, it entails celebrating their efforts to participate and learn. Supportive learning activities are tailored to students' current language and literacy capacities or "zones of proximal development" (Vygotsky, 1978) in the second language, and they provide affective and interactional support, or "scaffolding" (Applebee, 1984; Greenfield, 1984) for the students' efforts to learn new oral and written discourse. To illustrate, scaffolding could be added to a full group story-reading session by having ESL students at different levels of English proficiency answer questions about the story in different ways: beginning students by pointing to pictures of characters and events (e.g., "Quan, point to Cinderella"), intermediate students by using words or phrases and simple sentences (e.g., "Edries, how many stepsisters did Cinderella have? Were they nice or mean?"), and advanced students by using full sentences and narratives (e.g., "Amparo, what did the fairy godmother do to the pumpkin?").

6. Variety. Organize instruction to include a variety of learning activities and language forms and uses. Organizing for variety entails exposing ESL students to the diversity of oral and written English that they will be asked to use in the everyday world as well as in the classroom. This criterion should be employed in conjunction with all of the previous ones; thus, organizing for variety means including many different kinds of collaboration, learning purposes, student interests, and familiar and unfamiliar student experiences within classroom learning activities.

7. Integration. Organize instruction to integrate the various resources available for supporting ESL children's language and literacy development so that each resource works with and supports the others. Organizing for integration entails putting together many learning resources which have traditionally been kept apart in the classroom, including integrating the students' in-school and out-of-school experiences; integrating subject-matter or content instruction and language instruction; integrating the language processes of listening, speaking, reading, and writing; and integrating the students themselves.

The seven criteria outlined above are

very broad and also overlap considerably with each other. They are meant to be taken and applied as a group rather than individually, and indeed it would be quite difficult to organize instruction to take one criterion into account without also applying many or all of the other criteria. In this way, the seventh criterion of integration really encompasses all of the other six criteria. With this in mind, let's review some of the most successful techniques that have been developed to apply these criteria in support of ESL children's learning in both language and grade-level classrooms within the critical areas of integration mentioned above. Because this discussion is very broad in nature, additional resources for exploring these topics are listed in Appendix A.

INTEGRATING CONTENT AND LANGUAGE AND INTEGRATING THE FOUR LANGUAGE PROCESSES

One of the most important insights that has emanated from the recent work in children's second language and literacy development is that children use their skills in each of the four language processes of listening, speaking, reading, and writing to support their learning of the other processes. Heath (1985) describes this as children "tying-in" their oral and written language learning. Similarly, research conducted with both adult and child students in language and grade-level classrooms (Cuevas, 1984; DeAvila & Duncan, 1984; Genesee, 1987; Krashen & Biber, 1988) suggests that second language students can learn both oral and written second language skills within learning activities that are primarily organized around subject-matter or content topics, but which include specific modifications in the ways that the activities are conducted. (This is sometimes referred to as "sheltered" instruction.) These two important types of integration—integrating content and language instruction and integrating the four language processes —can be simultaneously addressed by mak-

ing adaptations in teacher talk, the curriculum, and the classroom environment.

Adapting Teacher Talk

The discourse (oral and written) that is used for instruction in any content area can also be used by ESL students to learn English if certain modifications are made in that language to make it accessible to them. Krashen and Terrell (1983) refer to this modified and accessible language as "comprehensible input." According to Krashen and Terrell, comprehensible input is novel language that is "just beyond" ESL students' current comprehension capacities. It is also language that is meaningful and interesting to students and language which they can immediately use to accomplish goals. Enright (1986), Genesee (1987), and others have summarized the various ways in which both successful language teachers and grade-level teachers adapt their own classroom discourse to make it comprehensible and useful:

Nonverbal Adaptations. Teachers add nonverbal meaning to their instructional language through gestures, pantomimes or nonverbal illustrations of meanings, and facial expressions.

Contextual Adaptations. Teachers add contextual aids to their instructional language, such as visual aids (e.g., pictures, blackboard sketches, real-life objects or "realia") and auditory aids (e.g., recorded sounds or recorded speech).

Paraverbal Adaptations. Teachers adapt the paraverbal dimension of their instructional language to make it more comprehensible by speaking clearly, slowing down the rate of their speech, and pausing between major idea units. They vary their volume and intonation to accentuate meaning (e.g., "That's a big pizza! A *big* [waving hands in big circle] pizza!"). They also use vocalizations to carry meaning (e.g., panting like a dog to illustrate the word "dog").

Discourse Adaptations. Teachers adapt the overall organization of their instructional language to make it more comprehensible by *framing* different topics/idea units within specific utterances (e.g., "Okay, you have decided what kind of fish you want to buy. Good. Now let's discuss the equipment that we'll need"). They also *rephrase* their utterances (e.g., "Now let's discuss the kind of equipment we'll buy. The kinds of things we need to make the aquarium run. Motors and stuff"), and they *repeat* their utterances in meaningful ways (e.g., "Yeah, that's a great *aquarium!* What a super picture of our *aquarium*. It even looks like the *aquarium* has real glass!").

Successful teachers of second language students also make a number of adaptations in the ways that they call on and interact with students during instruction which helps to make the ongoing classroom discourse into comprehensible input:

Elicitation Adaptations. Teachers vary their ways of calling on individuals and on the group so that everyone is involved in instruction. For example, they call on students by name, they ask for volunteers to respond, they call on the whole group, and they have open elicitations in which anyone can speak up.

Questioning Adaptations. Teachers vary their questions according to the proficiency and social style of their students (as in the previous Cinderella story-reading example). They also monitor their ESL students' progress over time and "raise the ante" by asking more difficult questions of these students as they become able to answer them.

Response Adaptations. Teachers adapt their responses to students' utterances to provide further comprehensible input and to encourage further student language use by using *confirmation checks* (e.g., "You decided on guppies and catfish, right?" and *clarification requests* (e.g., "I didn't get the kinds of fish you said. You said catfish and what else?").

They also *rephrase* student responses and/or *expand* on those responses to provide further input to the speaker and the group (e.g., "All right, Tam! You picked guppies and catfish. Swimming little fish for the water and crawling muddy fish for the bottom. Great!"). Teachers also give "extra chances" to students who don't respond to an elicitation through strategies such as *pausing* to give the student(s) plenty of time to speak, through *prompting* (e.g., "What fish did you pick, Yolanda? Your list of fish—read it"), and through *repeating* the elicitation. Teachers also give extra chances to students who *do* respond to an elicitation by inviting them to say more.

Correction Adaptations. Teachers adapt their corrections of second language students' utterances by focusing on the message that the student wants to convey—that is, its meaning and its intelligibility. Teachers correct either by modeling the correct utterance for the student (often this is done in the context of rephrasing and expanding upon the student's utterance) or by explicitly showing the student his or her error and providing feedback as to how to repair it (e.g., providing correct syntax or correct pronunciation). This latter strategy, however, is done in a way that will *support* students and not embarrass them—for example, correcting them individually and away from the group.

Finally, the most important discourse adaptation that successful teachers of second language students make is that they vary the *types of learning activities* that they employ in class so that teacher talk does not dominate the class discourse. These teachers use small group, paired, and independent/interactive activities in addition to full group lectures and question-answer sequences and student seatwork. They also vary the ways that these different activities are organized—for example, using student-directed pairs and discussion groups and learning center groups as well as teacher-directed pairs and instructional groups and discussion groups. This diversity of grouping ensures that students receive many opportunities to receive comprehensible input from many sources and to use it in many ways. This idea will be discussed again later in the chapter.

Adapting the Curriculum

Both the content-driven curriculum of grade-level classrooms and the language-driven curriculum of language classrooms can be adapted to integrate content and language instruction and the four language processes. Crandall and her colleagues (Crandall, Spanos, Christian, Simick-Dudgeon, & Willetts, 1987) call grade-level classrooms where the curriculum has been adapted in this manner "language-sensitive content classes" and language classrooms where the curriculum has been adapted in this manner "content-enriched ESL classes," and they provide classroom vignettes to illustrate these two varieties of integrated curricula in action. Snow and her colleagues (1989) and Rathmell (in press) also provide examples of integrated curricula in use in various kinds of classrooms. The following are some strategies for adapting the curriculum and the learning activities within it to integrate language and content instruction and the four language processes:

Mediate the Language Dimension of Every Classroom Activity. Whether ESL students are engaged in a science experiment, a writing activity, or finding out their assigned class jobs for the week, they can learn English and learn more subject matter if the language of the activity is being structured appropriately and mediated for them. In addition to the adaptations in teacher talk that have already been discussed, mediating the language dimension includes "warming up" students for an activity by drawing on their own background experience and interests in introducing and discussing the activity. It also involves presenting the key vocabulary and concepts of the activity before it begins as well as providing an overview of the activity and a clear outline or plan for what is to

happen so that ESL students will have a framework for understanding and participating fully in the activity. This may also include providing supplemental materials for the activity (e.g., a step-by-step plan for doing the science experiment, or a report format and a vocabulary list for the writing activity) and/or adapting the published materials used in the activity (e.g., providing a topical outline or summary narrative for a text selection for students to read before reading the actual selection). Short, Crandall, and Christian (1989) and Addison (in press) have developed several techniques for adapting materials in this way. In addition, mediating the language of a learning activity involves monitoring students' progress throughout the activity and summarizing, clarifying, and redirecting them both linguistically and conceptually whenever needed. In the full group setting, this entails seating ESL students where they will have the most access to instruction and where their visibility will serve as a constant *reminder* to teachers to adapt their discourse and to mediate the activity. In the small group and individualized setting, this entails frequently "checking in" with ESL students to assess their progress and provide redirection and additional instruction as necessary—and to teach ESL students' peers to perform these functions as well.

Use a Variety of Tasks Across a Variety of Contexts. Cummins (1984) suggests that there are two key dimensions of any language activity, including those found in grade-level and language classrooms: the "contextual" dimension and the "cognitive" dimension. Cummins also provides a framework (made up of four quadrants) in which any communicative activity can be categorized depending upon the amount of contextual support that is provided in relation to the language of the activity (from "context-embedded" to "context-reduced") and the degree of active cognitive involvement required by the speaker within the activity (from "cognitively undemanding" to "cognitively demanding"). Cummins hypothesizes that even the cognitive dimension of a given activity is largely language-dependent, however, since it depends on the degree to which the "linguistic tools" the learner employs within the task have become "automatized" (1984, p. 139).

Chamot and O'Malley (1987) have classified various classroom language and content activities within Cummins's framework, from the simplest ("context-embedded" and "cognitively undemanding") activities, such as playing a game, to the most challenging ("context-reduced" and "cognitively demanding") activities, such as writing a research report. Chamot and O'Malley also point out that "academic discourse," or the oral and written language tasks that are employed in subject-matter instruction at any level, tend to fall into the abstract, "context-reduced" and "cognitively demanding" category. Thus, a key strategy for adapting the curriculum to support ESL students' learning is to ensure that all new content and the discourse that is related to it is taught within a *variety* of learning activities, beginning with concrete, "hands-on" activities which allow students to experience the new material with lots of ties to the immediate context and their own knowledge, and moving toward using the new material in abstract and "language-only" ways. As an illustration, a unit on leadership and on the characteristics of successful public speaking might begin with a learning activity in which students watch videotapes or listen to recordings of famous speeches (e.g., John F. Kennedy's inaugural address, Martin Luther King's "I have a dream" speech) and derive the characteristics of the speech that make it so moving and successful. The students would then eventually move into a learning activity in which they write and deliver their own speeches which incorporate the rhetorical characteristics derived from the earlier activity. Adapting the curriculum in this way would also entail introducing and teaching new concepts through activities which embed it in the four types of purposeful language previously identified ("share," "fun," "fact," and "thought" discourse).

Develop Integrated, Thematic Units. A third way to integrate content and language instruction as well as the four language processes which encompasses both of the other strategies is to design and carry out integrated or thematic units. Integrated units are sets of learning activities which allow students to explore many dimensions of a single topic using all four language processes and a variety of subject-matter emphases. Integrated units can be designed around any topic of the teachers' or students' choosing. Units can center on a current event (e.g., a space shuttle unit) or a piece of children's literature (e.g., a unit on *The Jolly Postman or Other People's Letters;* Ahlberg & Ahlberg, 1986) or on a subject-matter topic already within the curriculum (e.g., "Our Digestive System" or "Georgia: The Peach State"). Integrated units also embed instruction in specific language and subject-matter skills within activities primarily designed to learn about the unit topic. To illustrate, a thematic unit centering on fish and underwater environments might have composition instruction embedded in learning activities within the unit, such as writing letters to fish experts and area aquariums to get information, writing research reports on various kinds of fish, writing a "sea adventure" or a fantasy story about being a fish, writing and sending thank-you letters to petstore personnel who contributed items for a class aquarium, recording and writing up observations of the class aquarium, and writing and performing a "fishy" theatrical production. Similarly, integrated thematic units embed instruction in several different content areas within activities related to the unit topic. Thus, the fish unit might include an activity on what fish need to live (science); an activity on planning and purchasing the components of a class aquarium (mathematics, science); an activity on sailing legends and sailor songs (history, music); an activity on sea explorers and their routes and discoveries throughout history (social studies, history, geography); and an activity on collecting and trying out seafood recipes from various cultures around the world (social studies, health, science, mathematics).

In addition to incorporating all four of the language processes and several content areas together, integrated units also combine students' interests with school curriculum goals and objectives. Because integrated units can be developed around any topic, students can also be directly involved in choosing the topic and in brainstorming, developing, and implementing the actual set of activities that constitute the unit. Further resources for designing integrated, thematic units and actual collections of units are listed in the "Integrated Curriculum and Instruction" section of Appendix A.

Adapting the Classroom Environment

Another resource that can be productively adapted to integrate language and content instruction and the four language processes within the classroom is the actual physical environment in which instruction occurs. The classroom furniture, materials, and even the walls can create numerous opportunities for ESL students to learn English speech and print during informal times throughout the day when no instructor is immediately present. Here are three broad strategies for adapting the classroom environment to integrate language and content and the four language processes:

Make the Environment Language-Rich. Language-rich classrooms are filled with lots of wonderful things to experience, listen to, think about, and talk and read and write about! A movie poster invitingly displayed near the hall door almost inevitably leads to informal student discussions about it—and this English practice could be going on while the teacher is getting the class lined up for lunch! A task card suggesting writing activities related to the movie (e.g., "You be the critics!") could turn the poster into a small group or independent writing activity. Similarly, the walls, shelves, and library of the classroom can be filled with materials related to a particular integrated unit theme to support students' learning explorations of that theme both during formal unit activities and during informal and unstructured class times.

Creating a language-rich classroom environment should include filling the room with a *variety* of materials for students' use. This variety should include *realia* (e.g., a science table, a display of papers and labels and photos of billboards collected on an "English search" for environmental print) and *authentic reading and writing materials* (e.g., novels and storybooks, magazines, word-processing software, travel posters, forms and schedules) in addition to textbooks and exercise books. This variety should also include *materials that are familiar to ESL students* and which relate to their own linguistic and cultural backgrounds (e.g., books and/or other authentic print written in the students' first language, items brought in from students' homes, English books and posters and other materials focusing on the cultural backgrounds and traditions of the ESL students). Finally, this variety should also include an abundance of materials which *encourage* rather than *limit* students' use of speech and print. For example, writing materials should be available in many places around the room, tape recorders and/or record players and headphones should be available and accessible, and reference books, literature, and other printed materials should be openly stored and attractively displayed to invite their use by student readers and researchers.

Incorporate Functional Print into the Environment. Functional print is real-world print that is directly used to accomplish a concrete purpose. Functional print is also usually related to a specific material, such as directions on medicine bottles, or a specific task, such as job application forms. Classroom activities and materials can support ESL students' English literacy development when functional print is added to them. One way of incorporating functional print into the environment is to label classroom materials ("magic markers," "writing materials") and activity areas (e.g., "book nook," "meeting area"). Another way is to post written instructions to accompany daily classroom activities (e.g., directions for using the listening center or a new learning center, suggestions for what to do after finishing an assigned activity early). Incorporating functional print into the environment might also include turning over classroom routines to students and letting them use functional print to accomplish these tasks. For example, students could "take roll" themselves by finding the date and their name on a class "Attendance Chart" and signing in each day. Restroom passes, lunch procedures, even book club purchases could also be turned into functional print activities to be administered by the students themselves. In order to extend the use of classroom functional print to students at all levels of English reading development, illustrations or rebus writing (print in which pictures appear in place of key words in the text) can also be added to posted directions and other forms of functional print. Zeigler, Larson, and Byers (1983) have compiled several sample rebus charts and suggestions for adapting and using them in elementary school classrooms.

Make the Environment Student-Owned. Another way to use the environment to integrate content and language instruction and the four language processes is to tailor the environment to student rather than to adult needs. This includes incorporating materials brought in by students into the environment and learning activities (e.g., doing a science research activity to follow up on a butterfly found over the weekend). It includes constantly displaying students' work and even using students' work as curriculum (e.g., making a student's just-published fantasy tale the reading selection for the day in a basal reading group or a full group story-reading session). It also includes arranging materials and furniture to make them maximally accessible and functional for students (e.g., hanging bulletin boards and displays at

"child's eye level," or having boxes of class crayons around the room in addition to or in place of individual child crayons). Finally, it includes organizing space and materials for students' autonomous use, such as having a student message board or mailbox, student "social" areas for free conversation, and even "free time" for individually chosen student learning projects.

INTEGRATING THE STUDENTS THEMSELVES

Recent work in the fields of educational research and second language development research has yielded another key resource for supporting ESL children's English language and literacy development at school: the children themselves! Studies conducted in both monolingual, English-speaking classrooms (D. W. Johnson, R. Johnson, J. Johnson, & Anderson, 1976; Sharan, 1984; Slavin, 1983) and multilingual classrooms (Cohen, 1986; Kagan, 1986) have demonstrated the positive effects that students of various abilities and backgrounds can have on one another's learning when they are placed together in pairs and small groups to work on learning tasks with teacher supervision and support (this is often referred to as "cooperative learning"). Well-organized and well-implemented cooperative learning programs can yield increased academic achievement, better social skills, improved interethnic relations, and more use of higher-order thinking skills (Kagan, 1986). In addition, studies of children's second language and literacy development at school (Edelsky, 1986; Gomez, 1987; Hester, 1984; D. M. Johnson, 1983; Urzua, 1987; Ventriglia, 1982) have documented the positive effects of peer interaction and cooperative learning on ESL students' oral and written English development.

Enright (1990) has summarized the learning potential of integrating ESL students with one another and with their native-English-speaking peers as the "five M's": motivating, meaningful, multiplicative, multidimensional, and multicultural. Peer interaction and cooperative learning tasks can be productively utilized in both grade-level and language classrooms to create learning activities which are inherently interesting and exciting for students (motivating); activities which incorporate authentic language and learning objectives into the group activity (meaningful); activities which multiply students' opportunities for receiving comprehensible input and for practicing new language and conceptual skills (multiplicative); activities which allow students to develop different skills (social, linguistic, cognitive) at the same time (multidimensional); and activities which by their very organization promote interethnic respect and understanding and which facilitate the students' use of their previously developed knowledge and expertise (multicultural). Thus, creating heterogeneous small group and paired learning activities in the classroom is an important technique for fulfilling all seven of the instructional criteria outlined in the introduction to this chapter. Three key strategies for accomplishing the integration of students within both grade-level and content classrooms are the following:

1. Incorporate a Variety of Groupings and Ways of Participating into Daily Instruction. In order for ESL students to obtain both sufficient language input and sufficient opportunities for using language to develop a full range of English language and literacy skills, it is important to vary the ways that students are grouped for learning as well as the ways that they are asked to participate and interact within those groupings. The classroom should reflect the same kinds of oral and written discourse that is found in the everyday world and it should in addition explicitly address the kinds of oral and written discourse that are utilized in the most formal academic settings. Thus, incorporating a variety of groupings and ways of participating into the curriculum entails deliberately using and discussing the three kinds of groupings and ways of participating (or participation structures) that still dominate U.S. schools:

full group teacher-led lectures, full group teacher-led question-answer sequences, and individualized and silent student seatwork (Goodlad, 1984; Sirotnik, 1983). But it also entails going beyond the use of these types of learning activities to deliberately incorporate small group activities, paired activities, and independent activities other than seatwork into the curriculum and into daily instruction. These additional groupings and ways of participating should also make use of students' already developed social styles and ways of participating (Mohatt & Erickson, 1982; Weisner, Gallimore, & Jordan, 1988) and, like all other learning activities, should be designed to support authentic learning goals and language uses.

As previously mentioned, one of the key types of learning activities which should be included in ESL students' grade-level and language classrooms is the student-led and small group, or cooperative learning activity. Cooperative learning activities can be organized to accomplish a number of types of learning *tasks* (e.g., discussing a topic, conducting a group research project, writing and performing a group skit, preparing for a test as a student study group). They can be organized to support a number of *ways of participating* and working on the target task (e.g., individual student roles such as group moderator and group recorder, equal student roles such as discussants' having to reach unanimous consensus regarding an issue with reasons for their position contributed by every group member). Cooperative learning activities can also be organized to create a number of different *kinds of student mixes* using a number of different kinds of student characteristics (e.g., homogeneously or heterogeneously grouping students by level of content knowledge, by level of interest, or by level of language ability). Cooperative learning groups can even vary *over time;* for example, groups could be formed for one time and task only, groups could be formed to meet every day until a specific project is completed, and groups could be formed to meet regularly throughout the entire school year. Additional resources for organizing and utilizing cooperative learning activities and for teaching students the skills needed to effectively learn and participate within these kinds of activities are listed in the "Integrating Students/Cooperative Learning" section of Appendix A.

2. Use the Classroom Environment to Support Student Collaboration and Sharing. The physical arrangement of furniture and materials in the classroom environment as well as the ways that it is changed around during class time for various types of learning activities can also support the integration of students and their learning resources. The day-to-day physical environment can be used to do this by including specific places for different kinds of language and literacy uses as well as specific social rules which govern those spaces within the room (e.g., a carpeted or otherwise marked area for full group meetings and activities, a "quiet only" library corner, a "social" area where informal conversation can occur, or a learning center spot where specific paired and small group collaborative activities take place and are governed by the posted rules for that week's center activities). Similarly, the classroom furniture itself should be as flexible and movable as possible (e.g., light, movable tables and chairs rather than heavy and awkward desks) in order to permit quick and easy changes in the room's arrangement for different learning activities (e.g., tables pushed back and chairs in rows for a student theatrical performance, tables in a U shape for a class debate, individual students seated at tables in rows for a listening activity or for a test). Whenever possible, the classroom environment should change to fit the curriculum and students' needs and not vice versa.

3. Develop a Sense of Community in the Classroom. Perhaps the most important ingredient in the successful integration of students within any classroom is the establishment of an ongoing sense of community within the class. Classroom communities are places where every class member encourages and supports the learning efforts of every other class member, and where individual class members have a responsibility for the community's (the class's) work and success in addition to their own work and success. Classroom communities are also places where the experiences, capacities, interests, and goals of every classroom member are simultaneously utilized for his or her benefit and for the benefit of every other member of the class. Thus, in classrooms with ESL students, developing a sense of community entails creating a *pluralistic* classroom community, a place in which every student's previous language and cultural experiences are celebrated by the group and used by both the individual student and the group to support new learning. This in turn entails learning as much as possible about the students in the class and their backgrounds and interests in order to take this information into account in planning and conducting instruction.

It should be noted that a sense of community in the classroom, like classroom cooperation, must be deliberately *taught* to students and reviewed with them throughout the school year. This might include discussing what a community is and what it means to be a member of a community; developing a community identity (e.g., a community name, mascot, slogan, song); recording the community's history (e.g., a class scrapbook or archives or weekly community letters to members' homes); developing rules and responsibilities for community members (e.g., class jobs, class projects); and continually modeling what it means to act as a community member. Enright and McCloskey (1988) present several strategies for developing pluralistic classroom communities in classes with ESL students. Additional resources for creating a sense of community in the classroom can also be found in the "Integrating Students/Cooperative Learning" section of Appendix A.

CONCLUSION

This chapter has summarized several of the recent developments in the education of school-age ESL students and the techniques that are currently being proposed to support these students in their English language and literacy development in both language classrooms and grade-level classrooms. The theme of *integration* has been the touchstone of this work, the idea that all of the educational resources that are available to ESL students and their teachers should work together to support these students' learning. As the student population in our schools continues to become more linguistically and culturally diverse throughout this century, it will also become increasingly critical for all of the educators who are involved in the education of ESL students to integrate *their* efforts in this regard as well. It will be through the sharing of ideas and resources, through communicating often, and even through working side by side in the same classrooms that ESL teachers and their grade-level counterparts will best be able to continue to meet the needs of our ESL student population. Thus, in order to facilitate the efforts of those educators who are reading this chapter to share its teaching insights with other educators, a synthesis of these ideas is presented in Appendix B. Perhaps this list can serve as one more way of integrating the educational services that we provide for ESL children.

DISCUSSION QUESTIONS

1. How do children approach the second language and literacy development task? What are some of the key criteria that teachers can keep in mind to support ESL students in accomplishing this task?

2. What are some of the ways that classroom discourse can be adapted to support ESL students' English language development? Adaptations in teacher talk? Adaptations in teacher–student interaction? Adaptations in the classroom environment?

3. How can the content or subject-matter curriculum be mediated to allow ESL students to learn English as well as concepts?

4. What are integrated or thematic units? How are they useful in supporting second language and literacy development?

5. What is cooperative learning? What are some of the dimensions of cooperative learning activities that can be varied in order to provide students with a range of language and content learning opportunities?

SUGGESTED ACTIVITIES

1. Videotape or audiotape yourself or a colleague during one or two lessons. Review the tape(s) a few times and assess how well teacher talk is being adapted to also serve as comprehensible input for ESL students.

2. Plan an activity centering on authentic printed materials (e.g., students' own compositions, the newspaper, a videotaped television show, other functional print). Use the seven instructional criteria presented in the introduction of this chapter to do this.

3. Make a map (or maps) of your classroom or a classroom you have observed and a list of the furniture that is being used in the room. Then draw in some new ways of arranging the spaces and furniture in the room to add variety to the classroom discourse and to support student collaboration as much as possible.

4. Plan a thematic unit with five to eight activities centering on a topic from a school curriculum or a topic that students are already interested in pursuing. Use the seven criteria presented in the introduction to this chapter to do this.

5. Take one activity that you or a colleague usually does as a full group activity and transform it into a cooperative learning activity. Or, plan a new cooperative learning activity (or activities) to support a current curriculum unit or objective.

6. Share and discuss the "Dos and Don'ts" list presented in Appendix B with a colleague who works with ESL children. Add to or revise the list based on your own beliefs.

SUGGESTIONS FOR FURTHER READING

Chamot, A. U., and J. M. O'Malley (1987)
The Cognitive-Academic Language Learning Approach: A Bridge to the Mainstream. *TESOL Quarterly, 21*(2), 217–249.

> Sets forth an integrated view of content-based language instruction and strategies for carrying it out. Particularly helpful is the categorization of the various kinds of academic discourse tasks that ESL students encounter at school.

Enright, D. S., and M. L. McCloskey (1988)
Integrating English: Developing English Language and Literacy in the Multilingual Classroom. Reading, MA: Addison-Wesley.

> Statement of a rationale and model for an integrated approach to second language and literacy instruction. Includes chapters on developing an integrated/thematic curriculum, providing oral and written discourse, and developing multicultural classroom communities. Also includes two complete thematic curriculum units.

Hudelson, S. (1984)
Kan yu ret an rayt en Ingles: Children Become Literate in English as a Second Language. *TESOL Quarterly, 18*(2), 221–238.

> Hudelson uses extensive samples of second language learners' own writing to illustrate her review of what recent research tells us about how children develop their reading and writing capacities in their second language and the implications of this information for organizing the classroom literacy environment and language/literacy instruction.

Jaggar, A., and M. T. Smith-Burke, eds. (1985)
Observing the Language Learner. Newark, DE: International Reading Association.

> Appealing and sensible recommendations for observing children's oral and written language development which can be put to work immediately in first and second language classroom settings.

Johnson, D. M., and D. H. Roen, eds. (1989)
Richness in Writing: Empowering ESL Students. White Plains, NY: Longman.

> A collection of articles addressing many of the most important current topics in the area of second language composition development, including computer writing networks, individual differences in ESL children's writing, and developing appropriate writing tasks and assignments for ESL students.

Kagan, S. (1986)
Cooperative Learning and Sociocultural Factors in Schooling. In *Beyond Language: Social and Cultural Factors in Schooling Language Minority Students* (pp. 231–298). Los Angeles: Evaluation, Dissemination, and Assessment Center, California State University.

> Synthesis of the major research findings in cooperative learning (including interethnic cooperative learning) and of the major techniques developed to accomplish successful cooperative learning.

Lindsfors, J. W. (1987)
Children's Language and Learning (2nd ed.). Englewood Cliffs, NJ: Prentice-Hall.

> This excellent introduction to the field of children's language development includes chapters centering on teaching second language learners and speakers of regional and social dialects of English.

Newman, J. M., ed. (1985)
Whole Language: Theory and Use. Portsmouth, NH: Heinemann Educational Books.

> A potpourri of articles dedicated to presenting well-conceived and successful whole language instructional practices as well as the theory upon which the practices are based.

Wallace, C. (1988)
Learning to Read in a Multicultural Society. New York: Prentice-Hall.

> Examines all of the critical dimensions of second language reading developing in theory and practice, including the social context of reading, the reading text and the reading event. Also provides some illuminating case studies of ESL "learner-readers."

APPENDIX A

Annotated Bibliography of School-Age ESL Resources

Overviews of School-Age Second Language Development

Genesee, F. (1987)
Learning Through Two Languages: Studies of Immersion and Bilingual Education. New York: Newbury House.

> Reviews Canadian and U.S. immersion and bilingual education programs and the research conducted on these programs, and describes the central characteristics of successful immersion programs.

McLaughlin, B. (1985)
Second Language Acquisition in Childhood, Vol. 2: School-Age Children. Hillsdale, NJ: Erlbaum.

A careful examination of the research centering on children's second language development once they begin their schooling, including this development within different school programs.

Ovando, C. J., and V. P. Collier (1985)
Bilingual and ESL Classrooms: Teaching in Multicultural Contexts. New York: McGraw-Hill.

A broad overview of current school-age second language teaching issues and methods.

Tough, J. (1985)
Talk Two: Children Using English as a Second Language in Primary Schools. London: Onyx Press. (U.S. Distributor: Heinemann Educational Books, Portsmouth, NH.)

This noted first language development educator applies many of her theories to working with children developing language number two. The book includes specific teaching ideas as well as an appendix of pictures and instructions for surveying children's oral English use.

Integrated Curriculum and Instruction

Barnitz, J. G. (1985)
Reading Development of Nonnative Speakers of English. Orlando, FL: Harcourt Brace Jovanovich.

Useful overview of teaching strategies for developing different aspects of ESL, from improving comprehension to developing awareness of syntax and orthography.

Calkins, L. M. (1986)
The Art of Teaching Writing. Portsmouth, NH: Heinemann Educational Books.

Describes the developmental changes that children undergo as writers, the teacher's role in students' writing development, the use of writing conferences, reading–writing connections, and writing across the curriculum.

Cullinan, B. E., ed. (1987)
Children's Literature in the Reading Program. Newark, DE: International Reading Association.

A rich collection of articles about using real books and literature to teach reading and language across the curriculum. There are sections specifically devoted to primary, middle, and upper grades.

Gamberg, R., W. Kwak, M. Huthings, and J. Altheim (1988)
Learning and Loving It: Theme Studies in the Classroom. Portsmouth, NH: Heinemann Educational Books.

Written by teachers who use thematic curricula in their classrooms for teachers who wish to do the same. There are hints for preparing, scheduling, and

evaluating thematic studies as well as for securing materials and school and community participation. Also includes six sample thematic units.

Hannah, G. G. (1982)
Classroom Spaces and Places. Belmont, CA: Pitman Learning.

Terrific resource for planning new ways to use the physical classroom environment and its furniture to create different kinds of learning environments. There are also lots of sets of clear directions for making classroom furniture, dividers and organizers and storage and display components.

Johnson, T. D., and D. R. Louis (1987)
Literacy Through Literature. Portsmouth, NH: Heinemann Educational Books.

Collection of strategies and ideas for using real children's literature and storybooks to develop literacy. Each idea is illustrated in connection with an actual piece of children's literature.

Loughlin, C. E., and M. D. Martin (1987)
Supporting Literacy: Developing Effective Learning Environments. New York: Teachers College Press.

A thorough portrayal of the ways that the classroom environment can be used to support children's language and literacy development. The book is replete with specific teaching ideas.

Mohan, B. A. (1986)
Language and Content. Reading, MA: Addison-Wesley.

Deals with important issues of conceptualizing and carrying out a program of coordinated language and subject-matter instruction.

Moss, J. F. (1984)
Focus Units in Literature: A Handbook for Elementary School Teachers. Urbana, IL: National Council of Teachers of English.

Useful sets of learning activities and reading selections centering on specific themes. Second language teachers will find the unit centering on "Literature Around the World" to be particularly helpful.

Spann, S., and M. B. Culp (1975)
Thematic Units in Teaching English and the Humanities. (Also *First, Second and Third Supplements,* under the same title and publisher.) Urbana, IL: National Council of Teachers of English.

Four collections of actual thematic teaching units for secondary students which embed the teaching of literature and communicative arts within a diverse array of topics, from advertising to the family to sports to death.

Integrating Students/Cooperative Learning

Banks, J. A. (1988)
Multiethnic Education: Theory and Practice. Boston: Allyn and Bacon.

> Comprehensive review of the major theoretical issues in the area of multicultural education and ways to reform the curriculum and the schools to better achieve truly pluralistic education.

Cohen, E. G. (1986).
Designing Groupwork: Strategies for the heterogeneous classroom. New York: Teachers College Press.

> Clear explanation of the rationale for cooperative group work and ways to plan group work and to prepare students for the activities. Also provides specific suggestions for multilingual classrooms.

Johnson, D. W., R. T. Johnson, E. J. Holubec, and P. Roy (1984)
Circles of Learning: Cooperation in the Classroom. Alexandria, VA: Association for Supervision and Curriculum Development.

> Concise yet thorough summary of central concerns in implementing cooperative learning groups in the classroom.

Kagan, S. (1985)
Cooperative Learning: Resources for Teachers. Laguna Niguel, CA: Spencer Kagan Resources for Teachers.

> A practical collection of materials, games, worksheets, and teaching ideas centering on developing and using cooperative learning.

Kendall, F. E. (1983)
Diversity in the Classroom: A Multicultural Approach to the Education of Young Children. New York: Teachers College Press.

> Provides many concrete ways to promote multiculturalism in the early childhood classroom using the environment, and the students and their families.

Morian, J. E. (1974)
Classroom Learning Centers: Planning Organization, Materials and Activities. Belmont, CA: David S. Lake.

> Guide for creating and using classroom learning centers, with suggested plans for centers in reading, math, science, language arts, and social studies.

APPENDIX B

Some Dos and Don'ts for the Teacher with ESL Students

DO	*DON'T*
1. Use clear, normal speech in communicating with ESL students.	1. Use unnatural speech with ESL students such as baby talk, monosyllables, or shouting.
2. Use nonverbal cues (such as gestures, pictures, and concrete objects) in your teaching to assist ESL students' comprehension.	2. Assume that ESL students always understand what you are saying or that they are already familiar with school customs and procedures (even if they act as if they do!).
3. Make sure that ESL students are seated where they can see and hear well. Provide them with maximum access to the instructional and linguistic input that you are providing. Involve them in some manner in all classroom activities.	3. Separate and isolate students away from the rest of the class—physically, socially, or instructionally.
4. Fill your classroom environment with print and with interesting things to talk about and read and write about. Creating a language-rich environment will allow your ESL students to learn even when you aren't directly teaching them.	4. Limit your ESL students' access to authentic, "advanced" materials (like library books or magazines) in the belief that these materials are too "hard" for them. If the materials are interesting, students at all levels will be able to use them to learn English.

5. Keep in mind that ESL students are developing communication skills in oral and written English as they are being exposed to content instruction. Try to highlight the English in all classroom activities (even routines). Focus on developing the ability to communicate rather than on the ability to memorize and repeat vocabulary items and grammatical segments.

6. Encourage ESL students' efforts to participate by celebrating their contributions and searching out new opportunities for them to take part directly in learning activities.

7. Provide opportunities for ESL students to *use* the language and concepts that you are teaching them in meaningful situations. Include a variety of ways of participating in your instruction (such as paired activities, learning centers, cooperative groups, and independent work) in addition to full group instruction.

8. Treat ESL students as full members of the classroom community. Help them to feel comfortable and integrate them into the class as quickly as possible. Refer to them often, and make it clear to them (and to the class) that you expect them to work and learn just like everyone else. Then ask for more and more participation and work as these students become able to accomplish it.

9. Encourage all of your students to work with and to help out their ESL peers. Assign a "buddy" to each ESL student to assist them in learning their way around the school and the classroom. Use cooperative learning groups to encourage peer language teaching and learning.

10. Learn as much about your ESL students as you can. The more you know about these students and their backgrounds, the easier it will be to incorporate them into your classroom.

5. Treat English as a separate subject to be taught apart from the rest of the curriculum and/or only at specific times.

6. Put ESL students on the spot by asking them to participate (e.g., give an answer in front of the rest of the class) before they are ready. Beware of sanctioning or correcting students in front of their peers, which may lead to decreased participation and learning.

7. Give ESL students worksheets and other assignments which drill meaningless language elements and language skills in isolated contexts.

8. Expect ESL students to complete age-appropriate, grade-level assignments before they have an adequate command of English. Give them the time they need to learn the language of their classwork without letting them avoid or opt out of that classwork completely.

9. Forget that while you may be faced with a few students who cannot speak your language, ESL students' entire environment is filled with people who cannot speak their language. In addition to English instruction, they will need support and understanding from those around them.

10. Confuse low English-speaking proficiency or lack of knowledge of the classroom culture with uncooperativeness and other antisocial behavior. If students can't understand what you want them to do or have never done it before, they will have difficulties in carrying out your wishes.

(10. *continued*)

There is a difference between students who are *unwilling* to do a task and those who are *unable* to do it.

11. Try to find ways to incorporate what you are learning about your ESL students into your classroom so that their experiences can be used to enrich the lives of all of your students.

11. Confuse low English-speaking proficiency with low intelligence or lack of experience. Most ESL students are normal cognitively and bring the same rich set of feelings, experiences, and ideas to the classroom as their English-speaking peers. They also often bring many first language and literacy skills to the classroom which can be used to develop new English and literacy skills.

12. *Relax!* Your ESL students have a specific need but not an insurmountable disability. With a *little* bit of patience, kindness, and determination, and a willingness to help on your part, you will be rewarded with a whole *lot* of hard work, learning, and love on the part of your ESL students!

Adult Education[1]

Sharon Hilles

Adult education commonly refers to public education for adults which does not fall within the mainstream credit/degree objective programs offered for adults by universities or colleges. Adult education is primarily funded by state, local, and (sometimes) federal governments, and is delivered by adult schools and community colleges and sometimes university extensions. Adult education has several purposes. First, it allows students who were unable to complete their high school educations, for whatever reasons, to get their diplomas. Second, it provides a resource for those who desire to pursue vocational training or continue their education after graduating from high school or university, but not in the setting of a college or graduate school. Finally, in recent years, the major burden of adult education has been teaching English as a Second Language (ESL) to an ever-increasing immigrant population in the United States. For this reason, adult education has, to a great degree, become synonymous with ESL. In this chapter we shall concern ourselves primarily with this aspect of adult education. It should be remembered, however, that adult education has other functions as well, not the least of which is assisting our society in the technological transition into the 20th century. As Margaret Mead pointed out, "No one will live all his life in the world into which he was born, and no one will die in the world in which he worked in his maturity" (quoted in Cotton, 1968, p. 25).

Adult and continuing education have had a long tradition in the United States, even though they have waxed and waned in popularity and status over the years. (For an excellent review of the literature, see Cotton, 1968; McIntire, 1988.) It has been suggested that perhaps the earliest example of adult education in the United States is Benjamin Franklin's Junto groups in 1727 (Knowles & Klevins, 1976, p. 12; McIntire, 1988, p. 20), which provided weekly discussions of intellectual subjects for adults. Josiah Holbrook's Lyceums in 1826 "encouraged teachers to participate in the acquisition of useful knowledge and helped the advancement of public schools. Lyceum meetings were similar to county teacher inservice institutes and topics frequently included attempts to improve teaching methodology" (McIntire, 1988, p. 20). Various other programs grew up following the Civil War, including an abundance of correspondence courses, which were very popular and widely accepted by the public. According to Knowles and Klevins (1976), the main thrust of early adult education was remedial. This began to change in 1919 when adult education was recognized as "a permanent national necessity, an inseparable aspect of citizenship" (p. 13). Between World War I and World War II, adult education passed through stages, from being informed by highly idealistic notions characterizing it as "a means of bringing about social reform, reconstruction and progress" to the more conservative stance that "the country could be better served if the ideals were modified to that which could be judged realistic" (p. 13). After World War II, government and philanthropic groups began to participate in adult

and continuing education, and in 1965 the Bureau of Adult and Vocational Education was formed as a part of the U.S. Office of Education. The number of students enrolled in adult programs has increased steadily since 1924.

According to McIntire (1988, p. 48), adult education currently serves a diverse population, including the following:

1. Students who did not have an opportunity to attend during the traditional elementary and/or secondary range.
2. Students who dropped out of school.
3. Immigrants who are learning English as a second language, acquiring basic skills in English, or obtaining a high school diploma in English.
4. Students acquiring vocational training skills.

Savage (1984) points out that adult ESL learners may also include students with a variety of literacy skills, from "preliterate," which she defines as "those who speak a language for which there is no written form or whose written form is rare (e.g., Hmong, Mien)," to illiterates, semiliterates, and students from non-Roman alphabets.[2] In the academic year 1986–1987, the breakdown of students enrolled in the Los Angeles Unified School District's adult classes was as follows:

1.	Elementary and basic skills	1,342
2.	High school diploma	8,168
3.	ESL	208,728
4.	Handicapped	11,369
5.	Vocational	115,419
6.	Parenting	4,865
7.	Gerontology	22,655
8.	Citizenship	1,320
9.	Other	72,266
	Total	446,132

Nonnative speakers of English are present in all of the above categories, though classes in ESL are often a steppingstone to other adult programs. In California, ESL classes are typically of two types: visa programs and resident programs. The former are restricted to students who are in the United

States on student visas. These students must be present in a classroom a specified number of hours per week and must be making reasonable progress toward a degree objective in order to retain their visas. They are allowed up to two years to master English before beginning their higher education. Most visa students plan to return to their respective countries after finishing their higher education in the United States. In California, there are a limited number of public schools which have visa programs. Resident ESL programs, on the other hand, are numerous. These programs do not—indeed, may not—serve those who hold student visas; in fact, many of the students in resident programs are not in the United States with any type of visa at all. This category includes a number of both "economic" and political refugees, and their presence in adult school classrooms is invariably a reflection (and often a precursor) of global events. Residents are usually and understandably older than visa students and compose the vast majority of students in categories 1, 2, 3, and 8 above.

ADULT LEARNERS

Whether they are ESL students or native speakers, visa students or residents, adults are different from "typical" or "traditional" K–12 students in that they bring a great deal of life experience and cognitive maturity to the classroom which their younger counterparts do not. In many cases they have borne and reared children, earned a living, seen life and death, and, all too often, survived extreme political and economic hardship. Adult students have a maturity and an understanding of priorities that many younger students might not. According to Knowles (1976), adults not only can but need to take responsibility, to some degree, for their own learning. "Evidence is beginning to accumulate, too, that what adults learn on their own initiative they learn more deeply and permanently than what they learn by being taught. In fact, there is strong evidence from both psychother-apeutical and developmental psychological research that a prime characteristic of adultness is the need and capacity to be self-directing" (Knowles, 1976, p. 181). In other words, unlike children, adults need to and will participate in their own learning. Whether this participation is manifested in a positive way or seeks less agreeable avenues depends largely on the degree to which the learning situation matches their cultural expectations and perceived needs, and the degree to which the teacher allows students to truly participate in their own learning. Something as simple as informally surveying students and allowing them to say whether they feel they have mastered a concept before going on to the next is one way of letting students participate in their own learning. Adults will, to some degree, "direct" their own learning agendas, and if this is not somehow accommodated by the teacher, the self-direction may take the form of challenging the teacher or syllabus in class, by simply leaving the class and attempting some other avenue of learning, or by filtering out what they perceive as nonessential. This difference between adult and child learners is so crucial that Knowles and Klevins (1976) maintain that the term *pedagogy* should not apply to adults because the word "taken literally from its roots means the leading of children, the implication thereof being that the learner is guided within a rather rigid system. A basic problem with pedagogy is that most teachers have known only how to teach adults as if they were children" (p. 14). Knowles and Klevins argue that "a more explicit and realistic term which may be applied to adult education is *andragogy*. From its root, it denotes the leading of man; or the art or science of helping adults learn" (p. 14). Though the term has never really caught on in the literature, their point is well taken. Without question there are numerous differences between adults and children; much too frequently, however, inexperienced adult ESL teachers (unconsciously) think of their students as children, perhaps because of their limited English proficiency. The results are often a disastrous paternalistic attitude, baby talk, which presents an unnatural, not to mention insulting, model of spoken English, and serious misunderstandings.

In addition to being mature and self-directed, adult learners are often, of necessity, more focused. McIntire (1988) points out that "because time is such a valuable commodity, participating in educational programs is often a personal sacrifice. Typically, adults can devote only limited time to their educational endeavors, which often translates into their being dedicated students who take learning seriously" (p. 47). According to his survey, approximately three-quarters of adult ESL students work 40 hours or more per week, a dedicated and focused group, indeed.

Finally, adult learners are most often voluntary learners. Unlike their younger counterparts, who are required by law or by their parents to be in school until a particular age, adult learners are in school because they want to be, a desire which is almost always inconvenient and often interrupted by family and job responsibilities and commitments. As a result, adult learners tend to have little patience with classes which they perceive are not furthering their own educational agendas. As Paul Davis (personal communication) has pointed out, "Adult learners vote with their feet. If they feel a class isn't meeting their needs to some acceptable degree, they walk."

A TYPICAL ADULT EDUCATION SETTING

Part of the challenge of teaching adult school ESL is the diversity. Iwataki (1981) describes the typical adult ESL classroom as follows:

Picture a classroom of some 30 or more students, ranging in age from 18–80. The learners come from heterogeneous language and experiential backgrounds . . . this is a voluntary, not a captive audience, found in churches, recreation centers, vacant elementary, secondary school bungalows, or classrooms unoccupied at night. (p. 24)

Heterogeneous classes are certainly characteristic of the adult school classroom, and part of its unique challenge. This notwithstanding, there does exist at least a statistically typical adult ESL student and classroom in each neighborhood. Let us take Belmont Community Adult School, the largest adult school in California in terms of absolute population, as a case in point. Belmont is an inner-city school in Los Angeles, established in 1925. The typical Belmont student is a single male Hispanic, between the ages of 21 and 29, who is employed full time and has had between an eighth-grade and a high school education.

Large ESL classes (often over 50 students) are characteristic of many adult schools. The typical Belmont ESL student feels that his teachers are "excellent," that there is adequate opportunity for him to get individual help from his teachers, and that the traditionally large ESL class size does not significantly interfere with his learning (Belmont Community Adult School Application for Accreditation, April 1988). Although LAUSD and union regulations specify that classes need not contain more than 49 students, classes must be closed when they cease to be cost-efficient. This is usually at about 21 students. Because attrition is a natural factor of adult ESL, and because teachers are often reluctant to turn students away, classes tend to be considerably larger than the prescribed 49 students.

Large classes make for an excitement and for group dynamics that smaller classes simply can't produce. Students clearly enjoy the social aspect. Adult school is, of course, a place to learn English, but it is also a place to get together with friends, establish new relationships, and even form and nurture romances. New ESL teachers often notice the social aspect and mistakenly assume that students attend school for social rather than educational reasons; as a result they do not take their teaching responsibilities seriously, but rather try to provide an entertaining social atmosphere in order to maintain class numbers. Perhaps a word of warning based on long years of experience might be in order: Students attend night school as long as they perceive that they are learning. When that perceived learning ceases, so does their attendance. No matter how entertaining or charming the teacher may be, students can always have more fun at home.

Adult school is also important in another sense. In his book on "America's underprepared," Rose (1989) recounts his ESL students' concerns with how their children were doing in school. They wanted to talk to their children's teachers, "but felt funny about seeing the teacher for their English was so bad and . . . well . . . who were they to presume to talk to the teacher about what she does?" Rose and his colleagues were also concerned that they weren't doing enough for their adult students, but their supervisor pointed out that the ESL classes were "bringing them comfortably into the schools, breaking down some of the intimidating barriers that traditionally keep them far away, distant from the places where their kids were learning how to read and write . . . there's more to look for here than just an increase in vocabulary" (Rose, 1989, pp. 130–131). All too often we forget that many of our students are parents, or will be parents in the near future. Perhaps school was inaccessible to them in their native lands, but it will be a central and not necessarily an altogether pleasant experience for their children. It is vital for all concerned that immigrant parents be brought "comfortably into the schools."

Students in a particular community adult school will usually reflect the (changing) ethnicity of the neighborhood. As immigrant populations tend to concentrate in a particular area, it is not unusual to see that concentration reflected in a particular community adult school. Belmont is no exception. Its student body (81 percent Hispanic, 10 percent Asian, 9 percent other) reflects the composition of the neighborhood. Over the past six years, the Hispanic population in Los Angeles has increased by approximately 37 percent and the Asian population by 10 per-cent, while the white population has decreased by 35 percent. Belmont Community Adult School has an active student body of approximately 8,500 at any one given time, with an enrollment of about 33,500 over the course of an academic year; about 60 percent of the students are enrolled in ESL classes.

ADULT SCHOOL TEACHERS

At Belmont in 1988, there were 66 day classes and 73 night classes staffed by 128 teachers. Seventy-two percent of the teachers were part time, working 10 hours or less each week, making them ineligible for district benefits. In fact, the majority of adult teachers in the Los Angeles Unified School District (LAUSD) fall into this category. As per district policy, only tenured teachers are allowed to work more than a 12-hour assignment in ESL. The typical ESL teacher at Belmont is female, is between the ages of 36 and 45, and has a bachelor's degree. Her adult school assignment is 10 hours per week. Although she teaches ESL at night, she usually has day employment outside of the educational field. She participates in district-sponsored workshops and in-service training and belongs to at least one professional organization. According to Hurst (1985), ESL teachers in general have good rapport with their students, and are remarkably attuned to what they perceive to be their students' needs and aspirations. The Belmont teacher does not, however, typically read professional journals or recent publications on second language acquisition, TESL pedagogy, or methodology.

According to McIntire (personal communication), if an ESL teacher is happy and content in her work, she is more of a "people person than a subject matter person." In other words, ESL teachers find interpersonal relationships with their students more deeply satisfying than the intellectual stimulation provided by the subject matter they are teaching. Iwataki (1981) warns that "those who teach ESL to adults need to be made of sturdy stock.

They need special qualities of understanding, cultural sensitivity, adaptability, stamina and resourcefulness to help them cope with the realities of the adult ESL classroom. Furthermore, they need to possess full command and knowledge of the subject area—the English language" (p. 24). Due to the current credentialing procedures in California, the last point is probably the typical ESL teacher's weakest area. The state simply requires a baccalaureate for the Basic Education Designated Subjects Credential. Individual districts are then allowed to set up their own specific standards for ESL teaching. The LAUSD requires only a minimum of 8 semester units in English (and 12 units in any foreign language, linguistics, or speech) to obtain a temporary credential to teach ESL. No formal training in TESL is required. This profile, of course, is changing as more and more universities produce TESL professionals who enter the ranks of adult education.

Hurst's comment regarding the unusual sensitivity of ESL teachers should come as no surprise. There is ample evidence that affective factors are more important in adult second language learning than in any other learning environment. Why this should be so is only speculation at this point.[3] The phenomenon is nonetheless widely recognized and has led many professionals such as Marianne Celce-Murcia to comment that "not everyone is meant to be an ESL teacher. Perhaps by inclination and personality some are more suited to computer programming or to some other profession" (personal communication). In any case, warmth, compassion, empathy, and kindness seem to be constant qualities in good ESL teachers.

Sensitivity to student cultures is also important. In a recent study of bilingual classrooms in the San Francisco Bay Area, Fillmore et al. (1985) found that Hispanic children did better in an environment in which they were allowed liberal peer interaction, whereas Chinese students did better in a classroom which was relatively quiet and the main interaction was with the teacher.

Whether these findings concerning cultural differences generalize to the adult ESL classroom has yet to be verified empirically, but intuitively it seems to be the case that Hispanic students are more comfortable with peer interaction and a noise level which might not be acceptable to other ESL learners. In some cases it appears that peer interaction is the preferred method of constructing meaning. For example, directions such as "Open your books to page 8," presented to advanced Hispanic students bimodally (that is, both written on the board and spoken), are often met with queries among students *in English* of "What page?" The problem does not seem to be that the students don't understand, but rather that meaning is not comfortably taken directly from a written source or from the teacher; instead it is negotiated verbally, through peer interaction. Colleagues have commented on the same response to directions written for ESL students in their native language. Although a sign is posted in Spanish which directs Spanish-speaking students to a certain room, they often still seem to prefer to arrive at a meaning through discussion with each other of what they have read rather than taking the meaning directly from the written word. This is a phenomenon documented among other groups (cf. Heath, 1983). Taking meaning directly from print and acting on that meaning is a skill that is learned; its absence reflects differing socialization patterns, not a cognitive deficit. It is important, therefore, that teachers be sensitive to their students, their needs, and their cultural differences, both in and out of the classroom. Some of our students have not had years of socialization to a school classroom. They may display behavior which new teachers might find inappropriate, such as using a noisy pencil sharpener during a teacher presentation, or opening or closing doors or windows without permission. In some classes teachers need to be tolerant of the noise generated by students as they negotiate meaning through peer interaction or of students' difficulty in silently following written or spoken instructions.

UNDERESTIMATING RESIDENT ESL STUDENTS

The emotional satisfaction in teaching adult school is legendary among ESL professionals. Because we often assume that emotional and intellectual satisfaction are incompatible, and perhaps because of the students' educational backgrounds, we often tend to underestimate resident students. It is widely assumed that residents have little interest in, or aptitude for, "more academic" approaches to ESL, and should be taught "the way children learn"—by speaking first with little emphasis on reading and writing. Instruction in grammar should be avoided in favor of more practical "survival English"—learning how to ride a bus or fill out a job application. To my knowledge there is no evidence supporting the assertion either that residents do not have the interest or ability to master ESL through a more sophisticated approach or that adults learn a second language "the way children do." In fact, there is ample anecdotal and preliminary empirical evidence to the contrary. Students routinely complain about teachers who do not have a direction in their program that the students can easily identify. It is essential that students feel they are making progress, and often this progress translates into moving from one grammatical concept to another which seems to follow logically. Moreover, many students expect formal grammar instruction to be a part of language learning, whether they are particularly good at it or not, and they suspect teachers of being incompetent who cannot provide at least minimal explanation.

Most students who enroll in an adult school already possess a vast storehouse of knowledge. They frequently arrive in this country with an extensive network of family and friends who have come before them. They are quickly tutored in how to take a bus, use the laundromat, make a call from a pay phone, and buy a money order. According to McIntire (1988), most adult school students have jobs; moreover, they get those jobs through friends, or through sheer luck, rather than through newspaper ads or other more conventional avenues. Most of them are "surviving," and doing it quite well.

One colleague pointed out the irony of teaching "survival" English *only* (and the key word here is *only*). When she made a factual mistake in her lesson on taking the bus in Los Angeles, several of her students promptly corrected her. At that point she realized that she had been teaching something about which she had no practical knowledge. She had never even been on a bus in Los Angeles. On the other hand, most of her students had not only come to school by bus that night, they also knew, from experience, how to get to work, the park, the house of a friend, or a specialty shop in the San Fernando Valley. They knew bus routes all over the city—something she could only imagine. The students had accepted the superfluous lesson with grace; as teachers we would all do well to accept a lesson from them with equal grace: don't underestimate resident students. The point here is not that survival English has no place in the ESL classroom, for of course it does; it is part of the adult ESL teacher's responsibility to teach skills that will help students do what McIntire (personal communication) calls "access the system." These kinds of skills are essential. That which has no place in the ESL classroom is the paternalistic assumption that students are capable of nothing else. Basic science, math, and social science concepts make excellent vehicles for grammar, conversation, pronunciation, reading, and writing lessons. Following Freire (1970a, 1970b) in spirit if not in letter, the students themselves and their concerns are valid, relevant, and perhaps even essential content for lessons. We might even appropriate Hirsch (1987) to the extent that we make our materials more substantive rather than less. For example, in teaching uses of the present tense, a teacher might use sample sentences such as "Water boils at 100°C" or

"Water freezes at 32°F" rather than "John takes a shower every day." These types of sentences spark conversation such as the differences between the Fahrenheit and Centigrade temperature scales, as well as providing interesting bits of information, fragmented though it may be, which students seem to truly appreciate. In fact, any of the teaching suggestions offered in this volume, with varying degrees of modification, would be appropriate for adult ESL classes. Modifications might include providing context or background information (schema) for an exercise that university students might not need, or revising the activity so that no out-of-class work is required. ESL resident students seldom have time for homework.

As for the second assumption mentioned above regarding the nature of adult second language learning, there is no empirical evidence that adults learn a second language the way children learn a first, and there is ample anecdotal and suggestive logical and empirical evidence that this is not the case (cf. Bley-Vroman, 1985; Hilles, in press, and sources cited therein; Richards, 1985).

ADULT SCHOOL PROGRAMS VERSUS TRADITIONAL PROGRAMS

Because of the nature of adult learners outlined above, McIntire (1988) points out that adult schools have traditionally been more responsive to student needs than most educational programs, and the courses offered reflect the changing concerns and needs of the community. Adult classes usually meet at night, and often on Saturdays. In the 1988–1989 academic year, to meet the requirements of amnesty students, some classes in the LAUSD were conducted literally around the clock at Evans Community Adult School. The last class of the day met from 9:00 p.m. to midnight. The first class was from midnight to 2:00 a.m., followed by a class which met from 2:00 a.m. to 6:00 a.m., and so on throughout the day and night. In 1986–1987, when over 30,000 students were turned away from ESL classes because there were no funds for teachers, classrooms, etc., LAUSD's adult education division produced an 80-lesson ESL series for television "in response to a request from the Board of Education to provide ESL instruction to persons who could not be accommodated in overcrowded classrooms" (Figueroa, Walker, Varon, & Johnson, 1988).

Another way in which adult schools are different from traditional schools and reflect community needs is in open enrollment, a procedure which has grown out of the constant change and flux which is characteristic of immigrant communities in the Southwest. Open enrollment or entry allows students to enroll in and then leave a class at any time up to the last week of class during the quarter. This is necessary because there are constantly new arrivals and sudden departures in any immigrant community. Job schedules also change, making it necessary for students to switch from night to day classes, or vice versa. The attrition rate is high; it is interesting to note that students surveyed by McIntire identified changing job or family responsibilities rather than educational dissatisfaction as the reason for their having left school (McIntire, personal communication). As a result of these and other factors, the complexion of any one ESL class is constantly changing. The challenge, of course, is to maintain class standards and retain students while accommodating a constant stream of new students, some of whom have never been in an American school, or indeed in any school, before. As a result of open enrollment, some schools have a multilevel "holding" class which accepts all newcomers, tests them, and teaches basic skills until an opening is available at the appropriate level. Most ESL teachers find constant newcomers part of the adult school challenge; regular and consistent review, in greater depth than might be expected in a class without open enrollment, is one solution. Contrary to what one might expect, such review is always welcomed by the veteran students and goes a long way toward orienting new ones. Some teachers also assign student hosts to help the newcomers find their way around the school and to explain classroom procedures, school rules, and schedules. Surprisingly enough, according to many adult ESL teachers, open enrollment is more of a problem in principle than in fact, and once accepted by the teacher as a variable which he/she has to factor into classroom operations, it is of little consequence.

MULTILEVEL CLASSES

Multilevel classes are also a challenge in adult ESL, especially at branch locations. A ''branch'' is a site which is responsible to and administered by a central school, but which typically has only one or two classes, though of course it can have many more. Branches are often located in makeshift schoolrooms in churches, community centers, libraries, or sometimes even hospitals or businesses. There are frequently not enough students at a branch location to support an entire class at any one level. Therefore, one teacher may have a single class in which there are very advanced students as well as some who are unable to write their own names. In many ways, branch locations are much like the old one-room schoolhouse. The task of teaching such a diverse group to speak English might seem an impossible one, but most teachers experienced in teaching multilevel classes would not give up their assignments for a more traditional group. They all agree that timing and planning are the most important factors in handling a multilevel class. The first

step is to divide students into more or less homogeneous groups. One, two, or three groups are normal. The second task is to structure activities so that the teacher can spend equal time with each group. For example, if the class can be divided into three groups—beginning, intermediate, and advanced—the schedule might look something like the one in Figure 1 below.

Notice that the opening activity has the whole class together. The activity might include learning vocabulary items, pronunciation practice, or learning a popular song or a folk song. These are all activities in which students with a wide range of proficiencies can participate on a more or less equal footing. Bob Rumin (personal communication) suggests bringing in a shoe box with several items from around the house in it. Sometimes the teacher brings items from a particular room, such as a knife, fork, can opener, spatula, saucer, saucepan, and wooden spoon. Students from around the room are allowed to remove an item without looking, which makes the activity fun and holds the interest of the students. Then each student is asked to tell the class what he or she has. If the student can't answer, the teacher elicits help from the entire class. If no one in the class knows, the teacher provides the lexical item. After the proper item has been elicited, it is written on the board, and the teacher models the pronunciation several times. He/she then allows students to repeat while constantly calling their attention to the item being held by their classmate. As the list progresses and becomes longer, the teacher asks the student holding the item to stand up. The task becomes more

	Beginners	Intermediate	Advanced
9:00–9:15	Teacher-directed	Teacher-directed	Teacher-directed
9:15–9:45	Teacher-directed	Desk work	Group work
9:45–10:00	Break	Break	Break
10:00–10:15	Desk work	Group work	Teacher-directed
10:15–10:45	Group work	Teacher-directed	Desk work
10:45–11:25	Teacher-directed	Teacher-directed	Teacher-directed

FIGURE 1. *Schedule for a multilevel class.*

and more lively as the teacher calls off items more quickly and students stand up and sit down, often at the encouragement of their classmates. For variety, a student may volunteer to come to the front of the room and pronounce and identify each of the objects. It is suggested that items be reviewed frequently, but after items from the house are exhausted, including cleaning supplies, items from business or children's small toy animals may be substituted.

After the opening activity, students divide into groups according to level. It is essential that students know exactly what to do at this point. They need to know where in the room to go and exactly what activity to begin with. Early training is the key to success at this point. Teachers have found that time spent directing students to their proper groups during the first few days of class will be well invested and result in smooth transitions later. A schedule of class activities for each group should be posted in each group area. Adhere stringently to the schedule for the first few weeks, and it will become automatic for the students. It is not unusual for a teacher actually to take a kitchen timer to class and set it for each activity. Some have watches with alarm clocks, and some bring in bedside alarm clocks. Getting students used to transition between activities is most important. Once the routine has been established, veteran students can help new students get used to the routine.

Pedagogically the idea is that all students spend opening and closing time with the teacher, and one-third or one-half of the remaining time (depending on the number of groups) in teacher-directed activities. Each teacher-directed lesson should lead to individual desk work, which can then move naturally into communicative group work. Advanced students may be able to work from written instructions, but most students will need instructions from the teacher supplied during the teacher-directed lesson, which can be reinforced by the posted schedule. Sometimes advanced students can also help beginning students under teacher super-vision. Teachers agree that multilevel classrooms are challenging, but definitely manageable, as long as the students are properly grouped and sufficient time is devoted to learning the class routine.

TESTING

Adult ESL has traditionally been lax in placing students, so that classes are often composed of students with varying degrees of proficiency, but all of whom are from the same family or social group, or are particularly fond of a certain teacher. According to McIntire (1988, p. 31), "Forty percent of immigrant students believed they were placed in the wrong grade level by school officials, which suggests that many immigrant students 'waste time' in classes which are inappropriate to their specific needs." In schools in which multilevel grouping is not dictated by necessity, it is most efficient to work toward some sort of evaluation metric so that students can be placed with others of like proficiency. Fortunately, adult schools without serious placement procedures are becoming a thing of the past.[4]

At Belmont, for example, all entering students take a placement test. In the upper levels, they are tracked according to language strengths and deficiencies. They are offered classes in grammar, reading, listening and speaking, and writing. Students take two classes a night. Those who are weak in grammar but strong in reading might take two grammar classes, or a reading class at one level, and a grammar class at a lower level. Over the course of several years, this system changed the structure of the school's ESL program from a pyramid configuration, with the majority of students at lower levels, to a columnar configuration. In other words, the attrition rate decreased as more and more students moved on to the upper levels, and fewer students dropped out. The school also developed exit tests for each level so that students with like proficiency tended to remain grouped. It is often felt (erroneously) that ESL student egos are so fragile that they could not possibly be submitted to actual testing. The Belmont experience seems to indicate otherwise. Observation suggests that students expect and respect formal testing and are challenged rather than overwhelmed by the event. In fact, it is not unusual for attendance to be particularly high on nights during which testing is scheduled, and for some students to insist on remaining in a level, regardless of test results, until they meet their own criteria for passing. The fact that students appreciate honest and valid testing should come as no surprise and is very much in keeping with the adult learner profile outlined earlier. Of course, it is certainly questionable, on the face of it, whether a paper-and-pencil test is a valid measure of language at all. Surely a Communicative Test (Wesche, 1987) would be closer to the ideal. Unfortunately, sheer numbers discourage a direct, communicative test in most schools.

Recently many adult schools have moved over to competency-based programs, which in theory should require competency-based exams. McIntire (1988, p. 15) defines competency-based education as "Curriculum based on predetermined competencies identified as necessary for adults to function successfully. Students must demonstrate mastery of these competencies to successfully complete a class or a program." The idea, then, is that a student might be required to be able to enroll his/her child in school, write an excuse to the teacher, report the child's health and immunization history, and similar details, in order to pass a unit. According to McIntire, "An underlying philosophical tenet of competency based education is the belief that a student must achieve skills rather than 'earn credits.' Thus, adults may attend a class for a short or for an extended period of time in order to satisfactorily demonstrate the attainment of competencies. . . . Success is measured in the mastery of specific competencies rather than through hours of attendance, commonly referred to as 'seat time' " (p. 37). The problem with respect to ESL is that imposing such "communicative" goals

early on can possibly have long-term negative effects on students in that the more formal aspects of language such as grammar or pronunciation tend to be completely ignored in favor of competencies or communication, possibly resulting in pidginization and fossilization of the learners' interlanguage (Celce-Murcia & Hilles, 1988; Higgs & Clifford, 1982; but for another view cf. also Dulay, Burt, & Krashen, 1982; Terrell 1977.)

THE VALUE OF ADULT EDUCATION

It is often assumed that education has historically been the key to social mobility among *all* immigrant groups. Many students believe, and many teachers perpetuate the myth, that education, including ESL, is the key to economic success. According to Sowell (1983), this is not necessarily the case. "Plausible as this may seem, the evidence does not support it. The Chinese, the Japanese, and the Jews were all rising economically before any significant proportion of them even completed high school. *After* they had achieved a measure of prosperity through business success (including farming, in the case of the Japanese) *then* they could afford to send their children on to college and postgraduate education to become doctors, scientists, and other well-paid professionals. To groups without the entrepreneurial backgrounds of the Jews, Chinese, and Japanese, education is of course more important as an avenue of upward mobility" (p. 198). These findings are borne out by McIntire (1988). The workplace is vitally important for our students, and often the ESL class has to take a backseat to overtime or training for a new job. As Iwataki (1981) points out, adult ESL students have as their frame of reference "not the school but their families, jobs, their outside responsibilities" (p. 24). Adult ESL teachers need to be aware of the importance of economic factors in the lives of their students. For many, upward mobility will be achieved, not by them, but by their children and their grandchildren. This is mentioned not to discourage, but to encourage realistic goals and expectations, and as a reminder that as adults, ESL students have their own priorities. Moreover, many of our students will come to the classroom already speaking a pidginized, "fossilized" English. Quite honestly, their prognosis for mastering *nativelike* English and assimilating into the mainstream culture is not particularly bright (Celce-Murcia & Hilles, 1988; Higgs & Clifford, 1982; McIntire, 1988). However, if they learn enough English to survive, their children and grandchildren will most likely be able to take advantage of the upward mobility that education can bring. This should in no way be construed as suggesting that adult school teachers ought not aim for targetlike proficiency in their students; rather it is meant to temper their expectations so that they are realistic and do not demand an insuperable task (and often a subsequent failure) of the students. The by-products of education which our students routinely *do* experience also need to be considered. In addition to bringing students "comfortably into the classroom," adult school is in many cases the first positive contact many immigrants have with American social institutions. Increased self-esteem, cultural awareness, tolerance, and a positive experience with American schools and teachers are important epiphenomena of adult ESL classes, and their significance cannot be overstated. Both the immigrant community and the community at large benefit greatly from such effects, even if the students do not achieve nativelike mastery of English. According to McIntire (personal communication), the real goals of adult education in general, and ESL in particular, are "bolstering self-esteem, providing appropriate instruction/remediation and helping students access the system."

CONCLUSION

Limited assignments, large multilevel classes, extensive bookkeeping, and students with less than a high school education combined with frequently underprepared teachers seems to be a sure recipe for pedagogical disaster; yet teachers are routinely effusive when describing their adult ESL experience, as are the students. Teachers who come to work "exhausted" speak about renewed energy and of taking several hours to "wind down" after an adult ESL class because the experience is so exciting and intense. The bond between ESL student and teacher is nothing short of remarkable, and the satisfaction teachers experience is truly profound. It has been said (Bob Rumin, personal communication) that the last bastion of genuine respect for teachers—and, indeed, for education in general in the United States—is the adult ESL classroom. Dale McIntire (personal communication) describes it as "what you thought education was going to be when you first decided to become a teacher." The consensus among those who have worked in this setting seems to be that it is among the most rewarding and interesting teaching assignments possible. It is sad, indeed, that lack of job security, and of full-time employment and benefits should also characterize the teaching assignment of many of our best qualified and experienced adult ESL teachers.

NOTES

1. I would like to thank Sadae Iwataki, Dale McIntire, Andre Sutton, and Marianne Celce-Murcia for their very helpful comments, suggestions, and discussions regarding earlier drafts of this chapter. The responsibility for any errors or omissions, of course, is mine.

2. These students present a particular set of challenges to the ESL teacher. The reader is referred to Savage (1984) as well as to the chapter by Haverson in this volume for very helpful and practical suggestions.

3. But see Schumann, 1990, for an interesting and possible explanation.

4. It should be noted that a special 1984 edition of *Night and Day with ESL,* a publication of Adult ESL Programs, Adult/Regional Occupational Centers/Programs Education Division of LAUSD, urged teachers to test adult ESL students and offered tests as well as training in administering them to interested schools. Such in-service options seem crucial for improvement in the overall quality of adult ESL.

DISCUSSION QUESTIONS

1. What are some characteristics of adult learners which set them apart from more traditional students?

2. How could you exploit these differences in your approach to adult ESL?

3. How are adult school students different from university students?

4. In what way do you think those differences should/do affect your approach to adult school students?

5. When do adult classes usually meet? Why? What challenges do such hours present to the adult ESL teacher?

6. It's not unusual when students and teachers are close to the same age for romantic feelings to occur, on one side or the other, or mutually. What are the ethics (if any) involved? Should a teacher date a student? Why or why not? How do you think such a situation should be handled from a teacher's point of view? from that of a student? from that of an administrator?

SUGGESTED ACTIVITIES

1. What are some life skills you think an adult needs to learn? How could you go about teaching them in an interesting and creative way?

2. Based on other readings in this book or on some of the suggested readings, find some teaching suggestions that appeal to you. Work out a lesson to teach the following to adult ESL students:

a. present tense
b. pronunciation of final /d/ in English
c. writing an absence excuse to a child's teacher
d. reading a child's report card

3. Part of a grammar lesson might be a controlled or manipulative phase in which students simply manipulate structures. This phase would precede a communicative exercise in which the students would actually practice the structure in a communicative context. Imagine that you are teaching the present perfect to an intermediate adult ESL class. Following the suggestions in this chapter, make up a list of sentences that could be used for the controlled exercise portion of the lesson.

4. Plan in detail a 2 1/2-hour lesson for a multilevel ESL class. Decide the proficiency of each level. What will your opening exercise(s) be? Why will this exercise be a good one for students at different levels? How will you time the rest of the lesson? How will you move students from one activity to another? How will you assure that when the teacher is with one group, he or she will not be needed by another?

5. Visit an adult ESL class. Keep a running written account of what you see. Describe the teacher, the students, the lesson, the room. What are the students doing during the teacher directed portion of the lesson? What is the noise level in the room? What do students seem to be talking about when they are talking to each other? Do they seem comfortable with the teacher? Upon what do you base your answer? Does the teacher talk down to the students? Is he or she equally attentive to male and female students? Older and younger ones? Students from different countries? Does the lesson seem appropriate to the level of the students?

6. From your observations in activity 5, do there seem to be differences between various student skills? In other words, did you find evidence that some students may have greater passive understanding than productive ability? Did students seem better at manipulative exercises than at actual communication or vice versa? Describe the differences found and then outline a program to remedy these differences or provide an argument as to why these differences cannot/need not be remedied.

SUGGESTIONS FOR FURTHER READING

Celce-Murcia, M., and D. Larsen-Freeman (1983)
The Grammar Book: an ESL/EFL Teacher's Course. New York: Newbury House.

Celce-Murcia, M., and S. Hilles (1988)
Techniques and Resources in Teaching Grammar. New York: Oxford University Press.

Ilyin, D., and T. Tragardh, eds. (1978)
Classroom Practices in Adult ESL. Washington, DC: TESOL.

Larsen-Freeman, D. (1986)
Techniques and Principles in Language Teaching. New York: Oxford University Press.

Long, M. and J. Richards, eds. (1987)
Methodology in TESOL. New York: Newbury House.

Richards, J., and T. Rodgers (1986)
Approaches and Methods in Language Teaching. Cambridge: Cambridge University Press.

Rose, M. (1989)
Lives on the Boundary. New York: Free Press.

V
Skills for Teachers

This book ends with a section devoted to the ESL teacher. What do teachers need to know in order to perform their job professionally and effectively? What are the skills all too frequently left undiscussed in an ESL methods course or a methods textbook? In the first chapter Purgason shows how lesson plans and units can be prepared and structured, offering some sound ideas and procedures to follow. Skierso's chapter then gives a detailed overview of textbook evaluation and selection, a stock from which the teacher can adapt instruments and techniques so that thought and care can inform decision making in this area. The chapter by Brinton on using media in language teaching shows teachers the pedagogical usefulness of media and how numerous technical and non-technical resources can be used to enhance the teaching-learning process. The Schrecks then give teachers an introduction to computer-assisted language learning, a new area which is becoming increasingly important in modern instructional programs. Cohen's chapter on language testing covers many issues (test types, test items, test administration, reliability, validity); every language teacher should have a good general overview of this area. Finally, Crandall reminds ESL teachers of all the resources they can exploit to keep up to date. The field is growing rapidly, and a big part of any ESL teacher's responsibility is to keep abreast of new developments.

Planning Lessons and Units

Katherine Barnhouse Purgason

INTRODUCTION

A teacher who wants to learn how to plan lessons can approach the problem on two levels. On one level are the issues of how to plan: taking various elements, putting them together in sequence, and recording all this in an appropriate format. On another level are the issues of what to plan. At this level we are really dealing with the question "What is good language teaching?" Although a complete answer to that question is the subject of this entire book and beyond the scope of this chapter, it is worth beginning the discussion of planning lessons and units with a review of what is considered to be good language teaching. Synthesized from Johnson and Morrow (1981, pp. 59–66), Omaggio (1986, pp. 35–36), and Richards (1990, pp. 15, 38–48), the following considerations underlie planning.

1. What is taught is defined by student needs.
   a. All activities are clearly related to something the learners will need to do with English in the real world.

2. What is taught is defined by real language use.
   a. Materials are authentic whenever possible.
   b. Discourse beyond the sentence level is used.
   c. Students learn a range of language functions.
   d. Proficiency necessary for the students' target context is the goal.
   e. Students "do" rather than "learn about."
3. Sound principles of learning are followed.
   a. Teaching reflects sound theory of learning, language learning, and the learning of specific language skills.
4. Lessons are structured for maximum learning.
   a. Objectives are defined.
   b. Activities or tasks to attain the objectives are set.
   c. Learners are informed of the objectives and clearly instructed in how to do the activities.
   d. Class time is used for learning;

learners are actively engaged in tasks.
  e. Student progress is monitored.
  f. Feedback appropriate to the task is given.
5. The classroom atmosphere and interaction are positive.
  a. Students interact well with the teacher and each other.
  b. Students and teacher expect success.
  c. Students gain satisfaction on a variety of levels, cognitive and personal.
6. Learning is student-centered.
  a. Learners are encouraged to express their own meaning.
  b. Learners take active roles in their own learning. The teacher's primary role is that of facilitator.
  c. Students are encouraged to develop personal good language learning strategies. (See Oxford, 1990, for a good discussion of this topic.)
  d. Autonomy is encouraged.
7. Activities reflect actual communication—that is, they have the following characteristics:
  a. Information gap: one person in the exchange knows something the other(s) do not.
  b. Choice: participants choose both what they will say and how they will say it.
  c. Feedback: participants evaluate communication according to how well the aims of the communication have been accomplished.
8. Activities balance accuracy and fluency.
9. Activities encourage interaction, both between learners and texts and among learners.

A CONTEXT FOR PLANNING

Given this foundation, let's return to the first level. Why plan a lesson? Research into teachers' planning processes (Haigh, 1981; Pennella, 1985) reveals various functions that teachers attribute to their plans. There are four major ones. (1) A plan can be a mechanism for decision making, helping the teacher think about content, materials, sequencing, timing, and activities. It can be the means by which a teacher gets familiar with the information, personalizes the activities, or solves other instructional problems. (2) At the level of what actually happens in the class, a plan can be a reminder or map, enabling a teacher to confidently face the students, concentrating on their responses to the material, rather than mentally groping for what to do or say next. It provides some security in the sometimes unpredictable atmosphere of a classroom. (3) A plan can become part of a log of what will be or has been taught. It can thus be used for testing or for comparing what has been taught with an earlier needs assessment or with the work of another class. If one is teaching several sections of the same class, this log can ensure that everything has been covered. (4) At the managerial level, a plan can help a substitute teacher take over or can provide a supervisor with a guide for observation or course evaluation.

A teacher setting out to plan a lesson or unit may or may not have any resources available. In the best of situations, one has a complete syllabus and a good textbook or set of books, including a comprehensive teacher's manual. In the worst, there is no overall plan for the class, there may be a text but it is probably irrelevant to the students' needs, and there are no supplementary materials. The time spent on lesson planning will vary depending on which end of the resource continuum teachers find themselves.

Planning with a Syllabus and a Text

Having a good syllabus, a teacher's manual, and a text that matches your students' needs is a tremendous help to a teacher, but it cannot eliminate the need for planning entirely. A teacher will still have to look over the entire book to see what is covered and when. You need to know, for example, that chapter 2 presents only one way of making a request and that other ways will be covered in chapters 7 and 12. Whatever the length of the "lesson" or "unit" in the text, you will need to choose what can be covered in one class period with your particular students. You may choose to adjust the order of activities, postponing vocabulary work until the end of the reading, for example, even though the text has it at the beginning. With some texts, you'll have to delete activities that don't fit class objectives. With even the best texts, you'll have to supplement: review activities, explanations, community-based assignments, or whatever the text may lack. Since no text is designed with your particular class in mind, you'll have to personalize and localize activities and bring in visual aids or authentic materials to make the material relevant and up to date. For example, if your text has a London map exercise, substitute or add an activity using a map of the city or campus where you are teaching.

There are lots of decisions to be made about how to use a book, from such things as whether the students should listen to a passage with their books closed or open to whether students should respond chorally or individually (Stevick, 1986). Lesson planning can be facilitated when the teacher is aware of a wide range of these options.

Planning with Few Resources

If you do not have a satisfactory syllabus or an adequate textbook, lesson planning is more involved. You will need to think about who your students are and what they need English for. (See the chapters by Peck and Johns, in this volume, for guidance on doing such a needs assessment.) You will need to translate needs into long-term goals and then into short-term objectives. If you can produce a list of objectives, with some quantifications of what percentage of time should be spent on each one, you will be able to check to see that the daily lesson plans are actually going in the right direction.

You will need to decide on a general focus for your class: grammatical structures (e.g., modals, present perfect), language functions (e.g., introducing oneself, requesting help), competencies or life skills (e.g., sending a money order, making a telephone call), study skills (e.g., listening for the main idea, scanning for particular information), content (e.g., medical English, citizenship training), tasks (e.g., reading a map, interpreting a timetable) or a combination. You will need to decide which of the four language skills your students need—reading, writing, listening, speaking—and whether any component skills require special attention—grammar, vocabulary, pronunciation. You will need to choose relevant contexts (e.g., gene transfer or tenant–landlord relations). Finally, you will need to choose activities that can accomplish your objectives, ranging from role-play to guided writing, from pooling information in order to solve a problem to skimming a reading for the main idea. (Even if you have a syllabus and text that has made the decisions already, you should be aware of these choices.)

Constraints

In any kind of teaching situation, there are a number of practical constraints that affect lesson planning. These constraints restrict the choices we have concerning what to teach and how to teach it in any given lesson. One is time—the length of the term and the class, the frequency of the class, the time of day the class meets.

Another set of constraints involve the students: their level, whether the class is mixed or homogeneous, large or small. Student variables also include the age, motivation, interests, and personalities of the students. Their educational background in general and language learning background in particular will affect planning decisions. Responsibilities students have, such as work or other classes, should be considered.

Other constraints involve physical conditions—crowded rooms, fixed desks, poor lighting, noisy halls, erratic electricity—or availability of resources such as paper or tape recorders. Finally, requirements such as an institutional grading policy or national exams may also constrain our lessons.

THE SHAPE OF A LESSON

It is difficult to say, "This is what a lesson should look like." A reading lesson will look very different from a speaking lesson. A lesson planned for a 50-minute academic class will be very different from a lesson for a three-hour adult school class. In simple terms, however, we can say that a lesson should have a beginning, a middle, and an end (Lewis & Hill, 1985).

The beginning can consist of a warm-up or attention-getter, to bring students from wherever they have been to the language class, and/or an orientation to the task at hand. The orientation may be a question ("Has your house ever been burglarized?") or a statement ("I want to tell you a story about being late") or anything to spark the students' interest and draw them into the next activity.

The end can be a brief summary, a comprehension check, a review, or an assignment that lets the students see how the class activity relates to their real life—anything to give a sense of closure (besides the bell ringing).

What you do in the middle will depend on what you are teaching and your approach to teaching. The typical sequence of "presentation, practice, communication" may fit many low-level oral skills classes, but it does not apply to a process-based writing class, for example. If you are using the Language Experience Approach for beginning readers, your lesson will look different from a reading lesson focused on a sight-word approach to recognizing common signs and notices.

Principles

Whatever the shape of your particular lesson, some general principles apply to all planning. Lessons need variety. Grouping is one aspect of the class that can be varied, moving students from whole class to small group activities. Teacher-centered activities can alternate with activities where students are more active and responsible. Skills can be alternated (depending on course goals): Move from a receptive listening exercise to a productive speaking exercise, for example, or from an intense test situation to a relaxing low-pressure game. Apply the principle of variety to series of lessons, too. If one day has been spent on accuracy-oriented practice activities, add variety by planning some fluency-oriented communication activities the next day. Variety will not only keep the class lively but will meet student needs better, since students bring such a range of learning styles to the class (Henak, 1984). Variety also contributes to pace (Omaggio, 1986). With slow learners who can't progress through material very quickly, especially, variety is the best way to give at least an impression of a faster pace.

Plan your lessons with classroom management issues in mind. Maclennan (1987) claims that lessons which may be "good" in terms of language-teaching principles may not work because of management issues, such as whether the class needs to be "settled down" or "stirred up" at a particular moment. A quiet group of students meeting after lunch may need to be stirred up with an activity such as brainstorming. A rowdy class that has been doing a lot of oral pair work may need to be settled by an individual writing activity. By being aware of which effect an activity is likely to have on a class and by planning in advance an appropriate sequence of activities, teachers can reduce the number of on-the-spot management decisions.

For experienced teachers, one word or a sentence in a plan may trigger a whole routine, but novice teachers may need to be more explicit in their planning, especially with such things as transitions, instructions, or explanations. If you are teaching a new group of students, using a new activity, or dealing with unfamiliar content, write out detailed notes for yourself to ensure that one activity flows from the other, or that students know exactly what they are to do, or that you don't waste a lot of words on an explanation that is over your students' heads.

Using the Plan

The purpose of a plan is to help you, not bind you. If an activity isn't working or if something else comes up in class, set your plan aside. If you find that spontaneous, off-the-cuff teaching is hard for you, plan alternative activities ahead of time.

A plan has to work in the midst of teaching, so choose an appropriate mechanism for using your plan. You might try standard-sized paper because it fits nicely into file folders, note cards because they are easy to hold, sticky notes attached to the pages of the text, or colored pencil notes in the margins. It may be that writing down ideas before class is enough to put them in your head and you don't need to carry a plan around with you. Use whatever format gives you the information in a usable form—for both present and future purposes.

If a plan is not only for your personal use, but also for a principal or a supervisor, use a format that is easy for them to follow. One suggestion is in Appendix A. The plan begins with background information about the students, class, and textbook. Thinking through this kind of information will help teachers at the beginning of a term assess some of the constraints they must take into account when planning lessons. If a lesson plan is to be handed in to someone else, the background information will help them understand the teacher's decisions.

The second section of the plan covers recent work. Considering what students have done recently will help a teacher provide balance and variety. It is also helpful to list the overall objectives of a class or a unit, though they are usually provided by the syllabus or text.

The core of the lesson plan is the procedures section. Here the teacher can plan exactly what will be done in the class. Since most teachers think of their class in terms of

"what am I going to do" (Walter 1984), "Activities" is the first part of this section. The next part is "Grouping." Will the activity be teacher-centered with the students all together? Students working in pairs? Students working individually? "Objectives" are listed next. Each activity needs to have a reason. A teacher must think through why that activity is important to the students and what they will be able to do when they finish it. Writing down "Aids/materials" will help a teacher remember the right equipment, materials, page numbers, and so on. The next part covers "Language." Thinking about the language students will need to use in an activity accomplishes several things. If overall objectives are given in terms of language, it helps ensure that objectives are met. It also may ensure that students don't do activities that are over their heads linguistically. "The Procedures section" ends with "Possible problems" and "Estimated time." Teachers should think about anything that could go wrong, and try to prepare a solution for it ahead of time. Finally, although it is often difficult to estimate how long an activity will take, it is a good way to "walk through" the lesson in advance.

Three more sections round out the lesson plan. What happens if the electricity is off, or if the students don't have their books? Teachers who don't like to "wing it" should plan some alternatives in advance, noting them under "Contingency plans." While planning one lesson, ideas for future ones may come to mind—"Related future work." Finally, after every lesson, teachers should jot down how it went, how long each activity actually took, and how it could be improved in the section "Comments/self-evaluation."

A column format for all of the above information (Matthews, Spratt, & Dangerfield, 1985; see also Appendices B and C, sample lessons) is chosen because it provides easy access to quite a bit of information: How much variety is there in grouping? What materials need to be brought to class? Are objectives being met? What kind of time adjustments can be made? and so on.

CONCLUSION

Whatever form a lesson plan takes, it is an important tool that can help teachers make decisions, solve instructional problems, deal with classroom management issues, record progress, and be accountable to peers or supervisors.

DISCUSSION QUESTIONS

1. Discuss the principles of good language teaching outlined in the introduction to this chapter. Do you agree with them? What others would you add?

2. Does having a good syllabus and a teacher's manual mean that a teacher does not need to plan lessons? What will need to be considered in a plan under such circumstances?

3. When a teacher does not have access to a lot of resources such as a syllabus or adequate textbook, what preliminary decisions and choices will have to be made before planning actual units and lessons?

4. Which of the constraints discussed by the author, or any others, affect your lesson planning the most?

5. What is recommended as the general shape of a lesson? What is the purpose of a ''beginning?'' What are some effective beginnings that you have observed or used? Why bother with an ''ending?'' What are some examples of both good and poor endings to lessons?

6. How can lesson planning help with classroom management? with variety?

7. How much detail needs to be written into a lesson plan? How does this depend on the situation and the teacher?

8. How would the appearance of a lesson plan vary according to the following situations: (a) teacher will have a similar class next term, (b) teacher must hand in all plans to supervisor, (c) class involves extensive discussion of details in textbook?

SUGGESTED ACTIVITIES

1. Based on your own teaching experience or based on a visit to an ESL class and an interview with the teacher, write the information outlined in the ''Background'' section of the suggested lesson plan format. How would this information help you plan a lesson?

2. Look at a unit in a textbook you are using (or are familiar with). What decisions about the order of activities, inclusion of activities, supplements, and personalization need to be made?

3. Using the lesson plan format suggested in this chapter, write a plan for one of the following situations:

a. A unit on language related to health care
b. A unit on using the telephone in the United States
c. A unit on writing a resume
d. A lesson on the present perfect (or some other grammar point)
e. A lesson on apologizing (or some other function)
f. A lesson on yes/no question intonation (or some other pronunciation point)

4. After writing (and, if possible, teaching) a unit or lesson using the suggested format, what revisions would you suggest? Should any sections be added or eliminated? Would any changes in format make the plan easier to use?

SUGGESTIONS FOR FURTHER READING

Harmer, J. (1983)
The Practice of English Language Teaching (Chap 11: Planning). London: Longman.

> Discusses principles behind lesson planning as well as background knowledge the teacher will need in order to plan. A detailed sample plan for a beginning adult class is provided.

Matthews, A., M. Spratt, & L. Dangerfield, eds. (1985)
At the Chalkface: Practical Techniques in Language Teaching (Chap. 6: Lesson Planning). London: Edward Arnold.

> Practical advice on what to put in a lesson plan and why, as well as a discussion of what may constrain planning. Other chapters in the anthology provide sample lessons.

Richards, J. C. (1990)
The Language Teaching Matrix. Cambridge: Cambridge University Press.

For the teacher interested in more information on specifying objectives, Richards outlines, evaluates, and gives examples for four types: behavioral, skills-based, content-based, and proficiency-based.

Stevick, E. (1986)
Images and Options in the Language Classroom. New York: Cambridge University Press.

Explores choices language teachers have in using materials and procedures. Exercises based on a variety of current ESL texts help teachers make choices that will enhance the effectiveness of what happens in the classroom. A good resource for the teacher concerned about *what* to put into a lesson plan.

APPENDIX A

Outline for a Lesson Plan

1. Background:
   a. Description of the students: level, linguistic/ethnic background, age, educational/language learning background, motivation, interests, personalities, out-of-class responsibilities
   b. Description of the class: time, length of term, frequency, size
   c. Description of the syllabus/texts (if any):
2. [Recent work]:
3. Overall objectives:
   These are usually provided by the syllabus or text.
4. Procedures:
   Activities:
   Grouping:
   Objectives:
   Aids/materials:
   Language:
   Possible problems:
   Estimated time:
   [Assignment]

5. [Contigency plans]:
6. Related future work:
7. Comments/self-evaluation:

APPENDIX B

A Sample Lesson: Adult ESL

1. Background
   a. Description of the students:
      Beginning level adults mostly from Mexico; ranging from 20 to 70 years old; some lively, some quiet; most left school before finishing high school; most work all day before coming—tired—to class.
   b. Description of the class:
      Forty to 50 students; attendance fluctuates; class meets 6:30 to 10:00 p.m. Monday through Thursday.
   c. Description of the syllabus/texts: *Real Life English* (Steck Vaughn), *Oxford Picture Dictionary*, and other supplementary materials.
2. [Recent work]:
   Since attendance varies so much, one class cannot build on another.
3. Overall objectives:
   Enable students to talk about their work.
4. Procedures:
   see below.
5. Related future work:
   Give Ss more practice with questions, asking about others' occupations; review with "I plan to _____" and "I want to _____."
6. Comments/self-evaluation:
   Students had difficulty describing what they did and often resorted to pantomime. Day 1 #1 took at least 1/2 hour. All the time estimates were based on a faster class. This actually took 3 days.

Procedures[a]

Activity	Grouping	Objective	Aids/materials	Language	Problems?	Time
DAY 1						
1. Find out what Ss do. Ask: "What do you do?" If necessary, give examples: "I am a teacher. I teach English. Jose is a cashier. He works at a gas station." Write Ss' answers on board in columns: Name Occupation	T-->Ss	Introduce topic, involve Ss with personal topic, get material for worksheet.	Blackboard	Oral: occupation vocabulary, BE and other verbs simple present w/ I (understand q's, produce short answers)	Ss won't know how to word their occupation: Ask other q's, e.g., "Where do you work?"	10 min
2. Practice the info from #1: T asks Ss questions: "What does Jose do? Who is a barber? Where does Lupe work? What does a gardner do?" etc. Where do you work? What do you do every day?	T-->Ss	Practice vocab, practice answering work-related q's, review listening for WH questions.	Blackboard	As in #1, but w/ *he, she*	Only the vocal Ss will get practice: Call on some Ss individually.	10 min
3. Picture dictionary. Ss count off and look at the picture associated w/ their number and make up a sentence to teach their word to the class. Ex: "#1 is a pharmacist. He makes and sells medicine."	1st: S 2nd: S -->Ss	Introduce more vocab, give Ss responsibility for learning vocab independently, have Ss help each other learn.	OPD pp. 84–86	Rdg, oral: as in #2	Ss will work at varying pace: Assign fast Ss several pictures. Ss will not be able to make sentences: Circulate to help when nec.	15 min

(continued on p. 428)

Activity	Interaction	Purpose	Materials	Skill	Pacing/Notes	Time
4. Workbook. Conferences on last week's writing asst.	S	Review vocab and sentence patterns, give T a chance to have individual time w/ Ss.	OPD Workbook pp. 34–37	Rdg, writ: as in #1,2	Ss will work at varying pace: Assign only 2 pages, let fast Ss do 3 or 4.	15 min
DAY 2						
1. Review occupations. Use OPD wall charts or other pictures and ask: "What does he/she do? Where does he/she work?"	T-->Ss	Warm class up, review vocab and short answers.	Large pix: occupations	Oral: as in Day 1 #2	See day #2	10 min
2. Review occupations. Ss in pairs, quiz each other. "A, look at the picture and tell B what that person is. B, check A's answer at the bottom of the page. Then switch roles."	S-->S	Review vocab.	OPD pp. 84–86	Oral: vocab	Ss won't cooperate: Move around class to confirm instructions and offer help.	15 min
3. Worksheets. Ss read about themselves and their classmates and fill in the blanks. Have one S write on transparency to do a quick answer check on OHP.	S	Interest Ss in reading with info about themselves, review vocab and sentence patterns	Worksheets based on info from Day 1, #1. Ex: Adel is a ___ at a gas station. He takes money from customers. OHP	Rdg, writ: as in Day 1, #2	Ss work at varying pace: Have fast Ss write original sentences too.	10 min

aT = teacher, S = student.

Procedures[a] (Continued)

Activity	Grouping	Objective	Aids/materials	Language	Problems?	Time
4. Occupation Bingo. Prep: Write 25 occupations on the board. Ss must write them at random in the blank squares on their bingo papers. Demo on board. Explain and demo rules. Play: Call out occupations (1st, just words, then in sentence context) and have Ss place their markers as they hear them.	T-->Ss	Review vocab, relax	Bingo papers, bingo markers (lima beans), blackboard	Writ. list: as in Day 1, #1,2.	Ss will be confused: Have some demo practice rounds using board.	15 min

[a]T = teacher, S = student.

Note: The above lesson is based on one prepared by Ellen Chervenick and is used with her permission.

APPENDIX C

A Sample Unit:
ESL Current Events Class

1. Background:
   a. Description of students:
      Advanced ESL students, preparing for university work in the U.S.; diverse nationalities, primarily Asian and Mideastern; motivated.
   b. Description of the class:
      Twelve students; one class out of an intensive day of five classes; meets 10:00–11:50 a.m. Monday through Friday.
   c. Description of the syllabus/text:
      Teacher developed handouts based on current media, especially newspapers, magazines, radio, and TV.
2. Recent work
   Students have completed units on the role of the media and on men's/women's roles. They have been introduced to some of the language and behavior appropriate in a discussion, in a debate, and in a speech/presentation.

3. Overall objectives
   Expand students' skills in reading, writing, listening, and speaking about current issues to prepare them in a general way for American university studies.

4. Procedures:
   See below.

5. Related future work:
   Could relate to a unit on citizens' roles in government or energy sources of the future.

6. Comments/self-evaluation:
   It might have been better to have the debate as the final activity; students seemed to lose steam after that. Maybe the letter writing activity wasn't very motivating because it seems like a lost cause to many. Look for more materials on the impact of protests. There wasn't enough time for all the groups to give their presentations on the short articles—reading could be done as homework to allow for more presentation time in class.

Procedures

Activity	Grouping	Objective	Aids/materials	Language	Problems?	Time
DAY 1						
1. Ss watch video on Hiroshima.	Ss	Get Ss interested in topic; provide discussion material.	Worksheet with vocabulary help and comprehension questions	Listening	Video breakdown; have photos, ad lib story in case.	25 min
2. Discussion: Do you remember this? How did you feel? Could it happen again today? etc.	Ss<-->Ss	Develop spontaneous speaking skills.	Discussion question sheet for teacher	Speaking	Ss won't talk: Call on Ss and use discussion question sheet.	25 min
3. Homework: Read article on two ways to prevent nuclear war—buildup and freeze.		Read for main ideas.	Article	Reading		
DAY 2						
1. Short discussion about article, any questions answered.	T<-->Ss	Ensure comprehension.	Article	Speaking, listening	None anticipated.	10 min
2. Students get into two groups (buildup and freeze) to prepare for debate.	[Ss][Ss]	Develop spontaneous speaking skills.	Additional material on the topic for interested Ss	Speaking	Remind Ss of debate format, if necessary.	40 min
DAY 3						
1. Debate (Video, if possible).	Ss<-->Ss	Formal speaking skills.	[Video]	Speaking	Take role of moderator, if necessary.	30 min
2. Discussion of debate.	T<-->Ss	Evaluate language, content, and behavior.		Speaking, listening	Need evaluation form?	20 min
3. Homework: Write a summary of the other side's opinion.	S	Encourage listening, critical thinking, written expression of opinions.		Writing		

Day / Activity	Grouping	Objective	Materials	Skills	Anticipated problems	Time
DAY 4						
1. Listen to several news reports on nuclear weapons in developing countries.	Ss	Listening for main ideas.	Worksheets	Listening	None anticipated.	25 min
2. Read and discuss sample letters to some nation's political leader arguing in support of/against their nuclear weapons policy.	T<-->Ss	Model opinion letter.	Sample letters OHP	Reading, speaking	None anticipated.	25 min
3. Homework: Write such a letter.	S	Written expression of opinion, letter format.		Writing	Ss will simply copy models: Provide data on various countries to ensure real composition.	
DAY 5						
1. Small groups read short articles on related topics—e.g., the world after a nuclear war, protests at nuclear power plants—and prepare summaries.	[Ss][Ss] [Ss][Ss]	Read for main ideas, summarize.	Articles	Reading, speaking	Summarizing may be difficult: Circulate to give help; prepare sample summaries.	25 min
2. Groups present their summaries to whole class.	Ss-->Ss	Oral presentation.		Speaking	One student will do all the work: Assign a speaker—others will	25 min

Textbook Selection and Evaluation

Alexandra Skierso

INTRODUCTION

Textbooks evoke a variety of emotions in their users. No teacher is entirely satisfied with the text used, yet very few manage to teach without one. Although some educators (O'Neill, 1982) feel that textbooks at best provide a base or core of materials as jumping-off points for the teacher and class, most teachers tend to follow the text's sequence, methodology, pacing, and vocabulary to the letter. As Ariew (1982) and Macian (1986) point out, both students and teachers use the examples, the written exercises, the oral work, and the explanations of grammatical material of the textbook and its accompanying materials (workbook and audiovisual aids) as their main source of guidance. If appendices and glossaries are included in the text, then it is used as a reference tool as well. "In addition, it may even be seen as a means of motivating students to pursue language study by offering glimpses of exotic situations in its illustrations and readings" (Ariew, 1982, p. 17).

The importance of the textbook in an English as a Second Language (ESL)/English as a Foreign Language (EFL) class makes the selection process crucial. Sometimes, it is the responsibility of teachers to select the textbook they will use in a given class. On the other hand, even in countries and school systems where the responsibility for the adoption of the textbook lies with the school board or the state, teachers still need to know on a daily basis how to evaluate the text in order to utilize its assets and compensate for its limitations in applying it to the needs of the students and the objectives of the class. In addition, at the end of the year, teachers might be asked to give their opinion as to the worthiness of the textbook. Most of the information given here would also be helpful in the preparation of such an evaluation.

PRELIMINARY INFORMATION

Before one even begins the process of evaluating textbooks or just looking for potentially appropriate texts, one needs to establish a basis of comparison. Certain preliminary information must be collected and explicitly stated. Please see the Preliminary Information Survey for Textbook Evaluation (Appendix A) for a concise, easy-to-use worksheet. The worksheet incorporates and expands on the outline of preliminary information presented by Daoud and Celce-Murcia (1979). In essence, background information is needed on the audience, the instructor, the course syllabus, and the institution.

Background Information on the Students

Who are the students? As a class, what is their age range, their sex distribution? Are the classes segregated or coeducational? What are their background languages and cultures; is it a homogeneous or heterogeneous group? Are they in the upper, middle, or lower socio-economic level? Is their environment urban, rural, or small town? Does their level of general education match their age group? What is their level of English proficiency—beginning, intermediate, or advanced? Do they have a positive or negative attitude toward the target language? This is generally brought about by historical or political factors or social conflicts—personal or community-wide. What are their reasons for studying English? Is it required or optional? What motivates them? Are the incentives academic (needed for higher learning), economic (helpful and necessary in attaining employment), communicative (as a language of wider communication or for survival), or for prestige? What English language skills will they need to use: listening/understanding, speaking, reading, and/or writing? Is it an ESL class, where English is the language of wider communication in the community? Or is English taught as a foreign language in an EFL class, or in one that is for special purposes (ESP)? And last but not least, what are the interests of the students with respect to their age and background? According to Dubin and Olshtain (1986), an inventory of suitable themes and topics is extremely important to the success or failure of a course in the classroom. "The topics to be included may come from questionnaires administered to potential students of similar age groups and interests as well as from open discussions with students at a similar level" (Dubin & Olshtain, 1986, p. 109).

Background Information on the Instructor

Who is the instructor? What is his/her linguistic background and preparation? Although this is an important dimension to consider when you are in a position to evaluate textbooks for a school or program in which you must decide what teaching materials others will use, it is just as important when you are selecting a suitable textbook for yourself. Are the instructors native speakers of English or are they nonnative? What kind of command do they have in English? As Ariew (1982) notes, since nonnative speakers learned the language in terms of grammatical rules and applications, they have little trouble stating and explaining them, giving some exceptions, and providing various mnemonic

devices to help their students remember them. But when it comes to providing examples, the nonnative teacher has a much harder time. Native speakers, on the contrary, have little trouble finding numerous examples. What is difficult for them to produce is the formulation of rules, since their language was acquired naturally: "The native . . . teacher does better with a text that provides clear and relatively more elaborate statements of grammatical usage and relationships, while the nonnative does better with a text that provides a wealth of examples" (Ariew, 1982, p. 18).

With regard to training and education, what kind of background and certification was attained by the instructors? Were they exposed to ideas concerning the nature of language and language learning? What are their attitudes toward the changing perceptions of accepted roles for teachers and learners? How much teaching experience do they have? The experienced teachers readily adjust and adapt different teaching materials to their students' needs and capabilities. The novice teacher "needs materials that are more complete and that fit the pedagogical objectives of the program very closely. . . . The beginning teacher needs a text that has many and varied exercises to choose from and materials that are heavily annotated with suggestions for their use" (Ariew, 1982, p. 18). As one looks at the background and preparation of the teachers, totally different text requirements emerge.

Course Syllabus

In the two sections above, we considered the players in the process of formal language acquisition: the "who." Now we will raise other questions in order to define the contents of the material and the method of their presentation: the "what" and "how," respectively. Whether predetermined either by the state, school board, or institution, or left to the teacher to decide, the following information concerning the basic linguistic, psychological, and pedagogical principles underlying modern methods of language teaching will have to be specified: first, the level of competency of the class (i.e., whether it is at the beginner, intermediate, or advanced level) will have to be determined, since the relative emphasis of each of the factors listed herein is contingent upon it. For example, what relative emphasis will be given to each of the four skills (listening, speaking, reading, and writing), and what tasks will each skill be needed for most (e.g., reading technical literature in physics)? How much emphasis will be given to each language area (grammar, vocabulary, pronunciation), and how much of the material will be used for reception or for both reception and production? How much attention will be given to mechanics such as penmanship, spelling, and punctuation? Is there a recommended method or approach for language teaching? If yes, what is it? What kind of exams or exercises are to be given—oral and/or written, objective, constrained, manipulative exercises, and/or subjective, open-ended, communicative essays? What cultural themes are to be presented? There is a general consensus that it is highly desirable that the culture and language presented in class and in a textbook be authentic and not contrived—that the dialogs, setting, and language be realistic, "that the samples of spoken language be those actually used by natives in face-to-face communication and that the samples of written language be those which could appear in, or are adapted from, real written material such as letters, reports, newspapers, and magazines" (Benevento, 1984, p. 5).

With regard to cultural topics, "the varied aspects of daily life in different social settings should be treated" (Benevento, 1984, p. 7). But how much culture should be presented and what kind? This sometimes presents a dilemma. For example, when presenting a unit on shopping to a group of students who live in a rural setting, and who may never get to see an American supermarket, should one present a typical American supermarket, with the type of customer–clerk interaction and the brands and types of goods one can find in a supermarket in the United States, or should one instead present a situation familiar to the learners (Dubin & Olshtain, 1986)? Perhaps sometimes, grading or sequencing from the familiar to the unfamiliar is appropriate in presenting authentic cultural content. But one must be cautious to use material which does not offend, insult, or tease the student population. The manner in which cultural content is portrayed evokes strong emotions, as noted in the following critique of an EFL text series:

Content that portrays Western institutions, values or life styles as ideals to be emulated is inappropriate and aims at acculturation rather than the teaching of culture. English is an international language but, definitely, is not an international culture. . . . [T]he foreign culture is different, probably interesting, but definitely not superior. (Zughoul, 1986, p. 7)

Institutional Data

In this section we try to define the total environment in which language study takes place (the "where") and the time element involved (the "when"). What are the national or institutional objectives for English instruction? Do the aims emphasize language recognition or both recognition and production? What are the aims for cultural acquisition—cross-cultural/global awareness or acculturation? Is English used as the medium of instruction in lectures and/or reading material? Is there a preferred dialect of English? Is there a formalized English achievement test; is it oral and/or written; does it mainly consist of manipulative exercises or communicative ones? How many students does a class comprise? How much time is allocated to the study of English? What kind of physical conditions are there in the institution? What is the size and shape of the classroom? Is there enough light? Is there enough blackboard space? Can the seating arrangements be changed to suit the lesson presented or are they fixed? Is there audiovisual support, and how extensive or modern is it? How much money has been allocated to the purchase of textbooks?

SURVEY ANALYSIS, AND JUDGMENT

Now that the stage has been set by the identification of the players and their roles, the contents of the script, the setting, and the time constraints involved, the ESL/EFL teacher is able to begin the evaluation of a given textbook. If, instead, the teacher is free to select his or her own text, a quick preliminary survey to try to find 5 to 10 texts which appear to be superficially appropriate for a given class should be undertaken.

The Survey (if applicable)

Much can be determined about the purpose of a book (its aims and objectives), the audience it purports to reach, its organization and method of presentation, as well as the range and kind of materials presented, by looking at the Introduction, the Table of Contents, the Text, and the Glossary or Index. Skim these sections of the texts to see which, on the surface, seem to agree with or include the previously specified preliminary requirements and then set them aside for further consideration.

Analysis

Although a text may seem to comply with the needs and interests of the students, the aims and goals of the course, the basic linguistic, psychological, and pedagogical principles of modern language teaching methods, and the time constraints involved, on close examination it may fail. Therefore, the second step requires an analysis, a careful examination, of the content of the textbook, the teacher's manual, and any supplementary material.

The following is a guide to textbook analysis. This guide presents in question format the checklist of items which will be evaluated in the next step, the judgment. This guide is especially beneficial to the novice for it provides the direction for the contents of the analysis. As you identify, describe, and record the data following the organization presented here, mark those items needed for textbook evaluation in your program.

GUIDE TO TEXTBOOK ANALYSIS

The Textbook
Bibliographical Data

- What are the title, level of proficiency, author(s), publisher, date of publication, number of volumes, number of pages, and price of the textbook?
- Is it self-contained or part of a series? Are there accompanying materials, such as a workbook, a teacher's manual, and audio-visual aids?
- What are the professional qualifications of the authors?

Aims and Goals

- What are the aims and goals of the text? What language skills and cultural understanding does the text intend to develop?
- What is the distribution of emphasis among the language skills (listening, speaking, reading, writing)? How much material is covered? Is the distribution of new teaching points evenly dispersed throughout the text, or do some lessons contain too much material, while others have too little?
- For whom is the text intended? Who are the learners? Who are the teachers?

Subject Matter

- What subject matter (topics, contexts) is covered? Is it presented through themes of interest, situations of necessity, and/or linguistic needs?
- What is the conceptual level (concrete vs. abstract)?
- How are the units and lessons organized?
- How (if at all) is culture presented? Is it integrated in the texts, dialogs, and exercises, or is it treated as supplemental or optional material? Is it free of biases?

- Which of these type(s) of texts does the text-book contain: dialogs "seeded" with cultural information and/or based on situations typical of the foreign culture, special cultural narratives, explanatory cultural notes, songs, poems, essays, biographies, letters, newspaper articles, jokes and anecdotes, folk tales, proverbs, legends, fables and myths, fiction by reputable writers, nonfiction, and plays?
- Are the texts authentic, edited, or totally contrived (especially composed for textbooks)? Are the samples of spoken language those actually used by natives in face-to-face communication? Are the samples of written language those which could appear in, or are adapted from, real written material, such as letters, poems, reports, stories, and newspaper and magazine articles? Where on the following authenticity scale, adapted from Rings's article, "Authentic Language and Authentic Conversational Texts" (1986, p. 207), do the texts rank? (Text types 1–10 are considered as authentic representations of conversational exchange.)

Authentic Conversation	1. Spontaneous conversations of native speakers having no knowledge of being monitored.
	2. Conversations in which one native speaker participant is aware of being recorded.
	3. Simulated role-play by native speakers.
	4. Well-written plays enacted by good actors/actresses.
	5. Excerpts from 1.
	6. Excerpts from 2.
	7. Excerpts from 3.
	8. Reenacted portions of 1.
	9. Reenacted portions of 2.
	10. Reenacted portions of 3.
Inauthentic Conversation	11. 1, altered.
	12. 2, altered.
	13. 3, altered.
	14. Plays whose dialog does not correspond to actual dialog.
	15. Conversations composed for texts and enacted by native speakers.
	16. Composed conversations printed in texts.

Vocabulary and Structures

Grammar

- What and how many teaching points are selected and emphasized?
- How are the grammar rules presented? Are they stated or unstated? Is an inductive or a deductive approach used, or do the authors use an approach which interrelates both the inductive and deductive approaches?
- How are the grammatical points sequenced?
- Are there summaries of verb forms (paradigms, conjugations) somewhere in the book?
- Are linguistic items introduced in meaningful contexts or unrelated to core content?

Vocabulary

- How is the vocabulary chosen? Is it based on frequency counts, thematic units, or communicative, sociocultural functions?
- Is attention paid to roots, inflectional endings (e.g., plurals, possessives, past tenses),

cognates, synonyms, antonyms, thematic groupings?
- How is the vocabulary introduced? In what context?
- Is the vocabulary summarized in some way (e.g., in a foreign-language dictionary section or in a bilingual list)?

Vocabulary and Structures

- What is the text's level of readability and does it match that of the students?
- Are the basic patterns and vocabulary included in the text sufficient for the level of complexity the text achieves or is required by the syllabus?
- What pedagogical considerations prompted the presentation and sequencing of nouns, verbs, sentence patterns, modifier structures, and vocabulary? Were they (a) simple to complex scheme, (b) functional load (i.e., the item's function is essential in communicating), (c) productivity in generating teaching points (e.g., "be" verbs are necessary in producing positive and negative sentences and short answers to "yes-no" questions), (d) frequency of occurrence, (e) ease and difficulty for individual students (predicted by contrastive analysis), (f) regular versus irregular patterns (i.e., teach the irregular first, so as to avoid overgeneralizations), (g) utility for classroom and community, (h) co-occurrence—that is, teach items that go together (e.g., here and there, adjectives and oppositions: "He is big"—"He is not small"), (i) universals (i.e., teach items which differentiate English from other languages—e.g., *do* insertion), and/or (j) error analysis?
- Is there evidence of language control—that is, are new structures carefully presented and explained before they appear in drills and presentation materials? Do some chapters present too much material and others too little, or is there an even distribution of grammatical and vocabulary material among the chapters?
- Are grammatical presentations clear and complete enough for the student to have a concise review?

- Are linguistic items introduced in meaningful situations (contexts) to facilitate understanding?
- Are new vocabulary and structures repeated and integrated in subsequent lessons in a cyclic pattern for reinforcement, and do they, when they reappear, do so in varying contexts and situations in order to portray their range of applicability?
- Is "standard English" (including idioms, but excluding substandard dialects, slang, and obscure regional idioms in nonadvanced texts) used?
- Does the writer use sentence structures that follow normal word order? Are they simple or complex sentences? Do the sentences and paragraphs follow one another in a logical sequence?
- Are connective words studied?
- Is punctuation covered?
- Does the text distinguish between British and American English with regard to vocabulary and grammatical structures?
- Does the text differentiate between formal and informal speech and writing patterns with regard to vocabulary and grammatical structures?

Exercises and Activities

- What kinds of exercises are provided? Translation, pattern practice (substitution), reading, writing (sentence completion, cloze, spelling, dictation, guided composition)?
- Do the exercises involve vocabulary and structures which build up the learner's repertoire? Are they graded to provide a progression from manipulation to communication? For example, where on the following scale for assessment of communicative potential, adapted from Dubin and Olshtain's *Course Design* (1986, pp. 98–99), do the exercises and activities fall?

Least Communicative
- *Exposure to New Information Only* (e.g., listening to a song, learning a story read aloud, watching on a TV program).

- *Mechanical Operations*
  (e.g., substituting, ordering, combining, adding, deleting, reading a memorized dialog, reading aloud with attention to pronunciation).
- *Communication with Physical Response*
  (e.g., following instructions, directions: drawing a picture, following a map route, constructing something via instructions).
- *Selective Transference of New Information*
  (e.g., filling in a chart, table, drawing a graph, copying information).
- *Application of New Information*
  (e.g., writing a letter in response to an ad, completing a form, answering an objective-type questionnaire, organizing main ideas in a logical sequence, gathering information outside class or from peers).
- *Creative Expression of New Information*
  (e.g., creating a questionnaire, writing a letter or paper, giving an oral report, taping or writing a message, providing information to others).
- *Negotiation of Interpreted New Information*
  Includes expression of, reaction to, and interpretation of new information (e.g., small discussion groups in the target language).

Most Communicative

- Do the exercises promote internalization by encouraging a student's active participation (e.g., writing summaries of stories, picture paraphrasing, paired or small conversation groups, games, and simulation activities such as role-playing and problem-solving)?
- Do the exercises refer to realistic activities and situations?
- Do they develop comprehension and test knowledge of main ideas, details, and sequence of ideas?
- Is there a pattern of review within lessons and do the exercises cumulatively test new material?
- Are there activities which provide for the development of study skills, such as skimming, note taking, outlining, looking up words in the dictionary?
- Along the following scale for assessing the cognitive potential (critical thinking) of exercises and activities adapted from Dubin and Olshtain's (1986, pp. 99–100) adaptation from Benjamin Bloom's *Taxonomy of Educational Objectives* and Norris Sanders's *Classroom Questions: What Kinds?*, where do the text's exercises and activities fall?

Cognitive Potential

Low
- Memorization: Recalling or recognizing information.
- Transcoding: Changing information into different symbolic form or language (e.g., scanning a text to find specific data to fill in a chart, map, or other graphic display; translating).
- Interpretation: Discovering relationships among facts, generalizations, definitions, values, and skills.
- Application: Identifying the issues and selecting and using the appropriate rules, methods, and theories to solve lifelike problems (e.g., simulation of a lifelike problem to be resolved through group interaction).
- Analysis: Solving a problem by identifying its constituent parts, and their interrelationships.
- Synthesis: Solving a problem by original, creative thinking.
- Evaluation: Making a judgment according to one's clearly stated standards.

High

- Are the instructions to the exercises clear and appropriate?

Layout and Physical Makeup

- What does the book look like? Is it attractive (i.e., cover, page appearance, binding)? Is it durable? Does its size seem convenient for the students to handle?
- What kind of type size is used? Are typefaces functional (i.e., present the organization of the units)? Are simple graphics (e.g., boxes, shadows, arrows, colors) used to clarify teaching points?
- Is there artwork and what kind? Who and what are pictured? Is the artwork varied? colorful? appealing? Is the artwork related to the text or is it only there for decoration? Do the pages look cluttered or is there an aesthetic balance of text and graphical material?
- Is there a table of contents? Does it indicate where to locate specific structures and their exercises? Is there an index of new vocabulary items and their location in the text? Are there appendices and other end matter with maps, verb summaries, a glossary?
- Is there a teacher's manual?

The Teacher's Manual

General Features

- Is a rationale provided regarding the text's objectives, methodology, subject matter, sequence of grammar points?
- Is there any set syllabus for that level?
- Is there an index locating the new vocabulary, structures, and topics found in the text?
- Are answers supplied for all the exercises in the text?
- Does the text assume that the teacher has near-native fluency and a great deal of experience, or does it provide information for the new and nonnative English-speaking teacher?

Supplementary Exercises for Each Language Skill

- What type and amount of supplementary exercises are presented for listening comprehension, speaking (pronunciation, intonation, and communication), reading, and writing? Are they authentic and accurate? Are they appropriate to the age, level, and background of the students? Would they be of interest to them? If the text is for students from a homogeneous language background, does it present a variety of opportunities to practice speaking and hearing the sounds most difficult for them to pronounce and distinguish?
- Does the manual provide achievement tests (with the answers) for the teacher to use?

Methodological and Pedagogical Guidance

- Does the manual provide the teacher with guidance on the teaching of language items and the four skills? What type and amount?
- Is the teacher expected to be experienced in language teaching or does the text offer clear and detailed advice for the novice to follow?
- Do the authors hold a particular bias on language teaching and methodology? What is it?
- Does the text conform to the methodological requirements determined to be suitable by the administrators or the teachers themselves? And, if not, can the exercises easily be adapted to conform to those requirements?
- Is the manual meaningful and helpful to the teacher without being too confining?
- Does the manual advise the teacher on the use of audiovisual aids?
- Does the manual present distinctions between British and American English with regard to pronunciation, vocabulary, and grammatical structure?
- If the text is for students from a homogeneous language background, does the manual present a contrastive analysis of the

sound system and word usage of English vis-a-vis the native language?

Linguistic Background Information

• Does the text assume or require that the teacher have near-native fluency, if not native fluency, or does the manual provide linguistic background information (perhaps derived from contrastive analysis or error analysis) on pronunciation, grammar, and vocabulary?

Overall Value

• Taking all criteria into consideration, how does the text rate?

Judgment

While it is the analysis step which helps organize the investigation of the myriad teaching points (both explicit and implicit), it is the third step, the judgment, by which books are deemed acceptable or not. To arrive at a final decision, the teacher must evaluate and grade certain quantitative and qualitative elements of the textbook, the teacher's manual (if there is one), and other accompanying material (if applicable). The suggested checklist in Appendix B is provided as a tool to be used in this judging process.

Instead of using any one of the evaluative guidelines published in recent years, I decided to develop a list of criteria based on various checklists. The list of features presented in the Evaluation Checklist was compiled by adapting and adopting the evaluative criteria suggested by many foreign language and second language educators. In fact, all items in the checklists presented by Daoud and Celce-Murcia (1979) and Prator (1977) were incorporated into this guideline, as well as the majority of the items in Mackey's checklist (1965). In parentheses after each question, the direct reference(s) for each item is given. In this way, the Evaluation Checklist also serves as a comprehensive quasi-review of the literature. For the sake of simplicity and

clarity, numbers have been used to refer to the references, the list of which is provided at the end of the checklist.

The overall framework of the guideline presented in this chapter rests on the precept that a textbook evaluation checklist should consist of a comprehensive set of criteria based on the basic linguistic, psychological, and pedagogical principles underlying modern methods of language teaching. These criteria "should be exhaustive enough to insure assessment of all characteristics of the textbook. And they should be discrete and precise enough to focus attention on one characteristic at a time or on a single group of related characteristics" (Tucker, 1978, p. 219).

Although this is a comprehensive checklist, it is not necessarily intended to be used in its entirety. What questions are and are not considered depend upon your teaching situation. For example, if you are teaching a course on the acquisition of reading or writing skills, then items pertaining to aural/oral skill acquisition can be disregarded. In addition, certain items or groups of items deemed more important than others may be attributed more weight, which, when taken into consideration, may change the course of the decision-making process and outcome. This, however, would be contingent upon the preliminary information collected in Appendix A.

The evaluative criteria in this guideline are organized as follows:

The textbook

A. Bibliographical data
B. Aims and goals
C. Subject matter
D. Vocabulary and structures
E. Exercises and activities
F. Layout and physical makeup

The Teacher's Manual

A. General features
B. Supplementary exercises
C. Methodological and pedagogical guidance
D. Linguistic background information

Overall Value

The following rating scale is suggested:

Excellent	4
Good	3
Adequate	2
Weak	1
Totally Lacking	0

One method of weighting items is to indicate either by number or letter which criteria are absolutely necessary to be included in a textbook and a teacher's manual, which criteria are beneficial and preferred, and which are not applicable. For example, the following weighting scale is recommended:

Item	Grade	Rate
Absolutely necessary, required	A	4
Beneficial, preferred	B	2
Not applicable	N	0

If the weighting of items is graded by number, these grades can be multiplied by the rating for a more comprehensive evaluation. In either case, though, the method of weighting helps ensure choosing the best possible text, given the students, teacher, teaching situation, time constraints, and language teaching principles, by individualizing the Textbook Evaluation Checklist.

In light of the findings in step two, the analysis, the teacher/rater evaluates the textbook for each question by making a check in the appropriate column. By having conducted the analytical recording of data prior to the evaluation process, subjective error, which is often the reason for differences of opinion among raters, is minimized to a great extent.

Although "coursebook assessment is fundamentally a subjective, rule-of-thumb activity, and that no neat formula, grid, or system will ever provide a definite yardstick" (Sheldon, 1988, p. 245), if an evaluation process integrating surveying, analysis, and judging were to be considered by three or more experienced teachers, the most suitable text for that particular, given situation would come to

light. Any rating disagreement(s) would become obvious by comparing the checklists of the raters, and via discussions and further examination of the text(s), reconciliation and consensus would become possible.

CONCLUSION

The heavy reliance on the textbook in the foreign language or second language classroom is a crucial issue. The fact that the teachers and students use the textbook and its ancillary materials as their central guiding force proves the importance of selecting an appropriate text. However, even if it is written with a specific course in mind, "a perfect text does not exist for any given course. . . . The important thing is to adopt a text whose perceived flaws are correctable, in the sense that the teacher can easily make the author's biases more harmonious with his own" (Ariew, 1982, p. 27). Of course, "the ultimate evaluation of a text comes with actual classroom use" (Daoud & Celce-Murcia, 1979, p. 306). Therefore, a re-evaluation of the selected text, perhaps using the identical checklist both times, would help the teacher to decide whether to continue using the adopted text or to look for a new one.

In any case, the search for a suitable text is endless; since every class is different, the objectives might be different, the teaching situation and setting might have changed, and what is considered proper language teaching principles today might be regarded as passé next year. The ESL/EFL teacher can keep current by visiting book exhibits at professional conventions, checking the new additions at the libraries and university bookstores containing ESL/EFL materials, and browsing through professional journals intended for the ESL/EFL teacher for textbook advertisements.

DISCUSSION QUESTIONS

1. If you have taught/are teaching ESL or EFL, how were/are the textbooks selected? Who was/is involved in the selection process? Was/is it an arbitrary or systematic procedure? Explain.

2. What do you think the optimal textbook selection process would be for several ESL/EFL instructors all instructing the same course and jointly responsible for selecting a textbook?

3. If you were to teach an ESL/EFL class for which there was a prescribed but totally inadequate textbook, what could or would you do?

4. If you have taught, are teaching, or will teach ESL or EFL, which items on the checklist (if any) do you feel are more important than others?

5. Do you think a checklist of universal criteria can or should be established? What do you think should be included in a checklist for textbook evaluation?

SUGGESTED ACTIVITIES

1. If you have taught, are currently teaching, or will soon be teaching an ESL/EFL class:

a. Describe in detail the type of class you had, have, or expect to have, as in the Preliminary Information Survey for Textbook Evaluation (Appendix A).
b. Evaluate the textbook you have used, are using, or will be using, according to the Guide to Textbook Analysis and the Evaluation Checklist (Appendix B).
c. Go to the library, find two or more suitable texts, and use the checklist (Appendix B) to evaluate the texts.
Which is the most appropriate text? Why?

2. Gather in groups of four, develop a scenario with regard to the type of class you expect to teach, the aims and goals of the students, the requirements of the syllabus, the setting, and the time allotted. Then proceed to act as a board to survey, analyze, evaluate, and select a textbook by using the checklists provided.

SUGGESTIONS FOR FURTHER READING

The following list of recently written articles and books are recommended for further reading to anyone interested in the evaluation and selection of language teaching textbooks:

Ariew, R. (1982)
The textbook as curriculum. In T.V. Higgs, ed., *Curriculum, Competence, and the Foreign Language Teacher. The ACTFL Foreign Language Education Series* (pp. 11–33). Hastings-on Hudson, NY: American Council on the Teaching of Foreign Languages. (ERIC Document Reproduction Service No. ED 210 908)

Benevento, J. (1984)
Choosing and Using Textbooks. Paper presented at the Annual Meeting of the American Council on the Teaching of Foreign Languages, Chicago, November 16–18. (ERIC Document Reproduction Service No. ED 253 080)

Dubin, F., and E. Olshtain. (1986)
Course Design: Developing Programs and Materials for Language Learning. Cambridge: Cambridge University Press.

Hetherington, A. (1985)
Assessing the suitability of reading materials for ESL students. *TESL Canada Journal/Revue TESL du Canada, 3*(1), 37–52.

Sheldon, L. E. (1988)
Evaluating ELT textbooks and materials. *English Language Teaching Journal, 42*(4), 237–246.

Williams, D. (1983)
Developing criteria for textbook evaluation. *English Language Teaching Journal, 37*(3), 251–261.

APPENDIX A

Preliminary Information Survey for Textbook Evaluation

A. Background Information on the Students

Age Range ___ | Sex Distribution: | ☐ Segregated | ☐ M ☐ F
| | ☐ Coed | ___ % of M/F

Background Languages | Background Cultures: Name and %
☐ Homogeneous: Name _____ | ___ % _____ | ___ % _____
☐ Heterogeneous: Names _____ | ___ % _____ | ___ % _____

Socioeconomic level | Environment | Language Setting (E = English)
___ Upper | ___ Urban | ☐ ESL: As a Second Language
___ Middle | ___ Rural | ☐ EFL: As a Foreign Language
___ Lower | ___ Small Town | ☐ ESP: For Special Purposes

Level of General Education | Proficiency Level in English
☐ Matches Students' Age |
☐ Below Age |
☐ Above Age | Beginning | Intermediate | Advanced

Attitude Toward Target Language | Incentives | Skills Needed
☐ Positive ☐ Neutral ☐ Negative | ☐ Academic | ☐ Listening
| ☐ Economic | ☐ Speaking
Reasons for Studying English | ☐ Communicative | ☐ Reading
☐ Required ☐ Optional | ☐ Prestige | ☐ Writing

Interests as per Age, Background:

B. Background Information on Teachers

Speaker of English | Proficiency or Command of English
☐ Native ☐ Nonnative | ☐ Poor ☐ Average ☐ Good

Training (Check All Training): | Year of Teacher
☐ Grammar School ☐ High School ☐ Teacher's College | Training
☐ Teacher's Certificate ☐ B.A. ☐ M.A. ☐ Ph.D. | ___

Number of Years of Teaching Experience ___

Attitude Toward Changes, Perceptions of Roles for Teachers and Learners
☐ Traditional ☐ Amenable to Change

C. Course Syllabus (Predetermined or Left to Teacher's Discretion)

Class Competency Level: ☐ Beginner ☐ Intermediate ☐ Advanced

Relative Emphasis Given to Each Skill (%) and Tasks Each Skill Is Needed for:
___ % Listening: _____
___ % Speaking: _____
___ % Reading: _____
___ % Writing: _____

Relative Emphasis Given to Each Language Area (%)	Percentage Used for:		Relative Attention Given to Mechanics
	Reception	Production	
___ % Grammar	_____ %	_____ %	___ % Penmanship
___ % Vocabulary	_____ %	_____ %	___ % Spelling
___ % Pronunciation	_____ %	_____ %	___ % Punctuation

Method(s) of Language Teaching: _____

Techniques of Evaluation or Examination
☐ Oral ☐ Objective, Constrained, Manipulative Exercises
☐ Written ☐ Subjective, Open-ended, Communicative Exercises

Cultural Content Exposure: Percentage and Type
__ % of Target Language: _____
__ % of First Language: _____
__ % Global Presentation: _____

D. Institutional Data

Institutional or National Objectives for English Instruction
☐ Language Reception ☐ Listening ☐ Reading
☐ Language Production ☐ Speaking ☐ Writing
☐ Cultural Recognition ☐ Global/Cross-cultural Awareness
☐ Cultural Production ☐ Acculturation

Role of English as Medium of Instruction: ☐ Oral ☐ Written

Preferred Dialect of English: ☐ British ☐ American ☐ Other (specify)

English Language Exam (Internal/External)
☐ Oral ☐ Objective, Constrained, Manipulative Exercises
☐ Written ☐ Subjective, Open-ended, Communicative Exercises

Class Size ☐ ⟨15 ☐ 15–28 ☐ 29–35 ☐ 35–50 ☐ ⟩50

Time Allocated to Study of English: _____ Yrs _____ Hrs/Wk

Type of Physical Environment/Support
Class Size: ☐ Too Small ☐ Adequate ☐ Too Large
Classroom Shape: ☐ Rectangle/Square ☐ Other
Lighting: ☐ Adequate ☐ Inadequate
Blackboard Space: ☐ Sufficient ☐ Insufficient
Seating Arrangement: ☐ Flexible ☐ Stationary
Audiovisual Equipment: ☐ Sufficient ☐ Insufficient
☐ Modern ☐ Outdated

Budget: ☐ Restricted ☐ Liberal

Remarks

APPENDIX B:

Evaluation checklist

(Reminder: This is a comprehensive checklist, not necessarily intended to be used in its entirety. Custom-make your own evaluation checklist by selecting the items which pertain to your program and situation as per the information collected in Appendix A.)

The Textbook

A. Bibliographical Data

	Rating	Weight
	Excellent Good Adequate Weak Totally Lacking	Required Preferred Not Applicable
1. *Author qualifications:* To what extent are the authors professionally qualified to write a foreign/second language textbook for your particular educational system and student population? (9,20,56)	4 3 2 1 0	A B N
2. *Availability of accompanying materials:* To what extent are accompanying	4 3 2 1 0	A B N

Column headers (Rating): Excellent, Good, Adequate, Weak, Totally Lacking → 4 3 2 1 0

Column headers (Weight): Required, Preferred, Not Applicable → A B N

materials (e.g., workbooks, audio-/videotapes, a teacher's edition, a teacher's guide, sample tests) available? (3,14,15,29,53,54) — 4 3 2 1 0 | A B N

3. *Completeness:* To what extent can the course be taught using only the student's book, or must all the attendant aids (e.g., cassettes) be used? (53) — 4 3 2 1 0 | A B N

4. *Quality of supplementary materials:* If there are workbooks and audio-/videotapes,

   a. to what extent is the material truly supplementary (and not mere duplications of the main text)? (3,6) — 4 3 2 1 0 | A B N

   b. to what extent are the tapes of professional quality (i.e., use authentic native or near-native speakers representing male and female adult as well as children's voices and/or actors, use voices speaking at an appropriate rate, with accurate intonation, avoiding extremes of high and low pitch, and reproduced with high fidelity? (9) — 4 3 2 1 0 | A B N

5. *Cost-effective:* To what extent does the price of the text (plus accompanying materials) seem reasonable and cost-effective (i.e., in terms of saving time, labor, and money)? (1,50,53,56,61,64) — 4 3 2 1 0 | A B N

B. Aims and Goals

Regarding Language Skills and Cultural Understanding

1. *Targeted students specifications:* To what extent do the specifications of the text's targeted audience (age range, culture, assumed background, grade level and background knowledge) match those of the students? (7,8,25,29,35,39,60) — 4 3 2 1 0 | A B N

2. *Matching to student needs:* To what extent do the aims and objectives of the text correspond to the needs and goals of the students? (8,17,19,25,29,37,41,52) — 4 3 2 1 0 | A B N

3. *Matching to syllabus requirements:* To what extent do the aims and objectives of the text correspond to those delineated in the syllabus (if there is one)? (3,5,17,20,39,53,57) — 4 3 2 1 0 | A B N

4. *Compliance with overall educational concerns:* To what extent does the text seem to be in tune with the broader educational concerns of the school system? (9,17,19,28,45,53,54) — 4 3 2 1 0 | A B N

5. *Feasibility:* To what extent are the amount and type of material to be covered realistic and adaptable toward the pace and time allotted for the course? (6,8,17,48,54) — 4 3 2 1 0 | A B N

C. Subject Matter

1. *Suitability and interest level:* To what extent does the subject matter cover a variety of topics suitable to the interests of the intended audience, as determined by age (youth, teenager, young adult, adult, middle age, old age), sex, socioeconomic levels (upper, middle, lower), environment (urban, rural, small town), and cultural orientation? (5,9,13,16,17,19,29,32,36,50) — 4 3 2 1 0 | A B N

2. *Ordering:* To what extent is the ordering of materials by topics or themes arranged in a logical fashion? (5,6,16,29,37) — 4 3 2 1 0 | A B N

3. *Variety of text types:* To what extent does the textbook contain an assortment of suitable text types (e.g., dialogs, essays, poetry, drama, folk tales)? (7,14,32,54,59) — 4 3 2 1 0 | A B N

4. *Content grading:* To what extent is the content graded according to the needs, — 4 3 2 1 0 | A B N

	Rating Excellent / Good / Adequate / Weak / Totally Lacking	Weight Required / Preferred / Not Applicable
background knowledge, and life-style of the students or the requirements of the existing syllabus (if there is one)? (5,9,16,17,18,29,33,35,37,59,64)	4 3 2 1 0	A B N
5. *Level of abstractness:* To what extent is the level of abstractness appropriate? (9,25,29,35,36,59)	4 3 2 1 0	A B N
6. *Register:* To what extent does the text teach the register appropriate for the needs of the students (e.g., formal or literary style vs. conversational style vs. technical style)? (6,14,17,37,49,53,57,65)	4 3 2 1 0	A B N
7. *Cultural sensitivity:* To what extent are ideological, political, and religious constraints taken into consideration? (5,17,65)	4 3 2 1 0	A B N
8. *Content accuracy, authenticity, currency:* To what extent is the material accurate, authentic, and current? How well are stereotypes, factual inaccuracies, oversimplification, and omissions avoided? How appropriate is the language used to the setting, characters, and relationships portrayed? (1,3,4,5,6,9,13,16,20,26,31,32,40,42,44,49,50,51,55,56,57,61,62)	4 3 2 1 0	A B N
9. *Cultural integration:* To what extent is the cultural content integrated in the texts, dialogs, and exercises? (6,14,32)	4 3 2 1 0	A B N

D. Vocabulary and Structures

Grammar

	Rating	Weight
1. *Number and sequence appropriacy:* To what extent is the number of grammatical points appropriate and how appropriate is their sequence? (2,6,10,11,16,19,29,37,38)	4 3 2 1 0	A B N
2. *Accuracy:* To what extent are the linguistic data accurate? (14,48,61)	4 3 2 1 0	A B N
3. *Clarity and completeness:* To what extent are the presentations clear and complete enough for the students to have available a concise review outside the classroom (e.g., models)? (3,9,56,64)	4 3 2 1 0	A B N
4. *Meaningful context:* To what extent are the linguistic items introduced in meaningful contexts? (6,16,22,37)	4 3 2 1 0	A B N

Vocabulary

	Rating	Weight
1. *Load suitability:* To what extent does the vocabulary load (i.e., the number of new words introduced every lesson) seem to be reasonable for the students of that level? (6,16,18,29,37)	4 3 2 1 0	A B N
2. *Appropriate context:* To what extent is vocabulary introduced in appropriate contexts? (6,18,19,37,48,55)	4 3 2 1 0	A B N

Vocabulary and Structures

	Rating	Weight
1. *Suitable readability level:* To what extent does the text's level of readability match that of the class? (29,34,36,39,55)	4 3 2 1 0	A B N
2. *Inclusiveness per text:* To what extent does the text include the basic patterns and vocabulary necessary for using the language up to the level of complexity/mastery the book achieves? (37,56,63)	4 3 2 1 0	A B N
3. *Inclusiveness per syllabus:* To what extent does the text include the basic patterns and vocabulary necessary for using the language up to the level of mastery required by the syllabus (if there is one)? (20)	4 3 2 1 0	A B N

The column headers (rating scale) read, from left to right: Excellent (4), Good (3), Adequate (2), Weak (1), Totally Lacking (0); and the weight headers: Required (A), Preferred (B), Not Applicable (N).

4. *Suitable sequence of progression:* To what extent does the presentation of vocabulary and structures move gradually from the simple to the more complex, except where functional load would indicate otherwise? (16,18,55,56) — 4 3 2 1 0 | A B N

5. *Adequate control of presentation:* To what extent are new structures controlled to be presented and explained before they appear in drills, dialogs, or reading material? (9,18,19,55) — 4 3 2 1 0 | A B N

6. *Balanced distribution:* To what extent is there an even distribution of grammatical and vocabulary material among the chapters (i.e., do some chapters present too much material and others too little)? (3,6) — 4 3 2 1 0 | A B N

7. *Presentation, practice, and recycling suitability:* To what extent does the presentation, practice, and recycling of new linguistic items seem to be appropriate for the level of language mastery (in L1 or L2) of the students? (1,29,39,43,53,64) — 4 3 2 1 0 | A B N

8. *Recycling for reinforcement and integration:* To what extent are new vocabulary and structures recycled in subsequent lessons for reinforcement, and integrated in varying contexts and situations in order to portray their range of applicability in English? (3,16,18,22,37,55,56,57) — 4 3 2 1 0 | A B N

9. *Standard language:* To what extent is standard English (sentence structures that follow normal word order—including idioms—sentences, and paragraphs which follow one another in a logical sequence) used? (9,16,29,49,56) — 4 3 2 1 0 | A B N

10. *Suitability of sentence length and syntactic complexity:* To what extent does the sentence length and syntactic complexity seem reasonable for the students of that level? (16,18,29,34,36) — 4 3 2 1 0 | A B N

11. *Cultural presentation:* To what extent does the text distinguish between British and American English with regard to vocabulary and grammatical structures? (19) — 4 3 2 1 0 | A B N

12. *Accessibility:* To what extent does the text make the structures and vocabulary presented easily accessible to the learner (e.g., summaries of verb forms via paradigms and conjugations, and summaries of new words and phrases via a foreign-language dictionary section or bilingual list)? (7,50,63) — 4 3 2 1 0 | A B N

E. Exercises and Activities

1. *Satisfaction of syllabus objectives:* To what extent do the activities meet the behavioral objectives delineated in the syllabus, curriculum? (18,20,28,33,56) — 4 3 2 1 0 | A B N

2. *Fulfillment of student objectives:* To what extent do the activities meet the behavioral objectives of the students? (5,19,25,29,41,47) — 4 3 2 1 0 | A B N

3. *Effectiveness:* To what extent are the activities provided the best calculated to achieve the stated objectives? (48,56) — 4 3 2 1 0 | A B N

4. *Sequencing toward communication:* To what extent does the text develop a progression from manipulative to communicative exercises? (14,18,20,35,46,48) — 4 3 2 1 0 | A B N

5. *Meaningful communication:* To what extent do the exercises promote — 4 3 2 1 0 | A B N

meaningful communication by referring to realistic activities and situations? (3,5,6,16,18,64,65)

6. *Communicative development:* To what extent do the exercises involve vocabulary and structures which build up the learner's repertoire and develop his/her ability to communicate increasingly independent of text or teacher direction? (9,16,18,35,58) — 4 3 2 1 0 | A B N

7. *Internalization via active participation:* To what extent do the exercises and activities promote internalization of learned material by providing exercises which encourage a student's active participation? (5,6,14,20,23,35,65) — 4 3 2 1 0 | A B N

8. *Promotion of critical thinking:* To what extent do the exercises and activities promote critical thinking (i.e., interpretation, application, analysis, synthesis, and evaluation)? (5,9,18,20,25,29,36) — 4 3 2 1 0 | A B N

9. *Instructional clarity and appropriacy:* To what extent are the instructions to the exercises and activities clear and appropriate? (5,14,17) — 4 3 2 1 0 | A B N

10. *Stereotype-free content:* To what extent are the exercises and activities free of stereotypes? (5,13,24,26,32,42,50) — 4 3 2 1 0 | A B N

11. *Suitability and interest level:* To what extent do the exercises and activities match the age, level, background, and interests of the students? (19,25,41,52,60,65) — 4 3 2 1 0 | A B N

12. *Provision for review:* To what extent does the book provide a pattern of review within lessons and cumulatively test new material? (9,16,17,18,37) — 4 3 2 1 0 | A B N

13. *Development of study skills:* To what extent do the activities provide for the development of study skills, such as skimming, note taking, outlining, looking up words in the dictionary? (2,33) — 4 3 2 1 0 | A B N

F. Layout and Physical Makeup

1. *Motivational attractiveness:* To what extent is the text attractive and appealing to the intended student population? (1,3,9,18,25,30,35) — 4 3 2 1 0 | A B N

2. *Suitability of durability, book and type dimensions:* To what extent is the size convenient enough, and the type size appropriate for the learners? (1,9,16,18,29) — 4 3 2 1 0 | A B N

3. *Organizational clarity and function:* To what extent is the material clearly organized (i.e., with functional typefaces, a detailed table of contents—which includes location of structures and their respective exercises—an index of new vocabulary items and their location, appendices and other end matter with maps, verb summaries, a glossary, etc.)? (3,7,9,19,29,53) — 4 3 2 1 0 | A B N

4. *Effectiveness in presentation:* To what extent are simple graphic devices (e.g., boxes, shading, color, arrows) effectively used to clarify the presentation of grammatical structures? (3,9,29) — 4 3 2 1 0 | A B N

5. *Relativity, linkage, and integration:* To what extent is the artwork directly related to the subject matter and printed near enough to it to assist the learner in understanding the printed text? (3,6,7,9,16,18,45,63) — 4 3 2 1 0 | A B N

6. *Stereotype-free, accurate, authentic portrayal:* To what extent is the artwork unbiased (free of stereotype), yet accurately and authentically conveying the culture content? (9,32,42) — 4 3 2 1 0 | A B N

7. *Suitability of artwork:* To what extent is the artwork geared to the age level and interests of the students? (9,32) — 4 3 2 1 0 | A B N

8. *Illustrative clarity and simplicity:* To what extent are the illustrations clear, simple, and free of unnecessary details that may confuse the learner? (16) — 4 3 2 1 0 | A B N

9. *Motivational atmosphere:* To what extent do the illustrations create a favorable atmosphere for practice in reading and speaking by depicting realism and action? (2,16,26,48) — 4 3 2 1 0 | A B N

The Teacher's Manual

A. General Features

1. *Guide to rationale:* To what extent does the manual help the teacher understand the rationale of the textbook regarding the text's objectives, methodology, subject matter, sequence of grammar points, etc.? (16,34,60) — 4 3 2 1 0 | A B N

2. *Guide to syllabus:* To what extent does the manual guide the teacher to any set syllabus for that level? (16) — 4 3 2 1 0 | A B N

3. *Guide to contents:* To what extent does the manual guide the teacher to the contents and location of the new vocabulary, structures, and topics found in the text via indexes? (16) — 4 3 2 1 0 | A B N

4. *Answer guide:* To what extent does the manual provide correct or suggested answers for the exercises in the student's text? (16,53) — 4 3 2 1 0 | A B N

5. *Guide for new and nonnative English-speaking teachers:* To what extent does the manual provide information for the new and nonnative English-speaking teacher? (3,17,30,53,60) — 4 3 2 1 0 | A B N

B. Supplementary Exercises for Each Language Skill

1. *In aural skills, effective listening, and comprehension practice:* To what extent does the manual provide effective material for training the students in listening and understanding the spoken language? (3,16) — 4 3 2 1 0 | A B N

2. *In oral skills, adequate, effective, and appropriate presentation and practice in pronunciation and intonation:*

    a. To what extent does the manual provide effective material for training the students in pronunciation and oral expression? Is there enough practice? In addition to descriptions of how the sounds are produced, are there practice exercises using the sounds in isolated words, in expressions, and in sentences? (3,16,56,64) — 4 3 2 1 0 | A B N

    b. To what extent is the presentation of the sounds of the foreign language complete? Does it include intonation patterns as well as presentations on the individual sounds? (3,56) — 4 3 2 1 0 | A B N

    c. To what extent is the presentation appropriate for the students? Is it not too technical? (3,9,56,57) — 4 3 2 1 0 | A B N

3. *In grammar, adequate integrative reinforcement via varied oral exercises:* To what extent does the manual suggest adequate and varied oral exercises for reinforcing points of grammar presented in the textbook? (16,37,48,50) — 4 3 2 1 0 | A B N

4. *In grammar, practice in meaningful situations:* To what extent does the manual offer meaningful situations and a variety of exercises for teaching structural units (grammar)? (16,22,37,64) — 4 3 2 1 0 | A B N

5. *In vocabulary development, effective drills and exercises:* To what extent does the manual provide effective drills and exercises that enable the teacher to assist the students in building up their vocabulary? (3,16) — 4 3 2 1 0 | A B N

6. *In reading skills, effective questions testing comprehension:* To what extent does the manual provide effective questions to help the teacher test the students' reading comprehension? (9,16)   4 3 2 1 0   A B N

7. *In reading, adequate graded material for practice:* To what extent does the manual provide adequate graded material for additional reading practice? (34)   4 3 2 1 0   A B N

8. *In writing, adequate graded material for practice:* To what extent does the manual provide adequate graded material for additional writing practice? (16)   4 3 2 1 0   A B N

9. *In all materials, authenticity, accuracy, and stereotype-free content:* To what extent are the supplementary materials authentic, accurate, and free of stereotypes and biases for the teaching of: 4 3 2 1 0   A B N

    a. listening comprehension

    b. speaking

    c. reading

    d. writing

     (9,13,16,20,24,26,32,42,50,56)

10. *In all materials, suitability, interest level, and goal fulfillment:* To what extent do the supplementary materials match the age, level, background interests, and aims of the students? (16,17,19)   4 3 2 1 0   A B N

11. *In aural/oral skills, contrastive analysis* (if applicable): If the text is written for students of a particular language background, to what extent does it provide a variety of aural/oral exercises to help the students practice hearing and speaking the sounds most difficult for them to distinguish and pronounce? (48,56,64)   4 3 2 1 0   A B N

12. *In all materials, sample achievement tests:* To what extent does the manual provide ready-to-give achievement tests (with answers) for the convenience of the teacher? (7,9,42,53)   4 3 2 1 0   A B N

C. Methodological and Pedagogical Guidance

1. *General:* To what extent does the manual provide guidance for the teacher on the teaching of language items and skills? Is the teacher expected to be experienced in language teaching or does the text offer clear and detailed advice for the novice to follow? (17,33,37,60,64)   4 3 2 1 0   A B N

2. *Per lesson type:* To what extent does the manual help the teacher with each new type of lesson introduced? (16,37,65)   4 3 2 1 0   A B N

3. *Per lesson:* To what extent does the manual provide lesson summaries and suggestions to help the teacher review old lessons and introduce new lessons? (16,53)   4 3 2 1 0   A B N

4. *Flexibility in lesson presentation:* To what extent does the manual advise about how to present the lessons in different ways? (20,53,65)   4 3 2 1 0   A B N

5. *Speaking skills:* To what extent does the manual provide practical suggestions for teaching pronunciation and intonation? (9,16,64)   4 3 2 1 0   A B N

6. *Prereading skills:* If it is for a beginning text, to what extent does the manual provide guidance to the teacher in presenting practice in prereading skills, such as visual identification of alphabet letters (especially those symbols   4 3 2 1 0   A B N

	Rating	Weight
	Excellent 4, Good 3, Adequate 2, Weak 1, Totally Lacking 0	Required A, Preferred B, Not Applicable N

which may be confused or not known by the students), identification of the sounds represented by the letters (with special attention to the sounds which may be troublesome), reading in left-to-right directionality (if applicable)? (21,55,57)

Item	Rating	Weight
7. *Vocabulary development:* To what extent does the manual provide guidance to the teacher in presenting practice in word identification skills and vocabulary development (e.g., identifying roots, inflectional endings, cognates, synonyms, antonyms, and theme groupings)? (18,29,55)	4 3 2 1 0	A B N
8. *Grammar in context:* To what extent does the manual offer a variety of techniques for teaching structural units in meaningful situations (e.g., notional/functional and semanticogrammatical categories)? (22,57,64)	4 3 2 1 0	A B N
9. *Reading and writing comprehension (R/WC): connectives:* To what extent does the manual provide suggestions for the teaching of connective words (e.g., conjunctions such as "if," "but," "and," prepositions such as "to," and markers of time, cause and effect, or consequence, such as "however," "moreover," "thus")? (18,21,29,55)	4 3 2 1 0	A B N
10. *R/WC: figurative, idiomatic, similar expressions:* To what extent does the manual provide guidance for the teacher in the presentation of figurative language, idiomatic expressions, and words and expressions similar to ones in his/her native language? (55)	4 3 2 1 0	A B N
11. *R/WC: punctuation, stress, intonation:* To what extent does the manual provide guidance to the teacher in presenting punctuation and how changes in stress and intonation may alter meanings? (55)	4 3 2 1 0	A B N
12. *Reading methods:* To what extent does the manual provide suggestions to help the teacher introduce new reading passages? (16,64)	4 3 2 1 0	A B N
13. *Writing skills:* To what extent does the manual provide guidance to the teacher for introducing various types of written work? (16,64)	4 3 2 1 0	A B N
14. *Evaluation of written work:* To what extent does the manual provide guidance to the teacher for evaluating written work and identifying their students' most serious mistakes? (16,45)	4 3 2 1 0	A B N
15. *Integration of language skills:* To what extent does the manual provide suggestions to the teacher for presenting exercises and activities which integrate all four language skills? (6,12,20)	4 3 2 1 0	A B N
16. *Adopt- or adaptability of methodology:* To what extent does the manual conform to the methodological requirements determined to be suitable by the administrators or the teachers themselves; and, if not, to what extent can the material be exploited or modified as required by local circumstances? (17,53)	4 3 2 1 0	A B N
17. *Flexibility (eclectic) in approach:* To what extent is the manual meaningful and helpful to the teacher without being too confining? Is it eclectic in approach? (1,19,27,33,37,47,53,65)	4 3 2 1 0	A B N
18. *Individualizing instruction:* To what extent does the manual provide guidance for the teacher on individualizing instruction? (9)	4 3 2 1 0	A B N
19. *Contrastive analysis* (if applicable): If the text is for students from a homogeneous language background, to what extent does the manual present a contrastive analysis of the sound system and word usage of English and the native language? (48,56)	4 3 2 1 0	A B N

	Rating	Weight
	Excellent / Good / Adequate / Weak / Totally Lacking	Required / Preferred / Not Applicable

20. *Cultural presentation:* To what extent does the manual provide guidance on the distinctions between British and American English with regard to pronunciation, vocabulary, and grammatical structures? (19) — 4 3 2 1 0 | A B N

21. *Audiovisual aids:* To what extent does the manual advise the teacher on the use of audiovisual aids, and suggest creative substitutions for situations where audiovisual equipment is unavailable? (9,16) — 4 3 2 1 0 | A B N

22. *Teacher's aids:* To what extent are teacher's aids such as tapescripts (if applicable) and suggestions for their effective use, "technical notes" (especially in the case of ESP textbooks), vocabulary lists, and structural/functional inventories provided in the manual? (53) — 4 3 2 1 0 | A B N

D. Linguistic Background Information

For the Nonnative-speaking Teacher

1. *Contrastive analysis for pronunciation:* To what extent does the manual provide contrastive information for the teacher on likely pronunciation problems? (16,64) — 4 3 2 1 0 | A B N

2. *Explanation on vocabulary and structures:* To what extent does the manual provide understandable explanations for the teacher on English vocabulary items and structures? (16) — 4 3 2 1 0 | A B N

3. *List of cognates:* To what extent does the manual provide lists of cognate words (true and false cognates) for the teacher? (16) — 4 3 2 1 0 | A B N

4. *Denotation of likely grammatical problems:* To what extent does the manual provide information on grammar to help the teacher explain grammatical patterns presented in the lessons and anticipate likely problems (i.e., data from contrastive analysis and error analysis)? — 4 3 2 1 0 | A B N

5. *Cultural information:* To what extent does the manual provide information on cultural items of interest? (9) — 4 3 2 1 0 | A B N

Overall Value

Overall suitability, appropriacy, adequacy and effectiveness: In light of the needs of the students, the objectives of the syllabus, the given educational setting and time constraints, the funding, the broad educational concerns, the principles of modern language teaching, and the background and experience of the teacher, to what extent is the textbook, teacher's manual, or other items suitable, appropriate, adequate, pedagogically effective, and cost-effective? — 4 3 2 1 0 | A B N

References Noted in Checklist

1. Alberta Department of Education, Edmonton, Language Services Branch, 1986
2. Allwright, 1981
3. Ariew, 1982
4. Arizpe & Aguirre, 1987
5. Auerbach & Burgess, 1985
6. Benevento, 1984
7. Bertoletti & Dahlet, 1984
8. Bruder, 1978
9. California State Board of Education, Sacramento, 1983
10. Carney & Lide, 1976
11. Celce-Murcia & Rosensweig, 1979
12. Chastain, 1976

13. Clausen, 1982
14. Cowles, 1976
15. Danesi, 1976
16. Daoud & Celce-Murcia, 1979
17. Davison, 1976
18. Dosi, 1983
19. Dubin & Olshtain, 1977
20. Dubin & Olshtain, 1986
21. Ebel, 1980
22. Finnemann, 1987
23. Fong, 1979
24. Freudenstein, ed., 1978
25. Frymier, 1977
26. Gaff, 1982
27. Grittner & Welty, 1974
28. Harrison, Prator, & Tucker, 1973
29. Hetherington, 1985
30. Holmes, 1976
31. Hornburger, 1977
32. Joiner, 1974
33. Kahn, 1978
34. Krause, 1976
35. Macian, 1986
36. Macian & Harewood, 1984
37. Mackey, 1965
38. McIntosh, 1979
39. Msosa, 1982
40. NCTE Task Force, 1971
41. Newton, 1979
42. Papalia, 1976
43. Payne, 1975
44. Pfister & Borzilleri, 1977
45. Prator, 1968
46. Prator, 1972
47. Prator, 1976
48. Prator, 1977
49. Rings, 1986
50. Rivers, 1968
51. Saville-Troike, 1976
52. Shapira, 1976
53. Sheldon, 1988
54. Steiner, 1973
55. Stieglitz, 1982
56. Tucker, 1978
57. Walz, 1986
58. Wardhaugh, cited in Mockridge-Fong, 1979
59. Waterman, 1952
60. Watt & De Jong, 1984
61. West, 1960
62. Weston & Stein, 1978
63. Williams, 1982
64. Williams, 1983
65. Zughoul, 1986

The Use of Media in Language Teaching[1]

Donna M. Brinton

As a tool for language learning/teaching, media have undoubtedly always been present, and have facilitated the task of language learning for both instructed and noninstructed learners. It is certain, for example, that children learning a first or second language grasp the meaning of words from the objects which surround them, and that native speakers of a language when attempting to communicate with nonnative speakers (both inside and outside the classroom) make use of the here and now or objects in the immediate environment (cf. Hudelson, 1984; Pica et al., 1987; Wesche & Ready, 1985) to contextualize language, thus facilitating comprehension of the message.

In terms of the second language classroom, the extent to which media are used has varied widely, depending on the methodology selected. In some methods, media have figured prominently as a force which drives the curriculum. In the St. Cloud (or Audio-Visual) Method, which was developed primarily for the teaching of French as a foreign language (Bowen et al., 1985; Stevick, 1976), all language items were introduced to learners via contextualized, audiovisual presentations (usually filmstrips or slide shows with an accompanying sound track). The underlying assumption or approach of this method was that language is an acoustic-visual whole which cannot be separated from its constituent elements. Similarly, in the Silent Way (Larsen-Freeman, 1986), the sound-color charts and rods form a central visual component of the method, allowing the teacher to present and elicit language while at the same time providing the students with tools for creative construction of language and communicative situations.

Yet in other methods, media are relegated more to the design or procedure level.[2] In the Communicative Approach (Larsen-Freeman, 1986, Morrow, 1981), for example, much emphasis is placed on the need for real-life objects or texts (e.g., maps, railroad timetables, application forms) to lend authenticity to the communicative situation, while in the Natural Approach (Krashen & Terrell, 1983) magazine pictures are used as an elicitation device in the Listening Comprehension and Early Production stages, and charts, maps, and props are used to motivate and enhance communicative interchange in later stages of acquisition. Finally, in experiential approaches to language learning (see the chapters by Eyring and Hawkins in this volume), language teaching media are often taken out of the hands of the teacher and placed in the hands of the students, such that students involved in project work might be expected to produce a scripted sound-slide show or a voice-over video documentary on the topic under investigation as their final class product.

Whatever the approach, language teachers seem to universally agree that media *can* and *do* enhance language teaching, and thus in the daily practice of language teaching we find the entire range of media (from non-mechanical aids such as flashcards and magazine pictures all the way up to sophisticated mechanical aids such as video cameras and computers) assisting teachers in their jobs, bringing the outside world into the classroom, and, in short, making the task of

454

language learning a more meaningful and exciting one. Keeping this fact in mind, then, let's examine the parameters of instructional media used in the language classroom.

MEDIA: A DEFINITION

Just as we often differentiate the teaching of "large 'C' culture"—i.e., the great literature, art, and other contributions of a society—from that of "small 'c' culture"—i.e., the customs and habits of a people—(Chastain, 1988), it is germane here to differentiate between "large 'M' media" and "small 'm' media." Certainly, as with culture, media means many different things to different people. The most immediate connotation of the term "media," at least as related to language teaching, is that of the "large M media"—of technological innovations in language teaching, of mechanical paraphernalia, and of glossy, polished audiovisual aids—with all the media anxiety that these can conjure up in teachers. However, to date there is no evidence that such glossy audiovisual aids are any more effective than teacher-made, nonmechanical aids (e.g., paper plate hand puppets, butcher paper verb charts, and the like) or props (e.g., cereal boxes, campaign buttons, travel pamphlets, bumper stickers) which have been adapted for classroom teaching purposes. I would therefore like to suggest that all these aids—mechanical and nonmechanical, glossy and nonglossy, pedagogical and nonpedagogical, commercial and teacher-made alike—constitute valuable contributions to the profession of language teaching, and should thus be part of our definition of language teaching media.

A RATIONALE FOR THE USE OF MEDIA IN LANGUAGE TEACHING

In addressing teachers on the subject of media, I tend to assume that the issue of why we should use media in the teaching of second or foreign languages is a superfluous one,

and that I am addressing the already converted. All too frequently, however, I am snapped out of this illusion by snatches of conversation I overhear in classroom hallways or at professional gatherings. These comments, made by colleagues regarding their inability or unwillingness to use audiovisual aids in their respective classrooms, fall roughly into the following "categories":

Statement 1: I'm all thumbs. I can't use media.

Statement 2: My school district has no budget for media.

Statement 3: I have no time to prepare media materials of my own.

Statement 4: The syllabus I teach from is too tightly structured to allow for media materials to be brought into the classroom.

Statement 5: I teach advanced levels (alternately, composition, or reading) and therefore don't need to use media.

Before proceeding to formulate a rationale for using media in the language teaching classroom, let us first examine the underlying fallacies of the above statements.

The first two statements, I believe, can be dealt with summarily by realizing that those who have made such statements are subscribing to the aforementioned "large M" definition of media. That is, these individuals are assuming that classroom media materials are by definition (1) mechanical (and therefore unavailable, unwieldy, and/or anxiety-provoking) and (2) commercial (and therefore costly and inaccessible). In fact, as I have already pointed out, classroom media need be none of the above—they can be nonmechanical, unthreatening to both teachers and students, teacher-produced rather than commercial, and cheap, or even free!

The fallacies which underlie statements 3 through 5 are somewhat more complex. On the surface, statement 3, i.e., the time factor, presents a somewhat viable argument against using media. Certainly, if one disregards the many attractive commercially available media materials which teachers can select from (see Appendix B for a partial list of these) and assumes that statement 2 also holds true in this case, the preparation of teacher-made media materials *does* demand an investment of time and energy above and beyond that of normal lesson planning. However, this statement neglects to take into account the fact that *any* lesson preparation is time-consuming, and that many media lessons, such as the preparation of vocabulary flashcards or the selection of magazine pictures to elicit and practice a particular structure of the language, do not require exhaustive amounts of time. Additionally, and perhaps more importantly, the statement ignores the "payoff" that can result from the hours spent preparing or assembling simple classroom media materials (e.g., a set of prespecified role assignments typed on 3 × 5 index cards to set up a role-play situation, or a collection of menus from local restaurants for a lesson on food items). In fact, this payoff, which is realized in terms of the teacher's recycling these same materials again and again with different student audiences (and even for different teaching purposes), is often far greater than the payoff of time invested in more traditional classroom lesson planning.[3]

Concerning statement 4, I believe that this is based on a commonly held misunderstanding of media as "extraneous" to normal lesson activities. In other words, proponents of this view fail to recognize that media can form a viable point of departure for achieving lesson objectives. In fact, rather than taking up additional class hours, the use of media which are designed with a particular student population and teaching objective in mind can often help to *economize* the teaching task. This is achieved in the sense that the media appeal to students' senses and help them process information (Hartnett, 1985), thus reinforcing the teaching point and saving the teacher unnecessary explanation.

Finally, those who hold the view expressed in statement 5 are neglecting the fact, grounded in the very definition of language, that language skills are not isolated entities, and that as language teachers we need to build bridges between skills. We can do so by creating a unified context in which the teaching of various skills is effectively integrated around media. For example, we can structure multiskill thematic units[4] requiring students to synthesize information from a variety of sources (e.g., a listening passage, a reading passage, and an interview assignment in which they poll native speakers for their opinions on a topic) and then write up the product of this synthesis as a term paper.

Undeniably, media help us to motivate students by bringing a slice of real life into the classroom and presenting language in its more complete communicative situation. Media can also provide a density of information and richness of cultural input not otherwise possible in the classroom, they can help students process information and free the teacher from excess explanation, and they can provide a contextualizer and solid point of departure for classroom activities.

In sum, we can propose the following arguments as a rationale for using media in the language teaching classroom:

- Given the role media play in the world outside the classroom, students expect to find it inside the classroom as well. Media thus serve as an important motivator in the language teaching process.
- Audiovisual materials provide students with content, meaning, and guidance. They thus create a contextualized situation within which language items are presented and practiced.
- Media materials can lend authenticity to the classroom situation, reinforcing for students the direct relation between the language classroom and the outside world.
- Since the learning styles of students differ (Reid, 1987), media provide us with a way of addressing the needs of more visual and auditory learners.
- The role which input plays in language

learning is virtually uncontested (Krashen, 1987). By bringing media into the classroom, teachers can expose their students to multiple input sources. Thus, while decreasing the risk of the students' becoming dependent on their teacher's dialect, they can also enrich their language learning experience.

- With reference to schema theory (Shank & Abelson, 1977), which proposes that we approach new information by scanning our memory banks for related knowledge, media can help students to call up existing schemata and therefore maximize their use of prior background knowledge in the language learning process.
- Finally, research suggests that media provide teachers with a means of presenting material in a time-efficient and compact manner, and of stimulating students' senses, thereby helping them to process information more readily (Mollica, 1979).

CLASSROOM MEDIA: AN OVERVIEW

At the height of the audiolingual era, if we had asked the average second or foreign language teacher to designate those media which they felt were appropriate for the teaching of languages, we would no doubt have received a fairly large range of responses, with the blackboard and other simple classroom aids along with the audiotape medium (and the ubiquitous language laboratory) dominating the responses. Today, needless to say, that range of responses would be even larger, as the ever-expanding horizons of technology present us with exciting new advances such as computer-assisted instruction, satellite transmission, and interactive video programming.

Despite these expanding horizons, we find today that rather than abandoning the more traditional, or small *m*, media and shifting allegiance to the newer, more technological innovations, language teachers are simply incorporating new technology into their rep-

ertoire of teaching aids, with many using sophisticated videodisk players alongside the less sophisticated (but tried and true) flannelboard or overhead projector. In attempting to provide an overview of the range of media available to classroom teachers today, it is perhaps best to stick with the traditional classification of "nontechnical" and "technical" media, as listed below.[5]

Nontechnical media

This category presents obvious advantages in settings where electricity is unreliable or where technical resources are scarce. Other obvious advantages of the forms of media included in this category are their cost, availability, and accessibility or user friendliness. Items which belong in this category typically include:

> blackboards/whiteboards
> magnetboards/flannelboards/pegboards
> flashcards/index cards
> wall charts, posters, maps, scrolls
> board games
> mounted pictures/photos
> cartoons/line drawings
> objects/realia
> pamphlets/brochures/leaflets/flyers
> equipment operation manuals
> puppets
> newspapers/magazines

Technical media

Although these forms of media are costlier and less user-friendly than the nontechnical media, they carry with them a larger degree of "psychological reality" in that they can bring the outside world in all its permutations into the classroom. In fact, since students in today's language classes tend to surround themselves with technology in their daily lives, they may grow to expect it in the language classroom as well. Items which belong in this category typically include:

> audiotapes, audio recorders/players
> records/record players
> videotapes/video players

radio/television

telephones/teletrainers

films/film projectors

computer software/hardware

overhead transparencies/overhead projectors

language lab/multimedia lab

opaque projectors

slides, filmstrips/slide and filmstrip projectors

In considering the above classification system, it is important to make a few further distinctions—namely, whether the media being used belong to the category of software (consumable media items) or hardware (equipment), commercially produced or teacher-produced, and authentic or nonauthentic materials—all of which have their proper place in the language teaching classroom.[6]

Finally, we must also consider the purpose to which these media are being put—i.e., to aid in presentation, to provide practice or stimulate communicative interaction, or to provide feedback (as in the case of audio/videotaping student oral products). To embark at this point on a description of the possible uses of all the above forms of media is beyond the scope of this article. However, to take but one example, the blackboard, we can see how even this simple medium can function effectively at the various stages of a lesson. In the presentation stage, for example, the blackboard can be used for verb paradigms, time lines, or other graphic or visual cues to elucidate a teaching point, while matrices or grids written on the blackboard can serve as elicitation tools. Similarly, in the practice stage, maps, stick figures, and other line drawings can function as contextualizers for a given activity. Finally, in the communication stage, the blackboard can be used to storyboard student ideas in a group-produced narrative, or to cluster and map student concepts as they are being developed.

Suffice it to say, then, that each form of media presents unique advantages—be it the availability and immediacy of feedback which the blackboard or whiteboard can supply, the economy of time which pre-prepared overhead transparencies can provide the teacher, or the richness of authentic input the film or video medium can offer. Ultimately, each medium leaves its own imprint on the teaching/learning process, and it is up to the teacher to decide which one to select in order to teach a given point.

GUIDELINES FOR USING MEDIA IN THE CLASSROOM

Given the range of classroom media (both hardware and software) discussed above, it is not surprising that language teachers are literally overwhelmed by the choices available to them. As Penfield (1987, p. 1) rightfully asserts, "too often [media] are neglected because teachers are not always certain how to adapt these rich and complex learning materials to students' needs and language competencies." Clearly, guidelines for use are in order.

In fact, guidelines for the selection, adaptation, development, and implementation of media materials do not differ radically from the kinds of guidelines we find mentioned more universally regarding lesson planning and textbook evaluation (see, e.g., the chapters by Purgason and Skierso in this volume). Thus, such issues as the appropriateness of the materials for the target audience, their technical and pedagogical quality, their teaching objective, and the pre/post procedures to be used all play as important a role in the selection and use of *audiovisual* media in the classroom as they do in that of conventional *print* media. Further, and this point cannot be stressed enough, media materials should not be viewed simply as extraneous to the lesson, or as contingency plans. Rather, they should be planned as carefully as the lesson itself, and should form a central (if not *the* central) component of the lesson—one which is interwoven with the other lesson components, such as the reading text, the writing assignment, or the speaking task.

A FRAMEWORK FOR STRUCTURING MEDIA LESSONS

The framework presented below[7] is intended to put the application of media to language teaching into some unified perspective and to assist teachers in structuring media lessons. In constructing this framework, I've divided up the typical "lesson" into four stages—the *information and motivation stage,* where the topic and relevant background information are presented; the *input stage,* where the teacher ensures comprehension of the item or item(s) presented; the *focus stage,* where the students practice the tasks and are provided with guided opportunities to manipulate items until they feel comfortable and confident; and the more open-ended *transfer stage,* in which students are given opportunities to use language more communicatively, i.e., to offer personal comments or share experiences relating to the general context defined by the media materials.[8] Figure 1 presents the framework.

In applying this framework, teachers need to be aware that the above points in the framework outline *options* available to teachers in designing and implementing media lessons, and are not intended to represent step-by-step procedures which must be followed. As is characteristic of the learning/teaching process, with its cyclical nature, the stages interconnect and overlap, yet in some sense each stage retains its essential characteristics. Teachers should also be aware that media can play a role at *any* or *all* of the four stages of the lesson, and that a variety of media might be used in these stages to complement each other and to achieve the designated teaching objective.

I. Information and motivation stage: Getting *into* media
II. Input stage: Working *from* media
  1. Teacher presents/elicits vocabulary
  2. Teacher presents/elicits structures
  3. Teacher presents/elicits functions
  4. Teacher presents/elicits concepts
  5. Teacher presents/elicits content
III. Focus stage: Working *with* media
  1. Teacher models language items/procedures
  2. Students practice items in context
    a. Drill
    b. Elicitation
  3. Students manipulate language/content
    a. Note taking
    b. Information transfer
    c. Pair work/small group work
IV. Transfer stage: Working *out of* media
  1. Class discussion
  2. Students interact, using context set by media materials as a point of departure
    a. Role-play/sociodrama
    b. Problem-solving activity
    c. Information gap activity
    d. Game
  3. Task-based assignment
  4. Follow-up writing assignment
  5. Sharing of personal experience
  6. Field trip

Figure 1. *A framework for structuring media lessons.*

SAMPLE MEDIA LESSONS

The following sample lessons, selected to illustrate a range of available media (both mechanical and nonmechanical), demonstrate how the above framework can be applied in making decisions about media use for language teaching purposes.[9] Note that numbers in square brackets indicate the relevant parts of the framework which have been applied in designing each lesson.

Sample Lesson 1: The "Ugly Lamp" (magazine picture)

Audience: Beginning-level adult students enrolled in an intensive language/visa program; intermediate-level EFL students.

Teaching Objective: To provide students with the language needed to express pleasure/displeasure; request an exchange for unwanted items.

Media: Mounted magazine picture of woman holding an ugly lamp (see Figure 2).

Skills: Speaking, vocabulary, writing.

Time: 2 class periods (1 hour each) plus follow-up (15 minutes).

Procedures:

1. Teacher introduces the concept of gift giving and receiving. If appropriate (e.g., holiday time), students may want to share information about what they are giving to friends or wish to receive [I.].
2. The teacher introduces the magazine picture of the ugly lamp, eliciting explicit vocabulary (e.g., lampshade, bow, frown) [II.1.] and structures (present progressive, descriptive adjectives) [II.2.].
3. The students and teacher examine the picture more closely, and the teacher asks questions which elicit more implicit vocabulary [II.1.] and structures [II.2.]. For example: "Who do you think gave the woman this gift? (sister-in-law, elderly relative); "Where do you think Aunt Harriet *might* have bought the lamp?" (She *might* have bought it from a thrift shop/garage sale/etc.).
4. Teacher presents language functions relevant to giving and receiving gifts [II.3], and provides students with guided practice [III.2.a.]. In pairs (gift giver and receiver), students practice the sequence of giving the gift, opening it, and expressing thanks [III.3.c.].
5. For homework, as follow-up writing practice, students write a letter to the giver of the gift thanking him/her [IV.4.].
6. On a subsequent day, the context is recycled, and the language necessary for returning unwanted items to a store and requesting cash/an exchange is presented [II.4.] and practiced [III.2.a.].
7. Students role-play the situation [IV.2.a.].
8. As a culminating activity, students bring in unwanted items they have received and share their reactions to receiving these gifts with their classmates [IV.5.].

Wing Au Yeung

Figure 2

Sample Lesson 2: Computer Hardware/Software Ads (mounted advertisements from magazines and journals)[10]

Audience: Advanced ESL/EFL students enrolled in EAP courses at the university; students enrolled in university-bound programs (e.g., advanced students in intensive language institutes).

Teaching Objective: To introduce, practice, and reinforce the task of writing formal definitions for academic purposes; secondary objectives include reading practice involving skimming and scanning, speaking in small groups, in-class writing, and follow-up writing error detection.

Media: Mounted advertisements of computer hardware and software products with accompanying text from magazines and journals.

Skills: Writing, grammar (sentences of definition), reading, and speaking.

Time: 90 minutes plus additional follow-up as desired.

Procedures:

1. Students are led in a brief discussion of where we are apt to find academic definitions of items—e.g., in textbooks, product manuals, journals, and magazines [I.].
2. Teacher reviews previously covered material—i.e., the structure of sentences of definition [II.2.].
3. Teacher distributes Xeroxed copy of a computer hardware or software advertisement. Together, the class members identify the item being advertised, and locate any information relevant to writing a concise sentence definition of the product [III.2.b.]. [Note: This advertisement and the subsequent mounted advertisements should be carefully selected so that there is no overt sentence definition of the product. The ad should, however, contain the necessary information for students to draw from in writing their definition.]
4. Together, students construct a complete sentence definition of the product. The teacher writes this definition on the blackboard [III.1.], stressing the previously studied formula for definitions, as in the following example:

An [X] is a [Y] that [Z]

[X]	[Y]	[Z]
SPECIFIC TERM	GENERAL CLASS	CHARACTERISTICS
Software Bridge	is a software program	that converts documents from one word-processing program to another without losing formatting specifications.

5. Students are next divided into small groups of three or four students, with each group receiving one mounted advertisement for a computer software or hardware item. Using the pattern provided, each group of students works for roughly four or five minutes to construct a sentence definition of the product [III.3.c.]. At the end of this time period, the groups pass their ads to another group, with each group receiving a new ad. This process continues until all groups have seen all ads, and students in each group have had a chance to write appropriate sentences of definition for each product.
6. With the help of the teacher, students now pool their answers. Students decide for themselves the most useful information to include [IV.1.], and the teacher writes the agreed-

upon definition on the board under the headings indicated above. Errors in spelling, sentence structure, etc., can be dealt with at this stage by eliciting peer correction.

7. On a subsequent day, the teacher can recycle the material in a more game-like atmosphere [IV.2.d.], either by giving students names of fictional products and having them compete to write the "best" definition of the product, or by having students play a "sort and unscramble" game in which students are given mixed-up items from categories X, Y, and Z on separate strips of paper and asked to put the items together to form sentence definitions.

Sample Lesson 3: Over-the-Counter Drugs[11]

Audience: Beginning or intermediate-level adult/community education students.

Teaching Objective: To develop an awareness of the availability, use and abuse of over-the-counter preparations; to increase reading for specific information skills; to expand topic-related vocabulary.

Media: Packages/containers of over-the-counter drug preparations (e.g., headache remedies, cold medications); information grid (see Figure 3; pp. 464–465).

Skills: Reading, vocabulary, and speaking.

Time: 2 class periods (1 hour each).

Procedures:

1. Teacher introduces concept of over-the-counter (OTC) drugs; elicits from students information on the types of OTC products they typically use [I.].
2. Common complaints (e.g., headache, allergy, cold sores, constipation) are reviewed [II.1.].
3. Teacher introduces information grid, and demonstrates the procedure students are to follow via the example (Sudafed) [III.1.]. Terms in the grid are explained [I.1.].
4. Students are divided into small groups of four or five and OTC products are distributed to each group.
5. Students work in groups to transfer information into the grid [III.3.b.].
6. Once all student groups have completed the task, they share their results with the class at large.
7. Students discuss previous experiences they have had with OTC drugs (side effects experienced, etc.) [IV.5.]
8. As a follow-up, each student is assigned a symptom (e.g., warts, fever blisters, heartburn) and told to go to the drug store and find three products intended to remedy this condition. They are to compare these products using the grid format and report back on their findings to the class on the following day [IV.3.].

PRODUCT NAME	SYMPTOMS	FORM	DOSAGE	FREQUENCY	AGE	TIME LIMIT	RESTRICTIONS	SIDE EFFECTS
1. Sudafed	cold hayfever allergy	tablet	12 yrs.-adult, 2 tablets 6-12 yrs., 1 tablet	every 4-6 hrs.	Adults and children 6-12	7 days	Not for children under 2 yrs. For children 2-6, use Sudafed syrup	nervousness dizziness sleeplessness
2.								
3.								

4.								
5.								
6.								

FIGURE 3. *Over-the-counter drugs chart.*

Sample Lesson 4: Postcard Description Activity (photographic postcards from various countries)[12]

Audience: Recently arrived international students living in the ESL context (any level).

Teaching Objective: To increase awareness of cultural stereotyping; to serve as a discussion stimulus for impressions formed of the United States, its people, and its culture.

Media: Picture postcards depicting stereotypical images of countries (one for each pair of students); a barrier (e.g., a notebook, manila folder) to separate students.

Skills: Speaking, cultural awareness, writing.

Time: 1 class period (1 hour) plus follow-up (10–15 minutes).

Procedures:

1. Teacher introduces the activity by discussing postcards in general, and the kinds of postcards which people send to their friends when they are on vacation [I.]. A model postcard (e.g., one depicting a Dutch girl wearing wooden shoes with a windmill and tulips in the background) may be shown to promote discussion.
2. Students are asked what kinds of postcards they have sent since arriving in the United States, who they have sent these to, and what kinds of messages they have written on them [II.4.].
3. Teacher explains/models the paired activity: Students are to get in pairs, with Student A receiving a postcard from a given country. They erect a barrier between them so Student B cannot see Student A's postcard. It is Student A's task to describe this postcard to Student B, without mentioning the name of the country [III.1.]. Student B then attempts to discover the identity of the country [IV.2.c.].
4. Once all students have completed the task, students share their postcards and the cultural stereotype depicted with the rest of the class.
5. Follow-up discussion ensues on the general topic of cultural stereotyping, with the teacher eliciting a definition of cultural stereotyping from the students [IV.1].
6. Teacher elicits cultural stereotypes of Americans, and organizes these on the blackboard under the headings "Positive" and "Negative" [II.4.].
7. Students discuss the possible harm of cultural stereotyping, and share some stereotypes held about their own cultures [IV.1.].
8. As a follow-up assignment, students are asked to bring in postcards from their country (alternately: postcards from the U.S.) and share further information [IV.5.]. Depending on class level and focus, they may be asked as well to write a brief paragraph defining cultural stereotypes [IV.4].

Sample Lesson 5: Radio Psychiatrist (phone-in broadcast taped off-air)[13]

Audience: High-intermediate to advanced international students enrolled in an intensive language institute or other visa program; advanced EFL students in the secondary or postsecondary context.

Teaching Objective: To expose students to authentic English; to help them gain insights into issues which concern Americans; to provide them with a forum for problem-solving activities.

Media: Advice column (Dear Abby, Ann Landers) on topic of audiotape (mounted on index cards); preprepared audiotape of phone-in radio psychiatrist show (possibly slightly edited).[14]

Skills: Reading, listening, speaking.

Time: 2–3 class periods (1 hour each).

Procedures:

1. Teacher introduces the lesson by asking students how people who are experiencing personal problems can get advice [I.4.]. What forums are available (e.g., advice columns, counselors, psychologists/psychiatrists)? Students are asked to name specific situations in which people might seek the advice of a psychiatrist.
2. The first half of the advice column is distributed to students, and topical vocabulary is discussed [II.1.].
3. In groups, students discuss the problem [III.3.c.] and write their "answer" to the person requesting advice [IV.4.]. They then share this with the class, and compare it with the actual answer written by the advice columnist [IV.1.].
4. In the subsequent class period, the teacher introduces the topic of radio talk-shows, and asks students what kinds of talk-shows they are familiar with [I.4.].
5. After a brief introduction to the topic of the taped phone-in call, students listen to the first half of the call—i.e., the caller's explanation of the problem. As necessary, difficult vocabulary is discussed [II.1.]. Depending on class level, the students may listen to this segment of the tape more than once, and may also work on answering prepared questions in groups [III.3.c.].
6. As in step 3 above, students are then asked to formulate their own answer to the predicament, and to predict the answer which the expert will give [IV.2.b.].
7. Students listen to the expert's advice (again, more than once if necessary), and subsequently discuss whether they feel this advice will be of assistance to the caller. They compare their own advice with that of the expert [IV.1.].
8. Optionally, on a third day, students can participate in a problem-solving [IV.2.b.] or role-play [IV.2.1.] activity, with situations prepared by the teacher. For each role-play, one student plays the role of the advice seeker, and one or more students can play the role of the advice giver.

Sample Lesson 6: People's Court (off-air videotape)[15]

Audience: High intermediate or advanced young adult or adult ESL students.

Teaching Objective: To increase listening comprehension in authentic situations and to introduce specialized vocabulary items; to provide a format for problem solving; to familiarize students with one aspect of the American judicial system.

Media: Videotape of "People's Court", a broadcast of actual small claims court proceedings, recorded off-air.

Skills: Listening, speaking, vocabulary, culture.

Time: 2 class periods (1 hour each).

Procedures:

1. The lesson is introduced by the teacher, who gives a brief introduction to the U.S. judicial system [I.], and explains the role of small claims court within this system [II.5.].
2. The program "People's Court" is explained, and relevant vocabulary (e.g., judge, plaintiff, defendant) is presented [II.1.]. Students are asked if they have ever watched this program, and are allowed to share their impressions of it [IV.5.].
3. Students view a selected case (broadcasts of "People's Court" typically consist of two cases) up to the point where the judge retires to make his decision. Class members consider the basic points of the case, judge the arguments of the plaintiff and defendant, and predict what the judge will decide [IV.2.b.].
4. Students then view the remainder of the tape, and compare their decision with that of the judge. They may wish at this point to suggest how the litigants could have improved their arguments, or discuss the testimony of the witnesses [IV.1.].
5. On a subsequent day, the teacher may present students with various situations which might be heard in small claims court (e.g., a dry cleaner who damaged someone's expensive dress, or a florist who delivered the wrong flowers to a wedding) and prepare the students for a role-play situation in which students take various roles (witnesses, plaintiff, defendant, bailiff, judge). Students are given time to practice the role-play prior to performing it [IV.2.a.].
6. Students perform the role-play, which is videotaped and then played back for feedback purposes. (If possible, the video products should be placed in a viewing facility so that students can review their performances outside of class.)
7. A follow-up to the video role-play can include an actual site visit [IV.6.] to a small claims court. (These visits should be scheduled in advance by the teacher; the courts are usually glad to accommodate.)
8. Following the field visit, a debriefing session is held, and students share their impressions [IV.1.].

CONCLUSION

As outlined above, instructional media come in an almost infinite variety of forms, and can play equally varied roles. The following are factors which should be considered when incorporating instructional media into our langauge teaching goals:

- Type of skill/concept to be presented.
- Student preference: the age, interests, expe-

riences, and learning style of the students concerned.

- Teacher preference: facility with equipment, familiarity/adroitness with the given medium, teaching style.
- Availability of software and hardware.
- Physical circumstances of the classroom/lab.

However, as Wright (1976, p. 65) notes, we should also keep in mind that "language teaching is a collective title for a variety of activities undertaken by different people in very different circumstances. There is consequently no single medium 'ideal for language teaching' as is so often claimed." Ultimately, availability and teacher creativity/adaptability will no doubt play the major role in determining to what extent media will be used, and which media will be selected.

In closing, I would like to encourage you to think creatively about ways to incorporate media into your language teaching endeavors, and to adhere to the following precepts: Use media materials when variety is called for, when they help you to reinforce the points you wish to make or serve as a contextualizer, when they expedite your teaching task and serve as a source of input, or when they help you to individualize instruction and appeal to the variety of cognitive styles in your classroom. But above all, use media to involve students more integrally in the learning process and make language learning a more authentic, meaningful process.

NOTES

1. This article replaces two articles in the 1979 edition of this text, "An Audiovisual Method for ESL" by James Heaton and "Language Teaching Aids" by Marianne Celce-Murcia. I am grateful to both authors for their ideas, from which I have borrowed liberally. I am also grateful to Marianne Celce-Murcia, Christine Holten, Linawati Sidarto, Mike Silverman, and Susan Ryan for their additional input on this article.

2. I refer here to the differentiation made by Richards and Rogers (1987a) among approach, design, and procedure, in which *approach* designates the underlying theories of language learning in a given methodology, *design*

refers to the form and function of the materials and activities used in the classroom, and *procedure* refers to the specific techniques employed.

3. It is strongly suggested that teachers share such materials, institute a materials library, and even collaborate in audiovisual materials preparation, since this can further ease the materials development burden and further increase the above-mentioned payoff.

4. See Edelhoff (1981) and Brinton, Snow, and Wesche (1989) for a discussion of such multiskills thematic units.

5. Far from exhaustive, this list is simply intended to give an idea of the range of media which are typically encountered in the second language classroom.

6. I use the term "authentic" here in its broad sense, to refer to materials which were *not* produced for language teaching purposes per se.

7. This framework is loosely adapted from a framework for using magazine pictures in the language classroom developed by McAlpin (1980).

8. These stages are based on Edelhoff (1981).

9. I have chosen here to highlight teacher-produced media lessons rather than commercial materials, since the latter are usually accompanied with teacher guidelines.

10. This idea was provided by Doug Beckwith, and is used with his permission.

11. This idea and the accompanying grid were provided by Jean Turner, and are used with her permission.

12. This idea was provided by Karen O'Neal, and is used with her permission.

13. This idea was provided by Wendy Saul and Atsuko Kato, and is used with their permission.

14. According to the guidelines established for off-air recording by nonprofit educational institutions, a broadcast program may be recorded off-air and retained by the educational institution for a period of up to 45 calendar days after the date of recording. Upon conclusion of this period, the off-air recording must be erased or destroyed (Penfield, 1987).

15. Used with the permission of Paula Van Gelder.

DISCUSSION QUESTIONS

1. Elsewhere in this volume, a number of language teaching methods (both traditional and innovative) have been discussed. At home, review these sections of the text and come prepared to discuss the role which media play in these methods. In which methods do you feel that media

play a central role (i.e., are part of the underlying approach of the method)? In which methods do media play a more peripheral role?

2. Examine the rationale for the use of media in language teaching given in this chapter. Which items in the list do you feel are the most convincing ones? Can you think of any others?

3. Select three items from the list of technical media and three items from those listed under non-technical media which you are likely to use in the language classroom. Draw up a list of the advantages and disadvantages of each. Can you think of specific teaching applications for these forms of media?

4. Is there a feasibility factor involved in the use of audiovisual media? In other words, are certain teachers or teaching situations limited to the types of media they can select? Why or why not?

SUGGESTED ACTIVITIES

1. Collect packaged food items which you have around your household, and design a survival-level grid activity similar to the one described in this article for over-the-counter medication. Keep in mind that the purpose of the grid is to provide students with guidance in selecting food items, and to train them in reading package labels for specific information.

2. Select a magazine picture or series of magazine pictures and apply the framework for designing media lessons discussed above. Bring this material to class and share with others your ideas on how you would use it. Be prepared as well to discuss your selection criteria.

3. Observe an ESL class. What was the objective of the lesson? What aids did the teacher use? Think of additional aids that would have improved the lesson.

4. Drawing on the suggestions given in the chapter by Skierso, develop a list of criteria for selecting and evaluating media materials.

SUGGESTIONS FOR FURTHER READING

The following sources contain a wealth of information for classroom teachers the use of instructional media for language teaching purposes:

Anderson, A., and T. Lynch (1988)
Listening. Oxford: Oxford University Press.

Allan, M. (1985)
Teaching English with Video. London: Longman.

Duncan, J. (1987)
Technology Assisted Teaching Techniques. Brattleboro, VT: Pro Lingua Associates.

Ely, P. (1984)
Bring the Lab Back to Life. Oxford: Pergamon Press.

Geddes, M., and G. Sturtridge, eds.
Practical Language Teaching, Volumes 1–8. London: George Allen & Unwin/Heinemann.

1. *Planning and Using the Blackboard* (1980). Mugglestone, P.
2. *Using the Magnetboard* (1980). Byrne, D.
3. *The Magazine Picture Library* (1980). McAlpin, J.
5. *Using Blackboard Drawing* (1980). Shaw, P., and de Vet, T.
6. *Photographic Slides in Language Teaching* (1981). Ayton, A., and Morgan, M.
7. *Video in the Language Classroom* (1982). Geddes, M., and Sturtridge, G.
8. *Using the Overhead Projector* (1982). Jones, J. R. H.

Holden, S., ed. (1978)
Visual Aids for Classroom Interaction. London: Modern English Publications.

Kamp, J. E., and D. C. Smellie (1989)
Planning, Producing, and Using Instructional Media, 6th ed. New York: Harper & Row.

Lonergan, J. (1984)
Video in Language Teaching. Cambridge: Cambridge University Press.

Penfield, J. (1987)
The Media: Catalysts for Communicative Language Learning. Reading, MA: Addison-Wesley.

Rixon, S. (1986)
Developing Listening Skills. London: Macmillan.

Tomalin, B. (1986)
Video, TV, and Radio in the English Class: An Introductory Guide. London: Macmillan.

Ur, P. (1984)
Teaching Listening Comprehension. Cambridge: Cambridge University Press.

Wright, A. (1976)
Visual Materials for the Language Teacher. London: Longman.

APPENDIX A

The materials listed below are useful teacher reference texts which contain additional suggestions for using instructional media to teach second languages.

Bassano, S., and M. A. Christison (1987)
Drawing Out. Hayward, CA: Alemany Press.

Bunn, C., and S. Seymour (1989)
Stepping Out: A Teacher's Book of Real-Life Situations. New York: Collier Macmillan.

Celce-Murcia, M., and S. Hilles (1988)
Techniques and Resources in Teaching Grammar. Oxford: Oxford University Press.

Ferrer, J., and P. Werner de Poleo (1983)
Bridge the Gap. Hayward, CA: Alemany Press.

Harmer, J. (1983)
The Practice of English Language Teaching. London: Longman.

Macdonald, M., and S. Rogers-Gordon (1984)
Action Plans: 80 Student-Centered Language Activities. New York: Newbury House.

Rinvolucri, M. (1984)
Grammar Games: Cognitive, Affective and Drama Activities for EFL Students. Cambridge: Cambridge University Press.

Sadow, S. A. (1982)
Idea Bank: Creative Activities for the Language Class. New York: Newbury House.

Wright, A. (1974)
1000 Pictures for Teachers to Copy. Reading, MA: Addison-Wesley.

APPENDIX B

The materials listed below are useful audiovisual packages which are commercially available for the teaching of English as a Second Language. This list is not intended to be an exhaustive one, but rather to give an idea of the range of materials available.

Alvarez-Martini, M. (1984)
The Rainbow Collection. Santillana.

Ashkenas, J. (1985)
Comics and Conversation: Using Humor to Elicit Conversation and Develop Vocabulary. Studio City, CA: Jag Publications.

Ballard, M. (1985)
The Magnetic Way into Language. Amherst, NY: Creative Edge.

Bunch, S., S. Cassidy, and K. Fisher (1983)
Teaching English Naturally (T.E.N.). Reading MA: Addison-Wesley.

Byrne, D. (1980)
First Book of Board Games. Hayward, CA: Alemany Press.

Chaille, D.
Picture Power Visuals. Bellflower, CA: Easy Aids.

Clark, R. C., ed. (1982)
Index Card Games for ESL. Brattleboro, VT: Pro Lingua Associates.

Educational Solutions
Silent Way Materials (Cuisenaire rods, sound-color charts, fidels, pictures, etc.). New York: Educational Solutions.

Ehrlichman, J. B. (1989)
Presto: A Language Learning Game. New York: Collier Macmillan.

Frauman-Prickel, M. (1985)
Action English Pictures. Hayward, CA: Alemany Press.

Fuchs, M. S. (1986)
Families: 10 Card Games for Language Learners. Brattleboro, VT: Pro Lingua Associates.

Hadfield, J. (1984)
Harrap's Communication Games: A Collection of Games and Activities for Elementary Students of English. Walton-on-Thames, Surrey: Nelson Harrap.

Hamel, P.
Picture Cards That Build Stories. Bellflower, CA: Easy Aids.

Jacot, Y. (1981)
See It—Say It. Reading, MA: Addison-Wesley.

Maley, A., and A. Duff (1975)
Sounds Interesting. Cambridge: Cambridge University Press.

Maley, A., and A. Duff (1979)
Sounds Intriguing. Cambridge: Cambridge University Press.

Maley, A., A. Duff, and F. Grellet (1980)
The Mind's Eye. Cambridge: Cambridge University Press.

Markstein, L., and D. Grunbaum (1981)
What's the Story: Sequential Photographs for Language Practice, Volumes I–IV. New York: Longman.

Moran, P. R. (1984)
Lexicarry: An Illustrated Vocabulary Builder for Second Language. Brattleboro, VT: Pro Lingua Associates.

Olsen, J. W.-B. (1984)
Look Again Pictures for Language Development and Life-skills. Hayward, CA: Alemany Press.

Palmer, A., and T. Rodgers (1985)
Back and Forth: Pair Activities. Hayward, CA: Alemany Press.

Silverson, S. K., M. Landa, and J. Smith (1983)
Speak Easy: English Through Video Mime Sketches. London: Longman.

Yedlin, J. (1981)
Double Action Picture Cards. Reading, MA: Addison-Wesley.

Computer-Assisted Language Learning

Richard Schreck and Janice Schreck

During the past decade the computer's use in educational settings has increased dramatically. Technological advances in both hardware (the physical equipment) and software (the programs of instructions that tell the computer what work to perform) continue to expand the capabilities that this powerful medium has to offer. Viewed as a new resource to help promote, enhance, and facilitate learning, the computer has fostered high expectations of more effective, more relevant, more motivating, and more innovative new learning experiences.

Yet the potential of computer-assisted instruction (CAI) in general, and of computer-assisted language learning (CALL) specifically, remains largely untapped and the expectations unfulfilled. At present, the major barrier to utilizing the full capabilities of this remarkable resource lies in the quality of available educational software. As in most other fields of education, the criticisms from CALL proponents and skeptics alike tend to focus on two distinct problems of courseware quality. One problem relates to internal quality: in a majority of currently available computer-delivered course materials, learners encounter inaccurate or incomplete content as well as frustrating operational difficulties. Some writers have estimated the prevalence of this unfortunate problem to be as high as 95 percent (Walker & Hess, 1984, p. 204). A second problem of quality relates to pedagogical relevance and integrity. In large measure, the types of learning experiences that current courseware most often provides appear to be those that are easiest to conceptualize and design, not necessarily those that would be most beneficial to the learner.

We believe that both of these problem areas can and will be remedied, but that the main impetus must come from within the field, primarily from teachers. Computers, after all, do not discriminate. They deliver both excellent and poor-quality courseware with equal and often embarrassing precision; they do exactly what they are told to do with the content and instructions that courseware designers give them. Realistically, very few teachers are likely to become extensively involved in designing CALL courseware themselves, but all teachers can and should have a participatory role in this evolving field. Rather than simply accepting whatever is available, ESOL professionals must be willing to (1) critically evaluate CALL courseware before incorporating it into their curricula, (2) elect to use only courseware that is instructionally sound and of the highest internal quality, and (3) demand more and better alternatives from courseware designers and publishers. We believe that during the 1990s the role that teachers are willing to play will have a profound impact on the future direction of CALL—on whether it becomes another costly and disappointing instructional gimmick or whether it begins to realize more and more of its truly unique potential.

This chapter first provides a brief introduction to selected computer-assisted language learning applications. Some are applications that educators are most likely to encounter because of current availability and widespread use; others are less widely available or currently undeveloped applications that we believe show great promise and that represent the type of application we hope will become more prevalent in the future. Second, we present some suggestions for evaluating CALL courseware. This is not meant to be an exhaustive discussion, for evaluation can take place on many levels. It is, however, intended as a starting point for educators who are considering incorporating any piece of courseware into their curriculum, and who want that courseware to provide a quality learning experience.

COMPUTER USES IN CALL

This discussion takes a broad view of computer applications in CALL. It includes applications in which the learning experience derives directly from the interaction between learner and computer. It also includes applications in which the computer, whether or not it is directly involved in the learning process, serves as a technical assistant (such as a word processor or a data manager) to either the learner or the instructor. Frequently, some of these direct and indirect applications are simultaneously integrated into a single computer-assisted learning situation.

In time, we expect that more of these computer functions will become more closely integrated with each other as well as with other technological resources, such as audio and video.

In reading through the following descriptions of computer applications it is important to keep in mind that, like all CAI, CALL is still in a very primitive stage. At present, costs or design constraints may prohibit the use of some of the following applications in many educational settings. In the future, however, many of these applications may seem startlingly naive. For such an evolving field, both in technology and in practice, we should certainly hope that this will be the case.

Interactive Tutorials

Computer-delivered tutorials are used primarily to introduce new information to the learner in a way that closely parallels how teachers and texts often present new instructional content. As in all other types of computer applications, the quality of the learning experience can vary widely from one piece of courseware to another. Poor-quality computer-delivered tutorials are often merely page-turning activities that force the learner into a passive role and that frequently rival the dullest, most pedantic presentations of more conventional media.

In contrast, high-quality tutorials actively engage the learner in a series of question-answer-feedback interactions that occur throughout an entire instructional presentation. Each question is intended to monitor the learner's understanding of the content, while each answer elicits appropriate and constructive feedback. As the learner progresses through the tutorial, related responses are often judged collectively, and these data are then used to determine further appropriate individualized activities—e.g., extra instruction in an area of difficulty, greater detail about a topic of interest, or the option to skip or review other segments of the tutorial.

In CALL/ESOL the tutorial format is especially well suited for individualized reading comprehension and study skills activities, particularly in special purpose content areas. As learners read through textual passages, the computer provides opportunities for numerous interactions, each incorporating constructive feedback. This allows learners to continuously monitor and adjust their own understandings of passages while they are reading.

For the future, we believe that it will eventually be possible for the tutorial's question-answer-feedback interactions to more closely resemble communicative dialog. In these dialogs the learner should be able not only to participate in but to initiate any of the computer–learner interactions and to ask for more information or clarification whenever desired.

Drill and Practice

Drill and practice exercises were among the earliest CALL applications and continue to account for a sizable proportion of available courseware. They also continue to generate a sizable proportion of the criticism directed at CALL. Historically, the reasons for their early appearance and widespread adoption arose from both machine and human limitations. On the one hand, even the earliest computers were very good at delivering this type of repetitious exercise; they needed very little memory to do so, thus the cost was not prohibitive. On the other hand, basic flashcardlike paired associate drill sequences were, and are, among the easiest to design and program, and in this simplistic format they required very little creative effort or imagination to produce or implement. Unfortunately, the majority of drill and practice applications in CALL have seldom transcended this level.

As their name implies, these exercises are intended to provide practice opportunities that help the learner become more proficient in recognizing, recalling, or applying information that has been previously introduced. It is not our intent to debate the relative pedagogical merits or drawbacks of drill and practice. There are many individuals, including learners themselves, who believe that practice is helpful in promoting certain aspects of language proficiency. For these people, quality computerized drill and practice sequences are capable of providing interactive individualized practice and constructive feedback that far surpass what the learner encounters in conventional workbook or flashcard activities. Courseware that permits instructors or learners to enter their own additional sets of practice items into a basic computerized drill routine may be especially useful. Learners who wish to practice forming irregular plurals or the simple past tense, for example, can proceed at their own pace through a designated set of items that, when mastered, can be replaced by a completely new set.

There is no reason, either, to assume that the mechanical computer routines that deliver drills of isolated words or phrases have not been or cannot be used in more meaningful and creative ways. Drill routines can and should provide practice for target words and phrases in context rather than only in isolation. Other CALL applications, such as games or simulations, frequently incorporate drill and practice routines, but these drills often go unnoticed because the entire presentation is interesting and motivating. Additionally, a wide variety of more communicative types of practice sequences are possible when audio and video capabilities are combined with these basic computer routines.

Simulations and Games

In general, a computer simulation or game presents a model of a real or imaginary situation in which the learner plays an active role in determining the situation's outcome. Such activities provide opportunities to learn a variety of procedures or problem-solving strategies and, additionally, how to apply them appropriately to produce desired results in different situations. As a simulation progresses, the situation changes in response to whatever courses of action the learner chooses to take. Choices usually are not designated as either right or wrong; they simply produce consequences. As in real life, the consequences of choosing a particular course of action may or may not be immediately apparent. Repeating the simulation making different choices may produce entirely different results. Sometimes the learner has the opportunity to define certain parameters, to select a particular role, or to set a specific level of challenge or difficulty. Simulations and games may involve only the learner and the computer, or they may include several participants, each with a particular role and set of choices.

Simulations are often incorporated in professional training activities in fields such as business and medicine. Learners can observe the probable consequences of various marketing or diagnostic decisions without the risk of causing the bankruptcy of an actual company or of endangering a real patient's life. The specific content of such simulations make them ideal for direct application in CALL/ESP.

A popular phenomenon among some CALL/ESOL professionals has been the attempt to use non-ESOL commercially sold computer games to encourage language practice. While the motivational characteristic of games has always been a major factor in using them as a vehicle for instruction, this feature cannot always be assumed. Many games are genuinely boring and provide far less opportunity or incentive for language practice than other vehicles clearly labeled instructional. In addition to being truly motivating, any game that has real value for CALL/ESOL should require the learner to use English rather than to manipulate nonlinguistic icons and should contain vocabulary that the learner will be able to use in real-life situations.

One of the concomitant benefits of simulations and games for CALL is their ability to facilitate group discussions among participants. As is the case with any well-focused activity, a group of learners may derive tremendous incentive to communicate among themselves if they are attempting to play a particularly motivating game or to solve an especially challenging problem.

Text-Building Applications

Text-building computer applications encompass a wide variety of learner–computer interactions in which the learner's primary role involves changing, reconstructing, or creating text. As English proficiency increases, greater emphasis can be placed on creating text. The best text-building applications incorporate both integrative and communicative features, requiring the learner to apply several types of linguistic knowledge concurrently and to understand, at least partially, the meaning of the text. The computer's capabilities allow a wide latitude in both the type and the amount of text manipulation that is possible. Becoming increasingly available is courseware that allows both the instructor and the learner to supply their own text and to choose the types of manipulations that will provide the most educationally appropriate individualized learning experiences.

Text Modification. In CALL text modification activities, the learner might punctuate text, change the tenses of verbs, rearrange random sentences into a coherent paragraph, or edit writing samples. Conventional editing on paper usually produces distracting marks and copy that is difficult to read unless completely rewritten. When the computer's word-processing capabilities are used instead, text modifications occur instantly with little effort; thus, the learner is free to focus attention more fully on textual meaning rather than on keeping track of isolated changes and rearrangements.

Text Reconstruction. These CALL applications most commonly appear in a modified cloze format and are most often associated with reading comprehension teaching or testing activities. Typically, an intact paragraph is displayed for a brief period of time, then every Nth word disappears and the learner fills in the resulting blank spaces. Quality courseware allows either the learner or the instructor to supply new passages and to make appropriate variations in the length of time the text is displayed, the number of words to be deleted, or the type of assistance (e.g., the first letter of a missing word) that the learner might receive. In other applications, the computer might delete larger or even complete portions of text that the learner would then have to recreate. Alternatively, a process of rational deletion may remove each word that belongs to a specific lexical category—e.g., prepositions or articles—so that learners can practice applying these items in context.

Text Generation. In text generation applications, it is the learner who produces the text. Traditional writing exercises are often greatly facilitated when the computer is used as a word-processing assistant. As suggested above, word processors provide better control over the mechanics of producing and printing text. Learners can be encouraged to experiment and to edit their own writing samples, because mechanical changes in text can be accomplished so quickly and easily. Usually the visual appearance of the final printed copy is additionally reinforcing. Some CALL labs maintain only word-processing software and serve exclusively as resource centers where learners produce and edit their own writing samples.

Another text generation CALL application takes advantage of the computer's message-delivery capability. Using electronic mail or electronic bulletin boards, learners can communicate among themselves, with instructors, or potentially with anyone else in the world who is linked to the same computer network. The texts of these messages are usually informal and, although perhaps initially written as part of a classroom exercise, they generally become increasingly spontaneous as learners become more accustomed to the ease with which they can send and receive information. The use of communicative messages can transfer to a wide variety of situations and take many different forms—e.g., a request for assistance from an instructor, a brief dialog among several individuals about a particular topic, or a problem-solving dialog that may continue over a period of several days or weeks. A particular advantage of this CALL application is that the instructor, as a communicative participant in the computerized message system, has the opportunity to model correct English usage and to provide immediate constructive feedback about the learner's linguistic output, all within the context of the communicative dialog itself. Also, the computer can maintain a file of all messages, thus preserving a complete longitudinal record of the learner's communicative linguistic output. This can serve not only as a basis for future learning experiences but for demonstrating growth in several areas of English proficiency over time.

Artificial Intelligence Applications

Efforts in the field of artificial intelligence (AI) are today still directed primarily at creating, rather than applying, sophisticated programs that will allow the computer to "understand" and interact with humans in ways that may be nearly indistinguishable from the ways that humans who are endowed with common sense and adaptability interact with each other. Although it may be some time before we can begin to try applying this technology in most educational settings, intelligent computer-assisted language learning (ICALL) holds such promise to so many CALL professionals that a brief mention is in order. ICALL applications will most likely arise primarily from two components of AI systems—natural language processing and student modeling.

In the field of computational linguistics, computer models are used to explore the structures of knowledge and the organization of processes that produce human language (see Winograd, 1983). If endowed with natural language-processing ability, a computer would be able to engage in conversations with learners just as a human might. It could also serve as a complete resource from which learners could request whatever information they wished about specific aspects of the language—e.g., regularities in forming plurals.

In the area of student modeling, computer models attempt to create the best possible learning experiences by incorporating the most desirable attributes of a human instructor and the unique background and problem-solving strategies of the individual learner (see Gable & Page, 1980). In general, the computer selects tasks for the learner, monitors the learner's attempts to carry out these tasks, uses this information to build a complex model of the learner, then uses this model to select further experiences or to suggest other problem-solving strategies that are appropriate for the learner. This model building is an ongoing process; as the learner's abilities and problem-solving strategies change, so too does the model.

The potential ICALL applications that may eventually derive from these two areas seem nearly limitless. Some features of AI are already incorporated in a very limited way in some CAI materials. Yet at this writing, access to more complete AI systems remains largely restricted due to the prohibitively high costs of both development and application.

Multimedia Applications

Many of the learning experiences mentioned in this chapter might be enhanced or expanded, or completely new experiences created, when the computer's capabilities are used in concert with other instructional media. As technology increases in both sophistication and affordability, interactive audio and video capabilities will most likely become standard features of basic computer systems. At the present time, however, combining the computer with relevant audio or video features usually involves either very expensive peripheral equipment or a simple noninteractive or not-very-interactive pairing with audio- or videocassettes.

As costs decrease, better interactive multimedia applications should become available. Interactive video is already a reality, albeit an expensive one. It features both sound and visual images, and is often used to produce very realistic simulations. Interactive audio, which can recognize, analyze, and manipulate the learner's speech as well as produce synthetic spoken feedback is still in its most rudimentary developmental stages. In the meantime, valid learning experiences may derive from less complex, more readily available audio capabilities. Speech from cassettes or audiodiskettes may be linked to computer programs, alone or in conjunction with textual or visual displays, to produce listening, speaking, and comprehension activities (see Wyatt, 1984, pp. 73–92). Also, the computer's voice-recognition capabilities may assist in isolating, monitoring, and modifying individual speech characteristics. For example, when the learner vocally produces a sentence, the computer can visually display a graph of the learner's rising and falling pitch along with a graph of the same sentence produced by a native speaker. The learner can compare the two and repeat the sentence with altered pitch until both graphs match (Loritz, 1984). During the past two decades, one of the major criticisms of most language laboratory activities has been their emphasis on practice without feedback (e.g., R. Allen, 1968, p. 59; Reed, 1970, pp. 25–28; Underwood, 1984, pp. 35–36). Incorporating the computer's feedback capabilities into many of these activities could permit far more instructionally valuable learning experiences to emerge.

Assessment, Data Collection, and Analysis

Computers are remarkably efficient at collecting information about a learner's performance, storing it, and later retrieving it in usable forms. For many years, computers have been used in formal language-testing situations to generate items, to score tests, and to analyze both individual and group performance usually for the purpose of assigning a learner to a specified achievement or proficiency level. Computers are additionally capable of administering tests or quizzes directly, thus eliminating the need for printed copies.

In educational settings the most familiar type of assessment, whether delivered in print or by computer, attempts to determine the learner's knowledge or proficiency in a particular area either before instruction begins or after instruction has ended. Far more difficult to accomplish, and therefore less typical, is assessment that attempts to determine what progress or difficulties might be occurring *during* the learning process. In this area the computer's capabilities can make an enormous contribution. Essentially, every single response the learner enters into the computer during instruction is a potential source of data. From these data the computer can isolate and analyze various aspects of the learner's daily performance to pinpoint specific areas of both progress and difficulty. A detailed error analysis, for example, may isolate a specific problem, offer the learner a selection of remedial interventions, and then analyze the chosen intervention's effectiveness in correcting the problem; adjustments can continue throughout the learning process whenever the performance data indicate. Learners also could be taught how to interpret their own data and to monitor their own progress so they can participate more fully in tailoring instruction to meet their own needs.

In addition to enhancing individualization of learning, assessment that occurs during the learning process may provide a significant corollary benefit. The cumulative body of data collected over time from many individual learners should begin to provide us with more substantive information about language and learning. The computer's capacity for data collection and analysis should allow us to track the process of language acquisition as it occurs. It should also allow us to better test our assumptions about how best to facilitate acquisition of another language—about which types of learning experiences are helpful and which are hindering, under what conditions, and for which learners. In essence, it should enable us to become much better teachers.

CALL COURSEWARE EVALUATION

The decision to incorporate CALL into the ESOL curriculum must also include a serious commitment to courseware evaluation. In the preceding descriptions of CALL applications, it is apparent that learning experiences delivered by computer differ in some significant ways from those delivered by conventional modes of instruction. Most of these differences relate in varying degrees to the dynamics of the interaction between the learner and the computer. It is primarily the nature of this learner–computer interaction, in conjunction with valid concerns about the present quality of most available courseware, that necessitates a much more thorough evaluation than is ordinarily required for traditional instructional programs and materials.

In comparison to conventional classroom instruction, computer delivery is far more learner-directed. It is the learner who initiates, continues, and ends an instructional sequence and who determines the pace and often the direction in which to proceed. Usually, the learner's attention is more directly focused on the instructional material because the computer requires more frequent responses and provides more immediate feedback than do typical classroom presentations. However, these self-directed and interactive characteristics of computer-delivered instruction function within parameters that are predetermined both by the courseware designer's input and by the computer's limitations. The computer lacks the abilities of a human instructor, for instance, who can interpret facial expressions that indicate confusion or distress, or who can clarify and explain poorly presented segments of otherwise acceptable material whenever the need arises.

In fact, few other modes of instruction are as self-contained and thus as potentially frustrating if the learning experiences they provide are of poor quality. The intent of CALL courseware evaluation is to ensure that the learner encounters not only relevant, accurate, and well-presented content but also the smoothest possible interactions with the computer. Courseware evaluation should attempt to determine quality in courseware content, instructional presentation, the interaction between the computer and the learner, and the relevance to learner and curricular goals and objectives.

We recommend a three-phase evaluation strategy. Using this strategy, the instructor/evaluator should be prepared to examine a single piece of courseware in three separate phases, each from a completely different perspective. In Phase 1 the evaluator should assume the role of subject matter expert—one who is knowledgeable about the courseware's content as well as about principles of learning and instruction. From this perspective, the first evaluation phase focuses entirely on the content's quality and on whether it is organized and presented in an instructionally sound manner. In Phase 2 the evaluator assumes the role of a learner, paying particular attention to the courseware's mechanical and aesthetic features and to the influence these features might have on the entire learning experience. Phase 3 requires the evaluator to resume the role of instructor or curriculum manager to examine the courseware's usefulness in meeting learners' needs and in fulfilling appropriate functions within the entire curriculum.

In conducting this type of evaluation, it is usually necessary to complete several passes through the courseware. The number of passes may vary widely from one piece of courseware to another, ranging from as few as 2 for a very simple program to 10 or more for those of greater complexity. Of course, poor quality is often immediately evident, and since the intent of the evaluation is to screen out this material, there is no need to proceed further once major flaws become apparent. In general, an initial pass should provide an overall view of content and organization. Subsequent passes allow more in-depth examination of specific areas.

Phase 1: Evaluating Content and Instructional Presentation

In most respects, the process of evaluating instructional content and presentation is no different for computer-delivered courseware than for material delivered via any other instructional medium. Goals and objectives should be clearly stated and should serve as useful, relevant guidelines to the instructional content. The content itself should be accurate, complete, and nontrivial. It should be arranged in meaningful, logical segments with appropriate emphasis on the most relevant or important information. It should be presented at an appropriate level of reading proficiency, learning difficulty, English proficiency, and cultural awareness. Principles of learning and instruction should be appropriately incorporated to facilitate content acquisition and mastery.

In addition to these standard evaluation concerns, there are several areas that require a more detailed analysis when instructional materials are delivered by computer. These areas include instructions, questions, learner responses, and feedback.

Instructions. In most cases, once a learner begins a computer session there should be no need for additional explanations or interpretations from a human instructor. The courseware should provide directions, instructions, and extra "HELP" displays that are clear, concise, and written at a level of difficulty no greater than that of the main content. Occasionally this information appears in a separate printed manual. Regardless of where it is presented, the evaluator should ensure that all information the learner will need to independently complete a computer session is accurate and complete.

Questions. Questions or prompts for learner responses should be frequent enough to ensure active, continued learner involvement. They should elicit learner input that focuses on the content the learner is expected to practice, acquire, or master rather than on trivial details. In addition to the content that a response is expected to contain, the requisite format that each response must take should be absolutely clear to the learner. Even with two simple choices—"1. Yes or 2. No"—the acceptable response format typically would be only one of several possibilities—e.g., the numeral "1" or "2," the letter "Y" or "N," or the word "yes" or "no." The learner should not have to guess which of these is required.

Answer Judging. The courseware must direct the computer to accept all reasonable responses. In traditional classroom instruction the human instructor can usually judge the accuracy of alternative answers on the spot without any advance planning. The breadth of the human knowledge and language base makes this possible. The computer's knowledge base, however, is only as extensive as the information humans select to give it in advance. With this limitation in knowledge and, as yet, natural language capability, courseware must be designed to anticipate in advance a variety of valid, alternative learner responses. For example, if the answer to a question is "Abraham Lincoln," then acceptable alternatives should include "Lincoln," "Abe Lincoln," "A. Lincoln," "President Lincoln," "His name was Abraham Lincoln," and (unless spelling or typing is one of the instructional objectives) "Licnoln." Good courseware often contains an internal check for misspelled words. In such cases the computer might respond to "Lincoln" with feedback such as "I think you have the correct answer, but please check your spelling" or "Did you want to type 'Licnoln' or 'Lincoln'?" Clearly, anticipating all acceptable alternatives is time-consuming and difficult. Thus, courseware designers frequently resort to restricting answer choices, often by asking only multiple-choice or true-false types of questions. As in conventional classroom instruction, there is generally a trade-off between the ease of answer judging on the one hand and, on the other, both the degree of relevancy in the questions and the extent of knowledge that the learner must demonstrate. Higher-quality courseware favors the latter.

In evaluating answer-judging capabilities it is important to determine how the courseware treats a range of different responses, from acceptable to partially acceptable to unacceptable. During the evaluation process, this will involve entering several different responses for each question or prompt. Although this procedure is quite time-consuming, it is extremely important. Answer judging must be accurate to ensure that specific responses produce the results intended in every interaction between the learner and the computer.

Feedback. Hand in hand with answer judging goes feedback. This, too, requires from courseware designers careful, advance planning. Each separate learner–computer interaction remains incomplete without feedback; some type of feedback must occur even if only to acknowledge that the computer received the learner's input. Feedback can take many forms, such as a simple movement of the cursor to the next line of text, movement to a selected segment of courseware, a printed message directly related to the learner's input, or an elaborate animated display following completion of a particularly difficult task.

One of the primary instructional advantages of the computer is its ability to provide feedback immediately after each response from the learner. Quality courseware maximizes this advantage by also incorporating other essential features of good feedback: It should be appropriate to the learner and the instructional task, it should relate directly to the learner's response, it should be easy for the learner to recognize and understand, and it should elicit from the learner a positive or neutral reaction rather than a negative one.

Equally important, good feedback must be informative and constructive. In addition to information about whether or not a response is accurate, the learner will want to know what it is, specifically, about the response that is accurate or inaccurate. If inaccurate, the learner should receive information about how to adjust or correct the response. Quality feedback provides different information, either in amount or in kind, each time the learner repeats an error. Thus, the learner receives new pieces of information to try to resolve the problem independently. Too frequently, however, courseware merely repeats the same feedback over and over a fixed number of times, then tells the learner the correct response. This not only creates frustration but also teaches an extraordinarily poor problem-solving strategy. It creates the expectation that if one guesses or presses random keys long enough, the correct response will eventually appear without any cognitive effort whatsoever. In contrast, constructive feedback that requires a continued effort to try to resolve difficulties is an outstanding means of fostering problem-solving strategies among learners.

Phase 2: Evaluating the Smoothness of the Learning Experience

There are a number of factors to consider in examining the smoothness of the learner's interaction with computer-delivered instruction. Most people think immediately of the obvious human–computer hardware interface. Clearly, some computers are more difficult to use than others. So too, learners and instructors will have varying degrees of expertise with the system available. Most often, however, human–machine difficulties can be overcome with a concise orientation for those who have had little or no experience with a particular system.

Far more important than the human–machine interaction is the learner's interaction with the courseware. The learning that takes place and the ultimate results of instruc-

tion are often influenced at a very basic level by extraneous courseware features, both mechanical and aesthetic. These features, viewed from the learner's perspective, are the focus of the second evaluation phase. In this review, the evaluator should be mindful of the learner's current level of skills and knowledge while looking for any features in the courseware presentation that might interrupt the flow of instruction or that might divert the learner's attention and thus interfere with the learning process.

Mechanical Features. Ideally, the learner should have access to several standard mechanical features for smooth progress through any piece of courseware. Such features serve the learner best when they are the most inconspicuous. In evaluating these features from the learner's perspective, note whether any of the mechanics involved in progressing through the courseware are likely to distract or impede the learner. Even slight distractions are undesirable; the learner's concentration should be directed solely to the instructional content, not to manipulating the mechanics that provide it.

All instructions about how to proceed through the courseware should be easily accessible or clearly displayed. There should also be consistency in key usage, kinds of responses, and forms of assistance and feedback. A learner should never have to guess which key to press or what type of response is required to proceed in a desired direction.

Key presses that perform specific duties are least distracting when they are simple and either typical of most computer programs or have a logical link to the function they perform. A [RETURN] or [NEXT] key that moves the learner to the next screen display is simple, familiar, and reasonable. A [HELP] or [H] key that brings a display of additional aid or hints onto the screen also meets these criteria. An [ESCAPE]-[X]-[3] keypress sequence for the ''HELP'' function, however, would be unfamiliar and cumbersome; further, it almost ensures that the learner will have to stop, try to remember it, look it up, or perhaps choose to forego any "HELP" displays altogether. A thorough evaluation requires that all designated keys be pressed to ensure that they operate as the instructions indicate. It is also extremely important to press a selection of supposedly inactive keys or various key sequences to be certain that they do not lead to unwanted displays or to program errors. This is a tedious but very necessary component of the evaluation process.

One primary advantage of CALL is its potential for individualization. At a very mechanical level, partial realization of this potential begins when learners are allowed maximum control over the pace, manner, and direction of their progress through the courseware. Ideally, learners should be able to move around in much the same fashion as they might in a book. They should be able to proceed both forward and backward, to branch to instructional segments according to their own preference, to retrieve menus, instructions, or additional assistance at any time, and to end an instructional sequence prior to completion. To determine the amount of learner control, the evaluator should simulate different strategies that potential learners might wish to use. For example, a learner might wait an exceptionally long time on various screen displays; if the computer program erases the screen and presents a new display without any input from the learner, then the principle of self-pacing is negated. Equally important is the courseware's allowance for skimming rapidly through the displays. If learners will be using the same courseware during several sessions, they should have the option to skip over familiar material such as displays of initial instructions.

Notable exceptions with respect to learner control occur in testing situations where it would be reasonable to restrict factors such as the amount of time allotted or to allow no choice but to complete the test in one session. In most instances, however, the learner should be allowed to skim an entire test, to change answers during the test, and to complete test items or segments in any order. These are all standard features of conventional paper-and-pencil quizzes or examinations yet are unfortunately lacking in many computer-delivered testing situations.

Aesthetic Features. To an instructor who is already familiar with the instructional content being presented, many surface features may seem to be little more than mere aesthetics, and the temptation is to view these as unimportant or a matter of personal taste. In fact, the more familiar we are with the basic content being presented, the more easily we sometimes become enamored with novelties and gimmick-laden presentations. Such a subjective approach misses the point that any evaluation of surface features must take place from the learner's perspective. What momentarily lifts away an instructor's boredom with a particular topic may be exactly what serves to disrupt the learner who is still struggling to understand or master it. Numerous examples exist of instruction that is faultless in content yet in presentation is so filled with instances of computerized cleverness that the learner is easily distracted, confused, or frustrated and finds it difficult to distinguish between the content that is relevant and the extraneous details that are not.

There are several aesthetic features commonly encountered in screen displays. None are inherently good or bad; none inherently enhance or detract. It is their use, judicious or otherwise, that gives them these qualities within any particular piece of courseware. Color, for example, may be used to highlight specific vocabulary items whenever they appear in context on a screen display. This seems to be an appropriate means of directing attention to the most important, most instructionally relevant areas of the screen. If different colors are deliberately assigned to different word groupings (e.g., yellow for adjectives, green for adverbs) and the distinction between these groups (adjectives vs. adverbs) is what the learner is attempting to master, this again seems an appropriate use of color. However, if colors are used to highlight relevant words but are assigned randomly and for the sole purpose of producing a more "interesting" screen display, then the use of color may not be merely irrelevant but may prove unnecessarily distracting to the learner. When a second or third color is introduced, the learner may justifiably conclude that there is an instructionally related reason for this when, in fact, there is none. Whether the learner spends a few seconds or several minutes to determine if there is a relevant instructional link, the addition of color merely for interest serves as a distractor, momentary or otherwise.

Similarly, surface features such as borders, underlining, boldface, or alternative type styles may unobtrusively assist the learner by identifying key pieces of information. The same features, used inconsistently, too frequently, or all at the same time, may produce a confusing or cluttered effect that proves unnecessarily distracting.

Of all of the aesthetic surface features, graphics and animation are the most frequently overused. Their appearance is often irrelevant to the information on the screen display and, although sometimes clever, they are often too clever, too cute, too juvenile, or too culturally biased. When used to provide or accompany feedback—e.g., a fireworks display for every correct answer—the novelty effect wears off almost immediately and the feedback becomes disgustingly patronizing. Adult learners may quietly tolerate such displays, but young children are often quite vocal in their resentment and may simply refuse to proceed. Additionally frustrating on many computer systems is the time it takes a graphic or an animated feature to appear on the screen. "Drawn" figures or lettering nearly always take longer to appear on the screen than do ordinary printed letters. Often the entire screen goes blank or all progress becomes frozen for a period of time while waiting for a completed figure to appear. Sometimes the entire process of drawing, shading, and lettering is visible; while this may actually prove interesting once or twice, particularly with complex drawings, by their third or fourth appearance even the finest, most relevant graphics turn into tedious and disruptive time lags. Quality courseware either does not contain these or provides an escape for the learner who wishes to proceed more rapidly, usually by allowing a simple keypress that will preempt the graphic and move the learner to the next step without interruption. A common assumption among novice courseware evaluators is that color, graphics, animation, or other novel devices must be present for CALL to be truly state of the art. In fact, some of the finest available courseware provides high-quality learning experiences solely via monochromatic displays and conventionally printed text.

Textual display, of course, also has its aesthetic component. Too much text on any single screen display is often difficult to read or remember. Indeed, a screen that is entirely filled with text looks not only cluttered but also overwhelming. Text should be centered, well spaced, or blocked into segments of meaningfully related content and activities. As mentioned previously, boldface and drawn letters may take significantly longer to appear on the screen than printed letters; consequently, such features might be better used to highlight spelling or vocabulary words on which the learner would be expected to pause momentarily than to set off titles or paragraph headings, which the learner would be expected to skim. Grammar, punctuation, spelling, and typographical errors seem almost too obvious to mention, yet their occurrence is frequent enough to warrant the conclusion that proofreading standards for computer screen displays still do not match those for conventional print media. Such blatant errors rightly or wrongly lead to assumptions of questionable instructional content. Additionally, even error-free text can have a significant impact on the learning experience. Depending on the form in which it appears, the same text may convey very different impressions to the learner. Even in conventional print, the words "no," "No," and "NO" connote degrees of meaning that may range from nonjudgmental disagreement to potentially harsh disapproval.

When combined with the computer's interactive nature, such text becomes extremely personal. As part of a feedback message, for example, learners frequently interpret "NO" as a shouted personal criticism. It is extremely important, then, that the form of the text agrees totally with the meaning it intends to convey.

Phase 3: Evaluating the Courseware's Value in the Curriculum

To be of real value, courseware that has reasonably met the concerns addressed in the first two phases of the evaluation must ultimately serve a useful purpose in the ESOL curriculum. In Phase 3 the evaluator, in the role of instructor or curriculum manager, should attempt to determine the likelihood that this will be the case.

Instructional intent, methodology, and any ancillary functions the courseware could potentially provide should already be clear from the information gained in Phase 1. Further, since the evaluation has progressed to this final phase, the evaluator has already ascertained that the courseware, in a general context, could accomplish its stated purposes reasonably well. At this point there are two remaining concerns: (1) the courseware's value in relation to the specific context in which it will be used, and (2) the courseware's value in relation to alternative means of instruction that purport to serve the same purposes.

The first concern may be addressed by estimating the degree to which the courseware meets the necessary criteria imposed by the evaluator's own instructional setting. Obvious considerations in selecting any instructional materials always include the degree to which they can meet specific learner needs as well as specific curricular goals and objectives. Other typical considerations, which may assume greater importance when the delivery system is the computer, include relative costs in proportion to instructional benefits, the requisite degree of access to essential physical equipment, and the amount of instructor or learner expertise necessary for successful implementation.

The second, equally important, concern may be addressed by comparing the courseware to other instructional materials, especially to those that are already in use in the instructional setting whether they are delivered by computer or, more likely, by traditional modes of instruction. The evaluator should consider all purposes or functions, both explicit and implicit, that the courseware ultimately will serve if it is adopted. For each of these, the courseware should be ranked among all other available materials and modes of instruction that might serve the same purpose.

To treat these two concerns, we suggest an approach that combines rating as well as ranking in a single procedure. This method uses a separate continuum (see Figure 1) for each purpose the courseware is expected to serve. The evaluator estimates the courseware's value with respect to a particular purpose, then places the courseware, along with all other means of instruction that could reasonably serve the same purpose, at various points along this continuum. It is often useful to enlist other colleagues who also work in the same instructional setting to independently perform these estimates as well. In general, because the courseware has passed through the first two evaluation phases, the evaluator should expect it to fall within the "adequate" to "excellent" range on nearly every continuum. However, it should also become evident how beneficial the courseware may be in comparison to other means of instruction.

When all of this information is combined, and all concerns unique to the specific instructional environment are accorded their appropriate weightings, the evaluator should be able to arrive at a reasonable judgment

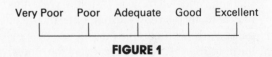

FIGURE 1

about the courseware's value. If adopted, follow-up evaluations will be necessary to ensure that any initial assessment of merit is, in fact, supported by actual application in various learning situations. The continuing need for comparative reviews will also be important as new alternatives become available.

DISCUSSION QUESTIONS

1. ESOL professionals have reacted to CALL with widely divergent responses ranging from unquestioning enthusiasm and adoption to total opposition and rejection. What accounts for such disparate attitudes?

2. What contributions can ESOL teachers make to the field of CALL? In what ways could these contributions affect the future of CALL? In what ways could they affect the future of ESOL?

3. In what ways does high-quality computer-delivered instruction differ from conventional classroom instruction of comparable quality? Describe two or three instructional activities that might best be delivered by computer; by a human instructor; by a textbook. For each activity, what are the characteristics that make it best suited for delivery via a particular instructional mode?

4. What factors contribute to poor internal quality of courseware? What features of a computer program might actually interfere with a student's learning? Which of these might also present problems in conventional classroom instruction?

5. What factors contribute to good internal quality of courseware? Which of these also apply to conventional classroom instruction?

SUGGESTED ACTIVITIES

1. From the point of view of the learner, make a pass through a piece of CALL courseware you have never used before. Was it clear and easy to use? Were there technical problems? If so, how many and what kind? Was the content presented in an interesting, creative way? Does the courseware merit further evaluation? For what instructional purposes?

2. Describe an ESOL setting in which you have taught or expect to teach. Would it be possible to use CALL in this setting? Would some use of CALL be fruitful? If so, for what purposes?

3. Interview ESOL students who have used CALL courseware. Summarize their reactions to CALL as a component of their curriculum. What problems have they encountered? In what ways do they believe that CALL has facilitated their language learning?

4. Interview a director of a computer lab or teachers who have used CALL courseware with their students. What problems have they encountered in incorporating CALL into their ESOL curricula? What contributions do they believe CALL has made to their students' learning? To their overall curricular goals and objectives?

SUGGESTIONS FOR FURTHER READING

Alessi, S. M., and S. R. Trollip (1985)
Computer-Based Instruction: Methods and Development. Englewood Cliffs, NJ: Prentice-Hall.

> A general text that includes thorough descriptions, accompanied by numerous examples, of computer applications in education. Includes particularly detailed chapters for people interested in designing and developing their own courseware.

Dalgish, G. (1985)
Current ESL Software. On Line: *TESOL Newsletter, 19* (1, 2, 3).

> A review that identifies shortcomings of specific ESL courseware packages. Although the courseware mentioned is now somewhat dated, this article infers desirable features of ESL courseware in general. Continuing evaluative updates of ESL courseware appear periodically in the On Line column of the *TESOL Newsletter,* as well as in the *CALICO Journal.*

Daum, D. A. (1988)
CALL in the ESL Curriculum. Calgary, Alberta: Canadian Center for Learning Systems.

> One of the more recent and selective annotated bibliographies of CALL books, articles, and courseware reviews. A good source for a beginning search of current CALL courseware.

Dunkel, P. (ed.) (1991).
Computer-assisted Language Learning and Testing: Research Issues and Practice. New York: Newbury House.

Higgins, J., and T. Johns (1984)
Computers in Language Learning. Reading, MA: Addison-Wesley.

Includes good discussion of various computer uses in ESOL with specific examples of creative courseware activities.

Pennington, M. C. (1989)
Teaching Languages with Computers: The State of the Art. LaJolla, CA: Athelstan.

Steinberg, E. R. (1984)
Teaching Computers to Teach. Hillsdale, NJ: Erlbaum.

For those who wish to design and develop their own courseware. Written with appropriate emphasis on principles of learning and instruction rather than on the intricacies of programming computer code.

Underwood, J. (1984)
Linguistics, Computers, and the Language Teacher: A Communicative Approach. New York: Newbury House.

Excellent discussion of CALL from the perspective of communicative language teaching.

Wyatt, D. H. (1984)
Computers and ESL. Orlando, FL: Harcourt Brace Jovanovich.

A thorough and clear introduction to computer applications in ESOL. Descriptions of practical CALL/ESOL activities are organized into useful categories of reading, writing, listening, speaking, and grammar.

Second Language Testing[1]

Andrew D. Cohen

INTRODUCTION

Testing is perhaps one of the more misunderstood areas of language teaching and learning. Students and teachers alike cringe when they hear the word "testing." Students see tests as a threat to their competence, because they are afraid that they will not perform well on them. Teachers often do not like to construct tests, and are not altogether satisfied with their results when they do. They are also suspicious of the standardized, professionally designed tests because they do not understand what these tests are really trying to measure. These attitudes are usually based on experience. In a survey of EFL teachers and students in Israeli public schools, Shohamy (1985) found a variety of misuses of tests, of which the following are just a sampling:

- Tests were used as punishment—e.g., because no one did the homework.
- Tests were administered instead of giving instruction.
- The tests were the exclusive measure for grading.
- Tests did not reflect what was taught.
- The tests were returned with a lack of corrections or explanations.
- The tests reflected only one testing method.
- There was a lack of teacher confidence in their own tests.
- The students were not adequately trained to take the tests.
- There was a substantial delay in the returning of the tests.

Given the above list, it is no wonder that both students and teachers alike are suspicious of tests. Fortunately, in the past few years, there has been a growing interest in improving the situation. The wave of interest in communicative language teaching, for example, has stimulated a parallel interest in more innovative and sensitive measures of speaking ability (see, e.g., Shohamy, 1988).

A more constructive view of language testing exists when (a) testing is seen as an opportunity for interaction between teacher and student, (b) students are judged on the basis of the knowledge they have, (c) the tests are intended to help students improve their skills, (d) the criteria for success on the test are clear to the students, (e) students receive a grade for their performance on a set of tests representing different testing methods (not just one), (f) the test-takers are trained in how to take tests—especially those involving unfamiliar formats, (g) the tests are returned promptly, and (h) the results are discussed (Shohamy, 1985).

This chapter will consider some key issues in language test construction. It is intended to better equip the ESL teacher both to understand and scrutinize tests prepared by others and to design their own tests such that they and their students will be satisfied. Beginning with a theoretical framework for types of tests and types of items, this chapter should help teachers determine just what kind of test they are constructing or reviewing, as well as give them insights into the types of items that are involved. What follows next is a discussion of approaches to testing reading comprehension. A discussion of approaches to testing the other skills—listening, speaking, and writing—is given in the appendix to this chapter. The chapter concludes with a discussion of test construction issues and test-taking strategies.

THEORETICAL FOUNDATIONS

Types of Tests

In order to properly construct or assess a test, it is helpful to have some explicit notion of what the test is testing and how it might be labeled. One way of referring to tests is according to those that deal with prediction of a student's performance, "prognosis," and those that assess the current level of accomplishments, "evaluation of attainment" (Clark, 1972). Prognostic tests include aptitude tests, which assume no prior study, and placement tests, which assume some prior study, however little. Tests of attainment include achievement tests, which assess the student's performance in a given course, and general proficiency tests, which assess a student's skill for real-life purposes.

Another more elaborate way to describe tests is according to their primary function—i.e., for administrative, instructional, or research purposes (Jacobs et al., 1981). In fact, the same test could conceivably be used for 12 different purposes: 5 administrative purposes (assessment, placement, exemption, certification, promotion), 4 instructional purposes (diagnosis, evidence of progress, feedback to the respondent, evaluation of teaching or curriculum), and 3 research purposes (evaluation, experimentation, knowledge about language learning and language use). The average test is not intended to be used for more than several purposes, and the major split is often between *proficiency* tests intended for administrative purposes and *achievement* tests for assessment of instructional results.

Current innovations in testing, however, would suggest that the same test could possibly merge these two different sets of purposes under certain circumstances—i.e., if assumptions of design and use are met. In other words, it is being suggested that tests used to differentiate people according to general level of ability and tests used for certifying the attainment of content be combined in one test (Henning, 1985). It is argued that by merging proficiency and achievement tests in this way, placement can be more in line with what is taught, passing from one level of instruction to the next can be contingent on actual learning, and the curriculum can be more sensitive to individual differences among students at every level.

Another distinction in testing is made between norm-referenced and criterion-referenced assessment. A test can be used, for example, to compare a respondent with other respondents, whether locally (e.g., in a class), regionally, or nationally. Classroom, regional, or national norms[2] may be established to interpret just how one student compares with another. A test can also be used to see whether a respondent has met certain instructional objectives or criteria, hence the term "criterion-referenced" assessment.

The work done by Canale and Swain (1980) in defining communicative competence has provided another set of criteria for describing tests. Tests are seen as tapping one or more of the four components making up the construct of communicative competence—namely, grammatical, discourse, sociolinguistic, and strategic competence. Grammatical competence encompasses "knowledge of lexical items and of rules of morphology, syntax, sentence-grammar semantics, and phonology" (Canale & Swain, 1980, p. 29). Discourse competence reflects the ability to connect sentences in stretches of discourse and to form a meaningful whole out of a series of utterances. While grammatical competence concerns itself with sentence-level grammar, discourse competence focuses on intersentential relationships. Sociolinguistic competence involves knowledge of the sociocultural rules of language and of discourse. Strategic competence refers to "the verbal and nonverbal communication strategies that may be called into action to compensate for breakdowns in communication due to performance variables or due to insufficient competence" (Canale & Swain, 1980, p. 30).

Classifying an Item

Tests usually consist of a series of items. An item is a specific task to perform, and can test one or more points or objectives. For example, an item may test *one* point, such as the meaning of a given vocabulary word, or *several* points, such as an item which tests the ability to obtain facts from a passage and then make inferences based on these facts. Likewise, a given objective may be tested by a series of items. For example, there could be five items all testing one grammatical point, say, tag questions. Items of a similar kind may also be grouped together to form *subtests* within a given test.

The Skill Tested

The language skills that we test include listening and reading, the more receptive skills on a continuum, and speaking and writing, the more productive skills. Nonverbal skills can be both receptive (e.g., interpreting someone else's gestures) and productive (making one's own gestures).

The Nature of the Item

Items can be more discrete or more integrative in nature, just as they can be more objective or subjective. A completely discrete-point item would test simply one point or objective, while an integrative item would test more than one point or objective at a time. Sometimes an integrative item is really more a procedure than an item, as in the case of a free composition which could test a number of objectives.

The objectivity of an item refers to the way it is scored. A multiple-choice item, for example, is objective in that there is only one right answer. A free composition may be more subjective in nature if the scorer is not looking for any one right answer, but rather for a series of factors, including, say, creativity, style, cohesion and coherence, grammar, and mechanics.

The Intellectual Operation Required

Items may call for different levels of intellectual operation (Valette, 1969, after Bloom et al., 1956). They can test for the following intellectual levels: (a) knowledge (bringing to mind the appropriate material); (b) comprehension (understanding the basic meaning of the material); (c) application (applying the knowledge of the elements of language and comprehension to how they interrelate in the production of a correct oral or written message); (d) analysis (breaking down a message into its constituent parts in order to make explicit the relationships between ideas, including tasks like recognizing the connotative meanings of words and correctly processing a dictation, and making inferences); (e) synthesis (arranging parts so as to produce a pattern not clearly there before, such as in effectively organizing ideas in a written composition); and (f) evaluation (making quantitative and qualitative judgments about material). It is thought that these levels demand increasingly greater cognitive control as one moves from knowledge to evaluation. It may be that effective operation at more advanced levels, such as synthesis and evaluation, would call for more advanced control of the second language.

The Tested Response Behavior

Items can test different response behavior. Respondents may be tested for fluency, for example, without concern for grammatical correctness. Or they could be told that the concern is for accuracy with respect to phonological or grammatical correctness. Some items may call for a speedy response to determine how effectively the respondent replies under time pressure.

Characteristics of Respondents

Items can be designed specifically to cater to populations with certain characteristics. For example, items may be written differently for different age groups (e.g., preschoolers, children, adolescents, adults; see Kennedy, 1972), for different socioeconomic levels, and for different ethnic or language groups (e.g., English-language items for Native Americans—or even more specifically for native speakers of Navajo). Both intentional and unintentional cultural bias has been iden-

tified in the way tests are designed and administered (see, e.g., Brière, 1973; Deyhle, 1987; Messick & Anderson, 1974).

Item Stimulus Format

The format for the item stimulus has to be determined. An item can have a spoken, written, or visual stimulus, as well as any combination of the three. A tester should be aware that a listening test in which respondents answer oral questions by means of written multiple-choice responses is testing reading as well as listening.[3]

Item Response Format

The item response format can be fixed, structured, or open-ended. Those with a fixed format include true/false, multiple-choice, and matching items. Those which call for a structured format include ordering (where, say, respondents are requested to arrange words to make a sentence, and several orders are possible), duplication—both written (e.g., dictation) and oral (e.g., recitation, repetition, mimicry), identification (e.g., explaining the part of speech of a form), and completion. Those calling for an open-ended format include composition—both written (e.g., creative fiction, expository essays) and oral (e.g., a speech)—as well as other activities, such as free oral response in role-playing situations.

Elements of Language to be Tested

Finally, as noted above with reference to communicative competence, items can test for grammatical, discourse, and sociolinguistic competence, as well as for whatever strategic competence respondents draw on when they lack the required competence. "Grammatical competence," here, includes phonology, morphology, syntax, knowledge of lexical items and semantics (Canale & Swain, 1980:29), as well as matters of mechanics (spelling, punctuation, capitalization, and handwriting).

TESTING LANGUAGE SKILLS

When the first version of this chapter appeared in 1979, the emphasis was largely on the testing of discrete language items. During the intervening years, greater emphasis has been put on more global assessment of language. The following discussion of reading assessment is intended to reflect more current thinking about testing. The appendix contains examples of approaches to testing other skills.

METHODS OF TESTING READING COMPREHENSION

Reading comprehension items or procedures require of learners that they use a certain type or types of reading, comprehend at a certain level or combination of levels of meaning, enlist a certain comprehension skill or skills, and do all of this within the framework of a certain testing method or methods. In this section, we will look at some of the choices available to the test constructor and considerations of concern to the test user.

Type of Reading

Items and procedures can be written so that they implicitly or explicitly call for a given type of reading. For example, a respondent can be given a lengthy passage to read in a limited time frame such that the only way to handle it successfully is to skim[4] or to scan,[5] depending on the task. A distinction is also made between scanning and "search reading," where in the latter case the respondent is scanning without being sure about the form that the information will take (i.e., whether it is a word, phrase, sentence, passage, or whatever) (Pugh, 1978, p. 53). A respondent could also be given a passage to read receptively.[6] Yet another approach is to have respondents read responsively, such that the written material acts as a prompt to them to reflect on some point or other and then possibly to respond in writing. Testing formats in which questions are interspersed within running text

may especially cater to such an approach, if the questions stimulate an active dialog between the text and the reader.

The type of reading task is raised here because it would appear to be neglected at times in the process of test construction. In other words, reading items and tasks are sometimes constructed without careful consideration as to how the respondent is to read them. It may even be of benefit for the test constructor to indicate explicitly to the respondent the type of reading expected. For example, a certain item could be introduced by the following:

Read the following text through rapidly (i.e., skim it) in order to get the main points. There will not be time to read the text intensively. When you have completed this reading, answer the questions provided—without looking back at the text. You will have 10 minutes for the exercise.

Level of Meaning

A test item or procedure can tap comprehension at one of four levels of meaning or at several levels simultaneously: grammatical meaning, propositional meaning, discoursal meaning, and writer's intent (adapted from Nuttall, 1982). Note, however, that these categories are presented as a rough rule of thumb, rather than as a hierarchy of discrete levels. *Grammatical meaning* deals with the meanings that words and morphemes have on their own. *Propositional meaning* refers to the meaning that a clause or sentence can have on its own—i.e., the information that the clause or sentence transmits. This meaning is also referred to as its "informational value." *Discoursal meaning* relates to the meaning a sentence can have only when in context. This meaning is also referred to as its "functional value." *Writer's intent* concerns the meaning that a sentence has only as part of the interaction between writer and reader. This is the meaning that reflects the writer's feelings and attitudes, and the intended effect of the utterance upon the reader.

The level of meaning that has perhaps gotten the most attention in the literature in recent years is the discoursal one, especially the perception of rhetorical functions conveyed by text. For example, an item may overtly or covertly require a respondent to identify where and how something is being defined, classified, exemplified, or contrasted with something else. Often such "discourse functions" are signaled by connectors or "discourse markers." Nonetheless, uninformed or unalert readers may miss these signals—words or phrases such as "unless," "however," "thus," "whereas," and the like. Research has shown that such markers need not be subtle to cause reading problems. Simple markers of sequential points ("first," "also," and "finally") may be missed by a reader as well as more subtle markers (see Cohen, Glasman, Rosenbaum-Cohen, Ferrara, & Fine, 1979).

Actually, a level that is worthy of more attention by teachers and other test constructors is that of writer's intent—especially author's tone. It would appear that nonnative respondents are slow to perceive humor, for example. Some years ago, when I was responsible for the English-as-a-Second-Language Placement Test at the University of California at Los Angeles, it included a humorous passage about the man who turns to the lady sitting next to him at a fancy banquet and informs her that he thinks the current speaker has nothing to say and should sit down. She asks if he knows who she is. When he says "no," she informs him that she is the speaker's wife. Then he asks her if she knows who he is. When she says "no," he says, "Good!" and gets up and leaves. The passage had a multiple-choice item inquiring whether the text was serious, sad, humorous, or cynical. Most of the 700 respondents responded that it was serious. This example would suggest that respondents may not be operating at the pragmatic level when they perform certain tasks on tests.

Comprehension Skill

A test constructor and user must be aware not only of levels of comprehension but also of individual skills tested by reading comprehension questions at one or more such levels of meaning. There are numerous taxonomies of such skills. Alderson (1987) offers one which reflects a compilation of others, and includes (1) the ability to recognize words and phrases of similar and opposing meaning, (2) the identifying or locating of information, (3) the discriminating of elements or features within context; the analysis of elements within a structure and of the relationship among them—e.g., causal, sequential, chronological, hierarchical, (4) the interpreting of complex ideas, actions, events, relationships, (5) inferencing—the deriving of conclusions and predicting the continuation, (6) synthesis, and (7) evaluation. We note that this taxonomy omits the reader–writer relationship—e.g., the author's distance from the text and the level of participation in the text that the author requires of the reader. With this taxonomy, as with others, the boundaries between skills are assumed to be discrete when, in reality, they may not be.

Testing Method

Besides considering the type of reading to be performed, the desired levels of meaning, and the comprehension skills to be tapped, the test constructor or user needs to give careful thought to the testing method. The challenge is to maximize the measurement of the trait—i.e., the respondent's ability, while minimizing the reactive effects of the method. In order to do this, it is useful to be informed as to the options for testing with each method and what these options yield. We will look at some of the innovative methods for testing reading—the cloze and the C-test, computerized adaptive testing, and communicative tests of reading comprehension. The testing of summarization skills is referred to in the appendix.

The Cloze and the C-Test

The origins of the cloze test date back farther than many would think—to 1897, in fact. At that time, Ebbinghaus proposed a series of tests that had one- or two-word deletions, rational deletion, and partial deletion from the beginning or end of words (Ebbinghaus, 1897). There is a controversy concerning the cloze test as to whether filling in cloze items is not just a matter of perceiving local redundancy but, rather, involves an awareness of the flow of discourse across sentences and paragraphs, as Oller (1979, chap. 12) maintains. Whereas recent research would suggest that traditional fixed-word deletion is more of a microlevel completion test (a measure of word- and sentence-level reading ability) than a macrolevel measure of skill at understanding connected discourse (Alderson, 1983; Klein-Braley, 1981), Chávez-Oller, Chihara, Weaver, and Oller (1985) have recently come out with yet another claim that cloze is sensitive to constraints *beyond* 5 to 11 words on either side of a blank, based on a reanalysis of earlier data.

As an alternative to the fixed-word deletion, researchers have turned to the rational deletion cloze, whereby words are deleted according to predetermined, primarily linguistic criteria—often stressing the area considered to be underrepresented, namely, macrolevel discourse links (Levenston, Nir, & Blum-Kulka, 1984). Research by Bachman (1985) with EFL university students found that the rational deletion approach sampled much more across sentence boundaries and somewhat more across clause boundaries within the same sentence than did the fixed-ratio cloze. He concluded that the rational deletion cloze was a better measure of the reading of connected discourse, but that the question still remains as to whether such tests "in fact measure the components of language proficiency hypothesized by the deletion criteria" (Bachman, 1985:550)—i.e., the flow of discourse across sentences and paragraphs within a text. Thus, the controversy continues.

A suggested alternative to the cloze test —namely, the C-test—has been proposed by Klein-Braley and Raatz (Klein-Braley, 1981; Klein-Braley & Raatz, 1984; Raatz, 1985; Raatz & Klein-Braley, 1982). In this proce-

dure, the second half of every other word is deleted, leaving the first and the last sentence of the passage intact. A given C-test consists of a number of short passages (maximum 100 words) on a variety of topics. This alternative eliminates certain problems associated with cloze, such as choice of deletion rate and starting point, representational sampling of different language elements in the passage, and the inadvertent assessment of written production as well as reading. With the C-test, being given a clue (half the word) serves as a stimulus for respondents to find the other half. The following is one passage within a C-test (from Raatz, 1985):

Pollution is one of the big problems in the world today. Towns a _____ cities a _____ growing, indu _____ is gro _____, and t _____ population o _____ the wo _____ is gro _____. Almost every _____ causes poll _____ in so _____ way o _____ another. T _____ air i _____ filled wi _____ fumes fr _____ factories a _____ vehicles, a _____ there i _____ noise fr _____ airplanes a _____ machines. Riv _____, lakes a _____ seas a _____ polluted b _____ factories and by sewage from our homes.

At present it would appear that the C-test may well be a more reliable and valid means of assessing what the cloze test assesses, but as suggested above, it is still not clear to what extent the C-test tests more than microlevel processing. Because half the word is given, students who do not understand the macro-context may still be able to mobilize their vocabulary skills adequately to fill in the appropriate discourse connector without indulging in higher-level processing.

Computerized Adaptive Testing (CAT)

Computerized adaptive testing (CAT) of reading comprehension implies an approach to testing whereby the selection and sequence of items depends on the pattern of success and failure experienced by the respondent. Most commonly, if the respondent succeeds on a given item, one of greater difficulty is presented, and if the respondent experiences failure, then an easier item is presented. The testing continues until sufficient information has been gathered to assess the particular respondent's ability. At present, such tests are mostly limited to objective formats, such as multiple-choice. CAT is known to be more efficient and more accurate than conventional fixed-length tests employing multiple-choice items (Tung, 1986).

Among the advantages of CAT are the following: Individual testing time may be reduced, frustration and fatigue are minimized, boredom is reduced, test scores and diagnostic feedback may be provided immediately, test security may be enhanced (since it is unlikely that two respondents would receive the same items in the same sequence), record-keeping functions are improved, and information is readily available for research purposes (Alderson, 1987; Larson & Madsen, 1985; Madsen, 1986; Meagher, 1987).

The main disadvantage is that CAT presumes that one major language factor or underlying trait is being measured at a time. Such a prerequisite runs counter to the existing theories of reading comprehension, which encompass multiple dimensions, such as world knowledge, language and cultural background, type of text, and reading styles (Canale, 1986b). The line of development that Canale would propose for CAT is that it move from simply mechanizing existing product-oriented reading comprehension item types to the inclusion of more process-oriented, interactive tasks that can be integrated into broad and thematically coherent language use/learning activities, such as "intelligent tutoring systems."[7]

Communicative Tests of Reading Comprehension

For years attention has been paid to so-called communicative tests—usually implying tests dealing with speaking. More recently, efforts have been made to design truly communicative tests of other language skills as well, such as reading comprehension. Canale (1984) pointed out that a good test is not just one which is valid, reliable, and practical in terms of test administration and scoring, but rather one that is acceptable—i.e., accepted as fair, important, and interesting by test-takers and test-users.[8] Also, a good test has feedback potential—rewarding both test-takers and test-users with clear, rich, relevant, and generalizable information. Canale suggests that acceptability and feedback potential have often been accorded low priority, thus explaining the curious phenomenon of multiple-choice tests claiming to assess oral interaction skills.

Some recent approaches to communicative testing were in part an outgrowth of Canale and Swain's theoretical framework presented above (Canale & Swain, 1980). The particular variety of communicative test that they dealt with has been referred to as a "storyline" test, a test with a line of development. In such a test, there is a common theme running throughout in order to assess context effects. The basis for such an approach is that the respondents learn as they read on, that they double back and check previous content, and that the ability to use language in conversation or writing depends in large measure on the skill of picking up information from past discussion and using it in formulating new strategies (Low, 1986).

Swain (1984), for example, developed a storyline test of French as a foreign language for high school French immersion students. The test consisted of six tasks around a common theme, "finding summer employment." There were four writing tasks (a letter, a note, a composition, and a technical exercise) and two speaking tasks (a group discussion and a job interview). The test was designed so that the topic would be motivating to the students and so that there would be enough new information provided in order to give the tasks credibility. Swain provided the respondents with sufficient time, suggestions as to how to do the test, and clear knowledge about what was being tested. There was access to dictionaries and other reference material, and opportunity to review and revise their work. Swain's main concern was to "bias for best" in the construction of the test—to make every effort to support the respondents in doing their best on the test.[9]

Brill (1986), for example, had 32 ninth-grade Hebrew speakers complete a communicative storyline test which included five tasks dealing with membership in a youth group. The tasks included writing a letter as a response to a friend interested in a youth movement the respondent belonged to, presenting questions to the group leader to get more information on the movement, preparing an announcement about the movement to post on bulletin boards, writing out a telephone request for information on how a local foundation could aid the movement, and writing out a telephone response to an invitation by a political group to join a demonstration of theirs. After completing the tasks, the students were then asked to compare their experience on this test and on the traditional multiple-choice one they had taken previously. They almost unanimously endorsed the communicative test as preferable because it was more creative, allowed them to express their opinions, was more interesting, taught them how to make contact with others, and investigated communication skills in addition to reading comprehension. For these reasons, they felt that it provided a truer measure of their competence than did the traditional test.

Canale (1985) viewed communicative tests such as that described above as "proficiency-oriented achievement tests" and offered five reasons supporting this view:

1. Such tests put to use what is learned. There is a transfer from controlled training to real performance.
2. There is a focus on the message and the function, not just on the form.
3. There is group collaboration as well as individual work, not just the latter.
4. The respondents are called upon to use their resourcefulness in resolving authen-

tic problems in language use as opposed to accuracy in resolving contrived problems at the linguistic level.
5. The testing itself is more like learning, and the learners are more involved in the assessment.

For sample items testing listening, speaking, and writing, see the appendix.

TEST CONSTRUCTION AND ADMINISTRATION

Inventory of Objectives

Test constructors first make an inventory of the objectives that they want to test. This involves distinguishing broad objectives from more specific ones. Important objectives are distinguished from trivial ones. Test items and procedures are then developed to assess these objectives separately or along with other objectives. Varying the type of items or procedures testing a particular objective, as well as their difficulty, helps distinguish one student's grasp of the area covered by the objectives from that of another student. As said at the outset, there is currently a premium being put on the use of multiple testing techniques in order to obtain a more representative sampling of a learner's language behavior.

The number of test items or procedures used to measure any given objective depends on several things. First, is the test intended to assess *mastery* of the objectives or simply some attainment? If mastery is being assessed, there should be a large enough sample of items to allow measurement of this. For example, including only one item on tag questions is unlikely to indicate to the testers that the respondent has a firm grasp of tag questions. But if the testers do not have the testing time to allow for, say, three items on tag questions, then they should at least be aware that they are not really testing for mastery. A respondent's correct answer on one item could be a result of guessing. Testers usually do not have the time to cover all the objectives they would like to, so instead they must satisfy themselves with a sampling of these behaviors.

If the test is designed for use in a course, then the objectives covered might be those most emphasized in the course and those of greatest utility value for the students as well. As mentioned at the outset, testers may need to resist the temptation to include difficult items of marginal importance simply because they differentiate between the better and poorer achievers.

Constructing an Item Bank

It is suggested that potential test items and procedures be selected and stored in an item bank. Before the advent of computer applications and sophisticated statistical procedures for processing items, test constructors would keep file cards of items. The use of computers allows for more rapid and more efficient handling of those kinds of items that lend themselves to computer applications. Whether computerized or not, an item bank would benefit from descriptive information on each item or procedure, such as the following:

1. The skill or combination of skills tested.
2. The language element(s) involved.
3. The item stimulus and item response formats.
4. Instructions as to how to give the item.
5. The section of the book or part of the course that the item relates to (if applicable).
6. The time it took to write the item (which gives an estimate of the time needed to prepare a series of such items for a test).

It is presumed that any item entered in the bank has been piloted on sample groups and reviewed. An item may seem easy or well written when it is generated but may exhibit glaring inadequacies upon later inspection.

Test Format

One basic issue of format is whether the test progresses to increasingly more difficult items or whether easy and difficult items and procedures are interspersed. There are arguments on both sides. If items get increasingly more difficult, the respondents may give up after a while and not attempt items after they encounter the first one that stumps them. Yet if respondents experience failure too frequently at the outset of a test because of difficult items, they may be discouraged from attempting the remainder of the items in a section. Thus, there may be a psychological advantage to pacing the items so that they become progressively more difficult. A compromise is to start the test with relatively easy items and then start interspersing easy and difficult items.

Another issue of format relates to multiple-choice items. Such items lend themselves to guessing. Increasing the number of alternatives (from, say, three to four) decreases the likelihood of getting the item right by chance alone. There is a 33 percent chance of getting a three-choice item right by guessing, and a 25 percent chance of guessing correctly on a four-choice item. This of course assumes that all choices are equally attractive to the respondent who does not know the answer to the item. This condition is not always met.

Instructions

The instructions should be brief and yet explicit and unambiguous. Examples may help, but may well hinder if they do not give the whole picture and yet become for the respondents a substitute for reading the instructions. Respondents may need training in how to take a particular kind of test. The respondents should be informed as to whether guessing incorrectly counts against them. They should also know the value of each item and section of the test. Finally, the time allowed for each subtest and/or for the total test should be announced. If speed is a factor for a subtest, the respondents should be made aware of this. Harris (1969), for example, discourages timed tests that leave more than 10 to 15 percent of the group behind.

Scoring

If an objective is tested by more than one item—say, five items—then it is possible to speak of mastery of the objective, at least according to that means of measuring it. (Again, the importance of using multiple measures of the same objectives is stressed.) If Juan gets four of the five items right, he has displayed 80 percent mastery of that objective, according to the test. The test may have a series of such items. If Juan's test performance is stated only in terms of his mastery of objectives, then the test is being used for criterion-referenced evaluation. What constitutes mastery of an objective is a difficult question to answer. Is it having four out of five items correct on that objective? What about three out of five? Further, what constitutes notable achievement? It could be that mastery of a certain objective reflects far more learning than mastery of another. For this reason, items covering one objective may be weighted more than items covering other objectives. For example, three questions asked after presentation of a lecture on a tape may count more than 10 short-answer multiple-choice reading or grammar items. Weighting also involves consideration of the ease of the task and the time spent on it.

The test constructor has to consider how long it will take to score particular types of items, as well as the easiest procedure for scoring (e.g., automated scoring by an optical scanner or a computer scoring vs. hand scoring). The more objective the scoring is for a particular item, the higher the scorer reliability is likely to be (i.e., the likelihood that two different scorers would come up with the same score for a particular respondent's test). For example, the scoring of a multiple-choice test would be considered more objective than that of an essay test, where the scorer's subjectivity would be expected to play more of a role.

Reliability

The reliability of a test concerns its precision as a measuring instrument. Reliability asks whether a test given to the same respondents a second time would yield the same results. At least three crucial factors relating to test reliability have been identified (Brière & Brown, 1971):

Test Factors. Such factors are types of items, content of each item, length of the total test (the longer, the more reliable). Harris (1969) provides an easy-to-calculate measure for estimating the reliability of a test based on the number of items, the mean, and the standard deviation (an index of variability). Formulas for more sophisticated measures are found in Henning (1987, pp. 80–85). Such measures call for correlating the odd-numbered items on the test with the even-numbered ones as a measure of interitem consistency. Other measures of internal consistency, such as Kuder-Richardson Formulas 20 and 21, call for more complex calculations. For most purposes, a reliability coefficient of 0.75 and up is good. A perfect coefficient is 1.0. Lado (1964, p. 332) offers different reliability coefficients for tests of different skills. For example, he suggests that in general terms acceptable reliability for a speaking test may be lower (0.70 to 0.79) than for a listening test (0.80 to 0.89) than for a reading test (0.90 to 0.99).

Situational Factors. The manner in which the examiner presents the instructions, the characteristics of the room (comfort, lighting, acoustics), outside noises, and other factors can have a bearing on how well the respondents perform on the test.

Individual Factors. These include (a) transient factors—such as the physical and psychological state of mind of the respondent (motivation, rapport with examiner), and

(b) stable factors—such as mechanical skill, IQ, ability to use English, experience with such tests.

Validity

Validity refers to whether the test actually measures what it purports to measure. Thus, the test must be reliable before it can be valid. Assuming that the test is producing a reliable measure of something, the question is then "What is that something?" and "Is it what the test is supposed to be measuring?"

Face Validity. This aspect of validity refers to whether the test *looks* as if it is measuring what it is supposed to measure. For this reason, Low (1985) refers to it as "perceived validity." For example, a test which measures a respondent's own English pronunciation by assessing the respondent's rating of another's pronunciation of English may not be readily accepted as a valid measure, nor may filling in blanks on a cloze test in order to assess reading skill. Such measures may appear to be too indirect. The fact that they are indirect may confuse and distract the respondent. Also, a test's title may be misleading. For example, a test entitled "Pragmatic Syntax Measure" may deal more with morphology than with syntax and may use stilted grammar-book English rather than the language of everyday situational interactions, as a pragmatic measure would be expected to.

Content Validity. This type of validity refers to the adequacy of sampling of content or objectives in a test. Sometimes even commercial tests constructed by experts fail to state what objectives are being covered in the test and which items specifically are testing each of these objectives. Valette (1977, p. 46) notes, "For the language teacher, the degree of test validity is not derived from a statistical analysis of test performance, but from a meticulous analysis of the content of each item and of the test as a whole."

Criterion-Related Validity. A test can be validated by seeing how closely respondents' performance on specific sets of objectives on a total test parallels their performance on another test which is thought to measure the same or similar activities.

1. *Concurrent Validity:* Validation is concurrent if test results are compared with results from another test given at about the same time. For example, a teacher may wish to see how student performance on a test that he or she constructs compares with student performance on some criterion measure of reading obtained from a commercial test of reading.
2. *Predictive Validity:* Validity is predictive if test results are compared with results from another test or another type of measure obtained at a later date. For example, a language aptitude test may be validated by a test of a student's achievement in the language class in which the student was placed on the basis of the aptitude test.

Construct Validity. This form of validity refers to the degree to which scores on a measure permit inferences about underlying traits. In other words, it examines whether the test is a true reflection of the theory of the trait being measured, in this case, language. As Shohamy (1985, p. 74) puts it, "the teacher should keep asking himself whenever he constructs a test, whether the tasks and items on the test are actually a reflection of what it means to know a language and to avoid those items which test something different than actual language knowledge."

Convergent Validity. Validity in testing a given construct, such as listening comprehension, may be attained by testing the same phenomenon in a variety of different ways. The classroom teacher can practice this kind of validation. The discussion of item types presented earlier in this chapter (and in the appendix) provides a number of techniques for testing the same objectives differently. Varying the item stimulus and response formats, as well as the discreteness and integrativeness of the items, can produce items testing the same objectives in different ways.

Item Analysis

Piloting the Test. If time and resources permit, a test should be piloted on a population similar to that for which it is designed. The pilot administration provides the test constructor with feedback on the items and procedures. On timed subtests, pilot respondents can be instructed to mark how far they got when the time ran out and then to go ahead and complete the test so that there is feedback on all the items in the test.

Item Difficulty. Item difficulty refers to the proportion of correct responses to a test item. A test which aims to differentiate among respondents should have items which, say, 60 to 80 percent of the respondents answer correctly. (If 15 out of 20 respondents answer an item correctly, the item difficulty is 75 percent.) If the purposes of the test is to determine whether nearly all students have achieved the objectives of, say, a course, then the item difficulty should be 90 percent or better.

Item Discrimination. The item discrimination index tells how well an item performs in separating the better students from the poorer ones. The index is intended to distinguish respondents who know the most or have the skills or abilities being tested from those who do not. Knowledge of the material is determined by the respondent's performance on the *total* test (i.e., all subtests combined).

An item discrimination level of .30 or above is generally agreed to be desirable. One way to calculate item discrimination is to distinguish the top 25 percent of the test papers and the bottom 25 percent (Harris, 1969). For example, if there are 20 papers, the top 5 and the bottom 5 are identified. These are labeled the "high" and the "low" groups, respectively. The others are called

"middle." There are three steps in the calculation. First, for any given item, the responses of the high and low groups are tabulated as "correct" or "incorrect." For example:

	No. of Respondents	Correct	Incorrect
High	5	4	1
Middle	(10)	(4)	(6)
Low	5	2	3

Second, the number of "lows" who answered correctly is subtracted from the number of "highs" who answered correctly. Third, the difference (here 2) is divided by the number of papers in the high or low groups (here 5). The result is the item discrimination coefficient (here, $2/5 = 0.40$). If there is an uneven number of papers in the high and low groups (e.g., 6 and 5), then the average (5.5) is used for calculations.

Another way to calculate item discrimination is by means of a point-biserial correlation, a measure of an item's reliability (Clark, 1972). A correlation is made between all respondents' performance on a given item (a dichotomous variable—right or wrong) and their performance on some more general criterion, usually scores on the test as a whole (a continuous variable). The higher the point-biserial correlation for a given item, the more the respondents getting a particular item right are also those who perform best on the total test (or other criterion measure). A correlation coefficient of .30 or better would make the item acceptable with respect to discrimination.

In-Class Item Analysis. The teacher can calculate item difficulty and discrimination for a test in class with the students' help (Valette, 1977, pp. 63–64). For item difficulty, the students can switch papers and then raise their hands if the item the teacher announces is incorrectly answered on the test they are correcting. The teacher keeps a tally. Obtaining item discrimination is more complex. The teacher must divide the papers into a high and a low stack (with or without a middle group) and then must ask for a show of hands from each group as to the number who got a particular item correct. The item discrimination coefficient is then calculated by means of the computational steps enumerated above.

Test Revision

If an item has a difficulty coefficient of lower than 60 percent or higher than 80 percent or so, and if the discrimination coefficient is below .30, then the item should probably be revised or eliminated. It is difficult to select or reject borderline items. Especially if the item analysis is performed on a small sample, only one or two responses will change the index considerably. There may be good justification for leaving an overly easy item in the test if, for example, it is a lead-off item used to give students encouragement to continue. Also, *where* an item appears in a test may effect performance on it. For example, students may do best on the items in the *middle* of an exam, after they have warmed up to the test and before fatigue sets in.

Multiple-choice items can be improved by examining the percent of respondents who selected each choice. If some distractors draw no responses or too many, then they should be omitted or altered. This task requires both rigor and intuition. For instance, it may be necessary to change the syntax or vocabulary of a distractor, or perhaps its semantic thrust. In piloting the test, it is possible to ask the respondents what their rationale was for choosing a particular distractor instead of the correct answer.

Ideally, the results of item analysis would be added to the information available on each item in the test constructor's item bank, if one has been established. If a particular test item comes under challenge by respondents or other examiners, it is useful to be able to check the item analysis information on the item. Perhaps it will turn out to be a borderline item that should probably not have been included in the test.

Test Administration Checklist

The following checklist of administration tips applies primarily to the administering of classroom tests and is intended as suggestive, not prescriptive. The "should"s of test administration will vary according to the testing situation:

- The room should have adequate ventilation or heat, light, and acoustics.
- If a tape recorder is to be used, it should be set up and tested in advance to make sure that it works well.
- The test administrator should assume an affable but stern posture. A few smiles help to put the respondents at ease but the sternness is necessary to make it clear that cheating is not allowed—unless cooperative effort among respondents is an integral part of the particular test or a portion of it.
- The time that the exam begins and the total time remaining for the test and/or subtests should be written on the blackboard.
- If the instructions are to be read aloud, they should be read slowly with no departure from the established wording. If questions arise, the tester can use paraphrasing but should not add anything substantive to the instructions (Harris, 1969).

Test-Taking Strategies

The strategies that respondents use in taking tests have implications both for the issue of test validity and "bias for best." Tests that are relied upon to indicate the comprehension level of readers may produce misleading results because of numerous techniques that readers have developed for obtaining correct answers on such tests without fully or even partially understanding the text. As Fransson (1984) puts it, respondents may not proceed via the text but rather around it. In effect, then, there are presumptions held by test constructors and administrators as to what is being tested, and there are the actual processes that test-takers go through to produce answers to questions and tasks. The two may not necessarily be one and the same. It may also be that the strategies the respondents are using are detrimental to their overall performance, or at least not as helpful as others they could be using.

Mentalistic measures using verbal report have helped determine how respondents actually take reading comprehension tests as opposed to what they may be expected to be doing (Cohen, 1984). Studies calling on respondents to provide immediate or delayed retrospection as to their test-taking strategies regarding reading passages with multiple-choice items have, for example, yielded the following results:

1. Whereas the instructions ask students to read the passage before answering the questions, students have reported either reading the questions first or reading just part of the article and then looking for the corresponding questions.
2. Whereas advised to read all alternatives before choosing one, students stop reading the alternatives as soon as they have found one that they decide is correct.
3. Students use a strategy of matching material from the passage with material in the item stem and in the alternatives, and prefer this surface-structure reading of the test items to one that calls for more in-depth reading and inferencing.
4. Students rely on their prior knowledge of the topic and on their general vocabulary.

From these findings and from others, there is emerging a description of what respondents do to answer questions. Unless trained to do otherwise, they may use the most expedient means of responding available to them—such as relying more on their previous experience with seemingly similar formats than on a close reading of the description of the task at hand. Thus, when given a passage to read and summarize, they may well perform the task the same way they did the last summary task, rather than paying close attention to what is called for in the current one. Often, this strategy works, but on occasion the particular task may require sub-

tle or major shifts in response behavior in order to perform well.

There appears to be a further insight to be gained from the test strategy literature, namely, that indirect testing formats—i.e., those which do not reflect real-world tasks (e.g., multiple-choice, cloze)—may prompt the use of strategies solely for the purpose of coping with the test format. More direct formats such as summarizing a text may be freer of such added testing effects. However, as long as the task is part of a test, students are bound to use strategies they would not use under nontest conditions. It is largely the responsibility of test constructors and of those who administer such tests to be aware of what their tests are actually measuring. Verbal report techniques can assist the test developer and user in obtaining such information.

Insights about the way in which respondents go about performing different testing tasks can be used to make informed decisions as to (1) the choice of testing format, (2) the choice and wording of instructions, and (3) the value and feasibility of coaching the respondents in how to take language tests. Work by O'Malley (1986) and others has already made use of research findings in designing training modules for the learning of test-taking skills.

NOTES

1. This is an updated version of a chapter of the same title, appearing in M. Celce-Murcia and L. McIntosh (eds.) (1979), *Teaching English as a Second or Foreign Language,* New York: Newbury House.

2. Sometimes teachers speak of using a "curve," which simply means that they evaluate a student's performance in comparison with that of other students in the same class or in other classes.

3. It would be possible to avoid this by having the multiple-choice alternatives presented orally as well.

4. Overall rapid inspection with periods of close inspection.

5. Locating a specific symbol or group of symbols—e.g., a date, a name of a person or place, a sum of money.

6. Discovering accurately what the author seeks to convey.

7. In intelligent tutoring systems, the computer diagnoses the students' strategies and their relationship to expert strategies, and then generates instruction based on this comparison.

8. This position is an endorsement of the need to take into account "perceived validity" (Low 1985), as discussed above.

9. The point here is that such cases of bias can be viewed as a good thing—as intentional bias. The aim would be to set up tasks that test-takers will be motivated to participate in, such as those that approximate real-life situations (Spolsky, 1985).

DISCUSSION QUESTIONS

1. Can you think of times when, as a student of a second or foreign language, one or more of the abuses of languages tests were "inflicted" upon you? Which ones? What was your reaction at the time? As a teacher of language, have you ever perpetrated any of those abuses yourself? What would be the appropriate remedies?

2. Have you ever used the same test for different administrative, instructional, or research purposes? Explain. Have you ever given exams that could serve both as tests of general proficiency and of achievement in a particular course of study?

3. What does it mean to say that an item may test for points that are not consistent with the test constructor's objective(s) for that item? How would such a reality be discovered and how might it be remedied?

SUGGESTED ACTIVITIES

I. Take an ESL/EFL test—either your own or someone else's—and review it, using the review checklist of questions provided below:
  1. Instructions
     a. Are the instructions for each section clear? Do all the items in a section fit the instructions for that section?
     b. Is the vocabulary in the instructions and in the items at the desired level of difficulty (or too hard—particularly in the instructions section)?
     c. Are there good examples of how to complete each section (where applicable)?
     d. In structured or open-ended sections, do the instructions indicate the approximate length of the response that is to be made?
     e. If the test is timed, or timed in certain sections, is the timing realistic?
     f. Are the respondents informed in the instructions as to whether the section is timed and how long they will have?
     g. Do the instructions indicate the value of the particular section with respect to the overall test score? Is the overall value of the test clear to the intended respondents? What is the purpose of the test?
     h. Is the method of administering the test/quiz carefully established (i.e., so that someone else would administer the test exactly as you would, if you were not able to give it or intended others to administer it)?
  2. Content
     a. (with reference to achievement tests) Is the test adequately covering the instructional objectives for the course? Is it testing material *not* taught/learned in the course? (Remember that a good test should reveal gaps in the instructor's teaching as well as in the students' learning.)
     b. Is the test testing the desired receptive/productive language skills? Has the test adequately isolated the desired skill (if this is what it purports to do)?
     c. Does the content of the test cover the intended aspects of communicative competence (grammatical, discourse, and sociolinguistic competence)? Is the test intending to get at *mastery* of a set (or sampled subset) of objectives or simply some attainment of these objectives? Is the actual test consistent with the expressed design?
     d. Is only one style (formal, casual, intimate) or dialect (standard or nonstandard) considered correct in one or all sections of the test? Are the respondents aware of this (with reference to the "Instructions" section above)? If the intent is to keep the language "conversational" in, say,

short-answer listening comprehension items, do the items reflect this intent?

e. Might some or many items be testing more points than you thought originally (if you constructed the test)? Would it then help to simplify these items or procedures so as to give greater prominence to exactly the points intended to be measured?

f. Are any of your sentences "linguistic curiosities" in an effort to test certain lexical and/or structural points (e.g., "My brother has something beautiful and I have nothing ugly"; from Rivers, 1981, p. 376)?

g. Does the test have the right title or might it mislead both the respondents and potential test administrators and interpreters of the results?

3. Item Format and Layout of the Test

a. Is the test as a whole too long or too short? (If too short, it may not be reliable.)

b. Is one objective or another being tested too much or too little? (Overtesting may start giving away the answers, and undertesting may not give enough diagnostic information.)

c. Are the items testing the same objective worded and spaced in such a way that one does not provide a giveaway for the others?

d. Are any items or sections clearly too difficult or too easy to answer? (Of course, item analysis helps answer this question. The difficulty of an item is often hard to determine on an a priori basis.)

e. Have the correct true/false and multiple-choice responses been adequately randomized so as not to set up a response pattern (e.g., all T/F items should not be "true" and all M-C items should not have either "b" or "c" as the correct answer)?

f. Are the items paced so that even the poorest student will experience at least a modicum of success at the outset?

g. Are the item response formats the most appropriate for what you want to test (e.g., would matching be a more efficient means of testing vocabulary,

say, than completion or multiple-choice, or would you wish to use several formats)?

h. Is the item stimulus format appropriate (e.g., should the stimulus be audiotaped, rather than written, or should both be used)?

i. How good is the layout?
(1) Is the technical arrangement of the items on the printed page easy to follow (e.g., are the multiple-choice alternatives horizontal or vertical, in the sentence itself, or to one side)?
(2) Is the spacing between and within items adequate?
(3) If dittoed, is the print legible?

j. Have the items been adequately reviewed by other native speakers (and nonnatives, if possible) to eliminate poor distractors and deceptive or confusing items?

4. Scoring

a. Have the methods for scoring the test or grading a procedure or section been adequately determined?

b. Are the items and/or sections weighed appropriately in scoring—i.e., do the weightings coincide with your notions about the most important objectives, the ones given the most emphasis in the class, the most useful elements?

II. Drawing on the suggestions in this chapter concerning the testing of reading comprehension, design a test of reading comprehension and write several sample items for it. Then review this test using the checklist in activity I.

III. Devise a way to test for strategic competence in test taking. Then try it out on a small group of respondents and discuss the results with others.

SUGGESTIONS FOR FURTHER READING

Alderson, J. C. (1987)
Innovation in Language Testing: Can the Micro-Computer Help? University of Lancaster, UK: Language Testing Update, Special Report No. 1.

Deals with computer-based English language testing

and includes a chapter of specific suggestions for objective item types—transformation, completion, combination, addition, rearrangement, correct/ incorrect editing, multiple-choice. Innovative testing possibilities for the computer are considered, in an effort to break down distinctions between testing and teaching. It is suggested that tests are potentially more user-friendly on the computer.

Alderson, J. C., et al., eds. (1987)
Reviews of English Language Proficiency Tests. Washington, DC: TESOL.

Provides descriptive and evaluative information on the major English-as-a-second-or-foreign-language tests in current use throughout the world.

Cohen, A. D. (1980)
Testing Language Ability in the Classroom. New York: Newbury House.

Deals with issues in language testing that other books had tended to neglect at that time, such as the issue of quizzes, the elicitation and response formats of items, the test-taking process, and the assessing of functional language ability. While the issues are addressed directly to language teachers, there is an effort to provide the research basis for these issues as well.

Harrison, A. (1983)
A Language Testing Handbook. London: Macmillan.

After defining types of tests, deals with the qualities of a good test and good test design for first and second language testing. Separate chapters are then devoted to placement, diagnostic, achievement, and proficiency tests. Also discusses marking and dealing with the results.

Henning, G. (1987)
A Guide to Language Testing. New York: Newbury House.

Primarily about issues in testing, such as types of measurement, measurement scales, data management, item analysis, and item banking. Discusses the analysis of test data in a sophisticated way, including coverage of Rasch Model as a form of latent trait measurement and discussion of reliability and validity in language testing.

Hughes, A. (1989)
Testing for Language Teachers. Cambridge: Cambridge University Press.

A recent practical guide for teachers, the book emphasizes that it is not enough to have test techniques to choose from. Rather, one needs to understand the principles of testing and how to apply them in prac-

tice. Drawing on currently available tests to illustrate points, the author makes his arguments interestingly and honestly.

Jacobs, H. L., S. A. Zingraf, D. R. Wormuth, V. F. Hartfiel, and J. B. Hughey (1981)
Testing ESL Composition: A Practical Approach. New York: Newbury House.

Deals first with the issue of why test for writing ability. Then proceeds to deal with each issue in turn, from presentation of the writing task to the learners to the evaluation of the results. The authors provide a writing profile for the purpose of more effective assessment of the results. The second portion of the book is actually a training manual offering step-by-step procedures for evaluating the learners' compositions. Sample compositions are provided as well.

Oller, J. W., Jr. (1979)
Language Tests at School. London: Longman.

Emphasizes differences between the pragmatically oriented approach that Oller advocates and discrete-point-oriented language-testing approaches. Provides detailed discussion of how to prepare, administer, score, and interpret pragmatic language tests. Among the pragmatic tests presented for use are dictation, various tests of oral language, varieties of the cloze procedure, and essay writing.

Shohamy, E. (1985)
A Practical Handbook in Language Testing for the Second Language Teacher. Tel Aviv, Israel: Tel Aviv University. (Available through Eric Cohen Book Seller, 5 Hankin Street, Ra'anana 43464, Israel.) (Revised version forthcoming, Oxford University Press.)

A most usable basic handbook for teachers on the process of producing language tests. It treats the planning, administering, and scoring of language tests, and the analysis and scoring of the results. The second section of the book provides numerous examples of ways of testing reading, listening, speaking, and writing.

Underhill, N. (1987)
Testing Spoken Language: A Handbook of Oral Testing Techniques. Cambridge: Cambridge University Press.

A basic introduction to oral language testing for teachers. Deals with aims and resources in testing, test types—including self-assessment, elicitation techniques—providing a rich assortment of techniques with some critique as well, marking systems —with an honest appraisal of some of the problems of assessors and their relative degrees of training, and test evaluation.

APPENDIX

Example Test Items for Measuring Listening, Vocabulary, Speaking, and Writing Skills

As pointed out in Cohen (1980, pp. 68–70), it is possible to combine different item stimulus formats (i.e., oral, written, nonverbal, or a combination) and item response formats (likewise oral, written, or nonverbal) in order to generate items. For this reason, lists of sample items in testing books may appear repetitious. For instance, a listening item and a reading item may actually have the same item stimulus (e.g., a written question) and differ only with respect to the way the multiple-choice responses are presented—say, orally, in the case of the listening item and in writing in the case of the reading item.

This appendix provides a brief sampling of some types of items that may be of benefit in testing depending upon the needs. Numerous textbooks on the market provide detailed sets of items (e.g., Clark, 1972; Finocchiaro & Sato, 1983; Heaton, 1975; Oller, 1979; Shohamy, 1985; Valette, 1977).

Testing Listening Skills

Discrimination of Sounds

a. The respondent indicates which vowel sound of three is different from the other two. (Taped stimulus): (1) sun, (2) put, (3) dug; (response choices): (a) 1, *(b) 2, (c) 3.

b. These sounds could be in sentence context. (Taped stimulus): (1) It's a sheep. (2) It's a sheep. (3) It's a ship. (Response choices): (a) 1, (b) 2, *(c) 3.

Intonation

a. The respondent is to indicate whether two phrases have the same intonation. (Taped stimulus): You're coming?/You're coming. (Response choices): (a) same, *(b) different.

b. The respondent must determine the meaning of the phrase from the intonation.

(Taped stimulus): Good morning! (Response choices): (a) happy to see employee, *(b) annoyed that the employee is late to work.

Listening for Grammatical Distinctions

The respondent has to listen carefully for inflectional markers—e.g., the respondent must determine whether the subject and verb are in the singular or the plural. (Taped stimulus): The boys sing well. (Response choices): (a) singular, *(b) plural, (c) same form for singular and plural.

Listening for Vocabulary

The respondent performs an action in response to a command (e.g., getting up, walking to the window) or draws a picture according to oral instructions (e.g., coloring a picture a certain way, sorting a set of objects according to instructions).

Auditory Comprehension

a. The respondent indicates whether a response to a question is appropriate. (Taped stimulus): How're you gonna get home? At about 3:30 p.m. (Response choices): (a) appropriate, *(b) inappropriate.

b. The respondent hears a statement and must indicate the appropriate paraphrase for the statement. (Taped stimulus): What'd you get yourself into this time? (Response choices): (a) What are you wearing this time? (b) What did you buy this time? *(c) What's your problem this time?

c. The respondents listen in on a telephone conversation between two people and at appropriate times must indicate what they would say if they were one of the speakers in the conversation. (Taped stimulus): Mother: Well, Mary, you know you were supposed to call me last week. Mary: I know, Mom, but I got tied up. Mother: That's really no excuse. Mary: (Response choices): (a) Yes, I'll call him. *(b) You're right. I'm sorry. (c) I've really had nothing to do.

d. The respondent hears a lecture, with all the false starts, filled pauses, and other features that make it different from oral recitation of a written text. After the lecture, there are taped multiple-choice, structured, or open-ended questions to be responded to in writing on the answer sheet.

e. Dictation can serve as a test of auditory comprehension if it is given at a fast enough pace so that it is not simply a spelling test (Cohen, 1980; Oller, 1979). The pace is determined by the size of the phrase groups between pauses, the length of the pauses, and the speed at which the phrase groups are read. Nonnative respondents must segment the sounds into words, phrases, and sentences. It has been found that they make errors of word inversion, incorrect word choice (through misunderstanding of grammar or lack of vocabulary), insertion of extra words, and omission of dictated words (Oller, 1972). More recent use of dictation as a measure of general listening ability involves scoring by unit, not by word (see Cziko & Nien-Hsuan, 1984).

Testing Vocabulary

a. Respondents receive sets of six words and three meanings and are instructed to choose the right word to go with each meaning. They are to write the number of that word next to its meaning (Nation, 1990):

1. apply
2. elect   _____ choose by voting
3. jump   _____ become like water
4. manufacture   _____ make
5. melt
6. threaten

b. Respondents receive a long list of words (e.g., 100) and are to indicate whether they know their meaning. The list consists of both real and imaginary words (nonexistent words which the respondent could not possibly know) (Meara & Buxton, 1987):

Tick the words you know the meaning of, e.g., milk √

gathering	forecast	wodesome	loyalment	
flane	crope	dismissal	sloping	
bluck	enclose	rehearsion	turmoil	etc.

c. Contextualized vocabulary: Asking respondents to indicate what a word means within the context of a given passage. The response could be open-ended or multiple-choice—e.g., What does *delinquent* means in line 7?
(Open-ended response): _____ .
(Multiple-choice response):
(a) naughty (b) haughty (c) sinful *(d) irresponsible.

Testing Speaking Skills

Whereas in the 1979 version of this chapter, speaking items were divided into those dealing with pronunciation, grammar, vocabulary, and pragmatics, in this version let us simply stress the importance of using varied measures of speaking, such that for each learner more than one type of speech interaction is tapped (e.g., reporting the contents of an article read in the native language, participating in group discussion on a common and possibly controversial theme, taking part in role-play, and lecturing).

Then it would be important to establish which speech functions are to be assessed in each type of interaction (e.g., reporting: ability to state the main ideas and express an opinion about them; discussion: arguing; role-play: the appropriate execution of the necessary speech acts—e.g., requesting, complaining, apologizing, complimenting; see chapter by Olshtain and Cohen in this volume for suggestions). Likewise, it is necessary to establish the topic of the interaction, the level of formality (informal, consultative, formal), the number of participants and their relative status, as well as their familiarity with each other. Each interaction is then rated on two scales, one for linguistic accuracy and the other for fluency (Shohamy 1988).

Testing the Interaction of Reading and Writing

An example of a test of reading and writing is that of summarizing. Summarization tests are complex in nature. The reading portion entails identifying topical information, distinguishing superordinate from subordinate material, and identifying redundant and trivial information. The writing up of the summary entails the selection of topical information (or generating it if it is not provided), deleting trivial and redundant information, substituting superordinate material, and restating the text so that it is coherent and polished (Brown & Day, 1983; Kintsch & van Dijk, 1978).

Given the lack of clarity that often accompanies such tasks, it may be useful to give specific instructions as to how to go about the summarization task. For example:

Instructions on How to Read:

- Read to extract the most important points—e.g., those constituting topic sentences signaled as crucial by the paragraph structure; points that the reader of the summary would want to read.
- Reduce information to superordinate points.
- Avoid redundant information—points off.

Instructions on How to Write:

- Prepare in draft form and then rewrite.
- Link points smoothly.
- Exact length of summary (e.g., 10 percent of original text, so 75 words for 750-word text).
- In own words.
- Be brief.
- Write legibly.

It may also be beneficial to give raters specific instructions as to how to assess the summaries:

- Check to see whether each important point is included (points that were agreed upon by a group of experts in advance).
- Check to make sure that these points are linked together by the key linking/integrating elements appearing on the master list.
- Points(s) off for each irrelevant point.
- Points off for illegibility.

Testing of Written Expression

Perhaps the main thing to be said about the testing of written expression is that it is a poor substitute for repeated samplings of a learner's writing ability while not under the pressure of an exam situation. The current process-oriented approach to writing would suggest that it is unnatural for a learner to write a single draft of a composition and submit it for a grade. Instead, learners prepare multiple drafts that are reviewed both by peers (in small groups) and by the teacher at appropriate moments. Hence, if writing is to be assessed on a test, it would be important to provide the learners with specific guidelines as to the nature of the task. For example:

Your boss has asked you to rough out an argument for why the factory employees should not get longer coffee breaks. Try to present your arguments in the most logical and persuasive way. Do not worry about grammar and punctuation at this point. There is no time for that now. Just concern yourself with the content of your ideas, their organization, and the choice of appropriate vocabulary to state your case.

It is also important for the person doing the assessment of the writing to pay attention only to those aspects of the task that learners were requested to consider.

Keeping Up to Date as an ESL Professional

JoAnn Crandall

INTRODUCTION

After you leave a graduate program in Teaching English as a Second or Foreign Language (TESL), you may find that you feel cut off and that you begin to lose touch with new developments in the field unless you take steps to keep up to date. There are a number of ways in which you can continue to grow as a teacher and to become better informed as an ESL professional. These include the following:

- Participating in professional associations concerned with the teaching of English or other foreign languages, including attending local, national, or international conferences.
- Subscribing to journals and regularly reading periodicals in the teaching of English and in related fields.
- Placing one's name on mailing lists of major ESL/EFL textbook publishers and information clearinghouses or resource centers.
- Offering to review texts for publishers or journals.
- Serving on textbook selection committees in your ESL program.
- Working on curriculum development or textbook preparation teams in your ESL program.
- Attending or giving in-service workshops and seminars for teachers.
- Participating in summer institutes or special graduate programs to augment and update your expertise.
- Participating in research projects, especially those which enable you to work with researchers and other professionals who are engaged in analyzing issues relevant to your classroom.
- Working collaboratively with professionals in other fields.

Let's look at these in a little more detail.

PROFESSIONAL ORGANIZATIONS

Professional organizations offer the best means of keeping in touch with others in one's own field. They provide, through both formal and informal channels, a number of ways to discuss issues and share ideas. These channels include publications, conferences, seminars and workshops, and professional committees. Publications range from books to journals to newsletters, each providing a different way of keeping informed about new research, new teaching strategies, new materials, or new issues in the field. Conferences also provide varied sources of information. Plenary addresses often discuss emerging questions, papers may analyze research results, demonstrations and workshops introduce techniques or strategies, and book exhibits provide an opportunity to examine new student and teacher resource texts. At these conferences, there are also numerous opportunities for getting into conversations with individuals who share many of your interests and concerns, often leading to long-term professional correspondence and friendship. There is perhaps no single experience with more potential for educating a seasoned professional than an international English language teaching conference. But even at the smaller national, regional, or local levels, these organizations and conferences are a great resource, sometimes providing even more useful information or assistance, since they are more in touch with immediate needs. In addition, professional associations increasingly are collaborating with universities and other educational institutions to provide an ongoing program of professional development activities, including summer institutes, short courses, and seminars, usually scheduled to permit teachers and others who are working to participate. These seminars and institutes can help revive a teacher who is feeling rather worn down after some time in the classroom.

Professional organizations also offer a means by which one can become more actively involved in improving the profession: in helping to set standards for teaching, in developing criteria for evaluating programs, and in recognizing particularly exemplary research or practice. These organizations also provide a means by which individuals who are especially interested in one aspect of the profession—for example, the use of computers or video in teaching, the development of materials, ESL for elementary or secondary students, or teacher education—can find others with similar interests with whom to talk.

While there are too many English language teaching professional associations to list, the following are among the largest and most important.

Teachers of English to Speakers of Other
   Languages (TESOL)
1600 Cameron Street, Suite 300
Alexandria, Virginia 22314
USA

The TESOL organization publishes *TESOL Matters*, the *TESOL Quarterly*, the *TESOL Journal*, special-interest-section newsletters, and a variety of professional books. It also hosts an annual conference and regularly sponsors a summer institute. In addition, there are over 71 TESOL affiliates around the world, which also publish journals, host con-

ferences, and serve as local forums for professional standards and issues.

International Association of Teachers of English
   as a Foreign Language (IATEFL)
3 Kingsdown Chambers, Kingsdown Park
Tankerton, Whitstable, Kent CT5 2DJ
England

IATEFL publishes the *IATEFL Newsletter* and makes available at reduced rates the following journals: *Modern English Teacher*, *Practical English Teaching*, the *ELT Journal*, *World Englishes*, and the *EFL Gazette*. Members can also belong to a number of special-interest groups. IATEFL hosts an annual conference and has a number of affiliates.

International Association of Applied Linguistics
   (AILA)
c/o American Association for Applied Linguistics
1325 18th Street, NW, Suite 211
Washington, DC 20036
USA

(Because AILA has no fixed secretariat, the easiest way to contact them is through one's national affiliate, such as AAAL (the American Association for Applied Linguistics) in the United States.) AILA is an international association made up of national associations of applied linguistics. It publishes *AILA News* and *AILA Review* (thematic occasional papers) and hosts a World Congress on Applied Linguistics in a different country every three years, which provides an excellent opportunity to become acquainted with the state of the art worldwide in research and practice in such areas as adult language learning, second language acquisition, language testing, language teacher education, language for special purposes, and multicultural education.

While participation in professional organizations dealing with the teaching of English might seem an obvious source of information, what may not be so clear is the role which related professional organizations can play in helping to broaden and deepen one's understanding of the nature of language teaching and learning. For example, attendance at a conference of reading or writing professionals or reading a journal concerned with second language acquisition or the teaching of another foreign language can offer insights which apply to ESL as well. Moreover, they can help bridge communication gaps between professionals who have much in common and much to share. These organizations exist in most parts of the world. In the United States, the International Reading Association (800 Barksdale Road, Newark, DE 19711), the National Council of Teachers of English (1111 Kenyon Road, Urbana, IL 61801), the American Council on the Teaching of Foreign Languages (6 Executive Boulevard, Upper Level, Yonkers, NY 10701), the Association for Supervision and Curriculum Development (125 North West Street, Alexandria, VA 22314), and the National Association for Foreign Student Affairs (1860 19th Street, NW, Washington, DC 20009) all provide interesting publications and conferences relevant to ESL professionals. The latter, NAFSA, in particular has a very active ESL group, the Association of Teachers of English as a Second Language (ATESL), which publishes newsletters, occasional papers, and books of interest to ESL professionals in higher education, particularly at American tertiary institutions.

Most of these organizations also have regional, state, or local affiliates which address more local issues and also provide opportunities to build professional relationships with those closer to home. Their conferences may be small or large, but they are likely to be very targeted to local needs.

PROFESSIONAL JOURNALS

An article, "Journals of Interest to TESOL Members," written by Diane Larsen-Freeman in the August 1985 issue of the *TESOL Newsletter* lists 47 journals relevant to the concerns of TESOL members. That list is still the most comprehensive and useful one available, providing subscription, manuscript submission, book review, and other information about each of the journals. It is impossible to list all 47 here. Instead, I have selected a few which are among the most relevant to a diverse group of ESL professionals.

APPLIED LINGUISTICS
Oxford University Press
Walton Street
Oxford OX2 6DP
England

Applied Linguistics is a joint publication of the American and British Associations for Applied Linguistics, published in cooperation with the International Association of Applied Linguistics. Articles include discussions of first and second language acquisition, language teaching methodology and testing, discourse analysis, and other topics of interest to applied linguists in diverse fields.

ELT JOURNAL
Oxford University Press
Walton Street
Oxford OX2 6DP
England

Formerly the *English Language Teaching Journal,* the *ELT Journal* is published in association with the British Council and IATEFL and is directed toward English language teachers around the world. It includes articles relating theory to classroom practice, reviews of new publications, and interviews with writers and teachers.

ENGLISH TEACHING FORUM
Room 312, 301 4th Street, SW
Washington, DC 20547
USA

The *Forum* is a journal "for the teacher of English outside the United States" and is published by the United States Information Agency for distribution by American embassies around the world. It is also available through the United States Government Printing Office in Washington, DC. Articles focus on practical issues in teaching and teacher education. Also included are short discussions of innovative teaching techniques.

ENGLISH FOR SPECIFIC PURPOSES
Pergamon Press Inc.
Maxwell House
Fairview Park
Elmsford, NY 10523
USA

Formerly known as *The ESP Journal,* this journal discusses research, program design, materials, teacher education, and other issues in the teaching of English for specific purposes. Book reviews and articles are written by professionals from around the world.

LANGUAGE LEARNING
178 Henry S. Frieze Building
105 South State Street
The University of Michigan
Ann Arbor, MI 48109-1285
USA

Language Learning is a "journal of applied linguistics" providing research and theoretical articles on second/foreign language acquisition and language learning, as well as book reviews, notes, and announcements. It is directed primarily to language researchers, but with articles of interest to language teachers as well.

LANGUAGE TEACHING
Cambridge University Press
32 East 57th Street
New York, NY 10022
USA

Language Teaching abstracts articles from over 400 journals, published in several languages, in the fields of applied linguistics, language studies, foreign languages, and English as a second or foreign language. Of special interest is the feature summary article, which presents a state-of-the-art overview of some aspect of language teaching. Bibliographies and book notices are also included.

LANGUAGE TESTING
Edward Arnold
41 Bedford Square
London WC1B 3DQ
England

Language Testing is an international journal concerned with issues of testing and assessment of second and foreign languages. Articles and research reports discuss testing theory and procedures; also included are reviews of tests.

RELC JOURNAL
SEAMEO Regional Language Centre
RELC Building
30 Orange Grove Road
Singapore 1025
Republic of Singapore

The *RELC Journal* is a publication of the Regional Language Centre in Singapore. Articles and book reviews relate to issues in the teaching and learning of second languages, many of which are particularly relevant to language educators in Southeast Asia.

STUDIES IN SECOND LANGUAGE
    ACQUISITION
Cambridge University Press
32 East 57th Street
New York, NY 10022
USA

Each year, one issue of *Studies in Second Language Acquisition* is devoted to a particular theme; the other two issues are broadly concerned with theoretical and research topics in second/foreign language acquisition and learning.

TESL TALK
Citizenship Development Branch
Ministry of Citizenship
77 Bloor Street West, 5th Floor
Toronto, Ontario M7A 2R9
Canada

While intended primarily for teachers of immigrants in Canada, the journal contains numerous practical articles for ESL teachers of children and adults.

TESOL JOURNAL
TESOL
1600 Cameron Street, Suite 300
Alexandria, VA 22314
USA

Available only through membership in TESOL, the *Journal* publishes practical articles on teaching and classroom research. It is designed to meet the needs of those working directly with ESL and EFL students. It contains a review section focusing on classroom materials.

TESOL QUARTERLY
TESOL
1600 Cameron Street, Suite 300
Alexandria, VA 22314
USA

TESOL Quarterly, which is available only through membership in TESOL, publishes scholarly articles of interest to researchers, teacher educators, curriculum developers, and teachers of English around the world. It also publishes book reviews, lengthier review articles, book notices, and brief research reports and summaries. Also included is a forum for debate on issues which have been raised previously in the *Quarterly.*

Other periodicals which deserve mention include the *TESOL Matters* (which contains information on meetings, conferences, and publications, as well as numerous short, practical articles), *Cross Currents* (a journal which is particularly concerned with cross-cultural issues in English language teaching), the *JALT Journal* and *The Language Teacher* (publications of the Japan Association of Language Teachers, the latter having thematic issues dealing with particular topics in English and other foreign language teaching), and the *TESL Reporter* (which publishes articles of particular relevance to ESL/EFL classroom teachers).

In addition, associations of professionals in the fields of reading, writing, foreign languages, and curriculum development publish journals and magazines which are of relevance of ESL professionals. Some of these include *Educational Leadership* (of particular interest to teacher educators and curriculum developers), *Foreign Language Annals* and *The Modern Language Journal* (both intended for teachers of other foreign languages, but with articles of interest to ESL/EFL professionals),

Reading Research Quarterly and *The Reading Teacher* (published by the International Reading Association), *Research in the Teaching of English* (published by the National Council of Teachers of English), and the *Annual Review of Applied Linguistics* (an annual state-of-the-art compendium of annotated bibliographies on important trends and issues in the field of applied linguistics, published by Cambridge University Press).

PUBLISHERS AND CLEARINGHOUSES

To keep up to date on new textbooks, teacher reference materials, or other theoretical or practical information relevant to you as an ESL professional, you will also want to ask that your name be placed on the mailing lists of all major ESL/EFL publishers and information clearinghouses to receive regular mailings from them.

The expanding role of English as an international language has led to the development of an unprecedented quantity of English language teaching materials, published by a wide range of publishers. It is impossible to list them all here. What follows is a list of those which produce diverse types of relevant ELT publications. The addresses given are all in the United States. However, publishers often have several addresses around the world, and if you are living outside of the United States, you will want to see if the company has an office closer to you or even a marketing representative in your own country.

Addison-Wesley Publishing Company
World Language Division
Jacob Way
Reading, MA 01867

Cambridge University Press
32 East 57th Street
New York, NY 10022

Harcourt Brace Jovanovich
2nd Floor International Division
Orlando, FL 32887

Heinle & Heinle Publishers, Inc.
20 Park Plaza
Boston, MA 02116

Longman, Inc.
95 Church Street
White Plains, NY 10601

Macmillan Publishing Company
866 Third Avenue
New York, NY 10023

McGraw-Hill Publishing Company
1221 Avenue of the Americas
New York, NY 10020

National Textbook Company
4255 West Touhy Avenue
Lincolnwood, IL 60646

Newbury House Publishers
10 East 53rd Street
New York, NY 10022

Oxford University Press
200 Madison Avenue
New York, NY 10016

Pergamon Press
Maxwell House
Fairview Park
Elmsford, NY 10523

Prentice-Hall Regents
College Division
Englewood Cliffs, NJ 07632

Random House, Inc.
201 East 50th Street
New York, NY 10022

Scott, Foresman and Company
1900 East Lake Avenue
Glenview, IL 60025

Silver Burdett & Ginn
250 James Street
Morristown, NJ 07960

Steck-Vaughn Company
PO Box 26015
Austin, TX 78755

University of Michigan Press
839 Greene Street
Ann Arbor, MI 48106

University of Pittsburgh Press
127 North Bellefield Avenue
Pittsburgh, PA 15260

CLEARINGHOUSES

There are also a number of information clearinghouses which can provide a variety of publications and answers to questions which may arise as you work in the ESL field. Some of these, such as the Educational Resources Information Center (ERIC) system, are long-standing; others develop as the need for them arises, only to dissolve when the issues are no longer as pressing or funding is no longer available. Some of the most useful include the following:

ERIC Clearinghouse on Languages and
    Linguistics
Center for Applied Linguistics
1118 22nd Street, NW
Washington, DC 20037
USA

The ERIC Clearinghouse on Languages and Linguistics is one of 16 U.S. government-funded educational clearinghouses. Its major objective is to make available to practitioners and researchers current information and resources on topics in language teaching and learning and, more broadly, in applied linguistics. It abstracts and summarizes articles from journals, conferences, and other sources and inputs these into a computerized data base, from which searches are obtained and publications are derived. ERIC can provide computer searches to identify materials, reports, or papers dealing broadly with any aspect of language teaching and learning. ERIC also publishes state-of-the-art summaries in the Language in Education series; *Digests* on such topics as program models, language acquisition research, methodology, and teacher education; *Mini-Bibliographies* from the data base on practical issues in language teaching; and longer *Q & A* sheets, which summarize answers to questions that are commonly asked of Clearinghouse personnel. A new adjunct clearinghouse on Literacy Education has also been added to this clearinghouse.

Center for Applied Linguistics
1118 22nd Street, NW
Washington, DC 20037
USA

CAL is a research and service organization which operates a number of clearinghouses (such as the ERIC Clearinghouse listed above) and provides information and technical assistance in English language, foreign language, and bilingual education. CAL's work includes needs assessments, program evaluation, curriculum and materials development, testing, teacher education, and the use of technology in language education. The Center has a special interest in literacy and content-based language instruction.

Centre for English Language Teaching and
    Research
Macquarie University
Sydney
New South Wales 2109
Australia

This is a new national centre which combines the work of the National Curriculum Resource Centre with the Centre for English Language Teaching and Research. The Centre will conduct research, develop a computerized information retrieval service, provide technical assistance, and disseminate information on English language teaching.

Centre for Information on Language Teaching
    and Research
Regent's College, Inner Circle
Regent's Park
London NW1 4NS
England

CILT is an information center which houses an extensive collection of materials, especially those related to foreign language teaching and learning. It publishes a number of practical guides and information bulletins for the practicing teacher, and in collaboration with Cambridge University Press and the British Council, the journal *Language Teaching*. A twice-yearly "information pack" of diverse information which has been collected and stored at CILT is available to subscribers.

Modern Language Centre
Ontario Institute for Studies in Education
252 Bloor Street West
Toronto, Ontario M5S 1V6
Canada

The Modern Language Centre serves as a research and technical assistance centre which maintains the most extensive library collection in the field of language education in Canada. The Centre publishes a Language and Literacy Monograph series and other guides and books of interest to practitioners.

Regional Language Centre (RELC)
30 Orange Grove Road
Singapore 1025
Republic of Singapore

RELC is a center for research and information concerning theories, research, methods, and materials related to language learning and teaching, with special attention to language teaching in Southeast Asia. RELC publishes the *RELC Journal*, the proceedings of their yearly thematic conference on a state-of-the-art question in language teaching, and maintains one of the best libraries and information systems in applied linguistics in the world.

BOOK REVIEWS, TEXTBOOK SELECTION COMMITTEES, AND CURRICULUM DEVELOPMENT TEAMS

Both publishers and journal editors are continually in need of identifying professionals to review manuscripts or books. Publishers routinely require a textbook or teacher reference manuscript to be evaluated by several outside reviewers before deciding whether to publish a book. If you wish to serve as a reviewer, you should contact these publishers, usually through their ESL editors, to let them know that you are available. Indicate the particular skill or grade level you are interested in and your qualifications for doing so and you may find yourself involved regularly in keeping up to date, since you will be reading manuscripts before they are even published.

Journal editors, as well, often have difficulty finding individuals who will review new books. If you are interested in reviewing a book, perhaps one which you have used in your teaching or in your own teacher education, contact the book review editor of one of the journals listed above. At first, you may want to write reviews for a newsletter or publication of a local chapter of one of the ESL professional association affiliates. After one or two successful efforts, you may find that new books are being sent to you routinely for your review, and in the reviewing process, you are remaining current in the field.

Textbook selection committees—many language programs have such a committee—offer another source of professional growth. These committees usually request copies of several relevant, new publications from a number of publishers from which to make their final selections. By participating in these committees, you have an opportunity to keep current on the kinds of techniques and strategies that are being implemented in ESL/EFL textbook series and to enrich your own teaching, lesson planning, or materials-writing projects. You also have an opportunity to broaden your circle of ESL colleagues and to benefit from their different educational backgrounds and experiences.

You may find, after reviewing manuscripts and books and serving on textbook selection committees, that you want to write materials or books of your own or serve as a member of a curriculum writing team, preparing new materials for your own and other classes. In the process of researching, developing, and field-testing these materials, you will learn a great deal about what is current practice in other ESL/EFL classrooms and will undoubtedly adapt some of your own teaching accordingly. You will also have the opportunity of working closely with other professionals, learning from each other as you collaborate on the writing project.

WORKSHOPS, SEMINARS, INSTITUTES, AND GRADUATE PROGRAMS

Naturally, one of the best ways of keeping up to date is to participate in local, state, or even national inservice workshops or seminars. These seminars may be sponsored by a professional association, by a university teacher education or linguistics program, by a resource or technical assistance center, or by a department or ministry of education. They may even offer graduate credit or credit which can be applied to teacher certification. Of even greater importance, they can provide a forum for learning new ideas, sharing problems, and identifying promising ways of expanding one's teaching repertoire. Participation, in the beginning, may be as a student or learner in one of these programs; however, as time passes, you will find that you will also learn a great deal from presenting your ideas and helping others to understand some of the successful techniques or materials you have developed. By participating as a member of a panel or a small group of presenters, you can also learn from your colleagues in the process.

Deserving special mention are the summer institutes for students and teachers which are hosted by organizations such as TESOL or by universities. It is possible to enroll in three- or six-week intensive programs with ESL colleagues from many parts of the world, learning from them as well as from the instructor, in what is usually an informal, collaborative learning experience. The opportunity to participate in a summer institute is one that should not be missed; you are likely to emerge from the experience feeling renewed as a professional and reassured that you have chosen the right profession. You will also undoubtedly meet professional colleagues with whom you will correspond for many years to come.

RESEARCH AND
COLLABORATIVE PROJECTS

If you want to keep up to date and to learn something more about your own classrooms or students at the same time, you may want to undertake a research project of your own. This might involve simply studying a few students' progress in English very closely, perhaps keeping a log which captures your conclusions on a regular basis. You might also want to become involved in a larger research project, or one that is investigating particular questions. One way to do this is to contact university linguistics or education programs or educational research centers located near your school. You might be surprised to learn that many researchers working in universities or research centers have a difficult time identifying teachers with whom to collaborate or classrooms with which to work; they are likely to welcome your interest in some kind of a joint project, one that will have as its objectives something which can be applied to your classroom or your particular situation. This teacher–researcher collaboration is certain to help you keep up to date on theoretical issues in the field and may lead to your trying some different techniques in your classroom.

Other interesting and broadening collaborations can occur even within your own school. Learning what is expected of students and what kinds of materials and methods are used in the teaching of science, social studies, or mathematics can provide you with ideas for including more academic content and addressing more academic language in the ESL/EFL classroom. Similarly, the science, social studies, or mathematics teachers will become more sensitive to the nature of the language demands in their disciplines by observing your classes or working collaboratively with you. These collaborations can occur at elementary, secondary, or tertiary levels and they may spread across the curriculum. This can lead to collaborative research, collaborative curriculum development, and even team

teaching, all of which are likely to provide professionally rewarding experiences.

CONCLUSION

Ending a TESL training program is really the beginning of a lifetime of professional growth. Teaching is, in itself, a continual growth experience, since one often really "learns" something when asked to teach it. Furthermore, much of what is learned in a classroom is taught by the students, and there are new students in each new class. Moreover, if you have the opportunity of teaching different courses, different grades, or different levels, you will continue to grow as a professional. If you keep looking for better textbooks or materials or finding better techniques or strategies for meeting individual students' needs, you will also continue to grow.

There are so many ways that being an ESL professional is a growth experience. The suggestions provided in this chapter offer ways of ensuring even more growth and of "keeping up to date as an ESL professional."

DISCUSSION QUESTIONS

1. This chapter has discussed a number of ways in which ESL professionals can keep current in the field. Which do you believe will be most helpful to you? Why?

2. Are there other ways in which you can keep up to date? Get together with colleagues who are also preparing to become ESL teachers and see if you can identify other sources of information or means of sharing ideas.

3. Why is it important to belong to an ESL/EFL professional association? What kinds of professional development opportunities do they offer? If you cannot belong to one of these associations, are there other ways in which you can benefit from their services?

4. Why do you think that ESL professionals have difficulty in keeping current? What are some of the factors which might affect your ability to keep up to date as an ESL professional?

SUGGESTED ACTIVITIES

1. Even if you are not a member, attend one of the international, national, or local conventions of one of the ESL/EFL professional associations. Try to attend some plenary sessions, some papers and workshops, and the book exhibits. Also allow yourself time to get to know some of your colleagues, by attending social activities or engaging in informal discussion sessions.

2. With two or three colleagues, write to some of the major professional associations which might be of interest to you. Do not confine yourself only to ESL/EFL associations; consider writing to some which are involved in related, but relevant, concerns.

3. Visit or contact one of the information clearinghouses or resource centers in your area. Find out about the services they provide and the publications they offer, and have your name added to any mailing lists they maintain.

4. Develop a form letter to send to publishers describing your background and interests as an ESL/EFL professional. Leave enough room so that you can type in the name and address of the publisher. Then, mail this to as many publishers as you wish. If you send the letter to the ESL/EFL Editor, it can serve both to get your name added to the ESL/EFL publications mailing list and also to indicate your interest in serving as a manuscript reviewer.

5. Choose three of the journals listed in this chapter to examine more closely. What articles are included? Who is the intended audience? What kinds of information do they provide? Do you think the journal will be useful to you? In what ways?

SUGGESTION FOR FURTHER READING

Larsen-Freeman, D. (1985)
Journals of Interest to TESOL Members. *TESOL Newsletter, 19*(4), 15–22. (Note: as of 1991, the *TESOL Newsletter* has been replaced by *TESOL Matters*.)

References

Abraham, P., & Mackey, D. (1986). *Get ready: Interactive listening and speaking.* Englewood Cliffs, NJ: Prentice-Hall.

Adams, S. J. (1982). Scripts and the recognition of unfamiliar vocabulary: Enhancing second language reading skills. *Modern Language Journal, 66*(2), 155–159.

Addison, A. A. (in press). Interacting with text. In R. E. W-B. Olsen & J. W-B. Olsen (Eds.), *Approaching content.* Hayward, CA: Alemany Press.

Aebersold, J., Kowitz, J., Schwarte, B., & Smith, E. (1985). *Critical thinking, critical choices: Book 2. Listening and speaking.* Englewood Cliffs, NJ: Prentice-Hall.

Agard, F. B., & Dunkel, H. B. (1948). *An investigation of second language teaching.* Boston: Ginn.

Ahlberg, J., & Ahlberg, A. (1986). *The jolly postman or other people's letters.* Boston: Little, Brown.

Akinnaso, F. N. & Ajirotutu, C. S. (1982). Performance and ethnic style in job interviews. In J. Gumperz (Ed.), *Language and social identity* (pp. 119–144). Cambridge: Cambridge University Press.

Alberta Department of Education, Edmonton, Language Service Branch. (1986). *French as a second language: Supplementary learning resources.* (ERIC Doucment Reproduction Service No. ED 281 365)

Alderson, J. C. (1983). The cloze procedure and proficiency in English as a foreign language. In J. W. Oller, Jr. (Ed.), *Issues in languages testing research* (pp. 205–228). New York: Newbury House.

Alderson, J. C. (1987). *Innovation in language testing: Can the micro-computer help? Special report no. 1: Language testing update.* Lancaster: Institute for English Language Education, University of Lancaster.

Alderson, J. C., & Urquhart, A. H. (Eds.). (1984). *Reading in a foreign language.* New York: Longman.

Alexander, L. G., Kingsbury, R., & Chapman, J. (1978). *Take a stand.* New York: Longman.

Allen, H. B. (1965). Teaching the printed word: Reading and literature (overview). In H. B. Allen (Ed.), *Teaching English as a second language—A book of readings.* New York: McGraw-Hill.

Allen, H. B. (1966). *TENES: A survey of the teaching of English to non-English speakers in the United States.* Champaign, IL: NCTE.

Allen, J. P. B., & Widdowson, H. G. (1974). *English in focus.* Oxford: Oxford University Press.

Allen, R. (1968). A reassessment of the role of the language laboratory. *Journal of English as a Second Language, 14*(1), 74–79.

Allen, V. F. (1983). *Techniques in teaching vocabulary.* London: Oxford University Press.

Allwright, R. L. (1975). Problems in the study of the language teacher's treatment of learner error. In M. Burt & H. C. Dulay (Eds.), *On TESOL '75: New directions in second language learning, teaching, and bilingual education* (pp. 96–109). Washington, DC: TESOL.

Allwright, R. W. (1981). What do we want teaching materials for? *ELT Journal, 36*(1), 5–18.

Amoroso, H. C. (1985). Organic primers for basic literacy instruction. *Journal of Reading, 28*(5), 398–401.

Anderson, A., & Lynch, T. (1988). *Listening.* Oxford: Oxford University Press.

Anderson, G. J., & Walberg, H. J. (1974). Learning environments. In H. J. Walberg (Ed.), *Evaluating educational performance: A sourcebook of methods, instruments, and examples* (pp. 81–98). Berkeley, CA: McCutchan.

Anderson, J. R. (1982). Acquisition of cognitive skill. *Psychological Review, 89*(4), 369–406.

Andersson, B. V., & Barnitz, J. G. (1984). Cross-cultural

517

schemata and reading comprehension instruction. *Journal of Reading, 28*(2), 102–108.

Anthony, E. M. (1963). Approach, method, and technique. *ELT Journal, 17*(2), 63–67.

Antony, T. (1986). Characterizing student–student interaction. Nucleo: Central University of Venezuela.

Applebee, A. N. (1984). *Contexts for learning to write: Studies of secondary school instruction.* Norwood, NJ: Ablex.

Applebee, A. N. (1986). Problems in process approaches: Toward a reconceptualization of process instruction. In A. R. Petrosky & D. Bartholomae (Eds.), *The teaching of writing* (pp. 95–113). Chicago: National Society for the Study of Education.

Arapoff, N. (1969). Discover and transform: A method of teaching writing to foreign students. *TESOL Quarterly, 3*(4), 297–304.

Argyris, C., Putnam, R., & Smith, D. McL. (1985). *Action science.* San Francisco: Jossey-Bass.

Ariew, R. (1982). The textbook as curriculum. In T. V. Higgs (Ed.), *Curriculum, competence, and the foreign language teacher* (pp. 11–33). Skokie, IL: National Textbook Co.

Arizpe, V., & Aguirre, B. E. (1987). Mexican, Puerto Rican, and Cuban ethnic groups in first-year college-level Spanish textbooks. *Modern Language Journal, 71*(2), 125–137.

Arlington Public Schools, ESOL/HILT Program and Center for Applied Linguistics. (1987). Integrating styles and skills: An approach to lesson planning for the ESL classroom. (ERIC Reproduction Services No. ED 292 292)

Arndt, V. (1987). Six writers in search of texts: A protocol-based study of L1 and L2 writing. *English Language Teaching Journal, 41*(4), 257–267.

Arnold, N., & others (1987). *Integrating styles and skills: An approach to lesson planning for the ESL classroom.* Arlington Public Schools Center for Applied Linguistics, Washington, DC: Center for Language Education and Research. (ERIC Reproduction Services No. ED 292 292)

Arthur, B. (1968). Reading literature and learning a second language. *Language Learning, 18*(3–4), 199–210.

Arthur, B. (1970). On the art of choosing literature for foreign language teachers. *UCLA workpapers in teaching English as a second language, 4,* 6–10.

Arthur, B. (1979). Teaching English to minority groups. In M. Celce-Murcia & L. McIntosh (Eds.), *Teaching English as a second or foreign language* (pp. 270–276). New York: Newbury House.

Asher, J. J. (1965). The strategy of the total physical response: An application to learning Russian. *Modern Language Journal, 44*(3), 291–300.

Asher, J. J. (1969). The total physical response approach to second language learning. *Modern Language Journal, 50*(2), 3–17.

Asher, J. J. (1977). *Learning another language through actions: The complete teachers' guidebook.* Los Gatos, CA: Sky Oak Productions.

Asher, J. J. (1982). The total physical response approach. In R. W. Blair (Ed.), *Innovative approaches to language teaching* (pp. 54–66). New York: Newbury House.

Ashton-Warner, S. (1963). *Teacher.* New York: Simon & Schuster.

Ashworth, M. (1985). *Beyond methodology.* Cambridge: Cambridge University Press.

Asian Project (1972). *Bridging the Asian language and culture gap.* Vol. 7. Los Angeles City Schools, Division of Career and Continuing Education (ERIC ED 095 709).

Attinasi, J., Pedraza, P., Poplack, S., & Pousada, A. (1982). *Intergenerational perspectives on bilingualism: From community to classroom* (Final Report to National Institute of Education, NIE-G-78-0091). Language Policy Task Force, City University of New York, Center for Puerto Rican Studies.

Auerbach, E. R., & Burgess, D. (1985). The hidden curriculm of survival ESL. *TESOL Quarterly, 19* (2), 125–137.

Austin, J. L. (1962). *How to do things with words.* Oxford: Clarendon Press.

Ausubel, D. A. (1963). Cognitive structure and the facilitation of meaningful verbal learning. *Journal of Teacher Education, 14*(2), 217–222.

Ausubel, D. A. (1968). Educational psychology: A cognitive view. New York: Holt, Rinehart & Winston.

Avery, P., & Erlich, S. (Eds.). (1987). The teaching of pronunciation: An introduction for teachers of English as a second language. *TESL Talk, 17*(1). Ontario, Canada: Ministry of Citizenship and Culture.

Bachman, L. F. (1985). Performance on cloze tests with fixed-ratio and rational deletions. *TESOL Quarterly, 19*(3), 535–556.

Bailey, K. M. (1980). An introspective analysis of an individual's language learning experience. In R. Scarcella & S. D. Krashen (Eds.), *Selected papers of the 1980 Los Angeles second language acquisition research forum* (pp. 58–65). New York: Newbury House.

Bailey, K. M., & Celce-Murcia, M. (1979). Classroom skills for ESL teachers. In M. Celce-Murcia & L. McIntosh (Eds.), *Teaching English as a second or foreign language* (pp. 315–330). New York: Newbury House.

Baldauf, R. B., & Jernudd, B. H. (1983). Language of publications as a variable in scientific communication. *Australian Review of Applied Linguistics, 6,* 96–108.

Bamford, J. (1982). Three out for two in: Use listening texts. *JALT Newsletter, 6*(4), 18–19.

Barker, G., & Canale, M. (1986). *The evaluation process in cooperative problem-solving activities.* Toronto: OISE, Centre for Franco-Ontarian Studies.

Bar-Lev, Z. (1987). *Automatic Hebrew*. Unpublished manuscript, San Diego State University, Linguistics Department.

Bar-Lev, Z. (1988). *Foreign language pre-courses*. Unpublished manuscript. San Diego State University, Linguistics Department.

Bar-Lev, Z. (1989). *Pre-language: An initial method*. Unpublished manuscript, San Diego State University, Linguistics Department.

Barnes, R. (1982). *English language proficiency survey*. Commissioned by the United States Department of Education. Washington, DC: United States Census Bureau.

Bassham, C. (1989). *Deixis as a clue to distinctness in L2 production*. Paper presented at the 2nd Language Research Forum, University of California, Los Angeles.

Bates, M., & Dudley-Evans, T. (1976). *Nucleus*. London: Longman.

Baudoin, E. M., Bober, E. S., Clarke, M. A., Dobson, B. K., & Silverstein, S. (1977). *Reader's choice: A reading skills textbook for students of English as a second language*. Ann Arbor, MI: University of Michigan Press.

Baxter, J. (1980). The dictionary and vocabulary behavior: A single word or a handful? *TESOL Quarterly, 14*(3), 325–337.

Beck, A., & Foster, S. H. (1989). *Navajo-English as nativized dialect*. Paper presented at the 2nd Language Research Forum, University of California, Los Angeles.

Beck, A., Foster, S. H., & Selinker, L. (1989). *Acquiring markers of coherence in non-native written English*. Paper presented at the 2nd Language Research Forum, University of California, Los Angeles.

Beebe, L. M., & Takahashi, T. (1987). *Do you have a bag?: Status and patterned variation in second language acquisition*. Unpublished manuscript, Columbia University, Teachers College.

Beile, W. (1978). Towards a classification of listening comprehension exercises. *Audio-visual Language Journal, 16*(3), 147–153.

Bejarano, Y. (1987). A cooperative small-group methodology in the language classroom. *TESOL Quarterly, 21*(3), 483–504.

Belasco, S. (1971). The feasibility of learning a second language in an artificial unicultural situation. In P. Pimsleur & T. Quinn (Eds.), *The psychology of second language learning. Papers from the Second International Congress of AILA*. Cambridge: Cambridge University Press.

Bell, J., & Burnaby, B. (1984). *A handbook for ESL literacy*. Agincourt, Ontario: Dominie Press.

Belmont Community Adult School. (1988, April). *Application for Accreditation, Form C*. Los Angeles, CA.

Belyayev, B. V. (1964). *The psychology of teaching foreign languages* (R. F. Hingley, Trans.). New York: Macmillan.

Benevento, J. (1984, November). *Choosing and using textbooks*. Paper presented at the Annual Meeting of the American Council of the Teaching of Foreign Languages, Chicago. (ERIC Document Reproduction Services No. ED 253 080)

Bengur, B. (1973). *Selection of literature for the ESL classroom: A project involving student evaluation*. Unpublished MATESL thesis, University of California, Los Angeles.

Benson, M. (1985). Collocations and idioms. In R. Ilson (Ed.), *Dictionaries, lexicography and language learning* (ELT Document No. 120). Oxford: Pergamon Press.

Benson, M., Benson, E., & Ilson, R. (1986). *The BBI combinatory dictionary of English: A guide to word combinations*. Amsterdam: John Benjamins.

Bensoussan, M., & Golan, J. (1985). An advanced English course for students of mathematics. In J. M. Ulijn & A. K. Pugh (Eds.), *Reading for professional purposes: Methods and materials in teaching languages*. Leuven/Amersfoort: ACCO.

Berko, J. (1958). The child's learning of English morphology. In S. Saporta (Ed.), *Psycholinguistics: A book of readings* (pp. 359–375). New York: Holt, Rinehart & Winston.

Berman, R. (1975). Analytical syntax: A technique for advanced level reading. *TESOL Quarterly, 9*(3), 243–251.

Berry, C., & Bailey, D. (1983). *Video English*. London: Macmillan.

Bertoletti, M. C., & Dahlet, P. (1984). Manuels et materiels scolaires pour l'apprentissage du F. L. E. Ébauche d'une grille d'analyse [Study guides and instructional materials for learning French as a foreign language. Outline of a grid for analysis]. *Français dans le Monde, 186*, 55–63.

Bialystock, E. (1978). A theoretical model of second language learning. *Language Learning, 28*(1), 69–83.

Billups, L. H., & Rauth, M. (1987). Teachers and research. In V. Richardson-Koehler (Ed.), *Educators' handbook: A research perspective* (pp. 624–639). New York: Longman.

Blackburn, J. M. (1974). A French immersion course at the senior high school level: Panacea or illusion. *Orbit, 5*(3), 7–9.

Blair, R. W. (Ed.). (1982). *Innovative approaches to language teaching*. New York: Newbury House.

Blanton, L. L. (1987). Reshaping ESL students' perceptions of writing. *ELT Journal, 41*(2), 112–118.

Blatchford, C. H. (1979). *Directory of teacher preparation programs in TESOL and bilingual education* (5th ed.). Washington, DC: TESOL.

Bley-Vroman, R. (1985). *The logical problem of foreign language acquisition*. Unpubl. Ms.; Univ. Texas, Austin. (In Rutherford & Sharwood Smith, 1988).

Bliss, B. (1986). Literacy and the limited English population: A national perspective. *Issues of parent in-*

volvement and literacy. Washington, DC: Trinity College.

Block, E. (1986). The comprehension strategies of second language readers. *TESOL Quarterly, 20*(3), 463–494.

Bloom, B. S., & Krathwohl, D. R. (1977). *Taxonomy of educational objectives: The classification of educational goals; Handbook I: Cognitive domain.* New York: Longman.

Bloomfield, L. (1933). *Language.* New York: Holt, Rinehart & Winston.

Blum-Kulka, S. (1982). Learning to say what you mean in a second language: A study of the speech act performance of learners of Hebrew as a second language. *Applied Linguistics, 3*(1), 29–59.

Blum-Kulka, S., Danet, B., & Gherson, R. (1985). The language of requesting in Israeli society. In F. Forgas (Ed.), *Language and social situation* (pp. 113–139). New York: Springer-Verlag.

Blum-Kulka, S., & Olshtain, E. (1984). Requests and apologies: A cross-cultural study of speech act realization patterns (CCSARP). *Applied Linguistics, 5*(3), 196–213.

Blundell, J., Higgens, H., & Middlemass, N. (1982). *Functions in English.* Oxford: Oxford University Press.

Bodman, J. W. , & Lanzano, M. K. (1975). *No hot water tonight.* New York: Collier-MacMillan.

Bodman, J. W., & Lanzano, M. K. (1981). *Milk and honey: An ESL series for adults* (Book 2). New York: HBJ Center for Lifelong Education.

Bodman, J. W., & Lanzano, M. K. (1984). *Milk and honey: An ESL series for adults* (Book 4). New York: HBJ Center for Lifelong Education.

Bossert, S. T. (1988). Cooperative activities in the classroom. In E. Z. Rothkopf (Ed.), *Review of research in education* (Vol. 15, pp. 225–250). Washington, DC: American Educational Research Association.

Bourdieu, P., & Passeron, J. C. (1977). *Reproduction in education, society, and culture* (R. Nice, Trans.). Beverly Hills, CA: Sage.

Bowen, J. D. (1972). Contextualizing pronunciation practice in the ESOL classroom. *TESOL Quarterly, 6*(1), 83–94.

Bowen, J. D. (1975). *Patterns of English pronunciation.* New York: Newbury House.

Bowen, J. D., Madsen, H., & Hilferty, A. (1985). *TESOL techniques and procedures.* New York: Newbury House.

Boyd, J. R., & Boyd, M. A. (1982). *Before book one: Listening activities for prebeginning students of English.* Englewood Cliffs, NJ: Prentice-Hall.

Braddock, R., Lloyd-Jones, R., & Schoer, L. (1963). *Research in written composition.* Champaign, IL: NCTE.

Branvold, D., Chang, L. L., Pribst, G., & Bennion, J. (1986). Effectiveness of the interactive videodisk workstation in use in English language center at Brigham Young University. *CALICO Journal, 4*(2), 25–39.

Brazil, D., Coulthard, M., & Johns, C. (1980). *Discourse intonation and language teaching.* London: Longman.

Breen, M. (1984). Process syllabuses for the language classroom. In C. J. Brumfit (Ed.), *General English syllabus design: Curriculum and syllabus design for the general English classroom* (EFL Documents 118, pp. 47–60). Oxford: Oxford University Press.

Breen, M. P. (1987a). Learner contributions to task design. In C. N. Candlin & D. F. Murphy (Eds.), *Language learning tasks* (pp. 23–46). Englewood Cliffs, NJ: Prentice-Hall.

Breen, M. P. (1987b). Contemporary paradigms in syllabus design. Part I. *Language Teaching, 20*(2), 81–92.

Breen, M. P. (1987c). Contemporary paradigms in syllabus design. Part II. *Language Teaching, 20*(3), 157–174.

Breen, M. P., Candlin, C., & Waters, A. (1979). Communicative materials design: Some basic principles. *RELC Journal, 10*(2), 1–13.

Brewster, E. T., & Brewster, E. (1976). *Language acquisition made practical.* Pasadena, CA: Lingua House.

Bridgeman, B., & Carlson, S. B. (1984). Survey of academic writing tasks. *Written Communication, 1*(2), 247–280.

Brière, E. J. (1973). Cross-cultural biases in language testing. In J. W. Oller, Jr., & J. C. Richards (Eds.), *Focus on the learner: Pragmatic perspectives for the language teacher* (pp. 214–227). New York: Newbury House.

Brière, E. J., & Brown, R. H. (1971). Norming tests of ESL among Amerindian children. *TESOL Quarterly, 5* (4), 327–333.

Bright, J., Koch, K., Ruttenberg, A., & Terdy, D. (1982). *An ESL literacy resource guide: A handbook for ESL/ adult educators in Illinois.* Arlington Heights, IL: Illinois Statewide English as a Second Language/ Adult Education Service Center.

Brill, H. (1986). *Developing a communicative test of reading comprehension and determining its effectiveness.* Unpublished manuscript. Hebrew School of Education, Jerusalem.

Brinton, D., Snow, M. A., & Wesche, M. B. (1989). *Content-based second language instruction.* New York: Newbury House.

Brock, C. A. (1986). The effects of referential questions on ESL classroom discourse. *TESOL Quarterly, 20*(1), 47–60.

Brooks, N. (1969). Teaching culture abroad: From concept to classroom technique. *Modern Language Journal, 53*(5), 320–324.

Brown, A. L., & Day J. D. (1983). Macrorules for summarizing texts: The development of expertise. *Journal of Verbal Learning and Verbal Behavior, 22*(1), 1–14.

Brown, D. F. (1986). *A world of books: An annotated reading list for ESL/EFL students*. Washington, DC: TESOL.

Brown, D. S. (1974). Advanced vocabulary teaching: The problem of collocation. *RELC Journal, 5*(2), 1–11.

Brown, D. S. (1980). Eight C's and a G. *RELC Journal, 11*(Suppl. 3), 1–17.

Brown, G. (1977). *Listening to spoken English*. London: Longman.

Brown, G. (1987). Twenty-five years of teaching listening comprehension. *English Teaching Forum, 25*(1), 11–15.

Brown, G., Currie, K. L., & Kenworthy, J. (1980). *Questions of intonation*. London: Croom Helm.

Brown, G., & Yule, G. (1983a). *Discourse analysis*. Cambridge: Cambridge University Press.

Brown, G., & Yule, G. (1983b). *Teaching the spoken language*. Cambridge: Cambridge University Press.

Brown, H. D. (1987). *Principles of language learning and teaching* (2nd ed.). Englewood Cliffs, NJ: Prentice-Hall.

Brown, J. D. (1981). Newly placed students versus continuing students: Comparing proficiency. In J. C. Fisher, M. A. Clarke, & J. Schachter (Eds.), *On TESOL '80—Building bridges: Research and practice in teaching English as a second language* (pp. 11–119). Washington, DC: TESOL.

Brown, P., & Levinson, S. (1978). Universals in language usage: Politeness phenomena. In E. N. Goody (Ed.), *Questions and politeness: Strategies in social interaction* (pp. 56–289). Cambridge: Cambridge University Press.

Bruder, M. N. (1978). Evaluation of foreign language textbooks: A simplified procedure. In H. S. Madsen & J. D. Bowen (Eds.), *Adaptation in language teaching* (pp. 209–218). New York: Newbury House.

Bruffee, K. (1984). Collaborative learning and the "conversation of mankind." *College English, 46*(7), 635–652.

Brumfit, C. (1981). Review of Moscowitz (1978). *ELT Journal, 36*(1), 63–64.

Brumfit, C. (1984). *Communicative methodology in language teaching—The roles of fluency and accuracy*. Cambridge: Cambridge University Press.

Brumfit, C., & Johnson, K. (1979). *The communicative approach to language teaching*. Oxford: Oxford University Press.

Buckingham, T., & Peck, W. (1976). An experience approach to teaching composition. *TESOL Quarterly 10*(1), 55–66.

Burfoot, A. (1988, November). High energy. *Runner's World* (pp. 38–43).

Burkland, J., & Grimm, N. (1986). Motivating through responding. *Journal of Teaching Writing, 5*(2), 237–247.

Burling, R. (1966). Some outlandish proposals for the teaching of foreign languages. *Language Learning, 18*(1 & 2), 61–75.

Burling, R. (1978). An introductory course in reading French. *Language Learning, 28*(2), 105–128.

Burling, R. (1983). *Sounding right*. New York: Newbury House.

Buzan, J. M. (1972). *Teaching English as an additional language to older people: A case study*. Vancouver, Canada: Adult Education Centre, British Columbia University. (ERIC Document Reproduction Services No. ED 106 535)

Byrd, D., & Clemente-Cabetas, I. (1980). *React interact—Situations for communication*. New York: Regents.

Byrnes, H. (1984). The role of listening comprehension: A theoretical base. *Foreign Language Annals, 17*(4), 317–329.

California State Board of Education. (1983). *Invitation to submit for adoption in California basic instructional materials in the areas of: Art, music, bilingual-bicultural, English as a second language, and foreign language, 1983–1984*. Sacramento: California State Department of Education. (ERIC Docuument Reproduction Service No. ED 239 417)

California State Department of Education (Bilingual Education Office). (1986). *Beyond language: Social and cultural factors in schooling language minority students*. Los Angeles: Evaluation, Dissemination and Assessment Center, California State University, Los Angeles.

California State Department of Education. (1987). *English language arts framework*. Sacramento: California State Department of Education.

Calkins, L. M. (1983). *Lessons from a child*. Exeter, NH: Heinemann Educational Books.

Canale, M. (1984). Considerations in the testing of reading and listening proficiency. *Foreign Language Annals, 17*(4), 349–357.

Canale, M. (1985). *Proficiency-oriented achievement testing*. Toronto: Franco-Ontarian Centre and Curriculm Department, Ontario Institute for Studies in Education.

Canale, M. (1986a). On some theoretical frameworks for language proficiency. In H. Byrnes & M. Canale (Eds.), *Defining and developing proficiency: Guidelines, implementations, and concepts* (pp. 28–40). Lincolnwood, IL: National Textbook Company.

Canale, M. (1986b). The promise and threat of computerized adaptive assessment of reading comprehension. In C. W. Stansfield (Ed.), *Technology and language testing* (pp. 29–45). Washington, DC: TESOL.

Canale, M., & Swain, M. (1980). Theoretical bases of communicative approaches to second language teaching and testing. *Applied Linguistics, 1*(1), 1–47.

Candlin, C. N. (1984). *Implementing process curricula in ESL: The issue of "task."* Paper presented at the 18th annual TESOL convention, Houston, TX.

Candlin, C. N. (1987). Toward task-based learning. In C. N. Candlin & D. F. Murphy (Eds.), *Language learning tasks* (pp. 5–22). Englewood Cliffs, NJ: Prentice-Hall.

Candlin, C., Bruton, C., Leather, J., & Woods, E. (1981). Designing modular materials for communicative language learning; An example: Doctor-patient communication skills. In L. Selinker, E. Tarone, & V. Hanzeli (Eds.), *English for academic and technical purposes: Studies in honor of Luis Trimble* (pp. 105–134). New York: Newbury House.

Candlin, C. N., & Murphy, D. F. (Eds.). (1986). *Language learning tasks.* Englewood Cliffs, NJ: Prentice-Hall.

Candlin, C., Carter, G., Legutke, M., Samuda, V., & Hanson, S. (1988). *Experimental learning: Theory into practice.* Paper presented at the 22nd Annual TESOL Colloquim, Chicago.

Canute, M. (1988). The Canadian ESL helicopter. *TESL Talk, 18*(1), 50–66.

Carbo, M. (1987). Reading styles research: What works isn't always phonics. *Phi Delta Kappan, 68*(6), 431–435.

Carney, B. W., & Lide, F. (1976, November). *Wanted: Alternatives to the lesson format in elementary foreign language textbooks* (rev. ed.). Paper presented at the annual meeting of the American Council of the Teaching of Foreign Languages, Washington, DC. (ERIC Doucument Reproduction Service No. ED 185 799).

Carnicelli, T. A. (1980). The writing conference: A one-to-one conversation. In T. R. Donovan & B. W. McClelland (Eds.), *Eight approaches to teaching composition* (pp. 101–131). Urbana, IL: NCTE.

Carrell, P. L. (1984). Schema theory and ESL reading: Classroom implications and applications. *Modern Language Journal, 68*(4), 332–343.

Carrell, P. L., Devine, J., & Eskey, D. (Eds.). (1988). *Interactive approaches to second language reading.* Cambridge: Cambridge University Press.

Carrell, P. L., & Eisterhold, J. C. (1983). Schema theory and ESL reading pedagogy. *TESOL Quarterly, 17*(4), 553–574.

Carroll, J. B. (1955). *The study of language.* Cambridge, MA: Harvard University Press.

Carter, G., Legutke, M., & Thomas, H. (1987). *Experiential learning: Project work in language learning.* Paper presented at the 21st Annual TESOL Convention, Miami, FL.

Carter, G., & Thomas, H. (1986). "Dear Brown Eyes": Experimental learning in a project-oriented approach. *English Language Teaching Journal, 40*(3), 196–204.

Carter, R. (1987). *Vocabulary.* London: Allen and Unwin.

Carter, R., & McCarthy, M. (1988). *Vocabulary and language teaching.* London: Longman.

Catford, I. (1987). Phonetics and the teaching of pronunciation. In J. Morley (Ed.), *Current perspectives on pronunciation: Practices anchored in theory* (pp. 87–100). Washington, DC: TESOL.

Cazden, C. (1986). ESL teachers as language advocates for children. In P. Rigg & D. S. Enright (Eds.), *Children and ESL: Integrating perspectives* (pp. 9–21). Washington, DC: TESOL.

Celce-Murcia, M. (1979). Language teaching aids. In M. Celce-Murcia & L. McIntosh (Eds.), *Teaching English as a second or foreign language* (pp. 307–315). New York: Newbury House.

Celce-Murcia, M. (1980). Language teaching methods from the ancient Greeks to Gattegno. *Mextesol Journal, 4*(4), 2–13.

Celce-Murcia, M. (1981). New methods in perspective. *Practical English Teaching, 2*(1), 9–12.

Celce-Murcia, M. (Ed.). (1985a). *Beyond basics: Issues and research in TESOL.* New York: Newbury House.

Celce-Murcia, M. (1985b). Making informed decisions about the role of grammar in language teaching. *TESOL Newsletter, 29*(1), 4–5.

Celce-Murcia, M. (1987). Teaching pronunciation as communication. In J. Morley (Ed.), *Current perspectives on pronunciation: Practices anchored in theory* (pp. 5–12). Washington, DC: TESOL.

Celce-Murcia, M., & Hilles, S. (1988). *Techniques and resources in teaching grammar.* New York: Oxford University Press.

Celce-Murcia, M., & Larsen-Freeman, D. (1983). *The grammar book: An ESL/EFL teacher's course.* New York: Newbury House.

Celce-Murcia, M., & Rosensweig, F. (1979). Teaching vocabulary in the ESL classroom. In M. Celce-Murcia & L. McIntosh (Eds.), *Teaching English as a second or foreign language* (pp. 241–257). New York: Newbury House.

Chafe, W. (1976). Givenness, contrastiveness, definiteness, subjects, topics and point of view. In C. Li (Ed.), *Subject and topic* (pp. 25–56). New York: Academic Press.

Chall, J. S. (1983). *Stages of reading development.* New York: McGraw Hill.

Chall, J. S., Heron, E., & Hilferty, A. (1987). Adult literacy: New and enduring problems. *Phi Delta Kappan, 69*(3), 190–196.

Chamberlain, P. (1985). *Communicative syllabus for language education in the workplace at "illustrious restorations"—A retrospective design.* Unpublished manuscript.

Chamot, A. U. (1985). English language development through a content-based approach. In *Issues in English language development* (pp. 49–55). Rosslyn, VA: National Clearinghouse for Bilingual Education and the Georgetown University Bilingual Education Service Center.

Chamot, A. U., & O'Malley, J. M. (1987). The cognitive-academic language learning approach: A bridge to the mainstream. *TESOL Quarterly, 21*(2), 217–249.

Chastain, K. (1976). *Developing second language skills: Theory to practice* (2nd ed.). Chicago: Rand McNally.

Chastain, K. (1988). *Developing second language skills: Theory to Practice* (3rd ed.). San Diego, CA: Harcourt, Brace, Jovanovich.

Chaudron, C. (1977). A descriptive model of discourse in the corrective treatment of learners' errors. *Language Learning, 27*(1), 29–46.

Chaudron, C. (1982). Vocabulary elaboration in teachers' speech to L2 learners. *Studies in Second Language Acquisition, 4*(2), 170–180.

Chaudron, C. (1986). The role of error correction in second language teaching. *U H Working Papers in ESL, 5*(3), 44–82.

Chaudron, C. (1988). *Second language classrooms.* Cambridge: Cambridge University Press.

Chaudron, C., Crookes, G., & Long, M. H. (1988). *Reliability and validity in second language classroom research.* (Tech. Rep. No. 8). Honolulu: University of Hawaii, Center for Second Language Classroom Research, Social Science Research Institute.

Chaudron, C., & Richards, J. C. (1986). The effect of discourse markers on the comprehension of lectures. *Applied Linguistics, 7*(2), 112–127.

Chaudron, C., & Valcarel, M. (1988). *A process-product study of communicative language teaching* (Final report submitted to the Comite Conjunto Hispano-Norteamericano para la Cooperacion Cultural y Educativa, Madrid). Murcia, Spain: Universidad de Murcia, Escuela Universitaria de Magisterio.

Chavez-Oller, M. A., Chihara, T., Weaver, K. A., & Oller, J. W., Jr. (1985). When are cloze items sensitive to constraints across sentences? *Language Learning, 35*(2), 181–206.

Chenoweth, N. A. (1987). The need to teach rewriting. *ELT Journal, 41*(1), 25–29.

Chesler, S. A. (1976). Integrating the teaching of reading and literature. *Journal of Reading, 19*(5), 360–366.

Chomsky, N. (1957). *Syntactic structures.* The Hague: Mouton.

Chomsky, N. (1959). Review of Skinner's *Verbal Behavior. Language, 35,* 26–58.

Chomsky, N., & Halle, M. (1968). *The sound pattern of English.* New York: Harper & Row.

Claassen, J. (1984, June). *Classics for the gifted: Some practical strategies.* Paper presented at the international conference: Education for the Gifted "Ingenium 2000," Stellenbosh, Republic of South Africa. (ERIC Document Reproduction Service No. ED 292 224)

Clahsen, H. (1984). The acquisition of German word order: A test case for cognitive approaches to L2 development. In R. Andersen (Ed.), *Second language: A crosslinguistic perspective.* New York: Newbury House.

Clark, C., & Lampert, M. (1986). The study of teacher thinking: Implications for teacher education. *Journal of Teacher Education, 37*(4), 27–31.

Clark, J. L. D. (1972). *Foreign-language testing: Theory and practice.* Philadelphia: Center for Curriculum Development.

Clarke, D., & Nation, I. S. P. (1980). Guessing the meaning of words from context: Strategies and techniques. *System, 8*(3), 211–220.

Clarke, M. (1979). Reading in Spanish and English: Evidence from adult ESL students. *Language Learning, 29*(1), 121–150.

Clarke, M. (1980). The short circuit hypothesis of ESL reading. *Modern Language Journal, 64*(2), 203–209.

Clausen, J. (1982). Textbooks and (in) -equality: A survey of literacy readers for elementary and intermediate German. *Die Unterrichtspraxis, 15*(2), 244–253.

Clifford, R., & Higgs, T. V. (1982). The push toward communication. In T. V. Higgs (Ed.), *ACTFL Foreign Language Education Series: Vol. 13. Curriculum, competence, and the foreign language teacher* (pp. 57–79). Lincolnwood, IL: National Textbook Co.

Cohen, A. D. (1980). *Testing language ability in the classroom.* New York: Newbury House.

Cohen, A. D. (1984). On taking language tests: What the students report. *Language Testing, 1*(1), 70–81.

Cohen, A. D. (1987). Student processing of feedback on their compositions. In A. L. Wenden & J. Rubin (Eds.), *Learner strategies in language learning* (pp. 57–69). Englewood Cliffs, NJ: Prentice-Hall International.

Cohen, A. D., & Aphek, E. (1980). Retention of second language vocabulary over time: Investigating the role of mnemonic association. *System, 8*(3), 221–236.

Cohen, A. D., & Cavalcanti, M. C. (1990). Feedback on compositions: Teacher and student verbal reports. In B. Kroll (Ed.), *Second language writing: Research insights for the classroom.* New York: Cambridge University Press, pp. 155–177.

Cohen, A. D., Glasman, H., Rosenbaum-Cohen, P. R., Ferrara, J., & Fine, J. (1979). Reading English for specialized purposes: Discourse analysis and the use of student informants. *TESOL Quarterly, 13*(4), 551–564.

Cohen, A. D., & Hosenfeld, C. (1981). Some uses of mentalistic data in second language research. *Language Learning, 31*(2), 285–313.

Cohen, A. D., & Olshtain, E. (1981). Developing a measure of sociocultural competence: The case of apology. *Language Learning, 31*(1), 113–134.

Cohen, A. D., Olshtain, E., & Rosenstein, D. S. (1986). Advanced EFL apologies: What remains to be learned. *International Journal of the Sociology of Language, 62,* 51–74.

Cohen, A. D., & Robbins, M. (1976). Toward assessing interlanguage performance: The relationship between selected errors, learners' characteristics, and learners' explanations. *Language Learning, 26*(1), 45–66.

Cohen, E. G. (1986). *Designing groupwork: Strategies for*

the heterogeneous classroom. New York: Teachers College Press.

Cole, P. (1970). An adaptation of group dynamics techniques to foreign language teaching. *TESOL Quarterly, 4*(4), 358–360.

Coleman, A. (1929). *Teaching of modern foreign languages in the United States.* New York: Macmillan.

Coleman, A., & Fife, R. H. (1949). *An analytical bibliography of modern language teaching, Vol. III (1937–42).* New York: King's Crown Press.

Coleman, J. S. (1976). Differences between experiential and classroom learning. In M. T. Keeton & Associates, *Experiential learning* (pp. 49–61). San Francisco: Jossey-Bass.

Collier, V. P. (1987). Age and rate of acquisition of second language for academic purposes. *TESOL Quarterly, 21*(4), 617–641.

Colvin, R. J., & Root, J. H. (1981). *TUTOR: Techniques used in the teaching of reading.* Syracuse, NY: Literacy Volunteers of America.

Colvin, R. J., & Root, J. H. (1982). *READ: Reading evaluation—Adult diagnosis.* Syracuse, NY: Literacy Volunteers of America.

Commins, N. L. (1989). Language and affect: Bilingual students at home and at school. *Language Arts, 66*(1), 29–43.

Cooper, R. L., & Fishman, J. A. (1977). A study of language attitudes. In J. A. Fishman, A. L. Cooper, & A. W. Conrad (Eds.), *The spread of English* (pp. 239–276). New York: Newbury House.

Cooper, R. L., & Seckbach, F. (1977). Economic incentives for the learning of a language of wider communication: A case study. In J. A. Fishman, R. L. Cooper, & A. W. Conrad (Eds.), *The spread of English* (pp. 212–219). New York: Newbury House.

Corder, S. P. (1973). Pedagogic grammars. In W. E. Rutherford & M. S. Smith (Eds.), *Grammar and second language teaching: A book of readings.* New York: Newbury House, 1988.

Cornelius, E. T. (1953). *Language teaching.* New York: Thomas Y. Crowell.

Cotton, W. (1968). *On behalf of adult education: A historical examination of the supporting literature.* Boston: Center for the Study of Liberal Education for Adults.

Council on Interracial Books for Children. (1977). Ten quick ways to analyse books for racism and sexism. In J. M. Hornburger & B. Boatman (Eds.), *Teaching multcultural children* (pp. 48–52). Boston: Boston University. (ERIC Document Reproduction Service No. ED 139 045)

Cowan, G., & Cowan, E. (1980). *Writing.* New York: Wiley.

Cowles, H. M. (1976). Textbook materials evaluation: A comprehensive checksheet. *Foreign Language Annals, 9*(4), 300–303.

Craig, M. (1985). Community contact program. Course Project Report for course taken with Prof. Michael Canale, Communicative Competence 1338F, Livia De Gannaro, December 9.

Crandall, J. (Ed.). (1987). *ESL through content-area instruction: Mathematics, science, social studies.* Englewood Cliffs, NJ: Prentice-Hall Regents.

Crandall, J., & Burkart, G. S. (Eds.). (1984). ESP: Vocational ESL [special issue]. *ESP Journal, 3*(2).

Crandall, J., Spanos, G., Christian, D., Simich-Dudgeon, C., & Willetts, K. (1987). *Integrating language and content instruction for language minority students* (Teacher Resource Guide No. 4). Wheaton, MD: National Clearinghouse for Bilingual Education.

Crawford, J. (1989). *Bilingual education: History, politics, theory, and practice.* Trenton, NJ: Crane.

Crawford-Lange, L. (1987). Curricular alternatives for second-language learning. In M. H. Long & J. C. Richards (Eds.), *Methodology in TESOL: A book of readings* (pp. 120–144). New York: Newbury House.

Cray, E. (1988). Why teachers should develop their own materials. *TESL Talk, 18*(1), 69–81.

Cronin, M. (1987). *Test-taking of experts and novices in an undergraduate geography class.* Unpublished manuscript, San Diego State University.

Crookes, G. (1986). *Task classification: A cross-disciplinary review* (Technical Report no. 4). Honolulu: University of Hawaii, Social Science Research Institute, Center for Second Language Classroom Research.

Crookes, G. (1989). Planning and interlanguage variation. *Studies in Second Language Acquisition, 11*(4), 367–383.

Crookes, G., & Rulon, K. A. (1985). *Incorporation of corrective feedback in NS/NNS conversation* (Technical Report no. 3). Honolulu: University of Hawaii, Social Science Research Institute, Center for Second Language Classroom Research.

Crookes, G., & Rulon, K. A. (1988). Topic and feedback in native-speaker/non-native speaker conversation. *TESOL Quarterly, 22*(4), 675–684.

Cruickshank, D. R. (1987). *Reflective teaching.* Reston, VA: Association of Teacher Educators.

Cuevas, G. (1984). Mathematics learning in English as a second language. *Journal of Research in Mathematics Education, 15*, 134–144.

Culley, G., Mulford, G., & Milbury-Steen, J. (1986). A foreign language adventure game: Progress report on application of AI to language instruction. *Calico Journal, 4*(2), 69–87.

Cummins, J. (1979). Linguistic interdependence and the educational development of bilingual children. *Review of Educational Research, 49*(2), 222–251.

Cummins, J. (1980a). The cross-lingual dimensions of language proficiency: Implications for bilingual education and the optimal age issue. *TESOL Quarterly, 14*(2), 175–187.

Cummins, J. (1980b). The exit and entry fallacy in bilingual education. *NABE Journal, 4*(3), 25–60.

Cummins, J. (1981a). Age on arrival and immigrant second language learning in Canada: A reassessment. *Applied Linguistics, 2*(2), 132–149.

Cummins, J. (1981b). The role of primary language development in promoting educational success for language minority students. In California State Department of Education, Office of Bilingual Bicultural Education, *Schooling and language minority students: A theoretical framework* (pp. 3–49). Sacramento: Evaluation, Dissemination and Assessment Center, California State University, Los Angeles.

Cummins, J. (1984). *Bilingualism and special education: Issues in assessment and pedagogy.* Clevedon: Multilingual Matters.

Curran, C. A. (1960). Communinity language learning. In R. W. Blair (Ed.), *Innovative approaches to language teaching* (pp. 118–133). New York: Newbury House.

Curran, C. A. (1976). *Counseling-learning in second-language learning.* East Dubuque, IL: Counseling-Learning Publications.

Curtain, H. A., & Martinez, L. S. (1989). *Integrating the elementary school curriculum into the foreign language class: Hints for the FLES teacher.* Educational Report, Univerity of California, Los Angeles: Center for Language Education and Research.

Cziko, G. A., & Nien-Hsuan, J. L. (1984). The construction and analysis of short scales of language proficiency: Classical psychometric, latent trait, and nonparametric approaches. *TESOL Quarterly, 18*(4), 627–647.

Danesi, M. (1976). A critical survey of elementary and intermediate Italian textbooks, 1966–1975. *Modern Language Journal, 60*(3), 119–122.

Danesi, M. (1988). Neurological bimodality and theories of language teaching. *Studies in Second Language Acquisition, 10*(1), 13–31.

Daoud, A. M., & Celce-Murcia, M. (1979). Selecting and evaluating textbooks. In M. Celce-Murcia & L. McIntosh (Eds.), *Teaching English as a second or foreign language* (pp. 302–307). New York: Newbury House.

Davis, P., & Rinvolucri, M. (1988). *Dictation: New methods, new possibilities.* Cambridge: Cambridge University Press.

Davison, W. F. (1976). Factors in evaluating and selecting texts for the foreign-language classroom. *English Language Teaching Journal, 30*(4), 310–314.

DeAvila, E., & Duncan, S. (1984). *Finding out and descubrimiento: Teacher's guide.* San Rafael, CA: Linguametrics Group.

De Beaugrande, R. (1985). Sentence combining and discourse processing: In search of a general theory. In. D. Daiker, A. Kerek & M. Morenberg (Eds.), *Sentence combining: A rhetorical perspective* (pp. 61–75). Carbondale, IL: Southern Illinois University Press.

De Capua, A. (1989). *The transfer of native language speech behavior into second language: A basis for cultural stereotypes?* Bronxville, NY: Concordia College.

D'Eloia, S. (1975). The uses—and limits—of grammar. *Journal of Basic Writing, 1*(1), 1–26.

Deloria, V., Jr. (1988). *Custer died for your sins* (rev. ed.). Norman, OK: University of Oklahoma Press.

Denes, P., & Pinson, E. (1963). *The speech chain: The physics and biology of spoken language.* New York: Doubleday.

Devine, J., Carrell, P. L., & Eskey, D. E. (Eds.). (1987). *Research in reading in English as a second language.* Washington, DC: TESOL.

Dewey, J. (1938). *Experience and education.* New York: Macmillan.

Deyhle, D. (1987). Learning failure: Tests as gatekeepers and the culturally different child. In *Success or failure: Learning and the language minority student* (pp. 85–108). New York: Newbury House/Harper & Row.

Diaz, S. (1987, April). *CERRC (Community Educational Resource and Research Center): A model in action.* Paper presented at the University of California Linguistic Minority Project Conference, Los Angeles.

Diaz, S., Moll, L., & Mehan, H. (1986). Sociocultural resources in instruction: A context-specific approach. In *Beyond language: Social and cultural factors in schooling language minority students* (pp. 187–230). Los Angeles: Evaluation, Dissemination, and Assessment Center, California State University.

Dickerson, W. B. (1975). The WH question of pronunciation: An answer for spelling and generative phonology. *TESOL Quarterly, 9*(3), 299–309.

Dickerson, W. B., & Finney, R. H. (1978). Spelling in TESL: Stress cues to vowel quality. *TESOL Quarterly, 12*(2), 163–175.

Dinsmore, D. (1985). Waiting for Godot in the EFL classroom. *ELT Journal, 39*(4), 225–234.

Dirven, R., & Oakeshott-Taylor, J. (1984). Listening comprehension, Part I. *Language Teaching, 17*(4), 326–343.

Dirven, R., & Oakeshott-Taylor, J. (1985). Listening comprehension, Part II. *Language Teaching, 18*(1), 2–20.

Dixon, C., & Nessel, D. (1983). *Language experience approach to reading (and writing).* Hayward, CA: Alemany Press.

Dornic, S. (Ed.). (1977). *Attention and performance VI.* Hillsdale, NJ: Erlbaum.

Dornic, S. (1979). Information processing in bilinguals: Some selected issues. *Psychological Research, 40*(4), 329–348.

Dosi, S. (1983). *Evaluation of primary English books I and II for Tanzania* (African Studies in Curriculum Development and Evaluation, No. 124). Requirement for the postgraduate diploma in curriculum development, University of Nairobi, Kenya. (ERIC Document Reproduction Services No. ED 249 501)

Doughty, C., & Pica, T. (1986). "Information gap" tasks: Do they facilitate second language acquisition? *TESOL Quarterly, 20*(2), 305–325.

Doyle, W. (1979). Classroom tasks and students' abilities. In P. L. Peterson & H. J. Walberg (Eds.), *Research on teaching.* Berkeley, CA: McCutchan.

Doyle, W. (1980). *Student mediating responses in teacher effectiveness.* Final report, Department of Education, North Texas State University.

Doyle, W. (1983). Academic work. *Review of Educational Research, 53*(2), 159–199.

Dubin, F. (1986). Dealing with texts. In F. Dubin, D. Eskey, & W. Grabe (Eds.), *Teaching second language reading for academic purposes* (pp. 127–160). Reading, MA: Addison-Wesley.

Dubin, F., Eskey, D., & Grabe, W. (Eds.). (1986). *Teaching second language reading for academic purposes.* Reading, MA: Addison-Wesley.

Dubin, F., & Olshtain, E. (1977). *Facilitating language learning: A guidebook for the ESL/EFL teacher.* New York: McGraw-Hill.

Dubin, F., & Olshtain, E. (1981). *Reading by all means.* Reading, MA: Addison-Wesley.

Dubin, F., & Olshtain, E. (1986). *Course design: Developing programs and materials for language learning.* New York: Cambridge University Press.

Dubin, F., & Olshtain, E. (1987). *Let's stop putting vocabulary under the rug.* Paper presented at the 21st Annual TESOL Convention, Miami, FL.

Dubin, F., & Olshtain, E. (1990). *Reading by all means: All new edition.* Reading, MA: Addison-Wesley.

Duff, P. A. (1986). Another look at interlanguage talk: Taking task to task. In R. R. Day (Ed.), *Talking to learn: Conversation in second language acquisition* (pp. 171–187). New York: Newbury House.

Duke University. (1987). *CALIS: Computer Assisted Language Instruction.* Durham: Author.

Dulay, H., Burt, M., & Krashen, S. (1982). *Language two.* New York: Oxford University Press.

Duran, R. (1987). Factors affecting development of second language literacy. In S. Goldman & H. Trueba (Eds.), *Becoming literate in English as a second language* (pp. 33–55). Norwood, NJ: Ablex.

Early, M. M. (1985). *Input and interaction in content classrooms: Foreigner talk and teacher talk in classroom discourse.* Unpublished doctoral dissertation, University of California, Los Angeles.

Ebbinghaus, H. (1897). Über eine neue Methode zür Prüfung geistiger Fähigkeiten und ihre Anwendung bei Schulkindern. In S. Exner et al., *Zeitschrift für Psychologie und Physiologie der Sinnesorgane.* Leipzig: Barth.

Ebel, C. W. (1980). An update: Teaching reading to students of English as a second language. *Reading Teacher, 33*(4), 403–407.

Ebel, C. W. (1985). The teacher as a coach in the ESL classroom, *NASSP Bulletin, 69*(479), 77–81.

Edelhoff, C. (1981). Theme-oriented English teaching: Text-varieties, media, skills and project work. In C. N. Candlin (Ed.), *The communicative teaching of English: Principles and an exercise typology* (pp. 49–62). London: Longman.

Edelsky, C. (1982). Writing in a bilingual program: The relation of L1 and L2 texts. *TESOL Quarterly, 16*(2), 211–228.

Edelsky, C. (1986). *Writing in a bilingual program. Habia una vez.* Norwood, NJ: Ablex.

Edelsky, C., Draper, K., & Smith, K. (1983). Hookin' 'em in at the start of school in a "whole language" classroom. *Anthropology and Educational Quarterly, 14*(4), 257–281.

Edwards, H. P., Wesche, M. B., Krashen, S., Clement, R., & Kruidenier, B. (1984). Second language acquisition through subject matter learning: A study of sheltered psychology classes at the University of Ottawa. *Canadian Modern Language Review, 41*(2), 268–282.

Eisenstein, M. R. (1980). Grammatical explanations in ESL: Teach the student, not the method. *TESL Talk, 11*(4), 3–11.

Ekwall, E. E., & Shanker, J. (1983). *Diagnosis and remediation of the disabled reader.* Newton, MA: Allyn and Bacon.

Elbow, P. (1973). *Writing without teachers.* New York: Oxford University Press.

Elbow, P. (1985). The challenge for sentence combining. In D. Daiker, A. Kerek, & M. Morenberg (Eds.), *Sentence combining: A rhetorical perspective* (pp. 232–245). Carbondale, IL: Southern Illinois University Press.

Eley, V., & Lewis, D. (1976). *Learning center activities for beginning ESL language and reading development.* Long Beach, CA: Harris.

Ellis, R. (1985). Teacher-pupil interaction in second language development. In S. Gass & C. Madden (Eds.), *Input in second language acquisition* (pp. 69–85). New York: Newbury House.

Emig, J. (1971). *The composing process of twelfth graders.* Urbana, IL: NCTE.

Emmerich, P. J. (1977). A textbook selection checklist for bilingual situations. *Reading Improvement, 14*(4), 256–257.

English Language Center, Brigham Young University. (1990). *Expeditions into English: Listening/Speaking I. A beginning integrated skills series.* Englewood Cliffs, NJ: Prentice-Hall.

English Language Institute, University of Michigan. (1943). *An intensive course in English for Latin-American students.* Ann Arbor, MI: Wahr.

Enright, D. S. (1986). Use everything you have to teach English: Providing useful input to young language learners. In P. Rigg & D. S. Enright (Eds.), *Children and ESL: Integrating perspectives* (pp. 113–162). Washington, DC: TESOL.

Enright, D. S. (1991). Tapping the Peer Interaction Resource. In M. McGroarty and C. Faltis (Eds.), *Languages in School and Society* (pp. 209–231). Berlin: Walter de Gruyter.

Enright, D. S., & McCloskey, M. L. (1985). Yes, talking!: Organizing the classroom to promote second language acquisition. *TESOL Quarterly, 19*(3), 431–453.

Enright, D. S., & McCloskey, M. L. (1988). *Integrating English: Developing English language and literacy in the multilingual classroom.* Addison-Wesley.

Erdynast, A. (1981). *Field experience education and stage theories of development* (Occasional paper). John Duley, Ed. National Society for Internships and Experiential Education, Washington, DC.

Erickson, F., & Mohatt, G. (1982). Cultural organization of participation structures in two classrooms of Indian students. In G. Spindler (Ed.), *Doing the ethnography of schooling* (pp. 132–174). New York: Holt, Rinehart & Winston.

Erteschik-Shir, N. (1979). Discourse constraints on dative movement. In T. Givon (Ed.), *Syntax and semantics: Vol. 12. Discourse and syntax* (pp. 441–467). New York: Academic Press.

Eskey, D. (1983). Meanwhile, back in the real world . . . : Accuracy and fluency in second language teaching. *TESOL Quarterly, 17*(2), 315–323.

Eskey, D. (1986). Theoretical foundations. In F. Dubin, D. Eskey, & W. Grabe (Eds.), *Teaching second language reading for academic purposes* (pp. 3–24). Reading, MA: Addison-Wesley.

Eskey, D. (1987). Conclusion. In J. Devine, P. L. Carrell, & D. Eskey (Eds.), *Research in reading English as a second language* (pp. 189–192). Washington, DC: TESOL.

Eskey, D. (1988). Holding in the bottom: An interactive approach to the language problems of second language readers. In P. Carrell, J. Devine, & D. Eskey (Eds.), *Interactive approaches to second language reading* (pp. 93–100). New York: Cambridge University Press.

Eyring, J. (1988). *Project work in the ESL writing course: A case study.* Unpublished manuscript. University of California, Los Angeles.

Eyring, J. (1989). *Teacher experiences and student responses in ESL project work instruction: A case study.* Doctoral dissertation, University of California, Los Angeles.

Faerch, C. (1986). Rules of thumb and other teacher-formulated rules in the foreign language classroom. In G. Kasper (Ed.), *Learning, teaching, and communication in the foreign language classroom* (pp. 125–143). Aarhus, Denmark: Aarhus University Press.

Fairbanks, P., & Schmid, M. (1988). *Program description for Indian studies in the Cass Lake public schools.* Cass Lakes, MN: Cass Lake/Bena School District.

Fassman, P., & Tavares, S. (1985). *Fast forward: Longman intermediate listening series* (Book 2). White Plains, NY: Longman.

Fathman, A., & Whalley, E. (1990). Teacher response to student writing: Focus on form versus focus on content. In B. Kroll (Ed.), *Second language writing: Re-search insights for the classroom* (pp. 178–190). New York: Cambridge University Press.

Ferguson, C. A., & Heath, S. B. (Eds.). (1981). *Language in the USA.* Cambridge: Cambridge University Press.

Ferris, D., Kiyochi, E., & Kowal, K. (1988). *Second language vocabulary acquisition from extensive reading.* Paper presented at the 22nd Annual TESOL Convention, Chicago.

Figueroa, J., Walker, L., Varon, M., & Johnson, H. (1988). *Division of adult and occupational education 1986–87* (Annual Report). Los Angeles: Los Angeles Unified School District.

Fillmore, C. (1981). Ideal readers and real readers. In D. Tannen (Ed.), *Georgetown University Roundtable on languages and linguistics 1981.* Washington, DC: Georgetown University Press.

Fillmore, C., Ammon, P., McLaughlin, B., & Ammon, M. S. (1985). *Final report for learning English through bilingual instruction.* Unpublished manuscript, University of California, Berkeley and Santa Cruz.

Filosa, F. (1988, September). The greenhouse effect: When will it hit? *World Press Review,* pp. 27–29.

Finger, A. (1985). *Tune in tonight: Listening to the news.* New York: Newbury House.

Finnemann, M. D. (1987). Liberating the foreign language syllabus. *Modern Language Journal, 71*(1), 36–43.

Finocchiaro, M., & Sako, S. (1983). *Foreign language testing: A practical approach.* New York: Regents.

Fishman, A. (1988). *Amish literacy: What and how it means.* Portsmouth, NH: Heinemann.

Fishman, J. A. (1980). *Non-English language resource of the United States. Final Report to Department of Education* (Grant G-00-79-01816). Washington, DC.

Fishman, J. A. (1977). The spread of English as a new perspective for the study of "language maintenance and language shift". In J. A. Fishman, A. L. Cooper, & A. W. Conrad (Eds.), *The spread of English* (pp. 108–133). New York: Newbury House.

Flanders, N. (1970). *Analyzing teacher behavior.* Reading, MA: Addison-Wesley.

Flashner, V. (1987). *An exploration of linguistic dichotomies and genres in the classroom languages of native and non-native English-speaking children.* Unpublished doctoral dissertation, University of California, Los Angeles.

Fleming, D. C., Fleming, E. R., Oksman, P. F., & Roach, K. S. (1984). An approach to self-supervision for school practitioners. In C. A. Maher, R. J. Illback, & J. E. Zins (Eds.), *Organizational psychology in the schools: A handbook for professionals* (pp. 323–344). Springfield, IL: Charles C Thomas.

Flower, L. S. (1979). Writer-based prose: A cognitive basis for problems in writing. *College English, 41*(1), 19–37.

Floyd, P., & Carrell, P. (1987). Effects on ESL reading of teaching and cultural content schemata. *Language Learning, 37*(1), 89–108.

Foley, B. H. (1984). *Now hear this: Listening comprehension for high-beginners and intermediates*. New York: Newbury House.

Foley, B. H. (1985). *Listen to me: Beginning listening comprehension*. New York: Newbury House.

Foley, J. A. (1985). Reading skills in science and technology for the L2 student. In J. M. Ulijn & A. K. Pugh (Eds.), *Reading for professional purposes: Methods and materials in teaching languages*. Leuven/Amersfoort: ACCO.

Fox, L. (1983). *Passages: An intermediate/advance writing book*. New York: Harcourt Brace Jovanovich.

Fragiadakis, H. (1988). Description and evaluation of training course for international graduate students instructors. (ERIC Document Reproduction Service No. ED 292 294)

Fransson, A. (1984). Cramming or understanding? Effects of instrinsic and extrinsic motivation on approach to learning and test performance. In J. C. Alderson & A. H. Urquhart (Eds.), *Reading in a foreign language* (pp. 86–121). London: Longman.

Fraser, B. J. (1986). *Classroom environment*. Dover, NH: Croom Helm.

Freedman, S. W. (1987). *Response to student writing*. Urbana, IL: NCTE.

Freire, P. (1970a). *Pedagogy of the oppressed*. New York: Continuum.

Freire, P. (1970b). *Cultural action for freedom*. Cambridge, MA: Harvard Educational Review.

Freire, P. (1973). *Education for critical consciousness*. New York: Seabury Press.

Freudenstein, R. (Ed.). (1978). *The role of women in foreign-language textbooks: A collection of essays. Collection d' "etudes linguistiques" No. 24*. Ghent, Belgium: Federation International des Professeurs de Langues Vivantes. (ERIC Document Reproduction Services No. ED 209 914)

Fried-Booth, D. (1982). Project work with advanced classes. *ELT Journal, 36*(2), 98–103.

Fried-Booth, D. (1986). *Project work*. Oxford: Oxford University Press.

Fries, C. C. (1945). *Teaching and learning English as a foreign language*. Ann Arbor: University of Michigan Press.

Fröhlich, M., Spada, N., & Allen, P. (1985). Differences in the communicative orientation of L2 classrooms. *TESOL Quarterly, 19*(1), 27–57.

Fry, E. (1975). *Reading drills for speed and comprehension* (2nd ed.). Providence, RI: Jamestown.

Frymier, J. (1977). *Annehurst curriculum classification system: A practical way to individualized instruction*. West Lafayette, ID: Kappa Delta Pi.

Gable, A., & Page, C. V. (1980). The use of artificial intelligence techniques in computer-assisted instruction: An overview. *International Journal of Man-Machine Studies, 12*, 259–282.

Gaff, R. (1982). Sex-stereotyping in modern language teaching—An aspect of the hidden curriculum. *British Journal of Language Teaching, 20*(2), 71–78.

Gagne, R. (1965). *The conditions of learning*. New York: Holt, Rinehart & Winston.

Gaies, S. J. (1982). NS-NNS interaction among academic peers. *Studies in Second Language Acquisition, 5*(1), 74–81.

Gaies, S. J. (1985). *Peer involvement in language learning*. Englewood Cliffs, NJ: Prentice-Hall.

Gairns, R., & Redman, S. (1986). *Working with words: A guide to teaching and learning vocabulary*. Cambridge: Cambridge University Press.

Gallimore, R., Boggs, J. W., & Jordan, C. (1974). *Culture, behavior, and education: A study of Hawaiian-Americans*. Beverly Hills, CA: Sage.

Galyean, B. (1982). A confluent design for language teaching. In R. W. Blair (Ed.), *Innovative approaches to language teaching* (pp. 176–188). New York: Newbury House.

Gardner, R. C. (1979). Attitudes and motivation: Their role in second language acquisition. In H. R. Trueba & C. Barnett-Mizrahi (Eds.), *Bilingual multicultural education and the professional* (pp. 319–327). New York: Newbury House.

Gass, S., & Varonis, L. (1985). Task variation and non-native/non-native negotiation of meaning. In S. M. Gass & C. G. Madden (Eds.), *Input and second language acquisition* (pp. 146–161). New York: Newbury House.

Gatbonton, E., & Segalowitz, N. (1988). Creative automatization: Principles for promoting fluency within a communicative framework. *TESOL Quarterly, 22*(3), 473–492.

Gattegno, C. (1963). *Teaching foreign languages in schools the silent way*. New York: Educational Solutions.

Gattegno, C. (1976). *The common sense of teaching foreign languages*. New York: Educational Solutions.

Gebhard, A. O. (1973). Poetry-acid test of comprehension. *Journal of Reading, 17*(2), 125–128.

Geddes, M. & Sturtridge, G. (1979). *Listening links*. London: Heinemann Educational Books.

Geddes, M., & White, R. (1978). The use of semi-scripted simulated authentic speech and listening comprehension. *Audio-visual Language Journal, 16*(3), 137–143.

Genesee, F. (1987). *Learning through two languages: Studies of immersion and bilingual education*. New York: Newbury House.

Geography games. (1973). London: Longman.

Gilmore, P. (1985). Silence and sulking: Emotional displays in the classroom. In D. Tannen & M. Saville-Troike (Eds.), *Perspectives on silence* (pp. 139–162). Norwood, NJ: Ablex.

Goldenberg, C. N. (1987). Roads to reading: Studies of Hispanic first-graders at risk for reading failure. *NABE Journal, 11*(3), 235–250.

Gomez, B. (1987). *"Friends gotta talk": An ethnographic study of behavioral patterns exhibited by young children in the process of acquiring English as a second language.* Unpublished doctoral dissertation, Georgia State University, Atlanta.

Gonzalez, A. (1983). *A cooperative/interdependent technique for the bilingual classroom and measures related to social motives.* Unpublished manuscript, California State University, Psychology Department, Fresno.

Goodlad, J. I. (1984). *A place called school: Prospects for the future.* New York: McGraw-Hill.

Goodman, C. C. (1967). Learning to read English as a part of the oral approach. *Journal of the Reading Specialist, 4,* 96–98.

Goodman, K. S. (1965). A linguistic study of cues and miscues in reading. *Elementary English, 42,* 639–643.

Goodman, K. S. (1967). Reading: A psycholinguistic guessing game. *Journal of the Reading Specialist, 6*(4), 126–135.

Goodman, K. S. (1970). Behind the eye: What happens in reading. In K. S. Goodman & O. S. Niles (Eds.), *Reading process and program.* Champaign, IL: NCTE.

Goodman, K. S. (1973). *The psycholinguistic nature of the reading process.* Detroit: Wayne State University Press.

Goodman, K. S. (1979). The know-more and the know-nothing movements in reading: A personal response. *Language Arts, 56*(6), 657–663.

Goodman, K. S., & Goodman, Y. M. (1977). Learning about psycholinguistic processes by analyzing oral reading. *Harvard Educational Review, 47*(3), 317–333.

Goodman, K. S., Smith, E. B., Meredith, R., & Goodman, Y. (1987). *Language and thinking in school: A whole language curriculum* (3rd ed.). New York: Richard C. Owen.

Goodwin, J. (1988). Using audiotaped dialogue journals to improve pronunciation instruction. CATESOL Conference presentation. San Francisco, CA. April, 1988.

Gouin, F. (1880). *L'art d'enseigner et d'étudier les langues.* Paris: Librairie Fischbacher.

Grabe, W. (1985, April). *Reassessing the term "interactive"* (rev. ed.). Paper presented at the 19th Annual TESOL Convention, New York.

Graham, C. (1978). *Jazz chants.* New York: Oxford University Press.

Graham, C. (1986). *Small talk.* New York: Oxford University Press.

Graham, S., & Curtis, W. (1986). *Harbrace ESL Workbook.* San Diego: Harcourt Brace Jovanovich.

Greenbaum, P. (1985). Nonverbal differences in communication style between American Indian and Anglo elementary classrooms. *American Educational Research Journal, 22*(1), 101–115.

Greenberg, K. (1989). *Long term writing assessment: Its impact on curriculum and instruction at CUNY.* Paper presented at the 40th Annual Conference on College Composition and Communication, Seattle.

Greenfield, P. M. (1984). A theory of the teacher in the learning activities of everyday life. In B. Rogoff & J. Lave (Eds.), *Everyday cognition: Its development in social context* (pp. 117–138). Cambridge, MA: Harvard University Press.

Gregg, J., & Pacheco, B. (1981). Back to basic stories: Literature in a thematic ESL reading course. *ESL in Higher Education* [TESOL special-interest section newsletter], *3*(1), 1–4.

Grice, P. H. (1975). Logic and conversation. In P. Cole & J. L. Morgan (Eds.), *Syntax and semantics: Vol. 3. Speech acts* (pp. 41–58). New York: Academic Press.

Griffee, D. T., & Hough, D. (1986). *Hearsay: Survival listening and speaking.* Tokyo: Addison-Wesley.

Grittner, F. M., & Welty, S. (1974). Beginning German textbooks for the high school level (1969–1973): A description evaluation. *Modern Language Journal, 58*(7), 314–322.

Grossberg, D., & Debenedetti, J. (1984). Individualized instructional in Hebrew (Grant # OEG-71-4409). In *Teaching language in college. Communicative proficiency and cross-cultured issues. Proceedings of a SUNY-Albany Conference.* Albany, NY. (ERIC Document Reproduction Services No. ED 262 580)

Gudchinsky, S. (1973). *A manual of literacy for preliterate people.* Huntington Beach, CA: Summer Institute of Linguistics.

Gunter, R. (1974). *Sentences in dialog.* Columbia, SC: Hornbeam Press.

Hagen, S. A. (1988). *Sound advice: A basis for listening.* Englewood Cliffs, NJ: Prentice-Hall.

Haigh, N. (1981). *Research on teacher thinking.* Paper presented at the National Conference of the New Zealand Association for Research in Education. (ERIC Document Reproduction Service No. ED 213 657)

Hairston, M. (1982). The winds of change: Thomas Kuhn and the revolution in the teaching of writing. *College Composition and Communication, 33*(1), 76–88.

Halliday, M. A. K. (1970). Language structure and language function. In J. Lyons (Ed.), *New horizons in linguistics* (pp. 140–165). Middlesex, England: Penguin Books.

Halliday, M. A. K. (1973). *Explorations in the functions of language.* London: Edward Arnold.

Halliday, M. A. K. (1975). *Learning how to mean.* London: Edward Arnold.

Handscombe, J., et al. (1974). Individualizing the ESL program (or teaching in the ways in which students learn). *TESL Talk, 5*(1), 23–35.

Hargreaves, P. R. (1969). *A cultural analysis of William Golding's "Lord of the Flies."* Unpublished MATESL thesis, University of California, Los Angeles.

Harley, B. (1988). Effects of instruction on SLA: Issues and evidence. In R. Kaplan (Ed.), *Annual review of applied linguistics.* New York: Cambridge University Press.

Harley, B. (1989). Functional grammar in French immersion: A classroom experiment. *Applied Linguistics, 10*(3), 331–359.

Harmer, J. (1983). *The practice of English language teaching.* London: Longman.

Harris, D. P. (1969). *Testing English as a second language.* New York: McGraw-Hill.

Harris, M. (1989). Composing behaviors of one- and multi-draft writers. *College English, 51*(2), 174–191.

Harrison, W. W., Prator, C. H., & Tucker, G. R. (1973). *English-language policy survey of Jordan* (prepublication version). Arlington, VA: Center of Applied Linguistics.

Hart, L. (1983). *Human brain and human learning.* New York: Longman.

Hartnett, D. (1985). Cognitive style and second language learning. In M. Celce-Murcia (Ed.), *Beyond basics: Issues and research in TESOL* (pp. 16–33). New York: Newbury House.

Hatch, E., Flashner, V., Hawkins, B., Motoike, W., Jacobs, M., & Wheeler, B. (1987). *A classroom research project at Encinita Elementary School: A presentation of linguistic/cognitive findings by researchers and observations from a school administrator and teachers.* Panel presentation at University of California Linguistic Minority Project Conference, University of California, Los Angeles.

Hatch, E., & Hawkins, B. (1987). Second language acquisition: An experiential approach. In S. Rosenberg (Ed.), *Advances in applied psycholinguistics, Vol 2: Reading, writing and language learning* (pp. 241–283). Cambridge: Cambridge University Press.

Hatch, E., Polin, P., & Part, S. (1974). Acoustic scanning or syntactic processing. *Journal of Reading Behavior, 6*(3), 275–285.

Hauptmann, P. C., Wesche, M. B., & Ready, D. (1988). Second language acquisition through subject-matter learning: A follow-up study at the University of Ottawa. *Language Learning, 38*(3), 433–475.

Haverson, W. W. (1986). Adult illiteracy: Implications for parent involvement. In *Issues of parent involvement and literacy.* Washington, DC: Trinity College.

Haverson, W. W., & Haverson, S. H. (1987). *Celebration: Festivities for reading!* Hayward, CA: Alemany Press.

Haverson, W. W., & Haynes, J. (1982). *Literacy training for ESL adult learners.* Washington, DC: Center for Applied Linguistics.

Hawkins, B. (1985). *Complaints: Nonnative speakers learn from native speakers.* Paper presented at the Second Language Acquisition Research Forum, Los Angeles.

Hawkins, B. (1988). *Scaffolded classroom interaction in a language minority setting.* Unpublished doctoral dissertation, University of California, Los Angeles.

Hayes, J. (1982). *The day it snowed tortillas: Tales from Spanish New Mexico.* Santa Fe: Trails West.

Hayes, M. F., & Daiker, D. A. (1984). Using protocol analysis in evaluating responses to student writing. *Freshman English News, 13*(10), 1–4.

Heath, S. B. (1983). *Ways with words.* Cambridge: Cambridge University Press.

Heath, S. B. (1984, November). Being literate in America: A sociohistorical perspective. In J. A. Niles (Ed.), *Issues in literacy: A research perspective* (pp. 1–18). Rochester, NY: National Reading Conference.

Heath, S. B. (1985). Literacy or literate skills? Considerations for ESL/EFL learners. In P. Larson, E. Judd, & D. S. Messerschmitt (Eds.), *On TESOL'84: A brave new world for TESOL* (pp. 15–28). Washington, DC: TESOL.

Heath, S. B. (1986). Sociocultural contexts of language development. In *Beyond language: Social and cultural factors in schooling linguistic minority students* (pp. 143–186). Los Angeles: Evaluation, Dissemination, and Assessment Center, California State University.

Heath, S. B., & Branscombe, A. (1985). Intelligent writing in an audience community: Teacher, students, and researcher. In S. W. Freedman (Ed.), *The acquisition of written language: Revision and response* (pp. 3–32). Norwood, NJ: Ablex.

Heaton, J. B. (1975). *Writing English language tests.* London: Longman.

Hecht, E., & Ryan, G. (1979). *Survival pronunciation: Vowel contrasts.* Hayward, CA: Alemany Press.

Heise, E. (1961). Let's talk sense about language teaching. *French Review, 35*(2), 176–184.

Henak, R. (1984). *Lesson planning for meaningful variety* (2nd ed.). Washington, DC: National Education Association.

Henderson, C., Portaro, B., & Wilensky, D. (1984). *Literacy supplement to ESL master plan.* San Francisco: San Francisco Community College District.

Henner-Stanchina, C. (1976). Two years of autonomy: Practice and outlook. In *Mélanges pedagogiques* (pp. 73–92). Nancy, France: Centre de recherches et d'applications pédagogiques (CRAPEL).

Henning, G. (1985). *Proficiency testing and achievement testing: A proposal of marriage.* Unpublished manuscript, University of California, Los Angeles.

Henning, G. (1987). *A guide to language testing.* New York: Newbury House.

Henriksen, B. (1988). Udvikling af sprogelevers pragmatiske bevidsthed: Et paedagogisk forsog engelskundervisning. In E. Hansen (Ed.), *Sproglig bevidsthed: Copenhagen studies in bilingualism* (Vol. 7, pp. 171–193). Copenhagen: Royal Danish School of Educational Studies.

Herbolich, J. B. (1979a). A note on negation in beginning

EFL textbooks. *Research in the Teaching of English, 13*(3), 281–283.

Herbolich, J. B. (1979b). Box kites. *English for Specific Purposes Newsletter, 29.* English Language Institute, Oregon State University.

Hernandez, A., & Melnick, S. L. (1974). *Modular sequence: ESL methods and techniques. TTP 001.13 evaluating and adapting materials. Teacher corps bilingual project.* Hartford, CT: Hartford University. *(ERIC Document Reproduction Service No. ED 095 141)*

Herron, C., & Tomasello, M. (1988). Learning grammatical structures in a foreign language: Modelling versus feedback. *French Review, 61*(6), 910–922.

Hester, H. (1984). Peer interaction in learning English as a second language. *Theory into Practice, 23*(3), 208–217.

Hetherington, A. (1985). Assessing the suitability of reading materials for ESL students. *TESL Canada Journal/Revue TESL du Canada, 3*(1), 37–52.

Higgs, T. V. (Ed.). (1984). *Teaching for proficiency: The organizing principle.* Skokie, IL: National Textbook Company.

Higgs, T. V., & Clifford, R. (1982). The push towards communication. In T. V. Higgs (Ed.), *Curriculum, competence, and the foreign language teacher* (pp. 57–79). Lincolnwood, IL: National Textbook Company.

Hilgard, E. R. (1956). *Theories of learning* (2nd ed.). New York: Appleton-Century-Crofts.

Hilles, S. (in press). Access to universal grammar in second language acquisition. In L. Eubanks (Ed.), *Point counterpoint: Universal grammar in the second language.* Amsterdam: John Benjamins.

Hillocks, G., Jr. (1986). *Research on written composition: New directions for teaching.* Urbana, IL: ERIC Clearinghouse on Reading and Communication Skills.

Hinofotis, F., & Bailey, K. (1980). American undergraduate reactions to the communication skills of foreign teaching assistants. In J. Fisher, M. Clarke, & J. Schachter (Eds.), *On TESOL '80: Building bridges: Research and practice in TESL* (pp. 120–133). Washington, DC: TESOL.

Hirsch, E. (1987). *Cultural literacy: What every American needs to know.* Boston: Houghton Mifflin.

Hochberg, J. (1970). Attention, organization and consciousness. In D. I. Mostofsky (Ed.), *Attention: Contemporary theory and analysis* (pp. 99–124). New York: Appleton-Century-Crofts.

Holdaway, D. (1985). *Stability and change in literacy learning.* Portsmouth, NH: Heinemann Educational Books.

Holm, W. (1989). On the role of a Navajo Tribal Educational Agency in Navajo education. *Journal of Navajo Education, 6*(3), 38–54.

Holmes, M. (1976). Intermediate English language texts. *Orbit, 7*(1), 22–23.

Horn, R. E., & Cleaves, A. (Eds.). (1980). *The guide to simulations/games for education and training* (4th ed.). Beverly Hills, CA: Sage.

Hornburger, J. M. (1977a). Criteria for selecting children's books which deal fairly with all groups of people. In J. M. Hornburger & K. Boatman (Eds.), *Teaching multicultural children* (p. 45). Boston: Boston University. (ERIC Document Reproduction Service No. ED 139 045)

Hornburger, J. M. (1977b). Short cuts to quality book selection. In J. M. Hornburger & K. Boatman (Eds.), *Teaching multicultural children* (pp. 46–47). Boston: Boston University. (ERIC Document Reproduction Service No. ED 139 045)

Hornby, A. S. (1948 edition; 1974 edition; 1980 edition). *Oxford advanced learner's dictionary of current English.* London: Oxford University Press.

Horowitz, D. (1986). What professors actually require: Academic tasks for the ESL classroom. *TESOL Quarterly, 20*(3), 445–462.

Hosenfeld, C. (1977). A preliminary investigation of the reading strategies of successful and nonsuccessful second language learners. *System, 5*(2), 110–123.

Hosenfeld, C. (1979, April). *Cindy: A learner in today's foreign language classroom.* Paper presented at the Northeast Conference on the Teaching of Foreign Languages, Washington, DC. (ERIC Document Reproduction Services No. ED 185 837)

Howatt, A. P. R. (1984). *A history of English language teaching.* Oxford: Oxford University Press.

Huckin, T. N., & Pesante, L. H. (1988). Existential "there." *Written Communication, 5*(3), 368–391.

Hudelson, S. (1984). Kan yu ret an rayt en Ingles: Children become literate in English as a second language. *TESOL Quarterly, 18*(2), 221–238.

Hudelson, S. (1987). The role of native language literacy in the education of language minority children. *Language Arts, 64*(8), 827–841.

Hudelson, S. (1989). A tale of two children: Individual differences in ESL children's writing. In D. M. Johnson & D. H. Roen (Eds.), *Richness in writing* (pp. 84–99). New York: Longman.

Hudson, T. (1982). The effects of induced schemata on the "short circuit" in L2 reading: Non-decoding factors in L2 reading performance. *Language Learning, 32*(2), 1–31.

Hughey, J. B., Wormuth, D. R., Hartfiel, V. F., & Jacobs, H. L. (1983). *Teaching ESL composition: Principles and techniques.* New York: Newbury House.

Huizenga, J. (1987). *From the start: Beginning listening* (Book 1). White Plains, NY: Longman.

Hulstijn, J., & Hulstijn, W. (1984). Grammatical errors as a function of processing constraints and explicit knowledge. *Language Learning, 34*(1), 23–43.

Hurst, M. M. (1985). *Do teachers know what students want to learn? A needs assesment of adult students of English as a second language.* Unpublished doctoral dissertation, University of Southern California.

Hutchinson, T., & Waters, A. (1987). *English for specific*

purposes: A learning-centered approach. Cambridge: Cambridge University Press.

Hymes, D. H. (1972). On communicative competence. In J. B. Pride & J. Holmes (Eds.), *Sociolinguistics; Selected readings*. (pp. 269–293). Harmondsworth, England: Penguin Books.

Hymes, D. H. (1981). Foreword. In C. A. Ferguson & S. B. Heath (Eds.), *Language in the USA*. (pp. v–ix). Cambridge: Cambridge University Press.

Iwataki, S. (1981). Preparing to teach in adult education programs. In J. C. Fischer, M. A. Clark, & J. Schachter (Eds.), *On TESOL '80: Building bridges: Research and practice in teaching English as a second language* (pp. 23–24). Washington, DC: TESOL.

Jacobs, G. (1988). Co-operative goal structure: A way to improve group activities. *ELT Journal, 42*(2), 97–101.

Jacobs, H. L., Zingraf, S. A., Wormuth, D. R., Hartfiel, V. F., & Hughey, J. B. (1981). *Testing ESL composition: A practical approach*. New York: Newbury House.

Jacobson, R. (1981). The implementation of bilingual instruction model: The new concurrent approach. In R. V. Padilla (Ed.), *Ethnoperspectives in bilingual education research, Vol. 3: Bilingual education technology* (pp. 14–29). Ypsilanti, MI: Eastern Michigan University.

Jacobson, R. (1989). Allocating two languages as a key feature of a bilingual methodology. In R. Jacobson & C. Faltis (Eds.), *Language distribution issues in bilingual schooling*. Clevedon, England: Multilingual Matters.

Jacobson, W. H. (1986). An assessment of the communication needs of non-native speakers of English in an undergraduate physics lab. *ESP Journal, 5*(2), 173–188.

James, M. O. (1987). ESL reading pedagogy: Implications of schema-theoretical research. In J. Devine, P. L. Carrell, & D. Eskey (Eds.), *Research in reading in English as a second language* (pp. 177–188). Washington, DC: TESOL.

Jerald, M., & Clark, R. (1983). *Experiential language teaching techniques: Resources handbook number 3*. Brattleboro, VT: Pro Linga Associates.

Johns, A. M. (1981). Necessary English: A faculty survey. *TESOL Quarterly, 15*(1), 51–57.

Johns, A. M. (1990). Coherence as a cultural phenomenon: Using ethnography in an academic milieu. In U. Conner & A. Johns (Eds.), *Coherence: Research and pedagogical perspectives*. Washington, DC: TESOL.

Johns, T. F. (1974). The communicative approach to language teaching in the context of a programme of English for Academic Purposes. In E. Roulet & H. Holec (Eds.), *L'enseignment de la competence de communication en langues secondes*. Neuchatel: CILA.

Johnson, A. D., & Pearson, P. D. (1978). *Teaching reading vocabulary*. New York: Holt, Rinehart & Winston.

Johnson, D. M. (1983). Natural language learning by design: A classroom experiment in social interaction and second language acquisition. *TESOL Quarterly, 17*(1), 55–68.

Johnson, D. W., Johnson, R. T., Holubec, E. J., & Roy, P. (1984). *Circles of learning: Cooperation in the classroom*. Alexandria, VA: Association for Supervision and Curriculum Development.

Johnson, D. W., Johnson, R. T., Johnson, J., & Anderson, D. (1976). The effects of cooperative vs. individualized instruction on student prosocial behavior, attitudes toward learning, and achievement. *Journal of Educational Psychology, 68*, 446–452.

Johnson, K. (1979). Communicative approaches and communicative processes. In C. J. Brumfit & K. Johnson (Eds.), *The communicative approach to language teaching* (pp. 192–205). Oxford: Oxford University Press.

Johnson, K., & Morrow, K. (Eds.). (1981). *Communication in the classroom*. London: Longman.

Johnson, P. (1981). Effects on reading comprehension of language complexity and cultural background of a text. *TESOL Quarterly, 15*(2), 169–181.

Johnson, P. (1982). Effects on reading comprehension of building background fluency. *TESOL Quarterly, 16*(4), 503–516.

Johnson, T. D., & Louis, D. R. (1987). *Literacy through literature*. Portsmouth, NH: Heinemann Educational Books.

Johnston, V. A. (1972). *Some effects of acoustic input on reading comprehension*. Unpublished MATESL thesis, University of California, Los Angeles.

Joiner, E. G. (1974). Evaluating the cultural content of foreign language texts. *Modern Language Journal, 58*(5-6), 242–244.

Jolly, D. (1984). *Writing tasks*. Cambridge: Cambridge University Press.

Jones, E. V. (1981). *Reading instruction for the adult illiterate*. Chicago: American Library Association.

Jones, K. (1974). *Nine graded simulations*. Ampthill: Management Games.

Jones, K. (1982). *Simulations in language teaching*. Cambridge: Cambridge University Press.

Jordan, C. (1983). Cultural differences in communication patterns: Classroom adaptations and translated strategies. In M. Clarke & J. J. Handscombe (Eds.), *On TESOL '82: Pacific perspectives on language, learning, and teaching* (pp. 285–294). Washington, DC: TESOL.

Jordan, I. K. (1989). *Sign language diversity: Communication and communicators*. Paper presented at the 23rd Annual TESOL Convention, San Antonio, TX.

Judd, E. L. (1978). Vocabulary teaching and TESOL: A need for reevaluation of existing assumptions. *TESOL Quarterly, 12*(1), 71–76.

Kagan, S. (1985). *Cooperative learning: Resources for teachers*. Laguna Niguel, CA: Spencer Kagan Resources for Teachers.

Kagan, S. (1986). Cooperative learning and sociocultural factors in schooling. In *Beyond language: Social and* cultural factors in schooling language minority students (pp. 231–298). Los Angeles: Evaluation, Dissemination, and Assessment Center, California State University.

Kahn, M. S. (1978). The selection of a textbook: Rationale and evaluation form. *Clearing House, 51*(5), 245–247.

Karlin, M., & Berger, R. (1971). *Experiential learning: An effective teaching program for elementary schools.* West Nyack, NY: Parker.

Kasper, G. (1984). Pragmatic comprehension in learner-native speaker discourse. *Language Learning, 34*(4), 1–20.

Kasper, G. & House, J. (1981). Zür Rolle der Kognition in Kommunikationkursen. *Die Neuren Sprachen, 80,* 42–55.

Kean, J. (1981). Grammar: A perspective. In V. Frosse & S. Straw (Eds.), *Research in the language arts, language and schooling* (pp. 163–180). Baltimore: University Park Press.

Keller, E., & Warner, S. T. (1979). *Gambits 1–3.* Hull, Quebec, Canada: Canadian Government Publishing Centre.

Keller, J. M. (1983). Motivational design of education. In C. M. Reigeluth (Ed.), *Instructional design theories and models* (pp. 386–433). Hillsdale, NJ: Erlbaum.

Kelly, L. G. (1969). *Twenty-five centuries of language teaching.* New York: Newbury House.

Kennedy, C. (1986). Formative evaluation as an indicator of student wants and attitudes. *ESP Journal, 4*(2), 93–100.

Kennedy, G. (1972). The language tests for young children. In B. Spolsky (Ed.), *The language education of minority children* (pp. 164–181). New York: Newbury House.

Kenworthy, J. (1987). *Teaching English pronunciation.* London: Longman.

Kintsch, W., & van Dijk, T. A. (1978). Toward a model of text comprehension and production. *Psychological Review, 85*(5), 363–394.

Kleifgen, J. A. (1988). Learning from student teachers' cross-cultural communicative failures. *Anthropology and Education Quarterly, 19*(3), 218–234.

Klein-Braley, C. (1981). *Empirical investigations of cloze tests: An examination of the validity of cloze tests as tests of general language proficiency in English for German university students.* Unpublished doctoral dissertation, University of Duisburg, West Germany.

Klein-Braley, C., & Raatz, U. (1984). A survey of research on the C-test. *Language Testing, 1*(2), 134–146.

Kleinmann, H. (1977). *Transformational grammar and the processing of certain English sentence types.* Unpublished MATESL thesis, University of California, Los Angeles.

Klinghammer, S. J. (1987). Teacher as researcher. *English for Foreign Students in English-speaking Countries Newsletter* [TESOL special issue], *5*(1), 2–3.

Knapper, T. B. (1977). Guidelines for administering effective text and materials selection. *Educational Technology, 17*(7), 32–34.

Knapton, J., & Evans, B. (1967). *Teaching a literature-centered English program.* New York: Random House.

Knowles, M. (1976). Contract learning. In C. Klevins (Ed.), *Materials and methods in continuing education.* Canoga Park, CA: Klevins.

Knowles, M., & Klevins, C. (1976). History and philosophy of continuing education. In C. Klevins (Ed.), *Materials and methods in continuing education.* Canoga Park, CA: Klevins.

Knowles, P., & Sasaki, R. (1980). *Story squares: Fluency in English as a second language.* Cambridge, MA: Winthrop.

Kochman, T. (1981). *Black and white styles in conflict.* Chicago: University of Chicago Press.

Kolb, D. (1984). *Experiential learning: Experience as the source of learning.* Englewood Cliffs, NJ: Prentice-Hall.

Kozol, J. (1985). *Illiterate America.* Garden City, NJ: Anchor Press/Doubleday.

Krahnke, K. (1987). *Approaches to syllabus design for foreign language teaching.* Washington, DC: Center for Applied Linguistics.

Kramsch, C. J. (1985). Classroom interaction and discourse options. *Studies in Second Language Acquisition, 7*(2), 169–183.

Krapels, A. R. (1990). A survey of second language writing process research. In B. Kroll (Ed.), *Second language writing: Research insights for the classroom* (pp. 37–56). New York: Cambridge University Press.

Krashen, S. D. (1982). *Principles and practice in second language acquisition.* Oxford: Pergamon Press.

Krashen, S. D. (1984). Immersion: Why it works and what it has taught us. *Language and Society, 12,* 61–64.

Krashen, S. D. (1984). *Writing: Research, theory and applications.* New York: Pergamon Institute of English.

Krashen, S. D. (1986). We acquire vocabulary by reading. In A. Papalia (Ed.), *Teaching our students a second language in a proficiency-based classroom.* Schenectady, NY: New York State Association of Foreign Language Teachers.

Krashen, S. D. (1987). Applications of psycholinguistic research to the classroom. In M. H. Long & J. C. Richards (Eds.), *Methodology in TESOL: A book of readings* (pp. 33–44). New York: Newbury House.

Krashen, S. D., & Biber, D. (1988). *On course: Bilingual education's success in California.* Sacramento: California Association for Bilingual Education.

Krashen, S. D., & Terrell, T. D. (1983). *The natural approach.* Hayward, CA: Alemany Press.

Krause, K. C. (1976). Do's and don'ts in evaluating textbooks. *Journal of Reading, 20*(3), 212–214.

Kreeft-Peyton, J. (1987). *Dialog journal writing with limited English proficient students* (Educational Report 7). Los Angeles: Center for Language Education and Research, University of California, Los Angeles.

Kroll, B. (1982). *Levels of error in ESL composition.* Unpublished doctoral dissertation. University of Southern California.

Kroll, B. (1990). The rhetoric/syntax split: Designing a curriculum for ESL students. *Journal of Basic Writing, 9*(1), 40–55.

Kroll, B. (Ed.). (1990). *Second language writing: Research insights for the classroom.* New York and Cambridge: Cambridge University Press.

Kuhn, T. S. (1970). *The structure of scientific revolutions.* Chicago: University of Chicago Press.

LaBerge, D., & Samuels, S. (1974). Toward a theory of automatic information processing in reading. *Cognitive Psychology, 6*(2), 293–323.

Labov, W. (1972a). Rules for ritual insults. In W. Labov (Ed.), *Language in the inner city: Studies in the black English vernacular* (pp. 297–353). Philadelphia: University of Pennsylvania Press.

Labov, W. (1972b). The social setting of linguistic change. In W. Labov (Ed.), *Sociolinguistic patterns* (pp. 260–325). Philadelphia: University of Pennsylvania Press.

Labov, W. (1982). Competing value systems in the inner-city schools. In P. Gilmore & A. A. Glatthorn (Eds.), *Children in and out of school: Ethnography and education* (pp. 148–171). Washington, DC: Center for Applied Linguistics.

Labov, W. (1983). Recognizing black English in the classroom. In J. Chambers, Jr. (Ed.), *Black English: Educational equity and the law* (pp. 29–55). Ann Arbor, MI: Karoma.

Labov, W., Cohen, P., Robins, C., & Lewis, J. (1968). *A study of nonstandard English of Negro and Puerto Rican speakers in New York City.* Philadelphia: U.S. Regional Survey.

Lado, R. (1964). *Language teaching: A scientific approach.* New York: McGraw-Hill.

Lado, R. (1965). Memory span as a factor in second language learning. *International Review of Applied Linguistics, 3*(2), 123–129.

Lambert, W. (1961). *A study of the roles of attitudes and motivation in second language learning* (Project Report No. SAE-8817). Montreal, Canada.

Lambert, W., & Tucker, G. (1969). White and Negro listeners' reactions to various American-English dialects. *Social Forces, 8,* 463–468.

Lane, H. (1964). Programmed learning of a second language. *International Review of Applied Linguistics, 4,* 249–301.

Larsen-Freeman, D. (1986). *Techniques and principles in language teaching.* Oxford: Oxford University Press.

Larsen-Freeman, D. (1990). Grammar. In R. Kaplan (Ed.), *Annual review of applied linguistics X.* Cambridge: Cambridge University Press.

Larsen-Freeman, D., & Celce-Murcia, M. (1985). Defining the challenge in language teaching. Paper presented at the Annual TESOL Conference. New York, March, 1985.

Larsen-Freeman, D., & Long, M. (1990). *An introduction to second language acquisition research.* London: Longman.

Larson, D. N. (1984). *Guidelines for barefoot language learning.* St. Paul, MN: CMS.

Larson, J. W., & Madsen, H. S. (1985). Computerized adaptive language testing: Moving beyond computer assisted testing. *CALICO Journal, 2*(3), 32–36.

Latimer, B. I. (Ed.). (1977). Criteria for judging books involving Black people. In J. M. Hornburger, & K. Boatman (Eds.), *Teaching multicultural children* (pp. 42–44). Boston: Boston University.

Lazaraton, A., & Riggenbach, H. (1987). *A task-based approach to oral proficiency testing.* Unpublished UCLA ESL service course research report, University of California, Los Angeles.

Leap, W. L. (1981). American Indian languages. In C. A. Ferguson & S. B. Heath (Eds.), *Language in the USA* (pp. 116–144). Cambridge: Cambridge University Press.

Lebauer, R. S. (1984). Using lecture transcripts in EAP lecture comprehension courses. *TESOL Quarterly, 18*(1), 41–54.

Lebauer, R. S. (1988). *Learn to listen; listen to learn: An advanced ESL/EFL lecture comprehension and note-taking textbook.* Englewood Cliffs, NJ: Prentice-Hall.

Legutke, M. (1987). *Experiential learning: Project work in language learning-project airport.* Paper presented at the 21st Annual TESOL Convention, Miami, FL.

Lehrer, A. (1974). *Semantic fields and lexical structure.* Amsterdam: North Holland.

Leinhardt, G., & Greeno, J. G. (1986). The cognitive skill of teaching. *Journal of Educational Psychology, 78*(2), 75–95.

Leki, I. (1986). *ESL student preferences in writing error correction.* Paper presented at the Southeast Regional TESOL Conference, Atlanta, GA.

Leki, I. (1990). Coaching from the margins: Issues in written response. In B. Kroll (Ed.), *Second language writing: Research insights for the classroom.* New York: Cambridge University Press.

Lentulay, R. (1976). The clockwork orange experiment. In *Seminar-workshop II on Russian for non-academic uses and the academic curriculum.* Bryn Mawr, PA: Bryn Mawr College Department of Russian.

Levenston, E. A., Nir, R., & Blum-Kulka, S. (1984). Discourse analysis and the testing of reading comprehension by cloze techniques. In A. K. Pugh & J. M. Ulijn (Eds.), *Reading for professional purposes* (pp. 202–212). London: Longman.

Levin, L. (1972). *Comparative studies in foreign language teaching.* Stockholm: Almqvist and Wiksell.

Levinson, S. (1983). *Pragmatics.* Cambridge: Cambridge University Press.

Lewis, M., & Hill, J. (1985). *Practical techniques for lan-*

guage teaching. Hove, England: Language Teaching Publications.

Liberman, I. Y., & Shankweiler, D. (1979). Speech, the alphabet and teaching to read. In L. B. Resnick & P. A. Weaver (Eds.), *Theory and practice of early reading* (Vol. 2, pp. 109–134). Hillsdale, NJ: Erlbaum.

Lindstromberg, S. (1985). Schemata for ordering the teaching and learning of vocabulary. *ELT Journal, 39*(4), 235–243.

Liski, E., & Puntanen, S. (1983). A study of the statistical foundations of group conversation tests in English. *Language Learning, 33*(2), 225–246.

Liu, N., & Nation, I. S. P. (1985). Factors affecting guessing vocabulary in context. *RELC Journal, 16*(1), 33–42.

Long, M. H. (1977). Teacher feedback on learner error: Mapping cognitions. In H. D. Brown, C. A. Yorio, & R. H. Crymes (Eds.), *On TESOL '77: Teaching and learning English as a second language: Trends in research and practice* (pp. 278–293). Washington, DC: TESOL.

Long, M. H. (1980). *Input, interaction, and second language acquisition.* Unpublished doctoral dissertation, University of California, Los Angeles.

Long, M. H. (1983a). Does second language instruction make a difference? A review of research. *TESOL Quarterly, 17*(3), 359–382.

Long, M. H. (1983b). Training the second language teacher as classroom researcher. In J. E. Alatis, P. Strevens, & H. H. Stern (Eds.), *Applied linguistics and the preparation of second language teachers: Towards a rationale.* Washington, DC: Georgetown University Press.

Long, M. H. (1985). The design of classroom second language acquisition: Towards task-based language teaching. In K. Hyltenstam & M. Pienemann (Eds.), *Modelling and assessing second language acquisition* (pp. 77–99). London: Multilingual Matters.

Long, M. H. (1988, June). *Focus on form: A design feature in language teaching methodology.* Paper presented at the National Foreign Language Center/European Cultural Foundation Conference on Empirical Research on Second Language Learning in Institutional Setting, Bellagio, Italy.

Long, M. H., Adams, L., McLean, M., & Castaños, F. (1976). Doing things with words: Verbal interaction in lockstep and small-group classroom situations. In R. Crymes & J. Fanselow (Eds.), *On TESOL '76: Selections based on teaching done at the 10th annual TESOL convention* (pp. 137–153). Washington, DC: TESOL.

Long, M. H., Brook, C., Crookes, G., Deicke, C., Potter, L. & Zhang, S. (1984). *The effect of teachers' questioning patterns and wait-time on pupil participation patterns in public high school classes in Hawaii for students of limited English proficiency* (Tech. Rep. No. 1). Honolulu: University of Hawaii, Center for Second Language Classroom Research, Social Science Research Institute.

Long, M. H., & Crookes, G. V. (1987). Intervention points in second language classroom processes. In B. Das (Ed.), *Patterns of classroom interaction in Southeast Asia* (pp. 177–203). Singapore, RELC.

Long, M. H., & Porter, P. (1985). Group work, interlanguage talk, and second language acquisition. *TESOL Quarterly, 19*(2), 207–228.

Long, M. H., & Richards, J. C. (Eds.). (1987). *Methodology in TESOL: A book of readings.* New York: Newbury House.

Long, M. H., & Sato, C. J. (1983). Classroom foreigner-talk discourse: Forms and functions of teachers' questions. In H. W. Seliger & M. H. Long (Eds.), *Classroom-oriented research in second language acquisition* (pp. 268–286). New York: Newbury House.

Longman (Publishers) (1973). *Geography Games.* Harlow.

Lopez, D. E. (1978). Chicano language loyalty in an urban setting. *Sociology and Social Research, 62,* 267–278.

Lopez, D. E. (1982). *Language maintenance and shift in the United States today: The basic patterns and their social implications. Vol. 3: Hispanics and Portuguese.* Los Alamitos, CA: National Center for Bilingual Research.

Loritz, D. (1984). *Computer-assisted diagnosis and instruction in L2 phonetics.* Paper presented at the 18th Annual TESOL Convention, Houston, TX.

Los Angeles City Schools, California Division of Career and Continuing Education. (1974). *Bridging the Asian language and cultural gap: A handbook for teachers. Vol. 7: Asian Project* (Grant No. OEG-71-4409). Washington, DC: Office of Education (DHEW). (ERIC Document Reproduction Service No. ED 095 709)

Lougheed, L. (1985). *Listening between the lines: A cultural approach.* Reading, MA: Addison-Wesley.

Low, G. D. (1985). Validity and the problem of direct language proficiency tests. In J. C. Alderson (Ed.), *Lancaster practical papers in English language education* (Vol. 6, pp. 151–168). Oxford: Pergamon.

Low, G. D. (1986). Storylines and other developing contexts in use-of-language test design. *Indian Journal of Applied Linguistics, 12,* 15–38.

Lozanov, G. (1978). *Suggestology and outlines of suggestopedy.* New York: Gordon and Breach Science Publishers.

Lozanov, G. (1982). Suggestion and suggestopedy. In R. W. Blair (Ed.), *Innovative approaches to language teaching* (pp. 146–159). New York: Newbury House.

Lozanov, G. (1988). *The foreign language teacher's suggestopedic manual.* New York: Gordon and Breach Science Publishers.

Lynch, A. (1982). "Authenticity" in language teaching:

Some implications for the design of listening materials. *British Journal of Language Teaching, 20*(1), 9–16.

Lynch, T. (1983). *Study listening*. Oxford: Oxford University Press.

Lyons, J. (1977a). *Semantics* (Vols. 1 & 2). Cambridge: Cambridge University Press.

Lyons, J. (Ed.). (1977b). *New horizons in linguistics*. Middlesex, England: Penguin Books.

MacDonald, B., Adelman, C., Kushner, S., & Walker, R. (1982). *Bread and dreams: A case study of bilingual schooling in the U.S.A.* Norwich, England: University of East Anglia, Center for Applied Research in Education.

Macian, J. L. (1986). An analysis of state adopted foreign language textbooks used in first- and third-year high school Spanish classes. *Foreign Language Annals, 19*(2), 103–118.

Macian, J. L., & Harewood, G. (1984). Textbooks: Do they match your students' learning needs? *OMLTA Journal,* pp. 54–63. (ERIC Document Reproduction Services No. ED 254 108)

Mackey, W. F. (1965). *Language teaching analysis*. Bloomington and London: Indiana University Press.

Maclennan, S. (1987). Integrating lesson planning and class management. *ELT Journal, 41*(3), 193–197.

Madden, J. F. (1980). Developing pupil's vocabulary-learning skills. *RELC Journal, 11*(Suppl. 3), 111–117.

Madsen, H. S. (1986). Evaluating a computer-adaptive ESL placement test. *CALICO Journal, 4*(2), 41–50.

Madsen, H. S. (1979). Innovative methodologies applicable to TESL. In M. Celce-Murcia & L. McIntosh (Eds.), *Teaching English as a second or foreign language* (pp. 26–38). New York: Newbury House.

Mage, T. (1978). Contrastive discourse analysis: EST and SST. In M. T. Trimble, L. Trimble, & K. Drobnic (Eds.), *English for specific purposes: EST* (pp. 154–166). Corvallis, OR: Oregon State University Press.

Mahon, D. (1986). Intermediate skills: Focusing on reading rate development. In F. Dubin, D. Eskey, & W. Grabe (Eds.), *Teaching second language reading for academic purposes* (pp. 77–102). Reading, MA: Addison-Wesley.

Maley, A., & Moulding, S. (1979). *Learning to listen.* Cambridge: Cambridge University Press.

Manes, J., & Wolfson, N. (1981). The compliment formula. In F. Coulmas (Ed.), *Conversational routine* (pp. 115–132). The Hague: Mouton.

Maring, G. H. (1978). Freire, Gray, and Robinson on reading. *Journal of Reading, 21*(5), 421–425.

Marshall, M. J. (1986). *Writing without tears: Advanced writing for academic success*. Urbana, IL: ERIC/RCS. (ERIC Document Reproduction Service No. ED 271 962)

Mason, J. M., & Au, K. H. (1986). *Reading instruction for today*. Glenview, IL: Scott, Foresman.

Master, P. (1985a). English for specific purposes: The development of ESP (Part 1). *CATESOL News, 17*(2), 15–19.

Master, P. (1985b). English for specific purposes: The development of ESP (Part 2). *CATESOL News, 17*(3), 12–15.

Matthews, A., Spratt, M., & Dangerfield, L. (Eds.). (1985). *At the chalkface*. London: Edward Arnold.

May, F. B., & Eliot, S. B. (1978). *To help children read: Mastery performance modules for teachers in training*. Columbus, OH: Charles E. Merrill.

McAlpin, J. (1980). *The magazine picture library*. London: George Allen & Unwin.

McArthur, T. (1981). *Longman lexicon of contemporary English*. London: Longman.

McCarthy, B. (1980). *The 4MAT system: Teaching to learning styles with right/left mode techniques*. Barrington, IL: EXCEL

McConochie, J. (Ed.). (1975). *Twentieth century American short stories*. New York: Collier Macmillan International.

McGee, D. (1977). *Reading skills for basic literacy*. Vancouver, BC: Vancouver Community College.

McGirt, J. (1984). *The effect of morphological and syntactic errors on the holistic scores of native and non-native compositions*. Unpublished MATESL thesis, University of California, Los Angeles.

McGroarty, M. (1989). The benefits of cooperative learning arrangements in second language instruction. *NABE Journal, 13*, 127–143.

McGroarty, M., Delgado-Gaitan, D., Romero, O., & Hurst, M. (1989). *Adult literacy and adult ESL* Research and Policy No. 2). Santa Barbara: University of California, Linguistic Minority Research Project.

McIntire, R. D. (1988). *Study of the instructional impact on adults enrolled in English as a second language classes with respect to employment*. Unpublished doctoral dissertation, Santa Barbara University.

McIntosh, L. (1979). Context and sequence in English grammar. In M. Celce-Murcia & L. McIntosh (Eds.), *Teaching English as a second or foreign language* (pp. 229–240). New York: Newbury House.

McKay, S. (1980). Teaching the syntactic, semantic and pragmatic dimensions of verbs. *TESOL Quarterly, 14*(1), 17–26.

McKay, S. (1982). Literature in the ESL classroom. *TESOL Quarterly, 16*(4), 529–536.

McKay, S. (1985). *Teaching grammar: Form, function and technique*. New York: Pergamon Press.

McKenna, E. (1987). Preparing foreign students to enter discourse communities in the United States. *ESP Journal, 6*(3), 187–202.

McKinley, C. A. (1974). *A study of ESL reading difficulties*. Unpublished MATESL thesis, University of California, Los Angeles.

McLaughlin, B. (1978). The monitor model: Some methodological considerations. *Language Learning, 28*(2), 309–332.

McLaughlin, B. (1987a). *Theories of second language acquisition*. London: Edward Arnold.

McLaughlin, B. (1987b). Reading in a second language: Studies with adult and child learners. In S. Goldman & H. Trueba (Eds.), *Becoming literate in English as a second language* (pp. 57–70). Norwood, NJ: Ablex.

McLaughlin, B., Rossman, T., & McLeod, B. (1983). Second language learning: An information-processing perspective. *Language Learning, 33*(2), 135–158.

McLeod, B., & McLaughlin, B. (1986). Restructuring or automaticity? Reading in a second language. *Language Learning, 36*(2), 109–123.

Meagher, R. S. (1987). *Computerized adaptive testing: Innovative approach to determine language proficiency*. ESOL/Bilingual Programs, Montgomery County Public Schools, MD.

Meara, P. M. (1981). Vocabulary acquisition: A neglected aspect of language learning. In Kinsella (Ed.), *Cambridge languages teaching surveys 3*. Cambridge: Cambridge University Press.

Meara, P., & Buxton, B. (1987). An alternative to multiple choice vocabulary tests. *Language Testing, 4*(2), 142–154.

Medley, D. M., & Mitzel, H. E. (1958). A technique for measuring classroom behavior. *Journal of Educational Psychology, 49*, 86–92.

Mellon, J. (1969). *Transformational sentence-combining: A method for enhancing the development of syntactic fluency in English composition*. Urbana, IL: NCTE.

Mercer, J. R. (1973). *Labelling the mentally retarded*. Los Angeles: University of California Press.

Mercer, J. R. (1979). *SOMPA technical manual*. New York: Psychological Corporation.

Mercer, J. R. (1983). Issues in the diagnosis of language disorders in students whose primary language is not English. *Topics in Language Disorders, 3*(3), 46–56.

Mercier, L. J. (1930). Is the Coleman report justified in its restatement of objectives for modern languages? *French Review, 3*, 397–415.

Messick, S., & Anderson, S. (1974). Educational testing, individual development, and social responsibility. In R. W. Tyler & R. W. Wolf, (Eds.), *Crucial issues in testing* (pp. 21–34). Berkeley, CA: McCutchan.

Meyer, V. (1985). The adult literacy initiative in the U.S.: A concern and a challenge. *Journal of Reading, 28*(8), 706–708.

Meyer, V. (1987). Lingering feelings of failure: An adult student who didn't learn to read properly. *Journal of Reading, 31*(3), 218–221.

Michaels, S. (1986). Narrative presentations: An oral preparation for literacy with first graders. In J. Cook-Gumperz (Ed.), *The social construction of literacy* (pp. 94–116). Cambridge: Cambridge University Press.

Milk, R. D. (1985). The changing role of ESL in bilingual education. *TESOL Quarterly, 19*(4), 657–672.

Miller, G. A. (1956). The magical number seven, plus or minus two. *Psychological Review, 63*(2), 81–97.

Minsky, M. L. (1975). A framework for representing knowledge. In P. H. Winston (Ed.), *The psychology of computer vision* (pp. 211–280). New York: McGraw-Hill.

Mitchell, R., Parkinson, B., & Johnstone, R. (1981). The foreign language classroom: An observational study. *Stirling Educational Monographs, 9*. Stirling, UK: University of Stirling, Department of Education.

Mittan, R. (1989). The peer review process: Harnessing students' communicative power. In D. M. Johnson & D. H. Roen (Eds.), *Richness in writing: Empowering ESL students* (pp. 207–219). New York: Longman.

Mockridge-Fong, S. (1979). Teaching the speaking skill. In M. Celce-Murcia & L. McIntosh (Eds.), *Teaching English as a second or foreign language* (pp. 90–101). New York: Newbury House.

Mohan, B. A. (1986). *Language and content*. Reading, MA: Addison-Wesley.

Mohatt, G., & Erickson, F. (1982). Cultural organization of participation structures in two classrooms of Indian students. In G. Spindler (Ed.), *Doing the ethnography of schooling: Educational anthropology in action*. New York: CBS College.

Mohr, M. M., & MacLean, M. S. (1987). *Working together: A guide for teacher-researchers*. Urbana, IL: NCTE.

Molinsky, S., & Bliss, B. (1980). *Side by side: English grammar through guided conversations*. Englewood Cliffs, NJ: Prentice-Hall.

Mollica, A. S. (1979). Print and non-print materials: Adapting for classroom use. In J. K. Phillips (Ed.), *Building on experience—Building for success* (pp. 157–198). Skokie, IL: National Textbook Company.

Montgomery, C., & Eisenstein, M. (1985). Real reality revisited: An experimental communicative course in ESL. *TESOL Quarterly, 19*(2), 317–334.

Moran, M. H., & Moran, M. G. (1985). *Research in technical communication* (pp. 313–52). Westport, CT: Greenwood Press.

Morgan, A. (1983). Theoretical aspects of project-based learning in higher education. *British Journal of Education Technology, 1*(14), 66–78.

Morgan, J., & Rinvolucri, M. (1986). *Vocabulary*. Oxford: Oxford University Press.

Morley, J. (1972). *Improving aural comprehension*. Ann Arbor: University of Michigan Press.

Morley, J. (1973). *Films for EFL practice: Listening, speaking, vocabulary building*. Ann Arbor: University of Michigan Press.

Morley, J. (1981). Using films and videos as English language instructional materials: Theoretical principles and pedagogical practices. *Nagoya Round Table Journal on Languages, Linguistics, and Literature, 4*(1), 1–17.

Morley, J. (1984). *Listening and language learning in ESL*. Englewood Cliffs, NJ: Prentice-Hall.

Morley, J. (1985). Listening comprehension. Student-controlled modules for self-access self-study. *TESOL Newsletter, 19*(6), 1; 32–33.

Morley, J. (1987a). Current directions in teaching English to speakers of other languages: A state of the art. *TESOL Newsletter, 21*(2), 16–20.

Morley, J. (Ed.). (1987b). *Current perspectives on pronunciation.* Washington, DC: TESOL.

Morley, J. (in press). *Consonants in context (Book 3): Extemporary speaking practice.* Ann Arbor: University of Michigan Press.

Morris, C. (1939). *Foundations of the theory of signs.* Chicago: University of Chicago Press.

Morrow, K. (1981). Principles of communicative methodology. In K. Johnson & K. Morrow (Eds.), *Communication in the classroom* (pp. 56–69). London: Longman.

Moskowitz, G. (1978). *Caring and sharing in the foreign language class.* New York: Newbury House.

Moskowitz, G., & Hayman, J. L. (1974). International patterns of first year, typical, and ''best'' teachers in inner-city schools. *Journal of Educational Research, 67*(5), 224–230.

Moustafa, M., & Penrose, J. (1985). Comprehensible input PLUS the language experience approach: Reading instruction for limited English speaking students. *Reading Teacher, 38*(7), 640–647.

Msosa, J. J. (1982). *An examination of the suitability and relevance of the prescribed textbook for English literature of junior certificate level in Malawi secondary schools* (African Studies in Curriculm and Evaluation, No. 50). Kenya: University of Nairobi. (ERIC Document Reproduction Service No. ED 234 000)

Munby, J. (1978). *Communicative syllabus design.* Cambridge: Cambridge University Press.

Mustapha, M., Nelson, P., & Thomas, J. (1985). Reading for specific purposes: The course for the faculty of earth sciences at King Abdulaziz University. In J. M. Ulijn & A. K. Pugh (Eds.), *Reading for professional purposes: Methods and materials in teaching languages.* Leuven/Amersfoort: ACCO.

Nadel, E., & Fishman, J. A. (1977). English in Israel: A sociolinguistic study. In J. A. Fishman, R. L. Cooper, & A. W. Conrad (Eds.), *The spread of English* (pp. 137–167). New York: Newbury House.

Nagle, S., & Sanders, S. (1986). Comprehension theory and secondary language pedagogy. *TESOL Quarterly, 20*(1), 9–26.

Nation, I. S. P. (1980). Strategies for receptive language learning. *RELC Journal, 11*(Suppl. 3), 15–23.

Nation, I. S. P. (1982). Beginning to learn foreign languages vocabulary: A review of the research. *RELC Journal, 13*(1), 14–36.

Nation, I. S. P. (1990). *Teaching and learning vocabulary.* New York: Newbury House.

National Dairy Council of America. (1971). *Food for life.* [Film]. Wexler Corporation.

National Defense Language Development Program, U.S. Office of Education (1964). *Completed research, studies, and instructional materials* (List No. 4 OE 12016-64). Washington, DC: U.S. Government Printing Office.

NCTE task force on racism and bias in the teaching of English: Criteria for teaching materials. (1971). *College English, 32*(6), 713–715.

Neisser, U. (1967). *Cognitive psychology.* New York: Appleton-Century-Crofts.

Nelson, G., & Winters, T. (1980). *ESL Operations.* New York: Newbury House.

Neu, J. (1986). American English business negotiations: Training for non-native speakers. *English for Specific Purposes, 5*(1), 41–58.

Neubert, G. A., & Binko, J. B. (1987). Teach-probe-revise: A model for initiating classroom research. *Teacher Educator, 22*(1), 9–17.

Neuleib, J., & Brosnahan, I. (1987). Teaching grammar to writers. *Journal of Basic Writing, 6*(1), 28–35.

Nevo, D. L., Weinbach, L., & Mark, N. (1987). *Final report on the pilot research on the evaluation of achievement in writing in elementary schools.* Tel-Aviv, Israel: Tel Aviv University.

Newkirk, T. (1989). The first five minutes: Setting the agenda in a writing conference. In C. M. Anson (Ed.), *Writing and response: Theory, practice, and research.* Urbana, IL: NCTE.

Newman, J. M. (Ed.). (1985). *Whole language: Theory and use.* Portsmouth, NH: Heinemann Educational Books.

Newmark, G., & Diller, E. (1964). Emphasizing the audio in the audio-lingual approach. *Modern Language Journal, 48*(1), 18–20.

Newton, A. (1985). A dimension of depth. *English Teaching Forum, 23*(1), inside front cover.

Newton, A. C. (1979). Current trends in language teaching. In M. Celce-Murcia & L. McIntosh (Eds.), *Teaching English as a second or foreign language* (pp. 17–26). New York: Newbury House.

Nichols, P. C. (1981). Creoles of the USA. In C. A. Ferguson & S. B. Heath (Eds.), *Language in the USA* (pp. 69–91). Cambridge: Cambridge University Press.

Nida, E. A. (1953). Selective listening. *Language Learning: A Journal of Applied Linguistics, 4*(3–4), 92–101.

Nida, E. A. (1957a). *Learning a foreign language.* New York: Friendship Press.

Nida, E. A. (1957b). Learning by listening. In R. Blair (Ed.), *Innovative approaches to language teaching* (pp. 42–53). New York: Newbury House.

Norris, W. E. (1970). Teaching second language reading at the advanced level: Goals, techniques, and procedures. *TESOL Quarterly, 9*(3), 243–251.

North, S. M. (1987). *The making of knowledge in composition: Portrait of an emerging field.* Upper Montclair, NJ: Boynton/Cook.

Numrich, C. (1987). *Consider the issues: Developing listening and critical thinking.* White Plains, NY: Longman.

Nunan, D. (1986, April). *Communicative language teaching: The learner's view*. Paper presented at the RELC Seminar, Singapore.

Nunan, D. (1988). *The learner-centered curriculum*. New York: Cambridge University Press.

Nunan, D. (1989). *Communicative task design*. Cambridge: Cambridge University Press.

Nurss, J. R., & Hough, R. A. (1985). Young children's oral language: Effects of task. *Journal of Educational Research, 78*(5), 280–285.

Nuttall, C. (1982). *Teaching reading skills in a foreign language*. London: Longman.

Ochs, E. (1988). *Culture and language development*. Cambridge: Cambridge University Press.

Ohannessian, S. (1960). *Interim bibliography on the teaching of English to speakers of other languages*. Washington, DC: Center for Applied Linguistics.

Ohannessian, S. (1965). ATESL Report. *NAFSA Newsletter, 16*, 7–13.

Oller, J. W., Jr. (1972). Dictation as a test of ESL proficiency. In H. B. Allen & R. N. Campbell (Eds.), *Teaching English as a second language* (2nd ed., pp. 346–354). New York: McGraw-Hill.

Oller, J. W., Jr. (1979). *Language tests at school*. London: Longman.

Oller, J., & Richard-Amato, P. (1983). *Methods that work*. New York: Newbury House.

Olshtain, E. (1983). Sociocultural competence and language transfer: The case of apology. In S. Gass & L. Selinker (Eds.), *Language transfer in language learning* (pp. 232–249). New York: Newbury House.

Olshtain, E., & Cohen, A. D. (1983). Apology: A speech act set. In N. Wolfson & E. Judd (Eds.), *Sociolinguistics and language acquisition* (pp. 18–35). New York: Newbury House.

Olshtain, E., & Cohen, A. D. (1987). *The learning of complex speech act behavior*. Tel-Aviv, Israel: Tel-Aviv University, School of Education.

Olshtain, E., & Weinbach, L. (1987). Complaints: A study of speech act behavior among native and nonnative speakers of Hebrew. In J. Verschueren & M. Bertucelli-Papi (Eds.), *The pragmatic perspective* (pp. 195–208). Amsterdam: John Benjamins.

Omaggio, A. (1986). *Teaching language in context*. Boston: Heinle and Heinle.

O'Malley, J. M. (1986). *Test-taking strategies for ESL students*. Rosslyn, VA: International Research Associates.

O'Malley, J. M., Chamot, A. U. & Walker, C. (1987). Some applications of cognitive theory to second language acquisition. *Studies in Second Language Acquisition, 9*(3), 287–306.

O'Neill, R. (1982). Why use textbooks? *ELT Journal, 36*(2), 104–111.

Orwell, G. (1946). *Animal farm*. New York: Harcourt Brace.

Ostler, S. (1980). A survey of academic needs for advanced ESL. *TESOL Quarterly, 14*(4), 489–502.

Owen, M. (1983). *Apologies and remedial interchanges*. Amsterdam: Mouton.

Oxford, R. (1990). *Language learning strategies: What every teacher should know*. New York: Newbury House.

Palmer, H. (1917). *The scientific study and teaching of languages*. Yonkers-on-Hudson, NY: World Book.

Papalia, A. (1976). *Learner-centered language teaching: Methods and materials*. New York: Newbury House.

Parker, D. (1986). *"Sheltered" English: Method and technique*. Paper presented at California Immersion/Second Language Institute, University of California, Santa Barbara.

Parry, K. J. (1987). Reading in a second culture. In J. Devine, P. L. Carrell, & D. Eskey (Eds.), *Research in reading in English as a second language* (pp. 61–70). Washington, DC: TESOL.

Paulston, C. B. (1972). Teaching writing in the ESOL classroom: Techniques of controlled composition. *TESOL Quarterly, 6*(1), 33–59.

Paulston, C. B., & Bruder, M. N. (1976). *Teaching English as a second language: Techniques and procedures*. Cambridge, MA: Winthrop.

Payne, C. H. (1976). In search of a method. *English Language Forum, 14*(1), 2–8.

Payne, R. M. (1975). *Universal textbooks and ESP*. Mexico City: Autonomous Metropolitan University. (ERIC Document Reproduction Service No. ED 117 953)

Pearson, P. D., & Johnson, D. D. (1978). *Teaching reading comprehension*. New York: Holt, Rinehart & Winston.

Penfield, J. (1987). *The media: Catalysts for communicative language learning*. Reading, MA: Addison-Wesley.

Pennella, M. (1985). *Mapping the instructional journey: The written public and private plans of secondary teachers of mathematics and English*. Paper presented at the 69th Annual meeting of the American Educational Research Association, Chicago. (ERIC Document Reproduction Service No. ED 262 001)

Pereyra-Suarez, E. (1986, May). *Individualized self-paced learning programs in foreign languages at San Jose State University*. Paper presented at the meeting of the Pacific Northwest conference on foreign languages, Vancouver, Canada. (ERIC Document Reproduction Services No. ED 276 295)

Perfetti, C. A. (1985). *Reading ability*. New York: Oxford Press.

Perren, G. E. (1963). Teaching English literature overseas: Historical notes and present instances. In J. Press (Ed.), *The teaching of English literature overseas*. London: Methuen.

Peterson, P. W. (1989). *A comparison of the propositional structures and amount of inferencing in written lecture summaries of native and non-native speakers*. Unpublished doctoral dissertation, University of Minnesota.

Pfister, G. G., & Borzilleri, P. A. (1977). Surface culture concepts: A design for the evaluation of culture material in textbooks. *Die Unterrichtspraxis, 10*(2), 102–108.

Philips, S. U. (1972). Participant structures and communicative competence: Warm Springs children in community and classrooms. In C. Cazden, V. John, & D. Hymes (Eds.), *Functions of languages in the classroom* (pp. 370–394). New York: Teachers College Press.

Philips, S. U. (1983). *The invisible culture*. New York: Longman.

Pica, T., & Doughty, C. (1985). Input and interaction in the communicative language classroom: A comparison of teacher-fronted and group activities. In S. M. Gass & C. G. Madden (Eds.), *Input and second language acquisition* (pp. 115–132). New York: Newbury House.

Pica, T., Holliday, L., Lewis, N., & Morgenthaler, L. (1988). *Comprehensible output in native speaker-nonnative speaker interaction*. Paper presented at the 22nd Annual TESOL Convention, Chicago.

Pica, T., & Long, M. H. (1986). The linguistic and conversational performance of experienced and inexperienced teachers. In R. R. Day (Ed.), *Talking to learn: Conversation in second language acquisition* (pp. 85–98). New York: Newbury House.

Pica, T., Young, R., & Doughty, C. (1987). The impact of interaction on comprehension. *TESOL Quarterly, 21*(4), 737–758.

Pienemann, M. (1984). Psychological constraints on the teachability of language. *Studies in Second Language Acquisition, 6*(2), 186–214.

Pienemann, M., & Johnston, M. (1987). Factors influencing the development of language profiency. In D. Nunan (Ed.), *Applying second language acquisition research* (pp. 45–141). Adelaide: National Curriculum Resource Centre.

Pike, K. (1945). *The intonation of American English*. Ann Arbor: University of Michigan Press.

Pike, K. (1959). Language as particle, wave, and field. *Texas Quarterly, 2,* 37–54.

Pimsleur, P. (1959). *Report of the conference on psychological experiments related to second-language learning*. Unpublished manuscript. (Available in mimeographed form from the Language Development Program, U.S. Office of Education)

Pimsleur, P., & Quinn, T. (Eds.). (1971). *The psychology of second language learning*. Cambridge: Cambridge University Press.

Piotrowski, M. (1986). Business as usual: Using the case method to teach ESL to executives. *TESOL Quarterly, 16*(2), 229–234.

Pittman, G. (1963). *Teaching structural English*. Brisbane, Australia: Jacaranda Press.

Politzer, R. L. (1970). Some reflections on "good" and "bad" language teaching behaviors. *Language Learning, 20*(1), 31–43.

Politzer, R. L. (1977). *Foreign language teaching and bilingual education: Implications of some recent research findings*. Paper presented at the Annual Meeting of the American Council on the Teaching of Foreign Languages, San Francisco.

Ponsot, M., & Deen, R. (1982). *Beat not the poor desk. Writing: What to teach, how to teach it and why*. Montclair, NJ: Boynton/Cook.

Poplack, S. (1979). *"Sometimes I'll start a sentence in Spanish y termino en Espanol": Toward a typology of code-switching* (Language Policy Task Force Working Paper No. 4). New York: City University of New York, Center for Puerto Rican Studies.

Porter, D., & Roberts, J. (1987). Authentic listening activities. In M. Long & J. Richards, *Methodology in TESOL* (pp. 177–187). New York: Newbury House.

Postovsky, V. (1970). *Effects of delay in oral practice at the beginning of second language learning*. Unpublished doctoral dissertation, University of California, Berkeley.

Postovsky, V. (1974). Effects of delay in oral practice at the beginning of second language learning. *Modern Language Journal, 58*(3), 229–239.

Pouwels, J. (1988). International potpourri: Foreign language for the gifted and talented in Arkansas. *Foreign Language Annals, 21*(2), 147–151.

Povey, J. F. (1972). Literature in TESL programs: The language and the culture. In H. B. Allen & R. N. Campbell (Eds.), *Teaching English as a second language: A book of readings* (2nd ed., pp. 185–191). New York: McGraw-Hill.

Povey, J. F. (1979). The teaching of literature in advanced ESL classes. In M. Celce-Murcia & L. McIntosh (Eds.), *Teaching English as a second or foreign language* (pp. 162–186). New York: Newbury House.

Prahbu, N. J. (1987). *Second language pedagogy*. Oxford: Oxford University Press.

Prator, C. H. (1972). Development of a manipulation-communication scale. In H. B. Allen & R. N. Campbell (Eds.), *Teaching English as a second language: A book of readings* (2nd ed., pp. 139–144). New York: McGraw-Hill.

Prator, C. H. (1976). In search of a method. *English Language Forum, 14*(1), 2–8.

Prator, C. H. (1977). *Suggested criteria for the selection of textbooks in teaching English as a second language*. Unpublished manuscript, University of California, Los Angeles.

Prator, C. H., & Celce-Murcia, M. (1979). An outline of language teaching approaches. In M. Celce-Murcia & L. McIntosh (Eds.), *Teaching English as a second or foreign language* (pp. 3–5). New York: Newbury House.

Prator, C. H., & Robinett, B. W. (1985). *Manual of Ameri-*

can *English pronunciation* (4th ed.). New York: Holt, Rinehart & Winston.

Press, J. (Ed.). (1963). *The teaching of English literature overseas.* London: Methuen.

Prince, D. (1984). Workplace English: Approach and analysis [special issue]. *ESP Journal, 3*(2), 109–116.

Procter, P. (Ed.). (1978 edition and 1988 edition). *Longman dictionary of contemporary English.* Harlow, England: Longman.

Pugh, A. K. (1978). *Silent reading.* London: Longman.

Quan, C. A. (1986). *Crisis intervention for the ESL teacher: Whose problem is it?* (ERIC Document reproduction. Service No. ED 271 951).

Raatz, U. (1985). Tests of reduced redundancy—The C-test, a practical example. *Fremdsprachen un Hochschule.* Bochum, West Germany: AKS-Roundbriefe 13–14:14–19.

Raatz, U., & Klein-Braley, C. (1982). The C-test—A modification of the cloze procedure. In T. Culhane et al. (Eds.), *Practice and problems in language testing 4.* Colchester: University of Essex.

Raimes, A. (1983a). *Techniques in teaching writing.* New York: Oxford University Press.

Raimes, A. (1983b). Tradition and revolution in ESL teaching. *TESOL Quarterly, 17*(4), 535–552.

Raimes, A. (1985). What unskilled ESL students do as they write: A classroom study of composing. *TESOL Quarterly, 19*(2), 229–258.

Raimes, A. (1986). *Teaching writing: What we know and what we do.* Paper presented at the 20th Annual TESOL Convention, Anaheim.

Raimes, A. (1987). Why write? From purpose to pedagogy. *English Teaching Forum, 25*(4), 36–41.

Raimes, A. (1988). *Grammar troublespots: An editing guide for ESL students.* New York: St. Martin's Press.

Ramani, E., Chacko, T., Singh, S. J., & Glendinning, E. H. (1988). An ethnographic approach to syllabus design: A case study of the Indian Institute of Science, Bangalore. *English for Specific Purposes, 7*(2), 81–90.

Rardin, J. P., & Tranel, D. D. (1988). *Education in a new dimension.* East Dubuque, Illinois: Counseling-Learning Publications.

Rathmell, G. (in press). What happens in the classroom. In R. E. W-B. Olsen & J. W-B. Olsen (Eds.), *Approaching content.* Hayward, CA: Alemany Press.

RCA/Colombia Pictures (1985). *We are the world: The video event.* Burbank, CA: RCA/Colombia Pictures Home Video.

Reed, J. (1970). Improving the effectiveness of language laboratory work. *Journal of Applied Linguistics and Language Teaching Technology, 3*(1), 25–37.

Reid, J. (1984). The radical outliner and the radical brainstormer: A perspective on composing processes. *TESOL Quarterly, 18*(3), 529–534.

Reid, J. (1989). English as a second language composition in higher education: The expectations of the academic audience. In D. M. Johnson & D. H. Roen (Eds.), *Richness in writing: Empowering ESL students* (pp. 220–234). New York: Longman.

Reid, J. M. (1987). The learning style preferences of ESL students. *TESOL Quarterly, 21*(1), 87–111.

Richard-Amato, P. (1988). *Making it happen.* New York: Longman.

Richards, J. C. (1976). The role of vocabulary teaching. *TESOL Quarterly, 10*(1), 77–89.

Richards, J. C. (1983). Listening comprehension: Approach, design, procedure. *TESOL Quarterly, 17*(2), 219–239.

Richards, J. C. (1984). The secret life of methods. *TESOL Quarterly, 18*(1), 7–23.

Richards, J. C. (1985). *The contexts of language teaching.* Cambridge: Cambridge University Press.

Richards, J. C. (1990). *The language teaching matrix.* Cambridge: Cambridge University Press.

Richards, J., & Bycina, D. (1985). *Person to person* (Book 2). Oxford: Oxford University Press.

Richards, J. C., Platt, J., & Weber, H. (1985). *Longman dictionary of applied linguistics.* London: Longman.

Richards, J. C., & Rodgers, T. S. (1986). *Approaches and methods in language teaching: A description and analysis.* New York: Cambridge University Press.

Richards, J. C., & Rodgers, T. S. (1987a). Method: Approach, design, and procedure. In M. H. Long & J. C. Richards (Eds.), *Methodology in TESOL: A book of readings* (pp. 145–160). New York: Newbury House.

Richards, J. C., & Rodgers, T. S. (1987b). Through the looking glass: Trends and directions in language teaching. *RELC Journal, 18*(2), 45–73.

Richterich, R. (1983). Introduction. In R. Richterich (Ed.), *Case studies in identifying language needs* (pp. 1–13). Oxford: Pergamon.

Richterich, R., & Chancerel, J. L. (1978). *Indentifying needs of adults learning a foreign language.* Strasbourg: Council for Cultural Cooperation of the Council of Europe.

Rico, G. L. (1986). Clustering: A pre-writing process. In C. B. Olson (Ed.), *Practical ideas for teaching writing as a process* (pp. 17–20). Sacramento: California State Department of Education.

Rigg, P., & Kazemek, F. (1983). Adult literacy in the USA: Problems and solutions. *Convergence, 15*(4), 215–221.

Rigg, P., & Kazemek, F. (1985). For adults only: Reading material for adult literacy. *Journal of Reading, 28*(8), 726–731.

Rings, L. (1986). Authentic language and authentic conversational texts. *Foreign Language Annals, 19*(3), 203–208.

Rivers, W. M. (1964). *The psychologist and the foreign language teacher.* Chicago: University of Chicago Press.

Rivers, W. M. (1966). Listening comprehension. *Modern Language Journal, 50*(4), 196–204.

References

Rivers, W. M. (1968). *Teaching foreign language skills.* Chicago: University of Chicago Press.

Rivers, W. M. (1972). *Speaking in many tongues: Essays in foreign-language teaching.* New York: Cambridge University Press.

Rivers, W. M. (1981). *Teaching foreign-language skills* (2nd ed.). Chicago: University of Chicago Press.

Robb, T., Ross, S., & Shortreed, I. (1986). Salience of feedback on error and its effect on EFL writing quality. *TESOL Quarterly, 20*(1), 83–93.

Robertson, D. (1983). *English language use, needs, and proficiency among foreign students at the University of Illinois at Urbana/Champaign.* Unpublished doctoral dissertation, University of Illinois, Urbana/Champaign.

Robinson, F. (1962). Effective reading. New York: Harper & Brothers.

Rooks, G. (1981). *The non-stop discussion workbook.* New York: Newbury House.

Rose, M. (1989). *Lives on the boundary.* New York: Free Press.

Rosier, P., & Holm, W. (1980). *The rock point experience: A longitudinal study of a Navajo school program* (Bilingual education series, No. 8). Washington, DC: Center for Applied Linguistics.

Ross, J. (1968). Controlled writing: A transformational approach. *TESOL Quarterly, 2*(4), 253–261.

Ross, M. (1984). Football red and baseball green. In A. Taylor (Ed.), *Short model essays* (pp. 293–304). Boston: Little, Brown.

Rossi-Landi, F. (1975). *Linguistics and economics.* The Hague: Mouton.

Rossner, R. (1985). The learner as lexicographer: Using dictionary in second language learning. In R. Ilson (Ed.), *Dictionary, lexicography and language learning.* Oxford: Pergamon Press.

Rowe, M. B. (1969). Science, soul, and sanctions. *Science and Children, 6*(6), 11–13.

Rudzka, B., Channell, J., Ostyn, P., & Putseys, Y. (1981). *The words you need.* London: Macmillan.

Rudzka, B., Channell, J., Ostyn, P., & Putseys, Y. (1985). *More words you need.* London: Macmillan.

Ruetten, M. K. (1986). *Comprehending academic lectures.* New York: Macmillan.

Rumelhart, D. E. (1977). Toward an interactive model of reading. In S. Dornic (Ed.), *Attention and performance* (pp. 573–603). New York: Academic Press.

Rumelhart, D. E. (1980). Schemata: The building blocks of cognition. In R. J. Spiro, B. Bruce, & W. F. Brewer (Eds.), *Theoretical issues in reading comprehension* (pp. 33–58). Hillsdale, NJ: Erlbaum.

Rumelhart, D. E., & Ortony, A. (1977). The representation of knowledge in memory. In R. C. Anderson, R. J. Spiro, & W. E. Montague (Eds.), *Schooling and the acquisition of knowledge.* Hillsdale, NJ: Erlbaum.

Rutherford, W. (1988). Functions of grammar in a language teaching syllabus. In W. E. Rutherford & M. Sharwood Smith (Eds.), *Grammar and second language teaching: A book of readings* (pp. 231–249). New York: Newbury House.

Rutherford, W. E. (1987). *Second language grammar: Learning and teaching.* London: Longman.

Rutherford, W. E., & Sharwood Smith, M. (Eds.). (1988). *Grammar and second language teaching: A book of readings.* New York: Newbury House.

Sapiens, A. (1982). *Instructional language strategies in bilingual Chicano peer tutoring and their effect on cognitive and affective learning outcomes.* Unpublished doctoral dissertation, Stanford, CA.

Saporta, S. (1961). *Psycholinguistics: A book of readings.* New York: Holt, Rinehart, & Winston.

Savage, L. (1984, January). *Teaching strategies for developing literacy skills in nonnative speakers of English.* Paper presented at the National Conference on Adult Literacy, Washington, DC.

Saville-Troike, M. (1976). *Foundations for teaching English as a second language: Theory and method for multicultural education.* Englewood Cliffs, NJ: Prentice-Hall. (ERIC Document Reproduction Service No. ED 153 458)

Saville-Troike, M. (1984). What really matters in second language learning for academic achievement? *TESOL Quarterly, 18*(2), 199–219.

Sayers, D. (1989). Bilingual sister classes in computer writing network. In D. M. Johnson & D. H. Roen (Eds.), *Richness in writing: Empowering ESL students* (pp. 120–133). New York: Longman.

Schachter, J. (1974). An error in error analysis. *Language Learning, 24*(2), 205–214.

Schachter, J., & Celce-Murcia, M. (1977). Some reservations concerning error analysis. *TESOL Quarterly, 11*(4), 441–449.

Schane, S. (1970). Linguistics, spelling and pronunciation. *TESOL Quarterly, 4*(2), 137–141.

Schank, R. C. (1975). The structure of episodes in memory. In D. G. Brobow & A. Collins (Eds.), *Representation and understanding* (pp. 237–272). New York: Academic Press.

Schank, R. C. (1982). *Reading and understanding: Teaching from the perspective of artificial intelligence.* Hillsdale, NJ: Erlbaum.

Schank, R. C., & Albelson, R. (1977a). *Scripts, plans, goals, and understanding: An inquiry into human knowledge structures.* Hillsdale, NJ: Erlbaum.

Schank, R. C., & Abelson, R. P. (1977b). Scripts, plans, and knowledge. In P. M. Johnson-Laird & P. C. Wason (Eds.), *Thinking: Readings in cognitive science* (pp. 421–432). Cambridge: Cambridge University Press.

Schärer, R. (1983). Indentification of learners' needs at Eurocentres. In R. Richterich (Ed.), *Case studies in identifying language needs* (pp. 106–116). Oxford: Pergamon.

Schechter, S. (1984). *Listening tasks for intermediate students of American English.* Cambridge: Cambridge University Press.

Schlesinger, I. (1968). *Sentence structure and the reading process*. The Hague: Mouton.

Schmidt, R. W. (1990). The role of consciousness in second language learning. *Applied Linguistics*, 11(2).

Schneider, W., & Schiffrin, R. M. (1977a). Controlled and automatic human information processing: I. Detection, search, and attention. *Psychology Review*, 84(1), 1–55.

Schneider, W., & Schiffrin, R. M. (1977b). Controlled and automatic human information processing: II. Perceptual learning, automatic attending, and a general theory. *Psychology Review*, 84(2), 128–190.

Scholfield, P. J. (1982). Using the English dictionary for comprehension. *TESOL Quarterly*, 16(2), 185–194.

Schumann, J. (1978). The acculturation model for second-language learning. In R. C. Gingras (Ed.), *Second language acquisition and foreign language teaching* (pp. 27–50). Washington, DC: Center for Applied Linguistics.

Schumann, J. (1986). Research on the acculturation model for second-language acquisition. *Journal of Multicultural Education*, 7(5), 379–392.

Schumann, J. (1990). *The role of the amygdala in mediating affect and cognition in second language acquisition*. Paper presented at the Georgetown University Roundtable, Washington, DC.

Scott, M. S., & Tucker, G. R. (1974). Error analysis and English language strategies of Arab students. *Language Learning*, 24(1), 69–97.

Scovel, T. (1969). Foreign accents, language acquisition, and cerebral dominance. *Language Learning*, 19(3 & 4), 245–254.

Seal, B. (1981). *In search of significant collocations*. Unpublished MATESL thesis, University of California, Los Angeles.

Seal, B. (1987). *Vocabulary builder 1*. London: Longman.

Seal, B. (1988). *Vocabulary builder 2*. London: Longman.

Searle, J. R. (1975). Indirect speech acts. In P. Cole & J. Morgan (Eds.), *Speech acts* (pp. 59–82). New York: Academic Press.

Semke, H. (1980). German cafe-theater: A venture in experiential learning. *Foreign Language Annals*, 13(2), 137–138.

Serpell, R. (1968). Selective attention and interference between first and second languages. *HDRU Reports*, University of Zambia.

Shapira, R. G. (1976). The role of attitude and motivation in language learning. In M. Celce-Murcia (Ed.), *ESL topics in research and methodology, vol. II* (prepublication version, pp. 118–136). Los Angeles: University of California, Los Angeles, Department of English, ESL Section.

Sharan, D. J. (1984). *Cooperative learning in the classroom: Research in desegregated schools*. Hillsdale, NJ: Erlbaum.

Sharpe, P. (1984). *Talking with Americans: Conversation and friendship strategies for learners of English*. Boston: Little, Brown.

Sharwood Smith, M. (1988). Applied linguistics and the psychology of instruction. In W. E. Rutherford & M. Sharwood Smith (Eds.), *Grammar and second language teaching: A book of readings* (pp. 206–223). New York: Newbury House.

Shaughnessy, M. (1977). *Errors and expectations: A guide for the teacher of basic writing*. New York: Oxford University Press.

Shavelson, R. J., & Stern, P. (1981). Research on teachers' pedagogical thoughts, judgements, and behavior. *Review of Educational Research*, 51(4), 455–498.

Sheldon, L. E. (1988). Evaluating ELT textbooks and materials. *English Language Teaching Journal*, 42(4), 237–246.

Shohamy, E. (1985). *A practical handbook in language testing for the second language teacher* (prepublication version). Tel Aviv, Israel: School of Education, Tel Aviv University.

Shohamy, E. (1988). A proposed framework for testing the oral language of second/foreign language learners. *Studies in Second Language Acquisition, 10*, 165–179.

Short, D. J., Crandall, J., & Christian, D. (1989). *How to integrate language and content instruction: A training manual*. Los Angeles: Center for Language Education and Research, University of California.

Shumaker, M. P. (1975). Literature and the teaching of reading. *Language Arts*, 52(7), 956–959.

Silva, T. (1990). ESL composition instruction: Developments, issues, and directions. In B. Kroll (Ed.), *Second language writing: Research insights for the classroom*. New York: Cambridge University Press, pp. 11–23.

Silva-Corvalan, C. (1983). Code-shifting patterns in Chicano Spanish. In L. Elias-Olivares (Ed.), *Spanish in the U.S. setting* (pp. 69–87). Rosslyn, VA: National Clearinghouse for Bilingual Education.

Simon, S. B., Howe, L. W., & Kirschenbaum, H. (1972). *Values clarification: A handbook of practical strategies for teachers and students*. New York: Hart.

Sims, J., & Peterson, P. W. (1981). *Better listening skills*. Englewood Cliffs, NJ: Prentice-Hall.

Sinclair, J. McH. (1966). Beginning the study of lexis. In C. E. Bazell, J. C. Catford, M. A. K. Halliday, & R. H. Robins (Eds.), *In memory of J. R. Firth* (pp. 410–430). London: Longman.

Sinclair, J. McH. (1984). The teaching of oral communication. *Speech and Language Learning*, 10, 1–11.

Sinclair, J. McH. (Ed.). (1987). *Collins COBUILD English language dictionary*. London: Longman.

Sinclair, J. McH., & Renouf, A. (1988). A lexical syllabus for language learning. In R. Carter & M. McCarthy (Eds.), *Vocabulary and language teaching*. London: Longman.

Sirotnik, K. A. (1983). What you see is what you get: Consistency, persistency, and mediocrity in classrooms. *Harvard Educational Review*, 53(1), 16–31.

Skierso, A. (1979). *An evaluation of the suitability of the major seventh-grade EFL textbook used in Israel.*

Unpublished MATESL thesis, University of California, Los Angeles.

Skinner, B. F. (1957). *Verbal behavior*. New York: Appleton-Century-Crofts.

Slager, W. R., & Marckwardt, A. H. (Eds.). (1975). *English for today: Book 6—Literature in English*. New York: McGraw-Hill.

Slavin, R. E. (1981). Synthesis of research on cooperative learning. *Educational Leadership, 38*(8), 655–660.

Slavin, R. E. (1983). When does cooperative learning increase student achievement? *Psychological Bulletin, 94*(3), 429–445.

Smith, F. (1973). *Psycholinguistics and reading*. New York: Holt, Rinehart & Winston.

Smith, F. (1978a). *Reading without nonsense*. New York: Teachers College Press.

Smith, F. (1978b). *Understanding reading, A psycholinguistic analysis of reading and learning* (2nd ed.). New York: Holt, Rinehart & Winston.

Smith, F. (1983) *Essays into literacy*. Exter, NH: Heinemann Educational Books.

Smith, S. (1988, October). *What am I going to teach? There's no book*. Paper presented at the 1988 MEX-TESOL Convention, Mexico City.

Smitherman, G. (1986). *Talkin and testifyin: The language of black America*. Detroit: Wayne State University Press.

Snow, B. G., & Perkins, K. (1979). The teaching of listening comprehension and communication activities. *TESOL Quarterly, 13*(1), 51–63.

Snow, M. A., & Brinton, D. M. (1988). Content-based language instruction: Investigating the effectiveness of the adjunct model. *TESOL Quarterly, 22*(4), 553–574.

Snow, M. A., Met, M., & Genesee, F. (1989). A conceptual framework for the integration of language and context in second/foreign language instruction. *TESOL Quarterly, 23*(2), 201–216.

Soar, R. M., & Soar, R. S. (1975). *Classroom behavior, pupil characteristics, and pupil growth for the school year and the summer*. Institute for Development of Human Resources, University of Florida.

Sowell, T. (1983). *The economics and politics of race*. New York: Quill.

Spack, R. (1984). Invention strategies and the ESL composition student. *TESOL Quarterly, 18*(4), 649–670.

Spack, R. (1985). Literature, reading, writing, and ESL: Bridging the gaps. *TESOL Quarterly, 19*(4), 703–725.

Spack, R., & Sadow, C. (1983). Student-teacher working journals in ESL freshman composition. *TESOL Quarterly, 17*(4), 575–593.

Sperling, M., & Freedman, S. W. (1987). A good girl writes like a good girl. *Written Communication, 4*(4), 343–369.

Spolsky, B. (1985). *Intentional and unintentional bias*. Ramat Gan: Bar-Ilan University, English Department.

Spradley, J. P. (1979). *The ethnographic interview*. New York: H. Holton.

Spradley, J. P. (1980). *Participant observation*. New York: H. Holton.

Squire, J. R., & Applebee, R. K. (1968). *High school English instruction today*. New York: Appleton.

Stafford, C. R. (1976). *A psycholinguistic analysis of ESL reading difficulties with teaching applications*. Unpublished MATESL thesis, University of California, Los Angeles.

Stanley, J. (1978). Teaching listening comprehension. *TESOL Quarterly, 12*(3), 285–295.

Stanovich, K. E. (1980). Toward an interactive-compensatory model of individual differences in the development of reading fluency. *Reading Research Quarterly, 16*(1), 32–71.

Staton, J. (1983). Dialog journals: A new tool for teaching communication. *ERIC/CLL News Bulletin, 6*(2), 1–6.

Staton, J., Shuy, R. W., Kreeft, J., & Reed, L. (1990). *Dialogue journal communication: Classroom, linguistic, social, and cognitive views*. Norwood, NJ: Ablex.

Steffensen, M. S., & Joag-Dev, C. (1984). Culture knowledge and reading. In J. Charles Alderson & A. H. Urquhart (Eds.), *Reading in a foreign language*. London: Longman.

Steiner, F. (1973). Sense and nonsense in foreign language textbooks. *Foreign Language Annals, 7*(1), 91–94.

Stern, H. H. (1983). *Fundamental concepts of language teaching*. Oxford: Oxford University Press.

Stern, S. L. (1977). *The teaching of contemporary American drama in advanced ESL*. Unpublished MATESL thesis, University of California, Los Angeles.

Stern, S. L. (1980). Drama in second language learning from a psycholinguistic perspective. *Language Learning, 30*(1), 77–100. (Reprinted as Why drama works: A psycholinguistic perspective. In J. W. Oller, Jr. & P. A. Richard-Amato (Eds.), (1983), *Methods that work* (pp. 207–225). New York: Newbury House.)

Stern, S. L. (1985). Teaching literature in ESL/EFL: An integrative approach. *Dissertation Abstracts International, 46*, 1547A–2176A. (University Microfilms No. DER85-13164)

Stevick, E. W. (1959). "Technemes" and the rhythm of class activity. *Language Learning, 9*(3), 45–51.

Stevick, E. W. (1971). *Adapting and writing language lessons*. Washington, DC: Foreign Service Institute.

Stevick, E. W. (1976). *Memory, meaning and method: Some psychological perspectives on language learning*. New York: Newbury House.

Stevick, E. W. (1980). *Teaching languages: A way and ways*. New York: Newbury House.

Stevick, E. W. (1986). *Images and options in the language classroom*. New York: Cambridge University Press.

Stevick, E. W. (1990). *Humanism in language teaching:*

A critical perspective. Oxford: Oxford University Press.

Stieglitz, E. L. (1982). A rating scale for evaluating English as a second language reading material. *Journal of Reading, 26*(3), 222–228.

Stitsworth, M. (1988). The relationship between previous foreign language study and personality change in youth exchange participants. *Foreign Language Annals, 21*(2), 131–137.

Stoller, F. (1986). Reading lab: Developing low-level reading skills. In F. Dubin, D. Eskey, & W. Grabe (Eds.), *Teaching second language reading for academic purposes* (pp. 51–76). Reading, MA: Addison-Wesley.

Strevens, P. (1977). Special-purpose language learning: A perspective. *Language Teaching and Linguistics Abstracts, 10*(3), 145–163.

Strevens, P. (1979). *Functional Englishes (ESP): The British perspective*. Unpublished manuscript.

Strevens, P. (1988). Language listening comprehension. *TESOL Quarterly, 12*(3), 285–295.

Sturtridge, G., & Herbert, D. (1979). *ELT guide to simulations*. London: British Council.

Svalberg, A. (1986). Teaching tense and aspect: A systematic approach. *ELT Journal, 40*(2), 136–145.

Swaffar, J. K. (1988). Readers, texts, and second languages: The interactive process. *Modern Language Journal, 72*(2), 123–149.

Swaffar, J. K., Arens, K., & Morgan, M. (1982). Teacher classroom practices: Redefining method as task hierarchy. *Modern Language Journal, 66*(1), 24–33.

Swain, M. (1984). Large-scale communicative language testing: A case study. In S. J. Savignon & M. S. Berns (Eds.), *Initiatives in communicative language teaching* (pp. 185–201). Reading, MA: Addison-Wesley.

Swain, M. (1985). Communicative competence: Some roles of comprehensible input and comprehensible output in its development. In S. M. Gass & C. G. Madden (Eds.), *Input in second language acquisition* (pp. 235–253). New York: Newbury House.

Swales, J. M. (1971). *Writing scientific English*. London: Nelson.

Swales, J. M. (1981). Aspects of article introductions (Research Report No. 1). Birmingham, AL: University of Aston.

Swales, J. M. (1985). *Episodes in ESP*. Englewood Cliffs, NJ: Prentice-Hall.

Swales, J. M. (1990a). Non-native speaking graduate students and their introduction: Global coherence and local management. In U. Conner & A. Johns (Eds.), *Coherence: Research and pedagogical perspectives*. Washington, DC: TESOL.

Swales, J. M. (1990b). *Genre analysis and its applications*. Cambridge: Cambridge University Press.

Swales, J. M., & Horowitz, D. (1988, March). *Genre-based approaches to ESL and ESP materials*. Paper presented at the 22nd Annual TESOL Convention, Chicago.

Swales, J. M., & Najjar, H. (1987). The writing of research article introductions. *Written Communication, 9*(2), 175–192.

Swan, M., & Smith, B. (Eds.). (1987). *Learner English: A teacher's guide to interference and other problems*. Cambridge: Cambridge University Press.

Swan, M., & Walter, E. (1985). *Cambridge English course* (Book 2). Cambridge: Cambridge University Press.

Sweet, H. (1964). *The practical study of languages*. London: Oxford University Press. (Original pub. 1899.)

Szöllösy, A. S. (1985). Types of texts: Means and levels in their comprehension. In J. M. Ulijn & A. K. Pugh (Eds.), *Reading for professional purposes: Methods and materials in teaching languages*. Leuven/Amersfoort: ACCO.

Taglieber, L. K., Johnson, L. L., & Yarborough, D. D. (1988). Effects of pre-reading activities on EFL reading by Brazilian college students. *TESOL Quarterly, 22*(3), 455–472.

Tannen, D. (Ed.) (1988). *Advances in discourse processes, Vol. 24. Linguistics in context: Connecting observation and understanding. Lectures from the 1985 LSA/TESOL and NEH institutes*. Norwood, NJ: Ablex.

Tansey, C., & Blatchford, C. H. (1987). *Understanding conversations*. Belmont, CA: Wadsworth.

Tarone, E., Dwyer, S., Gillette, S., & Icke, V. (1981). On the use of the passive in two astrophysics journal papers. *ESP Journal, 1*(2), 123–140.

Taylor, B. P. (1981). Content and written form: A two-way street. *TESOL Quarterly, 15*(1), 5–13.

Taylor, B. P. (1987). Teaching ESL: Incorporating a communicative, student-centered component. In M. Long & J. Richards (Eds.), *Methodology in TESOL: A book of readings* (pp. 45–60). New York: Newbury House.

Taylor, H. M. (1981). Learning to listen to English. *TESOL Quarterly, 15*(1), 41–50.

Temperley, M. S. (1987). Linking and deletion in final consonant clusters. In Morley (Ed.), *Current perspectives on pronunciation: Practices anchored in theory* (pp. 63–82). Washington, DC: TESOL.

Terkel, S. (1974). *Working*. New York: Avon Books.

Terrell, A. (1971, March). *Writing English lessons for the non academic adult*. Paper presented at the 5th Annual TESOL Convention, New Orleans. (ERIC Document Reproduction Service No. ED 052 655)

Terrell, T. (1977). A natural approach to second language acquisition and learning. *Modern Language Journal, 61*(7), 325–367.

Terrell, T. (1982). The natural approach to language teaching: An update. *Modern Language Journal, 66*(2), 121–132.

Terrell, T., Genzmer, H., Nikolai, B., & Tschirner, E. (1988). *KONTAKTE: A communicative approach*. New York: Random House.

Test of written English guide. (1989). Princeton, NJ: Educational Testing Service.

Tharp, R. G., & Gallimore, R. (1989). *Rousing minds to life: Teaching, learning, and schooling in social context*. Cambridge: Cambridge University Press.

Thonis, E. W. (1970). *Teaching reading to non-English speakers*. London: Collier Macmillan International.

Thorndike, E. L., & Lorge, I. (1944). *The teacher's word-book of 30,000 words*. New York: Columbia University Press.

Tikunoff, W. (1983). *An emerging description of successful bilingual instruction: An executive summary of Part 1 of the SBIF (Significant Bilingual Instructional Features) study*. San Francisco: Far West Laboratory for Educational Research and Development.

Tillit, B., & Bruder, M. N. (1985). *Speaking naturally*. Cambridge: Cambridge University Press.

Tizard, J., Schofield, W. N., & Hewison, J. (1982). Collaboration between teachers and parents in assisting children's reading. *British Journal of Educational Psychology, 52*, 1–15.

Tobin, K. (1987). The role of wait time in higher cognitive level learning. *Review of Educational Research, 57*(1), 69–95.

Tomasello, M., & Herron, C. (1988). Down the garden path: Inducing and correcting overgeneralization errors in the foreign language classroom. *Applied Psycholinguistics, 9*(3), 237–246.

Tomlinson, E., & Eastwick, J. (1980). Allons enfants. *Independent School, 40*(1), 23–31.

Topping, D. M. (1968). Linguistics or literature: An approach to language. *TESOL Quarterly, 2*(2), 45–100.

Torbert, W. (1972). *Learning from experience: Toward consciousness*. New York: Columbia University Press.

Troyka, L. Q. (1982). Looking back and forward. In K. L. Greenberg, H. S. Weiner, & R. A. Donovan (Eds.), *Notes from the national testing network in writing*. New York: City University of New York, Instructional Resource Center.

Trimble, L. (1985). *EST: A discourse approach*. Cambridge: CUP.

Trudgill, P. (1983). *On dialect: Social and geographical perspectives*. New York: New York University Press.

Trueba, H. T. (1989). *Raising silent voices: Educating the linguistic minorities for the 21st century*. New York: Newbury House.

Tucker, C. A. (1978). Evaluating beginning textbooks. In H. S. Madsen & J. D. Brown (Eds.), *Adaptation in language teaching* (pp. 219–237). New York: Newbury House.

Tung, P. (1986). Computerized adaptive testing: Implications for language test developers. In C. W. Stansfield (Ed.), *Technology and language testing* (pp. 11–28). Washington, DC: TESOL.

Twaddell, F. (1973). Vocabulary expansion in the ESOL classroom. *TESOL Quarterly, 7*(1), 61–78.

Uber-Grosse, C. (1988). The case study approach to teaching business English. *English for Specific Purposes, 7*(2), 131–136.

Ulijn, J. M., & Gorter, T. R. (1986). Language culture and technical-commercial negotiating. In H. Coleman (Ed.), *Working with language: A multidisciplinary consideration of language use in work contexts* (pp. 479–505). Berlin: Mouton de Gruyter.

Ulijn, J. M., & Pugh, A. K. (Eds.). (1985). *Reading for professional purposes: Methods and materials in teaching language*. Leuven/Amersfoot: ACCO.

Underhill, A. (1980). *Use your dictionary*. London: Oxford University Press.

Underhill, A. (1985). Working with the monolingual learners' dictionary. In R. Ilson (Ed.), *Dictionaries, lexicography and language learning*. Oxford: Pergamon Press.

Underhill, N. (1987). *Testing spoken language*. Cambridge: Cambridge University Press.

Underwood, G. N. (1983). Mid-South English, midwestern teachers, and middle-of-the-road textbooks. In J. Chambers, Jr. (Ed.), *Black English: Educational equality and the law* (pp. 81–96). Ann Arbor: MI: Karoma.

Underwood, J. (1984). *Linguistics, computers, and the language teacher: A communicative approach*. New York: Newbury House.

United States Department of Labor, and United States Department of Education (1988). *The bottom line: Basic skills in the workplace*. Washington, DC: Office of Public Information, Employment and Training Administration, U.S. Department of Labor.

United States General Accounting Office. (1987). *Bilingual education: A new look at the research evidence* (Briefing report to the chairman, House Committee on Education and Labor. GAO/PEMD-87-12BR.) Washington, DC: General Accounting Office.

Ur, P. (1984). *Teaching listening comprehension*. Cambridge: Cambridge University Press.

Ur, P. (1988). *Grammar practice activities: A practice guide for teachers*. Cambridge: Cambridge University Press.

Ure, J. (1969). Lexical density and register differentiation. In G. Perren & J. L. M. Trim (Eds.), *Applications of linguistics* (pp. 443–452). Cambridge: Cambridge University Press.

Urzua, C. (1987). You stopped too soon: Second language children composing and revising. *TESOL Quarterly, 21*(2), 279–304.

Valette, R. (1969). *Directions in foreign language testing*. New York: Modern Language Association.

Valette, R. (1977). *Modern language testing* (2nd ed.). New York: Harcourt Brace Jovanovich.

van Ek, J. A. (1976). *The threshold level for modern language learning in schools*. Council of Europe, London: Longman.

Van Doorslaer, M. P. (1972). *Reading problems and teaching literature in foreign languages*. Paper presented at the Rocky Mountain Language Association, Tucson, AR. (ERIC Document Reproduction Service No. 073 729) van Lier, L. A. W. (1988). *The classroom and the language learner: Ethnography and second language classroom research*. London: Longman.

Vann, R. J., Myer, D. E., & Lorenz, F. O. (1984). Error gravity: A study of faculty opinion of ESL errors. *TESOL Quarterly, 18*(3), 427–440.

Varonis, E. M., & Gass, S. (1985). Nonnative/nonnative conversations: A model for negotiation of meaning. *Applied Linguistics, 6*(1), 71–90.

Veltman, C. (1983). *Language shift in the United States*. The Hague: Mouton.

Venezky, R. L. (1970). *The structure of English orthography*. The Hague: Mouton.

Ventriglia, L. (1982). *Conversations of Miguel and Maria: How children learn a second language*. Reading, MA: Addison-Wesley.

Via, R. (1976). *English in three acts*. Honolulu: University of Hawaii Press.

Vorhaus, R. (1984). Strategies for reading in a second language. *Journal of Reading, 27*(5), 412–416.

Vygotsky, L. S. (1978). *Mind in society: The development of higher psychological processes*. Cambridge, MA: Harvard University Press.

Waggoner, D. (1988). Language minorities in the United States in the 1980's: The evidence from the 1980 census. In S. McKay & S. L. Wong (Eds.), *Language diversity: Problem or resource?: A social and educational perspective on language minorities in the United States*. New York: Newbury House.

Wagner, M. J., & Tilney, G. (1983). The effects of "superlearning techniques" on the vocabulary acquisition and alpha brainwave production of language learners. *TESOL Quarterly, 17*(1), 5–17.

Walberg, H. J. (1968). Teacher personality and classroom climate. *Psychology in the Schools, 5*(2), 163–169.

Walberg, H. J. (Ed.). (1974). *Evaluating educational performance: A sourcebook of methods, instruments, and examples*. Berkeley, CA: McCutchan.

Walberg, H. J. (1985). Classroom psychological environment. In T. Husen & T. N. Postlethwaite (Eds.), *International encyclopedia of education* (pp. 750–754). New York: Pergamon.

Walker, D. F., & Hess, R. D. (1984). Evaluation in courseware development. In D. Walker & R. D. Hess (Eds.), *Instructional software: Principles and perspectives for design and use* (pp. 204–215). Belmont, CA: Wadsworth.

Wallace, M. J. (1982). *Teaching vocabulary*. London: Longman.

Walsleben, M. C. (1975). *Improving advanced ESL students' reading comprehension: An analysis and evaluation of materials and procedures*. Unpublished MATESL thesis, University of California, Los Angeles.

Walter, L. J. (1984). A synthesis of research findings on teacher planning and decision making. In R. Egbert & M. Kluender (Eds.), *Using research to improve teacher education: The Nebraska consortium teacher education monograph No. 1* (pp. 54–63). Washington, DC: ERIC Clearinghouse on Teacher Education. (ERIC Document Reproduction Services No. ED 246 025)

Walz, J. (1986). Is oral proficiency possible with today's French textbooks? *Modern Language Journal, 70*(1), 13–20.

Waterman, I. R. (1952). When you choose a textbook. *Phi Delta Kappan, 33*(5), 267–271.

Watson, D. (Ed.). (1987). *Ideas and insights: Language arts K-6*. Urbana, IL: NCTE.

Watson, G. (1961). *What psychology can we trust?* New York: Bureau of Publications, Teachers College, Columbia University.

Watt, M., & De Jong, M. (1984). *A guide for selecting bilingual bicultural resource materials (Vol. II). Analysis and annotation of Dutch bilingual and bicultural resource materials*. Master of Education Project, University of Tasmania, Australia. (ERIC Document Reproduction Series No. ED 253 558)

Weathersby, B., & Henault, A. (1976). Cost effectiveness of programs. In M. T. Keeton & Associates, *Experiential learning* (pp. 131–149). San Francisco: Jossey-Bass.

Weaver, C. (1972). *Human listening: Processes and behavior*. New York: Bobbs-Merrill.

Weaver, C. (1980). *Psycholinguistics and reading: From process to practice*. Cambridge, MA: Winthrop.

Weaver, C. (1988). *Reading process and practice: From sociopsycholinguistics to whole language*. Portsmouth, NH: Heinemann Educational Books.

Weisner, T. S., Gallimore, R., & Jordan, C. (1988). Unpacking cultural effects: Native Hawaiian peer assistance and child-generated activity. *Anthropology and Education Quarterly, 19*(4), 327–353.

Weissberg, R. (1987, May). *Information transfer in the teaching of academic writing*. Paper presented at the Conference of the National Association for Foreign Students Affairs, Long Beach, CA. (ERIC Document Reproduction Service No. ED 292 100)

Wenden, A., & Rubin, J. (1987). *Learner strategies in language learning*. Englewood Cliffs, NJ: Prentice-Hall.

Wesche, M. (1987). Communicative testing in a second language. In M. Long & J. Richards (Eds.), *Methodology in TESOL: A book of readings* (pp. 373–394). New York: Newbury House.

Wesche, M. B., & Ready, D. (1985). Foreigner talk in the university classroom. In S. Gass & C. Madden (Eds.), *Input in second language acquisition* (pp. 89–114). New York: Newbury House.

West, G. K., & Byrd, P. (1982). Technical writing required of graduate engineering students. *Journal of Technical Writing and Communication, 12*(1), 1–6.

West, M. (1941). *Learning to read a foreign language*. London: Longman.

West, M. (1953). *A general service list of English words.* London: Longman. (Original work published 1936).

West, M. (1960). *Teaching English in difficult circumstances.* London: Longman.

Weston, L. C., & Stein, S. L. (1978). A content analysis of publishers' guidelines for the elimination of sex-role stereotyping. *Educational Researcher, 7*(3), 13–14.

Whelan, D. (1977). A somewhat polemical view of the teaching of Russian. *Slavic and East European Journal, 21*(2), 243–253.

Whitcut, J. (1979). Learning with LDOCE. London: Longman.

Widdowson, H. G. (1978). *Teaching language as communication.* London: Oxford University Press.

Widdowson, H. G. (1979). The national syllabus: Does it lead to communicative competence? In H. G. Widdowson, *Explorations in Applied Linguistics* (pp. 247–250). Oxford: Oxford University Press.

Widdowson, H. G. (1981). English for specific purposes: Criteria for course design. In L. Selinker, E. Tarone, & V. Hanzeli (Eds.), *English for academic and techinical purposes: Studies in honor of Louis Trimble* (pp. 1–11). New York: Newbury House.

Widdowson, H. G. (1988). Grammar, nonsense, and learning. In W. E. Rutherford & M. Sharwood Smith (Eds.), *Grammar and second language teaching: A book of readings* (pp. 146–155). New York: Newbury House.

Wiesendanger, K., & Birlen, E. (1979). Adapting language experience to reading for bilingual pupils. *Reading Teacher, 32*(6), 671–673.

Wigginton, E. (1989). Foxfire grows up. *Harvard Educational Review, 59*(1), 24–49.

Wilkins, D. A. (1976). *National syllabuses.* Oxford: Oxford University Press.

Williams, D. (1983). Developing criteria for textbook evaluation. *English Language Teaching Journal, 37*(3), 251–261.

Williams, R. (1982, July). *A publisher's attempts to make its content-field textbooks more readable: A case study in social studies.* Paper presented at the 19th Annual Meeting of the United Kingdom Reading Association, Newcastle-upon-Tyne, England. (ERIC Document Reproduction Service No. ED 222 876)

Williams, S. S. (1987). The politics of the black child's language: A study of attitudes in school and society. In W. A. Van Horne & T. V. Tonnesen (Eds.), *Ethnicity and language* (pp. 160–188). Milwaukee: University of Wisconsin Institute on Race and Ethnicity.

Willig, A. C. (1985). A meta-analysis of selected studies on the effectiveness of bilingual education. *Review of Educational Research, 55*(3), 269–317.

Willinsky, J. (1984). *The well-tempered tongue: The politics of standard English in the high school.* New York: Peter Lang.

Willis, D., & Willis, J. (1990). *The COBUILD English course.* London: Collins.

Wilson, L., & McCullough, V. (1986). Some transparency theory concepts applied to a language acquisition project. *CALICO Journal, 4*(2), 17–23.

Winitz, H. (1975). *Comprehension and problem solving as strategies for language training.* The Hague: Mouton.

Winitz, H. (Ed.). (1981). *The comprehension approach to foreign language instruction.* New York: Newbury House.

Winitz, H., & Reeds, J. (1973). Rapid acquisition of a foreign language (German) by the avoidance of speaking. *International Review of Applied Linguistics, 11*(4), 295–315.

Winograd, T. (1983). *Language as a cognitive process. Vol. I: Syntax.* Reading, MA: Addison-Wesley.

Wolfram, W., & Christian, D. (1976). *Appalachian speech.* Washington, DC: Center for Applied Linguistics.

Wolfram, W., & Christian, D. (1989). *Dialects and education: Issues and answers.* Englewood Cliffs, NJ: Prentice-Hall.

Wolfson, N. (1981). Invitations, compliments, and the competence of the native speaker. *International Journal of Psycholinguistics, 24*(4), 7–22.

Wolfson, N. (1983). Rules of speaking. In J. C. Richards & R. W. Schmidt (Eds.), *Language and communication* (pp. 61–87). London: Longman.

Wolfson, N. (1989). *Perspectives: Sociolinguistics and TESOL.* New York: Newbury House.

Wolfson, N., & Manes, J. (1980). The compliment as a social strategy. *Papers in Linguistics, 13*(3 & 4), 391–410.

Wong, R. (1987). Learner variables and prepronunciation considerations in teaching pronunciation. In J. Morley (Ed.), *Current perspectives on pronunciation* (pp. 17–28). Washington, DC: TESOL.

Wong Fillmore, L. (1983). The language learner as an individual: Implications of research on individual differences for the ESL teacher. In M. Clarke & J. Handscome (Eds.), *On TESOL '82: Pacific perspectives on language learning* (pp. 157–174). Washington, DC: TESOL.

Wong Fillmore, L. (1985). Second language learning in children: A proposed model. In *Issues in English language development* (pp. 33–42). Rosslyn, VA: National Clearinghouse for Bilingual Education.

Wong Fillmore, L., Ammon, P., McLaughlin, B., & Ammon, M. S. (1985). *Learning English through bilingual instruction. Final Report to National Institute of Education* (Rep. No. 400-80-0030). Berkeley: University of California. (ERIC Document Reproduction Series No. ED 259 579)

Woodworth, R. S. (1948). *Contemporary schools of psychology* (rev. ed.). New York: Ronald Press.

Wright, A. (1976). *Visual materials for the language teacher.* London: Longman.

Wright, A., Betteridge, D., & Buckby, M. (1984). *Games for language learning.* Cambridge: Cambridge University Press.

Wright, T. (1987). *Roles of teachers and learners.* Oxford: Oxford University Press.

Wyatt, D. H. (1984). *Computers and ESL.* Orlando, FL: Harcourt Brace Jovanovich.

Yalden, J., (1983). *The communicative syllabus: Evolution, design and implementation.* Oxford: Pergamon Press.

Yates, S. (1977). Commercial English: Some notes. In S. Holden (Ed.), *English for specific purposes* (pp. 65–66). London: Modern English Publications.

Yee, V., & Wagner, M. (1984). *Teacher talk; the structure of vocabulary and grammar explanations.* Honolulu: University of Hawaii, Department of ESL.

Yorio, C. A. (1971). Some sources of reading problems in foreign language learners. *Language Learning, 21*(1), 107–115.

Yorkey, R. (1974, July). *Practical EFL techniques for teaching Arabic-speaking students.* Paper presented at the Defense Language Institute, English Language Branch, Lackland Air Force Base. (ERIC Document Reproduction Service No. ED 117 990)

Yorkey, R. (1982). *Study skills for students of English* (2nd ed.). New York: McGraw-Hill.

Zamel, V. (1983). The composing processes of advanced ESL students: Six case studies. *TESOL Quarterly, 17*(2), 165–178.

Zamel, V. (1985). Responding to student writing. *TESOL Quarterly, 19*(1), 79–101.

Zamel, V. (1987). Recent research on writing pedagogy. *TESOL Quarterly, 21*(4), 697–715.

Zeigler, N., Larson, B., & Byers, J. (1983). *Let the kids do it* (Books 1 & 2). Belmont, CA: David S. Lake.

Zhang, S. (1988). Comments on Yael Bejarano's "A cooperative small-group methodology in the language classroom." *TESOL Quarterly, 22*(2), 347–349.

Zobl, H. (1985). Grammars in search of input and intake. In S. M. Gass & C. G. Madden (Eds.), *Input in second language acquisition* (pp. 329–344). New York: Newbury House.

Zughoul, M. R. (1986, April). *The prospective English language textbooks for the compulsory cycle in Jordan: Guidelines for the implementation phase.* Paper presented at the Conference on Compulsory Education, Amman, Jordan. (ERIC Document Reproduction Service No. ED 271 945)

Index

A small *n* following a page reference refers to the appearance of an entry in a note.

Cognitive academic language proficiency (CALP), 119, 120. *See also* Cummins's framework

Cognitive skills, 48

Cohen, A. D., 155, 156, 158–159, 162–163, 173, 257, 262n, 275, 309, 382, 490, 500, 503, 504, 505

Cohen, E. G., 394, 400

Cohen, P., 378

Coherence, 154

Cohesion, 154

Cole, L. R., 56

Coleman, A., 21n

Coleman, J. S., 348–349

Collie, J., 345

Collier, V. P., 374, 399

Collocation. *See* Grammar

Colvin, R. J., 187–188

Comenius, J., 4

Commins, N. L., 388

Communicative competence, 73, 125, 154–155, 217, 280, 316, 329, 377, 488, 489

Complaints, 157–158. *See also* Speech acts

Compliments, 158. *See also* Speech acts

Comprehensible input, 38–39, 55, 56, 108, 126, 316, 322, 389–390, 456–457

Computer-assisted language learning (CALL), 472–486
  activities, 230, 351, 381
  analysis and assessment, 477–478
  artificial intelligence (AI), 476–477
  computerized adaptive testing, 492–493
  evaluation of, 472–473, 478–485
  learning applications, 473–478

Conscientization. *See* Approaches, problem-posing

Content, 55, 119

Content-based instruction, 315–328, 381, 386–402
  activities, 320–322, 386–388
  adjunct model, 319–325
  classroom environment, 388, 393–394
  content-enriched FLES (foreign language in the elementary school), 317–318
  and cooperative learning, 394–396
  curriculum, 391–393
  historical overview, 315
  immersion model, 317
  instructional criteria, 387–389
  integrating skills, 319–320, 389–394
  lesson plan, 323–325
  rationale/objectives, 316, 322, 387
  role of the teacher, 325–326
  sheltered model, 318–319, 381, 389
  techniques, 322–323
  theme-based model, 318
  See also ESP; EST; Literature

Context, 171

Cook-Gumperz, J., 385

Corder, S. P., 292, 293

Cornelius, E. T., 21n

Correction. *See* Error Correction

Cotton, W., 403

Coulthard, M., 89

Counseling-learning community language learning. *See* Approaches

Cowan, E., 253

Cowan, G., 253

Cowles, H. M., 452n

Craig, M., 355

Crandall, J., 71, 327, 381, 391

Crawford, J., 379, 380, 385

Crawford-Lange, L., 41

Cray, E., 346, 354

Crittenden, J., 242

Crookes, G., 55, 56, 58, 59, 61

Cruickshank, D. R., 64, 66

Cuevas, G., 389

Culley, G., 352

Cullinan, B. E., 399

Culp, M. B., 399

Cultural differences, 156, 158, 162, 363, 367–369

Culture and cultural background, 127, 365, 366, 370, 434, 452, 466

Cummins, J., 111, 119, 316, 374, 377, 379, 380, 391–392

Cummins's framework, 391–392

Curran, C. A., 38, 43–44

Curriculum. *See* Approaches; Syllabuses

Currie, K. L., 89

Curtain, H. A., 317

Curtis, W., 274

Cziko, G. A., 505

Dahlet, P., 452n

Daiker, D. A., 257, 276

Dalgish, G., 485

Danesi, M., 346, 452n

Danet, B., 157

Dangerfield, L., 423, 424

Daoud, A. M., 432, 440, 442, 452n

Daum, D. A., 485

Davis, P., 93, 98, 405

Davison, W. F., 453n

Day, J. D., 506

DeAvila, E., 389

De Beaugrande, R., 270

Debenedetti, J., 364

De Capua, A., 158

Deen, R., 275

De Jong, M., 453n

Delayed oral response, 25, 28, 84, 108. *See also* Tasks, problem-solving

Delgado-Gaitan, D., 376

D'Eloia, S., 265, 268, 269

Deloria, V., Jr., 374

Denes, P., 85

de Sauzé, E. B., 4, 11

Devine, J., 214, 215, 231

Dewey, J., 347, 356

Deyhle, D., 489

Diaz, S., 380, 381

Jaggar, A., 398
James, M. O., 197
Jerald, M., 352–353, 354, 357
Jernudd, B. H., 71
Joag-Dev, C., 199
Johns, A. M., 72, 73, 216
Johns, C., 89
Johns, T., 486
Johns, T. F., 75
Johnson, D. D., 186
Johnson, D. M., 263, 387, 394, 398
Johnson, D. W., 394, 400
Johnson, J., 394
Johnson, H., 409
Johnson, K., 84, 91, 242, 352, 419
Johnson, L. L., 305
Johnson, P., 111, 119, 305
Johnson, R. T., 394, 400
Johnson, T. D., 182, 184, 399
Johnston, M., 48, 291
Johnston, V. A., 175
Johnstone, R., 49, 51
Joiner, E. G., 453n
Jolly, D., 158
Jones, E. V., 186, 194
Jones, K., 351
Jordan, C., 375
Jordan, I. K., 376
Jordan, J., 395
Journals. *See* Activities; Professional resources
Judd, E. L., 165, 297

Kagan, S., 262n, 382, 394, 398, 400
Kahn, M. S., 453n
Kamp, J. E., 470
Karlin, M., 351, 354
Kasper, G., 48, 111
Kaulfers, W. V., 11, 12
Kazemek, F., 186
Kean, J., 268
Keller, E., 63, 127, 136
Kelly, L. G., 10
Kendall, F. E., 400
Kennedy, C., 72, 76
Kennedy, G., 489
Kenworthy, J., 89, 137, 149n, 150
Kerek, A., 276
Kingsbury, R., 56
Kintsch, W., 109, 110, 506
Kirschenbaum, H., 364, 372
Kiyochi, E., 305
Kleifgen, J. A., 377
Klein-Braley, C., 492
Kleinmann, H., 268
Klevins, C., 403, 404
Klinghammer, S. J., 65
Knapton, J., 335
Knezevic, M. P., 215

Knoll, B., 249, 256, 263
Knowles, M., 403, 404
Koch, K., 185, 189
Kochman, T., 377, 378, 379
Kolb, D., 347, 348
Kowal, K., 305, 306
Kowitz, J., 121
Kozol, J., 184, 194
Krahnke, K., 74
Kramsch, C. J., 347
Krapels, A. R., 247
Krashen, S. D., 29, 49, 62, 108, 279, 305, 316, 318, 327, 380, 389, 412, 454, 457
Krathwohl, D. R., 488
Krause, K. C., 453n
Kreeft, J., 382
Kreeft-Peyton, J., 145
Kruidenier, B., 318, 327
Kuhn, T. S., 3
Kushner, S., 380
Kwak, W., 399

Labov, W., 374, 375, 376, 378
Lackstrom, J., 69
Lado, R., 111, 496
Lambert, W., 16, 369
Lampert, M., 65
Landa, M., 472
Lane, H., 16
Language Experience Approach (LEA). *See* Approaches; Experiential language learning; Reading
Language laboratory. *See* Listening, resource center
Language processing, 86–88, 108–110, 196–198
    bottom-up, 87, 92, 108–109, 112, 114–115, 117, 120, 170, 178, 196, 198, 219
    interactive, 109–110, 112, 115, 118, 121, 197, 219
    top-down, 87, 92, 109, 112, 115, 117–118, 120–121, 196–197, 198, 218
Language teaching
    guidelines for, 46–67
    historical overview, 3–9, 11–12, 13–17, 67–71
    and linguistics, 13–15
    and psychology, 15–17, 41–44
Lanzano, M., 70, 159
Larsen-Freeman, D., 11, 44, 45, 49, 279, 280, 281–283, 290, 294n, 295, 414, 415, 454, 516
Larson, B., 394
Larson, D. N., 30, 36, 44
Larson, J. W., 493
Latulippe, L. D., 215
Lazaraton, A., 133
Leap, W. L., 375
Learnability vs. functionality in language teaching, 35
Learner, role of, in language teaching, 6–8, 420. *See also* Activities; Approaches
Learning environment, 62–63, 188–189, 393–394, 396, 420, 481

Learning process, 283–285, 289
Learning styles, 363–364
Leather, J., 217
Lebauer, R. S., 119, 120, 121
Legutke, M., 348, 353–354
Lehrer, A., 298
Leinhardt, G., 65
Leki, I., 257
Lentulay, R., 29–30
Lesson planning, 323, 419–431, 456, 459
    context for, 420
    principles of, 422–423
    sample lesson plans, 206–208, 323–325, 357–359,
        425–431, 459–468
Levenston, E. A., 492
Levin, H., 49
Levinson, S., 157, 281
Lewis, D., 368
Lewis, J., 378
Lewis, M., 422
Lewis, N., 347
Liberman, I. Y., 186
Lide, F., 452n
Lindsfors, J. W., 398
Lindstromberg, S., 301
Lingua franca, 3–4
Linguistic minority groups, 372–385
    activities, 380–383
    approaches to teaching, 379–380
    dialect differences, 374–376
    goals for teaching, 376–377
    language shift within, 374
    language skill profiles, 374
    and minority literature, 380–381
    socialization patterns, 374–376, 378–379
    and standard English, 373
Linguistics, 13, 21
    applied, 14, 509
    descriptive/synchronic, 13
    Firthian, 5, 7, 8
    historical/diachronic, 13
    psycholinguistics, 16, 70–71, 110–111, 196, 218
    sociolinguistics. See Pragmatics; Speech acts
    See also Language teaching and linguistics
Liski, E., 58
Listening, 81–106, 106–122
    activities/tasks, 91–105, 114–115, 117–119,
        120–121
    developmental stages, 112–121
    global, 108–109, 111, 113–114, 116
    importance of, 82, 106–107
    information-processing model, 110–111
    interactional, 86, 87–88, 89
    interactive, 85
    and language function, 86–87
    and language processing. See Language processing
    as one-way communication, 85
    outcome categories, 93–103
    as the primary focus, 83, 84–85

to repeat, 83
resource center, 103–104, 145
role of, in language teaching, 6–8, 82–85
selective, 104, 108–109, 111, 113, 114, 116–117
as self-dialog communication, 85
testing of, 504–505
textbook evaluation, 449, 450
theories, 108–111
transactional, 86, 87–88, 89
as two-way communication. See Listening,
    interactive
to understand, 83–84
See also Approaches, comprehension-based
Literacy, 185–194
    first vs. second language, 188
    learner characteristics, 187–188
    learning environment, 188–189
    materials/activities, 189–191
    skills-based approach, 185–186
    strategies-based/whole language approach, 185,
        186–187, 346
    See also Reading; Writing
Literature, an integrated approach, 328–346
    and culture, 341–343
    and grammar, 331–332
    group activities, 340–341, 342–343
    historical overview, 329–330
    and oral skills, 337–341
    rationale for, 328–329
    and reading, 332–333
    selection of materials, 343–344
    and vocabulary, 330–331
    and writing, 333–337
    See also Content-based instruction; Reading
Liu, N., 305
Llanas, A., 243
Lloyd-Jones, R., 246, 248
Logan, G. E., 372
Lonergan, J., 470
Long, M. H., 44, 49, 54, 55–56, 58, 59, 60, 61, 64,
    109, 126, 280, 347, 415
Longman (Publishers), 351
Lopez, D. E., 374
Lorenz, F. O., 260
Lorge, I., 296–297
Loritz, D., 477
Lougheed, L., 119
Loughlin, C. E., 399
Louis, D. R., 182, 184, 399
Low, B., 51
Low, G., 493, 496, 501n
Lozanov, G., 38, 41–42, 44
Lynch, E. S., 215
Lynch, T., 85, 93, 105, 470
Lyons, J., 298

MacDonald, B., 380
Macdonald, M., 471
Mackey, W. F., 22, 440, 453n

Murphy, D. F., 74, 91
Music, role of, in language learning, 42, *See also* Activities
Mustafa, H., 77
Mustapha, M., 200
Myer, D. E., 260

Nagle, S., 110, 111, 122
Najjar, H., 70
Nation, I. S. P., 305–306, 309, 311, 505
Native language
  influences on second language, 137
  role of, in language teaching, 6–8
Natural approach. *See* Approaches
NCTE Task Force, 453n
Needs and needs assessment, 55, 126–127, 146–147, 219, 363–372, 419, 421, 479
  of adults, 363–364, 366–367
  of children, 365–366, 368–370
  in content-based instruction, 326
  in ESP, 67–71, 72–73
  in higher education, 367–368
  in literacy-level learners, 187–188, 189
  of older people, 366
  and placement in writing courses, 248–250
  See also Objectives; Aims of language instruction
Neisser, V., 173
Nelson, P., 200
Nessel, D., 179–180, 182, 184, 190, 194, 355
Neu, J., 70, 72
Neubert, G. A., 65, 66–67
Neuleib, J., 265
Nevo, D. L., 239
Newkirk, T., 262n
Newman, J. M., 185, 186, 398
Newmark, L., 82
Newton, A., 329, 453n
Nichols, P. C., 375
Nikolai, B., 84
Nida, E. A., 82, 108
Nien-Hsuan, J. L., 505
Nir, R., 492
Nonlinguistic messages. *See* Extralinguistic messages; Paralinguistic features
Norris, W. E., 331
North, S. M., 246
Notional/functional syllabus/approach. *See* Syllabuses
Numrich, C., 101
Nunan, D., 51, 54–55, 57, 59, 291
Nurss, J. R., 56
Nuttall, C., 215, 490

Oakeshott-Taylor, J., 122
Objectives
  of activities, 90–91, 202, 203, 204, 254
  of language instruction, 18–19, 47, 55, 126–127, 419–420, 421
  of materials, 479
  of tests, 494–495

See also Activities; Aims of language instruction; Needs and needs assessment
Ochs, E., 378
Ogden, C. K., 11, 13
Ohannessian, S., 21n
Oksman, P. F., 64–65
Oller, J., 44, 45, 492, 503, 504, 505
Olsen, J. W.-B., 472
Olshtain, E., 49, 155, 156–159, 162–163, 199, 215, 243, 262n, 433, 434, 437, 438, 442, 453n
Omaggio, A., 116, 119, 346, 419, 422
O'Malley, J. M., 47, 48, 57, 392, 398, 500
O'Neill, R., 48, 67, 432
Optimal habit reinforcement, 25, 28, 84. *See also* Tasks, problem-solving
Oral communication skills. *See* Speaking
Oral histories, 380, 388
Organization of classroom, 370–371, 348–355
  student-centered, 57–59, 126, 350–352, 353–355
  teacher-fronted, 57, 126, 349–350, 352–353
  See also Activities; Approaches
Orion, G., 151
Ortony, A., 219
Ostler, S., 216
Ostyn, P., 297, 307
Output, 38–39, 55, 56
Ovando, C. J., 399
Owen, M., 158
Oxford, R., 420

Pacheco, B., 329
Page, C. V., 477
Palmer, A., 82, 472
Papalia, A., 453n
Paralinguistic features, 88, 89, 389. *See also* Intonation; Rate; Rhythm; Stress
Parker, D., 381
Parkinson, B., 49, 51
Parry, K. J., 199
Part, S., 175
Passeron, J. C., 377
Paulston, C. B., 51, 268
Pavlov, I., 17
Payne, M., 453n
Pearson, P. D., 186
Peck, W., 353–354
Pedraza, P., 377
Peer support and interaction. *See* Activities, group work
Penfield, J., 458, 469n, 470
Pennella, M., 420
Pennington, M. C., 486
Penrose, J., 346
Pereyra-Suarez, E., 364
Perfetti, C. A., 197
Pesante, L. H., 197
Peterson, P. W., 120
Pfister, G. G., 453n
Philips, S. U., 378